The Crusades

The Crusades

An Encyclopedia

ALAN V. MURRAY

EDITOR

Volume IV: Q–Z

A B C • C L I O

Santa Barbara, California • Denver, Colorado • Oxford, England

Library of Congress Cataloging-in-Publication Data
The Crusades: an encyclopedia / edited by Alan V. Murray.
    p. cm.
    Includes bibliographical references and index.
    ISBN 1-57607-862-0 (alk. paper) — ISBN 1-57607-863-9 (ebook)
    1. Crusades—Encyclopedias. I. Murray, Alan V.

    D155.C78 2006
    909.07—dc22   2006019410

09 08 07 06   10 9 8 7 6 5 4 3 2 1

This book is also available on the World Wide Web as an eBook. Visit abc-clio.com for details.

ABC-CLIO, Inc.
130 Cremona Drive, P.O. Box 1911
Santa Barbara, California 93116-1911

Acquisitions Editor	Patience Melnik
Project Editor	Wendy Roseth
Production Editor	Anna Kaltenbach
Editorial Assistant	Alisha Martinez
Production Manager	Don Schmidt
Senior Media Editor	Ellen Rasmussen
Media Manager	Caroline Price
Media Resources Coordinator	Ellen Dougherty
File Coordinator	Paula Gerard

This book is printed on acid-free paper. ∞
Manufactured in the United States of America

Contents

Editorial Advisory Board
and Contributors

Contributors

Alfred J. Andrea
   University of Vermont
   Burlington, VT
   U.S.A.

Jeffrey Ashcroft
   University of St Andrews
   St Andrews, Scotland
   United Kingdom

Tomas Baranauskas
   The Lithuanian Institute of History
   Vilnius
   Lithuania

Malcolm Barber
   University of Reading
   Reading, England
   United Kingdom

Mário J. Barroca
   University of Oporto
   Porto
   Portugal

George Beech
   Western Michigan University
   Kalamazoo, MI
   U.S.A.

Jessalynn Bird
   Naperville, IL
   U.S.A.

Uta-Renate Blumenthal
   The Catholic University of America
   Washington, DC
   U.S.A.

Karl Borchardt
   Stadtarchiv Rothenburg
   Rothenburg ob der Tauber
   Germany

Michael Brett
   University of London
   London, England
   United Kingdom

Jochen Burgtorf
   California State University, Fullerton
   Fullerton, CA
   U.S.A.

Brian A. Catlos
   University of California, Santa Cruz
   Santa Cruz, CA
   U.S.A.

Niall Christie
   University of British Columbia
   Vancouver, British Columbia
   Canada

Geert H.M. Claassens
   Katholieke Universiteit Leuven
   Leuven
   Belgium

Leona F. Cordery
   Leopold-Franzens-Universität Innsbruck
   Innsbruck
   Austria

Michael D. Costen
   University of Bristol
   Bristol, England
   United Kingdom

Nicholas Coureas
   Cyprus Research Centre
   Nicosia
   Cyprus

Paul F. Crawford
   California University of Pennsylvania
   California, PA
   U.S.A.

Carlos de Ayala Martínez
   Universidad Autónoma de Madrid
   Madrid
   Spain

Gary Dickson
   University of Edinburgh
   Edinburgh, Scotland
   United Kingdom

Peter Edbury
   Cardiff University
   Cardiff, Wales
   United Kingdom

Susan B. Edgington
Queen Mary, University of London
London, England
United Kingdom

Axel Ehlers
Hannover
Germany

Sven Ekdahl
Polish-Scandinavian Research Institute
Copenhagen
Denmark

Taef El-Azhari
Helwan University
Cairo
Egypt

Michael R. Evans
University of Reading
Reading, England
United Kingdom

Marie-Luise Favreau-Lille
Freie Universität Berlin
Berlin
Germany

Mary Fischer
Napier University
Edinburgh, Scotland
United Kingdom

Kate Fleet
University of Cambridge
Cambridge, England
United Kingdom

Jean Flori
Centre d'Etudes Supérieures de Civilisation Médiévale
Poitiers
France

John France
University of Swansea
Swansea, Wales
United Kingdom

Luis García-Guijarro
University of Zaragoza
Huesca
Spain

Christopher Gardner
George Mason University
Fairfax, VA
U.S.A.

Deborah Gerish
Emporia State University
Emporia, KS
U.S.A.

John Gillingham
London, England
United Kingdom

Linda Goldsmith
Guildford County School
Guildford, England
United Kingdom

Aryeh Grabois
University of Haifa
Haifa
Israel

Bernard Hamilton
University of Nottingham
Nottingham, England
United Kingdom

Jonathan Harris
Royal Holloway, University of London
Egham, England
United Kingdom

Benjamin Hendrickx
Rand Afrikaans University
Auckland Park
Republic of South Africa

Carole Hillenbrand
University of Edinburgh
Edinburgh, Scotland
United Kingdom

Martin Hoch
Konrad-Adenauer-Foundation
Sankt Augustin
Germany

Natasha Hodgson
University of Hull
Hull, England
United Kingdom

Lucy-Anne Hunt
    Manchester Metropolitan University
    Manchester, England
    United Kingdom

Zsolt Hunyadi
    University of Szeged
    Szeged
    Hungary

Robert Irwin
    University of London
    London, England
    United Kingdom

Peter Jackson
    Keele University
    Keele, England
    United Kingdom

David Jacoby
    The Hebrew University of Jerusalem
    Jerusalem
    Israel

Nikolas Jaspert
    Ruhr-Universität Bochum
    Bochum
    Germany

Carsten Selch Jensen
    University of Copenhagen
    Copenhagen
    Denmark

Kurt Villads Jensen
    University of Southern Denmark
    Odense
    Denmark

Janus Møller Jensen
    University of Southern Denmark
    Odense
    Denmark

Philippe Josserand
    Université de Nantes
    Nantes
    France

Andrew Jotischky
    Lancaster University
    Lancaster, England
    United Kingdom

Tiina Kala
    Tallinn City Archives
    Tallinn
    Estonia

Katherine Keats-Rohan
    Linacre College, University of Oxford
    Oxford, England
    United Kingdom

Benjamin Z. Kedar
    The Hebrew University of Jerusalem
    Jerusalem
    Israel

Hugh Kennedy
    University of St Andrews
    St Andrews, Scotland
    United Kingdom

Beverly Mayne Kienzle
    Harvard University
    Cambridge, MA
    U.S.A.

Andreas Kiesewetter
    Pretoria-Maroelena
    Republic of South Africa

Klaus-Peter Kirstein
    UNESCO School
    Essen
    Germany

Juhan Kreem
    Tallinn City Archives
    Tallinn
    Estonia

Yaacov Lev
    Bar-Ilan University
    Ramat-Gan
    Israel

John H. Lind
  University of Southern Denmark
  Odense
  Denmark

Amnon Linder
  Public Record Office
  London, England
  United Kingdom

Peter Lock
  York St. John University College
  York, England
  United Kingdom

Kimberly A. LoPrete
  National University of Ireland, Galway
  Galway
  Ireland

Graham A. Loud
  University of Leeds
  Leeds, England
  United Kingdom

Michael Lower
  University of Minnesota
  Minneapolis, MN
  U.S.A.

Christopher MacEvitt
  Dartmouth College
  Hanover, NH
  U.S.A.

Thomas F. Madden
  Saint Louis University
  Saint Louis, MO
  U.S.A.

Christoph T. Maier
  University of Zürich
  Zürich
  Switzerland

Victor Mallia-Milanes
  University of Malta
  Msida
  Malta

Michael Matzke
  Historisches Museum Basel
  Basel
  Switzerland

Rasa Mazeika
  Toronto, Ontario
  Canada

Sophia Menache
  University of Haifa
  Haifa
  Israel

Alexander Mikaberidze
  ABC-CLIO
  Santa Barbara, CA
  U.S.A.

Laura Minervini
  Università di Napoli Federico II
  Naples
  Italy

Piers D. Mitchell
  Imperial College London
  London, England
  United Kingdom

Johannes A. Mol
  Fryske Akademy
  Leeuwarden
  Netherlands

Kristian Molin
  University of Nottingham
  Nottingham, England
  United Kingdom

John C. Moore
  Hofstra University
  Hempstead, NY
  U.S.A.

Rosemary Morris
  University of York
  York, England
  United Kingdom

Contributors

Alec Mulinder
    The National Archives
    London, England
    United Kingdom

Evgeniya L. Nazarova
    Russian Academy of Sciences
    Moscow
    Russia

Helen J. Nicholson
    Cardiff University
    Cardiff, Wales
    United Kingdom

David Nicolle
    University of Nottingham
    Nottingham, England
    United Kingdom

Marie-Adélaide Nielen
    Archives Nationales
    Paris
    France

Torben Kjersgaard Nielsen
    Aalborg University
    Aalborg
    Denmark

Peter S. Noble
    University of Reading
    Reading, England
    United Kingdom

Luís Filipe Oliveira
    Universidade do Algarve
    Faro
    Portugal

Peter Orth
    Monumenta Germaniae Historica
    Munich
    Germany

Johannes Pahlitzsch
    Johannes Gutenberg-Universität Mainz
    Mainz
    Germany

Aphrodite Papayianni
    University of London
    London, England
    United Kingdom

Linda M. Paterson
    University of Warwick
    Coventry, England
    United Kingdom

Jacques Paviot
    Université de Paris XII - Val de Marne
    Créteil
    France

Marcus Phillips
    Numismatic Chronicle
    London, England
    United Kingdom

Jonathan Phillips
    University of London
    Egham, England
    United Kingdom

James M. Powell
    Syracuse University
    Syracuse, NY
    U.S.A.

Denys Pringle
    Cardiff University
    Cardiff, Wales
    United Kingdom

John H. Pryor
    University of Sydney
    Sydney, NSW
    Australia

Jean Richard
    Académie des Inscriptions et Belles-Lettres
    Paris
    France

Samantha Riches
    Lancaster University
    Lancaster, England
    United Kingdom

Jeff Rider
  Wesleyan University
  Middletown, CT
  U.S.A.

Jürgen Sarnowsky
  Universität Hamburg
  Hamburg
  Germany

Alexios G.C. Savvides
  Aegean University
  Rhodes
  Greece

Sylvia Schein
  University of Haifa
  Haifa
  Israel

Iben Fonnesberg Schmidt
  University of Cambridge
  Cambridge, England
  United Kingdom

Elisabeth Schreiner
  Universität Salzburg
  Salzburg
  Austria

Anti Selart
  University of Tartu
  Tartu
  Estonia

Elizabeth Siberry
  Surbiton, England
  United Kingdom

Larry J. Simon
  Western Michigan University
  Kalamazoo, MI
  U.S.A.

Angus Stewart
  University of St Andrews
  St Andrews, Scotland
  United Kingdom

Harald Suermann
  Universität Bonn
  Eschweiler
  Germany

Daniella Talmon-Heller
  Ben-Gurion University of the Negev
  Beer-Sheva
  Israel

Heather J. Tanner
  The Ohio State University
  Mansfield, OH
  U.S.A.

Stefan Tebruck
  Universität Jena
  Jena
  Germany

Kathleen Thompson
  University of Sheffield
  Sheffield, England
  United Kingdom

R. M. Thomson
  University of Tasmania
  Hobart, Tasmania
  Australia

Klaus-Peter Todt
  Johannes-Gutenberg-Universität Mainz
  Mainz
  Germany

John Tolan
  Université de Nantes
  Nantes
  France

Christopher Tyerman
  University of Oxford
  Oxford, England
  United Kingdom

Brian Ulrich
  University of Wisconsin
  Madison, WI
  U.S.A.

William Urban
Monmouth College
Monmouth, IL
U.S.A.

Theresa M. Vann
Saint John's University
Collegeville, MN
U.S.A.

László Veszprémy
Institute of Military History
Budapest
Hungary

Darius von Güttner Sporzynski
University of Melbourne
Melbourne, Victoria
Australia

James Calder Walton
University of Cambridge
Cambridge, England
United Kingdom

Björn Weiler
University of Wales, Aberystwyth
Aberystwyth, Wales
United Kingdom

Dorothea Weltecke
Georg-August-Universität
Göttingen
Germany

Brett Edward Whalen
University of North Carolina
Chapel Hill, NC
U.S.A.

Rafal Witkowski
Adam Mickiewicz University
Poznań
Poland

List of Entries

List of Maps

List of Abbreviations

A.D.	Anno Domini		Lith.	Lithuanian
Arab.	Arabic		MLG	Middle Low German
Arm.	Armenian		MHG	Middle High German
b.	born		mod.	modern
B.C.	before Christ		MS	manuscript
c.	circa		n.s.	new series
ch.	chapter(s)		no(s).	number(s)
Cz.	Czech		OE	Old English
d.	died		OFr.	Old French
e.g.	for example		ON	Old Norse
ed.	edited by, edition		p(p).	page(s)
Est.	Estonian		pl.	plural
et al.	et alii		Pol.	Polish
Fig.	Figure		Port.	Portuguese
Finn.	Finnish		r	recto
fl.	floruit		rev. ed.	revised edition
fol(s).	folio(s)		Russ.	Russian
Fr.	French		s.v.	sub verbo
ft.	feet		ser.	series
Georg.	Georgian		sing.	singular
Ger.	German		Sp.	Spanish
Gr.	Greek		SS.	saints
Heb.	Hebrew		St.	saint
Hung.	Hungarian		Sw.	Swedish
i.e.	that is		Syr.	Syriac
It.	Italian		trans.	translated by
Lat.	Latin		Turk.	Turkish
Latv.	Latvian		v	verso
lb.	pound(s)		vol(s).	volume(s)

Preface

When, at the Council of Clermont in 1095, Pope Urban II called for an armed pilgrimage to liberate the Holy Land, he brought into existence a movement that was to have profound consequences for the history of Europe, the Near East, and North Africa for centuries to come. Hundreds of thousands of men and women took part in crusade expeditions to various goals, a huge number of them dying in the process. Millions of people lived as subjects of states that were brought into existence as a direct consequence of crusades to Palestine and Syria, to the Baltic lands, and to Greece and the islands of the eastern Mediterranean. Others served as members of religious orders established to protect pilgrims or ransom captives, while many more supported crusades through taxes and voluntary donations, or by prayers and participation in the liturgy of the Christian Church. Many of the political, economic, religious, and artistic consequences of the crusades are still apparent in the world that we live in.

This encyclopedia is intended as a reference work on the crusades from their origins in the eleventh century up to the early modern period. It comprises one thousand signed articles and translated texts, with a historical introduction by Professor James Powell. Articles are accompanied by bibliographies, and are thus intended to function as a first point of reference and orientation for users who wish to proceed further with their enquiries. The scope of the work is intentionally wide: it has long been accepted that the crusades were neither purely heroic manifestations of Christian valour nor cynical wars of aggressive colonialism; in more recent years historians have also recognized the diverse and changing nature of crusading, which gradually developed in scope from campaigns to defend the Holy Land, to take in wars of conquest or reconquest against Muslims in Iberia and North Africa and pagans in northeastern Europe, as well as heretics, Christians of the Orthodox faith, and even political enemies of the Roman Catholic Church.

The aim of the encyclopedia is to reflect the state of knowledge of the crusade movement as it is understood in historical scholarship at the beginning of the twenty-first century. It contains longer entries on the major crusade expeditions themselves; the various states that contributed to, were established by, or were targeted by crusading; sources for the history of the crusades; the main military religious orders; and key concepts and institutions connected with crusading. There are also a great number of shorter articles on persons and places. While an absolutely comprehensive treatment is not achievable in a work of this length, the reader will nevertheless find articles on all the major crusades of the eleventh to fourteenth centuries, on most of the military orders, and on all of the crusader states of Outremer, the Baltic lands, Frankish Greece, and Cyprus. There are also entries for all of the rulers of the kingdom of Jerusalem, the kingdom of Cyprus, the Latin Empire of Constantinople, the principality of Antioch, the county of Edessa, and (save one) the county of Tripoli. Within this overall framework, a particular emphasis has been given to the events, institutions, and personalities connected with crusade expeditions and the Frankish states of Outremer and their enemies in the period 1095–1291. Finally, it should be emphasized that in a publication bringing together the work of over a hundred scholars from some two dozen countries, the user should not expect a uniformity of approach or opinion, but will find a diversity of analysis and interpretation from different authors, even if the fortuitous nature of the A–Z sequence has permitted the editor, at least in one sense, to have the last word.

Many debts of gratitude are incurred in a work of the dimensions of this one. The encyclopedia first took shape in a series of conversations with Professor James Powell of Syracuse University and Dr. Robert Neville, then of ABC-CLIO, and I am grateful to them for their advice, as well as to the members of the Editorial Advisory Board, who readily provided assistance and counsel whenever it was requested of them. The authors of articles deserve thanks, not only for sharing their scholarship, but also for their forbearance in dealing with numerous queries and requests for alterations or clarifications, and not least for their patience in waiting for the work to see the light of day. Several board members and other contributors also deserve thanks for their readiness to step into the breach by agreeing to write articles for which, for whatever reason, no other author could be found. Much of the attractiveness of a work such as this derives from its illustrations, and I am particularly grateful to Professors Alfred Andrea, Benjamin Z. Kedar, and Graham Loud for generously allowing the use of photographs from their own collections, and to Dr. Janus Møller Jensen, Dr. Kristian Molin, and Dr. Samantha Riches for their help and advice in procuring images.

Among the staff at ABC-CLIO, a great deal is owed to the energy and enthusiasm of Wendy Roseth and to the good sense and experience of Martha Whitt, who supported the project during its most crucial stages, while Anna Kaltenbach and Vicki Moran in turn provided the care that brought it to publication. Significant contributions to the final product were also provided by Ellen Rasmussen, who undertook picture research; Bill Nelson (cartographer) and George Zirfas (graphic artist), who drew maps and genealogical tables to the editor's specifications; as well as Silvine Farnell and Kathy Streckfus (copyeditors), Mary Kay Kozyra and Lori Kranz (proofreaders), Tim Giesen (typesetter), and Heather Jones (indexer). Thanks are also due to Alison Miller and Patience Melnik, who acted as development editors during the initial stages of the project.

Lastly, I am grateful to Martina Häcker and Rhiannon Lawrence-Francis for their assistance in proofreading the final text.

— *Alan V. Murray*
Leeds, 5 July 2006

Q

Qal'at al-Hiṣn

See Krak des Chevaliers

Qal'at al-Rūm

See Hromgla

Qal'at al-Muslimūn

See Hromgla

Qalāwūn (1222–1290)

Mamlūk sultan of Egypt (1279–1290), and founder of a dynasty that lasted for 100 years. Qalāwūn's reign saw the Mamlūk victory in the Second Battle of Homs (1282), which ended the immediate Mongol threat to the eastern Mediterranean region and enabled the Mamlūks to concentrate their military efforts on the final destruction of the Frankish states of Outremer. He died while mounting an expedition against Acre (mod. 'Akko, Israel), which under his son and successor Khalīl ended the Frankish occupation of the Near East.

Qalāwūn was a Kipchak Turk by origin. In his twenties, he was purchased by a member of the household of al-Kāmil, Ayyūbid sultan of Egypt, for the price of 1,000 dinars, and hence came to be called al-Alfī, after the Arabic word for thousand. Later he served al-Ṣāliḥ Ayyūb as one of the Baḥriyya corps of soldiers, and became an emir under Sultan Baybars I. After Baybars's death, Qalāwūn succeeded to the throne following a brief power struggle,

and set about consolidating his position. This consolidation involved setting aside the *mamlūks* (slave soldiers) of Baybars in favor of his own, as well as some of the Ṣāliḥīs who had not previously held important positions. He also successfully confronted a revolt in Syria by Sunqur al-Ashqar with the support of the Bedouin leader 'Īsā ibn Muhannā.

In 1281, Qalāwūn faced a long-expected invasion of Syria by the Ilkhan Abaqa, who had sought to break Mamlūk power in the region. Qalāwūn's victory in the Second Battle of Homs (1282), followed by Abaqa's death shortly thereafter, left him free to continue the Mamlūk military campaign against Outremer, which was politically weak and divided. The sultanate had concluded a number of truces with individual Frankish powers; now, Qalāwūn simply found pretexts for declaring them void and eliminating his enemies one at a time.

In 1285, the sultan accused the Hospitallers of Margat of attacking Muslims, and after a brief campaign he took the stronghold in late May. He then moved against the castle of Maraclea, which Prince Bohemund VII of Tripoli ordered to be surrendered so as to preserve his own truce with the Mamlūks. In 1287, after an earthquake destroyed some of the fortifications at Laodikeia in Syria, Qalāwūn took the city, claiming that it was not covered by his truce with Bohemund, as the city lay outside the boundaries of the county of Tripoli. In 1289 Qalāwūn attacked Tripoli (mod. Trâblous, Lebanon), eventually storming the town and massacring much of the population. He then razed the city and ordered it rebuilt on a new site. In an attempt to save Acre, the last Christian possession in the area, Pope Nicholas IV called a crusade in February 1290, though many Western monarchs simply used the crisis to strengthen their economic interests in Egypt. During the preparations for his campaign against Acre, however, Qalāwūn died. The city's capture was left to his son Khalīl, whom he had successfully installed as heir.

–Brian Ulrich

Bibliography

Amitai-Preiss, Reuven, *Mongols and Mamluks: The Mamluk-Ilkhanid War, 1260–1281* (Cambridge: Cambridge University Press, 1995).

Holt, Peter M., *The Age of the Crusades: The Near East from the Eleventh Century to 1517* (London: Longman, 1986).

Irwin, Robert, *The Middle East in the Middle Ages: The Early Mamluk Sultanate, 1250–1382* (London: Croom Helm, 1986).

Northrup, Linda S., *From Slave to Sultan: The Career of al-Mansūr Qalāwūn and the Consolidation of Mamluk Rule in Egypt and Syria (678–689 A.H./1279–1290 A.D.)* (Stuttgart: Steiner, 1998).

Qilij Arslān I of Rūm (d. 1107)

'Izz al-Dīn Qilij Arslān I (Turk. *Izzüddin Kılıç Arslan I*) was the third ruler of Rūm (1092–1107), the sultanate established by a branch of the Saljūq dynasty in western Anatolia.

Qilij Arslān I was the son of Sulaymān I ibn Qutlumush, the founder of the Rūm sultanate. When Sulaymān died in combat at Shaizar in Syria (c. 1086) fighting against the Great Saljūq sultan Malik Shāh I and his brother Tutush I, ruler of Syria, the young Qilij Arslān was among the captives and spent some years in captivity in Baghdad, during which time his sultanate was ruled by his uncle Abu'l Qāsim (1086–1092). Qilij Arslān's liberation following Malik Shāh's violent death (1092) coincided with Abu'l Qāsim's death in Nicaea at the hands of Malik Shāh's agents, and so Qilij Arslān managed to ascend his throne. From the outset of his reign he established contacts with the ambitious emir of Smyrna (mod. İzmir, Turkey), Chaka, whose son-in-law he became, while his belligerent activities were directed against the Dānishmendids in eastern Anatolia.

In August 1096 Qilij Arslān's troops decimated the rabble of Peter the Hermit, who were the first crusaders to cross into Asia Minor. The following year, while he was engaged besieging Dānishmendid Melitene, Qilij Arslān's capital of Nicaea (mod. İznik, Turkey) was besieged by the combined armies of the First Crusade (1096–1099) and the Byzantines. The Byzantines became masters of the city and of the sultan's wife and family, despite his attempt to relieve the city (May–June 1097). However, the Byzantine emperor Alexios I Komnenos soon returned the captives to the sultan, who, now in coalition with the Dānishmendids, confronted the crusaders at Dorylaion (17 July 1097), suffering a grave defeat, while the Byzantines were restoring several of their Anatolian possessions.

Having lost his capital, Qilij Arslān selected Ikonion (mod. Konya, Turkey), which was to become his new headquarters early in the twelfth century, though it seems that the actual transferral of the new Rūm Saljūq capital was associated with his successors Malik Shāh II (1107–1116) or Mas'ūd I (1116–1155). He allied with the Dānishmendids in two victorious battles against the Crusade of 1101 at Mersivan and Herakleia (mod. Ereğli, Turkey); Bohemund I of Antioch was captured in these engagements and was released by the Dānishmendids in 1104.

In the last eventful period of his reign Qilij Arslān was persuaded by Alexios I (to whom he even sent mercenaries against the Norman invasion of Greece under Bohemund in 1107) to eliminate his father-in-law Chaka (c. 1105–1106), while the death of the Dānishmendid emir (c. 1104) caused him to resume his aggression against the latter's possessions. In 1106 he captured Melitene (mod. Malatya, Turkey) and Martyropolis (mod. Silvan, Turkey), and in 1107 he seized Mosul. However, when he attempted an invasion of Mesopotamia, he faced a massive coalition under the Great Saljūq sultan Muḥammad I (1105–1118) and was killed in action in a hotly contested battle at Khabur River on 3 July 1107, which was to assume legendary proportions in early Turkish epic.

–Alexios G. C. Savvides

See also: First Crusade (1095–1099); Crusade of 1101; Rūm, Sultanate of

Bibliography

Cahen, Claude, *Pre-Ottoman Turkey, c. 1071–1330* (London: Sidgwick & Jackson, 1968).

Demirkent, Isın, *Türkiye Selçuklu Hükündarı Sultan I. Kılıç Arslan* (Ankara: Türk Tarih Kurumu, 1996).

Savvides, Alexios G. C., "Kilij Arslan I of Rum, Byzantines, Crusaders and Danishmendids, A.D. 1092–1107," *Βυζαντινά* 21 (2000), 365–377.

Talbot-Rice, Tamara, *The Seljuks in Asia Minor* (London: Thames & Hudson, 1961).

Turan, Osman, *Selçuklular zamanında Türkiye tarihi, 1071–1318*, 2d ed. (İstanbul, Nakýplar Yayýnevi, 1984).

Wittek, Paul, *The Rise of the Ottoman Empire* (London: Royal Asiatic Monographs, 1938).

Qilij Arslān II of Rūm (d. 1192)

ʿIzz al-Dīn Qilij Arslān II (Turk. *Izzüddin Kılıç Arslan II*) was the sixth Saljūq sultan of Rūm (1156–1192), in whose reign the sultanate, centered on Ikonion (mod. Konya, Turkey), assumed a leading role in Anatolian affairs by defeating the Byzantines, annexing the two Dānishmendid emirates, and contracting an alliance with the Holy Roman Emperor and crusading leader Frederick I Barbarossa.

Qilij Arslān II was born around 1115, the son of Sultan Masʿūd I (d. 1156). Although his brother's claim to the succession was supported by Nūr al-Dīn, the ruler of Muslim Syria, Qilij Arslān II finally prevailed. Among his first tasks was to thwart a possible alliance between Nūr al-Dīn and Emperor Manuel I Komnenos of Byzantium, with whom he had signed an ineffectual treaty in 1158; for this reason he visited Constantinople in 1161–1162, where he was magnificently received for three months by Manuel and a new treaty was signed. However, this treaty was not observed, since in 1173/1174 the sultan signed another treaty with Byzantium's bitter Western enemy, Frederick I Barbarossa. Thus Manuel I decided to invade Anatolia, where he fortified the fortresses of Dorylaion and Choma-Soublaion (1175/1176), but, rejecting Qilij Arslān II's peace offer, he was eventually heavily defeated in September 1176 at Myriokephalon, in west-central Anatolia.

This victory enabled the sultan to expand his conquests at the expense of Byzantium until the mid-1180s. Meanwhile, between 1174 and 1177/1178, he succeeded in annexing the strongholds of the two Dānishmendid dynasties of Sebasteia (mod. Sivas, Turkey) and Melitene (mod. Malatya, Turkey). In the last years of his reign, when the Byzantines contracted alliances with Saladin (1184–1185 and 1189–1192) and the Rupenids of Cilicia solidified their grip on the Taurus-Antitaurus area, Qilij Arslān II faced difficulties with his nine ambitious sons, each of whom possessed an important Anatolian city as emir and aspired to the throne. Around 1189/1190 the eldest son, Quṭb al-Dīn, prevailed over his old and sick father at Ikonion, but with the advent of Frederick I at the head of the German army of the Third Crusade in Anatolia (1190), the Sāljuq capital was taken and, following Quṭb al-Dīn's death (c. 1191), it was restored to Qilij Arslān, who lived there until he died (August 1192) under the protection of his youngest and favorite son, Kay-Khusraw I, who succeeded him.

–Alexios G. C. Savvides

See also: Rūm, Sultanate of; Third Crusade (1189–1192)
Bibliography
Cahen, Claude, *Pre-Ottoman Turkey, c. 1071–1330* (London: Sidgwick & Jackson, 1968).
Rice, Tamara Talbot, *The Seljuks in Asia Minor* (London: Thames & Hudson, 1961).
Savvides, Alexios G. C., *Byzantium in the Near East: Its Relations With the Seljuk Sultanate of Rūm in Asia Minor, the Armenians of Cicilia, and the Mongols*, A.D. c. 1192–1237 (Thessaloniki: Byzantine Research Centre, 1981).
———, "Ο Σελτζούκος σουλτάνος Κιλίτζ Αρσλάν Β΄ και η μάχη του Μυριοκεφάλου, 1176 μ. Χ.," *Στρατιωτική Ιστορία* 8 (1997), 14–22.
Turan, Osman, *Selçuklular zamanında Türkiye tarihi*, 2d ed. (İstanbul, Nakýplar Yayýnevi, 1984).
Vryonis, Speros, Jr., *The Decline of Medieval Hellenism in Asia Minor and the Process of Islamization from the 11th through the 15th century* (Berkeley: University of California Press, 1971).

R

Radulph of Caen (d. after 1130)

Author of the *Gesta Tancredi*, a rhetorically sophisticated Latin account of the First Crusade (1096–1099) and the early years of Frankish Outremer, in prose with interspersed sections of verse (Lat. *prosimetrum*).

The *Gesta Tancredi* was composed between 1112 and 1118 and dedicated to Radulph's former teacher, Arnulf of Chocques, then Latin patriarch of Jerusalem (d. 1118). It survived in a single twelfth-century manuscript (MS Bruxelles, Bibliothèque royale Albert Ier, 5373) that was hardly known during the Middle Ages. Radulph was probably born around 1080. Since he served in the entourages of Bohemund I of Antioch (1107) and Tancred (1108) in Epiros and Syria and mainly relied on information supplied by them, the *Gesta* appears to be an appraisal of the Norman part in the events from 1099 to 1108.

The work shows a certain distance to the more popular histories of the First Crusade, of which Radulph may have known the *Gesta Francorum* as well as a first redaction of the *Historia Hierosolymitana* of Fulcher of Chartres. The inserted poems concerning the fighting at Dorylaion, Antioch, and Jerusalem introduce the Normans and their ambitious leaders rather like the heroes of classical epic.

–Peter Orth

Bibliography

Boehm, Laetitia, "Die Gesta Tancredi des Radulph von Caen: Ein Beitrag zur Geschichtsschreibung der Normannen um 1100," *Historisches Jahrbuch* 75 (1956), 47–72.

Elm, Kaspar, "*O Beatas idus ac prae ceteris gloriosas!* Darstellung und Deutung der Eroberung Jerusalems 1099 in den *Gesta Tancredi* des Raoul von Caen," in *Es hat sich viel ereignet, Gutes wie Böses: Lateinische Geschichtsschreibung der Spät- und Nachantike,* ed. Gabriele Thome and Jens Holzhausen (München: Saur, 2001), pp. 152–178.

"Gesta Tancredi in expeditione Hierosolymitana . . . auctore Radulfo Cadomensi," in *Recueil des Historiens des Croisades: Historiens Occidentaux,* 5 vols. (Paris: Académie des Inscriptions et Belles-Lettres, 1844–1895), 3:587–716.

The Gesta Tancredi of Ralph of Caen: A History of the Normans on the First Crusade, trans. Bernard S. Bachrach and David S. Bachrach (Aldershot, UK: Ashgate, 2005).

Glaesener, H., "Raoul de Caen, historien et écrivain," *Revue d'histoire ecclésiastique* 46 (1951), 5–21.

Pabst, Bernhard, *Prosimetrum: Tradition und Wandel einer Literaturform zwischen Spätantike und Spätmittelalter* (Köln: Böhlau, 1994).

Payen, Jean-Charles, "L'image du grec dans la chronique normande: Sur un passage de Raoul de Caen," in *Images et signes de l'Orient dans l'Occident médiéval* (Aix-en-Provence: CUERMA, 1982), pp. 267–280.

Rainald III of Toul

Count of Toul in Upper Lotharingia and participant in the First Crusade (1096–1099).

Rainald was the elder son of Frederick I, count of Astenois, and Gertrude, daughter of Rainald II, count of Toul. He and his brother Peter of Dampierre took part in the crusade in the army of their kinsman Godfrey of Bouillon, duke of Upper Lotharingia. Rainald was a prominent man of the second rank in the crusade, and commanded a division of the united crusader army at the Great Battle of

Antioch (28 June 1098). He returned home after the crusade, and died sometime before 1124.

–Alan V. Murray

Bibliography
Barthélemy, Anatole de, 'Le comté d'Astenois et les comtes de Dampierre-le-Château', *Revue de Champagne et de Brie* 16 (1888), 401–416; 17 (1889), 177–191; 18 (1890), 801–807; 19 (1891), 691–699.
Murray, Alan V., *The Crusader Kingdom of Jerusalem: A Dynastic History, 1099–1125* (Oxford: Prosopographica et Genealogica, 2000).

Rainald of Châtillon

See Reynald of Châtillon

Ralph of Caen

See Radulph of Caen

Ralph of Coggeshall

Abbot of Coggeshall and author of parts of the abbey's *Chronicon Anglicanum* dealing with the years 1187 to 1227.

Ralph was abbot of the Cistercian house of Coggeshall in Essex in southeast England, from 1206 until poor health forced his retirement in 1218. His portion of the *Chronicon Anglicanum* begins with the capture of Jerusalem by Saladin and devotes considerable attention to the Third Crusade (1189–1192). Not surprisingly, the English chronicler focused in particular on the exploits of King Richard I of England in the Holy Land, including his role in the capture of Acre (mod. 'Akko, Israel) on 12 June 1191, and his subsequent negotiations with Saladin.

Despite the lack of English participation in the Fourth Crusade (1202–1204), Ralph's membership in the Cistercian Order encouraged his considerable interest in events surrounding the capture of Constantinople (mod. İstanbul, Turkey) on 13 April 1204. The abbot reports in detail on the preparatory stages of the crusade, including the dramatic appearances by the crusade preacher Fulk of Neuilly at the Cistercian general chapters of 1198 and 1201. Together with his admiration for Fulk, Ralph's uncritical account of Constantinople's fall contributes to a relatively enthusiastic portrayal of the controversial Fourth Crusade. He also gives some information on the Albigensian Crusade

(1209–1229). Ralph presumably died in 1227 or shortly thereafter.

–Brett Edward Whalen

See also: Third Crusade (1189–1192)
Bibiliography
Contemporary Sources for the Fourth Crusade, trans. Alfred J. Andrea (Leiden: Brill, 2000), pp. 256–290.
Grandsen, Antonia, *Historical Writing in England,* vol. 7: *c. 550 to c. 1307* (Ithaca, NY: Cornell University Press, 1974), pp. 322–324.
Ralph of Coggeshall, *Chronicon Anglicanum,* ed. Joseph Stevenson, Rolls Series 66 (London: Longman, 1875), pp. 1–208.
Wagner, Kay, "La croisade albigeoise vue par le chroniqueur Raoul de Coggeshale: Une interprétation de l'histoire sous l'angle du 'patriotisme' anglais," *Heresis* 35 (2001), 83–89.

Ralph de Diceto (d. 1199/1200)

Author of a number of historical works, one of which (the *Ymagines historiarum*) contains important information about Outremer, especially from 1185 onward.

Although not a major source on the Third Crusade (1189–1192), Ralph's work contains valuable comparative information, of a high level of reliability. His surname, Diceto, probably refers to Diss in Norfolk, although this is not certain. After holding a number of ecclesiastical positions and studying at Paris, in 1180 he was elected dean of St. Paul's Cathedral, London. His important position assisted him in collecting information for his historical writings: for example, in 1196 William Longchamp, chancellor of King Richard I of England, sent him a copy of the supposed letter of the Assassin leader known as the Old Man of the Mountains to Leopold V, duke of Austria, giving an explanation of the assassination of Marquis Conrad of Montferrat in 1192. Ralph inserted this letter into his *Ymagines.* His own chaplain gave him details about the foundation of the English military order of St. Thomas of Acre. Some of the letters he recorded survive nowhere else. Although his information on Outremer was secondhand, his account was generally accurate because he either reproduced letters from the East in full or summarized them.

–Helen Nicholson

Bibliography
Gransden, Antonia, *Historical Writing in England,* vol. 1: *c. 550 to c. 1307* (1974).

Greenway, Diana E., "The Succession to Ralph de Diceto, Dean of St Paul's," *Bulletin of the Institute of Historical Research* 39 (1966), 89–95.

Ralph de Diceto, *Radulfi de Diceto decani Lundoniensis opera historica: The Historical Works of Master Ralph de Diceto, Dean of London*, Rolls Series 68, ed. William Stubbs (London: Longman, 1876).

Ralph of Domfront (d. c. 1146)

Latin patriarch of Antioch (1135–1140).

Born at Domfront in Normandy, Ralph was trained as a knight and later took holy orders. He went to Outremer, where by 1135 he had become archbishop of Mamistra (mod. Misis, Turkey) in Cilicia. When Bernard of Valence died the same year, Ralph was chosen to succeed him as patriarch of Antioch (mod. Antakya, Turkey) by popular acclaim. He did not seek papal ratification, and his enemies alleged that he did not consider the see of Antioch, founded by St. Peter, as subordinate to Rome. Pope Innocent II did not intervene because of the papal schism of 1130–1138. When Raymond of Poitiers, whom the barons of Antioch had invited to be the husband of the child heiress, Princess Constance, reached the city in 1136, Ralph agreed to solemnize the marriage against the wishes of the regent, Constance's mother Alice, if Raymond would do liege-homage to him. Raymond accepted this condition and became prince of Antioch, and Alice was forced into retirement. Yet Ralph's secular and ecclesiastical ambitions antagonized the prince and some of the senior clergy, who complained to the pope.

After the schism ended, Innocent II appointed Alberic, cardinal bishop of Ostia, to investigate the charges. The cardinal presided over a synod at Antioch from 30 November to 2 December 1140, at which Ralph's election was deemed uncanonical and charges of simony and fornication brought against him were upheld; he was deposed and imprisoned in chains in the monastery of St. Symeon on the Black Mountain of Antioch. He later escaped and reached Rome, where a pope (probably Lucius II) quashed his deposition, but he died—allegedly from poison—before he could return to Outremer.

–*Bernard Hamilton*

Bibliography

Cahen, Claude, *La Syrie du Nord à l'époque des croisades et la principauté franque d'Antioche* (Paris: Geuthner, 1940).

Hamilton, Bernard, "Ralph of Domfront, Patriarch of Antioch (1135–40)," *Nottingham Medieval Studies* 28 (1984), 1–21.

Hiestand, Rudolf, "Ein neuer Bericht über das Konzil von Antiochia 1140," *Annuarium Historiae Conciliorum* 20 (1988), 314–350.

Ralph of Merencourt (d. 1224)

Latin patriarch of Jerusalem (1214–1224) and papal legate.

Ralph originated from the village of Merencourt in Champagne, not far from Troyes. This place may be the same as the modern Saint-Benoît-sur-Vanne in the canton of Aux-en-Othe (dép. Aube, France). Having obtained a master's degree, from 1187 to 1190 Ralph served as assistant to the legal chambers of Count Henry II of Champagne. In the summer of 1190 he went to the Holy Land as notary to Henry when the count went there in the course of the Third Crusade (1189–1192). With the appointment of Henry as lord of the kingdom of Jerusalem, Ralph rose to the rank of notary to the lord of Jerusalem, while retaining responsibility for all matters relating to Champagne (5 May 1192–10 September 1197). After holding various other ecclesiastical offices in Palestine, Ralph became archdeacon of Tyre (1204) and then dean of the cathedral chapter of Acre (1206). At some point before 1215 (possibly as early as 1202) he was appointed as chancellor of the kingdom, and he was evidently also made bishop of Sidon between 1210 and 1214, being first attested in this office in the context of the royal coronation of John of Brienne in October 1210.

Ralph's abilities and his closeness to John of Brienne became evident when he traveled to the papal Curia on the new king's behalf and successfully advocated the legitimacy of his rule against charges brought by opposition nobles. It was therefore no surprise that John designated his chancellor as successor to Patriarch Albert of Jerusalem, who died in 1214. Ralph of Merencourt participated at the Fourth Lateran Council (November 1215). He was ordained patriarch by Pope Innocent III and resigned his office as chancellor. Between May 1218 and autumn 1221, Ralph took part in the Fifth Crusade (1217–1221) in Egypt.

After the defeat of the crusade by the Ayyūbids, the patriarch traveled to Brindisi with King John at the beginning of September 1222 to negotiate with the pope and Frederick II, Holy Roman Emperor and king of Sicily, about the future of the Holy Land, particularly the proposed marriage of Frederick to John's daughter Isabella II, the heiress to the kingdom of Jerusalem. As early as February 1223, Ralph stayed at the imperial court at Capua and took part in the Congress of Ferentino, where the emperor's forthcoming crusade and his marriage to Isabella were agreed upon. In May 1223, the pope appointed the patriarch as his legate for the patriarchate of Jerusalem, and the same year Ralph returned to the Holy Land. Ralph may have crowned Isabella II of Jerusalem, assuming that the coronation took place as early as 1224. He died the same year (before 15 December 1224).

–*Klaus-Peter Kirstein*

See also: Jerusalem, Latin Patriarchate of

Bibliography
Les Champenois et la Croisade, ed. Yvonne Bellenger and Danielle Quéruel (Paris: Aux Amateurs de Livres, 1989).
Eck, Thomas, *Die Kreuzfahrerbistümer Beirut und Sidon im 12. und 13. Jahrhundert auf prosopographischer Grundlage* (Frankfurt am Main: Lang, 2000).
Edbury, Peter W., "The Crusader States," in *The New Cambridge Medieval History,* vol. 5, ed. David Abulafia (Cambridge: Cambridge University Press, 1999), pp. 590–606, 934–938.
Hamilton, Bernard, *The Latin Church in the Crusader States: The Secular Church* (London: Variorum, 1980).
Housley, Norman, "The Thirteenth-Century Crusades in the Mediterranean," in *The New Cambridge Medieval History,* vol. 5, ed. David Abulafia (Cambridge: Cambridge University Press, 1999), pp. 569–589, 930–933.
Kirstein, Klaus-Peter, *Die lateinischen Patriarchen von Jerusalem* (Berlin: Duncker & Humblot, 2002).
Mayer, Hans Eberhard, *Die Kanzlei der lateinischen Könige von Jerusalem,* 2 vols. (Hannover: Hahn, 1996).
Powell, James M., *Anatomy of a Crusade, 1213–1221* (Philadelphia: University of Pennsylvania Press, 1986).
Richard, Jean, "Pouvoir royal et patriarcat au temps de la cinquième croisade, à propos du rapport du partriarche Raoul," *Crusades* 2 (2003), 89–104.

Ramla

Castle, town, and seat of a lordship in southern Palestine, located on the coastal plain between Jerusalem and Jaffa.

A city had been established at Ramla by the Umayyads as a successor to Christian Lydda (mod. Lod, Israel) around 715, but it was deserted when the armies of the First Crusade (1096–1099) occupied it on 3 June 1099. The leaders of the crusade installed Robert of Rouen as bishop and lord of Ramla-Lydda, providing him with a small garrison to defend the place. Their intention seems to have been to create an ecclesiastical lordship, as they had previously done at Albara

in northern Syria. Indeed, until around 1160 bishops of Lydda continued to style themselves bishops of Ramla. By May 1102, however, the city and its territory had been incorporated into the royal domain; a castle had been built in a part of the walled city and a castellan appointed. The strategic importance of the site is illustrated by the fact that three major battles against invading Egyptian forces took place in its vicinity, in September 1101, May 1102, and August 1105. After his defeat at the second of these, King Baldwin I of Jerusalem took refuge in the principal tower of the castle, escaping the following day just before it was burned and undermined by the Muslims.

From October 1106 onward, the castellan was Baldwin of Ramla, who later became a vassal of Hugh, count of Jaffa. Following Hugh's revolt against King Fulk in 1134, however, the county was divided, and Baldwin was subsequently made lord of Ramla. Around 1138, the lordship passed to his daughter, Helvis, who was assisted in running it by her husband, Balian, former castellan of Jaffa. When Helvis's younger brother, Renier, came of age around 1143–1144, the lordship passed to him, and it was possibly in anticipation of this that King Fulk granted Balian in 1141 the new castle of Ibelin (mod. Yavne, Israel). In 1146–1148, however, Renier died, and Helvis and Balian resumed control of Ramla. When Balian died in 1150, Helvis married Manasses of Hierges, who supported Queen Melisende against her son Baldwin III. As a result, in 1152, Baldwin captured Manasses in his castle of Mirabel and banished him, leaving Helvis to continue to administer Ramla with the help of her son Hugh, lord of Ibelin. On Helvis's death (1158–1160), Hugh became lord of Ramla, but in or soon after 1169 he departed for Santiago de Compostela. By 1171 he was dead, and Ramla was in the hands of his brother, Baldwin, who had been lord of Mirabel from around 1162. In 1186, Baldwin refused homage to the new king, Guy of Lusignan, and departed to Antioch, leaving his fief to another brother, Balian the Younger, husband of the dowager queen, Maria Komnene, and self-styled lord of Nablus. Balian led the defense of the city of Jerusalem against Saladin in 1187 and is last mentioned in 1193.

In the twelfth century, a small unwalled settlement of Franks and indigenous Christians developed outside the castle. The existence of a burgess court is attested by the jurist John of Jaffa. In 1177, the town was attacked and burned by the Muslims, having already been deserted by its inhabitants. It fell to Saladin in July or August 1187. The castle was

Tower of the Forty Martyrs, Ramla. (Library of Congress)

Mayer, Hans Eberhard, "Carving up Crusaders: The Early Ibelins and Ramlas," in *Outremer: Studies in the History of the Crusading Kingdom of Jerusalem,* ed. Benjamin Z. Kedar, Hans Eberhard Mayer, and R. C. Smail (Jerusalem: Yad Izhak Ben-Zvi Institute, 1982), pp. 101–118.

———, "The Origins of the Lordships of Ramla and Lydda in the Latin Kingdom of Jerusalem," *Speculum* 60 (1985), 537–552.

Pringle, Denys, *The Churches of the Crusader Kingdom of Jerusalem: A Corpus,* 3 vols. (Cambridge: Cambridge University Press, 1993–).

Ramla, First Battle of (1101)

A battle between King Baldwin I of Jerusalem and an Egyptian army commanded by Saʿad al-Dawla al-Qawā-misī, fought as part of concerted attempts between 1099 and 1105 by al-Afḍal, the vizier of Egypt, to regain the Fāṭimid possessions in Palestine lost to the army of the First Crusade in 1099.

The Egyptian army reached the Fāṭimid city of Ascalon (mod. Tel Ashqelon, Israel) in mid-May 1101 and advanced on Ramla, but retreated to Ascalon when Baldwin arrived with relieving forces. From May to August, there was a stalemate while the Egyptian army awaited reinforcements, and Baldwin was content to wait upon developments. On 4 September the Egyptians advanced upon Ramla. Baldwin had only 260 cavalry and 900 infantry at his disposal. He divided this force into five divisions and then attacked. The fighting was very fierce. The first two Frankish divisions were completely destroyed, and the third, suffering heavy losses, broke and fled back to Jaffa (mod. Tel Aviv-Yafo, Israel), pursued by the Egyptian left wing. Baldwin, commanding the reserve division, attacked and broke the Egyptian center, and the entire Egyptian army then fled back to Ascalon, pursued so closely by the Frankish army that most of the Egyptian force was subsequently destroyed.

–*Alec Mulinder*

Bibliography

Brett, Michael, "The Battles of Ramla (1099–1105)," in *Egypt and Syria in the Fatimid, Ayyubid and Mamluk Eras,* ed. Urbain Vermeulen and Daniel De Smet (Leuven: Peeters, 1995), pp. 17–39.

Röhricht, Reinhold, *Geschichte des Königreichs Jerusalem (1100–1291)* (Innsbruck: Wagner, 1898).

Runciman, Steven, *History of the Crusades,* 3 vols. (Cambridge: Cambridge University Press, 1951–1954).

destroyed in 1191, but the parish church was spared, possibly because it had already been converted into a mosque. By the Treaty of Jaffa (1192), the city was divided between the Franks and Muslims. In 1211–1212, the pilgrim Wilbrand of Oldenburg found it mostly destroyed, though it is unlikely to have been completely deserted. Although ceded to Emperor Frederick II in 1229, it would have been lost again in 1244. The Mamlīk sultan Baybars I took Ramla in 1266 and completed the rebuilding of the White Mosque, which had been started by Saladin. In 1395 the Franciscans established a hospice for pilgrims traveling to Jerusalem.

–*Denys Pringle*

Bibliography

Brett, Michael, "The Battles of Ramla (1099–1105)," in *Egypt and Syria in the Fatimid, Ayyubid and Mamluk Eras,* ed. Urbain Vermeulen and Daniel De Smet (Leuven: Peeters, 1995), pp. 17–39.

Ramla, Second Battle of (1102)

A defeat of a Christian force consisting of crusaders and Franks of Outremer under King Baldwin I of Jerusalem by an Egyptian army commanded by Sharaf al-Ma'ālī Samā' al-Mulk, a son of the vizier al-Afḍal.

In May 1102 the Egyptians besieged the town of Ramla in southwestern Palestine, plundering the surrounding lands. Spurred into a precipitate show of force, Baldwin gathered 700 cavalry, many of them recently arrived crusaders from the crusading expeditions of 1101–1102, and advanced toward Ramla. The battle took place at Yazur, 16 kilometers (10 miles) from Jaffa (mod. Tel Aviv-Yafo, Israel), on 17 May. The Egyptian army surprised Baldwin, who took a hasty decision to attack rather than retreat. The Christian force was surrounded and massacred. A few knights cut their way through to reach Jaffa, but most of the survivors were forced to take refuge in Ramla. Baldwin and a few companions escaped that night, and the following morning the Egyptians stormed the town. The surviving knights defended a tower, but all were quickly captured or killed. Christian casualties included Stephen, count of Blois, and Stephen, count of Burgundy. The defeat placed the kingdom of Jerusalem in great peril, but it was saved from collapse by Baldwin's decisive victory at the battle of Jaffa on 4 July 1102.

–Alec Mulinder

Bibliography

Mulinder, Alec, "The Crusade of 1101–1102" (Ph.D. diss., University of Wales at Swansea, 1996).

Brett, Michael, "The Battles of Ramla (1099–1105)," in *Egypt and Syria in the Fatimid, Ayyubid and Mamluk Eras,* ed. Urbain Vermeulen and Daniel De Smet (Leuven: Peeters, 1995), pp. 17–39.

Ramla, Third Battle of (1105)

A battle in southwestern Palestine between the forces of King Baldwin I of Jerusalem and an Egyptian army commanded by Sharaf al-Ma'ālī Samā' al-Mulk, a son of the vizier al-Afḍal.

At the beginning of August 1105, an Egyptian army of about 5,000 soldiers, composed primarily of Arab cavalry, Sudanese infantry, and mounted Turkish bowmen, together with allies from Damascus, gathered at Ascalon (mod. Tel Ashqelon, Israel). King Baldwin gathered his army of 500 horsemen and 2,000 infantry at Jaffa (mod. Tel Aviv-Yafo, Israel), and then advanced and met the allied Egyptian and Damascene army at Ramla, the battle occurring on 27 August 1105. The battle was closely contested, with the Egyptian infantry repelling repeated attacks by the Frankish cavalry. At one point a counterattack by the Damascene mounted archers caused great havoc in the Frankish ranks and nearly broke their army, but Baldwin attacked with his own division and routed the attackers. Many of the Egyptian cavalry on the Muslim left flank left the battle to try to plunder Haifa (mod. Hefa, Israel), without success, while the remainder of the cavalry were forced to retreat; despite these setbacks, the Egyptian infantry were able to withstand numerous mounted assaults and were only overcome following the collapse of their Damascene allies.

The Egyptian army retreated back to Ascalon. Having suffered many casualties, the Franks were unable to pursue the enemy and were content to plunder the Egyptian camp. The third battle of Ramla ended the last of the Fatimids' large scale attempts to reconquer Palestine from the Franks.

–Alec Mulinder

Bibliography

Brett, Michael, "The Battles of Ramla (1099–1105)," in *Egypt and Syria in the Fatimid, Ayyubid and Mamluk Eras,* ed. Urbain Vermeulen and Daniel De Smet (Leuven: Peeters, 1995), pp. 17–39.

Runciman, Steven, *History of the Crusades,* 3 vols. (Cambridge: Cambridge University Press, 1951–1954).

Ranculat

See Hromgla

Ravendel

A fortress, known in Arabic as Rāwandān (mod. Ravanda Kalesı, Turkey), about 40 kilometers (25 mi.) west of Turbessel (mod. Tellbaşar Kalesı, Turkey), on a commanding position on a tall conical hill above the upper Afrın Valley.

During the First Crusade the castle was captured by Baldwin of Boulogne with the support of the local Armenian population (1097–1098). It was first given to Baldwin's guide, Bagrat, but was taken away from him following intrigues and given, along with Turbessel, to Godfrey of Bouillon, who based himself there in the summer of 1098.

Ravendel was subsequently incorporated into the Frankish county of Edessa. It formed part of the lordship of Joscelin I of Courtenay during his tenure of Turbessel

(1101–1113) and thereafter belonged to the counts of Edessa. After Joscelin II's capture in 1150 it was transferred to a Byzantine garrison, but in 1151 it was taken by Nūr al-Dīn. The castle and its town had been expanded by the Franks; the castle was substantially rebuilt by Saladin, and it remained a military and administrative center under the Mamlūks, although it was depopulated during Timur's invasion (1400).

–*Angus Stewart*

Bibliography
Cahen, Claude, *La Syrie du Nord à l'époque des croisades et la principauté franque d'Antioche* (Paris: Geuthner, 1940).
Gardiner, Robert, "Crusader Turkey: The Fortifications of Edessa," *Fortress* 2 (1989), 23–35.
Morray, David, "Then and Now: A Medieval Visit to the Castle of al-Rāwandān Recalled," *Anatolian Studies* 43 (1993), 137–142.

Raymond I of Tripoli

See Raymond of Saint-Gilles

Raymond II of Tripoli (d. 1152)

Count of Tripoli (1137–1152).

The son of Count Pons of Tripoli and Cecilia of France, widow of Tancred of Antioch, Raymond succeeded to the county when his father was killed by the Damascenes in March 1137. He was by then married to Hodierna, sister of Queen Melisende of Jerusalem, by whom he later had a son, Raymond (III), and a daughter, Melisende.

In the summer of 1137 Raymond II was captured by Zangī while attempting to relieve the Tripolitan castle of Montferrand; the surrender of this strategic fortress was the price paid for his release by Raymond and his ally King Fulk of Jerusalem. Raymond subsequently made important grants to the Order of the Hospital, including the castle of Krak des Chevaliers and its territory. The arrival of the Second Crusade in 1148 brought about a threat to Raymond's rule in the person of Alphonse-Jordan, count of Toulouse, who claimed to be the rightful heir to the county of Tripoli as the son of its founder, Raymond of Saint-Gilles. The death of Alphonse-Jordan soon after his arrival in the Holy Land was blamed by his son Bertrand on Raymond, and the ill will between Raymond and the French crusaders contributed to Raymond's refusal to cooperate in the attack launched against

Damascus by the crusade armies and the Franks of Jerusalem in July 1148. In September Bertrand's troops seized the Tripolitan castle of Aryma, and Raymond called in the Muslim princes Unur of Damascus and Nūr al-Dīn, whose capture of Bertrand and destruction of his forces finally removed the Toulousan threat. Four years later, Raymond fell victim to attack by the Assassins, and he was succeeded by his son Raymond III.

–*Alan V. Murray*

Bibliography
Richard, Jean, *Le Comté de Tripoli sous la dynastie toulousaine (1102–1187)* (Paris: Geuthner, 1945).

Raymond III of Tripoli (d. 1187)

Count of Tripoli (1152–1187), lord of Tiberias (1174–1187), and twice regent of the kingdom of Jerusalem (1174–1176 and 1185–1186).

Raymond was the son of Raymond II of Tripoli and Hodierna, sister of Queen Melisende of Jerusalem. He was still a minor when his father was killed in 1152, and he took up the government of Tripoli in 1155. He was captured by Nūr al-Dīn in 1164 while participating in a combined Frankish attempt to relieve the town of Artah, and he spent the next ten years as a prisoner, during which time Tripoli was governed by his cousin King Amalric of Jerusalem. Raymond's captivity and his subsequent roles in the politics of the kingdom of Jerusalem meant that he was probably less involved in the affairs of his hereditary county of Tripoli than most of his predecessors.

Soon after being ransomed (by early 1174) Raymond acquired the lordship of Tiberias through marriage to Eschiva, widow of Walter of Saint-Omer. Thus on the accession of Amalric's underage son, the leper king Baldwin IV (July 1174), Raymond was holder of the greatest lordship in the kingdom of Jerusalem as well one of the closest male relatives of the king. Later the same year, he demanded and received the regency of the kingdom, which he exercised until Baldwin came of age (July 1176), when he returned to Tripoli.

In the spring of 1180, Raymond and Prince Bohemund III of Antioch led their armies into the kingdom, evidently with the aim of ensuring that a candidate amenable to them would be chosen as a new husband for Baldwin IV's widowed sister Sibyl, the heir to the throne. They were thwarted when the king had Sibyl married quickly to the Poitevin nobleman Guy of Lusignan. Despite a reconciliation with the king and Guy in 1182, Raymond came to be the leading figure among a growing number among the ruling class of Jerusalem (particularly the Ibelin family) who were implacably opposed to Guy becoming king. In 1185 the dying Baldwin IV, who by this time had also lost faith in Guy's abilities, appointed Raymond as regent for his nephew Baldwin V, Sibyl's son by her deceased first husband. Yet when the young king died in the summer of 1186, Raymond was outmaneuvered by his opponents, who had Guy and Sibyl crowned in Jerusalem. Fearing an attack on Tiberias, Raymond admitted Saladin's troops into the lordship, which seemed to confirm the suspicions of many that he intended to seize the throne himself, but he was forced into a new reconciliation with Guy by his own vassals in Tripoli and Tiberias after it became apparent that Saladin did not intend to renew his truce with the kingdom, which was due to expire in April 1187.

Raymond and his supporters were unable to persuade Guy to avoid giving battle to Saladin's great army that invaded Galilee in June 1187. At the ensuing disastrous encounter at Hattin (4 July 1187), Raymond managed to fight his way through the Muslim lines with his stepsons and made his way to Tripoli, where he fell ill and died in September 1187, regarded as a traitor by many of his fellow Franks. Having no children of his own, he conferred the county of Tripoli on Raymond, the elder son of his old ally Bohemund III of Antioch. The latter, however, appointed his younger son, Bohemund (IV), as ruler.

–Alan V. Murray

Bibliography
Baldwin, Marshall W., *Raymond III of Tripoli and the Fall of Jerusalem (1140–1187)* (Princeton: Princeton University Press, 1936).
Hamilton, Bernard, *The Leper King and His Heirs: Baldwin IV and the Crusader Kingdom of Jerusalem* (Cambridge: Cambridge University Press, 2000).
Richard, Jean, *Le Comté de Tripoli sous la dynastie toulousaine (1102–1187)* (Paris: Geuthner, 1945).

Raymond IV of Toulouse

See Raymond of Saint-Gilles

Raymond VI of Toulouse (1156–1222)

Count of Toulouse (1194–1222) at the time of the Albigensian Crusade (1209–1229).

Raymond ruled over the county of Toulouse itself (coterminous with the diocese of Toulouse), the Rouergue, Quercy, the Agenais, and the marquisate of Provence, as well as being acknowledged as overlord in Valence, Nîmes, the Vivarais, Anduze, Rodez, Lomagne, and Gourdon.

Raymond did nothing to counter the spread of the Catharism that had become widespread in his lands, and he tolerated the heretics. As a result he incurred the wrath of Pope Innocent III, and when one of Raymond's servants assassinated the legate Peter of Castelnau (15 January 1208), the pope launched the crusade. Raymond initially made peace with the crusaders but later saw his lands invaded. As a war leader he was ineffectual, and most of his lands fell to the crusaders, and his defeat by Simon of Montfort at the disastrous battle of Muret (12 September 1213) caused him to flee to England, and Toulouse itself was occupied by crusaders.

At the Fourth Lateran Council (November 1215) the political settlement made by Innocent III stripped Raymond of his lands, but he was invited back to Toulouse (September 1217) by the citizens and was present during the siege by Simon of Montfort. By the time of his death in 1222 he had passed responsibility for government to his son Raymond VII. He died excommunicate and was never buried.

–*Michael D. Costen*

Bibliography
Costen, Michael D., *The Cathars and the Albigensian Crusade* (Manchester, UK: Manchester University Press, 1997).
Roquebert, Michel, *L'Epopée Cathare*, vol. 1: *1198–1212: L'invasion* (Toulouse: Privat, 1970).

Raymond VII of Toulouse (1197–1249)

Count of Toulouse (1222–1249).

Raymond was the son of Count Raymond VI of Toulouse and Joan, daughter of King Henry II of England. Present at the battle of Muret in 1213 at which his father suffered a major defeat by the forces of the Albigensian Crusade (1209–1229), he went with his father to England and then to Rome for the Fourth Lateran Council (1215).

Over the next few years he campaigned ceaselessly, effectively functioning as ruler of the county of Toulouse, to which he formally succeeded on his father's death (1222). In 1223 he besieged Amalric of Montfort in Carcassonne and negotiated his withdrawal from the region. However, the French king Louis VIII intervened in the Languedoc, and in 1225 Raymond was faced with the king's overwhelming military superiority, which was maintained after Louis's untimely demise by the regency of Queen Blanche of Castile. Raymond accepted the terms of the Treaty of Meaux (12 April 1229); he continued to rule as count of Toulouse but recognized the overlordship of Louis IX. He lost control of his lands to the east of the Rhône and saw his only legitimate heir, Jeanne, married to Alphonse, the young king's brother.

As a result of the king's authority, Raymond was forced to accept the activities of the Inquisition throughout his lands from 1233 onward. An abortive rebellion in 1242 led to the Treaty of Lorris (1243), which confirmed his loss of power. Raymond's last years were filled with plans to get a male heir: he put away Jeanne's mother and sought to marry Sanchia of Provence, a project that failed, as did his plan to marry Beatrice of Provence. He died on 27 September 1249 near Rodez and was buried at Fontevrault with his mother.

–*Michael D. Costen*

Bibliography
Belperron, P., *La croisade contre les Albigeois et l'union du Languedoc à la France* (Paris: Perrin, 1942).
Costen, Michael D., *The Cathars and the Albigensian Crusade* (Manchester, UK: Manchester University Press, 1997).

Raymond of Aguilers

Participant in the First Crusade (1096–1099) and author of a Latin narrative of the expedition.

Raymond's purpose was set out in the preface to his work: he was recording on behalf of himself and one Pons of Balazun the deeds of the southern French army, led by Raymond, count of Saint-Gilles, and Adhemar, bishop of Le Puy. Although these notables were present at the Council of Clermont and among the first to take the cross in 1095, Raymond's narrative begins during the journey to Constantinople. The preface was written after the capture of Jerusalem (Raymond refers to the army as victorious); Pons, however, had been killed at Arqah (spring 1099), and so it appears that events were recorded as they happened. Since there is no indication that Raymond knew of the death of Saint-Gilles in 1105, his account was probably completed early in the 1100s. It is probable that he used a version of the anonymous *Gesta Francorum* for some details, but to all intents and purposes his work is firsthand and independent, ranking in importance alongside the *Gesta* and Fulcher of Chartres.

Everything known about Raymond of Aguilers derives from his book. He became a priest during the expedition,

and he served as chaplain to Raymond of Saint-Gilles, which gave him access to sound information and the councils of the leaders. Yet he was more interested in presenting the count of Saint-Gilles and the southern French in a good light, probably to counter rumors of cowardice circulating in France after the crusade. Above all, Raymond of Aguilers wished to defend the reputation of the relic known as the Holy Lance. He describes himself as one of the first to believe the visions of the pilgrim Peter Bartholomew, which revealed where the Holy Lance was to be found, and relates that he personally joined in the digging for the relic in the cathedral at Antioch (mod. Antakya, Turkey). His belief was unshaken by the ambiguous outcome of Peter Bartholomew's ordeal by fire, and his passionate advocacy unbalances his account. Nevertheless, Raymond's partisanship and his pious credulity are themselves important indicators of popular attitudes.

Raymond's work usually bears the title *Historia Francorum qui ceperunt Iherusalem* (The History of the Franks who Took Jerusalem), but its twentieth-century editors simply entitled it Raymond's *Liber* (book) from his own closing line. The original manuscript does not survive, but there are six copies dating from the twelfth and thirteenth centuries, the best of which is MS Paris, Bibliothèque nationale de France, lat.14378.

–*Susan B. Edgington*

Bibliography
France, John, "The Anonymous *Gesta Francorum* and the *Historia Francorum qui ceperunt Iherusalem* of Raymond of Aguilers and the *Historia de Hierosolimitano itinere* of Peter Tudebode: An Analysis of the Textual Relationship between Primary Sources for the First Crusade," in *The Crusades and their Sources: Essays presented to Bernard Hamilton*, ed. John France and William G. Zajac (Aldershot, UK: Ashgate, 1998) pp. 39–70.
Krey, August C., *The First Crusade: The Accounts of Eye-Witnesses and Participants* (Princeton: Princeton University Press, 1921).
Raymond of Aguilers, *Historia Francorum qui ceperunt Iherusalem,* trans. John H. Hill and Laurita L. Hill (Philadelphia: American Philosophical Society, 1968).
———, *Liber,* ed. John H. Hill and Laurita L. Hill (Paris: Geuthner, 1969).

Raymond Berengar IV of Barcelona (d. 1162)

Count of Barcelona (1131–1162), regent of Provence (1144–1157), and ruling prince of Aragon (1137–1162).

Raymond Berengar (Sp. *Ramon Berenguer*) was probably born around 1113, the son of Berengar III and Douce of Provence. Most famous for having brought about the dynastic union of Aragon and Barcelona (known as the Crown of Aragon) through his marriage to Petronilla of Aragon in 1137, Raymond Berengar was also a warrior who successfully fought the Muslims of western and southern Catalonia. In many ways, he continued the path laid out by his father. He fostered the Order of the Temple and enhanced his position in Provence through dynastic ties. The count's greatest military triumphs were the conquests of Tortosa, Lleida, and Fraga in 1148–1149, by which he incorporated the southern coastal areas later known as New Catalonia (Cat. *Catalunya Nova*) and gained territories that had separated Catalonia from Aragon. The Treaty of Tudellén of 27 January 1151, in which Alfonso VII of León-Castile and Raymond Berengar IV divided the Iberian Peninsula into zones for future conquest, bore witness to these successes. On his death, he was succeeded by his son King Alfonso II of Aragon.

–*Nikolas Jaspert*

Bibliography

Jaspert, Nikolas, "Bonds and Tensions on the Frontier: The Templars in Twelfth-Century Western Catalonia," in *Mendicants, Military Orders and Regionalism in Medieval Europe*, ed. Jürgen Sarnowsky (Aldershot, UK: Ashgate, 1999), pp. 19–45.

Schramm, Percy E., Joan F. Cabestany, and Enric Bagué, *Els primers comtes-reis: Ramon Berenguer IV, Alfons el Cast, Pere el Catòlic* (Barcelona: Vives, 1963).

Raymond of Poitiers (d. 1149)

Prince of Antioch (1136–1149) as consort of the Princess Constance.

Raymond was the second son of William IX, duke of Aquitaine, himself a notable crusader. In 1133, while still a young man at the court of King Henry I of England, Raymond received an offer from King Fulk of Jerusalem, who was then acting as regent of the principality of Antioch, to marry Constance, the daughter and heiress of Prince Bohemund II (d. 1131). Despite the opposition of Bohemund's cousin Roger II of Sicily, and his widow, Alice, Raymond made his way via Apulia to Antioch and was invested as prince upon his marriage to Constance in the second half of 1136. Raymond's accession brought a new southern French influence to the principality, whose ruling class had hitherto been predominantly Norman. As prince he commissioned the earliest literary work in French known to have been composed in Outremer: the poem *Les Chétifs*, dealing largely with the Crusade of 1101, in which his own father had taken part.

Raymond's status as an independent ruler was challenged by the Byzantine emperor John II Komnenos, who had sought Constance in marriage for his own son. John swept though Cilicia and laid siege to Antioch in the summer of 1137, reasserting long-standing Byzantine claims to the principality as former Byzantine territory. Raymond was obliged to become John's vassal, and he agreed to surrender his principality to direct Greek rule in exchange for Aleppo, Hama, Homs, and Shaizar if these territories could be conquered from the Muslims. Raymond's lack of cooperation in the joint Byzantine–Frankish invasion of Muslim territory launched the following year caused the emperor to abandon the siege of Shaizar in frustration and to withdraw to Cilicia. Raymond was able to see off another invasion by John in 1142, and he took the offensive against Byzantine Cilicia the next year. However, the increasing danger posed by the conquests of Zangī, as well as a further Byzantine invasion in 1144, forced Raymond to do homage to John's successor Manuel I Komnenos at Constantinople.

The arrival of the armies of the Second Crusade in Outremer (1148) brought Raymond great hopes of military assistance, particularly from King Louis VII of France, whose wife, Eleanor of Aquitaine, was Raymond's niece. However, he was unable to persuade Louis to join him in an attack on Aleppo, the power base of Nūr al-Dīn, and relations between the two men were further strained by Raymond's close relationship with and obvious influence over Eleanor. In consequence Raymond took no part in the attack on Damascus, which the crusade armies and the Franks of Jerusalem chose as their objective in June 1148, and the failure of this enterprise left Antioch as vulnerable as before. Raymond was killed in battle on 29 June 1149 while attempting to relieve the fortress of Inab from the forces of Nūr al-Dīn, who had the prince's skull mounted as a trophy for the caliph at Baghdad.

–*Alan V. Murray*

Bibliography

Beech, George T., "The Ventures of the Dukes of Aquitaine into Spain and the Crusader East in the Early Twelfth Century," *Haskins Society Journal* 5 (1993), 61–75.

Cahen, Claude, *La Syrie du Nord à l'époque des croisades et la principauté franque d'Antioche* (Paris: Geuthner, 1940).

Nicholson, Robert L., "The Growth of the Latin States, 1118–1144," in *A History of the Crusades,* ed. Kenneth M. Setton et al., 6 vols., 2d ed. (Madison: University of Wisconsin Press, 1969–1989), 1:410–447.

Phillips, Jonathan P., "A Note on the Origins of Raymond of Poitiers," *English Historical Review* 102 (1991), 66–67.

Raymond-Rupen of Antioch (d. 1222)

Prince of Antioch (1216–1219).

Raymond-Rupen was probably born in 1196, the son of Raymond, the eldest son of Prince Bohemund III of Antioch; his mother was Alice, niece of King Leon I of Cilicia (Lesser Armenia). He was raised in Cilicia after the death of his father in 1197.

Following the death of his grandfather. Bohemund III (1201), Raymond-Rupen should by rights have inherited the principality of Antioch. However, his uncle, Count Bohemund IV of Tripoli, arrived in the city of Antioch (mod. Antakya, Turkey) before him and was elected prince by its commune, which feared Armenian domination under Raymond-Rupen. Yet in 1216 the young Raymond-Rupen seized the city with the help of his great-uncle, Leon I, and was consecrated prince of Antioch. Raymond's rule in Antioch, though popular in the beginning, soon became an unwanted imposition. The citizens welcomed Bohemund IV back in 1219, and Raymond, having already alienated Leon, fled to Damietta in Egypt, where the Fifth Crusade (1217–1221) was in progress.

Following Leon's death in 1219 Raymond claimed the Cilician throne by right of his mother. He invaded Cilicia in 1221 but, after a few successes, was captured by Constantine of Lampron, regent for Leon's young daughter Isabella. He died in prison the following year.

–*Christopher MacEvitt*

Bibliography

Cahen, Claude, *La Syrie du Nord à l'époque des croisades et la principauté franque d'Antioche* (Paris: Geuthner, 1940).

Mutafian, Claude, *La Cilicie au carrefour des empires,* 2 vols. (Paris: Les Belles Lettres, 1988).

Runciman, Steven, *A History of the Crusades,* 3 vols. (Cambridge: Cambridge University Press, 1951).

Raymond of Saint-Gilles (d. 1105)

One of the leaders of the First Crusade (1096–1099) and later first count of Tripoli (1102–1105).

Raymond was born around 1041, the second son of Pons II, count of Toulouse, and Almodis of La Marche. Raymond inherited the lordship of Saint-Gilles (situated at the mouth of the Rhône), as well as lands in Provence; to these he was able to add an inheritance from his cousin Bertha, consisting of the marquisate of Gothia and the county of Rouergue. On the death of his childless elder brother William IV (1094), Raymond was the ruler of a vast aggregate of territory; he had already taken the title of count of Toulouse. His first marriage (probably dissolved on the grounds of consanguinity) produced one son, Bertrand (later count of Tripoli); around 1080 he married his second wife, Matilda, daughter of Roger I of Sicily. His third marriage, to Elvira, daughter of Alfonso VI of Castile, may well have been contracted in 1088 on the occasion of a campaign conducted by several French lords in Spain against the Almoravids, in which Raymond probably took part.

A resolute advocate of church reform, Raymond was one of the *fideles sancti Petri* (vassals of St. Peter) whom Pope Gregory VII had planned to take with him on his intended expedition to aid the Byzantine Empire, and Raymond evidently met Pope Urban II before the Council of Clermont. Certainly by November 1095 he had announced his intention to set out for the East, and by the time of his subsequent meeting with Urban, he must have been well informed about the pope's plans.

Raymond took command of an army drawn from the counts, bishops, and lords of southern France and Provence. He is not known to have alienated any of his own territories in order to finance his crusade, but he was nevertheless able to raise finances exceeding those of the other princes, and was even able to take some of them into his pay. Raymond's army left France in the autumn of 1096 and marched through Lombardy, Friuli, and Dalmatia, but encountered difficulties in crossing Croatia, despite an agreement he had concluded with King Constantine Bodin. After entering Byzantine territory at Dyrrachion (mod. Durrës, Albania), the crusader army was escorted by imperial Pecheneg auxiliaries, and there were clashes between the two forces. The crusaders stormed the city of Roussa on 12 April 1097, but were defeated by imperial troops at Rodosto after Raymond had gone on to Constantinople to negotiate with the Byzantine emperor, Alexios I Komnenos. Raymond refused to do homage to the emperor, but did agree to restore to him any formerly Byzantine cities that might fall into his hands during the crusade.

Raymond's army crossed the Bosporus on 28 April 1097, arriving at Nicaea (mod. İznik, Turkey) in time to intercept the relieving forces sent to the defenders of the city by Qilij Arslān I, sultan of Rūm. At Antioch (mod. Antakya, Turkey), Raymond insisted on a direct siege of the city rather than the blockade advised by the Byzantine general Tatikios, and he constructed a tower (known as La Mahomerie) in order to prevent enemy sallies from the Dog Gate (March 1098). He encouraged raids into the surrounding countryside to secure supplies for the besiegers, providing money for the establishment of a fund to replace horses lost on these occasions. After the capture of the city (3 June 1098), Raymond lent credence to the claims of the visionary Peter Bartholomew and was present at the discovery of the relic known as the Holy Lance in the Cathedral of St. Peter on 15 June. However, he disputed the possession of the citadel of Antioch with the Norman leader Bohemund of Taranto and insisted on maintaining a force of his own in the city. Subsequently Raymond made himself the spokesman of those who demanded that the city should be restored to the Emperor Alexios, even though he also subscribed to the appeal of the crusade leaders to Urban II to come to Antioch and take charge of the crusade (11 September 1098).

During the summer and autumn of 1098, Raymond proceeded to occupy the middle reaches of the Orontes Valley, taking the towns of Rugia, Albara (where he installed a bishop), and Ma'arrat al-Numan. These actions intensified his dispute with Bohemund, but the pressure of those crusaders impatient to reach Jerusalem persuaded Raymond to put himself at their head, and he left Ma'arrat in the attire of a pilgrim, leaving small garrisons in the places he had conquered, although Bohemund expelled the force he had left in Antioch. He obtained freedom of passage and supply facilities from the emirs of Shaizar and Homs, occupied Krak des Chevaliers, and besieged the town of Arqah for three months, hoping to compel the *qāḍī* (magistrate) of Tripoli (mod. Trâblous, Lebanon) to submit to him, but perhaps also to give the emperor time to join him. He was forced to raise the siege by Godfrey of Bouillon and Tancred, although he was able to secure a large money tribute from Tripoli.

When the crusade armies reached Jerusalem, Raymond took up a position on Mount Zion, from where he besieged the southwestern sector of the city. When Jerusalem fell on 15 July 1099, he took the surrender of the Fāṭimid garrison in the Tower of David and had them escorted back to Ascalon. Raymond had hoped to be made ruler of Jerusalem,

but eventually abandoned his claims, although he tried (in vain) to keep the Tower of David. He joined with Godfrey to repel the great Fāṭimid invasion of August 1099, and after the crusader victory outside Ascalon (12 August), the inhabitants of that city offered to surrender it to him; yet when Godfrey refused to accept this, Raymond withdrew, encouraging the Ascalonites to resist. He did the same at Arsuf, thus revealing his disappointment at being thwarted in his territorial ambitions in Palestine.

At the end of the summer of 1099, Raymond went north with crusaders who were returning home, although he had vowed to devote the rest of his life to the defense of the Holy City. He found Laodikeia in Syria (a city which he had previously restored to Byzantium) under siege by Bohemund I of Antioch and the Pisan followers of the papal legate Daibert; he forced them to withdraw and installed his own forces in the city. In the summer of 1100 Raymond traveled to Constantinople, and the next year he joined the Lombard army, which had arrived as part of the Crusade of 1101. Against Raymond's advice, the Lombards marched into the north of Anatolia, only to be defeated by the Turks at Mersivan. Raymond fled to Constantinople, abandoning the Holy Lance in the rout.

While attempting to return to Syria, Raymond was apprehended and imprisoned by the Normans of Antioch. The regent Tancred agreed to release him on condition that he would not attempt to take territory in the region of Antioch, and his followers abandoned Laodikeia, Albara, and the neighboring places. Raymond and his troops marched south with the survivors of the Crusade of 1101, capturing Tortosa (mod. Tartūs, Syria) on 18 February 1102 and inflicting a defeat upon the allied Muslim forces of Tripoli, Homs, and Damascus. Abandoning the aim of returning to Jerusalem, he proceeded to occupy the region of Tripoli instead, seizing Raphanea (mod. Rafanīyah, Syria), which threatened Homs. In order to blockade the city of Tripoli, he constructed a castle with Byzantine assistance, which he named Mont-Pèlerin. He took the title "count of Tripoli," founding several religious institutions around the castle, and on 28 April 1104 captured Gibelet to the south of the city. At the end of 1104, however, the Tripolitans attacked Mont-Pèlerin, and although they were repulsed, Raymond was severely wounded. Alphonse-Jordan, the only one of his sons with him in the East, was still a minor, and so Raymond entrusted the command of his troops to his cousin William-Jordan, count of Cerdagne; the relics he had accumulated were bequeathed to the abbey of La Chaise Dieu. Raymond died on 28 February 1105.

–Jean Richard

Bibliography

France, John, "The Departure of Tatikios from the Crusader Army," *Bulletin of the Institute of Historical Research* 44 (1971), 137–148.

Hiestand, Rudolf, "Saint-Ruf d'Avignon, Raymond de Saint-Gilles et l'église latine de Tripoli," *Annales du Midi* 96 (1986), 327–336.

Hill, John H., and Laurita L. Hill, *Raymond IV, Count of Toulouse* (Syracuse, NY: Syracuse University Press, 1962).

Richard, Jean, "Note sur l'archidiocèse d'Apamée et les conquêtes de Raymond de Saint-Gilles en Syrie du Nord," *Syria* 25 (1946–1948), 103–108.

———, "Le chartrier de Sainte-Marie Latine et l'établissement de Raymond de Saint-Gilles à Mont-Pèlerin," in *Mélanges d'histoire dédiés à la mémoire de Louis Halphen* (Paris: Presses Universitaires de France, 1951), pp. 605–612.

Riley-Smith, Jonathan, "Raymond IV of St Gilles, Achard of Arles and the Conquest of Lebanon," in *The Crusades and Their Sources: Essays Presented to Bernard Hamilton,* ed. John France and William G. Zajac (Aldershot, UK: Ashgate, 1998), pp. 1–8.

Reconquista

Only since the nineteenth century has the Christian conquest of the Iberian Peninsula from Muslim control been referred to as the *Reconquista,* that is, "reconquest." This has led some scholars to consider the term to be a modern attempt to justify colonization and subjugation by conferring supposedly higher values on the Christian expansion of the Middle Ages. Contemporary evidence does, however, show that the notion of regaining lost political and religious unity was indeed present among some Iberian Christians during the early Middle Ages: at the end of the ninth century, the memory of the vanished Visigothic kingdom was kept alive and its reestablishment propagated through a series of chronicles written during the reign of King Alfonso III of Asturias (866–910) by churchmen probably associated with his court. This Asturian "Neogothism" was an important basis for the Christian expansion of the tenth and eleventh centuries. It caused the borders to Islam to be regarded as only provisional and areas of future expansion to be repeatedly marked out by way of contracts between Christian powers.

The concept of Neogothism (of which the Muslims were aware, as Arab chronicles show) was only rarely linked to the notion of spiritually meritorious warfare. However, some early sources do exist, in which the Reconquista was justified on a religious basis. In certain Asturian and Leonese chronicles of the tenth and eleventh centuries, the conflict is presented as projected and thereby sanctified by God, as a fight to restore an incomplete ecclesiastical order, since the areas to be conquered had been Christian territories with a fully developed church structure before the Muslim conquest. According to these works, victories were attributable to God's care for his people, and Iberian Christians were associated with the Chosen People of the Old Testament. Until the end of the eleventh century, this opinion does not seem to have been common enough to have strongly influenced actions in the religious borderlands, nor did it attract foreign arms bearers to the Iberian Peninsula. The fronts were not as clearly laid out as often depicted: local rulers, whether Muslims or Christians, formed alliances in changing coalitions, and religion often played a secondary role. Christian rulers frequently preferred Muslim tribute payments (Sp. *parias*) to warfare, as Muslim chronicles clearly demonstrate. Only toward the end of the eleventh century did the notion of a sanctified, meritorious war on behalf of Christ against the Lord's foes, combined with the concept of the restoration of the Visigothic kingdom, begin to exert a strong influence on Christian actions. It was not until the beginning of the twelfth century that the Reconquista became a crusade, although even then cases of interreligious alliances and coexistence persisted.

The Reconquista should thus not be understood as an incessant religious war, but rather as a sequence of long periods of peace interrupted by shorter periods of crisis that were marked in varying degrees by religious ideals. Only the border zones were marked by frequent raids and devastation. Nor were Spain and Portugal formed out of the crucible of interreligious strife, although that strife did set the Iberian realms apart from most of Latin Europe.

Islamic Conquest and the Christian Realms of Iberia

The year 711 represents a turning point in the history of the Iberian Peninsula. In the early summer a Muslim army under Ṭāriq ibn Ziyād crossed the Strait of Gibraltar and defeated the Visigoths in the battle of Guadalete on 23 July 711. The invaders, mostly Arabs and islamized North Africans, rapidly succeeded in conquering nearly the entire Iberian Peninsula. The Muslims called the area they con-

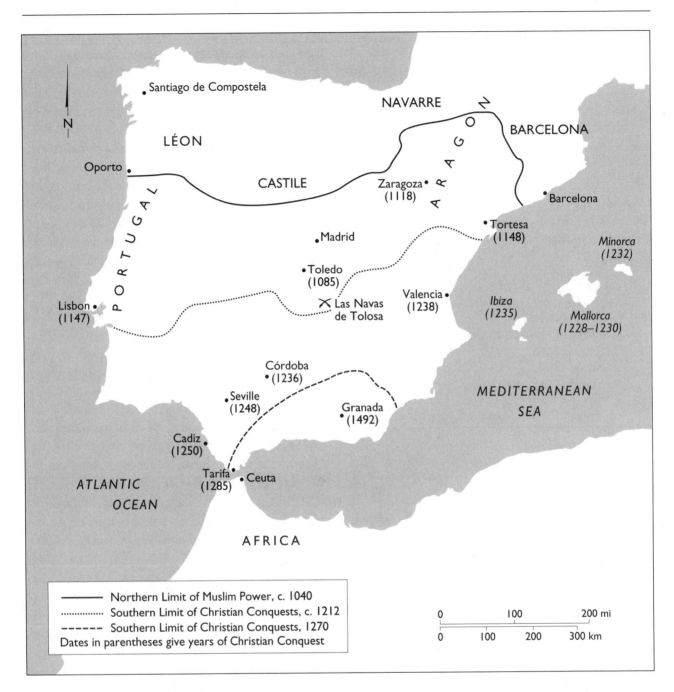

Progress of the Reconquista in Iberia

trolled al-Andalus ("Land of the Vandals") and raised the ancient bishopric of Córdoba to be the capital of their own emirate. With time the distance between this realm and the caliphate of Baghdad grew, and in the year 929 Emir 'Abd al-Raḥmān III (912–961) proclaimed the independent caliphate of Córdoba. The realm was far from homogenous: there were areas with a predominantly Berber and others with a mainly Arab Muslim population, and even within these communities one can define separate groups. Many Jews also lived in the peninsula, and the majority of the population, the subjected Christians (Mozarabs), may also be divided into the descendants of the Visigoths and of the Hispano-Romans.

Only the mountainous, inaccessible border zones in the extreme north of the peninsula remained under Christian rule. Here, five Christian realms developed between the eighth and the eleventh centuries: (1) In the area of Asturias–Cantabria, the kings of Asturias led the exiled Visigothic nobility. Toward the middle of the eighth century they expanded their rule to the west (Galicia) and east (Álava), and by the end of the following century they had crossed the river Duero (Port. Douro) in the south and conquered the town of León, to which the center of the realm, afterward known as the kingdom of León, shifted. (2) At its southeastern flank, the county of Castile gradually slipped from the control of the Leonese kings. By the beginning of the eleventh century, it had become fully established as an independent kingdom. (3) Further east, Navarre also developed into a principality of its own, which was ruled by kings from the beginning of the tenth century onward. (4) Aragon, once a county dependent on Navarre, escaped its control, rising to the status of kingdom after 1035. (5) The last of the five Christian realms was the county of Barcelona. It had been part of the Carolingian Empire, whose southern border it formed, together with a number of other Catalonian counties. In the course of the eleventh century, the count of Barcelona succeeded in becoming the dominant power of the southeastern Pyrenees.

These five realms—León, Castile, Navarra, Aragon, and Barcelona—experienced transformations during the High Middle Ages. On the one hand, the dynastic union between the rulers of Barcelona and Aragon (1137) brought forth the Crown of Aragon (or Aragonese-Catalan Crown). On the other hand, the county of Portugal became independent of León and achieved the rank of a kingdom in 1143. And finally, after a short-lived union (1038–1157), Castile and León were united once and for all in 1230. The existence of four independent kingdoms (Portugal, Castile-León, Navarre, and Aragon) impedes any general account of the "Spanish" history of the Middle Ages. Only with this complicated situation in mind can one attempt to describe the complex process known as *Reconquista*.

The Opening of the Reconquest to Non-Iberian Combatants

Until the second half of the eleventh century, the Christians' disputes with the Muslims were still a largely Iberian affair marked by the "neogothic" concept of reconquest, by limited religious zeal, and by border skirmishes of uncertain outcome. At the turn of the first millennium, the vizier and general al-Manṣūr billāh (Sp. *Almanzor*) achieved important military successes, but after his death (1002), the caliphate of Córdoba collapsed and disintegrated (1009–1031) into a number of petty Muslim realms (the so-called Taifa kingdoms). Some of these polities fought the Christians, while others preferred to sign treaties or make payments of tribute in return for peace. By so doing, these latter may have ultimately helped finance their own destruction, but the *parias* also show the synchronicity of coexistence and conflict typical for this period. In general the Christian frontier continued to expand south, and on 6 May 1085 King Alfonso VI of Castile-León succeeded in taking the old Visigothic capital, Toledo, without bloodshed by guaranteeing wide-ranging rights (which were soon abrogated) to the Muslim population. The historical figure who best represents the complexities of the Iberian eleventh century is Rodrigo Díaz de Vivar (d. 1099), better known to the modern world as El Cid. A vassal of Sancho II and Alfonso VI of Castile, Rodrigo fought against Christians, became involved in disputes between the Muslim rulers of Seville and Granada, and supported the Muslims of Zaragoza against the Christian king of Aragon. In 1094 he gained power over the Muslim town of Valencia, where he established an independent principality, which he successfully defended against attacks by Muslim opponents. The story of the Cid Campeador (from Arab. *sayyid,* "lord," and Lat. *campi doctor,* "victorious fighter") is only one example of the possibilities that the frontiers of the Iberian Peninsula offered to militarily and politically capable figures.

At this time, however, the struggle also began to draw Christians from beyond the Pyrenees. This change occurred for several reasons: increasing dynastic and feudal ties between the ruling Iberian lineages and noblemen from beyond the Pyrenees; the rising significance of Santiago de Compostela in Galicia as a center of pilgrimage that attracted a constantly growing stream of people, particularly from the eleventh century onward; and the papacy's mounting interest in the Iberian Peninsula. For a long time, the Roman church's influence was limited to the Carolingian-dominated eastern Pyrenees. But in the second half of the eleventh century, the zone widened: in 1064 for the first time, a notable contingent of French knights took part in the siege and conquest of an Aragonese town, Barbastro. Pope Alexander II supported this action by promising indulgences and depicting the siege as a war intended and justified by God. In 1068 the kingdom of Aragon placed itself under the protection of the Holy See and accepted the Roman liturgy. Soon Castile, León, and Navarre also followed the Roman rite, and prelates close to Rome took over important ecclesiastical functions after the conquest of Toledo. But the victory of 1085 also had unexpected military consequences: the hard-pressed Muslims called in co-religionists from the North African mainland to assist them: the Almoravids (Arab. *al-Murābiṭūn*), zealous Berbers particularly committed to the idea of religious warfare. On 23 October 1086 they gained a sweeping victory over Alfonso VI's forces at Sagrajas and soon thereafter began taking possession of al-Andalus. By 1095 they had conquered practically all the Taifa kingdoms in the peninsula; El Cid's Valencia also fell victim to their expansion (1102). An era in the history of the Iberian Peninsula had come to an end. That period had been marked by the predominantly secular and political character of the Reconquista. Now the logic of warfare became more dominated by religious issues on both sides, and the fronts hardened.

With the expansion of the Almoravids in Iberia (1085–1095), the second phase of the *Reconquista* began. It brought a religiously loaded form of warfare to al-Andalus that also affected Christian concepts and actions. The popes' commitment increased, and growing numbers of foreign arms bearers crossed the Pyrenees in order to fight against the Muslims. Some of them later took part in the First Crusade (1096–1099). Various factors caused the strangers to participate in the struggle, such as hope for booty or land, political considerations, and feudal ties to Iberian rulers. But the fights were also an expression of growing tensions between Islam and Christianity, which were being particularly aggravated on the Iberian Peninsula and which began to transcend the Pyrenees.

Reconquista and Crusade

During this period at the end of the eleventh century, at least some elements of the crusade movement become recognizable in the Iberian Peninsula: the religious nature of the struggle was stressed, the papacy's participation increased, indulgences were conferred, and foreign armed forces participated in the fighting. The situation in the Iberian Peninsula seems to have had a particularly strong effect on the papacy's attitude toward the use of force against Islam. The Iberian experience, however, neither led directly to the proclamation of the First Crusade, nor was it a crusade in its own right. Some of the latter's constitutive elements were still absent, such as the crusading vow, the taking of the cross, or the plenary indulgence (Lat. *remissio peccatorum*). At least regarding the indulgence, however, an important step was taken even before the conquest of Jerusalem: between 1096 and 1099, Pope Urban II specifically promised the Christians who contributed to the reestablishment of the Catalan town of Tarragona the *remissio peccatorum*. The conjunction between the fight against the Muslims and the plenary indulgence was thus first established in Iberia. In contrast, other features of the crusades entered the Iberian Peninsula as a result of the events in the Middle East. In the year 1101, for example, King Peter I of Aragon rallied his forces under the banner of the cross (Lat. *vexillum crucis*) when he fought against the Muslims before Zaragoza, where he named a locality after the war cry of the First Crusaders (*Júslibol*, after Lat. *Deus vult*, "God wills it").

In 1114, the Christians who participated in the conquest of the Balearic Islands were promised indulgences; a papal legate accompanied the expedition; and the participants marked themselves with the sign of the cross. During the conquest of Zaragoza under Alfonso I (the Battler) in the year 1118, foreign combatants were also called upon to assist their co-religionists and were promised indulgences. By this time at the latest, the Iberian wars had taken on the quality of a crusade, at least in the eyes of the papacy and the foreign combatants. It was only logical that in 1121 the arms bearers in Spain were explicitly assured identical indulgences to those of the crusaders in the Holy Land, and at the First Lateran Council of 1123, regulations were applied to those who took the cross to go to either Jerusalem or to Spain. In the Iberian Peninsula, too, the first crusade bull was issued in order to recruit new contingents. Almost at the same time as the establishment of the military orders in Outremer, military confraternities were founded in Aragon (Belchite, Monreal), which combined a form of life under monastic rules with warfare against the Muslims. Thus one can observe mutual influences between the Levant and the Iberian Peninsula. Both were seen as crusading areas.

Literary texts also contributed to fashioning and promoting the idea of Reconquista as crusade. Twelfth-century works like the *Chanson de Roland*, the *Rolandslied des Pfaffen Konrad*, and the so-called Pseudo-Turpin (*Historia Karoli Magni et Rotolandi*) represented the eighth-century Iberian campaign of the Emperor Charlemagne as a crusade, and a series of chansons de geste (epic poems) praised the feats of the Christians *in Hispania*. Only a few Hispanic sources, however, point to an authentic crusading ideal within the Iberian Christian population. This is hardly surprising: the same also applies to the inhabitants of Outremer after the establishment of the crusader kingdoms. For the local Christians, the struggle acquired the character of border warfare, marked by short incursions and raids. The Reconquista's domestic dimension was also the reason why Iberian Christian rulers apparently felt few reservations about concluding alliances with Muslims against co-religionists or treating the Muslim inhabitants of conquered towns honorably. Christian mercenaries fought for Muslim rulers, and the Iberian frontier was in many senses more permeable than many later historians would assert. The inconsistencies between crusading ideologies, political interests, and economic considerations are recurring elements of the Reconquista, which often antagonized foreign crusaders. Nevertheless, during important campaigns in particular, crusade propaganda and crusading enthusiasm can even be detected in the Iberian sources.

Particularly substantial participation of foreign crusaders occurred in the years 1147–1148 as a result of the diverse elements that made up the Second Crusade. At the same time as an attack on the Muslim state of Damascus launched from the kingdom of Jerusalem and a campaign against the pagan Slavs (Wends) beyond the river Elbe, the Iberian kings undertook a series of offensives against the weakened Almoravid Empire. In Portugal, Lisbon was taken in October 1147; in the same month the Castilian king conquered the important port of Almería; and shortly afterward (December 1148 and October 1149), the Taifas of Tortosa and Lleida (Lérida) capitulated to the Aragonese-Catalan ruler Count Raymond Berengar IV (1131–1162). For these campaigns, the monarchs sought and received the assistance of foreign contingents: the conquest of Lisbon was achieved thanks to the aid received by Afonso Henriques I of Portugal (1128–1185) from crusaders from England and the Rhineland on their way to the Holy Land. Some of the English crusaders participated in the conquest of Tortosa several months later; they were further supported by a Genoese fleet, which was crucial for the success of the enterprise. Certainly the campaigns of 1147–1148 represented the high point of foreign participation in the Reconquista.

During the following decades, the Iberian monarchs ensured that the influence of external forces diminished. This policy represents a substantial difference between the crusades in the Levant and those of the Iberian Peninsula: while the Franks of the East, few in number relative to the native population, actively sought and urgently required the assistance of their western co-religionists, the Iberian Christians did not depend on external support to a comparable degree. Foreign rulers did undertake crusading initiatives to Spain, including King Louis VII of France and King Henry II of England, who planned a joint expedition to the Iberian Peninsula in 1159. Nonnative crusaders also took part in several later campaigns (for example, in 1189 in Silves in Portugal, in 1212 leading to Las Navas de Tolosa, in 1217 in Alcácer do Sal in Portugal, and in 1309 at Gibraltar). But it is telling that the initiative of 1159 did not prosper, due to the fact that it was not coordinated with the native monarchs, who closely monitored later foreign activities. The many military orders founded during this period in the Iberian Peninsula (Calatrava, Alcántara, Santiago, et al.) helped keep alive the crusading ideal and undoubtedly included international elements; but they soon became strongly nationalized institutions and decidedly Iberian in scope. Thus the Reconquista's international resonance cannot be likened to that of the Eastern crusades, although this in no way contradicts the fact that the Iberian Peninsula was a crusading theater.

The Rise of the Almohads and the Reconquest of the Thirteenth to Fifteenth Centuries

By the late twelfth century, a new change of power had occurred in al-Andalus: the Almoravids were displaced by the Almohads (Arab. *al-Muwaḥḥidūn*). These were Sunnī reformers like the Almoravids, but belonged to a different Berber tribe. They were particularly critical of the Almoravids, whom they accused of religious laxity and error. By 1148 Morocco was subjugated with extreme violence, and by 1172 al-Andalus had also been conquered. The Almohads achieved their most important military success against the Christians on 9 July 1195 on the battlefield of Alarcos against the troops of Alfonso VIII of Castile (d. 1214). This defeat led the Christians to bury their internal disputes and take common action against the Muslims. They received strong support from Pope Innocent III, who promulgated crusade bulls in favor of the campaign and ordered both processions and prayers to be held far and wide. As a result, a substantial contingent of foreign (above all French) warriors enlarged the united armies led by the kings of Castile, Aragon, and Navarre. Although most of these crusaders withdrew their support when they were kept from plundering the castles that had capitulated, the local Christians triumphed over the Almohad army at Las Navas de Tolosa on 16 July 1212.

After this battle, the Muslims of al-Andalus were never again to achieve a major military success. For this reason Las Navas de Tolosa has been seen as a final turning point in the history of the Reconquista, even if this was hardly apparent to contemporaries. In fact, the expansion slowed down for a short period due to the untimely death of several of the chief political players. Also, Pope Innocent III attempted in 1213 to detach the Reconquista from the crusades to the East by breaking with the tradition of equating both struggles. But after a series of smaller campaigns of lesser importance, the expansion (once again fostered by papal indulgences) gathered momentum in the 1230s. Under King Ferdinand III, the Castilians conquered the most important Andalusian cities, among them Córdoba (1236) and Seville (1248). In the Aragonese-Catalan Crown, King James I the Conqueror (d. 1276) reaped similar successes: in 1228 the island of Mallorca was occupied; in 1238 the town of Valencia fell; and by 1235 and 1246, respectively, the Balearic Islands and the kingdom of Valencia had been subjugated. In Portugal the advance reached the coast of the Algarve by the year 1248. In barely twenty years, therefore, the realms of Portugal, Castile, and Aragon-Catalonia had nearly completed the conquest of al-Andalus. Only in the mountainous area around the Sierra Nevada in the extreme south could a Muslim lordship, the kingdom of Granada governed by the Naṣrid dynasty, remain intact, albeit as a vassal state to the kingdom of Castile. For over two centuries it maintained its position between the Muslim Marīnids in the south and the Christians in the north.

In the first half of the fourteenth century, the Reconquista flared up once more: an Aragonese-Castilian army wrested Gibraltar from the Marīnids in 1309, and on 30 October 1340 a Portuguese-Castilian force achieved an important victory at the river Salado. Foreign crusaders participated in both campaigns, thus acquiring crusading indulgences, and even in later decades, Christians repeatedly crossed the Pyrenees in order to fight the Muslims. But in the meantime these expeditions were strongly (though never exclusively) marked by chivalrous and courtly ideals. To many knights of the fourteenth and fifteenth centuries, honor and adventure counted just as much as the welfare of their souls. After the kingdoms of Aragon and Castile united under the joint rule of the Catholic Kings (Ferdinand II and Isabella I) in 1469, the kingdom of Granada, the last Muslim realm on Iberian soil, was subjugated in a ten-year war. With its fall on 2 January 1492 the Reconquista was ended. However, the idea lived on and served to justify the Spanish expansion to America.

Settlement and Interreligious Contacts

From a very early period, the Reconquista was accompanied by activities of colonization known as *repoblación* (resettlement). The majority of the settlers—Mozarabs from al-Andalus or co-religionists from the northern areas—came from the Iberian Peninsula, while foreigners, mostly Frenchmen, became established especially along the pilgrimage route to Santiago de Compostela. In several waves, the Christians moved into the conquered areas in the course of the eleventh to thirteenth centuries, attracted by liberal privileges included in the local law codes (Sp. *fueros*) conferred by the Christian monarchs. These zones were more or less densely inhabited by local Muslim and, to a far lesser degree, by Jewish communities. These newly subject populations were treated in very much the same way as in Outremer. In both areas, the treatment of the non-Christians was not tolerant in the modern sense but rather pragmatic. The frequently used Spanish term *convivencia* (that is, cohabitation, the peaceful coexistence of different religions in one territory) suggests a higher level of cooperation and exchange than the sources reveal. *Conveniencia* (convenience) better describes the interests that lay at the heart of religious coexistence both in Outremer and in the Iberian Peninsula. The Jews and even more so the Muslims under Christian rule (Mudéjars) were relegated to second-class status: they were required to pay a poll tax, were not permitted to carry weapons, and were obliged to dwell in special quarters. In Andalusia, for example, the subjected Muslims had to leave the cities, and their houses were distributed among the victors in the so-called *repartimiento* (repartition). Still, the Muslims of the Iberian Peninsula were mostly allowed to follow their religion and were granted personal safety and limited self-rule. Thus Muslims and Jews appear as subjects with specific (though repeatedly ignored) rights. Just as in Outremer, mission played a subordinated role in Iberia; however, legal restrictions and constant Christian pressure did lead to gradual acculturation and syncretism. Despite this tendency toward absorption, considerable Jewish and Muslim communities still existed at the end of the Reconquista in the year 1492. They fell victim to the Catholic Monarchs' zeal for confessional unity. Those Jews who did not convert to Christianity were expelled in 1492, and the Mudéjars were obliged to accept baptism shortly later. In the year 1609, the Christian descendants of former Muslims, known as Moriscos, were expelled from Spain.

–Nikolas Jaspert

Bibliography

Barbero, Aníbal, and Marcelo Vigil, *Sobre los orígenes sociales de la Reconquista* (Barcelona: Ariel, 1984).

Bishko, Charles J., "The Spanish and Portuguese Reconquest (1095–1492)," in *A History of the Crusades,* ed. Kenneth M. Setton, 6 vols. (Madison: University of Wisconsin Press, 1955), 1:396–457.

Bronisch, Alexander, *Reconquista und Heiliger Krieg: Die Deutung des Krieges im christlichen Spanien von den Westgoten bis ins frühe 12. Jahrhundert* (Münster: Aschendorff, 1998).

Bull, Marcus, *Knightly Piety and the Lay Response to the First Crusade: The Limousin and Gascony (ca. 970–1130)* (Oxford: Oxford University Press, 1993).

Burns, Robert I., "The Many Crusades of Valencia's Conquest, 1225–1289: An Historiographical Labyrinth," in *On the Social Origins of Medieval Institutions: Essays in Honor of Joseph F. O'Callaghan,* ed. Donald J. Kagay and Theresa M. Vann (Leiden: Brill, 1998), pp. 168–177.

Engels, Odilo, *Reconquista und Landesherrschaft: Studien zur Rechts- und Verfassungsgeschichte Spaniens im Mittelalter* (Paderborn: Aschendorff, 1989).

Henriet, Patrick, "L'idéologie de Guerre Sainte dans le haut Moyen Age hispanique," *Francia* 29 (2002), 171–220.

Goñi Gaztambide, José, *Historia de la bula de la cruzada en España* (Vitoria: Editorial del Seminario, 1958).

González Jiménez, Manuel, "Re-conquista? Un estado de la cuestión," in *Tópicos y realidades de la Edad Media,* ed. Eloy Benito Ruano (Madrid: Real Academia de Historia, 2000), pp. 155–172.

Jaspert, Nikolas, "Frühformen der geistlichen Ritterorden und die Kreuzzugsbewegung auf der Iberischen Halbinsel," in *Europa in der späten Salierzeit: Beiträge zu Ehren von Werner Goez,* ed. Klaus Herbers (Stuttgart: Steiner, 2001), pp. 90–116.

The Legacy of Muslim Spain, ed. Salma Khadra Jayyusi (Leiden: Brill, 1994).

Lomax, Derek, *The Reconquest of Spain* (London: Longman, 1978).

Martín Rodríguez, José Luis, "Reconquista y cruzada," *Studia Zamorensia,* ser. 2, 3 (1996), 215–241.

O'Callaghan, Joseph F., *Reconquest and Crusade in Medieval Spain* (Philadelphia: University of Pennsylvania Press, 2002).

Reilly, Bernard F., *The Medieval Spains* (Cambridge: Cambridge University Press 1988).

Recovery of the Holy Land

The loss of Christian Jerusalem to Saladin (1187) and even more so, the capture of Acre (mod. 'Akko, Israel) by the Mamlūks (1291) brought forth numerous projects intended to bring about the recovery of the Holy Land. These projects eventually gave rise to a new genre of crusade literature, namely memoranda or treatises "concerning the recovery of the Holy Land" (Lat. *de recuperatione Terrae Sanctae*).

Planning, often lasting years, had long been an essential preparation for crusades. However, it was only on the eve of the Second Council of Lyons (1274) that written plans or proposals appeared for the first time. This new development was a result of the bull of summons to the council, *Salvator noster* (31 March 1272), in which Pope Gregory X asked for suggestions as to how to keep the Holy Land once it was regained and restored. Some of the copies of the bull also contained a request for written advice concerning the planned crusade. The memoirs submitted to the council dealt little with the strategy of a crusade, but mainly with subjects such as its ideology, preaching, and financing. Those who did provide some advice on strategy, Humbert of Romans and Gilbert of Tournai, both supported the idea of small successive expeditions to the Holy Land, or "perpetual crusade" (Lat. *passagium particulare*), and opposed the traditional strategy of a large, general expedition (Lat. *passagium generale*). On the whole, crusade planning in this initial stage reflects a new strategy, whose main features were the creation of a permanent garrison in Outremer and the launching of small manageable expeditions, manned by professional soldiers, which would periodically succeed each other in the East.

Though the strategy advocated at the Second Council of Lyons marks the beginnings of a new period in crusade planning, it lacked some features that became popular after 1291. For example, the council made very little of European sea power as an important factor in any war against Islam. Gregory X was informed by experts such as William of Beaujeu, master of the Temple, and Humbert of Romans (and possibly Fidenzio of Padua) of the weakness of the Mamlūk sultanate at sea, but he envisaged a fleet of only 20 ships to be used solely for the crusade. It was therefore only after the fall of Acre, the last Christian possession in Palestine (1291), that the idea of an economic blockade of the Mamlūk ports was coupled with that of a special maritime police and of a *passagium particulare*. Also conspicuously absent from the crusade planning of Lyons II was the plan of the conquest of Egypt as the key to the reconquest of the Holy Land, even though this route had been pursued by crusades in the past. A written statement of this strategy appeared on the eve of the fall of Acre in *La Devise des chemins de Babiloine*, a military memoir addressed to the West by the Order of the Hospital (1289/1291).

One of the unintended results of the loss of the Holy Land in 1291 and the vigorous crusade policy of Pope Nicholas VI (1288–1292) was the inauguration of a new epoch in crusade literature. His request for advice (in the absence of a general council) stimulated the creation of a new branch of literature, the *de recuperatione Terrae Sanctae* memoranda. This new genre had much in common with previous crusade treatises such as those of Humbert of Romans or Gilbert of Tournai. Yet there is a meaningful difference between them. The early treatises may be described as working papers submitted for conciliar discussions and therefore mainly concerned with such topics as the ideology, preaching, and organization of the crusade. The memoranda composed after 1291 were practical guidelines, and, as such, were largely concerned with general strategy as well as with detailed plans to be followed. They reflect a new attitude to the crusade. As their authors were usually familiar with the strategy of war, the memoirs tended to transform the crusade into a minutely planned expedition.

The authors of the *de recuperatione* treatises can be divided into two major groups. The first consisted of people who had spent some time in the Levant and thus were recognized as experts: they included Fidenzio of Padua, Charles II of Anjou, Marino Sanudo Torsello, Philippe de Mézières, Emmanuel Piloti, Bertrandon de la Broquière, Giovanni Dominelli, and various masters of the military orders. Their treatises are characterized by their secular, highly professional, and practical strategic concepts of the crusade. The second group consisted of Europeans less acquainted with the Levant, who were often (but not always) sincerely interested in the promotion of a crusade, and were often writing at the request of a pope or a monarch. They included Ramon Llull, Pierre Dubois, William of Nogaret, Galvano of Levanto, William Durant, and William le Maire. Their treatises are more theoretical and pay more attention to the financial and European aspects of the crusade. As most of the authors in this group were churchmen, they gave special attention to the religious and sometimes missionary issues.

Three crusade plans written during the pontificate of Nicholas IV inaugurated the new trend in crusade planning and expressed the main features of crusade planning after 1291. Composed by the Franciscan Fidenzio of Padua, Ramon Llull, and Charles II of Anjou, king of Naples, they envisaged that Jerusalem would be won on the battlefields of Egypt, and thus returned to the thirteenth-century tradition. Whether they favored land or sea routes, none suggested a direct attack on the Holy Land, but proposed the establishment of bases from which a final attack should be launched after a blockade of Egypt. It was Christendom's naval power and its supremacy on the seas that would assure this victory.

Pope Clement V (1305–1314) announced his intention to organize a crusade in the encyclical that proclaimed his coronation. This announcement produced a number of treatises during his pontificate. With the exception of that of James of Molay, master of the Temple, they all focused on a maritime blockade of Egypt. The most influential was one formulated in the East (between September 1306 and summer 1307), possibly by Fulk of Villaret, master of the Hospital. It provided the plan of action for a papal-Hospitaller *passagium particulare*. Proclaimed on 12 August 1308, this *passagium* was seen by Clement V as intended to prepare, over a period of five years, the way for a general crusade by defending Cyprus and Cilicia and by preventing illegal commerce with the Muslims through a maritime blockade of Egypt. The expedition, consisting of 1,000 knights, 4,000 foot soldiers, and 40 galleys, was to depart on 24 June 1309. However, the project was only partly realized due to a lack of ships and funds. When it departed in the spring of 1310 it consisted only of some 26 galleys, 200–300 knights, and 3,000 foot soldiers. It assisted local Hospitallers in completing the conquest of Rhodes (mod. Rodos, Greece) and some of the adjacent islands, but failed to achieve its main aim: to stop illegal trade with the Mamlūk sultanate by means of a maritime blockade; its effect, therefore, on the military and economic standing of the Mamlūks was negligible. Another crusade that seems to have been organized according to a written plan was that of King Peter I of Cyprus, which culminated in the temporary capture of Alexandria (1365).

By 1336 the common features of crusade planning were the establishment of a general peace in Europe, the reform or unification of the military orders, an alliance with the Mongols, and the blockade of Egypt by forces of a *passagium particulere* as a necessary prologue to what was to become the grand finale—the general crusade. The years 1290–1336 were the golden age of the literary genre of the *de recuperatione Terrae Sanctae*. Its decline thereafter can be explained mainly as a result of the Hundred Years' War. However, new ideas still appeared. The contribution of Philippe de Mézières to crusade planning in his *Songe du vieil Pèlerin* (1389) was the conception of a new order of chivalry that should supersede all others and if possible incorporate them. In his opinion, the older orders had failed to accomplish their chief aim, the recovery of the Holy Land. In order to eliminate their vices, a new order was to be founded. It was to be an example of perfection, so that all might purify their actions from vices and shape their lives on its model. The new order was intended not only for the recovery of the Holy Land, but also its retention in Christian hands. It had to include all the knights and men-at-arms of Christendom in one large and holy fellowship. It was intended first of all to purify the West from all the evils that prevailed in it. This having been achieved, the new body would proceed to a preparatory campaign, which corresponds to the *passagium parvum* or *passagium particulare* suggested by other crusade planners. Then the *passagium generale* would follow, under the leadership of the kings of England and France, with every assurance of success in the conquest of the Holy Land.

The disastrous Crusade of Nikopolis (1396) marked the end of the crusades as an organized movement of Christendom against Islam for the deliverance of the Holy Land. In the tumult of new movements and a modern age, by the end of the fifteenth century the crusade for the salvation of the Holy Land sank into oblivion. Now and again projects to revive the holy war against the Ottoman Turks did emerge.

In 1515 Pope Leo X, King Francis I of France, and Emperor Maximilian I discussed a crusade, and Francis expressed his wish to lead a campaign for the reconquest of the Holy Land. Yet during the sixteenth century Western Christendom was so completely absorbed in the Reformation that the issue of the crusade was largely abandoned.

–*Sylvia Schein*

Bibliography
Atiya, Aziz S., *The Crusade in the Later Middle Ages* (London: Methuen, 1938).
Delaville le Roulx, Joseph, *La France en Orient au XIVe siècle: Expéditions du maréchal Boucicant* (Paris: Thorin, 1886).
Housley, Norman, *The Avignon Papacy and the Crusades, 1305–1378* (Oxford: Oxford University Press, 1986).
———, *The Later Crusades: From Lyons to Alcazar* (Oxford: Oxford University Press, 1992).
Jorga, N., *Philippe de Mézières, 1327–1405, et la croisade au XIVe siècle* (Paris: Bouillon, 1896).
———, "Un projet relatif à la conquête de Jérusalem, 1609," *Revue de l'Orient latin* 2 (1894), 183–189.
Kedar, Benjamin Z., and Sylvia Schein, "Un projet de "passage particulier" proposé par l'ordre de l'Hôpital 1306–1307," *Bibliothèque de l'Ecole des Chartes* 137 (1979), 211–226.
Leopold, Antony, "Crusading Proposals in the Fourteenth and Fifteenth Centuries," in *The Holy Land, Holy Lands, and Christian History*, ed. R. N. Swanson (Woodbridge, UK: Boydell, 2000), pp. 216–227.
———, *How to Recover the Holy Land: The Crusade Proposals of the Late Thirteenth and Early Fourteenth Centuries* (Aldershot, UK: Ashgate, 2000).
Schein, Sylvia, *Fideles Crucis: The Papacy, the West, and the Recovery of the Holy Land, 1274–1314* (Oxford: Oxford University Press, 1991).
Tyerman, Christopher J., *England and the Crusades, 1095–1588* (Chicago: University of Chicago Press, 1988).

Red Sea

During the period of the crusades, the Red Sea was a major artery for commerce and pilgrimage in the Islamic world, linking Egypt and North Africa with Arabia, East Africa, India, and the East Indies.

The Red Sea was a difficult route for navigation: classical geographers and travelers mention its erratic winds, currents, and hazards, while Muslim sources comment on the difficulties encountered in negotiating shallow waters, as well as the numerous rocks, coral reefs, and islands. Navigation from north to south was safest, and pilots would usually sail close to the shore and anchor at night. Sailing up the

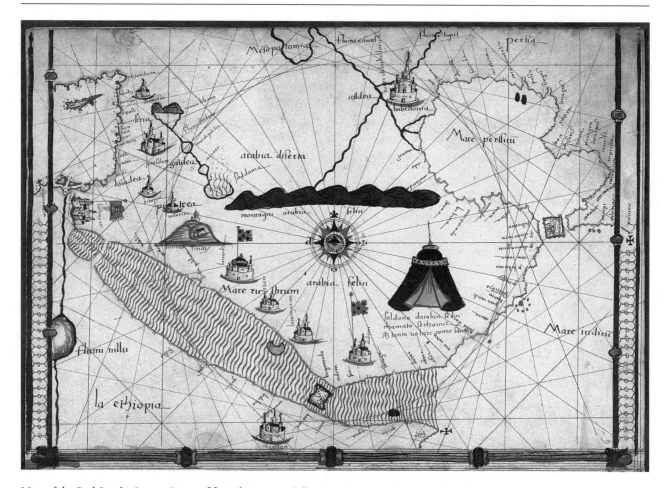

Map of the Red Sea, by Jacopo Russo, fifteenth century. (Alinari/Art Resource)

Red Sea against the prevailing wind was difficult, and because of this and irregular currents, ships from India and Africa rarely sailed to the northern end of the sea, but generally stopped at Jeddah in the Ḥijaz (western Arabia) and transshipped their goods on smaller local vessels for transport to the smaller ports on the Egyptian and Arabian coasts. As the port for Mecca, Jeddah also received considerable pilgrim traffic. The main Arab port town in the medieval period was ʻAydhāb on the western shore, which had an ideal position as a trade and pilgrimage center as it was located opposite Jeddah. ʻAydhāb was around 400 kilometers (250 mi.) (roughly 17–20 days' journey) from Qūṣ on the Nile, from where merchandise was transported by boat or pack animals to Lower Egypt. The port of Alexandria was the main point of contact with European Christian (mostly Italian) merchants, although much merchandise from the East (which included spices, textiles, and ceramics) also came by

land to ports in the Levant such as Acre (mod. ʻAkko, Israel), Tyre (mod. Soûr, Lebanon), and later, Ayas (mod. Yumurtalık, Turkey).

The first encounter of the Franks of Outremer with the Red Sea occurred in 1116 when King Baldwin I of Jerusalem led an expedition south as far as the head of the Gulf of ʻAqaba. The Franks established full control of this area by the second half of the twelfth century, fortifying the town of Aila and the nearby Ile de Graye (Pharaoh's Island). In 1161 it became part of the Frankish lordship of Transjordan, but was retaken by Saladin in 1170. The Gulf of ʻAqaba may have been used by some coastal shipping and fishing vessels, but it had no large-scale trade; the purpose of the Frankish occupation was to control the road, used by traders and pilrgrims, that went from Egypt through Sinai to the Hijaz. However, in late 1182 the lord of Transjordan, Reynald of Châtillon, had 5 prefabricated ships carried overland by camel from

Kerak (mod. Karak, Jordan) and assembled and launched in the gulf. In December 1182, 2 ships blockaded the Ile de Graye, while the others sailed south as far as 'Aydhāb, which they sacked, after having captured or destroyed 16 Muslim merchant ships, before crossing to the eastern shore.

This disruption to trade and pilgrimage unleashed panic in the Muslim world, which feared attacks on the holy cities of Medina and Mecca. As no naval forces were maintained by the Muslims in the Red Sea at that time, Saladin's brother al-'Ādil had a fleet of warships transported overland from Egypt, which broke the blockade of the Ile de Graye and hunted down the southern flotilla. The Franks, abandoning their ships and retreating inland, were defeated after a pursuit of five days (February 1183); Saladin had all prisoners executed in order to obliterate the Franks' knowledge of the sea's routes and navigation. Thereafter the Red Sea remained closed to Christian shipping until the appearance in the early sixteenth century of the Portuguese, who had reached the area via the Atlantic and the Indian Ocean.

–*Dionisius A. Agius and Alan V. Murray*

Bibliography

Abulafia, David, "The Role of Trade in Muslim-Christian Contact during the Middle Ages," in *The Arab Influence in Medieval Europe*, ed. Dionisius A. Agius and Richard Hitchcock (Reading, UK: Ithaca, 1994), pp. 1–24.

Hamilton, Bernard, *The Leper King and His Heirs: Baldwin IV and the Crusader Kingdom of Jerusalem* (Cambridge: Cambridge University Press, 2000).

Mayer, Hans Eberhard, *Die Kreuzfahrerherrschaft Montréal (Šōbak): Jordanien im 12. Jahrhundert* (Wiesbaden: Harrassowitz, 1990).

Tibbetts, G. R., *Arab Navigation in the Indian Ocean before the Coming of the Portuguese* (London: Royal Asiatic Society, 1971).

Relics: Constantinople

The extensive collection of relics in the city of Constantinople (mod. İstanbul, Turkey) when it was the capital of the Byzantine Empire made it a premier pilgrimage site, but in 1204 and shortly thereafter many of these sacred items were carried off as booty by the army of the Fourth Crusade (1202–1204).

Constantinople's relic wealth was well known in the West, as is witnessed by the twelfth-century French romantic epic *Le Pèlerinage de Charlemagne à Jerusalem et à Constantinople*, but there is no evidence to support the thesis that the cru-

saders decided to assault the city to gain its relics. Once they had secured the city, however, soldiers and clerics alike participated in widespread despoliation of Byzantium's churches.

The pillagers included Robert of Clari, who provides a wide-eyed account of Constantinople's relics in his chronicle *La Conquête de Constantinople*. Robert claims that in March 1204, when the crusaders realized that they would have to take the city again (this time for themselves), they swore upon relics that they would not break into any church or monastery. Abundant evidence makes it clear that these oaths proved ineffective in staying the hands of many crusaders from looting relics. Robert himself donated to the monastery of Corbie a crystal cross reliquary taken from Constantinople.

Robert's theft of relics was minor compared to that of the crusade's highest-ranking clerics. The booty of the crusade's chief prelate, Nivelon, bishop of Soissons, included the heads of seven saints (John the Baptist; the apostles Thomas, Thaddeus, and James; and saints Stephen, Blasius, and Dionysius the Areopagite) and the crown of St. Mark's head. Not to be outdone, Conrad, bishop of Halberstadt, collected a piece of the skull of St. John the Baptist and the head of James, the brother of Jesus, as well as major pieces of the apostles Peter, Paul, Andrew, Simon, Philip, and Barnabas. A portion of the head of John the Baptist also found its way into the hands of Doge Enrico Dandolo, who donated it to the church of St. Mark in Venice.

Although proud of their treasures, few of the pious thieves admitted their larceny. A Greek source charged Bishop Conrad with stealing relics, but at home Conrad publicly stated that all his relics were gifts from Emperor Alexios IV Angelos and various churchmen (presumably Byzantine ecclesiastics). Conceivably Conrad had received some relics from Alexios IV prior to January 1204 as a reward for his support of the young man's claim to the throne, but there is no reason to believe that Bishop Conrad did not participate in the general rush to collect purloined relics after the city fell to the crusaders. An exception to this cover-up was Martin of Pairis. Gunther of Pairis celebrated in prose and verse his abbot's pilfering of relics, justifying it on the grounds that the Greeks did not deserve to possess these sacred treasures because of their errors and sins. Martin had much to celebrate, inasmuch as he had brought back to his monastery numerous relics, including a trace of the Sacred Blood and a large piece of John the Baptist.

With all of this thievery, it is a wonder that Constantinople had any relics left after 1204, but it did, and they were still avidly sought. In 1238–1239 and 1241, the financially strapped Baldwin II, Latin emperor of Constantinople, sold the Crown of Thorns and assorted other relics associated with Christ's Passion to King Louis IX of France, who commissioned a royal chapel in Paris, the Gothic masterpiece known as Sainte-Chapelle, to house the treasures.

–*Alfred J. Andrea*

See also: Byzantine Empire

Bibliography

The Capture of Constantinople: The "Hystoria Constantinopolitana" of Gunther of Pairis, ed. and trans. Alfred J. Andrea (Philadelphia: University of Pennsylvania Press, 1997).

Contemporary Sources for the Fourth Crusade, ed. and trans. Alfred J. Andrea (Leiden: Brill, 2000).

Exuviae sacrae Constantinopolitana, ed. Paul Riant, 3 vols. (Genève: Leroux, 1877–1904).

The Journey of Charlemagne to Jerusalem and Constantinople, ed. and trans. Jean-Louis G. Picherit (Birmingham, AL: Summa, 1984).

Relics: The Holy Land

The discovery, acquisition, and veneration of sacred relics formed an integral part of the crusading experience in the Holy Land.

The importance of saints' remains and other holy objects for Christian pilgrims to Jerusalem and its environs dates back to at least the fourth century. This was a crucial period for the formation of a Christian sacred topography in Palestine, fostered by the ecclesiastical building program of Constantine I the Great, Roman emperor (312–337). Constantine's efforts included the construction of the Church of the Holy Sepulchre over the site of Christ's tomb, where (according to an almost contemporary legend) his mother, Helena, had discovered nails from the Crucifixion and a portion of the True Cross. The appeal of the latter relic is vividly illustrated by the Iberian pilgrim Egeria, who around 380 reported that zealous worshipers kissing the cross were known to bite off slivers of it. By the late fourth and early fifth centuries, the veneration of such physical relics associated with biblical events and places, popularized by St. Jerome among others, had come to occupy a prominent place in the pilgrimage experience of Western Christians.

The subsequent disruptions of authority in the western Roman Empire and the Muslim conquest of Palestine in the seventh century made long-distance pilgrimage to Jerusalem increasingly difficult. Local developments in the West, however, ensured that the cult of relics held a central position in Latin Christian piety. In particular, Carolingian rulers and prelates actively fostered and regulated the importance of saints' cults, mandating (among other efforts) the presence of a relic in every consecrated altar. With the decline of Carolingian authority in the late ninth and tenth centuries, accompanied by invasions of Europe's frontiers by Vikings, Magyars, and Muslim Arabs, saints' shrines emerged as powerful centers of local authority, bringing prestige, protection, and oblations to the religious institutions housing them, as well as healing miracles and other forms of intercession to their pilgrim devotees.

The brisk trade in holy remains that developed during the early Middle Ages, particularly between northern Europe and Rome, testifies to the religious, social, and economic significance that relics held among both the laity and the clergy. Nor were the relics of the Holy Land and other Eastern regions with a connection to the Bible or the age of the primitive church completely lost from view. Despite the difficulties, Western pilgrims continued to venerate the remains of saints and other holy objects at various sites in and around Jerusalem, as seen in the seventh-century pilgrimage account of the English traveler Arculf. In addition, pious travelers were more than willing to translate Eastern relics to new homes in the West, where they were seen as being safer from defilement by Muslims. The theft of St. Mark's remains from Alexandria and their removal to Venice in the year 827 is a well-known example of this phenomenon. Intensified European involvement in the Mediterranean region in the eleventh century, including mass pilgrimages to Jerusalem, undoubtedly encouraged a heightened sensitivity among Western Christians to the significance of the East and the Holy Land in particular as sources of relics. The increasing commercial activity of Italian cities in the Mediterranean also provided new opportunities for the westward translation of Eastern relics, such as the remains of St. Nicholas, which were translated from Myra (mod. Demre, Turkey) in Asia Minor to Bari in Apulia in 1087.

As pilgrims, the participants in the First Crusade (1096–1099) had a natural interest in holy relics. There are indications that contemporary Latins conceived of the entire Holy Land itself as a relic, imbued with sanctity by the blood of Christ and the remains of other biblical figures. Liberating this holiest of relics from the hands of the unbelievers quickly became a central theme of the crusading endeavor, particularly with regard to the Holy Sepulchre, the physical space where the central moment of Christian salvation was enacted. En route to Jerusalem, the crusaders would have had a striking preview of the Holy Land's sacred treasures when they passed through Constantinople (mod. İstanbul, Turkey), where such relics had been gathered for centuries.

As the crusading armies progressed through Anatolia and Syria, they soon obtained relics of their own that were associated with Eastern saints or the biblical past. These included the Holy Lance, discovered at Antioch (mod. Antakya, Turkey) on 14 June 1098, but there were a number of other, lesser relics acquired by pious Westerners during that march to Jerusalem, including relics of saints George, Cyprian, John Chrysostom, and Thecla. The capture of Jerusalem on 15 July 1099 was followed by another famous discovery: a relic of the True Cross uncovered in or near the Church of the Holy Sepulchre. Contemporary Latin historians were clear that the discovery of objects like the Holy Lance and the True Cross was a sign of God's favor toward the crusading armies, who had recovered the ultimate relic, the Holy Land, against overwhelming odds.

Following the First Crusade, crusaders returned home to Western Europe with relics in their possession, often the only objects of wealth accrued on their journey, which they bestowed upon local churches and monastic houses. Subsequent crusades and the continued Western presence in Palestine for much of the twelfth century meant that there were ample opportunities for crusaders, other pilgrims, and the new Latin inhabitants of the Holy Land to acquire additional relics. In some cases, this was a matter of discovering previously unknown remains, such as the relics of the biblical patriarchs Abraham, Isaac, and Jacob unearthed by a priory of Latin canons at Hebron in 1119. In other cases, such sacred treasures were stolen or otherwise acquired from Eastern Christian communities in the Holy Land or surrounding regions.

Regardless of the exact circumstances, ecclesiastical authors commemorating the discovery of Eastern relics or their transferal to the West represented these events as a clear sign of the Lord's favor toward Latin Christians, who had proven themselves more worthy of the saints' holy patronage than non-Latin Christians. Describing the acquisition of relics in this manner provided Western hagiographers with an opportunity to connect not only their respective communities but all of Latin Christendom with the narrative of sacred history, starting with the Bible or the days of the early church and leading down to the period of the crusades. This argument worked in both directions, however, as demonstrated by the Latin explanation for the defeat at the Horns of Hattin on 4 July 1187. This involved the loss of the church of Jerusalem's relic of the True Cross and was followed by the loss of the city of Jerusalem itself: Western churchmen unanimously attributed this shocking turn of events to the sins and shortcomings of their own people.

With the rise of Marian and Eucharistic devotion in the central and later Middle Ages, the cult of relics by no means vanished, but its centrality waned, as did the ecclesiastical celebration of relics brought from the Holy Land and other Eastern regions. During this same period, particularly during and after the thirteenth century, crusading in the eastern Mediterranean shifted toward different theaters of action than the Holy Land proper. At the same time Christian wars against Islam were increasingly validated by recourse to theories of just war, including the argument that Palestine, as a former possession of the Roman Empire, had been illicitly seized by the Muslims and was legally part of Christendom. Whatever the strategic realities and legal parsing, however, the recovery of Jerusalem as the ultimate Christian relic remained central to crusading ideology and propaganda.

–Brett Edward Whalen

See also: Pilgrimage

Bibliography

Brown, Peter, *The Cult of Saints: Its Rise and Function in Latin Christianity* (Chicago: University of Chicago Press, 1981).

Geary, Patrick J., *Furta Sacra: Thefts of Relics in the Central Middle Ages* (Princeton: Princeton University Press, 1990).

———, "Sacred Commodities: The Circulation of Medieval Relics," in *Living with the Dead in the Middle Ages,* ed. Patrick J. Geary (Ithaca, NY: Cornell University Press, 1994), pp. 194–228.

Murray, Alan V., "Mighty against the Enemies of Christ: The Relic of the True Cross in the Armies of the Kingdom of Jerusalem," in *The Crusades and Their Sources: Essays Presented to Bernard Hamilton,* ed. John France and William G. Zajac (Aldershot, UK: Ashgate, 1998), pp. 217–238.

Riley-Smith, Jonathan, *The First Crusade and the Idea of Crusading* (London: Athlone, 1986).

Whalen, Brett Edward, "The Discovery of the Holy Patriarchs: Relics, Ecclesiastical Politics and Sacred History in Twelfth-Century Crusader Palestine," *Historical Reflections* 27 (2001), 139–176.

Wilken, Robert, *The Land Called Holy: Palestine in Christian History and Thought* (New Haven: Yale University Press, 1992).

Reval

Reval (mod. Tallinn, Estonia) was the second-largest town in medieval Livonia after Riga. The name Revalia (Est. *Rävala*) originally designated the surrounding province.

At the beginning of the Baltic Crusades, the castle hill in Reval was an Estonian fortification adjoining a small port. In 1219 Danish crusaders, led by King Valdemar II, landed in Reval and started to build a castle; the modern Estonian name of the town probably derives from *Taani linn,* "the fortress or town of the Danes." On 15 June that year the Danes defeated a large Estonian army and subjected the surrounding country. The Order of the Sword Brethren captured Reval in 1227 but was forced to return it to Denmark in 1238 according to the Treaty of Stensby.

A town grew up at the foot of the castle hill, its development stimulated by Danish royal privileges. By the end of the thirteenth century, it had fortifications (which were later extended), two parish churches, a Dominican friary, and a Cistercian nunnery. The town was established as a corporation with an independent jurisdiction and was separate from the castle hill, which contained the castle of the bishops and the castle of the royal governor.

In 1346 Reval was sold together with the rest of North Estonia to the Teutonic Order. The royal castle was converted into a commandery of the order. German merchants and artisans dominated the legal and cultural life of the town. Although subject to the Livonian branch of the Teutonic Order, Reval was administered by a town council according to the Lübeck town law; its members normally belonged to the Great Guild of merchants. The local Estonian inhabitants, who constituted up to half of the population, participated actively in the economic life of the town and were prominent in some of the crafts and trades, such as stonebreaking and transport. The wealth of Reval derived from the great trade between Novgorod and the West. From the 1280s Reval belonged to the Hanseatic League, which dominated this commerce, and was able to prevent its eastern rival, Narva, from joining the league.

From the end of the fifteenth century Reval encountered many problems. The station of the German merchants in Novgorod was closed after its subjection by Muscovy in 1494, which adversely affected the Revalian economy. There were tensions with the nobility of Harria and Vironia over the migration of peasants to the town and increasing ethnic and social conflict between German and non-German segments of the urban population. As in other Hanseatic towns, the council expanded its power, suppressing the ambitions of the craft guilds to participate in government. In the 1520s the Reformation reached Reval; the town became Lutheran, but the castle district belonging to the bishop of Reval remained Roman Catholic until 1561. In that year, the town of Reval and the nobility of northern Estonia subjected themselves to Swedish rule.

–*Juhan Kreem*

Bibliography

Johansen, Paul, *Nordische Mission, Revals Gründung und die Schwedenansiedlung in Estland* (Stockholm: Wahlström & Widstrand, 1951).

Johansen, Paul, and Heinz von zur Mühlen, *Deutsch und Undeutsch im mittelalterlichen und frühneuzeitlichen Reval* (Köln: Böhlau, 1973).

Kala, Tiina, *Lübeck Law and Tallinn* (Tallinn: Tallinna Linnaarhiiv, 1998).

———, "Tallinna tekkeloo peegeldumine kirjalikes allikates," in *Keskus-Tagamaa-Ääreala: Uurimusi asustushierarhia ja võimukeskuste kujunemisest Eestis,* ed. Valter Lang (Tallinn: Ajalo Instituut, Tartu Ülikool, 2002), pp. 391–408.

Kreem, Juhan, "The Teutonic Order as a Secular Ruler in Livonia: The Privileges and Oath of Reval," in *Crusade and Conversion on the Baltic Frontier, 1150–1500,* ed. Alan V. Murray (Aldershot, UK: Ashgate, 2001), pp. 215–234.

———, *The Town and Its Lord: Reval and the Teutonic Order (in the Fifteenth Century)* (Tallinn: Tallinna Linnaarhiiv, 2002).

Mühlen, Heinz von zur, "Zur wissenschaftlichen Diskussion über den Ursprung Revals," *Zeitschrift für Ostforschung* 33 (1984), 626–673.

Nottbeck, Eugen von, and Wilhelm Neumann, *Geschichte und Kunstdenkmäler der Stadt Reval,* 2 vols. (Reval: Kluge, 1904).

Ritscher, Alfred, *Reval an der Schwelle zur Neuzeit,* vol. 1: *1510–1535* (Bonn: Kulturstiftung der Deutschen Vertriebenen, 1998).

Tallinna ajalugu 1860-ndate aastateni, ed. Raimo Pullat (Tallinn: Eesti Raamat, 1976).

Revel, Hugh

See Hugh Revel

Reynald of Châtillon (d. 1187)

Prince of Antioch (1153–1163) and later lord of Transjordan and Hebron (1177–1187).

A younger son of Hervé II of Donzy, Reynald took the cross before 1153, when he participated in the successful siege of Muslim Ascalon (mod. Tel Ashqelon, Israel). Later that year he married Constance, widow of Prince Raymond of Antioch, and became ruler of the principality. In 1155, acting on behalf of the Byzantine emperor Manuel I, Reynald attacked the Armenian prince T'oros, who had annexed Byzantine Cilicia. He recovered castles in the Amanus Mountains, but when Manuel failed to defray the costs of the campaign, gave them to the Knights Templar and joined with T'oros in an attack on the Byzantine island of Cyprus. When Manuel campaigned in northern Syria in 1158–1159, he required Reynald to perform a public ritual penance and to do homage to him, but Manuel's return to Constantinople meant that in practice Reynald's autonomy was not materially affected by this act.

In 1160 or 1161 Reynald was captured by the forces of Nūr al-Dīn and imprisoned at Aleppo for over fifteen years. During this time his wife died and his stepson Bohemund III attained his majority and became prince of Antioch (1163). After Nūr al-Dīn's death (1174), the regents for his son, seeking a Frankish alliance against Saladin, released Reynald along with Joscelin III of Edessa. Reynald, now a landless man (although retaining the courtesy title of prince), went to Jerusalem, where Joscelin's nephew, Baldwin IV, was king. Sent by Baldwin to Constantinople to renew a treaty against Egypt, Reynald was well received because he had become part of Manuel's extended kin group through the emperor's marriage to Reynald's stepdaughter, Mary of Antioch (1161). Manuel renewed the treaty with Jerusalem and almost certainly paid Reynald's ransom of 120,000 dinars.

Because of the success of this mission, Baldwin IV subsequently placed great confidence in Reynald; he arranged his marriage to Stephanie of Milly, widowed heiress of Transjordan (1176), and invested him with the lordship of Hebron, thus placing him in command of the southeastern defenses of the kingdom. Baldwin appointed Reynald his executive regent for a brief time while he was seriously ill in the summer of 1177, and Reynald was in command of the Frankish host at the battle on Mont Gisard when Saladin's invading army was decisively defeated on 25 November 1177. In 1180 Baldwin IV betrothed his younger sister, Isabella, to Reynald's stepson, Humphrey IV of Toron, and appointed Reynald as her guardian.

In 1180 Saladin made a two-year truce with Baldwin IV, but Reynald broke it by attacking caravans on the desert route from Damascus to Mecca. This was not an act of brigandage, but a successful attempt to prevent Saladin's forces from seizing Aleppo by diverting their attention to Transjordan. In 1182 Saladin launched a major attack on the Zangids in Iraq, who allied with the Franks of Jerusalem. In the winter of 1182–1183, Reynald launched a small war fleet in the Red Sea with the objective of capturing Aila and cutting Saladin's lines of communication between Egypt and Damascus. Part of the fleet attacked Arab merchant shipping, probably as a means of recouping the costs of the expedition. This initiative failed because of the speed with which al-'Ādil, governor of Egypt, transferred a fleet from the Mediterranean to the Red Sea. Reynald's forces were destroyed, though he evaded capture. Thereafter Saladin viewed Reynald as his most dangerous opponent. He built fortresses at Qal'at Guindi in the Sinai in 1182 and at Ajlun in 1184–1185 to restrict Reynald's movements, and twice unsuccessfully besieged Reynald's chief fortress of Kerak (1183, 1184).

During the succession crisis of 1186, Reynald supported Baldwin IV's elder sister, Sibyl, and her husband Guy of Lusignan (against his personal interests, since the alternative candidates were the princess Isabella and her husband, Reynald's stepson Humphrey). Saladin's official reason for invading the kingdom in 1187 was that Reynald had attacked one of his caravans during a truce, but that was merely the pretext for a war that had become inevitable. Reynald fought bravely at the battle of Hattin but was taken prisoner and had the doubtful distinction of being executed personally by Saladin, having first been offered and refused a reprieve if he would renounce the Christian faith.

–*Bernard Hamilton*

Bibliography

Cahen, Claude, *La Syrie du Nord à l'époque des croisades et la principauté franque d'Antioche* (Paris: Geuthner, 1940).

Hamilton, Bernard, "The Elephant of Christ: Reynald of Châtillon," in *Studies in Church History* 15 (1978), 97–108.

———, *The Leper King and His Heirs. Baldwin IV and the Crusader Kingdom of Jerusalem* (Cambridge: Cambridge University Press, 2000).

Hillenbrand, Carole, "The Imprisonment of Reynald of Châtillon," in *Texts, Documents and Artefacts: Islamic Studies in Honour of D. S. Richards,* ed. Chase F. Robinson (Leiden: Brill, 2003), pp. 79–101.

Mayer, Hans Eberhard, *Die Kreuzfahrerherrschaft Montréal (Šōbak): Jordanien im 12. Jahrhundert* (Wiesbaden: Harrassowitz, 1990).

Richard, Jean, "Aux origines d'un grand lignage: Des Palladii à Renaud de Châtillon," in *Media in Francia: Recueil de mélanges offert à Karl Ferdinand Werner* (Paris: Herault, 1989), pp. 409–418.

Schlumberger, Gustav, *Renaud de Châtillon, Prince d'Antioche, Seigneur de la terre d'Outre-Jourdain,* 3d ed. (Paris: Plon-Nourrit, 1923).

Reyse

A medieval German term (pl. *reysen*) that came to acquire the specialist meaning of a crusading campaign fought by the Teutonic Order and its Western allies in the Baltic region.

The Middle High German word written as *reyse, reysa, reise, reze,* and variants (mod. German *Reise*) covered a range of meanings, including "journey," "war," and "campaign." In the context of the crusades, it was used for the campaigns fought on a regular basis by the Teutonic Order in Prussia and Livonia against its pagan (and, in some cases, Russian Orthodox) enemies during the fourteenth and fifteenth centuries. As a result of international participation in the *reysen,* the term was also taken up by authors writing in languages other than German, such as Jean Froissart and Geoffrey Chaucer, and it also figures in some of the Latin writings of the order.

After the subjugation of Prussia and Livonia (by around 1290), the Teutonic Order concentrated on the struggle against the pagan Lithuanians. From 1304 onward, crusaders from the Western countries traveled to Prussia to take part in these campaigns, after over two decades that had seen very few "guests," as the order called the visiting knights. Whereas the earlier wars of the order had been supported only by nobles from north and central Europe (primarily Scandinavia and Germany), the campaigns of the fourteenth century witnessed an ever growing influx of guests from western and southern Europe (England, Scotland, the Low Countries, France, Spain, and Italy), in addition to the traditional areas. In 1328 John of Luxembourg, king of Bohemia (1311–1346), came to Prussia for the first time and inspired others by his example. In the same year, the first knights from the Low Countries and England visited Prussia, followed by Frenchmen (1335 at the latest) and Scots (from 1356). From 1343 there is occasional evidence for Italian knights in Prussia, and some Spanish guests arrived during the second half of the fourteenth century. Participation in a *reyse* became fashionable, with many guests going twice or sometimes even more. Several families, such as the Beauchamp family (earls of Warwick), established a tradition of going on a *reyse.* The rush diminished after the Crusade of Nikopolis (1396), but some knightly guests were still coming to Prussia until 1422/1423.

Reysen took place on an annual basis, in both winter and summer. They usually started around feast days of the Virgin Mary, the order's patroness. The *winter-reyse* began on the Feast of the Purification of Mary (2 February); the *sommer-reyse* began either on the Feast of the Assumption (15 August) or the Nativity of the Virgin (8 September). The winter campaign enjoyed great popularity for those seeking experience of warfare because during that season fighting was rare elsewhere in Europe. *Reysen* were announced by the grand master, but the command on campaign often lay with the order's marshal or minor commanders acting on the marshal's behalf. The guests chose their own subcommander. Crusader armies also included native Prussians and other christianized peoples acting as auxiliaries and scouts.

In character, the *reyse* was usually a raiding expedition that aimed at the devastation of the enemy's lands and the seizure of livestock and prisoners, but there were also sieges and campaigns to construct or reinforce castles, or conversely to destroy enemy strongholds. Pitched battles were an exception. The extent of the wilderness areas that lay between the territory of the order and its enemies meant that armies might have to journey over 160 kilometers (100 mi.) in order to reach worthwhile targets; for the same reason, they would carry up to a month's supplies with them.

The *reysen* proved to be highly attractive for the western European nobility. Combatants were often knighted on campaign, and their participation increased their knightly honor and fame. In the cathedral of Königsberg (mod. Kaliningrad, Russia), heraldic wall paintings attested the visits of many a knight. From the middle of the fourteenth century, the order added luster to the chivalrous character of the war by establishing its *Ehrentisch* ("table of honor") as a means of honoring those knights who had distinguished themselves in wars against the infidel.

The *reyse* showed distinct characteristics of a crusade. The war was described as a godly enterprise; participants came in fulfillment of vows, they were regarded as "pilgrims" (Lat. *peregrini*), and they received a plenary indulgence. This indulgence was derived from various crusade indulgences issued by the popes in favor of the order during the thirteenth century. There were, however, no additional papal crusade bulls in the fourteenth century. For this reason it has been argued that these campaigns "represented something new in crusading history . . .: a sort of 'ongoing' crusade" [Housley, *The Later Crusades,* p. 341]. Rather than having started because of a papal appeal, the *reyse* was entirely organized by the Teutonic Order, making use of a treasury of ancient crusade privileges.

–Axel Ehlers

Bibliography

Ehlers, Axel, "The Crusade of the Teutonic Knights against Lithuania Reconsidered," in *Crusade and Conversion on the Baltic Frontier, 1150–1500,* ed. Alan V. Murray (Aldershot, UK: Ashgate, 2001), pp. 21–44.

Housley, Norman, *The Later Crusades: From Lyons to Alcazar, 1274–1580* (Oxford: Oxford University Press, 1992).

Paravicini, Werner, *Die Preußenreisen des europäischen Adels,* 2 vols. (Sigmaringen: Thorbecke, 1989–1995).

City of Rhodes. (Pixel That)

Rhodes

The island of Rhodes (mod. Rodos, Greece) is the largest of the Dodecanese islands, strategically placed at the interface of the Aegean and Mediterranean seas. The town of the same name at the northeastern tip of the island is the largest settlement and the island's capital.

The island of Rhodes has been of considerable economic and naval importance since antiquity and proved to be more so as crusading interest moved from the Holy Land and Egypt to Asia Minor and the Aegean Sea; indeed, in 1316 the Catalan writer Ramon Llull recognized the importance of Rhodes as a crusading base. Before that the islanders took an active part in provisioning the First Crusade (1096–1099), and during the Third Crusade (1189–1192) both Richard I of England (1189) and Philip II of France (1192) stopped at Rhodes on their way, respectively, to and from the Holy Land. After the conquest of Constantinople by the forces of the Fourth Crusade (1202–1204), Rhodes nominally belonged to the empire of Nicaea, but in practice the island was ruled by the Gabalas family, which took a free hand in the collection of revenue and the conduct of affairs.

Emperor John III Vatatzes attempted to exert Nicaean control over the island by sending expeditions there in 1233 and 1244, but it was no easy task, since in 1234 Leo Gabalas, ruler of Rhodes (1204–1240), signed a treaty with the Venetians directed against Nicaea. Leo was able to pass some control of the island to his brother John, who was last recorded in 1249, when Nicaean control may be assumed to have been complete.

In 1278 the lordship of Nanfio and Rhodes was granted to the Genoese freebooter Giovanni de lo Covo, and once again the island came under the control of elements only nominally acknowledging Byzantine overlordship. In an agreement dated 27 May 1306, the Genoese lord of the island, Vignolo de' Vignoli, sold Rhodes, Kos, and Leros to the Order of the Hospital, reserving for himself one-third of the revenues from Kos and Leros and the *casale* (village) of Lardos on Rhodes. The order was seeking a base to replace its former headquarters in Acre (mod. 'Akko, Israel), lost to the Muslims in 1291, whereas Vignolo may have felt unable to exploit his lordships in the face of Venetian and Turkish

The Grand Vizier of Mehmed II conducting Turkish operations during the Siege of Rhodes (1480–1481). From *Histoire du Siege de Rhodes* (*Descriptio Obsidionis Rhodiae urbis*), by Guillaume Caoursin, c. 1483–1490. Ms.lat. 6067, f.50 v., Bibliothèque nationale de France, Paris, France. (Snark/Art Resource)

pressure. Certainly Rhodes had to be conquered by the Hospitallers, which suggests that Vignolo's control was limited.

On 23 June 1306, the Hospitaller grand master, Fulk of Villaret, left Limassol in Cyprus to conquer Rhodes with a small fleet of 2 galleys and 4 transports carrying 35 knights and 500 foot soldiers. The chronology of the conquest is unclear. Most of the island may have been in the hands of the Hospitallers by 1306, with the exception of Philerimos, which remained in Byzantine hands until 1310, when a crusading force arrived to assist the Hospitallers in their conquest. By 1320 the islands of Kos, Leros, Karpathos, and Kassos were conquered, the last two taken from the Venetians.

Rhodes became an entrepôt for trade with the West and the Turkish emirates of southwestern Anatolia, activities that the campaigns of the Hospitallers did not greatly inconvenience. Merchants from Florence, Narbonne, and Montpellier, transferring revenues from the European commanderies of the order to its Rhodian headquarters, provided banking facilities. Particularly close contact was maintained with Cyprus, Crete, and Sicily; merchants from France, Italy, and Spain were prominent in the commerce of the island, particularly in the export of sugar, which was refined in factories such as that excavated at Haraki and which was second in quality only to that of Cyprus.

The Hospitallers fortified and adorned the city of Rhodes with miles of walls and many monuments, such as the old and new hospitals and the Street of the Knights. The city became the center of the island, both for exporting its products and for distributing goods to the rest of the island. Relations with the indigenous Greek population seem to have been cordial and cooperative. It is generally assumed that in the Rhodian countryside Greeks were left very much to themselves; indeed, little is known of the landholding policies adopted by the Hospitallers. The fate of Vignolo's holding at Lardos is unknown.

Some of the coastal towers, such as those at Palati and Glyfada, bear armorial sculpture of the grand masters fixing both their dates and their builders, but other sites are built without dressed stones and have no armorial bearings, leaving open the questions of when they were erected and to whom they belonged. Many of the castles and coastal towers were built, refortified, or enlarged during the grand mastership of Peter of Aubusson (1476–1503). Plans drawn up in 1474 and revised in 1479 for places of refuge for the main centers of habitation in the island are a reflection of the growth and seriousness of Turkish raids on the island and the need to maintain the population base.

Raids turned to invasion with the first great siege of the city of Rhodes by the Ottomans (May–July 1480), for which we have a full and well-illustrated account by Guillaume Caoursin, vice-chancellor of the order. A further assault on Rhodes was prevented by the death of Sultan Mehmed II in 1481 and the disputed succession between Bayezid II and his brother Prince Cem (Djem), who fled to Rhodes in July 1482 and made a treaty with the grand master in return for protection. For his part, Bayezid II left the island unmolested as long as Cem was in Western hands. Cem died in 1495, leaving his family on the island, eventually to be executed in 1523.

Thereafter, Bayezid II was too preoccupied with other campaigns to concern himself with the capture of Rhodes. The respite thus gained was used to strengthen the fortifications of the city. The result, which is still visible today, incorporated the latest thinking in late medieval defense. The final Ottoman siege of Rhodes began on 28 July 1522, when a Turkish armada of 400 ships brought 200,000 troops, a large artillery train, and Sultan Süleyman I himself to the city. Despite being outnumbered almost thirty to one and decisively outgunned, the Hospitallers held out until the end of December and forced the sultan to offer terms that were eventually accepted. On 1 January 1523, the last grand master of Rhodes, Philippe de Villiers de l'Isle-Adam (1521–1534), the brethren of the order, and those Greek inhabitants who wished to go left the island for good.

The island remained in Turkish hands until 1911, when it passed to Italy. It became part of Greece in 1947.

–Peter Lock

See also: Hospital, Order of the; Ottoman Empire

Bibliography
Gerola, Guiseppe, "Monumenti mediovali delle Tredici Sporadi," *Annuario della Scuola Archeologica di Atene* 1 (1914), 169–356; 2 (1916), 1–66.
Kollias, Elias, *The Medieval City of Rhodes and the Palace of the Grand Master: From the Early Christian Period to the Conquest by the Turks (1522),* 2d ed. (Athens: Archaeological Receipts Fund, 1998).
Luttrell, Anthony, *Hospitallers in Cyprus, Rhodes, Greece and the West, 1291–1440* (London: Variorum, 1978).
———, *The Hospitallers of Rhodes and Their Mediterranean World* (Aldershot, UK: Ashgate, 1992).
———, *The Hospitaller State on Rhodes and Its Western Provinces, 1306–1462* (Aldershot, UK: Ashgate, 1999).
———, *The Town of Rhodes, 1306–1356* (Rhodes: City of Rhodes Office for the Medieval Town, 2003).
Nicholson, Helen, *The Knights Hospitaller* (London: Boydell, 2001).
Poutiers, Jean-Christian, *Rhodes et ses Chevaliers, 1306–1523: Approche historique et archéologique* (Araya: Imprimerie Catholique, 1989).
Sørensen, Lone Wriedt, and Peter Pentz, *Results of the Carlsberg Foundation Excavations in Rhodes, 1902–1914: Lindos,* 4/2 (Copenhagen: National Museum of Denmark, 1992).
Spiteri, Stephen C., *Fortresses of the Cross* (Valletta: Heritage Interpretation Services, 1994).
Triposkoufi, Anna, and Amalia Tsitouri, eds., *Venetians and Knights Hospitallers: Military Architecture Networks* (Athens: Hellenic Ministry of Culture, 2002).

Richard I the Lionheart (1157–1199)

King of England (1189–1199) and one of three leaders of the Third Crusade (1189–1192).

Born on 8 September 1157, Richard was the second surviving son of Henry II, king of England, and Eleanor of Aquitaine. He joined the family rebellion against his father in 1173–1174 but thereafter governed Aquitaine on the king's behalf with the title of count of Poitou, winning a considerable reputation as military leader and determined ruler. When his elder brother, Henry "the Young King," died in 1183, Richard became the principal heir to England and the Angevin family's vast possessions in France. From then on, relations with both his father and the new king of France, Philip II, were tense. Richard was widely praised for being the first prince north of the Alps to take the cross in response to the fall of Jerusalem to Saladin in 1187. Yet by doing this without consulting his father, he exacerbated the political tensions, which meant that neither Richard nor the kings of France and England had actually left for the East by the time Henry II died (6 July 1189).

Installed as duke of Normandy on 20 July, then anointed king of England at Westminster on 3 September, Richard focused all his energies on the crusade. The religious obligation to recover the patrimony of Christ coincided with family duty to restore the kingdom of Jerusalem to his cousins, the junior branch of the Angevin family, and its king, Guy of Lusignan, who had been one of his own Poitevin subjects. Richard took over the treasure accumulated by his father, including the yield of the Saladin Tithe, but set out to increase the size of his war chest by all possible means. He reorganized the government of England, taking large sums from those who received the offices and privileges they bid for; this was standard practice, but the scale and speed of Richard's operations were unprecedented.

To his younger brother John, lord of Ireland, Richard gave great estates in England, while assigning the castles to ministers he trusted, first William de Longchamp and then Walter de Coutances. This did not prevent John from rebelling in 1193 while Richard was a captive, but probably nothing could have done so. Richard also took care to secure his frontiers. Conferences with William the Lion, king of the Scots, and Welsh princes were successfully concluded. Alone of all the major French princes, his old enemy Raymond V of Toulouse had not taken the cross, so to protect his southern dominions, Richard promised to marry Berengaria, daughter of King Sancho VI of Navarre. These negotiations had to

ꝓ̃es Henry le secund regna Richard sun fiz. x. aūnz e demy si entrepayz and de la terre seynt fuit puis del dulȝ de Oustriȝ par eyde del Roy Phylype de fraunce. e fuit reynt hors de prison put cent mil lyuers de argent. e pur cel taunt un fu cent les Chaliȝ de Engleterre pris. des Eglyses e vendus. Puis fuit trez de un quarel de Arblast al Chastel de Chalezun. dūt cuū vers sur sez: X pe tui calicis: preto sit preda calittis.

Two scenes from a life of Richard I of England, fourteenth century. On the left Richard is shown languishing in prison in Germany; on the right he is mortally wounded in the shoulder by a crossbowman at Chalus. (HIP/Art Resource)

who had been kept in close confinement by King Tancred since the death of her husband, William II (1189). However, Tancred withheld both her dower and the legacy that William II had bequeathed as a crusade subsidy to Henry II, and that Richard now claimed as his.

When rioting broke out in Messina, Richard's troops took the city by force (4 October). Two days later, Tancred agreed to pay 20,000 ounces of gold in lieu of Joanna's dower, plus a further 20,000 that Richard promised to settle on Tancred's daughter when she married his nephew Arthur of Brittany (d. 1203), who was now declared his heir presumptive. In return, Richard agreed that while in Sicily he would help Tancred against any invader, a provision directed against threats from Henry VI, Holy Roman Emperor. In March 1191, Berengaria, escorted by Richard's mother, Eleanor, arrived. Philip now had to release Richard from the betrothal to Alice, fearing that Richard would produce witnesses to testify that she had been his father's mistress. From now on, Philip's crusade was directed as much against Richard as against Saladin. He sailed from Messina a few hours before Berengaria arrived and, on reaching Acre, threw his weight behind Guy of Lusignan's bitter rival, Conrad of Montferrat.

On 10 April Richard's 200 ships left Messina. Some ships, including the one carrying Joanna and Berengaria, were blown off course and eventually anchored off Limassol on Cyprus. Isaac Doukas Komnenos, the self-proclaimed Greek emperor of Cyprus, plundered two wrecked ships and evidently intended to take Joanna and Berengaria captive. When the rest of the fleet arrived, Richard led a daring amphibious assault, capturing Limassol on 6 May. That night, he had the crusaders' horses disembarked, and at dawn the Cypriot army camp fell to a surprise attack. When peace talks broke down, Richard set about the conquest of the island. When he captured Isaac's daughter, the emperor surrendered. By 1 June Richard was master of the island. Whether or not the conquest of Cyprus had been planned (as seems likely) during the winter months in Messina, it was a strategic masterstroke, vital to the survival of Outremer.

Richard finally joined the Christian army besieging Acre on 8 June 1191 and at once opened negotiations with Saladin. Confronted by Richard's siege equipment and galleys, the exhausted Muslim defenders of Acre capitulated on 12 July. The crusaders massacred most of their prisoners on 20 August when Saladin did not keep to the agreed terms regarding ransoms for their release. Richard and Philip

be kept secret because Richard had been betrothed to Alice, King Philip's half-sister, since 1169. Humiliating Philip by discarding her now would have meant the end of the crusade before it started.

Richard and Philip finally left Vézelay on 4 July 1190, having agreed that they would share equally the gains made on crusade. Richard had arranged to rendezvous at Marseilles with the huge fleet that he had raised in England, Normandy, Brittany, and Aquitaine. When the fleet was delayed, he hired ships to send one contingent ahead to the siege of Acre (mod. 'Akko, Israel) and made a new rendezvous at Messina in Sicily, where he arrived on 23 September. The customary winter closure of Mediterranean shipping lanes meant that he and Philip now had to stay there until the spring. While in Sicily, Richard secured the release of his sister Joanna, divided the booty between themselves, to the exclusion of Leopold V, duke of Austria, and others. On 28 July the two kings adjudicated the competing claims to the kingdom, awarding it to Guy for his lifetime and thereafter to Conrad. However, Philip, repeatedly outshone by a king whose war chest had been replenished in Cyprus, left for France on 31 July, leaving his troops under the command of Hugh III, duke of Burgundy. In Leopold and Philip, Richard had made two enemies, and they returned to the West ahead of him.

The crusaders began their march to Jerusalem on 25 August. The pace was slow, but Saladin could not break their disciplined advance. On 7 September he risked battle at Arsuf; but Richard's tactical control brought victory when the crusaders were on the brink of defeat. On 10 September the crusaders reached Jaffa (mod. Tel Aviv-Yafo, Israel). They needed a rest, and Jaffa's walls, which Saladin had dismantled, had to be rebuilt. Richard was already thinking in terms of the thirteenth-century strategy that the keys of Jerusalem were to be found in Egypt. Nearly all the troops, however, were passionately in favor of the direct route. After rebuilding the castles on the pilgrims' road from Jaffa, the army reached Beit Nuba, 19 kilometers (12 mi.) from Jerusalem, soon after Christmas. But although the crusader war of attrition had forced Saladin to disband the bulk of his troops, he stayed in Jerusalem. The crusaders' own logistical problems meant that even if they managed to take the city, they did not have the numbers to occupy and defend it; many crusaders, having fulfilled their pilgrim vows, would at once go home. An army council decided to move on Ascalon (mod. Tel Ashqelon, Israel), a step in the direction of Egypt that Hugh of Burgundy refused to take.

Richard entered Ascalon unopposed on 20 January 1192, but while rebuilding its walls, he was forced to return to Acre to deal with an attempted coup by Conrad of Montferrat. The coup made it clear that once Richard had gone, Guy would be no match for Conrad. In April 1192 Richard summoned a council, which offered the throne to Conrad and compensated Guy by selling him Cyprus for a down payment of 60,000 bezants. But Conrad was assassinated on 28 April. Inevitably Richard's enemies blamed him, an accusation lent plausibility by the marriage of Conrad's widow, Isabella, to Richard's nephew and ally Henry of Champagne (5 May). Yet Henry was also King Philip's nephew, well placed to reconcile the factions. On 22 May Richard captured Darum, an ideal base from which to disrupt the caravan route between Syria and Egypt.

Bowing to popular demand, Richard made another attempt on Jerusalem. By 29 June the entire crusader army was at Beit Nuba again. But once again, an army council, faced by reality, decided to withdraw and target Egypt instead. Duke Hugh left the army. Richard reopened negotiations with Saladin; he was at Acre when he was taken by surprise by the news that the Muslims had launched an attack on Jaffa. His galleys reached Jaffa just in time for him to lead an assault onto the beach and into the town. Four days later he beat off a dawn attack on his camp outside Jaffa in circumstances that humiliated Saladin and confirmed Richard's legendary status. Richard fell ill, but Saladin's troops were war-weary. A three-year truce was agreed on 2 September. Richard had to hand back Ascalon and Darum; Saladin granted Christian pilgrims free access to Jerusalem. Many crusaders took advantage of this facility, but not Richard. He was not well enough to set sail until 9 October 1192. He had failed to take Jerusalem, but the entire coast from Tyre (mod. Soûr, Lebanon) to Jaffa was now in Christian hands, as was Cyprus. Considered as an administrative, political, and military exercise, Richard's crusade had been an astonishing success.

In December 1192 Richard was seized on his journey home by Leopold of Austria, who later handed him over to Emperor Henry VI. Richard's provisions for government during his absence stood up well to this unforeseeable turn of events. John's rebellion was contained and a huge king's ransom raised. Once the emperor had received 100,000 marks, and hostages for the amount (50,000 marks) still outstanding, Richard was freed (February 1194). But by then Philip had captured some important frontier castles in France; Richard devoted the remainder of his life to recovering them. This task, which involved building the great fortress of Château-Gaillard, was almost complete when he was fatally wounded at Chalus. He died on 6 April 1199 and was buried at Fontevraud.

To pay for his wars Richard made heavy financial demands on his subjects everywhere, not just in England. On crusade Richard was, in the words of a German chronicler, greater in wealth and resources than all other kings. In planning and organizing wars on the scale of the crusade or the recovery of his dominions in France, he was a cool and patient strategist, as much a master of sea power as of land forces. Friends and enemies alike testified to his individual prowess and valor; these qualities at times endangered his life, but they impressed enemy troops as well as his own. In his lifetime he was already known as *Cœur de Lion* ("Lionheart"). Understanding the value of this reputation, he preached what he practiced; the letters in which he inflated his own achievements were intended for wide circulation.

According to King Philip's panegyrist, Guillaume le Breton, had Richard been more God-fearing and not fought against his lord, Philip, England would never have had a better king. The Arab chronicler Ibn al-Athīr judged him the most remarkable ruler of his time for courage, shrewdness, energy, and patience. His reputation as a crusader meant that he became a legend in his own lifetime and for many centuries was regarded as the greatest of all kings of England. But from the seventeenth century onward, that same reputation served to highlight his long absences from England and led to the view that he was woefully negligent of his kingdom's welfare.

–John Gillingham

Bibliography

Flori, Jean, *Richard Coeur de Lion: Le roi-chevalier* (Paris: Payot, 1999).

Gillingham, John, *Richard I* (New Haven, CT: Yale University Press, 1999).

Görich, Knut, "Verletzte Ehre. König Richard Löwenherz als Gefangener Kaiser Heinrichs VI.," *Historisches Jahrbuch* 123 (2003), 65–91.

Kessler, Ulrike, *Richard I. Löwenherz: König, Kreuzritter, Abenteurer* (Graz: Styria, 1995).

Markowski, Michael, "Richard Lionheart: Bad King, Bad Crusader?" *Journal of Medieval History* 23 (1997), 351–365.

Mayer, Hans Eberhard, "Die Kanzlei Richards I. von England auf dem Dritten Kreuzzug," *Mitteilungen des Instituts für Österreichische Geschichtsforschung* 85 (1977), 22–35.

Pringle, R. Denys, "King Richard I and the Walls of Ascalon," *Palestine Exploration Quarterly* 116 (1984), 133–147.

Turner, Ralph V., and Richard R. Heiser, *The Reign of Richard Lionheart: Ruler of the Angevin Empire, 1189–1199* (Harlow: Longman, 2000).

Richard of Cornwall (1209–1272)

Leader of an English expedition to the Holy Land in 1240–1241 in the wake of that of Thibaud IV of Champagne; later titular king of the Romans (1257–1272).

The second son of King John of England, Richard was named after his illustrious crusading uncle, King Richard I, the Lionheart. He was created earl of Cornwall by his older brother, King Henry III, in 1227.

Richard's crusade took place in the context of the political situation in England, which had been disturbed by the revolt of Richard Marshal in 1233. Richard took the cross in 1236 alongside Gilbert Marshal, in order to seal a reconciliatory alliance with the Marshal family, also marrying Gilbert's sister Eleanor. The crusade aimed to coincide with the end in 1239 of a ten-year truce with Egypt. Pope Gregory IX granted Richard the use of money raised from vows that had been redeemed by cash payments and from legacies intended for the aid of the Holy Land. This grant was unprecedented, a significant moment in the evolution of crusade finances, as redemptions had previously been granted to individual crusaders, not to a commander.

The proposed English crusade was nearly blown off course by papal politics, and in particular the conflict between Richard's brother-in-law, Emperor Frederick II, and Pope Gregory IX. Fearing that Richard's presence in Outremer would further the ambitions of Frederick II (whose son Conrad IV was titular king of Jerusalem) in the East, Gregory attempted to block Richard's departure, or at least to direct his crusade to the defense of the Latin states in Greece or of papal interests in Italy. However, in an oath taken at Northampton in November 1239, the English barons swore not to be turned aside from Outremer. Ironically, Frederick was scarcely more enthusiastic to see English or French armies intervening in "his" kingdom of Jerusalem, but Richard and the emperor grew closer diplomatically after the former's departure, and Richard seems to have been granted a measure of authority to act in Frederick's name in the East.

Richard's presence in the East was characterized by diplomacy and construction rather than battle. The defeat of Thibaud IV of Champagne by the Egyptian Ayyūbids at Gaza (1239) and internal dissension within the kingdom of Jerusalem made any offensive by the crusaders impossible. Richard contented himself with assisting in the reconstruction of the fortifications at Ascalon (mod. Tel Ashqelon, Israel) and concluding a treaty with Sultan al-Ṣāliḥ Ayyūb of Egypt confirming the Christian possession of Jerusalem. The impression of Richard's diplomatic achievements was exaggerated by his own skillful propaganda, as well as by his achievement in securing the release of French prisoners taken at Gaza. In reality, his efforts could be seen as undermining those of Thibaud before him, who had sensibly negotiated with the Ayyūbid sultan of Damascus, al-Ṣāliḥ Ismāʿīl. Although junior to al-Ṣāliḥ of Egypt, only the Damascene sultan was realistically able to dispose of territory in Palestine.

Richard never returned to the East, but his involvement in crusading and his relations with Frederick II may explain his later involvement in affairs overseas. He repeatedly turned down papal offers of the crown of Sicily between 1247 and 1254, but assumed the title of king of the Romans in 1257, in an ambitious attempt to make himself Holy Roman Emperor. He met Pope Innocent III at Lyons in 1250, as part of negotiations concerning Henry III's proposed crusade, which was later subsumed in papal plans for Henry to intervene in Sicily. Richard later played an important role as advisor to his nephew Edward (the future King Edward I) in the latter's crusade of 1270–1272.

–*Michael R. Evans*

Bibliography

Denholm-Young, Noel, *Richard of Cornwall* (Oxford: Blackwell, 1947).

Lloyd, Simon, *English Society and the Crusades* (Oxford: Oxford University Press, 1988).

Tyerman, Christopher, *England and the Crusades* (Chicago: University of Chicago Press, 1988).

Weiler, Björn, "Image and Reality in Richard of Cornwall's German Career," *English Historical Review* 113 (1998), 1111–1142.

Richard of Devizes

Monk of the Benedictine house of St. Swithun's at Winchester and author of a chronicle of the reign of Richard I of England between 1189 and 1192. He possibly also wrote sections of the annals of Winchester down to 1202.

Noted for its wry humor and colorful anecdotes, Richard's chronicle includes an account of the Third Crusade (1189–1192), which is based on unattributed second-hand information and is sometimes inaccurate. The chronicle breaks off abruptly at the end of the crusade. His lively one-liners have done much to shape modern views of King Richard I and his times. He recorded the king stating that he would sell London (to raise money for the crusade) if he could find a buyer; he described Berengaria of Navarre, the king's bride-to-be, as more wise than beautiful (although he had probably never set eyes on her); and he noted that the king refused to visit Jerusalem on pilgrimage because he would not accept from non-Christians what he could not obtain as a gift from God. It is more likely that the king was advised against the visit for security reasons. The chronicler's work is readable and amusing, but his crusade mate-

rial must be weighed against more reliable sources.

–*Helen Nicholson*

Bibliography

Cronicon Richardi Divisensis de tempore Regis Richardi Primi: The Chronicle of Richard of Devizes of the Time of King Richard the First, ed. John T. Appleby (London: Nelson, 1963).

Gransden, Antonia, *Historical Writing in England, vol. 1 c. 550 to c. 1307* (Ithaca, NY: Cornell University Press, 1974).

Richard of the Principate (d. 1112/1114)

A participant in the First Crusade (1096–1099) and later regent of the county of Edessa.

Richard (also known as Richard of Salerno) was born around 1060, a younger son of William, lord of the principality of Salerno, and a grandson of Tancred of Hauteville, the ancestor of the most distinguished family in Norman Italy. Excluded by elder brothers from the possibility of succession to family commands in Salerno and Sicily, he joined the Italian contingent in the First Crusade commanded by his cousin Bohemund of Taranto.

During the crusade, Richard served as an interpreter at the siege of Antioch, presumably having learned Arabic in childhood through exposure to the translation school in Salerno, and was twice taken prisoner: by the Greeks after crossing the Adriatic Sea (in late 1096), and by his fellow-crusader Baldwin of Boulogne at Tarsos (in summer 1097). By 1100 he had become second-in-command to Bohemund, but in the same year both men were captured by the Dānishmendid Turks near the Black Sea, who then turned him over to the Emperor Alexios in Constantinople.

Richard traveled extensively after he and Bohemund were freed in 1103: he donated a set of silver chains to the shrine of Saint-Leonard-du-Noblat in the Limousin to celebrate their release from captivity, and he arranged Bohemund's marriage to Princess Constance at the court of King Philip I of France. He ruled the county of Edessa as regent for the captive Baldwin II (1104–1108) before becoming lord of Marash (mod. Kahramanmaraş, Turkey) in Cilicia, the northernmost Frankish lordship in the Near East. His son Roger succeeded to the principality of Antioch in 1112.

–*George T. Beech*

Bibliography

Beech, George, "A Norman-Italian Adventurer in the East: Richard of Salerno, 1097–1112," in *Anglo-Norman Studies,* XV, ed. Marjorie Chibnall (Woodbridge, UK: Boydell, 1993), pp. 25–40.

Richard of Salerno

See Richard of the Principate

Riḍwān (1081–1113)

King (Arab. *malik*) of Aleppo and northern Syria (1095–1113), with the title Fakhr al-Mulūk ("Glory of the Kings").

Riḍwān was the eldest of five sons of the Saljūq king of Syria, Tutush I. During his struggle for the Saljūq sultanate, Tutush appointed Aytakin in 1094 as *atabeg* for Riḍwān and married him to Riḍwān's mother. When Tutush was killed in Persia (1095), Riḍwān and his brother Duqāq engaged in a conflict for power that plunged Syria into a civil war lasting until 1099. Each brother was aided by his own ambitious atabeg. Riḍwān ruled Aleppo (his capital) as well as Antioch (mod. Antakya, Turkey), Homs (mod. Ḥims, Syria), and Hama. He failed in two attempts to capture Duqāq's capital, Damascus, in 1096. As a result, he took an unprecedented step for a Sunnī ruler, and accepted an offer of the Egyptian vizier, al-Afḍal, by which he was to adopt the Fāṭimid Shī'ite doctrine in return for political support. On 7 September 1097 the name of the Fāṭimid caliph replaced that of the 'Abbasid caliph in the *khuṭba* (Friday sermon) in Aleppo, but after four weeks the Saljūq sultan persuaded Riḍwān to return to the Sunnī faith.

By this time, the armies of the First Crusade (1096–1099) had arrived in the northern dominions of Aleppo. Riḍwān did not intervene to save the city of Antioch, nor did he participate in the relief expedition mounted by Karbughā of Mosul, fearing his presence in Syria. Until 1103, Riḍwān avoided any serious hostilities against the Franks of Antioch or Edessa, a consequence of his economic difficulties and strife with his rebellious atabeg. Tancred, regent of Antioch from 1101, did not attack Riḍwān, as he was more afraid of other powers, such as the Byzantine Empire. Riḍwān was very keen on a modus vivendi with Antioch and in May 1103 agreed to pay a large annual tribute to protect his realm. He made no attempt to coordinate his policies with the Turcoman rulers of Upper Mesopotamia and Iraq in their wars with the Franks in the county of Edessa, even after the heavy defeat of the Franks at the battle of Harran in 1104. Riḍwān maintained the modus vivendi with the Franks during 1105–1110, but broke the peace when the Saljūq sultan started to send massive armies against the Franks in Syria, and plundered Antiochene territory.

The economy of Aleppo suffered from Tancred's retalia-tory attacks, and its citizens, who were losing confidence in Riḍwān, sent an embassy to the sultan urging him to promote *jihād* (holy war) against the Franks. When an army sent by Sultan Muḥammad Tapar arrived at Aleppo in 1111, Riḍwān closed the city's gates against it. Distrusting the loyalties of his subjects, Riḍwān imposed a curfew with the aid of the Assassins, a minority Ismā'īlī sect, until the sultan's forces withdrew. In his last years, Riḍwān was still paying a large annual tribute to Roger of Antioch to safeguard his kingdom. He died after an illness on 10 December 1113. He was succeeded by his son Alp Arslān, with the *mamlūk* (slave soldier) Lu'Lu' as regent.

–*Taef El-Azhari*

Bibliography

Eddé, Anne-Marie, "Ridwan prince d'Alep de 1095 à 1113," *Revue des études islamiques* 54 for 1986 (1988), 101–125.

El-Azhari, Taef, *The Saljūqs of Syria during the Crusades, 463–459 A.H./1070–1154 A.D.* (Berlin: Schwarz, 1997).

Riga

Riga (mod. Rīga, Latvia) was the principal town and bish-opric (later archbishopric) of medieval Livonia. It was founded in 1201 by the third bishop of Livonia, Albert of Buxhövden (Bekeshovede), as his new ecclesiastical center for the continuing Christianization and colonization of the region.

In the second half of the twelfth century German merchants had begun visiting the coasts of Livonia on an annual basis to trade with the local tribes. A frequently used anchoring place and market seems to have been a small Livonian settlement some 16 kilometers (c. 10 mi.) up the river Düna. The settlement was located near a small stream called Rigebach and inhabited mainly by fishermen and foresters. It was easily reached by the larger German vessels, and only a short way upstream the river became unnavigable for this type of ship. It was at this location that Riga was founded.

In 1186 a German cleric by the name of Meinhard became the first bishop of Livonia. Two years earlier he had settled in the village that became known as Üxküll (mod. Ikšķile, Latvia), some 30 kilometers (c. 19 mi.) further upstream. A church and a castle were built there, but Üxküll soon proved to be too isolated a place for a bishopric. On several occasions Meinhard found himself beleaguered in his church by hostile Livs, and in 1198 his successor, Bishop Bertold, died in battle when he and his crusaders tried to subdue the Livs after having been chased out of Üxküll the previous year. This may be one reason why Albert of Buxhövden, shortly after his appointment as bishop in 1199, decided to move the episcopal see to a more accessible location. The marketplace near the Rigebach seemed to be the ideal place.

Through papal privileges and a skillfully exploited trading monopoly, Albert was able to attract the first merchants to his new town. At first there were no more than a few hundred individuals, but ten years later the number of townspeople had grown considerably, predominantly through German merchants' settling in the town and profiting from trade in the region. With the rising number of townspeople the physical size of the city also grew until the early 1230s, when it seems to have reached the extent it retained for the rest of the medieval period. By this time it had strong, defensible stone walls.

Initially much of the work in Riga seems to have been carried out by crusaders from the West. From the beginning Albert was dependent on these armed pilgrims, both for the ongoing crusades against the pagans and also for the foundation of his town. Albert himself spent month after month in northern Germany gathering crusaders for new campaigns. Most of these crusaders would sail from Lübeck to Gotland and then continue to Riga. Here they arrived in the early spring or late autumn, prepared to spend a season in Livonia fighting for the church.

Not surprisingly, ecclesiastical institutions dominated Riga and its surroundings in the early years, making the chronicler Henry of Livonia exclaim that Riga was truly a city of God. A cathedral, several churches, and a hospital were soon built, and both Premonstratensians and Cistercians came to the region within the first ten years to take part in the mission: in 1205 a Cistercian monastery was founded at nearby Dünamünde (mod. Daugavgrīva, Latvia), and from 1210 the former Augustinian canons at the cathedral kept the Rule of the Premonstratensians. Also important was the founding of the Sword Brethren in 1202. Initially they were a small military order, numbering only a handful of knights until 1210. Soon, however, they came to have a central role in the continuous conquests in Livonia, with their master taking charge of most military campaigns in the region. This dominant position soon created tensions with the bishop and the civic authorities, which lasted until the order was almost wiped out in battle in 1236.

Skyline of the medieval town of Riga, in modern Latvia. (Steve Raymer/Corbis)

As a frontier settlement and the center of the crusading movement in Livonia, Riga had to be prepared to withstand attacks from hostile neighbors. Initially the crusaders constituted the only major fighting force available to the bishop in times of hostility, but by 1206 the numbers of townspeople living in Riga already seem to have risen to such a level that they could muster a fighting force of their own. The chronicler Henry of Livonia mentions that in that year a combined force of Sword Brethren, townspeople, and pilgrims (that is, crusaders) joined the armed servants of the bishop in an attack on Livs and Lithuanians who were plundering around Riga. From then on the townspeople took part in several campaigns in Livonia. This continual military engagement may explain why in 1226 the town was given one-third of the conquered territory in Livonia when the papal legate William of Modena divided the land between the various secular and ecclesiastical powers in the region. The other two-thirds were divided between the bishop and the Sword Brethren.

From Riga's beginnings, its growth had been dependent on the predominantly German merchants who settled in the town. They soon became the dominant group among the burgesses and also made up the majority of the town council. Even though the bishop (later archbishop) continued to be lord of the town, more and more rights were granted to the burgesses. The merchants in Riga continued to expand their commerce with the local population as well as with Russian trading centers to the east. This traffic secured a steady flow of goods (for example, wax and furs) that brought great wealth to the town and soon helped integrate Riga into the Hanseatic League.

In 1246 Albert Suerbeer became the first archbishop of Prussia, Livonia, and Estonia, and some years later he turned Riga into an archiepiscopal see. His time as archbishop was characterized by an evolving conflict with the Teutonic Order on the matter of regional supremacy. In 1237 the Teutonic Knights had absorbed the few remaining Sword Brethren and thereby established themselves firmly in Livonia. This conflict also affected the townspeople in Riga, inasmuch as they found themselves competing with the Teutonic Knights for the control of land and trade in the region. Thus, the townspeople supported the archbishop and in 1297 expelled the Teutonic Knights from Riga with the aid of the Lithuanian grand prince Vytenis. After years of juridical quarrels, however, the Teutonic Knights reconquered Riga by force in 1330.

In the later part of the fourteenth century the Teutonic Knights extended their dominance in Riga even further. In the 1390s a member of the order was elected archbishop, and the cathedral chapter was then periodically incorporated into the order until the incorporation became permanent in 1452. However, this did not prevent renewed hostilities between the Teutonic Order and the town of Riga, and another war was fought between 1482 and 1491. Due to its importance as a major port and as an administrative and religious center, Riga continued to be of great strategic importance in the crusades against the Lithuanians and later against the united kingdom of Poland-Lithuania, as well as in the later conflicts between Livonia and the Russians.

–Carsten Selch Jensen

Bibliography

Benninghoven, Friedrich, *Rigas Entstehung und der frühhansische Kaufmann* (Hamburg: Velmede, 1961).

Christiansen, Eric, *The Northern Crusades,* 2d ed. (London: Penguin, 1997).

Hellmann, Manfred, "Livland und das Reich: Das Problem ihrer gegenseitigen Beziehungen," *Sitzungsberichte der Bayerischen Akademie der Wissenschaften, Philosophisch-historische Klasse* 6 (1989), 3–35.

Jähnig, Bernhardt, "Die Anfänge der Sakraltopographie von Riga," in *Studien über die Anfänge der Mission in Livland,* ed. Manfred Hellmann (Sigmaringen: Thorbecke, 1989), pp. 123–158.

Jensen, Carsten Selch, "Urban Life and the Crusades in North Germany and the Baltic Lands in the Early Thirteenth Century," in *Crusade and Conversion on the Baltic Frontier, 1150–1500,* ed. Alan V. Murray (Aldershot, UK: Ashgate, 2001), pp. 75–94.

Rigord

Author of the *Gesta Philippi Augusti;* the only writer contemporary with the Third Crusade (1189–1192) to give an account of it from the point of view of Philip II Augustus, king of France.

Rigord's chronicle survives in only two manuscripts. It was an independent work, not commissioned by the king and sometimes critical of him. Rigord was a medical man by profession, who became a monk at the abbey of Saint-Denis near Paris before 1189. He began to write his history before 1186, and was the first to give Philip II the title Augustus. His references to the crusade mainly concern the king: a brief description of the events of 1187, Philip's preparations for the crusade, the course of the crusade from his departure for the East to the capture of Acre (mod. 'Akko, Israel), and the king's return to France, which Rigord attributes to Philip's severe illness and distrust of King Richard I of England, his fellow crusader. As he was writing a history of the king of France and not the king of England, he says no more of the crusade, except to criticize Richard for its outcome. His work was used by Guillaume le Breton and later French historians. He died soon after 1205.

–Helen Nicholson

Bibliography

Baldwin, John W., *The Government of Philip Augustus: Foundations of French Royal Power in the Middle Ages* (Berkeley: University of California Press, 1986).

Lewis, P. S. "Some Provisional Remarks upon the Chronicles of Saint-Denis and upon the *(Grandes) Chroniques de France* in the Fifteenth Century," *Nottingham Medieval Studies* 39 (1995), 151–153.

Cœuvres de Rigord et de Guillaume le Breton, historiens de Philippe-Auguste, ed. Henri-François Delaborde (Paris: Renouard, 1882)

Rimini, Golden Bull of

The basic charter of the lordship of the Teutonic Order in Prussia, issued by Frederick II, Holy Roman Emperor and king of Sicily, at Rimini in central Italy.

The charter conferred on the order all territorial rights (concerning ground, water, forests, mining, customs, markets, taxes, coinage, safe passage, and jurisdiction, comparable to the privileges of the princes of the empire) over the territories still to be conquered from the heathen Prussians. Its date has recently been debated: though the charter reads March 1226, Sylvain Gouguenheim, drawing on studies by

Holy Roman Emperor Frederick II confirms privileges of the Teutonic Order and charges the order with the conquest of Prussia. Facsimile of the Golden Bull of Rimini, 1226. (Bildarchiv Preußischer Kulturbesitz/Art Resource)

Tomasz Jasinski, has argued that the charter was renewed and changed in 1234/1235. Its importance is beyond question, and the order used it extensively in later disputes with the Prussian estates and Poland.

–*Jürgen Sarnowsky*

See also: Baltic Crusades; Teutonic Order
Bibliography
Gouguenheim, Sylvain, "L'empereur, le grand maître et la Prusse. La bulle de Rimini en question (1226/1235)," *Bibliothèque de l'Ecole des Chartes* 162 (2005), 381–420.
Kluger, Helmuth, *Hochmeister Hermann von Salza und Kaiser Friedrich II* (Marburg: Elwert, 1987).

Robert II of Flanders (d. 1111)

Count of Flanders (1093–1111) and one of the leaders of the First Crusade (1096–1099).

Robert was born in the third quarter of the eleventh century, the eldest son of Robert I the Frisian, count of Flanders, and Gertrude of Holland. In 1087 he was entrusted with the government of Flanders when his father undertook a pilgrimage to the Holy Land. Around that time he married Clementia, daughter of Count William I of Burgundy, and in 1093 he succeeded his father as count of Flanders.

In September 1096 Robert II and a large Flemish contingent joined the armies of Duke Robert Curthose of Normandy and Count Stephen of Blois and journeyed through France, Italy, and the Balkans, arriving at Constantinople (mod. İstanbul, Turkey) in December 1096. On 26 December 1097, during the siege of Antioch (mod. Antakya, Turkey), he commanded a foraging expedition that encountered a Turkish relief army at Albara (mod. al-Bārah, Syria). Facing fearful odds, the crusaders attacked the center of the Turkish army, which was driven away; had the Turks been able to go on, the continuation of the crusade might well have been threatened. At the siege of Jerusalem (June–July 1099) Robert was in charge of logistics. The last time he fought during the crusade was at the victory over the Fāṭimids at Ascelon (12 August 1099), but before returning he reconciled Godfrey of Bouillon and Raymond of Saint-Gilles and also settled a dispute between Raymond and Bohemund I of Antioch. Robert was back in Flanders by early spring of 1100. He died at Meaux (France) on 5 October 1111, leaving two sons, Baldwin VII (who succeeded him as count) and William.

–*Jan Anckaer*

Bibliography

De Hemptinne, Thérèse, "Les épouses des croisés et pèlerins flamands aux XI et XII siècles: L'exemple des comtesses de Flandre Clémence et Sibylle," in *Autour de la Première Croisade: Actes du Colloque de la Society for the Study of the Crusades and the Latin East (Clermont-Ferrand, 22–25 juin 1995),* ed. Michel Balard (Paris: Publications de la Sorbonne, 1996), pp. 83–99.

De Smet, J. J., *Mémoire sur Robert de Jérusalem, comte de Flandre à la première croisade,* Mémoires de la Classe des Lettres de l'Académie Royale des Sciences et Belles-Lettres de Belgique 1 (Bruxelles: Académie Royale, 1848).

Knappen, Marshall M., "Robert II of Flanders in the First Crusade," in *The Crusades and Other Historical Essays Presented to Dana C. Munro by His Former Students,* ed. Louis J. Paetow (New York: Crofts, 1928), pp. 79–100.

Robert Burgundio (d. 1149)

Master of the Templars (1136/1137–1149).

Robert, a son of Rainald Burgundio of Craon and Ennoguena of Vitré, belonged to the Angevin high nobility. After several years in the service of the count of Angoulême and at the court of the dukes of Aquitaine, he dissolved his engagement to the heiress of Chabannes and Confolens and traveled to Outremer. Robert had probably joined the Templars by 1125; he became seneschal of the the order and traveled to the West (1132–1133/1134), where he received important donations on its behalf, including the castle of Barberà in Spain. After the death of Hugo of Payns (1136/1137), Robert became the second master of the order.

Robert returned to the West in 1138. On 29 March 1139, Pope Innocent II issued *Omne datum optimum,* the Templars' most important papal privilege, naming Robert as its recipient. William of Tyre listed Robert among the participants of the Second Crusade's general curia held in Acre (mod. 'Akko, Israel) on 24 June 1148 and gave an unusually friendly assessment of him. Robert died on 13 January 1149 and was succeeded by Everard of Barres.

–Jochen Burgtorf

Bibliography

Barber, Malcolm, *The New Knighthood: A History of the Order of the Temple* (Cambridge: Cambridge University Press, 1994).

Jessee, W. Scott, "The Family of Robert the Burgundian and the Creation of the Angevin March of Sable and Craon," *Medieval Prosopography* 16 (1995), 31–60.

Robert of Clari (d. after 1216)

Chronicler of the Fourth Crusade (1202–1204) and the early years of the Latin Empire of Constantinople up to 1216.

Robert of Clari was probably born around 1180; he was a poor knight whose tiny fief was situated at the modern Cléry-lès-Pernois (*département* Somme, France). He first appears in sources from 1202 when, with his father Gilo, he witnessed a gift from their lord Peter of Amiens to the abbey of St. John of Amiens.

Clari went on crusade as a follower of Peter of Amiens. He names himself twice in his narrative: once during the attack by the crusaders on Constantinople (mod. İstanbul, Turkey) on 12 April 1204, and once at the end, when he testifies that he was an eyewitness to the events that he has described. His account is firsthand until the spring of 1204, but he does not seem to have been in the army defeated by the Bulgarians at Adrianople (mod. Edirne, Turkey) in 1204, either because he had already returned to France or because he was waiting to do so at Constantinople. He was still alive in 1216 when the news reached France of the death of the Latin Emperor Henry, which he mentions at the end of his chronicle. He brought back many relics from Constantinople, which he gave to the abbey of Corbie.

Clari is not always accurate in his dates, placing the negotiations of the crusade leaders with the Venetians after the death of the count of Champagne and the choice of Boniface of Montferrat as his replacement. His work is designed to instruct his audience, which would have been even less well informed than he. He includes long digressions on the political history of Byzantium to explain the feuds between the different Greek factions and the house of Montferrat. He also gives much space to descriptions of churches and palaces and, in particular, to the relics and the marvels to be found there. Clari's account is particularly valuable as it gives the viewpoint of the poor knights in the ranks of the crusade army. He is sharply critical of the greed of the leading crusaders and the *hauts homs* (men of high rank). He saw the defeat at Adrianople as God's punishment for this greed. His vivid account of the maneuvering of the crusader squadrons when confronted by the army of Emperor Alexios III Angelos outside Constantinople shows how jealous the different factions were of each other and how near they came to defeat. Clari's chronicle complements that of Geoffrey of Villehardouin and provides a completely different perspective on the events of the crusade until mid-1204.

Clari's style is vivid and full of life. Very aware of his audience, he makes every effort to explain difficult words and events. He had clearly taken some trouble to discover the political and historical background to events in Constantinople, and all his digressions are there to help his listeners understand his narrative. He struggles to find the vocabulary adequate for the task, which results in some repetition. His syntax is unsophisticated, with overlong sentences, but he is eager to communicate and does so with a vigor that contrasts with the much more detached style of Villehardouin.

–Peter S. Noble

Bibliography

Bagley, C. Patricia, "Robert de Clari's *La Conquête de Constantinople*," *Medium Aevum* 40 (1971), 109–115.

Dembowski, Peter F., *La Chronique de Robert de Clari: Etude de la langue et du style* (Toronto: University of Toronto Press, 1963).

Dufournet, Jean, *Les écrivains de la IV croisade: Villehardouin et Clari* (Paris: Société d'Edition d'Enseignement supérieur, 1973).

Pauphilet, Albert, "Sur Robert de Clari," *Romania* 57 (1931), 281–311.

Robert de Clari, *La Conquête de Constantinople,* ed. Philippe Lauer (Paris: Champion, 1924).

———, *The Conquest of Constantinople Translated from the Old French of Robert of Clari,* trans. Edgar H. McNeal (New York: Columbia University Press, 1936).

———, *La Conquête de Constantinople,* ed. and trans. Peter S. Noble (Edinburgh: British Rencesvals Publications, 2005).

Robert of Constantinople (d. 1228)

Latin emperor of Constantinople (1221–1228).

The second son of Peter of Courtenay, emperor of Constantinople, and Yolande of Flanders, Robert was crowned emperor in Constantinople (mod. İstanbul, Turkey) on 25 March 1221, after a period of regency following the death of his father (1217). Robert renewed peace with Theodore I Laskaris, emperor of Nicaea, but the planned marriage with Theodore's daughter Eudokia was not realized. In 1224 the Latins were defeated at Poimanenon by John III Vatatzes, the new emperor of Nicaea, who imposed humiliating peace conditions. Robert, a man inclined to pleasures, generally neglected state affairs, and his reign was disastrous for the Latin Empire. When the barons mutilated the face of the young Frenchwoman he had married in secret, Robert left Constantinople. He died in the Morea, probably in January 1228.

–Benjamin Hendrickx

Bibliography

Longnon, Jean, *L'empire latin de Constantinople et la principauté de Morée* (Paris: Payot, 1949).

Wolff, Robert L., "The Latin Empire of Constantinople, 1204–1261," in *A History of the Crusades,* ed. Kenneth M. Setton, 2d ed., 6 vols. (Madison: University of Wisconsin Press, 1969–1989), 2:187–274.

Robert Curthose (d. 1134)

Duke of Normandy (1087–1106) and one of the leaders of the First Crusade (1096–1099).

Born around 1154, the eldest son of William I of England and Matilda of Flanders, Robert was the subject of unflattering portraits by the chroniclers Orderic Vitalis and William of Malmesbury, who revealed that his father nicknamed him Curthose (Lat. *Curta Ocrea,* "short boots") because he was short and plump.

A pawn in his father's politics from an early age, Robert was consistently denied any responsible role as he became older. Charming, generous, and skilled with words, he lacked the overriding drive and ruthlessness with which his father and brothers forged their great successes in circumstances just as difficult as those facing Robert when he inherited Normandy on his father's death in 1087. For all his genuine piety, the crusade undoubtedly presented him with a welcome escape from his difficulties. He had fought a bitter and largely unsuccessful war for control of Normandy with his brother William II Rufus, king of England, to whom he now mortgaged the duchy for 10,000 silver marks. Accompanied by a sizable contingent of knights from northern France, he traveled to the East with Stephen of Blois, Alan IV of Brittany, and Robert II of Flanders (who left them at Bari). Their leisurely journey took them through Italy, where they met Pope Urban II at Lucca. After wintering in southern Italy, they reached Constantinople in May 1097 and joined the siege of Nicaea (mod. İznik, Turkey) on 3 June.

Robert displayed considerable qualities as a soldier and a commander during an attack by the Turks at Dorylaion on 30 June. He was one of four princes who led the vanguard on the march to Antioch (mod. Antakya, Turkey), and was again in the vanguard at the battle for the Iron Bridge controlling access to Antioch on 20 October. Although he retired to Laodikeia (mod. Al-Lādhiqīyah, Syria) and did not share all the privations of the army investing Antioch, he sent it food supplies obtained from Cyprus. He was in Antioch to help repel a Turkish attack on the citadel on 11 June 1098, and for the defeat of Karbughā and fall of Antioch on 28 July. The subsequent deadlock over the march to Jerusalem was broken when Raymond of Saint-Gilles took several leaders, including Robert, into his pay for the continued march (13 January 1099). After the capture of Jerusalem, Robert played a key role in the defeat of Fāṭimid forces before Ascalon (mod. Tel Ashqelon, Israel) on 12 August.

Robert is never implicated in the bitter disputes that broke out among some of the princes, and he is even assigned the role of mediator by Orderic Vitalis. He returned to Normandy via Sicily, where he married Sibyl of Conversano, a cousin of Bohemund I of Antioch; her dowry permitted him to redeem his duchy from his brother Henry I, now king of England. Robert's new prestige as a crusader did not prevent him being as ineffectual against Henry as he had been against William II. Captured by Henry at the battle of Tinchebray in 1106, he spent the rest of his life as a prisoner, dying in 1134 at Cardiff castle, six years after the death of his only legitimate son, William Clito. One of his natural sons, also called William, served Baldwin I of Jerusalem and became lord of Tortosa (mod. Tartūs, Lebanon) in the county of Tripoli.

–K. S. B. Keats-Rohan

Bibliography

Aird, William M., "Frustrated Masculinity: The Relationship between William the Conqueror and His Eldest Son," in *Masculinity in Europe*, ed. Dawn M. Hadley (Harlow: Longman, 1999).

Christelow, Stephanie Mooers, "'Backers and Stabbers': Problems of Loyalty in Robert Curthose's Entourage," *Journal of British Studies* 21 (1981), 1–17.

David, Charles W., *Robert Curthose, Duke of Normandy* (Cambridge: Harvard University Press, 1920).

France, John, "The Normans and Crusading," in *The Normans and Their Adversaries at War: Essays in Memory of C. Warren Hollister*, ed. Richard P. Abels and Bernard S. Bachrach (Woodbridge, UK: Boydell, 2001), pp. 87–101.

Green, Judith A., "Robert Curthose Reassessed," in *Anglo-Norman Studies*, XXII, ed. Christopher Harper-Bill (Woodbridge, UK: Boydell, 2000), 95–116.

Robert the Monk

See Robert of Rheims

Robert of Rheims

Author of the *Historia Iherosolimitana,* a Latin history of the First Crusade (1096–1099).

According to the apology (Lat. *sermo apologeticus*) Robert placed at the beginning of the work, he attended the Council of Clermont (November 1095) and wrote his *Historia* while a monk at the Benedictine abbey of St. Remi in Rheims. It is unlikely that he can be identified with a former abbot of St. Remi (d. 1122), who was expelled in 1096 or 1097 and went on the First Crusade himself.

No consensus has been reached about the *Historia*'s date of composition—whether it was finished by 1107 or written between 1110 and 1118—or its relationship to other sources. However, the nine books of the *Historia* follow the anonymous *Gesta Francorum* in their account of the years 1095–1099, framed by descriptions of Jerusalem and concentrating on the heroic fighting in Antioch (mod. Antakya, Turkey): the Council of Clermont (with a version of Pope Urban II's famous speech) and the story of Peter the Hermit (book 1); the march of the various contingents to Constantinople (mod. İstanbul, Turkey) and their disputes with the Byzantine emperor (book 2); the progression of the crusade from Constantinople to Antioch (book 3); the siege of Antioch (books 4–7); minor campaigns of the crusaders and tensions among them (book 8); and the capture of Jerusalem, the election of Godfrey of Bouillon, and the battle of Ascalon (book 9).

Robert gives a polished account with rhythmical and rhymed sentences and refined speeches; he intersperses verses to introduce and summarize chapters and, like other prosimetrical historians of the First Crusade (Fulcher of Chartres, Guibert of Nogent, Radulph of Caen), inserts poems, mostly to illustrate fighting emotively. The chronicle betrays Robert's special interest in topography, evident in his descriptions of Jerusalem, Constantinople, and Antioch. Naturally, Robert depicts the heroism of the crusaders and emphatically praises the deeds of Bohemund of Taranto and Godfrey of Bouillon, but above all, he explains the success of the First Crusade as a manifestation of God's will and power: "Hoc enim non fuit humanum opus, sed divinum" (This was not a human enterprise, but a divine one ["Robert Monachi historia Iherosolimitana," 3: 723]).

Robert's narrative soon became the most popular and the most frequently copied history of the First Crusade, surviving in over 100 manuscripts. It was first printed in 1472. The editors of the *Recueil des Historiens des Croisades* worked from twenty-two manuscripts but relied especially on a twelfth-century manuscript now in the Bibliothèque nationale de France [MS Paris, Bibliothèque nationale de

France, lat.5129]. Manuscripts of the *Historia* are often accompanied by a letter of the Byzantine emperor Alexios I Komnenos to Count Robert I of Flanders asking for military aid.

At least three Latin versifications derived from the *Historia*. Two originated in Germany: Metellus of Tegernsee's *Expeditio Ierosolimitana* (1146/1165) and Gunther's *Solimarius* (fragment of uncertain date; before 1186); the third is the fragmentary *Solymis* by the Italian Giovanni Maria Cattaneo (d. 1529/1530). In the later Middle Ages the *Historia* achieved even greater influence through translations into French, Italian, and, above all, German (five translations in the fifteenth and sixteenth centuries), while the growing threats from the Turks were reflected in Latin prose redactions or adaptations: Thomas Ebendorfer's *De duobus passagiis Christianorum principum* on the First and the Third Crusades (written 1454–1456) probably remained largely unknown, in a single manuscript, but the *Historiarum decades* of Flavio Biondo (d. 1463) became the standard account of the First Crusade, particularly of Urban's speech at Clermont, until the end of the sixteenth century.

–*Peter Orth*

Bibliography

Cronin, James E., "And the Reapers Are Angels: A Study of the Crusade Motivation as Described in the *Historia Iherosolimitana* of Robert the Monk" (Ph.D. diss., New York University, 1973).

Historia Hierosolymitana von Robertus Monachus in deutscher Übersetzung, ed. Barbara Haupt (Wiesbaden: Steiner, 1972).

Kraft, Friedrich, *Heinrich Steinhöwels Verdeutschung der Historia Hierosolymitana des Robertus Monachus: Eine literarhistorische Untersuchung* (Straßburg: Trübner, 1905).

Marquardt, Georg, *Die Historia Hierosolymitana des Robertus Monachus: Ein quellenkritischer Beitrag zur Geschichte des 1. Kreuzzugs* (Königsberg: Liedtke, 1892).

Orth, Peter, "Papst Urbans II. Kreuzzugsrede in Clermont bei lateinischen Schriftstellern des 15. und 16. Jahrhunderts," in *Jerusalem im Hoch- und Spätmittelalter: Vorstellungen und Vergegenwärtigungen, Konflikte und Konfliktregelung,* ed. Dieter Bauer, Klaus Herbers, and Nikolas Jaspert (Frankfurt am Main: Campus, 2001), pp. 367–405.

———, "Zur *Solymis* des Giovanni Maria Cattaneo," *Humanistica Lovaniensia* 50 (2001), 131–141.

Pabst, Bernhard, *Prosimetrum. Tradition und Wandel einer Literaturform zwischen Spätantike und Spätmittelalter* (Köln: Böhlau, 1994).

"Roberti Monachi historia Iherosolimitana," in *Recueil des Historiens des Croisades: Historiens Occidentaux,* 5 vols. (Paris: Académie des Inscriptions et Belles-Lettres, 1844–1895), 3:717–882.

Robert the Monk's History of the First Crusade: Historia Iherosolimitana, trans. Carol Sweetenham (Aldershot, UK: Ashgate, 2005).

Russo, Luigi, "Ricerche sull'*Historia Iherosolimitana* di Roberto di Reims," *Studi Medievali,* ser. 3, 43 (2002), 651–691.

Robertus Monachus

See Robert of Rheims

La Roche Family

A Burgundian family from La Roche-sur-l'Ognon, northeast of Besançon. Its members rose to prominence during the Fourth Crusade (1202–1204) and subsequently as lords of Athens and Thebes in central Greece, later bearing the title dukes of Athens.

Otho of La Roche is recorded in the Burgundian contingent before the walls of Constantinople at the end of the Fourth Crusade but is not listed among the prominent nobles of Burgundy who took the cross at Cîteaux in September 1201. Otho served in the army of Boniface of Montferrat in late 1204 as it invaded mainland Greece. He may have been granted Athens at this time, but it is unclear whether he also received Thebes then, or in 1209 or 1211 as a reward for his support of Emperor Henry of Constantinople against the Lombard lords of Thessalonica. In April 1209 Otho was certainly at the siege of Akrokorinth, and like Geoffrey I of Villehardouin he went from there to attend Henry at Ravennika. In June 1209 he welcomed Henry to his lordship of Athens and took part as lord in the ceremonials enacted there. Thereafter, Otho built up his lordship in central Greece: he wrote to Pope Innocent III, who addressed him from 1208 onward as *dominus Athenarum* (lord of Athens); possibly built up the Propylaia as a ducal palace; and in 1217 granted the monastery at Daphni to the Cistercian monastery of Bellevaux in Burgundy. Otho maintained close links with Burgundy throughout the twenty-six years he was absent on crusade and in Greece. In 1225 he returned to his native Burgundy, where he died by 1234.

Otho was succeeded in Burgundy by his son Otho II, and in Athens by his nephew Guy I, who had been in Greece with his uncle since 1211. Guy was the son of Pons of Flavigny, and it was his descendants who were to further the family interests in Frankish Greece, either as lords of Athens and Thebes, or as lords of Damala and Veligosti, Moreote fiefs that had been granted to Otho by the Villehardouin dynasty of Achaia in return for his support during the siege of Akrocorinth. Guy I ruled Athens and Thebes until his death in 1263. He was active in his resistance to Villehardouin claims and was granted the title of duke of Athens by King Louis IX of France in 1260. He was succeeded by his sons John (d. 1280) and William (d. 1287).

William's son Guy II (Guyot) was the last of the La Roche dukes. He was able and ambitious and, at his untimely death in 1308, seemed set to enhance the status of the dukes of Athens within Frankish Greece. He left no direct heir, and the succession passed to the Brienne family, into which his aunt Isabella had married in 1277. The family name continued with Reynaud, lord of Damala, who was killed at the battle of Halmyros in 1311.

–Peter Lock

See also: Athens, Lordship and Duchy of

Bibliography
Lock, Peter, *The Franks in the Aegean* (London: Longman, 1995).
Longnon, Jean, *Les Compagnons de Villehardouin* (Genève: Droz, 1978).
Miller, William, *The Latins in the Levant* (London: Murray, 1908).
———, *Essays on the Latin Orient* (Cambridge: Cambridge University Press, 1921).
Setton, Kenneth, *The Papacy and the Levant,* vol. 1 (Philadelphia: American Philosophical Society, 1976).

Roger I of Sicily (d. 1101)

Count of Sicily (1061–1101); conqueror of the island from its Muslim rulers.

The youngest of the twelve sons of Tancred of Hauteville, a minor baron from the Cotentin region of western Normandy, Roger followed his elder brothers to southern Italy around 1056/1057, at about the time when his brother Robert Guiscard became the overall leader of the south Italian Normans, who had already conquered inland Apulia and northern Calabria. Roger assisted Robert in the conquest of southern Calabria (1057–1060), and led a first, reconnaissance, raid on the island of Sicily in the autumn of 1060. Subsequently he undertook the conquest of the island from its Muslim rulers, in a series of campaigns last-

ing thirty years from 1061 onward. The northeast of the island, including the key port of Messina, was soon conquered, and a major defeat inflicted on the Muslims at Cerami (June 1063), but subsequent progress was slow, hampered by a shortage of troops, difficult terrain, problems with the indigenous Greek Christians, and Roger's frequent absences on the south Italian mainland. Palermo was eventually captured (with Robert Guiscard's help) in 1072, Trapani and most of western Sicily by 1077, Syracuse in 1086, and Agrigento in 1087. Only the southeast was now left, and the last town in Muslim hands there, Noto, surrendered in 1091. The last decade of Roger's life was devoted to the consolidation of Christian rule on the island, and of his rule in Calabria, the latter in alliance with his nephew Roger Borsa, duke of Apulia (1085–1111). Roger refused to take part in the First Crusade (1096–1099); he may well have been reluctant to jeopardize the stability of his rule in Sicily, where the majority of the population remained Muslim.

–G. A. Loud

Bibliography
Loud, Graham A., *The Age of Robert Guiscard: Southern Italy and the Norman Conquest* (Harlow: Longman, 2000).
Norwich, John Julius, *The Normans in the South* (London: Longman, 1967).
Ruggero il Gran Conte e l'inizio dello stato normanno (Roma: Centro di Ricerca Editore, 1977).

Roger II of Sicily (d. 1154)

Count (1105–1130) and subsequently king of Sicily (1130–1154).

Younger son of Count Roger I, Roger II succeeded his elder brother Simon as count in 1105. On the death of his cousin William (1127), he also became duke of Apulia and thus ruler of most of mainland southern Italy. Roger took advantage of the papal schism of 1130 to secure the consent of Anacletus II (the pope who held Rome) to his coronation as the first king of Sicily in Palermo cathedral on Christmas Day 1130. The early years of the new kingdom were difficult, since Roger was faced with the hostility of rebel barons on the mainland, of the German and Byzantine emperors (both of whom considered southern Italy to be rightfully part of their dominions), and of Pope Innocent II, the eventual victor in the schism. Nevertheless, by 1140 Roger had defeated

Roger II, king of Sicily (1095–1154). Byzantine mosaic from the Church of Martorana, Palermo. (Bettmann/Corbis)

his opponents, successfully united southern Italy under his rule, and secured Innocent's reluctant recognition of his kingship. His fleet conducted operations against Muslim pirates in the Mediterranean, capturing Jerba in 1135, and in 1146–1148 his forces conquered Tripoli, Mahdia, and other towns in Tunisia from their Muslim rulers, although they remained in Sicilian hands for little more than a decade. Roger's motives in this conquest appear not to have been religious but pragmatic: to secure Sicilian trade and tribute, taking opportunist advantage of internal divisions among the North African Muslims.

Roger also played a significant role in the failure of the Second Crusade (1147–1149) in the East. His war with Byzantium led the Emperor Manuel I Komnenos to conclude a truce with the Turks of Asia Minor shortly before the cru-

sade's arrival, and his fleet attacked Greece while it was under way. Louis VII of France subsequently returned from Outremer via the kingdom of Sicily, and, unlike the Germans, appears to have had good relations with Roger, but attempts to involve the Sicilian ruler directly in the crusade, both in 1145–1146 and in 1149–1150, were unsuccessful.

–G. A. Loud

Bibliography

Abulafia, David, "The Norman Kingdom of Africa and the Norman Expeditions to Majorca and the Muslim Mediterranean," in *Anglo-Norman Studies,* VII: *Proceedings of the Battle Conference 1984,* ed. R. Allen Brown (Woodbridge, UK: Boydell, 1985), pp. 26–49.

Houben, Hubert, *Roger II of Sicily: A Ruler between East and West* (Cambridge: Cambridge University Press, 2002).

Wieruszowski, Helene, "The Norman Kingdom of Sicily and the Crusades," in *A History of the Crusades,* ed. Kenneth M. Setton, 6 vols., 2d ed. (Madison: University of Wisconsin Press, 1969–1989), 2:3–42.

Roger of Antioch (d. 1119)

Ruler of the principality of Antioch (1113–1119) in succession to Tancred.

Roger of Salerno, as he was originally known, was a son of Richard of the Principate and a sister of Tancred. He succeeded Tancred as ruler of Antioch on the latter's death in 1113. It is disputed whether Roger ruled in his own right or as regent for the young Bohemund II (born 1108), who was in Italy. However, Roger was accused of usurpation only by Fulcher of Chartres; other chroniclers treat him as the rightful ruler and refer to him as "prince."

The first crisis of Roger's reign was a massive series of earthquakes in 1114–1115. He demonstrated admirable qualities of leadership in his organization of the repairs to the city of Antioch (mod. Antakya, Turkey) and surrounding towns. In 1115, after careful reconnaissance and after making an alliance with the Turkish leaders Ṭughtigin of Damascus and Īlghāzī, Roger campaigned against Bursuq of Hamadān. He did not wait for support from King Baldwin I of Jerusalem or Count Pons of Tripoli, his Christian allies, but launched a surprise attack on Bursuq's camp on 14 September 1115. The ensuing battle of Tell Danith was an overwhelming victory for Roger and the high point of his reign. Bursuq died a few months later, and Antioch was established as a formidable political and military force in northern Syria. However, Roger tried to repeat his success in June 1119, by attacking a Turkish army led by Īlghāzī, without waiting for Baldwin II of Jerusalem and Pons of Tripoli. The defeat that followed wiped out the Antiochene army and is known evocatively as the battle of *Ager Sanguinis* (the Field of Blood). Roger himself was killed in the fighting.

The principality of Antioch now lay wide open to conquest, but the Turks failed to follow up their victory, and the city held out until King Baldwin II arrived to take charge. He assumed the regency of the principality until Bohemund II achieved his majority in 1126.

–*Susan B. Edgington*

Bibliography
Asbridge, Thomas S., "The Significance and Causes of the Battle of the Field of Blood," *Journal of Medieval History* 23 (1997), 301–316.
———, *The Creation of the Principality of Antioch, 1098–1130* (Woodbridge, UK: Boydell, 2000).
Cahen, Claude, *La Syrie du Nord à l'époque des croisades et la principauté franque d'Antioche* (Paris: Geuthner, 1940).
Stevenson, W. B., *The Crusaders in the East* (Cambridge: Cambridge University Press, 1907).

Roger of Howden

English royal clerk and parson of Howden (Yorkshire), who wrote an eyewitness account of the Third Crusade (1189–1192). His first chronicle, the *Gesta Regis Henrici Secundi et Ricardi Primi* (formerly attributed to Benedict of Peterborough), covers the years from 1170 to 1192. It was revised and continued in the *Chronica,* a chronicle stretching from 732 to 1201.

English constitutional tradition led to a one-sided view of Howden, as a historian of administration and law, while ignoring other aspects of his career and interests. He was a religious man who was worried about heresy and interested in miracles, prophecies, and the coming end of the world. The most widely traveled of all English chroniclers, his many journeys in the service of both kings of England and bishops of Durham took him to Scotland, France, Rome, Sicily, and the Holy Land. During the Third Crusade, he joined the fleet of King Richard I at Marseilles in August 1190 and remained until after the capture of Acre (mod. 'Akko, Israel), leaving on 25 August 1191 to keep an eye on Richard's rival, Philip II of France. His *Gesta Regis* is in effect a crusade diary of those thirteen months, which he revised, in the light of subsequent events, in the *Chronica.*

Howden's crusading experience and enthusiasm informed his judgments. He became more critical of Henry II; although he regretted the heavy taxation of Richard's later years, he praised his piety, generosity, prowess, and generalship. He probably died around the year 1202.

–*John Gillingham*

Bibliography
Chronica Magistri Rogeri de Hoveden, ed. William Stubbs, 4 vols., Rolls Series 51 (London: Longman, 1868–1871).
The Chronicle of the Reigns of Henry II and Richard I, Known Commonly under the Name of Benedict of Peterborough, ed. William Stubbs, 2 vols., Rolls Series 49 (London: Longman, 1867).
Gillingham, John, "Roger of Howden on Crusade," in *Medieval Historical Writing in the Christian and Islamic Worlds,* ed. David O. Morgan (London: School of Oriental and African Studies, 1982), pp. 60–75; repr. in Gillingham, *Richard Coeur de Lion* (London: Hambledon, 1994).

Roger of Les Moulins (d. 1187)

Master of the Order of the Hospital (1177–1187).

Roger was a member of the order in Outremer by March 1175 and master two years later. He traveled to the West twice: to Sicily on Hospitaller business in April 1179, and again in 1184 as part of a delegation soliciting help against Saladin. In 1183 he and the Hospitallers fought against Saladin with the army of Jerusalem under the regent, Guy of Lusignan. Roger witnessed Baldwin IV's will in 1185, which named the king's nephew (Baldwin V) as heir and appointed Count Raymond III of Tripoli as regent.

After Baldwin V died in 1186, Baldwin IV's sister Sibyl claimed the throne, flouting the terms of the will. Roger supported the faction in the kingdom (led by Raymond) that was opposed to Sibyl and her husband, Guy of Lusignan; at their coronation in Jerusalem, he refused to surrender his key to the treasury containing the royal crowns, finally throwing it away. It was retrieved by Gerard of Ridefort, master of the Temple, and the coronation proceeded. Roger was killed fighting against Saladin's troops at the battle at the springs of Cresson (1 May 1187). Roger's death left the Hospitallers without a master until the election of Warner of Nablus, former prior of England and grand commander of France, in 1189.

–*Theresa M. Vann*

Bibliography

Ligato, Giuseppe, "Il magister ospedaliero Ruggiero des Moulins nella crisi finale del regno latino di Gerusalemme (1182–1187)," *Antonianum: Periodicum philosophico-theologicum trimestre* 71 (1996), 495–522.

Riley-Smith, Jonathan, *The Knights of St. John in Jerusalem and Cyprus* (London: St. Martin's, 1967).

Sire, H. J. A., *The Knights of Malta* (New Haven: Yale University Press, 1994).

Rognvald Kali Kolsson (d. 1158)

Earl of Orkney (1136–1158) and leader of a crusade to the Holy Land in 1151–1153.

Born around 1099, Kali Kolsson, as he was originally known, belonged to a family that had ruled Orkney as a semi-independent earldom under the Norwegian Crown since the tenth century. Although he was born and grew up in Norway, Kali had a claim to the earldom of Orkney through his mother Gunnhild, sister of the martyred earl St. Magnus I Erlendsson (d. 1115). In 1129 Kali's title to half of Orkney was recognized by Sigurd, king of Norway, and at this time he adopted the name of Rognvald, after an eleventh-century earl. Rognvald contracted an alliance with William the Old, bishop of Orkney, and Maddad, earl of Atholl, who was married to Margaret, sister of the ruling earl, Paul II Hakonsson (1123–1136). This alliance enabled Rognvald to mount a successful invasion of Orkney in 1135, capturing and disposing of Earl Paul. Rognvald's rule as earl was marked by his promotion of the cult of St. Magnus, notably in the construction of a new cathedral dedicated to him at Kirkwall.

In 1150 Rognvald decided to embark on an expedition to the Holy Land. He left Orkney in the charge of Maddad's son Harald, whom he had accepted as joint earl in 1138. Rognvald's decision was influenced by one Eindredi Ungi, a Norwegian with extensive experience in the East, who evidently hoped to recruit Norsemen for service in the Varangian units of the Byzantine emperor. The timing of the expedition suggests that it may also have been connected with wider (but ultimately fruitless) efforts in 1150 to launch a new crusade in response to the advances of Nūr al-Dīn in northern Syria. Rognvald's crusade is described somewhat confusedly in the *Orkneyinga Saga*, but its itinerary can be reconstructed with reasonable certainty. Crusaders from Orkney and Norway, including Bishop William and Eindredi, sailed from Orkney with 15 ships in the summer of 1151, and, after a short stay in Galicia, on to southern France. They wintered in Narbonne,

giving military assistance to Aimery, count of Narbonne, against his enemies. Eindredi went on to Constantinople (mod. İstanbul, Turkey), but Rognvald and the others sailed for the Holy Land in early 1152, capturing en route a Muslim ship of the type known as a dromon. These proved to be the only warlike activities of the Orkney crusaders. In August 1152 they visited Jerusalem and the river Jordan, and returned home via Constantinople, Italy, Denmark, and Norway. Rognvald arrived in Orkney by Christmas 1153 to find the earldom being disputed between Harald Maddadsson and Paul II's nephew, Erlend III Haraldsson (1151–1154). A period of civil war between the three earls ended in 1154 when Rognvald and Harald joined forces and captured and killed Erlend. Four years later Rognvald himself was killed as the result of a feud while hunting in Caithness.

–Alan V. Murray

Bibliography

Macquarrie, Alan, *Scotland and the Crusades, 1095–1560* (Edinburgh: John Donald, 1997).

The Orkneyinga Saga, ed. and trans. Alexander B. Taylor (Edinburgh: Oliver and Boyd, 1938).

Taylor, Alexander B., "Studies in the Orkneyinga Saga," *Proceedings of the Orkney Antiquarian Society* 11 for 1932–1933 (1933), 45–49.

Thomson, William P. L., *History of Orkney* (Edinburgh: Mercat, 1987).

Rolandslied des Pfaffen Konrad

Middle High German version of the Old French *Chanson de Roland,* written by an author recorded as *der phaffe Chunrat* (Conrad the Priest) for Henry the Lion, duke of Saxony and Bavaria.

The *Rolandslied* injects a twelfth-century German ideology of empire and crusade into the ancient epic of Charlemagne's war against the Muslims of Spain, reflecting Henry's renewal of Carolingian holy war against the pagan Slavs and the church's sanction of it as crusade from 1147.

Conrad may be the ducal chaplain *Conradus* recorded in charters of the 1170s: a Swabian priest, conversant with Henry's politico-religious goals, and charged with the literary representation of his quasi-royal status and crusading aspirations. The commissioning of the *Rolandslied* was part of a lavish program of secular and religious patronage centered upon Henry's palace and court church in Braunschweig and their associated artifacts. Conrad's epilogue extols Henry's imperial lineage and his conquest and conversion of the heathen.

In the poem, the Emperor Karl and his warrior-bishop Turpin summon and preach a crusade, pledging spiritual rewards. Roland and the knights eagerly take the cross, in warfare simultaneously serving theocratic emperor and heavenly king. Death in battle confers not warrior glory but a martyr's crown. The heathen, spurning baptism, and the traitor Genelun, seduced by basely secular concerns, are consigned to hell as children of the devil. Conrad's portrayal of Karl reproduces twelfth-century hagiographical images of the Emperor Charlemagne. Roland's and Oliver's austere redemptive chivalry seems inspired by Bernard of Clairvaux's preaching of the Second Crusade (1147–1149) and his writings for the Templars.

One complete illustrated manuscript (MS Heidelberg, Universitätsbibliothek cpg. 112) and six fragments, all written shortly before or after 1200, testify to the *Rolandslied*'s contemporary impact. It profoundly influenced Wolfram von Eschenbach's *Willehalm* (1210/1220). Around 1225 the poet known as Der Stricker modernized Conrad's narrative, which in this form remained popular until the end of the Middle Ages, especially among the Teutonic Knights.

–Jeffrey Ashcroft

Bibliography

Ashcroft, Jeffrey, "Konrad's Rolandslied, Henry the Lion, and the Northern Crusade," *Forum for Modern Language Studies* 22 (1986), 184–208.

———, "Magister Conradus Presbyter: Pfaffe Conrad at the Court of Henry the Lion," in *Literary Aspects of Courtly Culture*, ed. Donald Maddox and Sara Sturm Maddox (Cambridge: Brewer, 1994), pp. 301–308.

Dozoby, Maria, "The Meaning of *Virtus*: Heroic Vocabulary in Konrad's *Rolandslied*," *Archiv für das Studium der neueren Sprachen und Literatur* 224 (1987), 241–253.

Geith, Karl-Ernst, *Carolus Magnus: Studien zur Darstellung Karls des Großen in der deutschen Literatur des 12. und 13. Jahrhunderts* (Bern: Francke, 1977).

Ott-Meimberg, Marianne, *Kreuzzugsepos oder Staatsroman? Strukturen adeliger Heilsversicherung im deutschen Rolandslied* (München: Beck, 1980).

Priest Konrad's Song of Roland, trans. J. W. Thomas (Columbia, SC: Camden House, 1994).

Das Rolandslied des Pfaffen Konrad, ed. Dieter Kartschoke (Stuttgart: Reclam, 1993).

Roman van Cassant

See Dutch Literature

Roman van Saladin

See Dutch Literature

Romania

See Frankish Greece

Romanos IV Diogenes (d. 1072)

Byzantine emperor (1068–1071).

Romanos was originally a member of the landed aristocracy of Anatolia. Although convicted of plotting against the dowager empress, Eudokia Makrembolitissa, Romanos came to the throne when she pardoned and married him (January 1068). As emperor Romanos was unable to send help to the remaining Byzantine territory in southern Italy, where Bari fell to the Normans in 1071. He attempted to counter the growing Turkish threat against the eastern parts of the empire with campaigns in 1068–1069, but Turkish incursions continued. While campaigning in Armenia in 1071 he encountered a large Turkish army under the command of the Saljūq sultan Alp Arslān; after betrayal by some of his commanders and the flight of many of his troops, Romanos was defeated and captured at the battle of Mantzikert (26 August 1071). On news of the defeat the Doukas family led a revolt against him in Constantinople. After his release from captivity Romanos was pursued by their forces to Cilicia, captured, tonsured as a monk, and subsequently blinded. He died of his injuries on 4 August 1072.

–Rosemary Morris

Bibliography

Angold, Michael, *The Byzantine Empire, 1025–1204: A Political History*, 2d ed. (New York: Longman, 1997).

De Vries-Van Der Velden, Eva, "Psellos, Romain IV Diogénés et Mantzikert," *Byzantinoslavica* 58 (1997), 274–310.

Rotrou II of the Perche (d. 1144)

Count of the Perche (1099–1144), who fought in the First Crusade (1096–1099) and in at least two campaigns against the Muslims in Spain.

Rotrou was born around 1075, the only son of Geoffrey, count of Mortagne (Orne), and Beatrix, daughter of Hilduin of Mondidier and Roucy. From the closing years of the eleventh century the family preferred to call themselves counts of the Perche.

Rotrou joined the 1096 expedition to Jerusalem, probably as a member of the entourage of Robert Curthose, duke of Normandy. He is known to have fought at the siege of Nicaea (mod. İznik, Turkey) in 1097, while literary sources such as the *Chanson d'Antioche* suggest that he fought alongside Bohemund of Taranto at the battle of Dorylaion, so it is possible that he had separated himself from the Norman ducal forces. At the siege of Antioch (mod. Antakya, Turkey) he commanded one of the divisions that broke out of the city in June 1098. He presumably followed the expedition to its culmination at Jerusalem in July 1099, returning to western France in the next year to find that his father had died during his absence and that his mother had preserved his inheritance. The cartulary of the family foundation of Saint-Denis of Nogent-le-Rotrou describes Rotrou's ceremonial return to its precincts and the reception of palm leaves that he brought from the Holy Land.

At some point in the 1100s Rotrou was invited by his cousin King Alfonso I of Aragon to join his campaigns against the Muslims. Rotrou probably remained in the Iberian Peninsula for only one campaigning season, but in the early 1120s he returned for a much longer period as governor of the recently reconquered town of Tudela in the Ebro Valley. He finally left this post at or shortly before the death of King Alfonso (1134), leaving his rights in the area to his niece, Margaret of L'Aigle, and her husband, García Ramírez, who subsequently became king of Navarre. A letter from another niece, whose name is recorded only as "B," was preserved among the archives of the abbey of St. Victor in Paris; in it she begged her uncle to return to his duties, since his absence might encourage his enemies against the Christians. Rotrou made a final visit to Tudela in January 1142, perhaps to commemorate the death of his niece Queen Margaret of Navarre in that year.

A late tradition preserved at the abbey of La Trappe, founded by Rotrou, suggests that he made further visits to the Holy Land. It asserts that the count presented La Trappe with relics that he had collected on his second pilgrimage shortly before he set off on a third pilgrimage. Nearly a century later Rotrou's grandson Bishop William of Châlons-en-Champagne, the last count of the Perche of the house of Rotrou, was to refer proudly to his grandfather's presence at the siege of Antioch in a family genealogy.

–*Kathleen Thompson*

Bibliography

Laliena Corbera, Carlos, *"Larga stipendia et optima praedia:* Les nobles *francos* en Aragon au service d'Alphonse le batailleur," *Annales du Midi* 112 (2000), 149–169.

Nelson, Lynn, "Rotrou of Perche and the Aragonese Reconquest," *Traditio* 26 (1970), 113–133.
Thompson, Kathleen, "Family Tradition and the Crusading Impulse: The Rotrou Counts of the Perche," *Medieval Prosopography* 19 (1998), 1–33.

Rotrou Dynasty

See Perche, Counts of

Ruad

The waterless island of Ruad (mod. Arwād, Syria), situated off the Syrian coast near Tortosa (mod. Tartūs, Syria), was fortified by the Franks in the period of the crusades.

Ruad appears to have been held by the Byzantines after their loss of the coast to the Arabs until its capture by Caliph Mu'āwiya (d. 680). The Arab geographer al-Idrīsī in the mid-twelfth century describes a strongly built church on the island, which at that time must have belonged to the county of Tripoli. The capture of Ruad was the main success of Saladin's naval campaign of 1179–1180, demonstrating his revival of the Egyptian fleet.

The island was again in the hands of the Franks in the thirteenth century and has achieved fame as their last stronghold in Outremer: it held out after the fall of Acre (mod. 'Akko, Israel) in 1291 and was captured by the Mamlūks only in 1302. However, there is confusion over the exact chronology of events. It is unlikely that the island had been continuously occupied by the Franks; rather, it was probably reoccupied and refortified by Cypriot, Templar, and Hospitaller forces attempting to link up with an aborted Mongol invasion of Syria in late 1300. A Templar garrison was left, which launched raids against the coast, until in 1302 the Mamlūks dispatched a force, including 20 galleys sent from Egypt, to retake the island. Many Templars were killed, and some were taken prisoner (according to one source, more than 2,000). Its fortifications destroyed, the island was left abandoned.

–*Angus Stewart*

Bibliography

Deschamps, Paul, *La défense du comté de Tripoli et de la principauté d'Antioche* (Paris: Geuthner, 1973).
The Memoirs of a Syrian Prince: Abu'l-Fida, Sultan of Ḥamāh (672–732/1273–1331), trans. P. M. Holt (Wiesbaden: Steiner, 1983).

Rügen

A large island in the southwestern Baltic Sea, separated from the mainland by a long strait (the Strelasund), which was subjected to Danish rule in the course of the crusades in the twelfth century.

Rügen was inhabited by a Wendish (Slavic) tribe known as the Rane or Rugians. They had an important trade settlement at Ralswiek; their princes lived at Garz; the fortress-temple of Arkona in the north was the site of Svantevit, the main pagan idol in the region.

In the ninth century, according to the chronicler Helmold of Bosau, monks from Corvey in Westphalia introduced Christianity and established an oratory on Rügen, consecrated to St. Vitus, the patron saint of Corvey. However, Christianity seems to have been eradicated during pagan uprisings in 983 and later. Rügen was the most important target of Danish raids against the Wends. It seems to have been first subjected to Danish rule during the reign of King Erik I Ejegod (1095–1103) and linked to the newly established archbishopric of Lund. This was why, when Bishop Otto of Bamberg targeted Rügen on his second mission among the Baltic Slavs (1127), he asked the Danish archbishop Asser for permission, which Asser was unwilling to grant.

The Danish kings seem to have lost control over the island by this time, but in 1136 Erik II Emune is reported to have conquered Arkona, reintroducing Christianity but letting the Rugians retain their idol Svantevit, which they continued to venerate. Another crusade, led by King Valdemar I, reached the island in 1168. Arkona was taken on St. Vitus's Day (15 June), the statue of Svantevit was cut down and dragged through the town, and Bishop Absalon of Roskilde immediately began to establish a church organization. It has been suggested that Svantevit was actually the object of an independent Christian veneration of St. Vitus and that the image of the pagan idol, so vividly depicted by Helmold and Saxo Grammaticus, was created to justify the attack as a crusade. However, it is known that in 1201 Absalon left two cups taken from the idols of the Rugians to a niece in his testament, which indicates the existence of pagan veneration.

Valdemar I secured papal confirmation of the conquest and persuaded the pope to subordinate Rügen to the bishopric of Roskilde rather than the archbishopric of Lund. After 1168 the newly baptized Rugian princes were allowed to rule the island under Danish supremacy. The descendant of one of these, Vitslav, participated in a Danish crusade to Estonia in 1219, where he was instrumental in securing a Danish victory over the Estonians at Reval (mod. Tallinn, Estonia). In 1325 Rügen was subjected to the Pomeranian princes but continued to be linked to the bishopric of Roskilde.

–*John H. Lind*

See also: Baltic Crusades; Denmark
Bibliography
Bistum Roskilde und Rügen, ed. Bertil Wiberg (Roskilde: Roskilde Stiftsblad, 1987).
Herrmann, Joachim, *Ralswiek auf Rügen: Die slawisch-wikingischen Siedlungen und deren Hinterland,* 2 vols. (Lübstorf: Archäologisches Landesmuseum für Mecklenburg-Vorpommern, 1997–1998).
Neumünster, Peter, "Die slavische Ostseeküste im Spannungsfeld der Nachbarmächte (bis 1227/1239)," in *Zwischen Reric und Bornhöved,* ed. Ole Harck and Christian Lübke (Stuttgart: Steiner, 2001), pp. 37–55.

Rūm, Sultanate of

A sultanate in Anatolia (Asia Minor), with its capital first at Nicaea (mod. İznik, Turkey) and then at Ikonion (mod. Konya), ruled by a branch of the Saljūq family from 1080/1081 to 1307/1308. The name Rūm, deriving from the Bilad al-Rūm of Muslim authors, relates to the formerly "Rhomaic" (i.e., Byzantine) territories of Anatolia.

The sultanate's foundation and consolidation period is intertwined with the careers of the able Sulaymān I ibn Qutlumush, who perished fighting against a large Great Saljūq coalition in 1085 or 1086, and with Qilij Arslān I, who lost his capital of Nicaea to the Byzantines in 1097 during the First Crusade (1096–1099). The latter faced the Crusade of 1101 in coalition with the Dānishmendids, winning two important victories at Mersivan and Herakleia, but met his death in Syria against the Saljūq ruler Riḍwān of Aleppo in 1107. By the early twelfth century, the Saljūqs of Rūm had moved their capital to the Cappadocian town of Ikonion, from which comes the alternative appellation of their state as Sultanate of Konya.

For most of the twelfth century, the sultans of Rūm had to wage wars against their Anatolian rivals, the Turkophone Dānishmendids of Caesarea in Cappadocia (mod. Kayseri) and Sebasteia (mod. Sivas), as well as against the Byzantines. They also faced attacks by the armies of the Second Crusade

(1147–1149) and the Third Crusade (1189–1192). Under the Komnenian emperors Alexios I and John II (c. 1112–1140), the Byzantines succeeded in wresting from the Saljūqs a significant section of their former western and northwestern Anatolian possessions. However, it was in the following period that Saljūq-Byzantine relations went through fluctuating phases, especially in the reigns of Qilij Arslān II of Rūm and Manuel I Komnenos of Byzantium. In 1161–1162 the sultan was magnificently received in Constantinople, but the treaty concluded was soon proven a dead letter, for in 1173/1174 Qilij Arslān II made a pact with Byzantium's bitter enemy, the Holy Roman Emperor Frederick I Barbarossa. Shortly afterward the sultan thwarted Manuel I's invasion of Rūm (1174–1175) by defeating him at the battle of Myriokephalon in September 1176.

Qilij Arslān II crowned his successes by annexing the two Dānishmendid emirates in 1174–1177/1178, though his final years were spent in agonizing strife, as his sons bickered over the succession. In the course of the Third Crusade, Qilij Arslān II lost his capital to the armies of Frederick I and soon afterward died a broken man, naming as his successor one of his younger sons, Kay-Khusraw I. It was during that period that Byzantium failed to exploit its contacts with the Zangids; a firm alliance with Nūr al-Dīn (d. 1174) might have prevented its defeat at Myriokephalon, while a more effective collaboration with Saladin (with whom the last Komnenos, Andronikos I, and the first Angelos, Isaac II, signed treaties between 1184/1185 and 1192) might have led to a gradual reconquest of Asia Minor, most of which had been lost to the Rūm Saljūqs by the late twelfth century.

The sultanate's history from the late twelfth to the late thirteenth century is treated in detail by the *Saljuq-nama* of Ibn Bībī, a Persian court chronicler at Ikonion, whose work is complemented by Ibn al-Athīr and the major Byzantine chroniclers of the period. From this period dates another important aspect of Byzantine-Saljūq relations: the frequently attested social, institutional, cultural, and artistic contact and interplay between Rūm Saljūqs and Anatolian Christians, mostly evidenced by the phenomenon of mixed marriages, prove that both were not only opponents in battlefields but also partakers of a common cultural heritage.

In his first reign Kay-Khusraw I attempted to expand his territories at the expense of Byzantium, but he was temporarily toppled by his brother Rukn al-Dīn Sulaymān Shah II, who continued his brother's policy, and also attacked Cilician Armenia and Georgia, but died suddenly while preparing a major expedition in the Caucasus. Meanwhile the exiled Kay-Khusraw I, who had found refuge in Byzantium in 1197–1203/1204, was reinstated at Ikonion. Since his Byzantine benefactors, the Angeloi, had been toppled in 1204, he became hostile toward their successors at Nicaea, the Laskarids, as well as to the latter's allies, the Cilician Armenians. He succeeded in capturing the important southern Anatolian port of Attaleia (mod. Antalya) in 1207, but in 1211 the Saljūqs were defeated at Antioch on the Maeander by the Laskarids and their Italian mercenaries, and Kay-Khusraw I was killed in action.

The operations of Kay-Khusraw's successors were directed mainly against the Grand Komnenoi of the empire of Trebizond, from whom Kay-Kawūs I (1211–1220) took Sinope in 1214, but the Saljūq army of Kay-Qubādh I (1220–1237) failed to capture Trebizond in 1222–1223 (a previous unsuccessful attempt having taken place in 1205–1206). Kay-Qubādh also faced attacks from John III Doukas Vatatzes of Nicaea between 1222/1225 and 1231, while he also led an expedition against Crimea (1227/1228) and participated in an eastern alliance that defeated the Khwārazm Shāh Jalāl al-Dīn Mangubirtī in 1231. The brunt of the imminent Mongol invasion of Anatolia, however, was reserved for Kay-Qubādh's successor, Kay-Khusraw II, shortly after an internal religious insurrection led by Baba Isḥāq (1240/1241) had threatened the Rūm throne. On 26 June 1243 the Mongol Ilkhans under Baidju crushed the forces of the Rūm Saljūqs and their Latin and Trapezuntine allies at Satala (mod. Köse Dagh). It was now too late for the Nicaean-Saljūq alliance (August 1243) to be effective, and from then onward the Rūm sultanate declined to the status of a protectorate of the Mongol Ilkhanid empire, in which most of the sultans were mere puppets in the hands of Ilkhanid governors. The period from the mid-thirteenth century, with a long list of ineffectual Saljūq nominal sultans, witnessed a gradual spread of Turcoman emirates (*beylik*s) in Anatolia. The most powerful of these developed into the Ottoman empire.

–*Alexios C. C. Savvides*

See also: Crusade of 1101

Bibliography

Cahen, Claude, *Pre-Ottoman Turkey, c. 1071–1330* (London: Sidgwick & Jackson, 1968).

———, *Turcobyzantina et Oriens Christianus* (London: Variorum Reprints, 1974).

———, *La Turquie pré-ottomane* (Istanbul: Isis, 1988).

Kafesoğlu, İbrahim, *History of the Seljuks,* ed. Gary Leiser (Carbondale: Southern Illinois University Press, 1988).

Köprülü, Mehmed Fuad, *The Seljuks of Anatolia: Their History and Culture according to Local Muslim Sources* (Salt Lake City: University of Utah Press, 1992).

Langdon, J., *Byzantium's Last Imperial Offensive in Asia Minor, 1222 or 1225 to 1231* (New Rochelle, NY: Caratzas, 1992).

Rice, Tamara Talbot, *The Seljuks in Asia Minor* (London: Thames & Hudson, 1961).

Savvides, Alexios G. C., *Byzantium in the Near East: Its Relations with the Seljuk Sultanate of Rūm in Asia Minor, the Armenians of Cilicia and the Mongols,* A.D. c. *1192–1237* (Thessaloniki: Byzantine Research Centre, 1981).

————, *Βυζαντινοτουρκικά μελετήματα* (Athinai: Herodotos, 1991).

————, "Comneni, Angeli, Zengids and Ayyubids to the Death of Saladin," *Journal of Oriental and African Studies* 3–4 (1991–1992), 231–235.

————, "Acropolites and Gregoras on the Byzantine-Seljuk Confrontation at Antioch-on-the-Maeander," *Journal of Oriental and African Studies* 8 (1996), 73–82.

————, *Οι Τούρκοι και οι Βυζάντιο* 1 (Athinai: Domos, 1996).

————, "Ο Σελτζούκος σουλτάνος Κιλίτζ Αρσλάν Β" και η μάχη του Μυριοκεφάλου, 1176 μ. Χ.," *Στρατιωτική Ιστορία* 8 (1997), 14–22.

————, "Kilij Arslan I of Rum, Byzantines, Crusaders and Danishmendids," *Βυζαντινά* 21 (2000), 365–377.

————, "Suleyman Shah of Rūm, Byzantium, Cilician Armenia and Georgia, A.D. 1197–1204," *Byzantion* 73 (2003), 96–111.

Turan, Osman, *Selçuklular zamanında Türkiye tarihi,* 2d ed. (İstanbul, 1984).

Vryonis, Speros, Jr., *The Decline of Medieval Hellenism in Asia Minor and the Process of Islamization from the 11th through the 15th century* (Berkeley: University of California Press, 1971).

————, *Studies on Byzantium, Seljuks and Ottomans* (Malibu, CA: Byzantina & Metabyzantina, 1981).

Yıldız, Hakkı, "Seljuks of Anatolia," in *A Short History of the Turkish-Islamic States (excluding the Ottoman state),* ed. M. D. Yıldız, E. Merçil, and M. Saray (Ankara: Turkish Historical Society: 1994), pp. 120–135.

Russia (Rus')

The first mention of the Old Russian state or "Russian Land" (Russ. Russkaya zemlya) occurs in 862 in the Russian *Primary Chronicle (Povest' vremennykh let)* of Nestor. The compiler of this work relates that the elders of the eastern Slavic tribes had summoned three Varangians (i.e., Scandinavians) called Rurik, Sineus, and Truvor to establish order among them and to rule their lands. Without denying the appearance of Rurik as a fact, historians now date the foundation of Rus', to use the medieval name, to the eighth century, as the economy and political relations of the native peoples had developed by this time.

Ancient Rus' was a confederation of a number of towns with subject lands that were governed by princes of the Rurikid family (Russ. *Ryurikovichi*), whose senior member was the prince of Kiev (mod. Kyiv, Ukraine). It was on the initiative of a prince of Kiev, Vladimir the Great (d. 1015), that the Russian princes adopted the Orthodox form of Christianity in 988. By the beginning of the twelfth century, the Russian princes had extended their political influence into the lands of neighboring non-Slavic pagan peoples of the eastern Baltic Region. The region known as Northwestern Rus' included the Novgorodian Land (Russ. Novgorodskaya zemlya) together with the Finnic regions of Karelia, Ingria and Votia, and the Pskovian Land (Russ. Pskovskaya zemlya). The preface of the *Primary Chronicle* (dated to 1113) lists those who were required to pay tribute to Russia: the *Chud'* (Estonians), *Neroma* (possibly the northeastern Estonians), the Livs, *Letigola* (Lettgalians), *Zimigola* (Semgallians), *Kors'* (Curonians), and *Litva* (Lithuanians). Although by this time the Russian state had fragmented into different (and sometimes hostile) principalities, the princes had preserved their influence in the eastern Baltic lands. According to the *First Novgorodian Chronicle* and the chronicle of Henry of Livonia, at the beginning of the thirteenth century, the Estonians and the northern Lettgallians were tributaries of the Novgorodian state, while the Russians of Polotsk (mod. Polatsk, Belarus) came for tribute in the lands of the Livs and the Lettgallians around the river Düna (Russ. *Zapadnaya Dvina*, Latv. *Daugava*).

Rus' and the Crusaders in the Baltic Region

From their inception, the Western crusades to the eastern Baltic region were detrimental to Russian interests. Initially Russian control over the Düna area was recognized in the West; thus in 1184 the canon Meinhard came to Polotsk in order to persuade its prince to permit his preaching of the Latin (Roman Catholic) faith to the Livs of the Düna region. Meinhard was accompanied by German merchants who were interested in establishing fortified trading stations on the lower reaches of the Düna. Their proposal to build stone fortresses in the lands of the Livs suited the prince of Polotsk. By the 1180s the Livish regions had become a target for Lithuanian raids, while Polotsk had become entangled in internal wars in Russia and the prince could not defend his subjects in the Baltic region. He therefore allowed Meinhard to preach in return for constructing fortresses that would protect the Livs against Lithuanian attacks. However, the Orthodox Church and Russian merchants were displeased by the growing influence of German merchants and by the establishment in 1186 of a Livonian bishopric with Meinhard as its first bishop, which was named in a bull of Pope Clement III of 1 October 1188 as "the bishopric of Üxküll in Ruthenia [i.e., Russia]" [*Liv-, Esth- und Curländisches Urkundenbuch nebst Regesten,* ed. Friedrich G. von Bunge et al., 15 vols. (Reval: Kluge und Ströhm, 1853–1914), 10:11].

Russian control of Livonia began to crumble with the appearance of a new bishop, Albert of Buxhövden (1198–1229), who had obtained papal permission for annual crusades to Livonia. In 1208–1209 the crusaders conquered the Orthodox Lettgallian principalities of Koknese (Ger. *Kokenhusen*) and Jersika (Ger. *Gerzike*), whose rulers were vassals of the prince of Polotsk. In 1212 Prince Vladimir of Polotsk was forced to give up his rights to tribute from the Livs. In 1216 the Russians of Polotsk were ready to invade Livonia, but the campaign was canceled because of the sudden death of Prince Vladimir. By the late 1230s the crusaders had extended their authority along the Düna as far as the lands inhabited by Russians.

It was only in 1210 that the Russians of Novgorod attempted to assert their authority over the lands of the Estonians and northern Letgallians, after the crusaders and the Order of the Sword Brethren (established in 1202) had invaded Estonia. The aim of the Novgorodian incursions into Estonia in 1210 and 1212 was to force the still pagan natives to accept conversion to the Orthodox form of Christianity and to concede the rights of Novgorod to take tribute. However, the Novgorodians failed to convert the Estonians, and there was also confrontation between Novgorod and Pskov: in 1210 a detachment from Pskov took part in the crusaders' campaign against southwestern Estonia.

In 1216–1221 the Novgorodians and Pskovians fought against the crusaders in Livonia, but met little success because of their uncoordinated actions. The long history of raiding between Estonians and Russians hampered any immediate military alliance between them; it was not until 1222, when the greater part of Estonia had been occupied, that the Estonians and Russians allied against the crusaders. Although the Novgorodians sent troops to help defend several fortresses of the Estonians, the allies were unable to withstand the crusaders and the large numbers of native inhabitants who were by now subject to the new rulers of Livonia. The last fortress to hold out was Dorpat (mod. Tartu, Estonia), defended by Estonians and a Russian detachment led by Prince Vetseke, the former ruler of Koknese. On 15 August 1224 Dorpat was captured by storm after a siege of two weeks. All but one of the Russian defenders were killed.

In 1224 the Russians concluded a peace treaty with the bishop of Riga and the Sword Brethren. The Novgorodians and Pskovians gave up political control of the territories of the Estonians and Lettgallians, but retained the right to take tribute from the natives; in the early 1280s the Pskovians were still known to come for tribute to the Lettgallian land of Adzele. The Livonian-Russian border was fixed along the line of the river Narova and lakes Peipus and Pskovskoye.

The Western powers in Livonia intended to extend their authority into the Russian lands, pressing in two directions: toward Pskov and along the southern shore of the Gulf of Finland into the lands of the Finnic peoples subject to the Novgorodian state. The papacy planned to found a new bishopric in Northwestern Rus' with Pskov as its center. The main role in the realization of these projects was to be taken by the Livonian church and the Sword Brethren, whose prospects were improved by a Lithuanian offensive against the principality of Polotsk and the rout of the Russian troops by the Mongols in the battle of Kalka. Letters of Pope Honorius III addressed to the Christians of Russia (16 November 1224) and the kings of Russia (17 January 1227) called on them to adopt the Latin faith in order to support the struggle against the pagans. In his second letter the pope had in mind the princes of Novgorod, Pskov, Smolensk, and Polotsk, but it went unheeded.

In the late 1220s the Livonians planned to take advantage of the confrontation between Pskov and Novgorod.

The Crusaders' War against Northwestern Rus'
After the establishment of the bishopric of Dorpat (1225), lands close to the Russian border were given to Dietrich, brother of Bishop Albert of Riga and of Bishop Hermann of Dorpat, and to other members of their family. This region

was intended as a springboard for the invasion of Russia. After a new conflict broke out between Pskov and Novgorod in 1228, the Pskovians concluded a defense treaty with the Livonians in expectation of an attack by Yaroslav Vsevolodovich, the prince of Novgorod. This, together with opposition from the citizens of Novgorod, forced the prince to call off the campaign. In 1233 Prince Yaroslav, son of Prince Vladimir of Pskov (d. 1227), together with disgraced nobles from Novgorod and vassals of the bishop of Dorpat, besieged Izborsk, but were defeated. Yaroslav was captured and held captive in Pereslavl'-Zalesskii until 1235. In the same year the Livonians desolated the town of Tesov near Novgorod; in response the Novgorodians invaded the bishopric of Dorpat and gained a victory over the vassals of the bishop and the Sword Brethren (1234). In 1236 a detachment of 200 warriors from Pskov took part in the crusaders' offensive against Lithuania, which was ended with their defeat in the battle of Saule (22 September 1236).

In 1240–1241 four consecutive military expeditions were launched against Northwestern Rus'. Some historians hold to the theory of a prearranged offensive from Livonia, Sweden, and Denmark. However, the written sources suggest that these were separate undertakings, which were intended to take advantage of the military-political situation in Russia after large areas of the country had fallen prey to the Mongol invaders in 1238.

In July 1240 a Swedish naval force entered the mouth of the river Neva, planning to build a fortress at the confluence of the river Izhora. They hoped to find support among the elders of the Ingrian (Izhorian) people, who were dissatisfied with the authority of Novgorod. By chance coastal watchers of the Orthodox Izhorian elder Pelgusii, who was loyal to Novgorod, observed the Swedes at sea. The Novgorodians managed to mount a surprise attack and smashed the Swedes in battle on 15 July 1240. The Novgorodian commander, Prince Alexander Yaroslavich, was later known as Nevskii after this victory.

In September 1240 a united Livonian army together with a detachment under Prince Yaroslav Vladimirovich captured Izborsk, and after seven days' siege Pskov surrendered (15 September 1240). The invaders remained for a year and a half, from time to time desolating villages in Novgorodian territory. In the winter of 1240–1241 the Teutonic Knights of Livonia invaded the territory of the Votians and built the fortress of Kopor'e with the consent of the native elders, who had agreed to adopt the Latin faith. In the beginning of 1241, Livonians (possibly vassals of the bishopric of Riga) occupied the Novgorodian lands in the region of the river Luga and the fortress of Tesov. The situation was complicated, since Prince Alexander Nevskii had left Novgorod for Pereslavl'-Zalesskii in the summer of 1240 after a dispute with the citizens, and returned only in 1241. Toward the end of 1241, an armed force consisting of Novgorodians, Izhorians, Karelians, and the inhabitants of the Ladoga region dislodged the Teutonic Knights from Kopor'e. Some of the knights were taken prisoner, while the elders of the Votians who had gone over to the Livonians were hanged. In March 1242 Pskov and Izborsk were freed from the invaders. On 5 April 1242 the crusader army was smashed on the ice of Lake Peipus. Now facing the threat of a Russian offensive, the Livonians signed a peace treaty with Prince Alexander, forswearing all claims to any lands within the territory of the Novgorodian state.

The papacy and the rulers of Livonia did not give up the idea of annexing and converting the Russian territories. Two letters of Pope Innocent IV are known from 21 January and 15 September 1248, which appealed to Prince Alexander Nevskii to adopt the Latin faith and build a Roman Catholic cathedral in Pskov. Alexander was tempted by the prospect of obtaining the help of the Teutonic Order in the war with the Mongols. The pope's legate to Russia, John of Piano Carpini, had met Yaroslav Vsevolodovich, prince of Vladimir, at Qaraqorum in Mongolia in 1246. John had assured the pope of Yaroslav's willingness to convert, although it cannot be established whether his assurance was correct, as the prince was poisoned soon after their meeting. Negotiations conducted with Alexander by Albert Suerbeer, the archbishop of Riga, failed because Alexander was firmly against conversion.

The next attempt of the Livonian crusaders to gain a foothold in Northwestern Rus' occurred in the 1250s. In 1253 Livonian troops attacked the Pskovian Land, but retreated without a fight. Soon after that the Novgorodian host and the united Pskovian-Karelian army pushed across the river Narva and devastated the Estonian province of Vironia. The Russians were not only concerned about Livonian attacks, but were also evidently attempting to stop the infiltration of secular and ecclesiastical emissaries from Livonia. This assumption can be confirmed by letters of Pope Alexander IV to the archbishop of Riga (19 March and 3 August 1255), which relate that according to the king of Denmark's vassals in North Estonia, some natives in the Finnic lands of the

Novgorodian state had been converted. In 1256 a Swedish army came to the Narva and started to build a fortress on the right bank of the river, but retreated when it heard of the advance of Prince Alexander's troops.

In 1261 the Lithuanian king Mindaugas and Prince Alexander negotiated about a combined offensive against the crusaders. This was probably planned for the spring of 1262, but it was postponed when Alexander had to travel to the khanate of the Golden Horde to prevent a punitive campaign against his lands by the Mongols. It was only in autumn 1262 that the Russian host nominally led by Prince Dmitrii, the son of Alexander, invaded Livonia. As Dmitrii was too young to exercise command, decisions were made by his uncle, Prince Yaroslav Yaroslavich, and other princes. They plundered the country around Dorpat, burned its suburbs, and besieged the fortress before withdrawing. In 1267, having heard of Livonian plans to establish a new bishopric at Kopor'e, the Novgorodians attacked the fortress of Wesenberg (mod. Rakvere, Estonia), but withdrew after sustaining losses.

At the end of February 1268 the Russians assembled a large army and launched an offensive across the Narva. Having signed a treaty with the rulers of Livonia, the Novgorodians were confident that they would only be opposed by the nobles of Danish North Estonia, and were therefore surprised by the appearance of a Livonian military force. On 18 February 1268 there was a battle at the river Kegol near Wesenberg, which ended with great losses for both armies. The Russians withdrew, but the Livonians started to prepare for a new campaign, mustering forces in Livonia and north Germany. The rulers of Livonia and the Danish archbishopric of Lund agreed that all conquered Russian lands should be united within the diocese of Dorpat. In May 1269 the Livonian forces came to Pskov and besieged the fortress for a week (19–25 May), but after relief came from Novgorod, the Livonian master of the Teutonic Order signed a peace agreement with Prince Yurii. However, this was only a respite before a new offensive into Russia. In January 1270 war broke out between the Lithuanians and the Livonians, and on 16 February 1270 the Livonian master, Otto von Lutterberg, was killed in the battle of Karusen. At the same time a large Russian force mustered in Novgorod with the aim of attacking Reval; it included a detachment under Amragan, the *baskak* (representative of the khan) of the Golden Horde. Unable to fight on two fronts simultaneously, the Livonians asked Prince Yaroslav of Novgorod for a peace treaty, in which they forswore all claims to any lands of Northwestern Russia beyond the Narva. In addition, a trade agreement was concluded between Novgorod and the merchants of Lübeck and Riga.

Rus' and Livonia in the Later Middle Ages

There is no evidence for any plans for conversion or establishment of a Latin bishopric within the territory of Northwestern Rus' after the 1270s. Nevertheless, the peace treaty and the increase in trade connections between the Russian, Livonian, and Western merchants did not prevent fresh attacks on Russia by the Livonians. Two offensives against Pskov occurred in 1299 and 1323, and in 1343 Izborsk was attacked. In 1294 the Russians destroyed the fortress of Ottenburg, which had been built by the North Estonian vassals on the right bank of the Narva. There were also retaliatory Russian attacks across the Livonian border. Frontier wars occurred sporadically during the fourteenth and fifteenth centuries.

The Swedes and the Livonian branch of the Teutonic Order from time to time organized raids into the lands along the southern shore of the Gulf of Finland up to Lake Ladoga and also into Karelia. In 1300 the Swedes constructed the fortress of Landskrona at the mouth of the Neva and left a detachment there, which was expelled by the Novgorodians a year later. In 1443 the Teutonic Knights fought a war with the Novgorodian state that went badly for them: it ended with the Treaty of Narva (1448), which confirmed the existing Russian-Livonian border. A peace treaty between the Novgorodian state and the archbishopric of Livonia was signed in 1474.

From the middle of the fifteenth century, the government of Novgorod was concerned by resistance from Pskov and by the threat of annexation to the Muscovite state, and consequently tried to avoid military conflicts with Livonia. Indeed, Novgorod tried to negotiate Livonian assistance against Pskov and Moscow, but no treaty was signed. Muscovy annexed Novgorod in 1478 and Pskov in 1510. In 1469 Ivan III, grand prince of Muscovy, invaded Livonia after Russian merchants had been imprisoned in Dorpat. In 1501–1502 there was war between Muscovy and an alliance consisting of the Livonian branch of the Teutonic Order and the grand duchy of Lithuania, which went badly for the allies. In 1558 Muscovy declared war on Livonia, which hastened the destruction of the Livonian ecclesiastical states.

–*Evgeniya L. Nazarova.*

See also: Baltic Crusades; Russian Sources

Bibliography

Ammann, Albert M., *Kirchenpolitische Wandlungen im Ostbaltikum bis zum Tode Alexander Newskis: Studien zum Werden der Russischen Orthodoxie* (Roma: Pont. Institutum Orientalium Studiorum, 1936).

Angermann, Norbert, "Livländisch-russische Beziehungen im Mittelalter," in *Wolter von Plettenberg und das mittelalterliche Livland,* ed. Norbert Angermann and Ilgvārs Misāns (Lüneburg: Nordostdeutsches Kulturwerk, 2001), pp. 129–143.

Fennell, John, *The Crisis of Medieval Russia, 1200–1304* (London: Longman, 1993).

Kazakova, Nataliya A., "Борьба Руси с агрессией Ливонского ордена в первой половине XV в.," Ученые записки ЛГУ Исторических наук 32 (1959), 3–33.

———, "Русь и Ливония 60-х – начало 90-х годов XV века," in Международные связи России до XVII в , ed. Aleksandr A. Zimin and Vladimir T. Pashuto (Moskva: Izdatel'stvo Akademii nauk SSSR, 1961), pp. 306–338.

Matuzova, Vera I., and Evgeniya L. Nazarova, Крестоносты и Русь: Конец XII в. – 1270. Тексты, переводы, комментарии (Moskva: Indrik, 2002).

Nazarova, Evgeniya L., "Регион Запаной Двины в епоху смены политического влияния," in Контактные зоны в истории Восточной Европы, ed. Aleksandr M. Nekrasov (Moskva: Institut Rossiskoi istorii, 1995), pp. 71–82.

———, "К вопросу о литовско русском союзе," in Староладожский сборник , ed. Adrian A. Selin (Sankt-Peterburg: Staroladozhskii muzei-zapovednik, 1998), pp. 12–19.

———, "Крестовый поход на Русь в 1240 г. Организация и планы," in Восточная Европа в исторической ретроспективе ed. Tatyana N. Dzhakson and Elena A. Mel'nikova (Moskva: Yazyki russkoi kul'tury, 1999), pp. 190–201.

———, "The Crusades against Votians and Ingrians in the Thirteenth Century," in *Crusade and Conversion on the Baltic Frontier, 1150–1500,* ed. Alan V. Murray (Aldershot, UK: Ashgate, 2001), pp. 177–197.

Pashuto, Vladimir T., Героическая борьба русского народа за независимость в XIII в. (Moskva: Gosudarstvennoe izdatel'stvo politicheskoi literatury, 1956).

Ramm, Boris Ya., Папство и Русь в X-XV вв . (Moskva: Izdatel'stvo Akademii nauk SSSR, 1959).

Selart, Anti, "Confessional Conflict and Political Cooperation: Livonia and Russia in the Thirteenth Century," in *Crusade and Conversion on the Baltic Frontier, 1150–1500,* ed. Alan V. Murray (Aldershot, UK: Ashgate, 2001), pp. 151–177.

Russian Sources

Various narrative sources in Russian provide significant information concerning the wars fought by the Russians against the crusaders in the eastern Baltic region.

The most important Russian source is the *Novgorodskaya pervaya letopis' (First Novgorod Chronicle)*. It exists in two versions, which survive in five different manuscripts. The Older Version (*Starshyi izvod*) is contained in the Sinodal'nyi manuscript (MS Moscow, State Historical Museum, 786). This manuscript covers events from 1016 up to 1352, but 128 folios at the beginning and several in the middle of the manuscript (dealing with events of the years 1273–1298) have been lost. The full text of the chronicle (beginning with the year 854) can be reconstructed from the Younger Version (*Mladshyi izvod*), which survives in four manuscripts, the oldest of which is the Comissionnyi manuscript in the collection of the Archeographical Commission (Institute of History, St Petersburg, no. 240), dating from the mid-fifteenth century.

The compilation of the text of the Sinodal'nyi version dealing with events up to 1234 was begun in the second part of the thirteenth century and completed in the middle of the fourteenth century. The chronicle tells of the attempts of the Novgorodians to preserve their political authority in Livonia against the crusaders. The accounts of the Russian campaigns against Livonia in 1212, 1214, 1217, 1218, 1222, and 1223 correspond with the testimony in the chronicle of Henry of Livonia about Russian raids in 1210, 1212, 1216–1217, 1218, 1221, and 1223. In the opinion of Russian scholars, where the dates differ, those given by Henry are to be preferred. The siege and capture of the fortress of Dorpat (mod. Tartu, Estonia) in 1224 are mentioned in passing in the *First Novgorod Chronicle.* By contrast, the accounts of Russian struggles against the Livonian attempts to annex parts of the Novgorodian state in the period between the 1230s and 1260s are more informative and important for the history of the Baltic Crusades. Some of the events described are also known from the Livonian sources: the occupation of Pskov (1240–1242), the crusades into the lands of the Finnic peoples of the Novgorodian state (1241), the battle on the ice of Lake Peipus (1242), the siege of Dorpat (1262), the battle of Wesenberg (1268), and the failed attempt to capture Pskov (1269). The chronicle also contains much exclusive information. This includes the military actions of the vassals of the bishop of Dorpat together with the Russian prince Yaroslav Vladimirovich in the 1230s, the attack of the

Russian and Karelian hosts against Dorpat (1253), the invasion by Livonian and Swedish troops of the lower reaches of the river Narva (1256) and the response to it by the Russians and Karelians (1256/1257), the peace treaty between Russians and the Livonians in 1270, and the defense of Pskov against the Livonians (1299 and 1323). The Comissionnyi manuscript also relates that in 1294 the Novgorodians expelled the North Estonian vassals of the Danish Crown who had started to build a fortress on the eastern bank of the river Narva; a folio that may have contained this evidence has been lost from the Sinodal'nyi manuscript. Both versions also contain much evidence about the wars between the Russians and the Teutonic Order in Livonia in the frontier region (from the 1280s onward), as well as the invasions of the order and the Swedes into the areas of the river Neva, Lake Ladoga, and Karelia.

Important original information is contained in the *Zhitie Alexandra Nevskogo* (*Life of Alexander Nevskii*), a hagiographical life of Alexander Yaroslavich, prince of Novgorod. It survives in more than 500 manuscripts (written between the end of the fourteenth and the end of the eighteenth centuries), which comprise fifteen versions. Opinions as to the time and place of its composition vary between the late 1260s and early 1280s. The *Life* may have been written by a monk of the monastery of the Nativity of Our Lady in Vladimir. The author drew on the annals of Novgorod and Vladimir, as well as on information recorded by someone who belonged to the entourage of Alexander Yaroslavich between the late 1230s and the prince's death in 1263. The *Life* contains exclusive information about the visit of the legation of the Teutonic Order led by Andreas von Felben to Novgorod and the theological disputation between Prince Alexander and the envoys of the pope. Information about the battle at the river Neva (1240) is given in greater detail than in the *First Novgorod Chronicle* and forms the main part of the *Life*.

Events in the *Life* are ordered correctly, but in keeping with the genre of the text are not dated. In the fifteenth century, the text of the *Life* was included in the Younger version of the *First Novgorod Chronicle*. The information in this chronicle was in turn used in later chronicles of Novgorod, Pskov, and Northeastern Russia. The *Life of Alexander Nevskii* also formed part of the fourteenth-century collection known as the *Slovo o pogibeli Zemli Russkoi* (*Account concerning the Loss of the Russian Land*). Some information about the wars between the Livonians and Pskovians (from the 1280s to the end of the fifteenth century) is found in the *First, Second* and *Third Chronicles of Pskov* (fifteenth–seventeenth centuries). This information derives from the earlier annual records made in Pskov and also from the *Povest' o Dovmonte* (*The Story of Dovmont*). The *Story* was written in the fourteenth century, soon after the death of Daumantas (Russ. *Dovmont*), the Lithuanian prince who ruled in Pskov in 1266–1299. During the years of his government, the principality of Pskov achieved its greatest independence from Novgorod, and the composition of the work was more of a political than a literary act. In writing this work the author imitated the *Life of Alexander Nevskii*. The text contains useful information, with particularly interesting and detailed accounts of the defense of Pskov in 1269 and 1299.

–*Evgeniya L. Nazarova*

See also: Baltic Crusades; Russia (Rus')

Bibliography

Begunov, Yurii K., Памятник русской литературы XIII в. Слово о погибели земли Русской (Moskva: Nauka 1965).

The Chronicle of Novgorod, 1016–1471, trans. R. Michell and N. Forbes, Camden Third Series, 25 (London: Camden Society, 1914).

Die erste Novgoroder Chronik nach ihrer ältesten Redaktion (Synodalhandschrift) 1016–1330/1352, ed. Joachim Dietze (München: Sagner, 1971).

Князь Александр Невский и его эпоха, ed. Yurii K. Begunov and Anatolii N. Kirpichnikov (Sankt-Peterburg: Nauka, 1995).

Matuzova, Vera I., and Evgeniya L. Nazarova, Крестоносцы и Русь: Конец XII в. – 1270. Тексты, переводы, комментарии (Moskva: Indrik, 2002).

"Новгородская первая летопись старшего и младшегс изводов," ed. Arsenii N. Nasonov, Mikhail N. Tikhomirov, and Boris M. Kloss, in Полное собрание русских летописей, 3 (Moskva: Yazyki russkoi kul'tury, 2000).

Okhotnikova, Valentina I., Повесть о Довмонте (Leningrad: Nauka 1983).

"Псковские Летописи," ed. Arsenii N. Nasonov and Boris M. Kloss, in Полное собрание русских летописей, 5:1–2 (Moskva: Yazyki slavyanskoi kul'tury, 2000–2003).

S

St. Sabas, War of (1256–1258)

A conflict between the Genoese and the Venetian merchant communes in Acre (mod. 'Akko, Israel) that escalated into a civil war that embraced the whole of the kingdom of Jerusalem.

The conflict developed out of rival claims by the Genoese and the Venetians to the monastery of St. Sabas, which lay on the boundary between their respective quarters in the city, and was fueled by their competition for the maritime trade of the Mediterranean. Early in 1256 the Genoese seized the monastery and attacked the Venetian quarter with the support of the Pisans. They were repulsed, but siege engines were set up with which the Italians bombarded each other.

The kingdom of Jerusalem was divided by the conflict. John of Arsuf initially backed the Genoese, while some barons, led by John of Jaffa, favored the Venetians. Philip of Montfort, lord of Tyre and Toron, used the opportunity to expel the Venetians from Tyre (mod. Soûr, Lebanon) and allied himself with the Genoese. In July 1257 the Pisans changed sides to join Venice. The fraternities in Acre sided with the Venetians, as did the Templars and the Teutonic Knights, while the Hospitallers supported the Genoese. The communes from southern France opposed the Genoese, and consequently the Catalan communes backed them.

The Venetians gained ground when John of Jaffa successfully manipulated the regency laws to bring Plaisance of Antioch to power in the kingdom of Jerusalem. As *bailli* (regent) she ordered the Crown vassals to support Venice. Both sides were reinforced by new arrivals from Europe, and the struggle continued both on land and at sea. A Venetian fleet under the command of Lorenzo Tiepolo broke the Genoese blockade of Acre and regained possession of their quarter. In June 1258 Philip of Montfort, with the support of the Hospitallers, led an army south to attack Acre while the Genoese launched an assault from the sea. The Venetian and Genoese fleets clashed, and the latter were defeated, losing many men and galleys, and Philip and the Hospitallers were forced to withdraw.

The position of the Genoese in Acre had become untenable, and they abandoned the city in favor of Tyre. The conflict had destroyed much of Acre, damaged its trade, and exacerbated the factional divisions within Outremer.

–*Linda Goldsmith*

Bibliography
Richard, Jean, *The Latin Kingdom of Jerusalem* (Amsterdam: North Holland, 1979).

Safad

See Saphet

Sakkala

A province of medieval Livonia corresponding to the southwestern part of modern Estonia. Sakkala was delimited to the north by the river Nawwest (mod. Navesti, Estonia), to the east by Lake Wirzjärw (mod. Võrtsjärv), and to the west by massive swamps. The main provincial centers according to the chronicle of Henry of Livonia were Fellin (mod. Viljandi) and Leole (mod. Lõhavere).

Raids into Sakkala by the German crusaders based in and around Riga began in 1208 and were met by counterattacks from the Estonian inhabitants in the province. One of the chieftains of Sakkala, Lembitu of Leole, was singled out by Henry of Livonia as one of the fiercest enemies of Riga. He emerged as one of the heroes of Estonian national historiography in modern times. In 1215, after the capture of Leole and Fellin, the population of the province was baptized. However, resistance was not broken until 1217, when the crusaders defeated the Estonian forces in the battle of Fellin, in which Lembitu lost his life.

The new German administration, with its center in Fellin, suffered a serious blow from an Estonian uprising in January 1223, but Sakkala was finally subjected by the Order of the Sword Brethren in August that year. The province became one of the core areas of the Livonian branch of the Teutonic Order after it incorporated the remnants of the Sword Brethren in 1237.

–Juhan Kreem

Bibliography
Kenkmann, Rudolf, "Über die Lage des Pala-Flusses: Ein Beitrag zur Topographie Mittelestlands im 13. Jahrhundert," *Sitzungsberichte der Gelehrten Estnischen Gesellschaft* 1931 (Tartu: Gelehrte Estnische Gesellschaft, 1932), pp. 202–251.
Tarvel, Enn, "Sakala ja Ugandi kihelkonnad," *Keel ja Kirjandus* (1968), pp. 543–550.

Saladin (1138–1193)

Vizier (1169–1171) and sultan of Egypt (1174–1193), the main Muslim opponent of the Franks of Outremer in the fourth quarter of the twelfth century. His original name was Yūsuf ibn Ayyūb; the name Saladin is a European corruption of his honorific Arabic title Ṣalāḥ al-Dīn ("goodness of the faith").

Saladin was a Kurd who was born at Tikrit (in mod. Iraq) in 1138. His family originated in Dvin in the Caucasus (near mod. Yerevan, Armenia), but employment opportunities brought members of the family to Iraq. Saladin's father, Najm al-Dīn Ayyūb, and uncle, Asad al-Dīn Shīrkūh, served as governors of Tikrit on behalf of the Saljūq sultan Muḥammad ibn Malik Shāh. However, in 1138 they had to flee from Tikrit following a murder committed by Shīrkūh. They both found employment at the court of ʿImād al-Dīn Zangī, emir of Mosul. For some years the careers of the two brothers took separate courses, but from 1154 they were both in Damascus in the service of Zangī's son Nūr al-Dīn, ruler of Muslim Syria. Saladin spent his formative years in Damascus: for a short period he served as chief of police, but he was mostly known as Nūr al-Dīn's highly skilled polo-playing companion.

Between 1164 and 1169, Nūr al-Dīn found himself obliged to intervene militarily in Egypt in order to counter invasions of the country mounted by the Franks of Jerusalem in alliance with the Byzantines. Saladin accompanied the expeditionary force commanded by Shīrkūh, gaining his first military experience at the battle of Babayn and the defense of Alexandria (1167).

On the death of Shīrkūh (26 March 1169), Saladin became commander of Nūr al-Dīn's forces in Egypt and was also appointed as vizier, governing in the name of the Fāṭimid caliph. The period from this point up to the death of the caliph al-ʿĀḍid (September 1171) saw the consolidation of Saladin's power, the undermining of the Fāṭimid state, and the growth of tension with Nūr al-Dīn. Saladin bought the loyalty of the officers of the Syrian army in Egypt by rewarding them with rural and urban property. His personal standing was much strengthened with the arrival of his father and older brothers from Damascus. His brother, Tūrān Shāh, fought and destroyed the Fāṭimid infantry regiments in Cairo, thus curtailing the ability of the Fāṭimid regime to oppose Saladin. Saladin's father, Najm al-Dīn Ayyūb, governed provinces of Egypt, and his nephew, Taqī al-Dīn, emulated Saladin by establishing educational and religious institutions that emphasized the new Sunnī character of Egypt. In the struggle against the Fāṭimid state Saladin was assisted by Sunnī Muslims within the Fāṭimid administration, who had a deep dislike for the incompetent and religiously abhorrent Shīʿite regime. Among these, the cooperation of Qāḍī al-Fāḍil, head of the Fāṭimid chancery, proved invaluable.

The death of al-ʿĀḍid in 1171 brought the tension between Saladin and Nūr al-Dīn into the open: Nūr al-Dīn now realized that Saladin and his Ayyūbid kinsmen had developed a taste for power in Egypt, but found himself unable to enjoy the fruits of the military investment he had made in sending his armies there. This tension, although it did not burst into open conflict, continued until the death of Nūr al-Dīn in 1174.

Following the death of his formal overlord, Saladin set out to conquer Syria from the hands of Nūr al-Dīn's young heirs. This intra-Muslim war was presented in Qāḍī al-

Fāḍil's propaganda as having a different motive: the desire to wage holy war on the Franks. Damascus, Homs, and Hama came under Saladin's rule in 1174. However, it was only after two battles against Zangid forces, in 1175 and 1176, that Saladin was able to conquer Aleppo in 1183. Mosul remained a Zangid possession, while recognizing Saladin's sovereignty and contributing forces to his campaigns (1186). Other victories by Saladin included the conquest of the Artūqid towns of Mayyafariqin, Mardin, and the fortress of Amida (mod. Diyarbakir, Turkey) in 1183. Saladin's expansion at the cost of other Muslim dynasties took place intermittently, interspersed with wars against the Franks of Outremer and clashes with the Assassins, who were regarded as Muslim heretics.

In 1177, Saladin suffered a disastrous defeat at the hands of the Franks in the battle of Mont Gisard in southern Palestine. However, he was able to recover from this and successfully fought the battle of Marj Uyun (1179). Special animosity developed between Saladin and the lord of Transjordan, Reynald of Châtillon, who intercepted pilgrim caravans to Arabia and launched a naval raid in the Red Sea aimed at the holy city of Mecca, which was defeated by Saladin's forces in Egypt. Saladin's invasions of the kingdom of Jerusalem in 1182 and 1183 were quite futile; in 1183, for example, the refusal of the Franks to be dragged into an all-out battle led to a stalemate and forced him to withdraw from the kingdom.

The campaign of 1187 was marked by Saladin's vast numerical superiority and tactical mistakes committed by the Franks. On 27 June, Saladin rounded the southern tip of Lake Tiberias and on 30 June took up a position to the northwest at Kfar Sabt. This well-watered place controlled one of the roads from Saforie, where the Franks had concentrated, to Tiberias (mod. Teverya, Israel). On 2 July Saladin left most of his army at Kfar Sabt and attacked Tiberias with his personal guard. The town was quickly taken, but Eschiva of Galilee, the wife of Raymond III of Tripoli, held out in the strongly fortified citadel. On 3 July the Franks left Saforie in an attempt to relieve Tiberias. Saladin's army seized the springs of Tur'ān as they left, cutting the Franks off from water supplies; the nearest springs were at the Horns of Hattin, but these had also been seized by Saladin's troops. Saladin made effective use of his numerical superiority, attacking the rear of the Frankish army, held by the Templars, from the high ground of Tur'ān. At this point King Guy of Jerusalem decided to establish a camp, and the Franks

Painting of Saladin (1138–1193) by Cristofano (di Papi) dell'Altissimo (1552–1605). (The Art Archive/Galleria degli Uffizi Florence/Dagli Orti)

endured a night of thirst on the arid plateau (3–4 July). In the ensuing battle, Raymond of Tripoli and some of his troops were able to escape the Muslim encirclement, but the Frankish army, although it fought gallantly, finally collapsed, with the majority of the Franks killed or taken prisoner. Saladin spared King Guy, but executed Reynald of Châtillon along with the Templar and Hospitaller captives. Vast numbers of prisoners were sent to Damascus. Saladin took full advantage of this victory and went on to capture the city of Jerusalem (20 October 1187) and numerous other territories held by the Franks in Palestine and Syria in intense campaigns in 1187–1189, which occasionally continued into the winter months as well. Only Tyre (mod. Soûr, Lebanon) and Tripoli (mod. Trâblous, Lebanon) remained in Christian hands, but this was enough for the Franks, aided by crusader forces, to begin their attempt at reconquest.

During the Third Crusade (1189–1192), one of Saladin's major problems, the lack of adequate naval power, came to the fore. Saladin built a fleet, but it was much smaller than the European fleets operating in the eastern Mediterranean and performed poorly in combat, notably at Tyre in 1187. This naval shortcoming contributed greatly to Saladin's failure in the battle for Acre (mod. 'Akko, Israel) from September 1189 to July 1191. Although the Third Crusade failed to re-conquer Jerusalem, Saladin suffered further military setbacks, losing the port of Jaffa (mod. Tel Aviv-Yafo, Israel) and being defeated at the battle of Arsuf (7 September 1191). Fearing for the safety of Egypt, he decided to dismantle the fortifications of Ascalon (mod. Tel Ashqelon, Israel). The truce of 2 September 1192, known as the Treaty of Jaffa, confirmed what the Franks held and gave the two sides a much needed respite, but events had taken a heavy toll on Saladin's health: he died on 3 March 1193, after an illness lasting only a few days.

Saladin's great achievements in fighting the holy war had already become a myth during his lifetime, obliterating almost every feature of his personality and deeds that did not tally with the myth. Only rarely, if at all, is the nonmythical Saladin discernible from what is recorded about him. The myth of Saladin was created and propagated by a group of three historian-admirers; Qāḍī al-Fāḍil, 'Imād al-Dīn al-Iṣfahānī, and Bahā' al-Dīn ibn Shaddād, who also served him in various capacities and accompanied him on campaigns. Saladin's critics were few, and even they could not deny his real achievements. We are basically left with Saladin's depiction by his historian-admirers, and these accounts must be examined on their own merits.

Saladin is portrayed as a religious person who scrupulously performed the rites of Islam, and there is nothing unbelievable in this description. Medieval people, both humble and high-born, were deeply religious, and for many the strict observance of religious rites was a way of life. Far more problematic is the description of Saladin's religious beliefs and inclinations, since these are presented as conforming to the Sunnī orthodoxy of his time. We can certainly ask ourselves whether Saladin was indeed much concerned with theological problems such as God's attributes, or whether the views attributed to him by his historian-admirers were the reflections of their own inner religious world rather than his.

No less questionable are the descriptions crediting him with great interest in religious learning and the sessions of transmission of Prophetic traditions. It is true that Saladin and his extended family were linguistically and culturally fully Arabicized with Saladin being fluent in both Kurdish and Arabic. The religious education of his many sons was important to him, and he tried to provide them with the best available. Attendance at sessions of the transmission of traditions, however, was not only a personal religious act. It had public implications and was politically useful in forging ties with the religious class, which was a group that rendered intermediary services between the ruling military elite (mostly Kurdish and Turkish) of Egypt and Syria and the subject populations.

Participation in public sessions was only one minor aspect of Saladin's manifold relations with the religious class. The establishment of law colleges supported by vast pious endowments was a far more significant aspect of these relations. In this respect Saladin's religious policy lacked originality, since it was the continuation of a pattern that had evolved in the eleventh and twelfth centuries in the Iranian world and the Near East. The main problem is, however, the depiction of Saladin as an unselfish warrior of the holy war. This image was propagated long before there were any real achievements and was used to justify wars against Muslims. By the time of him, the manipulation of the holy war for political purposes was common, and the fact that it was used in Saladin's propaganda should not necessarily automatically discredit him. Judging from the tenacity with which he fought the Third Crusade, Saladin's commitment to the ideology of the holy war was deep and real. Given the prevailing mood of those times, this is hardly surprising.

It must be admitted that the real qualities of Saladin's character, or to put it differently, the charisma that won him the admiration of his contemporaries, Muslims and foes alike, elude us. His financial and material generosity toward members of the ruling elite is widely reported and must have been a very basic trait of his character. He is also characterized as humanely generous and attentive to the plight of captured and suffering enemies. This characterization prevailed in spite of the well-known executions of prisoners-of-war carried out on his orders and his quite callous attitude toward his own men in captivity. His failure to ransom the captured garrison of Acre, eventually executed by the crusaders, subsequently affected his relations with his emirs. Leaving aside issues of personality, in his military and administrative policies Saladin rather unimaginatively adhered to the accepted norms of his day, but it must be said these served him well.

–Yaacov Lev

Bibliography
Ehrenkreutz, Andrew S., *Saladin* (Albany: State University of New York Press, 1972).

Frenkel, Yehoshua, "Political and Social Aspects of Islamic Religious Endowments (*Awqaf*): Saladin in Cairo (1163–73) and Jerusalem (1187–93)," *Bulletin of the School of Oriental and African Studies* 62 (1999), 1–21.

Gibb, Hamilton, A. R., *The Life of Saladin* (Oxford: Clarendon, 1973).

Humphreys, R. Stephen, *From Saladin to the Mongols: The Ayyubids of Damascus, 1193–1260* (Albany: State University of New York Press, 1977).

Kedar, Benjamin Z., "The Battle of Hattin Revisited," in *The Horns of Hattin*, ed. Benjamin Z. Kedar (Jerusalem: Yad Izhak Ben-Zvi Institute, 1992), pp. 190–208.

Lev, Yaacov, *Saladin in Egypt* (Leiden: Brill, 1999).

Lyons, Malcom Cameron, and D. E. P. Jackson, *Saladin. The Politics of the Holy War* (Cambridge: Cambridge University Press, 1982).

Minorsky, Vladimir, *Studies in Caucasian History* (London: Taylor's Foreign Press, 1953).

Möhring, Hannes, *Saladin und der Dritte Kreuzzug* (Wiesbaden: Steiner, 1980).

———, "Zwischen Joseph-Legende und Mahdi-Erwartung: Erfolge und Ziele Sultan Saladins im Spiegel zeitgenössicher Dichtung und Weissagung," in *War and Society in the Eastern Mediterranean, 7th–15th Centuries*, ed. Yaacov Lev (Leiden: Brill, 1997), pp. 177–225.

Richards, Donald S., "The Early History of Saladin," *The Islamic Quarterly* 17 (1973), 140–159.

Sivan, Emanuel, *L'Islam et la croisade* (Paris: Librairie d'Amérique et d'Orient, 1967).

Saladin in Literature

The Christian West regarded the Muslim ruler Saladin as the most important opponent of the Franks in Outremer, but he was also renowned for his generosity and chivalry, two virtues highly valued in the European chivalric ideal. This ambivalence guaranteed Saladin a protracted career in the western European literature of the Middle Ages (and beyond). The depiction of Saladin in literary texts combines historical elements with completely fictitious stories. This mixture presumably aims at giving plausible and acceptable form and explanation to a remarkable Muslim leader, whose conduct defied medieval Christian prejudices toward and perceptions of Islam. The substantial textual testimony (in Latin, French, English, German, Dutch, Italian, and Castilian) to Saladin's extraordinary reputation shows, over and above numerous idiosyncrasies, a number of more or less common elements.

Besides his generosity and chivalry, an alleged Christian descent (e.g., from the French noble house of Ponthieu) belongs to the common tradition of these texts (e.g., in the fourteenth- and fifteenth-century Old French and Middle Dutch *Saladin* romances). Several texts mention Saladin receiving an initiation in Christian chivalry; for example, in the Old French *Ordène de chevalerie* (1250/1300) his captive Hue de Tabarie eventually dubs him a knight. Saladin is sometimes credited with an incognito journey to western Europe, as well as amorous adventures with a French queen. But the efforts to rationalize the phenomenon of Saladin from a Western, Christian perspective are most explicitly illustrated in the stories about his innate inclination toward Christianity and his autobaptism. This literary tradition relates how, on his deathbed, Saladin organizes a dispute between a Muslim, a Jew, and a Christian. Persuaded by the last, he orders a bowl of water, baptizes himself, and dies convinced that he is a Christian. Though this kind of story is counterbalanced by negative judgments (such as allegations of political opportunism and cruelty), it remains remarkable that within the Christian framework of European medieval literature a Muslim receives such a positive portrayal.

The pinnacle of this literary career is perhaps found in Dante's *Divina Commedia*, where the poet places Saladin (as the only Muslim) in Limbo, together with, though set aside from, the great men of ancient times who are spared from hell. Saladin's special status is well illustrated in a fourteenth-century Middle Dutch exemplum that presents him as a notable example of *contemptus mundi* (literally, "disdain for the world," that is, worldly concerns) and wise preparation for life's inevitable end.

–*Geert H. M. Claassens*

See also: Saladin (1138–1193)
Bibliography
Jubb, Margaret, *The Legend of Saladin in Western Literature and Historiography* (Lewiston, NY: Mellen, 2000).

Saladin Tithe

A tax levied by Henry II, king of England, and Philip II Augustus, king of France, on their respective dominions in order to finance a crusade intended to recover the Christian possessions in the Holy Land overrun by Saladin, ruler of

Egypt and Muslim Syria, in the aftermath of the battle of Hattin (4 July 1187).

The tax was proclaimed when the two kings took the cross together in January 1188 and fixed at the rate of one-tenth of the value of revenues and movable goods, to be paid by all those not going on crusade, although the assessment excluded certain categories of property such as precious stones, as well as possessions required for professional purposes by knights (such as horses and weaponry) and clerics (such as books and vestments). Crusaders were exempt from the tax, and were entitled to receive the tithes paid by their vassals and tenants.

The tithe aroused much resentment in both realms, particularly as it was feared that it would create a precedent for future taxation. In Philip's lands it was collected by lay and ecclesiastical lords, with patchy results. Opposition was so great that Philip eventually suspended collection, rescinded the tithe on movables, and promised never to levy such a tax again. In England and in Henry's lands in France, collection of the tax was carried out by a system of committees and juries at parish level with the participation of royal officials, and those who failed to pay were threatened with excommunication. The taxes raised from Henry's dominions went to fund the expedition of his son Richard the Lionheart in the Third Crusade (1189–1192), and the more effective collection in the Angevin realm was one of the reasons why Richard's expedition was better financed than that of Philip.

–Alan V. Murray

Bibliography

Baldwin, John W., *The Government of Philip Augustus: Foundations of French Royal Power in the Middle Ages* (Berkeley: University of California Press, 1986).

Cazel, Fred. A., Jr., "Financing the Crusades," in *A History of the Crusades,* ed. Kenneth M. Setton et al., 6 vols., 2d ed. (Madison: University of Wisconsin Press, 1969–1989), 6:116–149.

Select Charters of English Constitutional History, ed. William Stubbs (Oxford: Clarendon Press, 1913).

Ṣalāḥ al-Dīn

See Saladin

Saljūqs

The Saljūqs (also spelled Seljuks) were a Turkish dynasty of Central Asiatic origin that conquered and ruled Persia, Iraq, and much of the Near East in the late eleventh and earlier twelfth centuries.

Origins: The Saljūqs in Central Asia

By the middle of the eleventh century, the Muslim world consisted of a patchwork of peoples and states in the lands of the former Arab Empire, united, and divided, by the religion of Islam. That world had been founded by the Arab conquests 400 years earlier, when the last of the barbarians to assault the Roman Empire, and the last of the heretics to challenge its faith, had invaded and unified a Near and Middle East previously partitioned between the empires of Rome and Persia. In the middle of the eleventh century, this world was in turn invaded by fresh barbarians: Berbers from the Sahara and Turcomans from Central Asia. Even more than the Arabs, these barbarians were nomads of the arid zone from the Atlantic to Mongolia; and, as in the case of the Arabs, their invasions were testimony to the attraction of the civilized world for the peoples on its periphery, who were drawn into its affairs by its wealth on the one hand, by its religion and its politics on the other.

At the end of the tenth century the emirate of the Sāmānid dynasty in Central Asia, an offshoot of the 'Abbāsid Empire, collapsed. Its territories were divided between the Turcoman Qarakhānids in Transoxania and the Ghaznawids in Khurasan and Afghanistan. Unlike the immigrant Qarakhānids, the Turcoman Oghuz (also known as Ghuzz), occupying the steppes beyond the Aral Sea, remained largely pagan. In the first half of the eleventh century, however, a Muslim fraction of the Oghuz, nomadic warriors in search of pasture and military service, moved south into Qarakhānid and then Ghaznawid territory. These were the Saljūq (Turk. *Selçük*) clan, named after their ancestor; and they came into conflict with both the Qarakhānids and the Ghaznawids, a dynasty founded by a Turkish *ghulām* (slave soldier, pl. *ghilmān*) in the service of the Sāmānids.

To justify his usurpation of power, Maḥmūd of Ghazna (998–1030) had turned to war upon the internal and external enemies of Islam, that is the Shī'ites in Iraq and Persia and Hindus of the Indian subcontinent. The Shī'ite Būyid dynasty in western Persia held power over the Sunnī 'Abbāsid caliphate at Baghdad; the Shī'ite Fāṭimids in Egypt claimed the caliphate for themselves. As recognized champions of the 'Abbāsids, Maḥmūd and his son Mas'ūd not only persecuted the Ismā'īlis, the followers of the Fāṭimids within their dominions, but set out to overthrow the Būyids

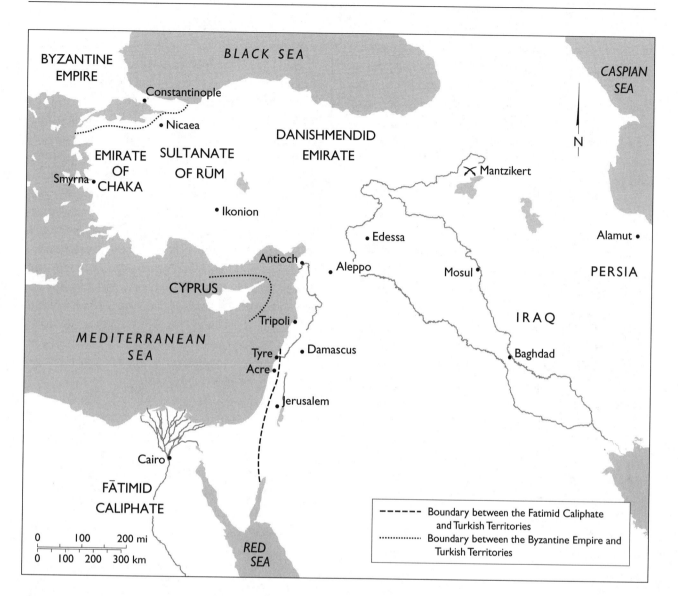

The Saljūq Sultanate (Western Half), including dependent Turkish Territories, in 1095

and ultimately the Fāṭimids. But their ambitions were cut short at the battle of Dandanqān in 1040, when Masʿūd's ponderous army was routed by the Saljūqs who had overrun the province of Khurasan. From the battlefield, the Saljūq leader Ṭughril Beg sent the news of his victory to Baghdad, thereby taking upon himself the championship of the ʿAbbāsid caliphate and Sunnī Islam.

The Establishment of the Saljūq Empire

With the Ghaznawids confined to Afghanistan and north-western India, their dominions in northeastern Persia were divided between Ṭughril and his brothers Chagrī and Mūsā Yabghū in a family dominion like that of the Qarakhānids in Transoxania. What might in consequence have remained yet another regional power, without pretensions or prospects, was transformed into a great new empire by this active championship. Leaving Chagrī to establish a local dynasty in Kirman in southeastern Persia, Ṭughril resumed the drive of the Ghaznawids to the west. Between 1040 and 1055 he took over the Būyid dominions in western Persia and Iraq, and between 1055 and 1060 secured Baghdad against the attempt of the Fāṭimids to win it for themselves. By the time of his death in 1063, he had married the daughter of the ʿAbbāsid caliph and received from him a plethora of titles: King of the East and the West, Pillar of the Faith, and so on. These confirmed him as the sultan, the hereditary ruler of the world on behalf of the caliph.

Ṭughril's nephew Alp Arslān (d. 1073) and Alp Arslān's son Malik Shāh I (d. 1092) ensured that this role did not die with him, but was justified by further conquest. In 1071 Alp Arslān routed the Byzantines at the battle of Mantzikert in Armenia, adding Anatolia not only to the Saljūq realm but to the Islamic world. Between 1078 and 1086 Malik Shāh I and his brother Tutush I took the bulk of Syria, while in the northeast, the Qarakhānids of Transoxania were forced into submission. The ambition to conquer Egypt was never pursued, but at the death of Malik Shāh I, Islam in Asia was predominantly under Saljūq rule.

Government, Institutions, and Armies

The Saljūq Empire was a family affair, divided among brothers and their sons in accordance with Turcoman custom, and exposed to their rivalry. But at the same time it was not a Turcoman empire in the sense of nomadic tribesmen ruling over settled populations. The princes were khans, or chieftains, to the nomads who followed them, but as heirs to the Ghaznawids and the Būyids, they were patriarchs in Max Weber's sense, rulers who relied less upon the folk than the household for their forces, and from the outset they depended upon the secretarial class of the Muslim world for their administration.

The Turcoman tribesmen who accompanied the Saljūqs into the Muslim world and migrated in search of pasture for their sheep through the highlands of Persia into Anatolia largely escaped, and indeed resisted, their control. The twin threats of devolution and dissidence were only overcome with the creation of a centralized regime by two great viziers (Arab. wazīr) brought up in the service of the Ghaznawids, al-Kundurī and Niẓām al-Mulk. They did so as politicians as well as administrators, whose powers of appointment and patronage created networks of clients around their own extensive households, and enabled them to command obedience from the Saljūqs themselves, from their colleagues, and from their subordinates. As politicians they lived dangerously between the confidence of the sultan and the royal ladies on the one hand, and the intrigues of their rivals on the other: Niẓām al-Mulk had al-Kundurī put to death, and before his own murder in 1092 was protesting his loyalty against the calumnies of his enemies. But for over thirty years they reined back the centrifugal forces underlying the supremacy of the King of the East and the West.

The Siyāsat-nāma (Book of Government) by Niẓām al-Mulk is a prescription for government that relies heavily upon Ghaznawid practice and example, not least for the acculturation of the Turks, who were to be trained up as ghilmān, loyal and disciplined warriors in the household of the prince. What has been called the despotic and monolithic Ghaznawid state could not be recreated; the household of the sultan was only the greatest of many such retinues, which gave each prince a greater or lesser degree of independence. Devolution was nevertheless kept in check by the size of his household, coupled with that of Niẓām al-Mulk himself, and by the appointment of its members as provincial governors and atabegs ("father dukes"), senior commanders who acted as tutors of junior princes, whose mothers they often married. It was more formally controlled by the use of the iqṭaʿ, a grant of revenue in payment for military service, which under the Saljūqs became a grant of local or provincial government. At the same time Niẓām al-Mulk set out to ground the pretensions of the sultan to the role of defender of the faith in more than titles and occasional warfare. In the name of Sunnī Islam, he founded the Niẓāmiyya at Baghdad, the most famous of a series of colleges of religious education designed to inculcate the true faith as well as to bring it under the patronage and control of the state. The foundation of such a *madrasa* (religious college) became a hallmark of the pious prince, concerned with his image in the public eye.

On their entry into the Islamic world, the Saljūqs were Turcoman nomads, fighting on horseback with composite bows and curved swords, but without armor, opposing their mobility to the more static formations of the armies they encountered. Over the next hundred years of warfare, the Turcomans acquired helmets and a certain amount of body armor, while the Saljūqs themselves adopted the style of the *ghulām,* the so-called slave soldier, recruited as a boy from the Turkish populations of Central Asia and trained up to be a fully armored cavalryman in the armies of the Islamic world from the ninth century onward. Their principal innovation was to provide him with the Turcoman bow in addition to sword and spear. Saljūq armies thus came to consist of squadrons of heavy household cavalry supported by Turcoman and other ethnic auxiliaries, with all the advantages of armor, archery, and mobility. Such squadrons under their individual commanders were nevertheless limited in size, and large armies were the exception. By the end of the Saljūq period, the term *ghulām* had been generally replaced by *mamlūk* (pl. *mamālīk*), most obviously in Egypt, where the Saljūq warrior was introduced by Saladin.

The Crisis of the Empire

The image of piety supplemented that of defender of the faith, employed by Ṭughril to create his empire, and to justify the power of a rank outsider over the Islamic world. That justification, however, at the expense of Shī'ite Islam, provoked a radical new challenge and a radical new threat. The *Siyāsat-nāma* barely mentions the Fāṭimids, nominal enemies who had evidently ceased to serve the Saljūq purpose of empire building. But it vehemently attacks the Ismā'īlīs, followers of the Fāṭimids under their leader Ḥasan-i Ṣabbāḥ, who in 1090 seized the castle of Alamut in northwestern Persia as a base for revolution. Directed against the Saljūqs as the champions of Sunnī Islam, the threat of insurrection not only forced the regime to go to war in the mountains, but in 1092 Ḥasan's alarming campaign of assassination may have claimed the life of Niẓām al-Mulk himself. Whoever arranged it, the murder of the great vizier was the beginning of the end for the empire he had striven to consolidate. The death of Malik Shāh I a few weeks later curtailed the sultan's

plan to depose the reigning caliph, and thus bring the 'Abbāsid caliphate completely under his control. Instead, it opened the way to a struggle for the succession from which the empire never fully recovered.

Malik Shāh I's sons Maḥmūd and Barkyārūq were minors, fought over by the factions at court, and challenged by their uncle Tutush I in Syria. Barkyārūq succeeded to the throne in 1094; Tutush was killed in 1095; but from 1097 to his death in 1105, the new sultan was challenged by his half-brothers Muḥammad Tapar (d. 1118) and Sanjar (d. 1157). The ensuing warfare divided the empire between Barkyārūq in Iraq and western Persia and his rivals in the northeast, and placed the contestants in the hands of the military. As the shifting loyalties of the atabegs came to dominate the conflict, Syria was abandoned to the sons of Tutush at Damascus and Aleppo, while the Saljūqs of Rūm (Anatolia) were left to fight off the Byzantines and crusaders at Ikonion (mod. Konya, Turkey). The unsuccessful attempt of the atabeg of Mosul, Karbughā, to relieve Antioch (mod. Antakya, Turkey) in 1098 was the most that was done to halt the progress of the First Crusade (1096–1099). In Persia itself, Ḥasan-i Ṣabbāḥ extended his mountain kingdom, while his assassins claimed their victims, and Shahdiz outside Isfahan fell into Ismā'īlī hands.

Decline of the Empire

The conflict ended with the death of Barkyārūq in 1105 and the accession of Muḥammad Tapar, under whom the unity of the empire was restored. Shahdiz was recovered in 1110, and the expansion of Alamut halted. Between 1110 and 1115 two attempts were made by the atabegs of Mosul on behalf of the sultan to organize a joint campaign in Syria against the Frankish states of Outremer. Both, however, failed in the face of Syrian hostility to any attempt to recover the country for the empire. Mosul itself, under successive atabegs, was semi-independent, while Diyar Bakr and Mayyafariqin on the upper Euphrates were taken over by the Turcoman Artūqid dynasty.

This shrinkage of the empire back toward the east was confirmed by the death of Muḥammad Tapar in 1118. The sultanate then passed to Sanjar, the fourth son of Malik Shāh I, who had governed Khurasan since 1097, and remained identified with this first conquest of the dynasty. Left to rule over western Persia and Iraq, the sons and grandsons of Muḥammad steadily lost control of their territory to their atabegs, whose principalities came to stretch from the

Great Saljūq Sultans

Tughril Beg	1055–1063
Alp Arslān	1063–1072
Malik Shāh I	1072–1092
Maḥmūd I	1092–1094
Barkyārūq	1094–1105
Malik Shāh II	1105
Muḥammad Tapar	1105–1118
Sanjar	1118–1157

Caspian Sea and the Caucasus through Mosul in northern Iraq to Luristan and Fars in western and southern Persia. By 1152 they had even lost Baghdad to the 'Abbāsids, who had taken advantage of Saljūq weakness to create their own state. In Khurasan itself, Sanjar's position was seriously weakened by defeat at the hands of the Qara Khitay in Transoxania in 1141, and collapsed in 1157, when he was defeated by Oghuz Turkish tribesmen, and died.

Like the Ghaznawids before them, the Great Saljūqs thus met their fate in the same region and at the hands of the same people whom they had led to the original victory at Dandanqān. Just as in 1040, their dominions in eastern Persia, including Kirman under the descendants of Ṭughril's brother Chagrī, were overrun by the victors, while an empty title passed to the line of Muḥammad in what was left of their empire in the west. From 1161 to 1191 their sultanate was under the control of the atabeg Eldigüz and his successors, whose power extended from Azerbaijan as far as Isfahan. It ended in heroic suicide, when Ṭughril III ousted the Eldiguzids, only to go to war with the formidable Khwārazm Shāh, and die in battle in 1194.

The great difference between the victory of the Oghuz in 1157 and the victory of the Saljūqs in 1040 was the absence of either a great religious or a great political cause. After the death of Sanjar, the Turks behaved as the Saljūqs might have done without the championship of the caliphate and Islam, and remained as a horde in eastern Persia; there was no mantle for their leader Malik Dinār to inherit. This failure on the part of the Great Saljūqs to maintain the ideal as well as the reality of universal empire is symptomatic of the growing conviction that might is right; in other words, that the ruler who had the power to govern had the authority to do so. It anticipated the coming of the pagan Mongols, and their ready acceptance by the counterparts of Niẓām al-Mulk in

the thirteenth century. It was left to the Zangids, the dynasty of the Saljūq atabeg at Mosul, gradually to rediscover the principle of religion for empire, and to their henchman Saladin to put it once again into practice.

–Michael Brett

Bibliography

Ayalon, David, *The Mamluk Military Society* (London: Variorum, 1979).

Bosworth, Clifford Edmund, "The Political and Dynastic History of the Iranian World (A.D. 1000–1217)," in *The Cambridge History of Iran,* vol. 5: *The Saljuq and Mongol Periods,* ed. J. A. Boyle (Cambridge: Cambridge University Press, 1968), pp. 1–202.

———, *The New Islamic Dynasties* (Edinburgh: Edinburgh University Press, 1996).

Cahen, Claude, "The Turkish Invasion: The Selchükids," in *A History of the Crusades,* ed. Kenneth M. Setton et al., 2d ed., 6 vols. (Madison: University of Wisconsin Press, 1969–1989), 1:135–176.

Humphreys, R. Stephen, *Islamic History: A Framework for Inquiry,* 2d ed. (London: Tauris, 1991).

Klausner, Carla L., *The Seljuk Vezirate: A Study of Civil Administration 1055–1194* (Cambridge, Mass.: Harvard University Press, 1973).

Lambton, Anne K. S., "The Internal Structure of the Saljuq Empire," in *The Cambridge History of Iran,* vol. 5: *The Saljuq and Mongol Periods,* ed. J. A. Boyle (Cambridge: Cambridge University Press, 1968), pp. 203–283.

Morgan, David O., *Medieval Persia, 1040–1797* (London: Longman, 1988).

Nicolle, David, *The Armies of Islam, 7th–11th Centuries* (London: Osprey, 1982).

Niẓām al-Mulk, *The Book of Government or Rules for Kings,* trans. Hubert Darke (London: Routledge and Kegan Paul, 1960).

Ẓahīr al-Dīn Nīshāpūrī, *The History of the Seljuq Turks,* trans. K. A. Luther, ed. C. E. Bosworth (Richmond, UK: Curzon, 2001.

Samogitia

Samogitia (Lith. *Žemaitija,* Pol. *Žmudz,* Ger. *Schmaiten*) was part of the Lithuanian lowlands north of the river Nemunas, a region of scattered settlements protected by dense forests and swamps from attacks by both crusaders and those Lithuanian grand princes of the highlands who attempted in vain to exercise authority there.

The Samogitians were the most fierce warriors of the Baltic region, and the most resolutely pagan. There were few important lords and few serfs, a fact that folklore and even

Polish literature later exploited to depict later generations as retaining the best qualities of the noble savage. The Samogitians were indeed great warriors who fought with courage, cunning, and conviction against overwhelming numbers, but they were also ruthless toward their foes, carrying away women and children into slavery and occasionally burning a knight alive in honor of their gods. Cultural conservatism, together with the swampy and forested nature of the land, slowed the development of agriculture; instead Samogitians raised cattle and horses, which could be easily hidden from enemy armies and added to by successful raids of their own.

The first conflicts in the course of the Baltic Crusades came early in the thirteenth century when Lithuanian raiders were conducting their annual plundering of Livonia and Estonian settlements, and their greatest victories came in defense of their lands against crusaders. In the fourteenth century, members of the Teutonic Order operating out of Prussia conducted more than seventy invasions into Samogitia and further up the river Nemunas into central Lithuania; they also attacked from Curonia and central Livonia. Many squires came in hope of being knighted in magnificent ceremonies. Crusader poets described Samogitian warriors lurking in the darkness outside the crusaders' celebrations, thirsting for revenge against those who had killed their people and burned their homes and crops, but unable to satisfy their rage.

Eventually Samogitian independence was traded away for peace by Grand Duke Vytautas of Lithuania (1386–1430) and Władysław II Jagiełło (Lith. *Jogaila*), king of Poland (1386–1434), who in 1398 assisted the grand master of the Teutonic Order in repressing the last resistance, and then confirmed his authority over the region in the Treaty of Sallinwerder. The grand master was criticized by churchmen for not rushing the population to the baptismal font, but he held to his policy of westernizing the economy first. A later effort to collect taxes led to the hostilities with Poland and Lithuania that ended in the battle of Tannenberg in 1410. Vytautas and Władysław introduced Christianity in 1413, sending a delegation of converts to the Council of Konstanz in 1415, and oversaw the creation of a diocese in 1417. Nevertheless, passive resistance prevented a thorough conversion until the Counter-Reformation.

–*William L. Urban*

See also: Baltic Crusades; Lithuania; Livonia; Mindaugas
Bibliography
Paravicini, Werner, "Die Preußenreisen des europäischen Adels," *Historische Zeitschrift* 48 (1981), 25–38.
Urban, William L., *The Samogitian Crusade* (Chicago: Lithuanian Research and Study Center, 1989).

St. Samuel

See Montjoie, Abbey of

San Germano, Treaty of (1230)

The agreement between Frederick II, Holy Roman Emperor and king of Sicily, and Pope Gregory IX that ended the conflict arising from Frederick's excommunication in 1227, which Gregory had pronounced because of Frederick's delays in going on crusade to the Holy Land.

The settlement was negotiated by Hermann von Salza, master of the Teutonic Order, and Cardinal Thomas of Capua, and confirmed by Frederick II at San Germano in Italy on 23 July 1227. It included the promise that those who had supported the papacy would be taken back into the emperor's favor; that Frederick would not enter the duchy of Spoleto or other papal lands; that episcopal elections in Sicily would conform to the rules laid out at the Fourth Lateran Council (1215); that the church in Sicily would be free from taxation, and its clergy exempt from royal jurisdiction; and that lands that had been seized from the military orders would be returned to them.

Various issues were not, however, fully resolved until 28 August, at Ceprano (on the borders between the kingdom of Sicily and the papal states), where two papal legates absolved Frederick from his sentence of excommunication. By that stage, some of the more stringent clauses had been modified in Frederick's favor. The ceremony was followed by a meeting between Frederick and Gregory at Anagni on 1 September, which symbolically ended Frederick's excommunication.

–*Björn K. U. Weiler*

See also: Baltic Crusades; Lithuania; Teutonic Order
Bibliography
Abulafia, David, *Frederick II. A Medieval Emperor* (Harmondsworth, UK: Penguin, 1988).
Die Actenstücke zum Frieden von San Germano, ed. Karl Hampe (Berlin: Weidmannsche Verlagsbuchhandlung, 1926).
Stürner, Friedrich, *Friedrich II.*, 2 vols. (Darmstadt: Wissenschaftliche Buchgesellschaft, 1994–2000).

Santiago de Compostela

A major pilgrimage center and bishopric (later archbishopric) in Galicia (northwestern Spain). The church of Compostela was built over the relics of the apostle St. James (Sp. *Santiago*), which were discovered at the beginning of the reign of King Alfonso II of León (791–842).

Compostela became the site of a bishopric and, from 1124 onward, an archbishopric, ranking alongside the other Iberian provinces of Toledo, Tarragona, and Braga. The reputation of the sanctuary soon drew a growing number of pilgrims, and by the twelfth century Compostela was one of the three major places of pilgrimage in Latin Christendom, alongside Rome and Jerusalem.

Santiago de Compostela is linked to the European crusading movement in four ways. First, St. James became an active agent of the Spanish *Reconquista* (reconquest of the peninsula from the Muslims) in the shape of Santiago Matamoros (St. James, slayer of Muslims), an iconographic model that associated the apostle directly with the war against the Muslims on the Iberian Peninsula. A series of extant paintings and sculptures show the saint as an armed and mounted pilgrim, trampling beaten Muslims underfoot. Consequently, Santiago also became the patron saint of the Hispano-American conquest, as illustrated in a number of place-names, such as Santiago de Chile and Santiago de Cuba. However, one must bear in mind that the figure of Santiago Matamoros only came into appearance at the middle of the twelfth century. During the High Middle Ages—the heyday of crusading—St. James was depicted as a pilgrim, not a fighter. Second, St. James was the patron saint of one of the major military religious orders of the Middle Ages, the Order of Santiago. This was, however, due to the personal relations between Pedro Gudesteiz, archbishop of Santiago de Compostela, and the first members of the confraternity from which the order originated. Nevertheless, the Order of Santiago remained closely tied to its saintly protector in iconography, liturgy, and the like. Third, Santiago de Compostela played an important role in the diffusion of the idea of crusading in the Iberian Peninsula. In the famous *Historia Compostelana,* Diego Gelmírez, archbishop of Santiago, transcribed a letter he wrote in 1125, in the days of his legation in the metropolitan provinces of Mérida and Braga, in order to convince fighters from the entire Iberian Peninsula to take arms in the name of Christ in order to open a road through al-Andalus that would lead to Jerusalem. The prelate clearly intended to associate the struggles of his compatriots with the crusade, and judging from the careful spreading of the letter, it seems the speech, however new it might have sounded in the kingdom of Castile, soon became familiar to most. Finally, one can discern direct contacts between the see of Santiago de Compostela and that of Jerusalem in the first decades of the twelfth century, which led to the establishment of confraternal ties between the two communities and mutual visits.

–*Philippe Josserand*

Bibliography

Díaz y Díaz, Manuel, "Las tres grandes peregrinaciones vistas desde Santiago," in *Santiago, Roma, Jerusalén: Actas del III Congreso Internacional de Estudios Jacobeos,* ed. Paolo Caucci von Saucken (Santiago de Compostela: Xunta de Galicia, 1999), pp. 81–97.

Fletcher, Richard, *Saint James's Catapult: The Life and Times of Diego Gelmírez of Santiago de Compostela* (Oxford: Clarendon, 1984).

Jaspert, Nikolas, "'Pro nobis, qui pro vobis oramus, orate.' Die Kathedralkapitel von Compostela und Jerusalem in der ersten Hälfte des 12. Jahrhunderts," in *Santiago, Roma, Jerusalén. Actas del III Congreso Internacional de Estudios Jacobeos,* ed. Paolo Caucci von Saucken (Santiago de Compostela: Xunta de Galicia, 1999), pp. 187–212.

Josserand, Philippe, "Croisade et reconquête dans le royaume de Castille au XIIe siècle. Eléments pour une réflexion," in *L'expansion occidentale (XIe-XVe siècles). Formes et conséquences. Actes du XXXIIIe Congrès de la Société des Médiévistes de l'Enseignement Supérieur* (Paris: Presses Universitaires de la Sorbonne, 2003), pp. 75–85.

Saint Jacques et la France, ed. Adeline Rucquoi (Paris: Editions Du Cerf, 2003).

Santiago, Order of

The Order of Santiago (St. James) was the most powerful of the Iberian military religious orders, originating as a confraternity of knights founded by King Ferdinand II of León in Cáceres in August 1170 in order to protect the southern part of his kingdom against the Muslim Almohads.

Despite later medieval legends that dated the order as far back as the mythical battle of Clavijo won by King Ramiro I of Asturias (d. 850) against the Moors, the birth of this institution occurred within the context of the reconquest of Iberia from the Muslims in the second half of the twelfth century. The appearance of a confraternity under the leadership of its master Pedro Fernández followed the pattern of other militias such as the *hermandad* (confraternity) of Belchite, founded by King Alfonso I half a century before in Aragon, or the more recent *hermandad* of Ávila in Castile, which eventually merged with the Order of Santiago.

The members of the new confraternity were known as the Brethren of Cáceres until January 1171. In that year they came to an agreement with Pedro Gudesteiz, archbishop of Santiago de Compostela, who became a member of the community as an honorary brother and in return received the master and his knights into his cathedral chapter. Although this pact did not last long, the brethren chose St. James (Sp. *Santiago*) as their patron and protector, whose fame helped them obtain donations. In 1173 Master Pedro Fernández obtained a bull of protection from the papacy for the community. He probably presented Pope Alexander III with the first version of the rule of Santiago, which received papal approval two years later in July 1175.

According to this rule, the membership of the order consisted of knight brethren, who were dedicated to fighting against the Muslims, and clerics, who followed the Rule of St. Augustine and most probably came from the Galician monastery of Loyo. Both clerics and knights bore the insignia of a red cross in the shape of a sword. These two parallel communities were under the authority of a master, who was elected from among the knights and governed the whole order with the assent of the general chapter. This institutional structure was inspired by the orders of the Temple and the Hospital, but also by the Order of Calatrava, founded in Castile in 1158.

The founder of the order, Ferdinand II of León, wanted to use the new militia to protect the southern border of his realm, which was threatened by Almohad incursions. Master Pedro Fernández, by contrast, had quite different aims: with the encouragement of the papacy, he tried to give his order a dimension that would not be restricted to León. In 1171 King Alfonso VIII of Castile granted it the castles of Mora and Oreja, whose location to the south and east of Toledo gave them a key role in the defense of that city. From Afonso I Henriques, king of Portugal, the order received the castles of Monsanto (1171) and Abrantes (1173) and was thus brought into the defense of the line of the river Tagus (Sp. *Tajo*). The expansion of the order beyond León can be seen from a confirmation by Pope Lucius III (1184), which mentions possessions in León, Portugal, and Castile, as well as Aragon, France, and Italy. The order thus turned into an international organization, which, even though most of its activity was focused on the Iberian Peninsula, still extended as far as the Holy Land, where the brethren were repeatedly asked to settle.

The Iberian Peninsula, however, remained the main theater of operations for the Order of Santiago, whose brethren, during the first fifty years of its existence, were busy fighting the Almohads under the direction of the various Hispanic kings. Against these powerful enemies, they first had to defend the line of the Tagus from Palmela and Alcácer do Sal, in the west, to Uclés, where the order officially settled after being granted the city by Alfonso VIII of Castile in 1174. The task was far from easy, and, in such a difficult context of division between the Christian realms, the order had to give up certain places: Cáceres (1174), Alcácer (1191), and even Montánchez, Trujillo, and Santa Cruz (1196), during the great Almohad offensive that occurred after the Castilian defeat at Alarcos. Despite their difficult situation, the brethren succeeded in preserving most of their estates in La Mancha by resisting the Muslim attacks of 1197 against Alarcón and Uclés. From such bases, it was possible for them to continue fighting and progressively resume offensive action until the great victory of Las Navas de Tolosa (16 July 1212), which opened the south of the peninsula to the Christian kingdoms.

The determination of the brethren of Santiago was instrumental in enabling Iberian Christendom to take advantage of the Almohad collapse. The order fought on every front. In Portugal its members decisively contributed in 1217 to the seizure of Alcácer, where they established their provincial seat, before participating in the integration of the Campo de Montiel and the towns of the Guadiana Valley into the kingdoms of Castile and León. They assisted in the conquest of the Taifa kingdom of Valencia, where King James I of Aragon was supported by Rodrigo Bueso, the commander of Montalbán. During the submission of the southern part of al-Andalus that took place during the reigns of Ferdinand III of Castile and Afonso III of Portugal, the Santiaguists relentlessly supported the monarchies until the mid-thirteenth century, as shown by the involvement of the master Pelayo Pérez Correa, who actively participated in the capture of Seville in 1248 and in the submission of the Algarve the next year.

Thanks to such military activity, the Order of Santiago underwent a great expansion from the second quarter of the thirteenth century. Numerous donations built up a near continuous bloc of estates extending from the estuary of the river Tagus, south of Lisbon, to that of the Segura, in the region of Murcia. Within these possessions, the order organized a system of commanderies and, in some places, established male and female convents as well as charitable foundations intended to welcome pilgrims, take care of lepers, and even to ransom captives. These elements all contributed to the prestige as well as the wealth of the order, whose influence reached a peak under the long mastership of Pelayo Pérez Correa (1242–1275), who acquired a level of power unprecedented among of his predecessors.

The wealth of the order came to be coveted, at a time when it was also tending to interfere in the domestic policies of the Christian kingdoms. At the instigation of Pelayo Pérez Correa, in 1272 it secretly supported the rebellion of those members of the Castilian nobility who were reluctant to accept the plans of monarchical centralization contemplated by King Alfonso X. Ten years later, the brethren openly rose up in arms against the king, who, at the end of his reign, was at war against his son, the future Sancho IV. As a leading but sometimes unruly element in politics, from the late thirteenth century Santiago in turn became the object of growing interference on the part of the Castilian monarchy, which more than ever needed to be certain of its cooperation. King Alfonso XI was able to manipulate the order to a greater degree than any of his predecessors: he succeeded in having important trials concerning the military orders brought under the jurisdiction of the royal courts, and he forced the Santiaguists to accept his mistress's brother, Alonso Méndez de Guzmán, as master of the order in 1338, even granting the office to the young Fadrique, his own natural son, four years later.

Until the mid-fourteenth century, the brethren regularly joined the campaigns fought by Castile for control of the strait of Gibraltar in an attempt to wrest from the Naṣrids of Granada and the Marīnids of Morocco the domination of maritime traffic between the Atlantic Ocean and the Mediterranean: they not only took part in the fighting but also contributed to the costly maintenance of several strongholds on the border. Yet the order also played an increasingly important part in internal conflicts within Iberian Christendom, particularly in the civil war that rent Castile between 1366 and 1369, during which brethren of Santiago were found in both opposing factions.

By the fifteenth century, there was a constant competition between the Crown and the local aristocracy for control of the Order of Santiago's most important offices. On several occasions in Castile, during the reigns of John II and Henry IV, such competition within the order degenerated into armed confrontation. Yet while most kings had been content with installing men they trusted as heads of the institution, a far more radical solution was implemented in the time of the "Catholic Monarchs," Isabella I of Castile (d. 1504) and Ferdinand II of Aragon (d. 1516). On the death of Master Alonso de Cárdenas (1493), they obtained from Pope Alexander VI the right to rule the order until their deaths. This measure was renewed under their successors, and it paved the way for the subsequent integration of Santiago's estates into the patrimony of the Spanish monarchy. In Portugal, where a branch of the order had become independent from the Castilian center in the early fourteenth century, a similar privilege was granted by the papacy to King John III in 1551. At this time in both kingdoms, Santiago entered a new period of its history, and first became a purely honorary noble corporation largely distant from any form of military action, before it was dissolved in the modern period, initially in 1874 by the first Spanish Republic, and definitively in 1931 after the abolition of the monarchy.

–*Philippe Josserand*

Bibliography

Ayala Martínez, Carlos de, *Las órdenes militares hispánicas en la Edad Media (siglos XII-XV)* (Madrid: Pons, 2003).

Josserand, Philippe, *Eglise et pouvoir dans la Péninsule Ibérique: Les ordres militaires dans le royaume de Castille (1252–1369)* (Madrid: Casa de Velázquez, 2004).

———, "Par-delà l'an mil. Le discours des origines dans l'ordre de Santiago au Moyen Age," in *Guerre, pouvoirs et idéologies dans l'Espagne chrétienne aux alentours de l'an mil,* ed. Thomas Deswarte and Philippe Sénac (Turnhout: Brepols, 2005), pp. 183–190.

Lomax, Derek, "The Order of Santiago and the Kings of León," *Hispania* 18 (1958), 3–37.

———, *La orden de Santiago, 1170–1275* (Madrid: Consejo Superior de Investigaciones Científicas, 1965).

Martín Rodríguez, José Luis, *Orígenes de la orden militar de Santiago, 1170–1195* (Madrid: Consejo Superior de Investigaciones Científicas, 1974).

Porras Arboledas, Pedro, *La orden de Santiago en el siglo XV: La provincia de Castilla* (Jaén: Caja Provincial de Ahorros de Jaén, 1997).

Sanudo Family

The Sanudo family rose to prominence in the thirteenth and fourteenth centuries as the Venetian dynasty that established and ruled the duchy of the Archipelago from the Greek island of Naxos. It included the chronicler Marino Sanudo Torsello (d. 1337), a prominent crusading publicist and historian of Latin Greece, as well as his namesake, the historian Marino Sanudo the Younger (d. 1533). The latter kept a very full *Diari* of events in Venice for a period of thirty-eight years as well as composing *Le Vite dei Dogi,* both of which are important sources for Venetian history.

The first Sanudo to be recorded by name was a certain John who was one of the signatories to the Treaty of Cittanova in 1009. According to the chronicler Andrea Dandolo, by the 1170s the family was regarded as one of the noblest of Venice, having possible associations with the ancient family of Candiani, one of the founding families of the city. The Sanudi were well connected in Venetian governing circles and also had established links in the Aegean through Marco Sanudo Constantinopolitani, who may have been the father or the grandfather of Marco Sanudo, the conqueror of the Archipelago. The latter's mother was a sister of Enrico Dandolo, whose election as doge the family backed in 1192.

Four members of the family were present on the Fourth Crusade (1202–1204). Probably with the support of his uncle, Enrico Dandolo (d. 1207), Marco (d. 1227) embarked on the conquest of the Cyclades, setting up the center of his island duchy on Naxos in 1204–1205 and expelling a Genoese force from Apalire in 1206. Besides Naxos, Marco occupied the islands of Paros, Antiparos, Melos, Siphnos Thermia, Ios, Amorgos, Kimilos, Sikinos, Syra, and Pholegandros. He was so well established by 1212 that he was able to respond to a call for assistance from the Venetian authorities on Crete to help suppress a rising on that island.

In the third generation, the Sanudi created island lordships on Melos, Nio, Paros, and Syra for their younger sons. Marriage alliances with them allowed other Latin families in Greece to gain material and dynastic interests in the Archipelago. The direct male line of the Sanudi died out in 1362 with the death of Duke Giovanni I. The title passed to his daughter Fiorenza, who, as the widow of Giovanni dalle Carceri, was already the regent of Negroponte. She died in 1371, and the duchy passed to her son Niccolo dalle Carceri, on whose murder in 1388 it passed to the Crispi family.

–Peter Lock

Bibliography

Boffito, Giuseppe, "Nuove lettere di Marino Sanudo il Vecchio," *La Bibliofilia* 42 (1940), 321–359.

Kunstmann, Friedrich, "Studien über Marino Sanudo Torsello den Älteren," *Abhandlungen der Bayerischen Akademie der Wissenschaften: Historische Klasse* 7 (1853), 695–819.

Laiou, Angeliki E., "Marino Sanudo Torsello, Byzantium and the Turks: The Background to the Anti-Turkish League of 1332–34," *Speculum* 45 (1970), 374–392.

Lane, Frederic C., *Venice: A Maritime Republic* (Baltimore: Johns Hopkins University Press, 1973).

Setton, Kenneth, *The Papacy and the Levant,* vol. 1 (Philadelphia: American Philosophical Society, 1976).

Tyerman, Christopher J., "Marino Sanudo Torsello and the Lost Crusade: Lobbying in the Fourteenth Century," *Transactions of the Royal Historical Society* 32 (1982), 57–73.

Sanudo, Marino (d. 1343)

Marino Sanudo, called Torsello, was a merchant, chronicler, historian, lobbyist, and crusade theorist and propagandist.

Sanudo was born about 1270 into a distinguished Venetian family, one branch of which ruled the island of Naxos in the Aegean Sea. After extensive experience of the eastern Mediterranean as a young man, Sanudo composed the *Conditiones Terrae Sanctae* (1306–1309), a scheme for an economic blockade of Egypt as a preliminary to military action against the Mamlūk sultanate. Refining and expanding his ideas, Sanudo produced the *Liber Secretorum* (or *Secreta*) *Fidelium Crucis,* presented to Pope John XXII in 1321. Its first book contained a revamped *Conditiones;* the second dealt with the preliminary military assault on Egypt by a professional force, to be followed by a general crusade (Lat. *passagium generale*); the third included a history of Outremer to the early fourteenth century, in its final version relying on William of Tyre, James of Vitry, Vincent of Beauvais, and Het'um the Armenian, as well as on original material, to which was appended a geographical description of the Holy Land and a summary of how a renewed kingdom of Jerusalem should be organized.

Although set within an overtly pious and revivalist frame, the *Secreta* constituted operational advice, not an appeal for action. Despite its apparent pragmatism, certain details remained contestably practical. With Sanudo's manuscripts, produced in his Venetian atelier, came detailed maps, some designed by the Genoese cartographer Pietro Vesconte. At least nineteen manuscripts of the *Secreta* survive.

To press his ideas, Sanudo exhaustively visited or corresponded with the courts of rulers interested in reviving the holy war in the East. Earlier than many in the West, Sanudo appreciated the danger posed by Turkish emirates in the Aegean, warnings that contributed to the anti-Turkish league of 1332–1334. Sanudo also wrote a continuation of the chronicle of Geoffrey of Villehardouin and an *Istoria del Regno di Romania* (1328–1333).

–Christopher Tyerman

Bibliography

Cardini, Franco, "I costi della crociata. L'aspetto economico del progetto di Marin Sanudo il Vecchio (1312–21)," *Studi in Memoria di Frederigo Melis,* 2 vols. (Napoli, 1978), 2:179–210.

Cerlini, A., "Nuovere lettere di Marino Sanudo il Vecchio," *La Bibliofilia* 42 (1940), 321–359.

Delaville Le Roulx, Joseph, *La France en Orient au XIVe siecle,* 2 vols. (Paris: Thorin, 1886).

Kunstmann, Friedrich, "Studien über Marino Sanudo Torsello den Älteren," *Abhandlungen der Bayerischen Akademie der Wissenschaften: Historische Klasse* 7 (1853), 695–819.

Leopold, Anthony, *How To Recover the Holy Land* (Aldershot, UK: Ashgate, 2000).

Magnocavallo, Arturo, *Marino Sanudo il Vecchio e il progetto di crociata* (Bergamo: Istituto Lombardo di Scienze e Lettere, 1901).

Sanudo, Marino, "Liber Secretorum Fidelium Crucis," in *Gesta Dei per Francos,* ed. Jacques Bongars, 2 vols. (Hannover: Typis Wechelianis, apud heredes Ioan. Aubrii, 1611), 2:1–288.

Tyerman, Christopher J., "Marino Sanudo Torsello and the Lost Crusade: Lobbying in the Fourteenth Century," *Transactions of the Royal Historical Society,* 5th ser., 32 (1982), 57–73.

Saphet

Saphet or Safad (mod. Zefat, Israel) was a Templar castle in the kingdom of Jerusalem, situated in Upper Galilee about 13 kilometers (c. 8 mi.) northwest of Lake Tiberias.

There are few visible remains of the castle, which stood on a prominent hilltop position commanding fine views over the surrounding country. It is now a public park. Excavations have recovered some evidence of crusader work and Mamlūk rebuilding.

The castle was originally constructed by the Templars but lost to Saladin in 1188. In 1240 it was restored to the Templars in the aftermath of the Crusade of 1239–1241 and rebuilt on a large scale. In 1266 the Mamlūk sultan Baybars I took the castle; he had apparently promised the defenders safe conduct, but 150 knights and 769 other members of the garrison were executed. The local Syrian Christians were allowed to go free. Saphet is best known for the account of the rebuilding of the castle after 1240 written for the bishop of Marseilles, Benedict of Alignan, who visited twice. It was Benedict who had persuaded the Templars to undertake the refortification. His account was probably written as a fundraising pamphlet and describes the strategic position of the castle and its design in some detail. It is the fullest account we have of the building of any castle in Outremer.

–Hugh Kennedy

Bibliography

Kennedy, Hugh, *Crusader Castles* (Cambridge: Cambridge University Press, 1994).

Pringle, Denys, "Reconstructing the Castle of Safad," *Palestine Exploration Quarterly* 117 (1985), 141–149.

Saracens

Saracens (Lat. *Sarraceni,* Fr. *Sarrasins*) was used in the period of the crusades as an indiscriminate term for Muslims. Originally designating one ethnic group in the Arabian Peninsula, by late antiquity it had become a synonym for Arabs, and it was employed by Latin chroniclers of the eighth and ninth centuries to describe the Muslim Arab invaders in the Mediterranean region. In the twelfth century, chroniclers of the First Crusade (1096–1099) and poets of the chansons de geste (Old French epic poems) applied the term to Turks, Arabs, and other Muslims, creating a colorful and wildly inaccurate portrait of Saracens who worshipped pantheon idols, the chief among them Mahomet. At the same time, theologians offered polemical refutations of the *Lex Sarracenorum* (Law of the Saracens), as they generally called Islam. The travel narratives and romances of the later Middle Ages often blend literary topoi of pagan Saracens with more realistic depictions of Islam. The term *Saracen* gradually fell into disuse by the seventeenth century, to be replaced by *Turk, Mohammedan,* and *Moslem.*

The origins of the Latin word *Sarracenus* are obscure; the hypothesis of its derivation from the Arabic *sharqiyyīn* (the plural of *sharqī,* "Easterner") is not universally accepted. Roman writers used the term to designate one ethnic group in eastern Arabia. By the third century, the term designated all of the nomadic Arabs of the peninsula. Some authors affirmed that the Saracens worshiped idols of stone. The theologian Jerome asserted that the Saracens were the descendants of Abraham through his handmaid Hagar and their son, the "wild man" Ishmael (Genesis 16:12); they thus

Crusader and Saracen jousting, fourteenth century. Detail from the Luttrell Psalter (MS London, British Library, Add.42130). (HIP/Art Resource)

should be properly called Hagarenes or Ishmaelites, but they falsely called themselves Saracens, claiming to be the descendants of Abraham's legitimate wife Sarah. This etymology was taken up by Isidore of Seville and many subsequent Latin authors. It no doubt seemed to fit the experience of those who chronicled the conquests and raids of the *Sarraceni* in the seventh and eighth centuries. Very few chroniclers showed any interest in the religion of these invaders, and those who did showed little awareness of the rise of Islam; they contented themselves with repeating what they found in Jerome and Isidore.

Hrotsvit (Roswitha), a nun at the abbey of Gandersheim at the turn of the millennium, presents the Saracens in the familiar guise of classical Roman idolaters. She depicts the Saracen King Abderahemen, that is the historical 'Abd al-Raḥmān III, caliph of Córdoba (912–961), as a tyrant who inflicts the death penalty on anyone who blasphemes his golden idols. Chroniclers of the First Crusade (1096–1099), notably Peter Tudebode, Radulph of Caen, and Raymond of Aguilers, depict the crusaders' Saracen adversaries as pagans who worship various idols, in particular Mahummet. Radulph of Caen goes so far as to assert that when the crusaders took Jerusalem, Tancred entered the Dome of the Rock and there found an idol of Mahummet, which he promptly destroyed. For these authors, the pollution of Jerusalem's holy places by the supposedly idolatrous rites of

the Saracens called for retribution. Fighting against pagans, crusaders could claim to be wreaking vengeance for the pagans' Crucifixion of Christ and their usurpation of his city; when the crusaders fell in battle, they could claim the mantle of martyrdom. The fight against paganism had a long history, from which Christianity was sure to emerge victorious.

The Old French *Chanson de Roland,* roughly contemporary with the chronicles of the First Crusade, describes in greater detail the idolatrous cult of the Saracens, devotees of an anti-Trinity of idols: Apolin, Tervagan, and Mahumet. Effigies of these gods adorn the standards of the Saracen troops; the Saracens invoke them in battle, and they destroy their idols when they fail to procure victory for them. Subsequent chansons de geste purvey this same image of Saracen paganism, and the word *sar(r)asin* is often used indiscriminately to designate all non-Christian enemies, from Africa, Scandinavia, or elsewhere. The twelfth-century epic *Floovant,* for example, refers to the Frankish king Clovis (d. 511) as a "Saracen" before his conversion to Christianity.

Many writers, in Latin and the various vernacular languages, use *Saracen* as a synonym for *pagan*. In English plays of the fourteenth centuries, the Romans are depicted as Saracens who worship idols of "Mahound." The poet William Langland, in *Piers Plowman,* refers to the Roman Emperor Trajan as a "Sarasene." Chroniclers refer to Lithuanian and Wendish pagans as Saracens. The image was so common

Saracen on horseback fighting in Sicily, late-thirteenth-century fresco, Tour Ferrande, Pernes-les-Fontaines, France. (The Art Archive/Dagli Orti)

that writers on Islam who knew better (from the twelfth century on) went to great pains to explain that the Saracens *were not* pagans.

For other medieval writers, *Saracen* was used to denote the Muslim; Islam was frequently referred to as the *Lex Sarracenorum* or *Lex Machometi* (Law of Muḥammad). These authors depict the Saracens not as idolaters, but as heretics, blind followers of the arch-heresiarch Mahomet.

A more ambivalent image of the imagined Saracen world is presented in romances of the thirteenth and fourteenth centuries, where the treasures of the East beckon and beautiful Saracen princesses are ready to help their Western heroes out of dangerous scrapes. Religious differences for the most part remain comfortably in the background, the

supposed paganism of the Saracens an occasional object of curiosity rather than animosity. Another genre that received increasing attention and elaboration in the fourteenth century was the narrative of real or imagined travels to the East. Here the Saracen world has become a distinct part of a larger entity: the Orient. As the traveler moves ever further east, from Latin Europe to the Byzantine world, through the Muslim lands, and perhaps into India, China, or the mythic islands inhabited by dog-headed men, fish-people, or Amazons, the world becomes progressively stranger and more wondrous. The Saracen is no longer the Other par excellence; for some of these authors, the Saracens' customs and religion now seem comfortably (or disturbingly) close to their own.

In the fourteenth century the boundaries between genres such as epic, romance, travelogue, and so on began to break down, at times producing strange blends. A good example of this is provided by the *Guerrino il Meschino* by Andrea da Barberino (d. 1431). At several points Andrea depicts Saracens worshiping Muḥammad as a god and as part of the standard idolatrous pantheon of the chansons de geste; yet elsewhere he distinguishes clearly between paganism and Islam and condemns Muḥammad as a false prophet. His descriptions of religious practices are more exotic than polemical. In the fifteenth century, as the Ottomans seized Constantinople (mod. İstanbul, Turkey) and pushed into the heart of Europe, the polemical view of the Muslim again returned to the fore, though now, rather than the Saracen, he was presented as the Turk.

–*John Tolan*

Bibliography

Camille, Michael, *The Gothic Idol: Ideology and Image-making in Medieval Art* (Cambridge: Cambridge Press, 1989).

Medieval Christian Perceptions of Islam: A Collection of Essays, ed. John Tolan (New York: Garland, 1996).

Ramey, Lynn, *Christian, Saracen and Genre in Medieval French Literature: Imagination and Cultural Interaction in the French Middle Ages* (New York: Garland, 2001).

Tolan, John, *Saracens: Islam in the Medieval European Imagination* (New York: Columbia University Press, 2002).

Saule, Battle of (1232)

A battle between the Order of the Sword Brethren and the Lithuanians, fought as part of a campaign by the Christians of Livonia to penetrate Samogitia, the most westerly part of pagan Lithuania.

In September 1236 Volkwin, master of the Sword Brethren, led some 3,000 men, consisting of troops of the order, native auxiliaries, German crusaders, and Russian allies from Pskov, starting from Riga and moving through the frontier wilderness area into settled Lithuanian territory. After several days of plundering, the army began an orderly withdrawal (21 September), but at a site called Saule in the sources, and now generally identified as modern Siauliai (in Lithuania), its retreat was blocked by Lithuanian forces assembling from throughout Samogitia.

The attempt of the Christian army to fight its way home through difficult terrain degenerated into a rout with heavy casualties, and Master Volkwin and most of the knight brethren of the order were killed covering the retreat (22 September). The decisive defeat ended Christian attempts to gain control of the Lithuanian-held territory between Livonia and Prussia, and the loss of at least half of the military strength of the Sword Brethren hastened the incorporation of the remnants of the order by the Teutonic Knights in 1237.

–*Alan V. Murray*

Bibliography

Benninghoven, Friedrich, *Der Orden der Schwertbrüder* (Köln: Böhlau, 1965).

Saxo Grammaticus

Author of the *Gesta Danorum,* a great Latin chronicle telling the history of the Danes from mythical times up to the final submission of Pomerania in 1185 during the reign of King Knud VI (1182–1202).

Saxo was born on Sjælland around 1150 into a noble family and studied at one of the schools in northern France. He probably became a canon at the cathedral in Lund, where Archbishop Absalon (1178–1201) commissioned him to write his work. He began it around 1190 at the latest but probably did not finish until shortly after 1208. It is dedicated to Absalon's successor as archbishop, Anders Sunesen (1201–1228), and to King Valdemar II of Denmark (1202–1241). Saxo is thought to have died around 1220.

The style and composition of the *Gesta Danorum* are based on those of classical authors. One of the most important purposes behind the chronicle was to show that Denmark was an independent nation as old as and equal to the Roman Empire. Saxo wrote his work during a time of Danish expansion in the Baltic area that began in the reign of King Valdemar I (1157–1182) and culminated with the conquest of Estonia in 1219 by Valdemar II. This expansion must be viewed as part of the crusades of the twelfth century, as Saxo also clearly indicates. Archbishop Absalon is described as a *pater patriae* ("father of his country") and as the main mover behind the expansion and extension of the faith to the heathen peoples living on the southern coast of the Baltic Sea collectively called the Wends. One of the high points of the chronicle is the account of the capture by Absalon and Valdemar I of the strong fortress of Arkona on the island of Rügen in 1168–1169 and the destruction of the great wooden statue of the heathen god Svantevit that was venerated there. However, the conflict itself is presented as a centuries-old, sharp antagonism between Danes and Wends. The Wends are heathen pirates, often described as inhuman beings who have always attacked the Danish kingdom; the war against them is therefore depicted as just. The Danes are described as fighting for peace and out of a burning love for their homeland: anyone attacking the Danes ought therefore to burn in hell forever.

The picture of an age-old conflict served to legitimize the wars of the Danish kings and church against the heathen Wends as being just and as crusades. The most frequent term used in the chronicle to describe the Danish expeditions (almost exclusively so for the period after 1100) is *expeditio,* one of the standard terms for crusade in the period. The work of Saxo must be seen in the same context as similar constructions of national history based on creations of age-old conflicts and diabolic images of the enemy in other frontier zones of Latin Christendom.

–*Janus Møller Jensen*

Bibliography

Archbishop Absalon and His World, ed. Karsten Friis-Jensen and Inge Skovgaard-Petersen (Roskilde: Roskilde Museums Forlag, 2000).

Friis-Jensen, Karsten, "Was Saxo Grammaticus a Canon of Lund?" *Cahiers de l'Institut du Moyen-Age grec et latin* 59 (1989), 331–357.

Jensen, Kurt Villads, "The Blue Baltic Border of Denmark in the High Middle Ages: Danes, Wends and Saxo Grammaticus," in *Medieval Frontiers: Concepts and Practices,* ed. David Abulafia and Nora Berend (Aldershot, UK: Ashgate, 2002), pp. 173–193.

Lind, John H., Carsten Selch Jensen, Kurt Villads Jensen, and Ane L. Bysted, *Danske korstog: Krig og mission i Østersøen* (København: Høst og Søn, 2004).

Saxo Grammaticus, *History of the Danes: Books I–IX,* ed. Hilda Ellis Davidson, trans. Peter Fisher, 2 vols. (Cambridge: Brewer, 1979–1980).

———, *Danorum Regum heroumque historia: Books X–XVI,* trans. Eric Christiansen, 3 vols. (Oxford: British Archaeological Reports, 1980–1981).

Schism of East and West

The roots of the schism, or division, between the Latin Church of the West and the Greek Orthodox Church of Byzantium predated the crusade era, but the first four major crusades (1096–1204) made the rupture clear and final. Pope Urban II set in motion the First Crusade (1096–1099) because he desired to aid his fellow Christians in the East and apparently hoped that this action would bring the Latin and Greek churches closer together under papal leadership. The opposite was the case.

Origins

Multiple factors—cultural, political, and ecclesiological—precipitated the schism. The most basic was ecclesiology: the manner in which the West and Byzantium envisioned the nature and functioning of the universal church. The central ecclesiological issue was papal primacy. Byzantine Christians regarded the pope as first among equals within a pentarchy consisting of the patriarchates of Rome, Constantinople (mod. İstanbul, Turkey), Alexandria, Antioch (mod. Antakya, Turkey), and Jerusalem. These were the collective guardians of the orthodox faith, as defined in the seven ecumenical councils that met between 325 and 787. Western Christians, especially after the mid-eleventh century, understood papal primacy to mean that submission to the unique authority of the Roman pope was *the* determinant of orthodoxy and membership in the universal church.

Although the ideology of radical papal primacy, as well as the crusades, arose out of the so-called Gregorian Revolution of the eleventh century, the Roman and Byzantine churches had moments of misunderstanding and separation long before then. They were temporarily divided during the Acacian Schism (484–519), when the papacy rejected the efforts of Emperor Zeno and Patriarch Acacius to accommodate the Monophysite Christians of Egypt, whose doctrine that Christ had a single, divine nature had been condemned at the Council of Chalcedon in 451. Two centuries later, the Iconoclastic Controversy (726–843) drove a deep wedge between papal Rome and imperial Constantinople, but even though the Byzantine Church was officially iconoclastic for most of these twelve decades, its lower clergy and laity shared the West's strong rejection of iconoclasm. When Empress Theodora permanently restored the practice of icon veneration in 843, the two churches reestablished communion.

Despite reunion, the Iconoclastic Controversy permanently widened an ever-growing cultural and political chasm. In its moment of crisis, the papacy turned to the Franks—a radical departure from earlier policies—and the result was the coronation of Charlemagne as the Holy Roman, or Western, emperor. It was Charlemagne's court that introduced the practice of adding the word *Filioque* ("and from the Son") to the phrase in the Nicene Creed "the Holy Spirit . . . who proceeds from the Father." Although the papacy initially rejected this Carolingian addition to the creed and did not accept it until around 1014–1015, the innovation became a matter of controversy between Eastern and Western Christians almost immediately.

Filioque figured prominently in the list of erroneous customs that Photios, patriarch of Constantinople, leveled against the Latin Church during the next major ecclesiastical breach, the Photian Schism (863–880). This controversy, although amicably resolved, pointed out the growing differences in ecclesiological ideologies and traditions that separated Eastern and Western Christians. Simply put, Pope Nicholas I's vision of papal primacy led him to intervene in the internal affairs of the Byzantine Church, namely, the issue of Photios's contested promotion to the patriarchate, and that intervention aroused resistance in Constantinople.

Photios died in communion with Rome, but the schism that bears his name was a prologue to greater misunderstandings engendered during the eleventh century in the wake of papal reform. The year 1054 is often identified as the definitive moment of schism owing to supposed sentences of excommunication that the churches of Rome and Constantinople laid on one another. In fact, the events of 1054 did not usher in a recognized and accepted split between these two churches, but they were symptoms of essential differences.

In 1050 Pope Leo IX and Patriarch Michael I Keroularios quarreled over the papacy's attempt to impose Latin practices on the Greek Christians of southern Italy and the patriarch's retaliatory action of forcing Byzantine rituals on Latin churches in Constantinople. Chief among the controverted issues were clerical celibacy, *Filioque,* the Latin practice of fasting on Sunday, and the Latin use of unleavened bread (Lat. *azymes*) for the Eucharist. Despite this disagreement, in 1054 Pope Leo sent several legates to Constantinople to arrange an alliance with Emperor Constantine IX Monomachos against the Normans of southern Italy. The legation's chief delegate, Cardinal Humbert of Silva Candida, soon engaged in heated debates with several Byzantine churchmen regarding their respective ecclesiastical traditions, and in the process both parties lost all sense of moderation. On 16 July 1054 Humbert laid on the altar of the Church of Hagia Sophia a bull excommunicating Michael and his supporters. The patriarch retaliated by convening a synod that excommunicated the legates. Neither excommunication was directed against an entire church, and there is no evidence of any sense of cataclysmic schism on either side, even though the two churches had, in fact, become separate entities.

The Period of the Early Crusades

In 1073, two years after the great defeat of the Byzantines by the Saljūq Turks at Mantzikert and the contemporaneous loss of Byzantium's last holdings in southern Italy to the Normans, Emperor Michael VII Doukas appealed to Pope Gregory VII for aid. In February 1074 Gregory sent a letter to William, count of Upper Burgundy, urging him to send troops to Italy to defend papal lands against the Normans, and then went on to note that once the Normans were pacified, Gregory hoped to cross to Constantinople to aid the Christians who were oppressed by Muslim attacks. The following month the pope issued a general summons to all Latin Christians to aid their siblings in the East, and in December Gregory informed King Henry IV of Germany that 50,000 men stood ready to march east with Gregory at their head. Nothing immediate came of this plan due to the Investiture Controversy that broke out in 1075–1076. The dream, however, of aiding fellow Christians in the East through armed intervention remained alive within papal reform circles until it was transformed into the First Crusade by Pope Urban II.

As early as 1089 Pope Urban and Emperor Alexios I Komnenos discussed closer ecclesiastical relations. Urban lifted a ban of excommunication that Pope Gregory had laid on Alexios and his predecessor for deposing Emperor Michael VII and requested that his name be entered into the diptychs of Constantinople, which listed all Orthodox prelates with whom the Byzantine Church was in communion. A synod convened by the emperor that year could find no reason for the omission (possibly the synod chose to be diplomatically ignorant) and invited the pope either to come to Constantinople to discuss their differences or to send a statement of faith. Showing an equal sense of diplomacy, Urban did not press the issue and sent no credal statement, probably realizing that *Filioque* would be a sticking point. He remained uncommemorated in the prayers of the Byzantine Church, but his relations with Alexios remained warm.

On the eve of the First Crusade, therefore, high-ranking church leaders in both Rome and Constantinople were aware that differences separated them, and that for some time they had not been in official communion. At the same time, they seem to have believed they still were members of the same Christian family and that their differences were not irremediable or the result of the other party's depravity. On the popular level there seems to have been even less awareness of separation. The crusades changed that.

A number of leaders of the First Crusade, including the papal legate Adhemar of Le Puy, sought to weld Byzantine and crusader forces into a single Christian army, but the military, logistical, and personal strains proved too great. Crusaders and Byzantine soldiers clashed in the Balkans and outside the gates of Constantinople, and once they were in Anatolia, misunderstandings multiplied. Antioch, a Byzantine Christian city, became a particular center of growing estrangement. Emperor Alexios's failure to come to the crusaders' aid during their long struggle to seize and then defend Antioch contributed to a growing sentiment within crusader circles that the Greeks were faithless. On their part, the Byzantines looked upon Bohemund of Taranto's conversion of Antioch into a crusader principality in 1098 and his forcing the Greek patriarch of the city into exile in 1100 and replacing him with a Latin churchman as evidence of Frankish perfidy. Rival Byzantine patriarchs-in-exile of Antioch became voices and rallying points against this invasion by Christians from the West, who were now perceived as less than orthodox. Bohemund I of Antioch further contributed to the growing hostility between Byzantines and Latins when he convinced Pope Paschal II in 1105 to authorize a crusade against Alexios I, a putative enemy of the Frankish states of Outremer. Although Bohemund's crusade of 1107 failed, it fomented new animosity between Byzantines and Latins.

The remainder of the twelfth century witnessed growing hostility and a deepening sense of schism on both sides. Many Westerners ascribed the failure of the Second Crusade (1147–1149) to Greek treachery. The massacre of Constantinople's Latin residents in 1182 and the alliance of Emperor Isaac II Angelos with Saladin during the early stages of the Third Crusade (1189–1192) only added to the Latin West's general belief that the Greeks were no better than the Saracens. On their part, Byzantines could point to the many instances of Western attacks on their lands and persons, including William II of Sicily's massacre of the Byzantines of Thessalonica in 1185, as proof of Western barbarism.

The Later Middle Ages

On the eve of the Fourth Crusade (1202–1204), specifically between the spring of 1198 and early summer 1202, eight missions and twelve letters passed between the Byzantine imperial court and the Curia of Pope Innocent III, as Emperor Alexios III Angelos and the pope tried to negotiate an alliance. The negotiations failed because Innocent demanded submission of the Byzantine Church to papal authority as a necessary prelude to any political accommodation.

The pope did not direct the Fourth Crusade against Constantinople and actually tried to prevent its diversion. However, when he learned of the city's capture and the installation of a Latin emperor, he rejoiced, perceiving it to be fitting punishment for the Greeks' willful separation from the Roman Church and a God-given opportunity to bring these fallen siblings back into the fold. Most Westerners seem to have agreed with this assessment. From the Byzantine perspective, the brutal sack of the city, the subsequent conquest of large areas of the Byzantine Empire by crusader-adventurers, and the papacy's largely unsuccessful but vigorous attempt to Latinize a captive Greek Church were all humiliating but temporary burdens to be borne.

In response, the Byzantines established several empires in exile. The most important was at Nicaea (mod. İznik, Turkey) in Asia Minor, where the Byzantine patriarchate of Constantinople was also reestablished. With rival Latin and Greek emperors and patriarchs residing in Constantinople and Nicaea, the schism was complete.

In 1261 the Nicaean emperor Michael VIII Palaiologos recaptured Constantinople, but the threat of attack by Westerners who wished to restore the Latin empire of Constantinople forced him into the policy of offering church union in return for the papacy's support. At the Second Council of Lyons (1274), imperial representatives submitted the Byzantine Church to the papacy. Virulent opposition within Byzantium and shifting fortunes in the West combined to defeat this union, which Emperor Andronikos II Palaiologos repudiated in 1282.

Another threat, this time from the Ottoman Turks, again drove a Byzantine emperor, John VIII Palaiologos, to offer church union in exchange for Western assistance. In 1439 at the Council of Florence, Patriarch Joseph II submitted to Roman papal authority. Once again, however, official imperial policy was defeated by popular opposition. Although the union existed on paper until its repudiation in 1484, it was a phantom union from the start.

The so-called union did produce the Crusade of Varna (1444), which failed to stem the Ottoman tide. Constantinople fell to the Ottoman Turks on 29 May 1453. Under Turkish rule the Byzantine Church grew ever more adamant in its determination to be a bulwark of Christian orthodoxy against the infidelity of its Muslim lords and the perceived heresies of the Latin West.

–Alfred J. Andrea

See also: Byzantine Empire; Constantinople, Latin Empire of

Bibliography

Awakumov, Georgij, *Die Entstehung des Unionsgedankens: Die lateinische Theologie des Hochmittelalters in der Auseinandersetzung mit dem Ritus der Ostkirche* (Berlin: Akademie, 2002).

Bârlea, Octavian, *Die Konzile des 13.–15. Jahrhunderts und die ökumenische Frage* (Wiesbaden: Harrassowitz, 1989).

Bayer, Axel, *Spaltung der Christenheit: Das sogenannte Morgenländische Schisma von 1054* (Köln: Böhlau, 2002).

Congar, Yves, *After Nine Hundred Years: The Background of the Schism between the Eastern and Western Churches* (New York: Fordham University Press, 1959).

Daly, William M., "Christian Fraternity, the Crusaders, and the Security of Constantinople, 1097–1204: The Precarious Survival of an Ideal," *Mediaeval Studies* 22 (1960), 43–91.

Dvornik, Francis, *The Photian Schism: History and Legend* (Cambridge: Cambridge University Press, 1948).

———, *Photian and Byzantine Ecclesiastical Studies* (London: Variorum, 1974).

Ebels-Hoving, Bunna, *Byzantium in Westerse Ogen, 1096–1204* (Assen: Van Gorcum, 1971).

Every, George, *The Byzantine Patriarchate, 451–1204,* rev. ed. (London: S.P.C.K., 1962).

———, *Misunderstandings between East and West* (Richmond, VA: Knox, 1966).

Geanakoplos, Deno J., *Emperor Michael Palaeologus and the West, 1258–1282* (Cambridge, MA: Harvard University Press, 1959).

Gill, Joseph, *The Council of Florence* (Cambridge: Cambridge University Press, 1959).

———, *Byzantium and the Papacy: 1198–1400* (New Brunswick, NJ: Rutgers University Press, 1979).

———, *Church Union: Rome and Byzantium (1204–1453)* (London: Variorum, 1979).

Kolbaba, Tia M., *The Byzantine Lists: Errors of the Latins* (Urbana: University of Illinois Press, 2000).

Nichols, Aidan, *Rome and the Eastern Churches: A Study in Schism* (Edinburgh: Clark, 1992).

Nicol, Donald M., *Byzantium: Its Ecclesiastical History and Relations with the Western World* (London: Variorum, 1972).

Papadakis, Aristeides, *Crisis in Byzantium: The Filioque Controversy in the Patriarchate of Gregory II of Cyprus (1283–1289)* (New York: Fordham University Press, 1983).

Runciman, Steven, *The Eastern Schism* (Oxford: Clarendon, 1955).

Setton, Kenneth M., *The Papacy and the Levant (1204–1571),* 4 vols. (Philadelphia: American Philosophical Society, 1976–1984).

Sherrard, Philip, *The Greek East and the Latin West: A Study in the Christian Tradition,* 2d ed. (Limni: Harvey, 1995).

Smith, Mahlon H., *And Taking Bread . . .: Cerularius and the Azyme Controversy of 1054* (Paris: Beauchesne, 1978).

Scotland

Despite its position on the northwestern periphery of Christendom, the kingdom of Scotland contributed to all major aspects of the crusading movement from the late eleventh to the early sixteenth centuries, although the nature of its contributions was often affected or even determined by its relationship with its more powerful southern neighbor, the kingdom of England.

The presence of Scots on the First (1096–1099) and Second (1147–1149) crusades is mentioned by several contemporary authors, including eyewitness sources, although none of their names are known; Lagmann, king of Man, who went to the Holy Land at the time of the First Crusade, and the Orkneymen who accompanied the crusade of Earl Rognvald Kali in 1151–1153 came from the western and northern isles that were still under Norwegian suzerainty, rather than from the kingdom itself.

King David I (1124–1153) established the orders of the Temple and the Hospital in Scotland but was dissuaded by his subjects from joining the Second Crusade himself; the orders were granted property in every burgh in the kingdom by David's grandson Malcolm IV (1153–1165). The Templars came to be organized in two commanderies (preceptories), at Balantrodoch (mod. Temple) in Midlothian and Maryculter in Kincardineshire, and the Hospitallers in one, Torphichen in West Lothian. Both orders in Scotland came under the authority of their respective English provinces, and most of the few knight brethren who resided in the kingdom in the twelfth and thirteenth centuries were Englishmen.

Some Scots, notably the nobleman Robert de Quincy, joined the Third Crusade (1189–1192), while King William the Lion (1165–1214) used the opportunity to buy the kingdom free of the English overlordship that had been imposed when he had been captured by Henry II in 1174 (the Treaty of Falaise), by a payment of 10,000 marks to Henry's son Richard the Lionheart, who was desperate to finance his own

King Robert Bruce encouraging his troops before the Battle of Bannockburn (June 23, 1314). (Bettmann/Corbis)

expedition to the Holy Land (the Quit-Claim of Canterbury, 1189). A greater number of Scots accompanied the Fifth Crusade (1217–1221), including two poets from Gaelic-speaking areas, Muiredhach Albanach Ó Dálaigh and Gille-Brigde Albanach, both of whom later composed poems telling of their journey to Damietta and Acre (mod. ʿAkko, Israel) and return via Greece and Italy. In 1247 Patrick, earl of March, took the cross to join the crusade of Louis IX of France to

Egypt, while his wife founded a Trinitarian house at Dunbar, thus augmenting the order's two existing Scottish foundations at Failford and Berwick. Earl Patrick died at Marseilles before embarkation the next year, but more Scots left for the Holy Land in 1250.

Correspondence with the papacy during this period shows how the Scottish monarchy and bishops repeatedly tried to prevent crusading taxation levied on the Scottish church from being used for the benefit of English crusaders, as had evidently often happened in the past. When a new crusade was preached in 1267–1268, Alexander III (1249–1286) prohibited the export of tax revenues that Henry III of England intended for the use of his sons Edward and Edmund. However, the years 1270–1272 saw the greatest response yet seen to a crusade by Scots, who sailed with Louis IX of France as well as with the two English princes. They included David of Strathbogie, earl of Atholl; Adam de Kinconquhar, earl of Carrick; and Ingram de Balliol with Louis; and David de Lindsay; Robert Bruce the Elder, lord of Annandale, and his son Robert; and Alexander de Balliol and his uncle Eustace de Balliol with the English princes. Many of those who survived the French defeat at Tunis appear to have joined Edward in Sicily and continued to the Holy Land.

The fall of Acre to the Egyptian sultan Khalīl in 1291 found Scotland in the throes of a succession crisis occasioned by the death of Margaret, granddaughter of Alexander III, in 1290, which was exploited by Edward I of England to impose his overlordship over the kingdom and to secure for himself the profits of crusading taxation raised there. In 1296, having defeated the new king, John Balliol (1292–1296), Edward I occupied Scotland in an attempt to annex it permanently to the English realm. In 1306 Robert I Bruce (1306–1329), son and grandson of the two Bruce crusaders of 1270–1272, was installed as king by the Scottish patriotic party and led resistance against English domination until Scottish independence was confirmed by the Treaty of Edinburgh-Northampton in 1328.

During this period the crusading idea figured prominently in the propaganda of both Scottish and English governments, particularly in their attempts to secure papal favor. Edward I pleaded his intentions to lead a new crusade once the political situation allowed and repeatedly complained to the pope of how Robert Bruce's clerical supporters had preached that it was just as meritorious to resist the English as it was to fight the Saracens in the Holy Land. In their own correspondence with the pope and the king of France, the Scottish leaders asserted the desire of their people and king to join a crusade, but only once the kingdom's freedom had been restored, an idea also contained in the famous statement of independence sent by the Scottish barons to Pope John XXII in 1320 (the Declaration of Arbroath).

Robert I's proclaimed desire to fight the enemies of Christendom was never realized, but on his death it found expression in the form of a proxy crusade led by his trusted companion Sir James Douglas, who took the king's embalmed heart on an expedition directed against Muslim Spain, possibly with the Holy Land as its ultimate goal. After the death of Douglas in battle at Teba in the kingdom of Granada in 1330, Robert's heart was retrieved and brought back to Scotland for burial at Melrose Abbey. The Templars and Hospitallers of Scotland had largely supported Edward I during the wars of independence, but the Templars were suppressed in 1312 by the English occupation regime in the course of the general dissolution of the order and the bulk of their properties handed over to the Hospitallers. After the victory of Robert I, who confirmed the Hospitallers' holdings in 1314, most of the order's officers seem to have been Scots, who often preferred to pay revenues directly to the central treasury of the order at Rhodes (mod. Rodos, Greece) rather than to the priory of England.

The resumption of aggression against Scotland by Edward III of England in 1333, which lasted until 1370, constituted a major bar to Scottish crusading activity, compounded by the English king's claims to the throne of France, Scotland's ally, which sparked off the Hundred Years' War. During a lull in hostilities many Scottish knights took part in the crusade of Peter I of Cyprus against Alexandria (1365) with the active encouragement of David II (1329–1371), who professed a keen interest in crusading and had met Peter at the English court in 1363.

Two of the Scottish crusaders of 1365, the brothers Walter and Norman Leslie, had previously been to Prussia, and it was the Baltic Crusades that constituted the main sphere of Scottish crusading activity from the mid-fourteenth century until the battle of Tannenberg (1410); during this period over seventy Scottish knights are known to have traveled to Prussia to take part in the campaigns of the Teutonic Order against pagan Lithuania, and as their names are known primarily from safe-conducts issued by the English government, the actual number of crusaders may have been higher than that documented in the surviving sources. Yet even in Prussia, crusading activity might be affected by the wider political situation, as in 1391, when fighting broke out between Scottish and English crusaders at Königsberg (mod. Kaliningrad, Russia), resulting in the death of Sir William Douglas, lord of Nithsdale.

Unlike the Bruce dynasty, the Stewarts, who succeeded in 1371, showed little interest in the crusade until the reign of James IV (1488–1513). By 1507 James was planning a pilgrimage to Jerusalem, an idea that during the next two years developed into a grand project to lead a crusade against the Turks. He had already begun the construction of a navy, which was to attain the size of 38 ships, and he now pursued a diplomatic initiative among the European powers with the aim of building a pan-Christian coalition. The project eventually foundered owing to the hostility to France of the Holy League formed by the papacy, England, Venice, and Spain. When Henry VIII of England invaded France in 1513, James moved against England in support of his ally, only to be defeated and killed at the battle of Flodden.

The following period, characterized by regency governments and factional disputes, saw the Hospitallers as the only remaining Scottish institution with an interest in the crusade, continuing to send recruits and money to their headquarters, initially at Rhodes and later at Malta. Walter Lindsay, preceptor of Torphichen (1532/1533–1546), compiled a rental listing of all the order's lands and rights in Scotland; however, as the Reformation swept through the kingdom, all of these were surrendered to the Crown in 1564 by his successor James Sandilands, who received them back as a hereditary barony. While a handful of Catholic Scots subsequently emigrated to join the order, the secularization of the Hospitaller lands in Scotland effectively ended the country's contribution to the crusading movement.

–Alan V. Murray

Bibliography

Cameron, Sonja, "Sir James Douglas, Spain, and the Holy Land," in *Freedom and Authority: Scotland c. 1050–c. 1650; Historical and Historiographical Essays Presented to Grant G. Simpson,* ed. Terry Brotherstone and David Ditchburn (East Linton: Tuckwell, 2000), pp. 108–117.

Ditchburn, David, *Scotland and Europe,* vol.1: *The Medieval Kingdom and Its Contacts with Christendom, c. 1215–1545* (East Linton: Tuckwell, 2000).

The Knights of St John of Jerusalem in Scotland, ed. Ian B. Cowan, P. H. R. Mackay, and Alan Macquarrie (Edinburgh: Scottish History Society, 1983).

Macdougall, Norman, *James IV* (Edinburgh: Donald, 1989).

Macquarrie, Alan, "The Ideal of the Holy War in Scotland, 1296–1330," *Innes Review* 32 (1981), 83–92.

———, *Scotland and the Crusades, 1095–1560* (Edinburgh: Donald, 1997).

McRoberts, David, "Scottish Pilgrims to the Holy Land," *Innes Review* 20 (1969), 80–106.

Murphy, G., "Two Irish Poems from the Mediterranean in the Thirteenth Century," *Éigse* 7 (1955), 71–77.

Scots Literature

See English and Scots Literature

Second Crusade (1147–1149)

A crusade launched in response to the capture of the Christian city of Edessa (mod. Şanlıurfa, Turkey) by the Muslims in 1144. Ultimately the campaign in the Levant failed, but by then it was only one part of a much wider offensive against the enemies of Christendom that came to encompass the Iberian Peninsula as well as the pagan lands to the east of the river Elbe. For this reason at least, the Second Crusade holds an important place in the history of the crusades.

Origins, Preaching, and Recruitment

On 24 December 1144 'Imād al-Dīn Zangī, the Muslim ruler of Aleppo and Mosul, captured the city of Edessa in Upper Mesopotamia. The news of this disaster quickly reached the rulers of Antioch and Jerusalem, and messengers were dispatched to western Europe to plead for help. The loss of the principal city of one of the four Frankish states in Outremer was the greatest calamity yet to affect the Latin East and provoked the largest expedition to the Holy Land since the First Crusade (1096–1099) almost fifty years previously.

The response of the West to the fall of Edessa was slow but, at least from the papal perspective, carefully planned. On 1 December 1145 Pope Eugenius III issued *Quantum praedecessores,* the first surviving papal encyclical to call for a crusade. This carefully researched document had three sections: an outline of recent events, an exhortation to take the cross, and an outline of the rewards and protection offered to crusaders by the church. The bull conveyed its message with clarity and emphasis and was designed to be easily understood when read out at large public gatherings. It relied strongly on the repetition of several key themes to reinforce its ideas. Eugenius laid great emphasis on linking the new campaign with the achievements of the First Crusade, and he urged potential recruits to live up to the deeds of their forefathers and to ensure that the present generation did not shame the memory of their predecessors. The offer of the remission of sins was repeated four times in the bull, which stated that those who died en route to the Holy Land were to be treated as martyrs and would find a place in heaven, thus allaying one worry of potential recruits.

Almost in parallel with the publication of this document, King Louis VII of France (1137–1180) announced plans to go

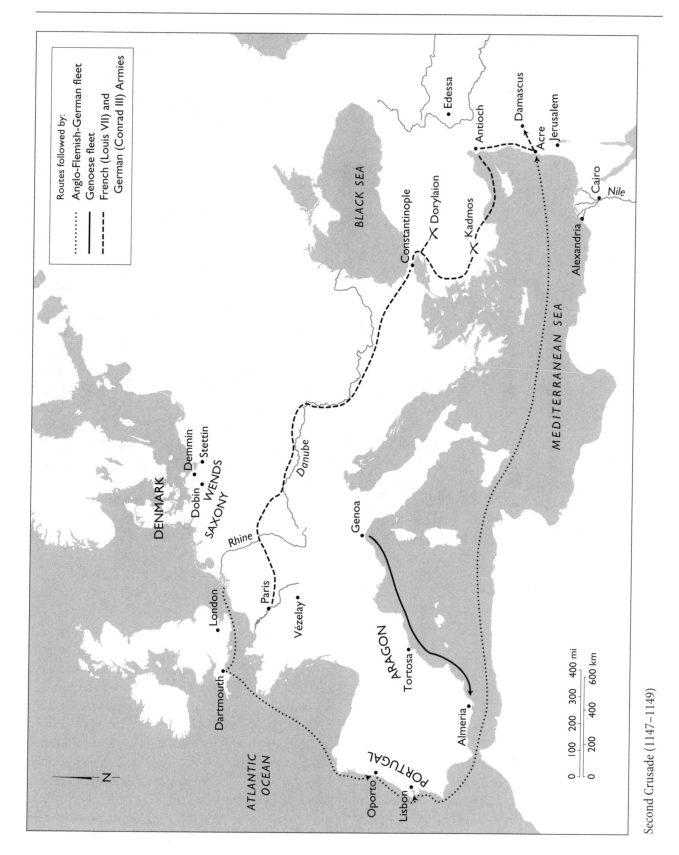

King Louis VII of France enters Constantinople during the Second Crusade, from *Grandes Chroniques de France,* Jean Fouquet (c. 1415/1420–1481). MS Paris, Bibliothèque nationale de France, 6465 f.202. (Snark/Art Resource)

to the East at his Christmas court at Bourges. However, Louis had experienced a difficult start to his reign, and there may well have been worries about disorder in his absence, particularly since he did not yet have a male heir. Prior to the Second Crusade no major European monarch had taken part in such an expedition, and in this sense the king's proposal was a step into the unknown. It seems unlikely that *Quantum praedecessores* had reached northern France by this time, and the French clergy were probably unwilling to proceed without papal authorization. Louis's plan was not declined outright, however, and it was agreed to postpone any formal commitments until a meeting at Vézelay at Easter 1146.

Troubles within the city of Rome caused Eugenius to delegate his former mentor, Abbot Bernard of Clairvaux, the foremost churchman of the age, to lead the preaching of the crusade. Bernard's passionate oratory, combined with the persuasive message of *Quantum praedecessores,* inflamed the audience at Vézelay, and people rushed forward to be signed with the cross. Over the next few months Eugenius and Bernard sent out numerous churchmen to urge the people of western Europe to help their fellow Christians in the East. They also dispatched letters, some of which survive and reveal the powerful language used to convince people to act. Bernard described the people of the West as a lucky generation, blessed to be offered the opportunity of such splendid spiritual riches, and he almost guaranteed the crusaders success.

The abbot also embarked upon a grueling preaching tour between August 1146 and March 1147 that took him through Flanders and the Low Countries, down the Rhine to Basel and Lake Constance, then northward to the Christmas court of King Conrad III of Germany (1137–1152), and finally back into France. Miracles and wondrous portents accompanied the abbot of Clairvaux, and he undoubtedly did much to raise the profile of the campaign. Yet it is plain that he was approaching a highly receptive audience whose intense religiosity and devotion to the holy places had been fueled in the decades since the capture of Jerusalem by waves of pilgrimage and smaller crusading expeditions. The construction of churches as copies of the Holy Sepulchre in Jerusalem and the emergence of the first military orders, with their growing landholdings across western Europe, were visible reminders of the land of Christ. As the stirrings of chivalric culture were felt among the knightly classes, the widespread memorialization of the deeds of the first crusaders in literature and song were constantly held out as an ideal for later generations to emulate.

As Bernard and his copreachers moved around Europe, a renegade Cistercian monk named Ralph attracted large crowds with his anti-Judaic preaching, urging people to destroy unbelievers at home. This message was coupled with the popular notion that the Jews' money (much of it made from the sinful practice of usury) should be seized and used for the crusade. The church hierarchy, which was often responsible for protecting Jewish communities, invoked biblical testimony to forbid these outbreaks of disorder and directed that the Jews should not be killed lest their souls be lost forever. Nonetheless, Jewish communities in northern France and, especially, in the Rhineland were attacked. Bernard had to travel to Ralph in person to insist that he desist from his wickedness and return to his cloister. With the chief troublemaker removed, the problem largely ended.

In the autumn of 1146 the crusade began to broaden its appeal beyond the initial approach to the French nobility. As Bernard moved through the lands of Conrad of Germany, Eugenius dispatched the papal bull *Divini dispensatione I* to the people of northern Italy, another part of Conrad's dominions. Bernard himself wrote to the people of Bavaria and eastern France encouraging them to take the cross but cautioned them to wait for proper leadership, rather than rushing eastward as the calamitous People's Crusades of 1096 had done. Given the high level of interest in Germany and the need for a suitable leader, it was natural that the pope would want to build upon recent positive relations between the Curia and the German monarchy and enlist the support of Conrad, the most powerful ruler in Latin Christendom.

Conrad is said to have refused to take the cross at first and was supposedly shamed into participating in the crusade after an impassioned speech from Bernard of Clairvaux. The only source for this episode is the *Vita* of Saint Bernard, and this may be somewhat slanted in outlook. In reality, Conrad probably wished to defer an absolute commitment to the campaign until a series of bitter regional disputes that afflicted his lands had been settled. Bernard is known to have worked hard to make peace across Germany, and once this was achieved Conrad was able to enlist for the crusade and prepare to head the large numbers of his subjects who wished to fight for Christ.

As the crusade to the Holy Land gathered momentum, the period between the summer of 1146 and the summer of 1147 saw the scope of the holy war broaden considerably to include the Iberian Peninsula and the Slavic lands to the east of Germany. The stimulus for this came from secular rulers who wished to exploit the contemporary crusading fervor both to advance the frontiers of Christianity and to enlarge their own lands. Such an agenda fitted in with the confident and outward-looking spiritual agenda of Eugenius and Bernard, and they were prepared to endorse or support such campaigns.

The Crusade in Iberia

The first ruler to approach the church hierarchy was probably Afonso I Henriques, king of Portugal (1128–1185). For several years he had been trying to capture the city of Lisbon (Port. *Lisboa*) from the Muslims, and now he saw a chance to enlist the assistance of those northern European crusaders who planned to sail around Iberia en route to the Levant. Bernard of Clairvaux came into contact with some of the Flemings who eventually took part in this campaign, and he probably wrote a letter of support to the king. No formal agreement was drawn up, but it seems that the prospect of a siege at Lisbon was a compelling reason for a fleet of some 165 ships from the Rhineland, Flanders, and the Anglo-Norman realm to set out from Dartmouth in May 1147, several weeks before the primary land forces started their march to the East. There is no surviving crusade bull for this expedition, although the presence of a churchman bearing a piece of the True Cross and the observations of some contemporary writers indicate that it was regarded as a part of the broader crusading enterprise.

In preparation for the arrival of this force Afonso Henriques captured the strategically important town of Santarém in March 1147. As the fleet reached northern Spain the king sent the bishop of Oporto to greet the crusaders and to convince them of both the spiritual value and the material advantage of fighting the enemies of Christ at Lisbon. A contract was agreed, and the siege began on 28 June. The crusaders and their allies made little progress at first, but, untroubled by Muslim relief forces and with plentiful supplies of food, they were able to persist. Assaults by siege towers and a mine were eventually sufficient to gain entry to the city, and Lisbon was taken on 24 October 1147. Most of the fleet chose to winter there before sailing on to the Holy Land in the spring to meet the main armies.

The conquest of Lisbon was not the only crusading activity in the Iberian Peninsula in 1147. Alfonso VII, king of León and Castile, also sought to link an expansion of his lands to the holy war. He proposed an attack on the Andalusian port of Almería, deep in the Muslim-held south. To secure the naval expertise of the Italian trading city of Genoa, he offered substantial commercial privileges, although given the intense religiosity of the age, the Italians must have been motivated by spiritual concerns as well. The siege lasted from August to October 1147, when Almería fell to the crusaders. Alfonso's grant to the Genoese demonstrates the combination of motives to good effect: the charter was given "because [the Genoese] captured the city for the honour of God and all of Christendom and the honour of Genoa" [J. B. Williams, "The Making of a Crusade": pp. 38–39].

In April 1148 Eugenius III encouraged Alfonso in his (ultimately unsuccessful) attack on the southern Spanish town of Jaén. The previous year the pope had described the conflict in Iberia in the same context as those in the Holy Land, reflecting an ongoing parity between the two theaters of war that dated back to expeditions to the Balearic Islands and the Iberian Peninsula from 1113–1114, 1117–1118, and 1123. At the time of the Second Crusade, therefore, the large-scale campaign to the Levant prompted a dramatic increase in the level of crusading activity in the peninsula.

The Genoese were also contracted to help Raymond Berengar IV, count of Barcelona, conquer Tortosa in north-

eastern Spain; once again they would receive considerable economic benefits in return, including one-third of the city, which fell to them on 30 December 1148. Almería was recaptured by the Muslims in 1157, but Lisbon and Tortosa remained permanently in Christian hands and marked the two most important and long-lasting achievements of the entire Second Crusade.

The Crusade against the Wends

The third and final theater of war represented the most radical aspect of the crusade. As the Germans prepared for the expedition to the Levant, a group of Saxon nobles approached Bernard of Clairvaux at an assembly at Frankfurt am Main and asked for his blessing to fight the pagan Wendish (that is, Slavic) tribes on their borders. Like the crusades in Iberia, this was motivated by a mixture of religious and territorial expansionism. The Germans claimed that the inhabitants of the island of Rügen had converted to Christianity only to lapse back to paganism. The leading men of northern Germany and Denmark also wished to expand their dominions. Bernard agreed to the proposal, and Pope Eugenius formally endorsed the idea in his bull *Divini dispensatione II* (April 1147), in which he confirmed that the conflict with the pagans would merit the same spiritual rewards as those in Iberia and the Holy Land. For decades the Saxons had fought against their pagan neighbors, but this was the first time that the struggle had been brought under the crusading banner. The behavior of the Rugians merited a severe response, and this may have been the reason behind Bernard's infamous statement "We utterly forbid that for any reason whatsoever a truce should be made with these peoples, either for the sake of money, or for the sake of tribute, until such a time, as by God's help they shall either be converted or wiped out" [Bernard of Clairvaux, *Opera*, ed. J. Leclercq and H. Rochais, 8 vols. (Roma: Editiones Cisterciences, 1955–1977), 8:433].

In the summer of 1147 an army of Danes and Saxons attacked Dobin and Malchow. At the former settlement the defenders accepted baptism; at the latter a temple and idols were burned. The crusaders then turned toward the Christian city of Stettin (mod. Szczecin, Poland), but when the inhabitants hung crosses from the walls, the army withdrew, and the campaign broke up. The island of Rügen itself was not attacked. The campaign had secured the token submission of one chieftain and gained some tribute but had hardly swept aside the forces of the unbelievers, and once under way it appeared more intent on simply extending the power of secular lords, regardless of their opponents' faith. Bitter arguments between two rivals for the Danish Crown and mistrust between the Saxons and the Danes also contributed to the mediocre outcome of this expedition.

The Crusade to the Levant

Through the autumn of 1146 and the spring of 1147 the crusaders of France and Germany gathered the money and equipment needed for the holy war. They decided to travel overland, a prospect that caused deep anxiety to the Byzantine emperor, Manuel I Komnenos (1143–1180), and induced him to write to the pope asking him to guarantee the good behavior of the crusaders as they crossed Byzantine territory.

The Germans left first. As they neared Constantinople (mod. İstanbul, Turkey) their poor discipline did much to antagonize the Greeks, although Conrad and Manuel (who were related through Manuel's wife, Bertha of Salzburg) remained on reasonable terms. Once they reached Constantinople, however, the Germans were swiftly ushered across the Bosporus and into Asia Minor.

In June 1147 Eugenius and Bernard presided over a great public ceremony at the abbey of Saint-Denis near Paris to mark the departure of King Louis. The French were more orderly in their approach to Constantinople, but serious tensions were generated by small-scale skirmishes with the Byzantines, coupled with a deeper antipathy based on doctrinal differences between the Orthodox and Latin churches, a recent Byzantine treaty with the Saljūq Turks, and Greek invasions of the principality of Antioch (ruled by Raymond of Poitiers, uncle of Queen Eleanor of France). One group of the crusaders advocated an immediate attack on Constantinople, but King Louis was not in favor of the idea. This hostility alarmed Manuel enormously, particularly because the Greeks' bitterest rivals, the Sicilians, had chosen to exploit the passing of the crusade by invading the Peloponnese. The Sicilians and the French were known to be on friendly terms, and Manuel feared a joint assault on his city. He used the promise of better markets to persuade the French to cross the Bosporus, and with this barrier between himself and the Westerners he felt more secure.

Unknown to the French, the German army had not, as planned, waited for them. Conrad had hoped for a quick victory over the Saljūqs of Rūm, and this overconfidence, prob-

ably together with treachery by his Greek guides, meant that in late October 1147 his army marched into a trap. The German forces were largely destroyed after a few days' march past Nicaea (mod. İznik, Turkey), although King Conrad himself escaped to join Louis.

The French crusaders skirted southwest toward the coastline at Ephesos (mod. Efes, Turkey), and then, moving inland in late December, they won a resounding victory over the Turks in the valley of the Maeander (mod. Menderes). In January 1148, however, as they traversed Mount Kadmos (mod. Honaz Dağı), the French became stretched out, and the vanguard lost sight of the remainder of the force. The Turks immediately exploited this and launched a devastating attack on the crusaders, killing large numbers of men and horses and taking valuable equipment. In the crossing of Asia Minor, therefore, both the German and the French armies suffered serious damage in terms of men, materials, and morale.

In March 1148 Louis arrived in the city of Antioch (mod. Antakya, Turkey), where Prince Raymond fully expected him to fight to regain Edessa. This had been the original intention of the crusaders, and it would also, of course, secure Raymond's own position against the Muslims of the region. Perhaps the recent imposition (1145) of Byzantine overlordship on Antioch, which meant that the crusaders' efforts in the area would indirectly benefit the Greeks, caused the king to change his mind. Many in the French army blamed the Byzantines for their misfortunes; furthermore, rumors of an affair between Raymond and Eleanor hardly helped matters, and in early May Louis led his men southward to the kingdom of Jerusalem.

King Conrad had wintered in Constantinople but gathered together his remaining men to fight in the Holy Land along with the French. In June 1148 at a great assembly at Palmarea, near Acre (mod. 'Akko, Israel), the crusaders and the Franks of Jerusalem and Tripoli decided to besiege Damascus. Until recently the Damascenes had been allied with Jerusalem, but the rise of Nūr al-Dīn of Aleppo and his growing rapprochement with Damascus meant that it was a sound strategic choice to attack the city. The Christian troops arrived at Damascus on 4 July 1148, but after achieving early progress through the dense orchards to the south of the city, they decided to move northward to try to achieve a quick breakthrough. There, however, they found no water, and with Nūr al-Dīn heading toward the city with a relieving army, they were compelled to withdraw.

Conclusions

After the exhortations of Abbot Bernard and the enormous hardship and expense of the campaign, the collapse of the siege of Damascus after only a few days was a humiliation to the Christians. Equally, it was a source of great delight and encouragement to their Muslim opponents, who saw that the rulers of the West were not invincible. The crusaders struggled to explain their reverse. Conrad III of Germany was adamant that the Franks of Outremer had been bribed by the Muslims into leading the crusader army astray. The Franks were also said to be unenthusiastic about the prospect of Westerners taking over Damascus for themselves while they remained unrewarded, in spite of the decades they had spent fighting the Muslims. For Bernard of Clairvaux, the reason behind the fiasco was the crusaders' failure to travel with the right intention: their motives must have been clouded by thoughts of greed and honor because with pure hearts they would have prevailed. The chronicler Henry of Huntingdon contrasted the defeat of the glory-seeking kings and nobles at Damascus with the success of the more humble forces at Lisbon.

The Second Crusade evolved into an ambitious and broad-ranging attempt to broaden Christendom on three fronts, yet it made real progress only in Iberia. The failure of the campaign in the Holy Land damaged the standing of the papacy, soured relations between the Christians of Outremer and the West for many years, and encouraged the Muslims of Syria to even greater efforts to defeat the Franks.

–Jonathan Phillips

Bibliography
Berry, Virginia, "The Second Crusade," in *A History of the Crusades,* ed. Kenneth M. Setton et al., 2d ed., 6 vols. (Madison: University of Wisconsin Press, 1969–1989), 1:463–511.

Cole, Penny J., *The Preaching of the Crusades to the Holy Land, 1095–1270* (Cambridge, MA: Medieval Academy of America, 1991).

Constable, Giles, "The Second Crusade as Seen by Contemporaries," *Traditio* 9 (1953), pp. 213–279.

Hoch, Martin, *Jerusalem, Damaskus und der Zweite Kreuzzug: Konstitutionelle Krise und äußere Sicherheit des Kreuzfahrerkönigreiches Jerusalem,* A.D. *1126–1154* (Frankfurt am Main: Lang, 1993).

Lilie, Ralph-Johannes, *Byzantium and the Crusader States, 1096–1204* (Oxford: Clarendon, 1993).

O'Callaghan, Joseph F., *Reconquest and Crusade in Medieval Spain* (Philadelphia: University of Pennsylvania Press, 2003).

Phillips, Jonathan P., *Defenders of the Holy Land: Relations between the Latin East and the West, 1119–87* (Oxford: Oxford University Press, 1996).

———, *The Second Crusade: Extending the Borders of Christianity* (New Haven: Yale University Press, 2007).

The Second Crusade: Scope and Consequences, ed. Jonathan P. Phillips and Martin Hoch (Manchester, UK: Manchester University Press, 2001).

The Second Crusade and the Cistercians, ed. Michael Gervers (New York: St. Martin's, 1992).

Williams, J. B., "The Making of a Crusade: The Genoese Anti-Muslim Attacks in Spain, 1146–8," *Journal of Medieval History* 23 (1997), 29–53.

Second Shepherds' Crusade

See Shepherds' Crusade, Second

Seghelijn van Jherusalem

See Dutch Literature

Sermons and Preaching

Sermons were preached on many different occasions in the course of a crusade. Propagandists preached in order to announce new crusades as well as to recruit participants and collect money for military campaigns. Often the departure of a crusader or a crusade army was also marked by sermons. During the campaigns, the clergy accompanying armies regularly preached sermons in order to sustain the participants' enthusiasm or to give them courage on the eve of a battle or in moments of crisis. Sermons thanking God were held after successful battles. In addition, sermons about the crusade were preached to those at home in the context of penitentiary processions and prayers in support of crusaders in the field.

Crusade sermons were preached by clerics of all levels of the ecclesiastical hierarchy from parish priests to cardinals and popes. From the thirteenth century onward, however, the bulk of crusade preaching was done by the members of the mendicant Franciscan and Dominican orders. Public preaching constituted one of their principal activities, and among other duties, they were commissioned by the popes to propagate the crusades throughout Latin Europe in a systematic manner. Considering the frequency of crusading between the twelfth and the sixteenth centuries, the number of different types of crusade sermons preached in various contexts during this time must have been considerable. Thus, sermons were not only an integral part of each crusade; they also played an important role in shaping and sustaining attitudes and responses to the medieval crusade movement.

Crusade sermons differed depending on their specific circumstance and purpose. They varied greatly in length, content, and complexity, ranging from short addresses to a crusade army in the field to elaborate sermons preached at various times in the run-up to a military campaign. Crusade recruitment sermons were preached in churches, in marketplaces, or in front of gatherings of knights and noblemen on the occasion of courtly festivities or tournaments. Preachers often moved from place to place within an assigned area of recruitment, making use of occasions at which people came together for other purposes, such as market days or church feasts. Preferred dates for crusade preaching were the feasts of the Invention of the Cross (3 May) and the Exaltation of the Cross (14 September), which provided a strong symbolic affinity in terms of crusade spirituality, and Lent, because of its strong penitential and Christocentric thrust. But crusade sermons, especially those aimed at eliciting financial support and prayers for crusade armies in the field, were also preached on a regular basis within ordinary church services throughout the year.

At times crusade propagandists were given special powers by the papacy to force parish priests to assemble their parishioners for a crusade sermon. In return, from the thirteenth century onward, attendance at recruitment sermons was rewarded by minor indulgences. This indicates that the dynamics of crowd psychology, especially peer pressure, was considered an important tool for enhancing the effectiveness of crusade preaching. Chronicle reports confirm that successful crusade propagandists showed extreme skill in provoking emotional responses by instilling their audiences with feelings of shame, contrition, anger, or rage. Sermons aimed at recruiting crusaders often took place in elaborate ceremonial settings accompanied by liturgical acts such as prayers, chants, processions, and sometimes the exposition of relics. In addition preachers often read out the papal bulls to their audiences, giving detailed information about the privileges and the terms of a particular crusade. After the sermons people solemnly took the vow by receiving the cross from the preacher, thus publicly demonstrating their transition to the status of crusader. More often than not crusade recruitment sermons were part of carefully planned and choreographed propaganda events.

Some crusade sermons were recorded in chronicles, such as Urban II's sermon at Clermont in 1095 or the sermons preached by Bishop Henry of Strasbourg in his home town in 1188 and Abbot Martin of Pairis in Basel in 1200. There are also reports of Baldwin of Canterbury's recruitment tour of Wales in 1188, Eustace of Fly's preaching in England in 1200–1201, Oliver of Paderborn's sermons in Frisia prior to the Fifth Crusade, and John of Capistrano's preaching of the cross in the fifteenth century. In addition we have a number of texts related to the preaching of the crusade against the Albigensian heretics at the beginning of the thirteenth century.

Generally speaking, however, crusade preaching was not the stuff of medieval chronicles, and other narrative accounts and evidence for the exact contents of individual sermons are limited. But there are a number of sermon texts, as well as tracts about preaching the crusade, that give an insight into the sets of ideas and the kinds of arguments that individual preachers would have drawn on. The most elaborate of these preaching aids was *De predicatione sanctae Crucis* by Humbert of Romans, a handbook for crusade preachers written in the 1260s, which gave practical information and listed numerous themes that might be used in crusade sermons. A shorter and less elaborate tract about preaching the cross to the Holy Land, the *Ordinacio de predicatione sanctae Crucis in Anglia,* was put together by an anonymous author in the first half of the thirteenth century.

Model sermons were written, copied, and used from the thirteenth century onward. These sermon texts were often derived from the authors' own crusade preaching and were adapted as models for the use of other preachers. Authors include famous crusade preachers, such as James of Vitry, Odo of Châteauroux, and Humbert of Romans, as well as some of the most prolific medieval sermon writers, such as Gilbert of Tournai and Bertrand of La Tour. Other preaching aids include *exempla* (illustrative stories to be included in a sermon) about the crusade, which appear in many late medieval *exempla* collections.

Depending on the occasion and the preacher's specific aims, crusade sermons varied in content. Judging from chronicle reports and model sermons, the preachers' messages usually portrayed crusading as a devotional and spiritual activity undertaken for the good of the participant's soul as well as a justified war against the enemies of the Christian religion. Sermons being a form of exegesis, preachers mainly talked about the crusade in theological terms and with reference to the Scriptures. Crusades were often compared to the wars of the Old Testament in which the Israelites fought against their enemies under the guidance of God. The crusade was thus described, and at the same time justified, as God's war fought in defense of and for the good of his church.

For participants or supporters, crusading was portrayed as a penitential activity through which an individual could establish a special relationship with God. This relationship was characterized by two main components: obligation and love. In as much as crusaders were perceived as soldiers fighting a war in the service of God or Christ, they were considered to be bound to God by the terms of feudal obligation. In return for this obligation, God rewarded crusaders by an indulgence for the forgiveness of their sins. Just as important for the characterization of the relationship between crusader and God was the model of love and friendship. Taking the cross was described as a spiritual quest for union with God through the bonds of mutual love. Crusaders were said to express their love of God by following him as "soldiers of Christ" or even to imitate Christ's act of redemption when dying in battle. Crusade preaching often dwelled at length on the spiritual and devotional aspects of the crusade. Crusading was first and foremost portrayed as a penitential activity, and participating or supporting the crusade was advocated as an effective way of dealing with the consequence of sin. This prevailing emphasis on the devotional and the penitential aspects of crusading can, in part, be explained by the strong pastoral thrust of crusade preaching from the thirteenth century onward.

For many, participation in the crusade consisted in supporting the crusade financially and by prayers rather than actually joining a crusade army. This meant that propagandists portrayed the crusade as profoundly relevant to people who might support the crusade movement for reasons that were not primarily connected to its military aspects. Participation in the crusade was thus advertised above all as a way of showing one's devotion to Christ and of cleansing one's soul from sin.

–*Christoph T. Maier*

See also: Bernard of Clairvaux (1090–1153); Communications

Bibliography

Bériou, Nicole, "La prédication de croisade de Philippe le Chancelier et d'Eudes de Châteauroux en 1226," in *La Prédication en Pay d'Oc (XIIe–début XVe siècle),* ed. Jean-Louis Biget (Toulouse: Privat, 1997), pp. 85–109.

Cole, Penny C., *The Preaching of the Crusades to the Holy Land, 1095–1270* (Cambridge, MA: Medieval Academy of America, 1991).

Edbury, Peter W., "Preaching the Crusade in Wales," in *England and Germany in the High Middle Ages,* ed. Alfred Haverkamp and Hanna Vollrath (Oxford: Oxford University Press, 1996), pp. 221–233.

Kienzle, Beverly Mayne, *Cistercians, Heresy and Crusade in Occitania, 1145–1229* (Woodbridge, UK: York Medieval Press, 2001).

Maier, Christoph T., *Preaching the Crusade: Mendicant Friars and the Cross in the Thirteenth Century* (Cambridge: Cambridge University Press, 1994).

———, *Crusade Propaganda and Ideology: Model Sermons for the Preaching of the Cross* (Cambridge: Cambridge University Press, 2000).

———, "Konflikt und Kommunikation: Neues zum Kreuzzugsaufruf Urbans II.," in *Jerusalem im Hoch- und Spätmittelalter: Konflikte und Konfliktregelungen—Vorstellungen und Vergegenwärtigungen,* ed. Dieter Bauer, Klaus Herbers, and Nikolas Jaspert (Frankfurt am Main: Campus, 2001), pp. 13–30.

Seljuks

See Saljūqs

Seventh Crusade

See Crusade of Louis IX to the East

Sgouros, Leo

Byzantine *archon* (ruler) of the Peloponnesian Argolid and Corinth, and leader of resistance against the Frankish conquest in southern and central Greece in the wake of the conquest of Constantinople by the Fourth Crusade (1204).

From around 1200 to 1204, Sgouros established a short-lived state comprising his inherited lands as well as Attica and Megaris, Boeotia, part of Negroponte, Phokis, Thermopylae, and parts of Thessaly, which soon brought him into conflict with Frankish forces attempting to annex Greek territories. He was awarded the high title of *sebastohypertatos* by the fugitive Alexios III Angelos, whose daughter Eudokia he married at Larissa, the northernmost part of his advance. However, he failed to check the advance of the Franks at Thermopylae and fled south to the fortress of Akrocorinth, where he sustained a siege of almost four years until his death (c. 1208).

A highly controversial figure, Sgouros has been variously characterized as an unscrupulous and ambitious local tyrant, and as a heroic defender of medieval Hellenism against the Frankish conquest.

–Alexios G. C. Savvides

See also: Byzantine Empire

Bibliography

Ilieva, Aneta, "The Phenomenon Leo Sgouros," *Etudes balkaniques* 26 (1990), 31–51.

Kordosses, Michael, *Η κατάκτηση της Νότιας Ελλάδας από τους Φράγκους* (Thessaloniki: Historikogeographika, 1986).

Niaves, Pavlos, "Λέων Σγουρός πατριώτης ή τύραννος?" *Βυζαντιναί Μελέται* 4 (1992), 333–357.

Savvides, Alexios G. C., "A Note on the Death of Leo Sgurus in A.D. 1208," *Byzantine and Modern Greek Studies* 12 (1988), 289–295.

Vlachopoulou, Photeine, *Λέων Σγουρός. Ὁ βίος και η πολιτεία του Βυζαντινού άρχοντα της βορειοανατολικής Πελοποννήσου στις αρχές του 13ου αιώνα* (Thessaloniki: Herodotos, 2002).

Shepherds' Crusade, First (1251)

The Shepherds' Crusade (Lat. *Crucesignatio pastorellorum*) of 1251 was an unofficial or popular crusade of poor shepherds and peasants from the Low Countries and northern France who set out with the declared aim of aiding and avenging King Louis IX of France and rescuing the Holy Land from the Muslims.

These unauthorized crusaders were known collectively as "shepherds" (Lat. *pastores,* Fr. *pastoureaux*). This was not only because there were many actual shepherds (including Roger, one of their leaders), cowherds, and dairy maids among the several bands of agrarian laborers, but also because shepherds claimed a privileged role in the Christian story, having been the first to see the Christ Child. The Annunciation to the Shepherds was sculpted above cathedral portals and dramatized in contemporary Nativity plays. Seeing themselves depicted in this way, ordinary shepherds could thus regard themselves as chosen by God. Often youthful, landless, mobile, and frequently in one another's company, shepherds constituted an ideal nucleus for a popular crusading movement, as they appear to have done in the Children's Crusade of 1212. In 1251, displaying banners of the Lamb and the Cross, traveling bands of armed shepherds asserted both their religious identity and their crusading intent. The crusade of the pastores probably originated in Flanders or Brabant toward Eastertide (16–23 April 1251), rapidly gathering recruits in the towns and villages of Hainaut, at Amiens in Picardy, and later at Rouen in Normandy. There they were joined by artisans and members of the urban underclass, who were often recent migrants from the countryside.

The circumstances out of which this popular crusade enthusiasm arose are reasonably clear. First of all, the miserable end of Louis IX's Egyptian crusade (1248–1254) and the king's subsequent captivity were no doubt widely known in Flanders. A large Flemish contingent had participated in Louis's crusade, including William of Dampierre, count of Flanders. After Louis was ransomed (6 May 1250), it is possible that some of his Flemish captains returned home. Pope Innocent IV's letter on Louis's incarceration (12–31 August 1250), intended for wide circulation, also urged public liturgies of supplication on Louis's behalf. Probably more important was the letter that Louis himself composed in Acre (10 August 1250) in which he refers to the Christian prisoners still being held in Egypt and announces his desperate need for more troops. In his letter Louis says that the men should depart for the Holy Land the next April or May. That date, corresponding as it does with the probable origins of the movement, is significant. Around that time as well, crusading excitement in the Low Countries was being fanned by the preaching of the papal crusade against Conrad IV, king of Germany. The Franciscan friar John of Diest may have been preaching this anti-Staufen crusade in Flanders in late March or early April 1251. Strong opposition to this preaching from Queen Blanche of Castile, Louis's mother and regent, may have triggered increased sympathy for and attention to the plight of her son. As with the Children's Crusade of 1212, popular enthusiasm generated by one crusade was readily deflected onto another, especially if the focus of the latter was the Holy Land. Speculation aside, what is important to emphasize is that popular crusades like that of the pastores frequently occurred in the midst of official crusade activities aimed at generating mass enthusiasm.

Once the pastores arrived at Paris (probably in early June 1251), their most prominent leader, the charismatic Jacob, known as "the Master of Hungary" and described as a runaway monk, was well received by Queen Blanche. Reportedly, she believed that the shepherds were intending to come to the aid of her son. But it was in Paris, apparently for the first time, that the pastores engaged in anticlerical violence. Perhaps it was the surprising reception that the queen gave them that, by seeming to confirm their providential status, destabilized them. In Paris they began to attack the clergy, while the Master of Hungary assumed the costume of a bishop and usurped clerical functions at the Church of St. Eustace. Starting out as an orthodox (although unauthorized) crusading venture, the shepherds had become a vast, rebellious, heretical mob. With his long beard and his pale, ascetic, and venerable appearance, together with a (supposed) letter from the Virgin Mary, the Master of Hungary swayed his followers as only a charismatic leader could. Two Englishmen, the chronicler Matthew Paris and the philosopher Roger Bacon, were intrigued by his understanding of crowd psychology. Matthew Paris was well informed about the movement, having interviewed the archbishop of Canterbury, who had been in France at the time, and Thomas of Sherborne, an English monk taken prisoner by the pastores. According to Matthew Paris, the Master of Hungary "infatuated" the people who heard him, whereas Bacon, who witnessed his spellbinding performance in Paris, spoke of "fascination" as the key to his success.

After Paris, most of the troops of shepherds headed southward. Violence erupted at Tours, where friars were attacked, and at Orléans, where scholars, students, and priests were robbed, beaten, and killed. At Bourges the pastores pillaged and persecuted the Jews with the connivance of local people. Probably it was at this point that Queen Blanche commanded that the shepherds be put down. The Master of Hungary was killed and many of his followers executed. Some shepherds made their way to Marseilles, Aigues-Mortes, Bordeaux, or even to Shoreham in England, but nearly all were apprehended, and many were hanged. The response of the clergy to the violence directed against them, oftentimes with the complicity of the local populace, was outrage and fear. The Franciscan chronicler Salimbene, who was in France at the time, was horrified by the violent attacks of the "innumerable host of Shepherds" upon his fellow mendicants because "they had preached the crusade [of Louis IX] and given men crosses to go beyond seas with the King" [Coulton, *From St. Francis to Dante*, p. 188]. He thus makes it clear that antimendicant sentiment, provoked by

the failure of the crusade the friars had preached, endeared the shepherds to the people, even when the result was anticlerical violence.

Clerical chroniclers, like the early fourteenth-century Dominican Bernard Gui, never forgot the pastores of 1251. As if in disbelief, he acknowledged that the common people rejoiced in the persecution of the clergy. To him, this was the most disquieting aspect of the Shepherds' Crusade of 1251. Thus the Second Shepherds' Crusade of 1320 stirred old memories and reawakened old fears.

–Gary Dickson

See also: Popular Crusades

Bibliography
Barber, Malcolm, "The Crusade of the Shepherds in 1251," in *Proceedings of the Tenth Annual Meeting of the Western Society for French History*, ed. J. F. Sweets (Lawrence: University of Kansas, 1984), pp. 1–23.
———, *Crusaders and Heretics, 12th–14th Centuries* (Aldershot, UK: Variorum, 1995).
Cohn, Norman, *The Pursuit of the Millennium*, 3d ed. (London: Random House, 1970).
Coulton, George G., *From St. Francis to Dante: A Translation of All That Is of Primary Interest in the Chronicle of the Franciscan Salimbene* (London: David Nutt, 1906).
Dickson, Gary, "The Advent of the *Pastores*," *Revue Belge de Philologie et d'Histoire* 66 (1988), 249–267.
———, *Religious Enthusiasm in the Medieval West: Revivals, Crusades, Saints* (Aldershot, UK: Ashgate, 2000).
———, "Medieval Christian Crowds and the Origins of Crowd Psychology," *Revue d'histoire ecclésiastique* 95 (2000), 54–75.
Jordan, William Chester, *Louis IX and the Challenge of the Crusade* (Princeton, NJ: Princeton University Press, 1979).

Shepherds' Crusade, Second (1320)

The popular crusade of 1320, whose participants were known in French as the *pastoureaux*, was the last and probably the most violent of the medieval crusades of the "shepherds."

Like the Children's Crusade (1212) and the First Shepherds' Crusade (1251), the crusade of the pastoureaux was unauthorized. Unlike the participants in those movements, however, the pastoureaux were named and condemned by the papacy. Terrified by the prospect of their arrival in Avignon, Pope John XXII ordered their dispersal (19 June 1320). As with other popular crusades, their collective name gives an inexact indication of their social composition. Actual shepherds probably formed the nucleus of the movement, but soon the multitudes flocking to join it included peasant laborers, craftsmen, the poor, and the socially marginal, both urban and rural, male and female. Although the French chroniclers refer to no knights in their ranks, a few nobles do appear in the Aragonese records. People of all ages participated, with youths of fourteen to sixteen particularly notable.

The movement lasted around four months. It originated in northern France, perhaps in Normandy, around Easter (20 March) 1320, reaching Paris by early May, then headed southward to Languedoc and Aragon, where, in the second half of July, it was crushed. In France as in Aragon the royal armies prevailed. Many of the pastoureaux were hanged. In the north, their leaders were reportedly a defrocked priest and a runaway monk, while in Languedoc no leaders are mentioned. At first, the pastoureaux professed crusading goals of fighting the infidels and regaining the Holy Land. In Paris, they may have believed that King Philip V of France, who had taken the cross, would lead them. An official crusade, planned since 1318, was still being discussed as recently as 17 February 1320. Royal propaganda thus aroused illusory expectations, inciting popular crusade enthusiasm. Memories of the "Crusade of the Poor" (1309) and the unsettling miseries of the great famine of 1315–1317 may have also played a part in the origins of the movement. From Paris onward this shepherds' crusade was characterized by anti-Jewish and anticlerical violence and civic disorder. Jews were offered baptism or death: Their goods were stolen, their debt records destroyed; they were then massacred—as, for example, at Verdun on the Garonne, Toulouse, or Monclus—or, like Baruch l'Allemand, forcibly baptized. What alarmed the Dominican chronicler Bernard Gui was that in their plundering of clerics and religious orders, the pastoureaux were often aided by local people, even the civic authorities. Crusading aims were eventually overshadowed by anti-Judaic and anticlerical rioting that carried more than a hint of sociopolitical rebellion.

−*Gary Dickson*

See also: Popular Crusades

Bibliography

Barber, Malcolm, "The *Pastoureaux* of 1320," *Journal of Ecclesiastical History* 32 (1981), 143–166. Reprinted in Malcolm Barber, *Crusaders and Heretics, 12th–14th Centuries* (Aldershot, UK: Variorum, 1995).

Dickson, Gary, "Encounters in Medieval Revivalism: Monks, Friars, and Popular Enthusiasts," *Church History* 68 (1999), 265–293.

Housley, Norman, *The Later Crusades, 1274–1580* (Oxford: Oxford University Press, 1992).

Nirenberg, David, *Communities of Violence: Persecution of Minorities in the Middle Ages* (Princeton, NJ: Princeton University Press, 1996).

Shī'ites

A term collectively applied to a number of Muslim sects that assert the primacy of the family of Muḥammad, as represented by the Prophet's son-in-law, 'Alī ibn Abī Ṭālib (d. 661) and his descendants.

The actual Arabic term is *shī'at 'Alī* (party of 'Alī), which seems to have been used as early as the civil war during 'Alī's caliphate (656–661). After 'Alī's death the Shī'ites continued to agitate on behalf of his family, and Shī'ite rebellions caused considerable concern for both the Umayyad (661–750) and 'Abbāsid (750–1258) caliphates.

Shī'ite doctrine is characterized most particularly by the recognition of the *imām*s: individuals regarded as the spiritual leaders of the Muslim community. Each *imām* was meant to guide the Muslim community, a task in which he was assisted by the teachings of the one who designated him and by a closer connection to God, achieved through *ilhām* (divine inspiration). Shī'ites believe that Muḥammad designated 'Alī as the first *imām,* with a number of *imām*s following him. Over time the Shī'ites split into a number of subdivisions, each with their own doctrines and practices. One of the main features distinguishing between them was the number of *imām*s they recognized. Some Shī'ite groups still recognize living *imām*s today, while others regard them as currently being hidden from the world. Several of these groups were important in the Muslim world during the period of the crusades.

The Ithnā'ashari Shī'ites, often known as the Twelvers, or Imāmis, recognize a line of twelve *imām*s, starting with 'Alī and passing down through his family. They believe that after the death of the eleventh *imām,* al-Ḥasan al-'Askarī (d. 874), his son, named Muḥammad, went into a state of *ghaybah* (occultation), communicating with the world through a line of four emissaries. After the death of the last of these in 941, the *imām* entered a state of *ghaybah kubra* (greater occultation). This will last until the end of time, when he will return as the *mahdī* ("guided one"), or messiah. During the period of the crusades, many Bedouin tribesmen of the Near East were Ithnāʿasharī Shīʿites.

The Ismāʿīlīs, sometimes known as the Seveners, were a Shīʿite sect that claimed that the sixth *imām,* Jaʿfar al-Ṣādiq (d. 765), had nominated his son Ismāʿīl as his successor. When Ismāʿīl died in 755 before his father, Ismāʿīl's supporters recognized his son Muḥammad as the seventh and final *imām,* maintaining that he would also reappear as the *mahdī* at the end of time. They existed in secret until the middle of the ninth century, before emerging as two movements known collectively as the Ismāʿīlīs. The first of these, known as the Qarmatians, attained particular prominence in eastern Arabia in the ninth and tenth centuries. However, it was the second movement, the Fāṭimids, that was particularly important in the history of the crusades. The heads of the Fāṭimid dynasty, diverging from earlier Ismāʿīlī thought, claimed to be both rightful caliphs and true living *imāms* descended from Muḥammad ibn Ismāʿīl. They established themselves at Kairouan in North Africa in 909 and then moved their power base to Egypt after conquering al-Fustāt in 969. They built Cairo, from which they ruled until 1171, when their caliphate was suppressed by Saladin.

The Assassins, or Nizārīs, owe their origins to a Persian propagandist of the Fāṭimids named Ḥasan-i Ṣabbāḥ (d. 1124), who in 1090 seized the fortress of Alamut in northern Persia. From there he began a program of Fāṭimid propaganda and political assassination. In 1094 the Fāṭimid caliph, al-Mustanṣir, died; he had nominated his eldest son, Nizār (d. 1095), to succeed him, but the palace administration ousted and murdered Nizār in favor of his more pliable brother al-Mustaʿlī (1094–1101). Ḥasan-i Ṣabbāḥ and his followers had sided with Nizār and became independent from the main Fāṭimid administration. During the years that followed, the Assassins established a hierarchical sect and continued to expand their sphere of influence, taking several fortresses in Persia and Syria. After 1162 the masters of the Persian Assassins claimed to be descendants of Nizār and hence the rightful *imāms,* a claim that they generally maintained until their Persian strongholds were destroyed by the Mongols in 1256. The Syrian Assassins survived slightly longer, the last of their fortresses falling to Baybars I, the Mamlūk sultan, in 1273.

In addition to the belief in the doctrine of the *imāms,* Shīʿite doctrine and practices show a number of other differences from those of Sunnī Muslims. In their interpretation of the *ḥadīth* (reports of the sayings and actions of the Prophet and his companions, constituting a source of Islamic law), they give greater importance to accounts attributed to ʿAlī and his family; they reject the use of consensus in their interpretation of the law but give reason a greater role in their theology; not surprisingly, they place greater emphasis on the teachings of the *imām*s, as passed down through the jurisprudents; and most importantly for the period of the crusades, for the Shīʿite groups that believe in a hidden *imām,* the offensive *jihād* (holy war) is considered to be suspended, as only the *imām* may lead it.

–Niall Christie

Bibliography

Daftary, Farhad, *The Ismaʿilis: Their History and Doctrines* (Cambridge: Cambridge University Press, 1990).

———, "The Ismaʿilis and the Crusaders: History and Myth," in *The Crusades and the Military Orders: Expanding the Frontiers of Medieval Latin Christianity,* ed. Zsolt Hunyadi and József Laszlovszky (Budapest: Department of Medieval Studies, Central European University, 2001), pp. 21–42.

Halm, Heinz, *Shiism* (Edinburgh: Edinburgh University Press, 1991).

Jafri, S. Husain M., *Origins and Early Development of Shiʿa Islam* (London: Longman, 1979).

Momen, Moojan, *An Introduction to Shiʿism: The History and Doctrines of Twelver Shiʿism* (New Haven: Yale University Press, 1985).

Rippin, Andrew, *Muslims: Their Religious Beliefs and Practices,* 2d ed. (London: Routledge, 2001).

Ships

The types of ships involved in the crusades at various times were referred to in contemporary sources by a wide variety of different names, and in most cases the types of vessels to which the terms corresponded are known reasonably well; however, there are exceptions that are sometimes difficult to categorize with certainty. This is particularly true of the Muslim world. Only a handful of scholars have addressed the issues, and none have examined the nature of the ships involved, their historical evolution, and their performance capabilities, issues that influenced, indeed governed profoundly the actual participation of naval forces in the crusades.

Terminology

The first Western fleet to sail to the East in the period of the crusades was probably that commanded by Guynemer of

Boulogne, who anchored off Tarsos (mod. Tarsus, Turkey) in September 1097. His vessels are characterized merely as *naves* by the chronicler Albert of Aachen, who was undoubtedly using the term as a generic for ships. The Genoese fleet that sailed in summer 1097 reportedly consisted of 12 *galee* (galleys of a new Western design) and 1 *sandanum*. The term *sandanum* was a Latinization of the Greek *chelandion*, for a transport galley. The Pisan fleet that left in summer 1099 reportedly numbered 120 *naves*, while that of the Venetians that sailed in summer 1099 had at least 30 *naves*. The fleet of Sigurd Jorsalfar, which left Norway in 1107, was said by Thórarin Stuttfeld to have consisted of 60 ships (ON *skip*). In 1123 the Venetian fleet that sailed for Outremer reportedly numbered 120 *naves* plus some small boats (Lat. *carabii*).

During the Third Crusade (1189–1192), a Northern fleet of 50 ships referred to as *cogas* (cogs) reached Acre (mod. 'Akko, Israel). The fleet of Richard I the Lionheart, king of England, consisted of ships variously called *esneccas* or *enekes*, *galees*, *naves* or *nefs*, *dromonz*, and *bucee*. For the Fourth Crusade (1202–1204) the Venetians supplied a battle fleet of 50 *galeae* (galleys) and a transport fleet consisting of *naves* for the men and *uissiers* for the horses. In 1217 Count William I of Holland led a fleet of *coccones* to Damietta in Egypt. For his Crusade of 1227–1229 the Holy Roman Emperor Frederick II prepared various fleets of ships described as *naves*, *galee*, *usseria*, *chelandre*, and *taride*. King Louis IX of France contracted with Marseilles and Genoa for squadrons of *naves*, *taride*, and *galee* for his Crusade of 1248–1254.

Byzantine sources of the crusade period mostly use classical Greek terms such as *trieres* (pl. *triereis*) or generic terms such as *naus* (pl. *nees*) or *ploion* (pl. *ploia*) for ships, although Anna Komnene and Niketas Choniates occasionally use *dromon* (pl. *dromones*), the term par excellence for Byzantine war galleys since the sixth century. From the late twelfth century a new term, *katergon* (pl. *katerga*), began to be used, displacing *dromon* and becoming the generic for war galleys during the late Byzantine Empire.

Arabic sources of the period use terms such as *qārib* (pl. *qawārib*) for small boats and also for galleys, *shīnī* (pl. *shawānī*) and *ghurāb* (pl. *'aghriba/ghirbān/'aghrub*) for galleys; *markab* (pl. *marākib*) and *qiṭ'a* (pl. *qiṭa'*) for vessels in general, but often with reference to war galleys; *safina* (pl. *sufun, safā'in*) for vessels in general, but often for transport ships; *musattah* (pl. *musattahāt*) for transport ships; *baṭsha* (pl. *buṭash*) for large sailing ships; *'ushari* (pl. *'ushāriyyāt*) for transport galleys, *tarrīda* (pl. *tarā'id*) for horse transports, and *ḥarrāqa* (pl. *ḥarrāqāt*) for fire ships, as well as loan words such as *shalandī* (pl. *shalandiyyat*) from the Byzantine *chelandion*, frequently used for Byzantine war ships but also for galleys built in Egypt.

Such words were rarely used in a technical or technological sense. Most authors were unfamiliar with the sea, were not writing for maritime audiences, and used approved or literary terms for ships even if they did know what particular types ought to be called. Generic terms such as *naves*, *nees*, or *ploia*, and *sufun/safā'in* or *marākib* were used for all types of ships in fleets. The Latin word *naves* was used for all ships of the Pisan and Venetian fleets in the First Crusade (1096–1099), even though they included galleys. But as well as its generic meaning, by the twelfth century the term *navis/naves* had acquired a specific reference in a Mediterranean context to lateen-rigged, round-hulled sailing ships.

Evolution of Ship Types

The historical evolution of ship types was continuous. A type could change in its fundamental technology and yet retain the same name, as in the case of the cog. Alternatively a name could become applied to a completely different type of ship, as occurred with *dromon* in its Latin and Arabic variants. By the twelfth century it was used for sailing ships that had nothing in common with Byzantine galleys.

In the centuries before the First Crusade, Mediterranean maritime commerce was carried on a cloud of small sailing ships. Judging from excavations of shipwrecks (the Yassı Ada ship of the seventh century, the Bozburun ship whose timbers were felled in 874, and the early eleventh-century Serçe Limani ship, all from within modern Turkey, and the thirteenth-century Contarina ship found near Venice), such ships averaged around 20 meters (c. 65½ ft.) in overall length, around 5 meters (c. 16½ ft.) maximum beam, and around 2–2.5 meters (c. 6½–8¼ ft.) depth in hold. They probably had single masts and lateen sails, were steered by two stern-quarter rudders, and carried multiple anchors because of their inefficient design and light weight. Smaller versions had only half-decks at bow and stern. Larger ones were fully decked with a small, low cabin at the stern, such as was the case with the Yassı Ada ship.

There certainly were large ships, such as the fine one sailing up the Bosporus that reportedly incensed the Byzantine emperor Theophilos (d. 842) when he learned that its owner was his wife Theodora, or the three-masted "pirate" *naus* reported by Anna Komnene during the First Crusade. Three-masted sailing ships certainly existed in the eleventh century, as is proved by a depiction on glazed Pisan *bacini,* which were glazed pottery bowls from the Muslim world placed on the facades of churches at Pisa and elsewhere to reflect sunlight and give the churches a glittering aspect. However, such large ships have left no trace in the documentary record before the thirteenth century.

In the Mediterranean, ships had always been built with strakes edge-joined: that is, with the planks of the hull joined edge to edge and not overlapping as in clinker construction. In classical antiquity, hulls had been shell-constructed from the keel out by holding the strakes together with closely spaced mortise-and-tenon joints pegged with treenails (wooden pegs). Frames were inserted only when hulls had been built to a point where they could be usefully positioned. This produced light and strong hulls but was extremely expensive in terms of the labor and carpentry skills required. By the fourth century (as evidenced in another wreck found at Yassı Ada), tenons had become less tightly fitting, wider but shorter, and spaced more widely apart. The evolutionary process was yet more clearly apparent in the seventh-century Yassı Ada wreck. The Bozburun wreck showed no signs of mortise-and-tenon edge-joining, and by the eleventh century, in the Serçe Limani wreck, skeleton construction over a framework of ribs and stringers had replaced shell construction.

Coating ships with a layer of pitch over the whole hull was replaced by driving caulking into the seams between the planks. The first usages of the Greek word for a caulker (*kalaphates*) occurred in sixth-century Egyptian papyri and appeared in Byzantium itself in the tenth century, in inventories for expeditions to Crete in the *De cerimoniis* attributed to Emperor Constantine VII Porphyrogennetos, which included linen for, and the cost of *kalaphateseos:* caulking. The first picture of caulkers working on a ship is in a manuscript of the *De materia medica* of Dioskorides Pedanios, probably made for Emperor Constantine VII (MS New York, Pierpont Morgan Library, 652 fol. 240r).

In northern Europe, ships were also shell-constructed, but there strakes were not edge-joined but rather clinker-overlapped. Up to the eleventh century, the sailing ship par excellence was the Norse *knörr* (ON, pl. *knerrir*). Two such ships, dated to around 1000, were among 5 ships excavated off Skuldelev in Roskilde Fjord (Denmark). The smaller was around 13.72 meters (45 ft.) long and around 3.20 meters

(10½ ft.) in beam, the larger around 14.94 meters (49 ft.) long and 4.57 meters (15 ft.) in the beam. Both had half decks forward and aft and an open hold amidships. The mast of the smaller was socketed into the kelson, with a stringer laid over the floor timbers and keel to provide fore-and-aft rigidity and to lock the floor timbers to the keel, while that of the larger was set in a complex mast-step. Both would have been steered by a starboard stern-quarter rudder. The larger may well have ventured out into the Atlantic Ocean, since it was heavily built with sturdy frames. Larger *knerrir* were primarily sailing ships, using what oars they carried only for entering and leaving harbor, for close maneuvering, and in emergencies.

The Skuldelev ships also included two long ships (ON *langskip*) like the famous ships excavated at Oseberg and Gokstad. The Oseberg ship (from around 800) and the Tune ship (from around 875) had dimensions of 21.4 meters (70¼ ft.) in length, 5.1 meters (16¾ ft.) in the beam, and 1.4 meters (4½ ft.) depth in hold and around 20.0, 4.6, and an unknown depth in hold respectively (65½ and 15 ft.). The Gokstad ship (of around 900) was 23.4 meters in length, 5.2 meters in the beam, and 1.9 meters depth in hold (76¾, 17, and 6¼ ft.). Those of the two Skuldelev ships were approximately 18, 2.6, and 1.1 meters (59, 8½, and 3½ ft.) and 30, 4.2 meters (98½ and 13¾ ft.), and unknown depth in hold, respectively. The Oseberg ship carried 15 pairs of oars, the Tune and smaller Skuldelev ships 12 pairs. The Gokstad ship carried 16 pairs of oars and the larger Skuldelev ship between 20 and 30 pairs. In Norse literature the terms *langskip* and "snake" (ON *snekkja,* pl. *snekkjur*) were interchangeable, although *snekkjur* may have been larger. As the length of northern longships began to increase, the largest became known as *drekar,* "dragon ships" (sing. *dreki*). Those such as the Gokstad ship and the larger Skuldelev ship would certainly have been capable of voyages to Outremer; however, whether Norse *langskip, snekkjur,* or *drekar* actually made such voyages is debatable. Crews would have been much more comfortable in *knerrir,* and there would have been no reason to use longships unless naval combat was expected.

In England *knerrir* became known as *céolas* (OE sing. *céol*), that is keels, perhaps reflecting originally the pronounced keels of Norse ships as opposed to keel-less Frisian hulks and cogs. By the eleventh century the Old English term *céol* was used commonly for sailing ships in the lower North Sea and English Channel. Another name that appeared increasingly from the eleventh century was *bussa/busse/bus/buza* (Lat.

bucia/bucius); however, whether the Mediterranean Latin *bucia/bucius* was adopted in the north or vice-versa is unclear. No descriptions of these terms permit attribution of particular characteristics to ships. Nor do illustrations name types until much later. By the thirteenth century ships like *knerrir* but with light and possibly demountable castles added at the stern, and sometimes the bow, appeared on town seals. Beam ends through the hull of some were probably deck beams. Such ships were probably the *buciae* in the English fleet of the Third Crusade, and according to Richard of Devizes, the *naves* of the English fleet, which were only half the size of the *buciae,* carried forty foot soldiers and forty horses as well as their supplies. The Norse *snekkja* was also imitated in England under the names *esnecca* or *esneke.* King Henry II had a sixty-oared *esnecca* that made the voyage to Outremer during the Third Crusade. Other flotillas of *snekkjur* and smaller oared ships from France, Flanders, and Denmark also participated.

From the sixth to late eleventh centuries, the warship par excellence in the Mediterranean was the dromon and its Muslim and Latin imitations, although Byzantines also developed the *chelandion,* originally an oared horse transport, which was also imitated. By the tenth century dromons had become biremes with two banks of 50 oars, one below and one above deck. A standard ship's complement (Gr. *ousia*) consisted of 108 men, excluding officers, marines, and specialists such as helmsmen and a carpenter. Around 31.5 meters (103 ft.) long, they carried two masts with lateen sails and had quarter rudders on both stern quarters. They also had fighting castles on each side just aft of the foremast and a foredeck at the prow, below which was housed their *siphon* for hurling Greek fire: this was a weapon that used a force pump to eject a stream of petroleum naphtha fuel that was set alight, creating a tongue of flame that could destroy enemy ships.

Monoreme dromons with only 50 oars were known as *galeai,* and it seems certain that the Latin *galea* developed from them. The earliest uses of the Latin term were by a group of eleventh-century Italo-Norman chroniclers, which suggests an adaptation of this ship type in southern Italy from Byzantine originals encountered there. Even though references to *galee* proliferated rapidly, however, they were never described in detail and all that is known about early *galee* is that they had fine lines and were fast. The earliest documents with construction details are from the Angevin kingdom of Sicily between 1269 and 1284.

Almost certainly, the oarage system was reconfigured so that two oarsmen could row from one bench position above deck. This made immeasurable difference to the oar mechanics, increasing oarsmen's combined power delivery markedly. No longer did one bank row below deck in stygian darkness and foul air. It also freed holds for supplies, water, spare gear, and armaments. No wonder that the *galea* spread rapidly in the West and came to be emulated in both the Byzantine and Muslim worlds.

The earliest datable illustrations of *galee* are three miniatures in the Madrid manuscript of the *Synopsis historiarum* of John Skylitzes, produced in Palermo around 1160 (MS Madrid, Biblioteca Nacional, vitr. 26–2). These clearly show bireme galleys with a different oarage system. One file of oars was rowed through oarports, but the other was worked above the gunwale. The same system is depicted even more clearly in an early thirteenth-century manuscript of the *Carmen ad honorem Augusti* of Peter of Eboli (MS Bern, Burgerbibliothek, 120).

This bireme oarage system became known as the *alla sensile* system. Two oarsmen each rowed single oars from the same bench above deck. Using a stand-and-sit stroke as opposed to the fully seated stroke of classical and Byzantine galleys, they threw their whole weight and the power of their legs into the stroke by falling back onto the bench. The inboard oar was pulled through an oarport in the outrigger, while the outboard oar was pulled against a thole, a pin set in the gunwale (Gr. *apostis,* It. *posticcio, apposticio*), to which an oar was held by an oar thong or grommet.

Such bireme galleys remained the norm throughout the main age of the crusades. There is no clear evidence for galleys using any other type of oarage system, and occasional literary references to triremes or to more than one oarsmen pulling each oar are either classical allusions or mistakes. Only in the early fourteenth century did Marino Sanudo Torsello report that: "in [. . .] 1290, two oarsmen used to row on a bench on almost all galleys which sailed the sea. Later more perceptive men realized that three oarsmen could row on each of the aforesaid benches. Almost everyone uses this nowadays" [Marino Sanudo Torsello, "Liber Secretorum Fidelium Crucis," in *Gesta Dei per Francos,* ed. Jacques Bongars, 2 vols. (Hannover: Typis Wechelianis, 1611), p. 57].

Standard bireme *galee* came to measure around 39.5 meters (129½ ft.) in overall length; they were longer than dromons because they mounted 108 rather than 100 oars and because the stand-and-sit stroke needed a distance

Thirteenth-century warships. Illustration from the *Cantigas de Santa Maria,* by King Alfonso X of Castile. (Bridgeman-Giraudon/Art Resource)

between any two tholes (Lat. *interscalmium*) of around 1.20 meters (4 ft.) rather than the 1 meter (3¼ ft.) for fully-seated oarsmen. Their beam was around 4.6 meters (15 ft.) at the deck amidships, and their depth in hold around 2 meters (6½ ft.). They still carried only two masts with lateen sails, the foremasts being almost 16 meters (52½ ft.) long with yards nearly 27 meters (88½ ft.) and the midships masts being 11 meters (36 ft.) long with yards of 20.5 meters (67¼ ft.). The stern-quarter rudders were 6 meters (19¾ ft.) long. By the later thirteenth century, standard crews on Angevin galleys consisted of 108 oarsmen, 2 masters, 4 helmsmen, 36 marines, and 2 ship's boys. Standard armaments included around 30 crossbows, 8 cases of quarrels (crossbow bolts),

40 shields, 200 lances, 10 halberds, 47 axes, 400 darts, 108 helmets and padded jackets for the oarsmen, 40 glass bottles for Greek fire and 100 pots of powdered quick lime, 2 iron grapnels, rigging cutters, and possibly iron rockets for shooting Greek fire.

Although no substantiable evidence suggests that any oarage system other than the *alla sensile* system was used until the late thirteenth century, a variety of names for galleys other than *galee* appeared sporadically in the sources: *sagene, sagittae, gatti,* and *garabi* in particular.

The term *sagena* appeared first for vessels of Muslim and Croatian corsairs in Byzantine sources. The type was developed among the Slavs on the east coast of the Adriatic Sea.

Sagitta (lit. "arrow") was also applied to corsair galleys, but to those of the Latin West. They were smaller than *galee* and presumably very fast, to judge by their name. Thirteenth-century Genoese documents refer to *sagittae* with 48, 58, 64, and 80 oars. *Gattus* was derived from the Arabic *qiṭ'a* and appeared mainly in late eleventh- and twelfth-century sources, referring to galleys larger than the norm. The ships were sometimes described as triremes, although that may have been a classicizing literary affectation. *Garabus* was again derived from Arabic: *ghurāb*, or possibly also *qārib*, since it is unclear whether these terms were not simply variants of the same name. *'Aghriba* were sometimes said to have carried 140 oars, and *garabus* may also have been applied to galleys larger than the norm. If they really did row 140 oars, then they must have been triremes.

Horse Transports

Byzantines had oared horse transports equipped with landing ramps as early as the ninth century and retained that capability into the twelfth. The chronicler William of Tyre reports Byzantine horse transports supplied for a combined Byzantine-Frankish attack on Egypt in 1169 as "also having accessible ports at the poops for embarking and disembarking them [horses], also with bridges by which ease of entrance and exit both of men and of horses might be attended to as usual" [William of Tyre, *Chronicon*, ed. Robert B. C. Huygens (Turnhout: Brepols, 1986), p. 927].

Muslims too were transporting horses on specialized *'ushāriyyāt* and *tarā'id* by the tenth century. Twelfth-century *tarā'id* could hold forty horses. The Venetians were apparently the first Latins to transport horses to Outremer in 1123, but it is unknown what types of ship they used. By this time the Normans of Sicily definitely could transport horses by galley, because during the Mahdia campaign (1087) 500 cavalry disembarked from beached ships to attack Muslim troops; only galleys could be beached.

Horses were transported in both sailing ships and galleys from the West to Outremer from 1129 up to the time of the Third Crusade. Venice used oared horse transports with stern-quarter ports and landing bridges for the Fourth Cru-

Table I: Primary specifications of Genoese 20-horse *taride* of 1246 and Angevin 30-horse *taride* of 1274–1281		
	Genoese	Angevin
Overall length	35.71m.	37.97m.
Depth in hold amidships	2.23m.	2.11m.
Beam on floor	3.35m.	3.56 or 3.69m.
Beam at wale	4.09m.	3.96 or 4.09m.
Beam of deck beams	–	4.88 or 5.01m.
Number of stern quarter ports	2	1 or 2
Length of foremast	19.34m.	17.40m.
Length of foremast yard	–	28.48m.
Length of midships mast	14.88m.	13.45m.
Length of quarter rudders	–	7.38m.
Number and length of oars	–	108 or 112m., half 7.38m., half 7.65m.
Length of landing bridges	–	3.69m.
Number of stalls	20	30
Length of stalls	–	1.98m.

sade (1202–1204), and both appeared among the miscellaneous fleets that reached Damietta during the Fifth Crusade (1217–1221). In 1224 Emperor Frederick II prepared a great fleet of 50 oared horse transports, each carrying forty horses, and in 1246 agents of King Louis IX of France contracted with Genoa for 12 *taride* to carry twenty horses each for his Crusade to the East.

The Byzantine term for an oared horse transport was *chelandion* while those of the Muslims had been *'ushari* and *tarrīda*. In the West *uscerius* and variants became the generic term for an oared horse transport, while *chelandion* became adopted as *chelandre* and variants and *tarrīda* as *taride/tarida*. Whether there was ever any real difference between Western *chelandre* and *taride* is debatable, but as the thirteenth century wore on, *tarida* became more common and *chelandre* disappeared.

Louis IX's contract of 1246 has the earliest specifications, and these may be compared to those of thirty-horse *taride* constructed for Charles I of Anjou between 1274 and 1281.

The Later Middle Ages

The twelfth and thirteenth centuries saw no innovation in the technology or construction of Mediterranean sailing *naves;* however, the length and beam, number of masts, and number of decks and depth in hold of some increased dramatically. By the mid–twelfth century, iconography depicted as a matter of course two-masted *naves* with multiple-tiered

Table II: Primary dimensions of 2-decked and 3-decked Genoese and Venetian crusader *naves*, 1246–1269

	2-decked *naves*	3-decked *naves*
Length of keel	18.7 m.	22.6 m.
Overall length	28.9 m.	35.2 m.
Depth in hold	3.45 m.	4.11 m.
Height of first deck	2.06 m.	2.91 m.
Height of second deck	–	2.03 m.
Height of corridoria part decks (calculated for 3-decked naves)	1.57 m.	1.76 m.
Height of bulwark	1.13 m.	1.18 m.
Height of stem- and sternposts above keel (calculated)	–	12.77 m.
Internal beam on floor (calculated)	1.7 m.	3.14 m.
Internal beam at first deck (calculated)	–	8.92 m.
Maximum internal beam (calculated)	7.75 m.	9.5 m.
Forecastle		
Talamus (number of)	1	–
Pontes (number of)	–	2
Suprapons (number of)	–	1
Sterncastle		
Paradisi (number of)	1	2
Castellum (number of)	1	–
Vanna (number of)	–	1
Supravannum (number of)	–	1
Length of quarter rudders (calculated)	13.98 m.	17.0 m.
Length of foremast (calculated for 3-decked naves)	29.3 m.	36.48 m.
Length of midships mast (calculated for 3-decked naves)	26.8 m.	34.25 m.
Length of foremast yard (calculated)	36.2 m.	46.8 m.
Length of midships yard (calculated)	33.3 m.	41.8 m.
Ship's boats (number of)		
Barca de canterio (52 oars)	–	1
Barche de parischalmo (32 or 34 oars)	–	2
Gondola	–	1
Deadweight tonnage (calculated)	323 tonnes	805 tonnes

sterncastles and substantial forecastles, such as the Genoese ship conveying Conrad of Montferrat to the Holy Land in the Paris manuscript of the *Annals of Genoa* [MS Paris, Bibliothèque nationale de France, suppl.lat.773]. By the thirteenth century, the mosaics of San Marco in Venice also showed three-masted ships. No documentary evidence for three-masted ships survives; however, it is available for two-masted ships provided by Genoa and Venice in 1246–1269 for the two crusades of Louis IX of France. The data vary

considerably but may be averaged out or calculated as laid out in the accompanying table.

With the amount of deck space legislated by Marseilles for each pilgrim or crusader, ships of the size of the average three-decked ship could carry around 500–550 passengers. One thirteenth-century Genoese ship, the *Oliva*, is known to have had a capacity of 1,100 passengers. Such ships were intercepted and captured by Saladin's squadrons in the 1170s and 1180s and were referred to in Arabic sources as *buṭash*. According to Arabic sources, one *baṭsha* wrecked off Damietta in 1181/1182 was carrying 2,500 passengers, of whom 1,690 were taken alive. The figures are probably exaggerated, but perhaps not by a great deal if the ship was indeed very large. They could also carry up to 100 horses, normally on the lowest deck, as revealed by a Marseillese contract of 1268 with Louis IX, which specified a fare of 25 shillings for passengers if horses were not stabled there. As the French chronicler Joinville remarked: "On the day that we entered into our ships, the port of the ship was opened and all the horses we wanted to take to Outremer were put inside, and then the port was closed again and plugged well, as when a cask is caulked, because, when the ship is on the high sea, the whole port is under water" [John of Joinville, *Vie de Saint Louis*, ed. J. Monfrin (Paris: Classsiques Garnier, 1998), p. 62].

Another Northern ship, the cog (MLG *kogge*), appeared in crusader fleets as early as the Second Crusade (1147–1149). Originally cogs had been flat-bottomed estuarine and river craft in Frisia, but in the early twelfth century cogs appeared that had flat floors and high sides, a radical new rudder hung off a straight sternpost, and straight stemposts, and that could hold the high seas. The wreck from Kolding Fjord (Denmark), dated to the late twelfth or thirteenth centuries, was around 18.3 meters (60 ft.) long and 6.1 (1³/4 ft.) meters wide, with a mast step around 1.98 meters (6¹/2 ft.) forward of midships. It had a flat bottom with edge-joined strakes and sides with clinker strakes. Traces of rust on the sternpost revealed a sternpost rudder rather than the Norse quarter rudder. One of the earliest depictions of such a cog is on the first seal of the city of Elbing (mod. Elbląg, Poland) in Prussia (1242). Whether they evolved from earlier Frisian cogs or whether this name was taken over by a completely new ocean-going craft is debatable.

Cogs of the new type appeared in northern fleets for the Third and Fifth Crusades. In 1217 Count William I of Holland left with a fleet of cogs to join the Fifth Crusade at Damietta. Ports were cut into their sterns to embark the horses, and when the horses were on board, the ports were covered and sealed with pitch and tar. The Mediterranean technology for embarking and disembarking horses by ramps through ports in the hull became adopted in northern Europe.

Maritime history was an evolutionary process. The bireme *galee,* one-decked and single-masted Mediterranean *naves,* and Norse *knerrir* and *snekkjur* of the age of the First Crusade were replaced 200 years later by trireme *galee,* multiple-decked and masted *naves,* and northern cogs.

–John H. Pryor

Bibliography

The Age of the Galley: Mediterranean Oared Vessels since Pre-Classical Times, ed. John Morrison (London: Conway Maritime Press, 1995).

Cogs, Caravels and Galleons: The Sailing Ship, 1000–1650, ed. Richard W. Unger (London: Conway Maritime Press, 1994).

Crumlin-Pedersen, Ole, "The Skuldelev Ships," *Acta Archaeologica* 38 (1967), 73–174.

A History of Seafaring Based on Underwater Archaeology, ed. George F. Bass (London: Thames and Hudson, 1972).

Pryor, John H., "The Transportation of Horses by Sea during the Era of the Crusades: Eighth Century to 1285 A.D.," *Mariner's Mirror* 68 (1982), 9–27, 103–125.

——, "The Naval Architecture of Crusader Transport Ships: A Reconstruction of Some Archetypes for Round-Hulled Sailing Ships," *Mariner's Mirror* 70 (1984), 171–219, 275–292, 363–386.

——, *Geography, Technology, and War: Studies in the Maritime History of the Mediterranean, 649–1571* (Cambridge: Cambridge University Press, 1988).

——, "The Naval Architecture of Crusader Transport Ships and Horse Transports Revisited," *Mariner's Mirror* 76 (1990), 255–273.

——, "The Galleys of Charles I of Anjou, King of Sicily: ca. 1269–84," *Studies in Medieval and Renaissance History* 14 (1993), 33–103.

Serçe Limanı: An Eleventh-Century Shipwreck, vol. 1: *The Ship and Its Anchorage, Crew, and Passengers,* ed. George F. Bass et al. (College Station: Texas A&M University Press, 2004).

Steffy, John R., *Wooden Ship Building and the Interpretation of Shipwrecks* (College Station: Texas A&M University Press, 1994).

Unger, Richard W., *The Ship in the Medieval Economy, 600–1600* (London: Croom Hill, 1980).

——, "Warships and Cargo Ships in Medieval Europe," *Technology and Culture* 22 (1981), 233–252.

Yassı Ada, vol. 1: *A Seventh-Century Byzantine Shipwreck,* ed. George F. Bass and Frederick H. van Doorninck, Jr. (College Station: Texas A&M University Press, 1982).

Shīrkūh (d. 1169)

A Muslim general who conquered Fāṭimid Egypt for Nūr al-Dīn ibn Zangī, the ruler of Muslim Syria.

The two Ayyūbid brothers Asad al-Dīn Shīrkūh and Najm al-Dīn Ayyūb were Kurds from Dvin in the Caucasus (in mod. Armenia), who migrated to Iraq, where from 1138 they served ʿImād al-Dīn Zangi, ruler of Mosul. Shīrkūh was a capable soldier, and he rose to high military responsibilities in the service of Zangī's son, Nūr al-Dīn.

In 1164, when Nūr al-Din decided to intervene in the internal affairs of the Fāṭimid state, Shīrkūh led the expedition to Egypt. Between 1164 and 1169, he campaigned three times in Egypt, fighting both Fāṭimids and Franks. His death paved the way for the rise to power of his nephew Saladin, son of Najm al-Dīn Ayyūb, who overthrew the Fāṭimids in 1171 and brought about the rupture in relations between the Ayyūbids in Egypt and Nūr al-Dīn in Damascus.

–Yaacov Lev

Bibliography

Lyons, Malcolm C., and D. E. P. Jackson, *Saladin. The Politics of the Holy War* (Cambridge: Cambridge University Press, 1982).

Sibṭ ibn al-Jawzī (1185/1186–1256)

Shams al-Dīn Abu'l-Muẓaffar Yūsuf ibn Qizoghlu, also known as Sibṭ ibn al-Jawzī, was a famous preacher and writer.

The son of a Turkish freedman and the daughter of another well-known preacher and writer, Ibn al-Jawzī (whence comes his name, "grandson of Ibn al-Jawzī"), he was actually brought up by his famous grandfather. After the latter's death in 1201 he went to Damascus, where he served the Ayyūbid rulers al-Muʿaẓẓam ʿĪsā, al-Nāṣir Dāwūd, and al-Ashraf Mūsā. He became known in particular for his preaching and was said to have moved his listeners to tears with his eloquence.

Sibṭ ibn al-Jawzī wrote a great universal history entitled *Mir'āt al-Zamān fī Ta'rīkh al-A'yān* (*Mirror of Time Concerning the History of Notables*), which includes an account of the crusading period up to his death. A number of other works have also been ascribed to him.

–*Niall Christie*

Bibliography

Hillenbrand, Carole, *The Crusades: Islamic Perspectives* (Edinburgh: Edinburgh University Press, 1999).

Sibṭ ibn al-Jawzī, "Extraits du Mirât ez-Zèmân," in *Recueil des Historiens des Croisades: Historiens Orientaux*, 5 vols. (Paris: Académie des Inscriptions et Belles-Lettres, 1884), 3:511–570.

———, *Mir'āt al-Zamān fī Ta'rīkh al-A'yān*, 2 vols. (Hyderabad: Dayrat al-Maʿārif al-Uthmānīyah, 1951–1952).

Sibyl of Jerusalem (d. 1190)

Queen of Jerusalem (1186–1190).

Sibyl was born before 1161, the eldest child of King Amalric of Jerusalem and his first wife, Agnes of Courtenay. Despite the annulment of her parents' marriage in 1163, she and her brother Baldwin (IV) were declared legitimate. After Baldwin became king (1174), his leprosy meant that a husband was needed for Sibyl, his heir, to assume the regency and father a male successor. In the autumn of 1176 Sibyl was married to William of Montferrat, but he died in June 1177, leaving a posthumous son, the future Baldwin V. At Easter 1180 Sibyl married a Poitevin nobleman, Guy of Lusignan; the reasons for the marriage are unclear, but it may have been precipitated by the advance of Bohemund III of Antioch and Raymond III of Tripoli on the kingdom, ostensibly to impose their candidate on Sibyl.

Guy's elevation was resented and led to factional strife. Baldwin IV had Baldwin V crowned in 1183, hoping that on his own death Sibyl and Guy would be kept from the throne. However, the young Baldwin V died in 1186, only a year after his uncle the king; while the High Court debated the succession in Nablus, Sibyl had herself crowned in Jerusalem and proceeded to crown Guy.

Sibyl was associated with Guy in his charters, but their rule ended with the defeat at Hattin in July 1187. After Guy's release from captivity by Saladin they both traveled to Tyre (mod. Soûr, Lebanon) but were refused access to the city by Conrad of Montferrat. They then laid siege to Acre (mod. ʿAkko, Israel), where Sibyl died of disease (25 July 1190) along with her two young daughters. These deaths left Guy without a secure claim to the throne and provoked renewed discord among the Franks over the kingship of Jerusalem.

–*Linda Goldsmith*

Bibliography

Edbury, Peter W., "Propaganda and Faction in the Kingdom of Jerusalem: The Background to Hattin," in *Crusaders and Muslims in Twelfth-Century Syria*, ed. Maya Shatzmiller (Leiden: Brill, 1993), pp. 173–189.

Hamilton, Bernard, "Women in the Crusader States: The Queens of Jerusalem, 1100–1190," in *Medieval Women*, ed. Derek Baker (Oxford: Blackwell, 1978), pp. 143–174.

Riley-Smith, Jonathan, "The Crusading Heritage of Guy and Aimery of Lusignan," in *Η Κύπρος και οι Σταυροφορίες / Cyprus and the Crusades*, ed. Nicholas Coureas and Jonathan Riley-Smith (Nicosia: Cyprus Research Centre, 1995), pp. 31–45.

Sicily, Kingdom of

The island of Sicily was conquered and settled by Muslim invaders from North Africa in the ninth century and was reconquered by the Normans of southern Italy in the period 1061–1091. Thereafter the island and various mainland territories came to form a kingdom that became one of the major powers in the Mediterranean region.

The Norman Kingdom

The Norman conquest was led by Robert Guiscard, duke of Apulia and Calabria, and his younger brother Roger. While Robert's participation was important in securing the northeastern part of the island (1061–1062) and Palermo (1072), the conquest was largely conducted by Count Roger, and rule over the island was left in his hands.

Certain features of the conquest foreshadowed the First Crusade: there was sporadic papal encouragement, and contemporary chroniclers stress that this was a holy war on behalf of Christendom. Yet while Pope Gregory VII suggested to Count Roger (in 1076) that he "should seek to spread the worship of the Christian name amongst the pagans" [*The Register of Pope Gregory VII, 1073–1083*, trans. H. E. J. Cowdrey (Oxford: Oxford University Press, 2002), p. 193], in practice many towns surrendered on terms that included the maintenance of Islamic worship and law, and the majority of the island's population remained Muslim until the late twelfth century. Roger I created six Latin bishoprics and founded a number of both Latin- and Greek-rite monasteries, but Christian immigration was slow (and largely went into the east of the island), and conversion slower. Western Sicily remained largely Muslim until the 1230s, when Frederick II transferred many of the remaining Muslims to northern Apulia.

The kingdom played little part in the early crusades to the Holy Land. Roger II, count (1105–1130) and then first king of Sicily (1130–1154), was primarily concerned with consolidating his new kingdom, particularly his rule over the southern Italian mainland. Once this had been achieved (by 1140), his forces conducted campaigns against Muslim North Africa (especially in 1146–1148) and Byzantium. Garrisons were established in several coastal cities in Africa, notably Mahdia (mod. al-Mahdiya, Tunisia), Tripoli (mod. Tarābulus, Libya), Gabès, and Sfax, but while attempts were made to attract Christian immigrants, the primary purpose of these conquests was to control the lucrative trade between Africa and Sicily. Given its involvement in these operations, the kingdom was unlikely to have resources to spare for involvement in the Levant. In addition, there were cordial diplomatic exchanges between Roger's court and the Fāṭimids of Egypt, and indeed the reorganization of the Sicilian administration in the 1140s drew on Fāṭimid practice.

While there had been a substantial southern Italian involvement in the First Crusade, thereafter interest in the Holy Land appears to have waned. Roger II's relations with the rulers of Outremer were poor. The marriage of his mother, Adelaide, to Baldwin I of Jerusalem in 1113 and Baldwin's subsequent repudiation of her left Roger, according to the chronicler William of Tyre, with a mortal hatred against the kingdom of Jerusalem. His unsuccessful claims to succeed his cousin Bohemund II of Antioch after 1130 meant that his relations with that principality were equally hostile. Furthermore, his attacks on the Byzantine Empire in 1147–1148 also contributed to the failure of the Second Crusade in the East.

The Apulian ports, especially Bari, Brindisi, and Otranto, as well as Messina on Sicily, were key embarkation points for pilgrims to the Holy Land, but few southern Italians went there themselves. After a first flush of enthusiasm following the First Crusade, endowments to Holy Land churches in the kingdom of Sicily were relatively few, although the Church of St. Mary of the Latins at Jerusalem did have a wealthy dependency at Agira on the island of Sicily. The military orders established themselves in the kingdom relatively late and (at least at first) on a limited scale. The Order of the Hospital (of St. John) had established separate provinces for Sicily and Apulia by about 1170, but the Templars only established a local organization within the kingdom between 1184 and 1196. The kings offered protection to them and to some of the churches of Outremer, but little material endowment. During the reign of William I (1154–1166) revolts and internal dissension within the kingdom as well as the continued threat of attack from the hostile German Empire contributed to the loss of the Sicilian colonies in North Africa to the Almohads in 1158–1160.

It was only under King William II (1166–1189) that the kingdom started to take a more active part in the crusading movement. An alliance was concluded with King Amalric of Jerusalem to carry out a joint attack on Egypt, although after Amalric's death (1174) the Jerusalemite expedition was abandoned and the Sicilians, forced to make the attempt alone, were defeated. The Sicilian fleet also attacked the Muslim-held Balearic Islands in 1182, primarily in response to Muslim piracy. However, Sicilian attention was then diverted once more toward Byzantium; a major invasion was launched in 1185 but miscarried, despite the capture of Thessalonica. This attack may well have contributed to the decision of the Byzantine emperor, Isaac II Angelos, to conclude an alliance with Saladin. However, the collapse of the kingdom of Jerusalem in 1187 revived interest in the fate of Outremer, and because of its geographical position and its powerful navy, Sicily was able to provide more immediate help to the embattled states in Outremer than other western kingdoms could. The Sicilian fleet (under Margaritus of Brindisi) played a crucial role in supplying and reinforcing the cities of Tyre (mod. Soûr, Lebanon), Tripoli (mod. Trâblous, Lebanon), and Antioch (mod. Antakya, Turkey) in 1187–1188.

Sicily under the Staufen Dynasty

The death of the childless William II in November 1189 led to a succession crisis and to the eventual conquest of the kingdom by Henry VI, Holy Roman Emperor from the

Staufen dynasty (whose wife, Constance, was Roger II's daughter) in 1194. Hence, direct Sicilian contribution to the Third Crusade (1189–1192) was limited. However, with the maritime route to the East becoming increasingly important, Sicily's role as a base for crusading became crucial. Richard I of England and Philip II of France stayed in Sicily during the winter of 1190–1191, and the vanguard of Henry VI's German crusade sailed from Apulian ports and Messina in 1197. Part of the Fourth Crusade (1202–1204) also sailed from these ports directly to the kingdom of Jerusalem, as did the English crusader Simon of Montfort in 1241.

Under Frederick II (king of Sicily 1198–1250), the son of Henry VI and Constance, the kingdom played a much more significant part in the crusade to the East than hitherto. Sicilian ships and troops under the counts of Lesina and Malta reinforced the Fifth Crusade in 1220–1221, and Frederick himself attempted to set off on crusade from Brindisi in 1227 but was forced back by illness, finally doing so in 1228. Frederick's marriage to Isabella II, the heiress of Jerusalem, in 1225 and the birth of their son, Conrad (IV), in 1228 strengthened the links between the kingdoms of Sicily and Jerusalem. From 1231 until 1243 (or perhaps 1242) Sicilian troops garrisoned Tyre, and their leader, Riccardo Filangieri, acted as Conrad's *bailli* (regent) in the kingdom of Jerusalem, although his authority was disputed by the Ibelin family and their supporters. In addition, the military orders received considerable endowment within the kingdom of Sicily in the early thirteenth century, not least from the Staufen rulers' patronage of the Teutonic Order. Henry VI granted the Teutonic Knights houses in Barletta and Palermo in 1197, and a separate province within the order, with four subject commanderies, was established for Apulia by 1225.

The kingdom was involved not only as a participant in the crusading movement but also as a target for crusading. The precedent was set by the crusade preached by Pope Innocent III, who was then the kingdom's regent acting on behalf of its infant king, Frederick, against the German adventurer Markward of Annweiler in 1199–1202. Markward's alliance with the Muslims of Sicily, then in revolt, was used as a justification for this crusade. Once Frederick began to rule the kingdom in person, his relations with the papacy became increasingly difficult and caused a renewal of such crusading activity. Frederick's excommunication by Pope Gregory IX in 1227, for failing to fulfill his crusade vow, led to an invasion of the kingdom by a papal army in 1229–1230. Whether or not this was actually a "crusade" is a moot point; the local chronicler Richard of San Germano expressly contrasted the papal troops, "the army of the keys" (that is, the keys of St. Peter, a papal symbol), with "the army of the crusaders" led by Frederick against them when he returned from the Holy Land; but certainly crusade taxation paid for the papal expedition, and remission of sins was offered to the participants. Frederick's second excommunication (1239) led to a renewal of crusade preaching against him and even to attempts to divert those who had taken vows to go to the Holy Land to fight against him. However, while papal agents attempted to undermine his rule within the kingdom, especially on the mainland, the major theater of military operations was in northern Italy.

After Frederick II's death (1250) there were sporadic, and unsuccessful, papal campaigns against his sons in Sicily. The coronation of his illegitimate son Manfred as king in 1258 led to a more sustained attempt to overthrow Staufen rule. The crusade was the means for this, using crusade preaching, especially by the mendicant orders, to secure recruits and crusade taxation to raise money. Attempts to transfer the kingdom to the younger son of Henry III of England failed because of the general dislike of the project, and especially of paying for it, among Henry's subjects. Sporadic negotiations to secure a settlement with Manfred also failed. Finally, in 1264 Pope Clement IV conferred the kingdom on Charles of Anjou, brother of Louis IX of France. As in the earlier case of Markward of Annweiler, Manfred's use of Muslim troops was one of the principal justifications of this policy. In 1266 Charles conquered the kingdom at the head of an army whose members received the full spiritual privileges accorded to those who had taken the cross.

The Angevin Conquest

As king of Sicily, Charles I of Anjou (1266–1285) pursued an ambitious and expansionary foreign policy in the Mediterranean. His involvement with Frankish Greece had been anticipated by Manfred, who had married the daughter of the despot of Epiros and in 1259 had sent troops to support Epiros and Achaia against the resurgent Empire of Nicaea, a project that was ended by the defeat of the allies at the battle of Pelagonia. By the Treaty of Viterbo (1267) Charles secured extensive rights in Greece, including suzerainty over Achaia (from Baldwin II, former Latin emperor of Constantinople), and the marriage of the heiress of the principality to his younger son, Philip, in 1271. Sicilian troops and money henceforth underpinned the defense of Frankish Greece against the Byzantines.

Charles also persuaded his brother Louis IX of France to divert his second crusade from the Holy Land to Tunis (1270). The motives for this were purely political, to ensure the continued payment of the tribute that the rulers of Tunisia had been accustomed to pay to the kings of Sicily since the time of Roger II. Finally, in 1277 Charles bought out the claims of Mary of Antioch to the kingship of Jerusalem, proclaimed himself king, and sent Roger of San Severino to Acre (mod. ʿAkko, Israel) to rule the kingdom as his representative. Mary's claims had never been accepted by the High Court of Jerusalem, but Roger was able to displace King Hugh (II of Cyprus) and take over. Meanwhile Charles was preparing to launch an expedition against Byzantium, which, even if not actually declared a crusade, had papal sanction, the support of crusade taxation, and the participation of those vowed to the crusade.

These ambitious plans were destroyed by a revolt in Sicily at Easter 1282, known as the Sicilian Vespers, that led to the takeover of the island of Sicily by King Peter III of Aragon and thereafter to the long-standing conflict between the two rival kingdoms of "Sicily": the island ruled by the Aragonese dynasty and the southern Italian mainland under the Angevins. Pope Martin IV declared Charles's attempts to reconquer Sicily to be a crusade, the king of France was drawn into the conflict, and crusade preaching and taxation boosted the Angevin military effort. Yet despite this support the campaigns were consistently defeated, and eventually King Charles II (1285–1309) admitted defeat at the Peace of Caltebellota in 1302.

Conclusions

Despite its key central position in the Mediterranean and the wealth and military (and especially naval) power of the kingdom created by Roger II, the Sicilian contribution to the crusades in the Holy Land was surprisingly limited and at times deleterious. The circumstances of its creation meant that its early rulers were above all concerned with ensuring its survival, until peace was finally made with the Holy Roman Empire in 1177. The presence of a very substantial Muslim population on the island also acted as a brake on any Sicilian crusade against the infidel, at least until immigration, some conversions, and later forcible relocation of Muslims to Apulia made the population of the island overwhelmingly Christian. Campaigns against North Africa were undertaken for

pragmatic reasons, not as part of a crusade, and those against the Byzantine Empire undermined Christian unity. The increased Sicilian involvement in the crusade from 1174 onward was hampered by domestic political problems and the conflict of the papacy with the Staufen rulers. Sicily became a target for the "political" crusades of the thirteenth century, and once Charles of Anjou became king, he used the crusade as a tool to further his own ambitions. Even as nominal king of Jerusalem, his real concern was with the Balkans and the Byzantine Empire, not the defense of his new kingdom. As the remains of the Christian states in Outremer were collapsing before the Mamlūks, the papacy was encouraging crusades against Christians within the Sicilian kingdom.

–G. A. Loud

Bibliography

Abulafia, David, "The Norman Kingdom of Africa and the Norman Expeditions to Majorca and the Muslim Mediterranean," in *Anglo-Norman Studies*, VII: *Proceedings of the Battle Conference 1984,* ed. R. Allen Brown (Woodbridge, UK: Boydell, 1985), pp. 26–49.

Dunbabin, Jean, *Charles I of Anjou* (Harlow, UK: Longman, 1998).

Housley, Norman, *The Italian Crusade: The Papal Angevin Alliance and the Crusades against Christian Lay Powers, 1254–1343* (Oxford: Oxford University Press, 1982).

Kennan, Elizabeth, "Innocent III and the First Political Crusade," *Traditio* 27 (1971), 231–249.

Loud, Graham A., "Norman Italy and the Holy Land," in *The Horns of Hattin,* ed. Benjamin Z. Kedar (Jerusalem: Israel Exploration Society, 1992), pp. 49–62.

Il Mezzogiorno normanno-svevo e le Crociate, ed. Giosuè Musca (Bari: Dedalo, 2002).

Strayer, Joseph R., "The Political Crusades of the Thirteenth Century," in *A History of the Crusades,* ed. Kenneth M. Setton et al., 2d ed., 6 vols. (Madison: University of Wisconsin Press, 1969–1989), 2:343–375.

Wieruszowski, Helene, "The Norman Kingdom of Sicily and the Crusades," in *A History of the Crusades,* ed. Kenneth M. Setton et al., 2d ed., 6 vols. (Madison: University of Wisconsin Press, 1969–1989), 2:3–42.

Siege Warfare

Siege technology was an aspect of medieval warfare that ranged in scope from very small-scale operations, as when some Byzantine local forces drove off nomad raiders by erecting a barricade of carts around their church, to massive endeavours involving thousands of troops and huge expenditure. It was a field in which Byzantine and Muslim supe-

Siege works and engines from the time of the Crusades. (Bettmann/Corbis)

riority over Western Europe was initially pronounced. Despite their tendency to rely on established tactics and weaponry, the Byzantines possessed very advanced siege machines. For example the earliest illustrations of a great crossbow mounted on a chassis comes from an eleventh-century Byzantine source, and the late thirteenth-century Western scholar Egidio Colonna attributed the *biffa* (form of trebuchet) with an adjustable counterweight to the Romans, by which he probably meant the Byzantines.

Christian Armies

The crusaders arrived in the Near East with less sophisticated traditions. In attack they might dig trenches to isolate the besieged from relief, form a *testudo* (a close group of men with their shields interlocked over their heads) to enable men to force a breach, and even pose as a band of lost travelers in an attempt to trick the night watchman at Shaizar (mod. Shayzar, Syria) to open his gate. While besieging Damascus in 1148, a crusader army found itself counter-besieged in its own camp by defending forces, but two generations later, a crusader cavalry charge broke a Muslim garrison unit that emerged from the besieged city of Acre (mod. 'Akko, Israel) to challenge them during the Third Crusade (1189–1192).

In defense, castles in Outremer had a minimal impact on full-scale invasions, though it took the Muslims a long time to reduce those that could not be taken by surprise. According to the Rule of the Hospitallers, the gates of castles near the frontier were closed after compline, the last service of the day, and were not to be opened until the following morning. The Arab writer Usāma Ibn Munqidh described how one group of crusader cavalry dismounted outside the gate of a twelfth century castle and used their lances as pikes to defend its entrance. On another occasion, those making a sortie included men riding mules, though whether they were mounted infantry or knights who lacked proper mounts is unclear. Some Frankish garrisons defended themselves so vigorously that anyone coming within range of their walls had to wear armor.

The crusaders came to the East with a tradition of wooden siege engines, which were vulnerable to the incendiary weapons of both Byzantines and Muslims. For example, the First Crusade (1096–1099) used a wooden tower on wheels or rollers during its attack on Albara (mod. al-Bārah, Syria); it had knights on top, while other armored men pushed it forward. The Franks' two wooden siege towers used during an attack on Tyre (mod. Soûr, Lebanon) in 1111–1112 contained rams suspended by ropes. Both were burned by the defenders. The *chats châteaux* (combined shelters and siege towers), used against Damietta during the crusade of King Louis IX of France to the East (1248–1254), enabled the besiegers to protect their miners attacking the base of a wall and also shoot at enemies defending the parapet of that wall. The troops inside wooden siege towers were said to have stored water and vinegar to douse fires. In turn crusader archers shot fire-arrows at the bundles of straw that defenders would hang in front of their walls as buffers against stones or rams.

Although the Franks did not use stone-throwing mangonels in such numbers as did their Muslim foes, they clearly had the latest versions, including *boves,* a type of mangonel with adjustable counterweights. Those defending Acre in 1291 could throw a stone whose weight has been translated as 45 kilograms (99 lb.) by some historians [D. P. Little, "The Fall of 'Akka in 690/1291: The Muslim Version," in *Studies in Islamic History and Civilization in Honour of Professor David Ayalon,* ed. M. Sharon (Leiden: Brill, 1986), pp. 159–181]. The Western European *espringal* was an anti-personnel weapon that came in various sizes, the best being made of beech, elm, or oak. Its torsion power was provided by twisted skeins or ropes of horse or cattle hair, and it could shoot a truly massive arrow.

The reconquest of the Iberian Peninsula (*Reconquista*) was primarily aimed at cities, several of which were so large or well fortified that sieges sometimes took years. Occasionally the final struggle was resolved by street fighting of almost modern savagery. Siege engineering in the Christian states of northern Iberia was, of course, greatly influenced by that of the Muslim south. For example, the Spanish *algarrada* came from the Arabic *al-'arrāda,* which was a small antipersonnel mangonel. The *manganell turquès* ("Turkish mangonel") mentioned in early thirteenth-century Aragon was probably a new form, perhaps with an adjustable counterweight.

Muslim Armies

Muslim armies used various siege techniques. Light troops went ahead to impose a blockade, and orchards outside the city were progressively destroyed in an attempt to induce surrender, while the besiegers defended themselves with palisades and entrenchments. A thirteenth-century military manual by the writer al-Harawī, based upon long established procedures, lists the sequence of events as follows: First the commander ordered his laborers to assemble siege machines. Then bombardment began with the smallest engines, followed by those of greater power to put the enemy under increasing psychological pressure. The besiegers were also to post units of cavalry an arrow-shot from each enemy gate as a precaution against sorties.

Saladin's siege train included a variety of specialist troops such as engineers, fire troops, flamethrower operators, surveyors, and assorted craftsmen. It is also clear that the Muslims did more mining than crusader or Frankish armies, and they used the originally Chinese tactic of erecting mounds of earth as firing positions for stone-throwing machines throughout the medieval period and well into the early mod-

ern era. Such machines gradually demolished the enemy's battlements so that defending archers lacked cover. Assault parties were commanded by the best officers, while the troops themselves carried fire weapons and tools to further demolish the enemy wall. A further variation was to use any numerical advantage to make small attacks against different parts of the wall and thus exhaust the garrison.

In defense, Muslim garrisons resorted to various stratagems, including psychological warfare: for example, they sent men with torches out of a postern gate by night, who then returned with their torches extinguished and emerged again, making the garrison appear more formidable. Local militias used their knowledge of surrounding orchards and gardens to destroy small groups of invaders, as happened during the crusader attack on Damascus in 1148. During the siege of Acre in the course of the Third Crusade, the son of a coppersmith surpassed professional fire-troops by designing a more effective way of shooting Greek Fire (the petroleum-based incendiary liquid, which is still widely, though perhaps wrongly, regarded as the "secret weapon" that enabled the Byzantine Empire to survive against repeated Arab-Muslim attacks during the early medieval period), thereby destroying the crusaders' siege engines. During this same siege, the defenders also used a grappling hook to ensnare one of the leading men in the army of Richard the Lionheart, hauling him up the wall.

The counterweight mangonel, or trebuchet, is generally considered to have been invented in the Middle East during the twelfth century, though there is evidence that a primitive counterweight *manjanīq* had been known in the Muslim area two centuries earlier. This "Persian" weapon was first illustrated and described in a military treatise written by Murdā al-Ṭarsūsī for Saladin. Nevertheless, the counterweight trebuchet did not have a major impact on siege warfare until the start of the thirteenth century.

Al-Ṭarsūsī also described well-established forms of man-powered *manjanīqs,* of which the "Arab" type was considered most reliable. It consisted of a wooden frame with a roof and three walls to protect a team of rope-pullers inside. The "Turkish" type required less timber and was simpler to erect, while the "Frankish" or "Rūmī" (i.e., Western or Byzantine) version had a more stable arm and axle. The smallest form (Arab. *lu'ab*) was mounted on a single pole and had the smallest payload and shortest range, but could shoot in any direction. By the late thirteenth century, some of the largest counterweight machines were prefabricated and transported to the scene of a siege in pieces. As elsewhere, most mangonels and other siege engines could also be used defensively from the top of fortified towers.

Apart from unclear references to a "black bull-like" *manjanīq* that shot large arrows rather than stones, and may therefore not have been a beam-sling weapon at all, there were several bolt-shooting machines. These included the great crossbow, which was sometimes mounted on a frame or pedestal. This weapon had been known for centuries; it was spanned by a windlass or other mechanical means. The *qaws al-ziyār,* known in Europe as the *espringal,* was another fearsome weapon spanned by a winch or windlass. It had two separate "bow arms" thrust through tightly twisted skeins of animal hair, silk, sinew, or a mixture of these. The monstrous version described by al-Ṭarsūsī had the power of twenty men, but even in fourteenth-century Morocco, it took eleven mules to carry a dismantled *qaws al-ziyār*. The ordinary *ziyār* appears to have been a development of the single-armed stone-throwing engine known in Late Roman times as an onager.

Mobile wooden sheds to protect men working rams were used by Islamic armies, as they were by crusader and Byzantine forces, but, like the *burj* (wooden siege tower), were ideal targets for Greek Fire and other forms of fire weapon. Perhaps for this reason, they largely fell out of use from the late thirteenth century. Other more common devices were screens and mantlets to protect sappers and miners, which were commonly used by virtually all medieval armies. One example used during the final siege of Acre by the Mamlūks in 1291 consisted of a large sheet of felt on a system of pulleys. It not only hid individual men but absorbed mangonel stones and crossbow bolts. The *zahafah* is more obscure, but may have been a fixed immobile wooden tower for archers.

Fire weapons became steadily more effective. In twelfth-century Syria, for example, clay and glass grenades were designed for different purposes, some apparently being antipersonnel weapons. Yet the decline of fire weapons from the end of the fourteenth century may have resulted from their own success in driving wooden and other inflammable targets from the battlefield.

Siege technology in the western Muslim world was virtually identical to that in the Near and Middle East and became particularly sophisticated under the Almohads in the later twelfth century. Here a commander sometimes had a *marqaba* (observation post) erected from which he could direct operations. Another notable feature of sieges in these western regions was the building of towns, complete with their own stone fortifications, next to the city under attack; the walls and minaret of one such "counter city" still stand at al-Manṣūra outside Tlemcen in North Africa. Otherwise the usual sequence of events was followed. Defenders fought outside their walls until convinced that the attackers could not be driven away. In fourteenth-century Granada, this stage was followed by walling up all gates except those needed for sorties. Particularly advanced semiexplosive pyrotechnics also appeared in North Africa and al-Andalus in the late thirteenth century, some of them possibly incorporating primitive gunpowder. Knowledge of saltpeter, essential in the making of gunpowder, already existed in the Middle East, and traces are said to have been found in ceramic grenades found at the sites of thirteenth- or even twelfth-century sieges. It was not, however, until the fourteenth century that gunpowder was used widely in siege warfare, not only in primitive guns but as rockets and as an incendiary substance.

–David Nicolle

Bibliography

Cathcart-King, David J., "The Trebuchet and Other Siege Engines," *Château Gaillard* 9–10 (1982), 457–469.

Chevedden, Paul E., "Fortifications and the Development of Defensive Planning in the Latin East," in *The Circle of War in the Middle Ages,* ed. Donald J. Kagay and L. J. Andrew Villalon (Woodbridge, UK: Boydell, 1999), pp. 33–43.

Ellenblum, Ronnie, "Frankish and Muslim Siege Warfare and the Construction of Frankish Concentric Castles," in *Dei Gesta per Francos,* ed. Michel Balard, Benjamin Z. Kedar, and Jonathan Riley-Smith (Aldershot, UK: Ashgate, 2001), pp. 187–198.

Finó, Jean-François, "Le feu et ses usages militaires," *Gladius* 9 (1970), 15–30.

———, "Machines de jet médiévales," *Gladius* 10 (1972), 25–43.

Hill, Donald R., "Trebuchets," *Viator* 4 (1973), 99–114.

Huuri, Kalervo, *Zur Geschichte des mittelalterlichen Geschützwesens aus orientalischen Quellen* (Helsinki: Societas Orientalis Fennica, 1941).

Liebel, Jean, *Springalds and Great Crossbows* (Leeds: Royal Armouries, 1998).

Marshall, Christopher J., *Warfare in the Latin East, 1192–1291* (Cambridge: Cambridge University Press, 1991).

The Medieval City under Siege, ed. Ivy A. Corfis and Michael Wolfe (Woodbridge, UK: Boydell, 1995).

Rogers, Randall, *Latin Siege Warfare in the Twelfth Century* (Oxford: Oxford University Press, 1992).

Sander, E., "Der Belagerungskrieg im Mittelalter," *Historische Zeitschrift* 105 (1941), 99–110.

Smail, Raymond C., *Crusading Warfare, 1097–1193* (Cambridge: Cambridge University Press, 1956).

Sourdel-Thomine, Janine, "Les Conseils du Sayh al Harawi à un prince ayyubide," *Bulletin d'études orientales* 17 (1961–62), 205–266.

al-Ṭarsūsī, Murḍā Ibn 'Ali Murḍā, "Un traité d'armurerie composé pour Saladin," ed. and trans. Claude Cahen, *Bulletin d'études orientales,* 12 (1947–1948), 108–126.

Udina Martorell, Frederic, *Ingenieria militar en las cronicas catalanas* (Barcelona: Datmau, 1971).

Siegfried von Feuchtwangen (d. 1311)

Grand master of the Teutonic Order (1303–1311), who was responsible for moving the order's headquarters from Venice to Marienburg (mod. Malbork, Poland) in Prussia.

In 1298 Siegfried was German master; a year later he acted as commander of Vienna. In mid-October 1303 he was elected grand master at a chapter in Elbing (mod. Elbląg, Poland). His predecessor Gottfried von Hohenlohe, who probably had been pressed to resign, did not acknowledge the new master and claimed the office for himself. Siegfried went to the order's headquarters at Venice to assert his authority and proceeded to arrange their transfer to Prussia. The reasons for this were pressing. Venice had become an insecure abode because of the town's conflict with the pope, and the brothers of the Teutonic Order, terrified by the recent suppression of the Templars, feared for the order's independence from secular powers. Siegfried therefore proposed a move to Prussia, which had been made more secure as a result of the order's occupation of the neighboring province of Pomerelia.

On 14 September 1309, Siegfried and his entourage entered Marienburg, where they established their new headquarters. From this time crusading in the Mediterranean region ceased to be an objective for the order. Siegfried died on 5 March 1311 at Marienburg. He was buried in the cathedral at Kulmsee.

–Axel Ehlers

Bibliography

Christiansen, Eric, *The Northern Crusades,* 2d ed. (London: Penguin, 1997).

Nieß, Ulrich, "Siegfried von Feuchtwangen," in *Die Hochmeister des Deutschen Ordens, 1190–1994,* ed. Udo Arnold (Marburg: Elwert, 1998), pp. 51–56.

Urban, William, *The Samogitian Crusade* (Chicago: Lithuanian Research and Studies Center, 1989).

Sigismund of Luxembourg (1368–1437)

King of Hungary (1387–1437), Germany (1410–1437), and Bohemia (1420–1437) and Holy Roman Emperor (1433–1437), Sigismund of Luxembourg was the leader of the Nikopolis Crusade (1396) against the Ottoman Turks and organizer of crusades against the Hussites in Bohemia (1420–1433).

Sigismund was the son of Charles IV of Luxembourg, Holy Roman Emperor and king of Bohemia, and Elisabeth of Pomerania. He acquired the Hungarian crown by marriage to the kingdom's last Angevin queen, Mary, daughter of King Louis I. After his wife's death, he survived a long political crisis (1397–1403) to rule the kingdom efficiently with unparalleled self confidence until his death. Hungary, which he accepted as his adopted country, offered a solid base for his far-reaching ambitions. He resided at Buda (mod. Budapest, Hungary) and Bratislava, although his court remained basically international.

Sigismund's outstanding executive ability and ambitious character became evident during his preparations for the Nikopolis Crusade (1396), the last large, pan-European crusade against the Turks, which he led personally. Although the campaign ended in spectacular defeat at the battle of Nikopolis (25 September 1396; according to some scholars 28 September) and a breathtaking escape for him, he never gave up his ambitions; within a few years he gained other important crowns: he was elected king of Germany (king of the Romans) on the death of Rupert of the Palatinate (1410) and of Bohemia on the death of his elder brother Wenceslas IV. Sigismund was the last Holy Roman Emperor (crowned 1433) who believed himself to be the lord of all Christian Europe both on a representative level and in reality, and behaved so. One of the most traveled rulers of his time, he tried to intervene personally in all parts of Europe in order to solve political problems with his admired charm, intellect, and talent for languages. He was interested in the technical and military novelties of his time, such as paper mills and the textile industry, and issued military manuals for the Holy Roman Empire and Hungary. His crusades against the Ottoman Empire and the Hussites were, like his commercial embargo against Venice, means intended to achieve his universal political goals.

Sigismund had several major political successes. He brought the Great Schism of the papacy to an end at the Council of Konstanz (1417); he ended the Hussite wars by diplomacy and compromise after sustaining a series of humiliating defeats; and he negotiated a peace between the Teutonic Order and the kingdom of Poland. He realized correctly that successful management of the Turkish problem was a necessary condition to his rule in Hungary, and from the beginning of his reign he led campaigns (many of them in person) to the frontier areas against the Turks and their local allies, sometimes spending lengthy periods there (e.g., 1426–1428). After a victory over Bosnia, he established the secular Order of the Dragon (1408), in order to bind the rulers of Serbia, Wallachia, and Bosnia into an anti-Ottoman coalition. His most enduring achievement was the establishment of a fortress system, centered on Belgrade, to defend the southern frontiers of Hungary; it proved effective until the capture of Belgrade by the Ottomans in 1521. Even at the age of sixty he went to war to recapture the castle of Golubac (1428), although he was defeated again. His diplomatic horizon extended to the Middle East, where he established relations and collaborated with the khanate of the Golden Horde against the Ottoman Turks.

–László Veszprémy

Bibliography

Hoensch, Jörg K., *Kaiser Sigismund: Herrscher an der Schwelle der Neuzeit, 1368–1437* (München: Beck, 1996).

Itinerar König und Kaiser Sigismunds von Luxemburg, 1368–1437, ed. Jörg K. Hoensch (Warendorf: Fahlbusch, 1995).

Mályusz, Elemér, *Kaiser Sigismund in Ungarn, 1387–1437* (Budapest: Akadémiai, 1990).

Sigismund von Luxemburg: Kaiser und König in Mitteleuropa 1387–1437, ed. Josef Macek, Ernő Marosi, and Ferdinand Seibt (Warendorf: Fahlbusch, 1994).

Das Zeitalter König Sigismunds in Ungarn und im Deutschen Reich, ed. Tilmann Schmidt and Péter Gunst (Debrecen: Debrecen University Press, 2000).

Sigurd Jorsalfar (1090–1130)

King of Norway (1103–1130) and leader of a seaborne crusade to the Holy Land.

Sigurd became joint king of Norway along with his brothers Eystein and Olaf after their father, King Magnus III Barelegs, was killed during a raid in Ireland (1103). Sigurd's decision to lead an expedition to the East fell in the third or fourth year of the kings' joint reign and was undoubtedly prompted both by the recent success of the First Crusade (1096–1099) and the experiences of Norsemen returning from travel—and in some cases military service—in Byzantium and Palestine.

The precise chronology of the Norwegian expedition is unclear. Sigurd and his followers seem to have left Norway between 1106 and 1108 and to have reached the Holy Land by 1110 at the latest. The Norwegian fleet of some sixty ships sailed first to England, where it overwintered, sailing on to Galicia in the spring. The crusaders spent a further winter in Spain, moving south along the Portuguese and Andalusian coasts the next spring; by the time they reached the Strait of Gibraltar they had defeated several Muslim forces on both land and sea and had captured a number of enemy vessels. The warlike, crusading character of the expedition was clearly confirmed when the fleet entered the western Mediterranean and carried out the first recorded attack by a Christian force on the Muslim-held Balearic Islands. The Norwegians landed on the island of Formentera, to the south of Ibiza, where they assaulted and stormed a cave fortress (probably a pirate base), capturing large quantities of booty, and they followed up this success with raids on the islands of Ibiza and Menorca (1108 or 1109). The fleet then proceeded to Sicily, where it made a lengthy stay, arriving at Jaffa (mod. Tel Aviv-Yafo, Israel) at the end of the summer sailing season.

The Norwegians were well received by King Baldwin I of Jerusalem, who presented Sigurd with a relic of the True Cross. After visiting Jerusalem and the river Jordan, they enlisted in Baldwin's efforts to reduce the Muslim-held cities of the Palestinian coast, providing the naval blockade during the siege of the port of Sidon (mod. Saïda, Lebanon), which surrendered in December 1110. Probably in early 1111 Sigurd and his followers sailed for Constantinople (mod. İstanbul, Turkey), where they handed over their ships to the Byzantine emperor Alexios I Komnenos and returned to Norway by the land route through Russia.

Sigurd's crusading exploits, which earned him his surname Jorsalfar ("Jerusalem-farer"), were celebrated in several Norse sagas (*Ágrip af Nóregskonunga sögum, Morkinskinna, Fagrskinna,* and Snorri Sturluson's *Heimskringla*) and are also mentioned in Latin sources. The deaths of the co-kings Olaf (1115) and Eystein (1123) left Sigurd as sole ruler of Norway; the remainder of his reign was largely peaceful.

–Alan V. Murray

Bibliography

Blöndal, Sigfús, and Benedikt S. Benedikz, *The Varangians of Byzantium* (Cambridge: Cambridge University Press, 1978).

Doxey, Gary B., "Norwegian Crusaders and the Balearic Islands," *Scandinavian Studies* 68 (1996), 139–160.

Simon of Montfort (d. 1218)

Participant in the Fourth Crusade (1202–1204), first leader of the Albigensian Crusade (1209–1229), and subsequently count of Toulouse (1216–1218).

Simon was born around 1160, a younger son of Simon of Montfort-l'Amaury, lord of Rochefort in the Ile-de-France, and Amice of Leicester. By 1200 he had established a solid reputation as a brave and gifted soldier of pious and virtuous disposition. When, therefore, together with his brother Guy of La Ferté-Alais (a veteran of the Third Crusade), he joined the Fourth Crusade in 1202, he could expect to play a leading role, but he was to be disappointed.

Committed to the ideal of the crusade as war against the infidel, Simon and his friend Abbot Guy of Vaux-de-Cernay opposed the diversion of the army against the Christian city of Zara (mod. Zadar, Croatia). Knowing that Abbot Guy had received a letter from Pope Innocent III forbidding an attack, and that the power of excommunication could be used to enforce this directive, he informed the defenders, and so provoked the resistance that led to the crusader attack on the city. Simon, Guy, and Engeran of Boves led the opposition to the treaty with the Greek prince Alexios Angelos; after it was concluded, they left the main crusade for Palestine, where Simon fought with distinction. On his return, he went to England, where he had been recognized as earl of Leicester in succession to his maternal uncle by 1206.

In 1209 Simon accepted an invitation from the duke of Burgundy to lead an army in the papal crusade against the

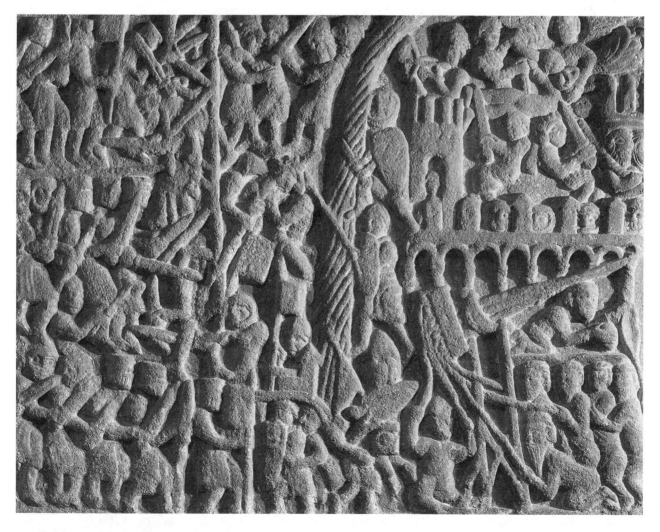

Detail of the sarcophagus of Simon of Montfort, thirteenth century, St. Nazaire, Carcassonne, France. (Erich Lessing/Art Resource)

Albigensians of the Languedoc. For a zealot such as Simon, the threat posed by the heretic, the enemy within, was even greater than that posed by the infidel. Simon's military prowess and undoubted bravery won admiration, but the callous brutality of the campaign shocked even contemporaries. In July 1209 he took Béziers, and Carcassonne soon afterward surrendered. Elected leader, and bearing the title of viscount in each place, he thereafter governed wisely. In 1210 he took Albi, and besieged Toulouse in 1211, finally defeating Count Raymond VI of Toulouse at Castelnaudry. At the battle of Muret (12 September 1213), he defeated a coalition led by King Peter II of Aragon, who was killed. However, resistance continued, and in 1215 Prince Louis (VIII) came to his aid. In April 1216 Simon did homage to King Philip II of France for all the lands formerly held by Raymond VI.

Simon was killed on 25 June 1218 during the siege of Toulouse, which had readmitted Count Raymond in September 1217. By his wife Alice of Montmorency, whom he had married around 1190, he left four sons and two daughters, including Simon, earl of Leicester.

–K. S. B. Keats-Rohan

See also: Jerusalem, (Latin) Kingdom of

Bibliography

Canet, Victor, *Simon de Montfort et la croisade contre les Albigeois* (Lille: Société de Saint-Augustin, 1891).

Dossat, Yves, "Simon de Montfort," in *Paix de Dieu et guerre sainte en Languedoc en XIIIe siècle,* ed. Marie-Humbert Vicaire (Toulouse: Privat, 1969), pp. 281–302.

Hamilton, Bernard, *The Albigensian Crusade* (London: Historical Association, 1974).

Keck, Christine, "L'entourage de Simon de Montfort pendant la Croisade albigeoise et l'établissement territorial des crucesignati," in *La Croisade albigeoise,* ed. Michel Roquebert (Carcassonne: Centre d'Etudes Cathares, 2004), pp. 235–243.

Oldenburg, Zoe, *Massacre at Montségur: A History of the Albigensian Crusade* (London: Minerva, 1968).

Roscher, Helmut, *Papst Innocenz III. und die Kreuzügge* (Göttingen: Vandenhoeck & Ruprecht, 1969).

Sumption, Jonathan, *The Albigensian Crusade* (London: Faber, 1978)

Sinai, Mount

The Greek Orthodox monastery of St. Catherine at Mount Sinai (mod. Gebel Mûsa, Egypt) was located at a site sacred to Jews, Christians, and Muslims, where, according to tra-

dition, the biblical prophet Moses ascended to bring down the Ten Commandments (Ex. 19–20).

The site began to attract Christian monks at an early date. In addition to its biblical associations, it was believed that the body of the martyr Catherine of Alexandria (d. 307) had been miraculously transported there. By the late fourth century it had a cenobitic community and several small churches; in the sixth century, the Byzantine emperor Justinian I had the present church and surrounding walls constructed to protect the monks from Bedouin raiders. Following the Islamic conquests of the seventh century, a provision in the testament attributed to Muḥammad protected the monastery, relieving it from the payment of taxes. Western interest in the monastery increased after Abbot Symeon, a Greek originating from Sicily, visited France in 1025, depositing relics of St. Catherine at Rouen and successfully diffusing the veneration of the saint in the West. Western pilgrims began to visit Sinai via the ports of Alexandria and Gaza.

After the First Crusade (1096–1099) and the resultant establishment of the kingdom of Jerusalem in Palestine, such visits increased, although the monastery remained outside Frankish-controlled territory throughout the period 1099–1291. A handbook for pilgrims, probably written during the reign of King Fulk of Jerusalem (1131–1143), alludes to the monks' illustrious reputation and widespread fame, on account of which no one dared to harm them. Nonetheless, when King Baldwin I wished to visit them during his expedition to 'Aqaba, the monks dissuaded him, fearing Muslim reprisals. The monastery's visitors included the future Templar master Philip of Milly, who was given a relic of St. Catherine.

The abbot of Mount Sinai, who also had the rank of a Greek Orthodox archbishop, was the only Orthodox prelate whom the Franks recognized as a full diocesan bishop; he was a suffragan of the Latin metropolitan of Petra. The abbot and monks nonetheless continued to recognize the jurisdiction of the Orthodox patriarchs of Constantinople. Euthymios, the Orthodox patriarch of Jerusalem, was resident in Sinai, dying there in 1222. The monastery had properties and daughter houses in areas under Latin control, such as Acre (mod. 'Akko, Israel), Laodikeia (al-Lathqiyah, Syria), Antioch (mod. Antakya, Turkey), Crete, and Cyprus, as well as two confraternities in Constantinople.

By 1291 Frankish rule had ended in Palestine, Syria, and Constantinople, but continued in Crete (to 1571) and Cyprus (1668). On account of this, the abbots of Mount

Sinai recognized papal jurisdiction, requesting the popes throughout the thirteenth and fourteenth centuries to protect their properties in Venetian Crete and Lusignan Cyprus. In Crete during this period, Latin nobles and prelates damaged and occupied the monastery's properties, forcing the monks to pay tithes and other exactions, in violation of the provisions of the Fourth Lateran Council (1215) and notwithstanding the attempts of Honorius III, Gregory IX, and John XXII to protect the monastery. In Cyprus the monastery had the church of St. Symeon in Famagusta (the chief port of the island), oratories in deserted areas of the island, and an annual income of one gold pound from market taxes. The monastery exported foodstuffs and clothing from Crete, but piracy was a problem, and in 1328 the pope ordered the punishment of John Saut, a Latin preying on the monastery's ships.

–*Nicholas Coureas*

Bibliography

Amantos, Konstantinos, Σύντομος Ιστορία της Ιεράς Μονής του Σινα (Thessaloniki: Etaireia Makedonikon Spoudon, 1953).

Coureas, Nicholas, "The Orthodox Monastery of Mt. Sinai and Papal Protection of its Cretan and Cypriot Properties," in *Autour de la Première Croisade: Actes du Colloque de la Society for the Study of the Crusades and the Latin East (Clermont-Ferrand, 22–25 juin 1995)*, ed. Michel Balard (Paris: Publications de la Sorbonne, 1996), pp. 474–483.

Hamilton, Bernard, *The Latin Church in the Crusader States: The Secular Church* (London: Ashgate, 1980).

Hofman, George, "Lettere pontifice edite et inedite," *Orientalia Christiana Periodica* 17 (1951), 298–303.

Al-Sinnabrāh, Battle of (1113)

A defeat of the army of Baldwin I of Jerusalem by a Turkish coalition led by Mawdūd, *atabeg* of Mosul, and Ṭughtigīn, *atabeg* of Damascus, who had launched a joint attack on the kingdom of Jerusalem at the instigation of the Saljūq sultan Muḥammad.

The combined Turkish armies invaded Galilee in late May 1113, whereupon Baldwin I summoned assistance from the principality of Antioch and the county of Tripoli, but without waiting for reinforcements to arrive, moved against the invasion with some 700 knights and 4,000 foot soldiers. Near the village of al-Sinnabrāh, south of Lake Tiberias, the Franks were lured into an ambush in which they suffered heavy casualties and then retreated to a hilltop position west of Tiberias (mod. Teverya, Israel) on 28 June 1113. Although joined there by contingents under Prince Roger of Antioch and Count Pons of Tripoli, Baldwin did not dare attack, and for the next two months much of the countryside of the kingdom was under the effective control of the Turks, who ravaged as far as Jaffa (mod. Tel Aviv-Yafo, Israel) and Jerusalem, finally withdrawing at the end of August, when the Frankish forces had been swelled by large numbers of pilgrims.

–*Alan V. Murray*

Bibliography

Röhricht, Reinhold, *Geschichte des Königreichs Jerusalem (1100–1291)* (Innsbruck: Wagner, 1898).

Sis

Sis (mod. Kozan, Turkey) was a fortress and town that was the capital of the Armenian kingdom of Cilicia (1198–1375). It lay at the foot of the Taurus Mountains on a tributary of the Pyramus (mod. Ceyhan Nehri).

The earliest mentions of Sis are as a frontier fortress during the wars between the Byzantines and the 'Abbāsid caliphs; it was captured by the Byzantines in 962. Mentions of Sis in the early crusade period are scarce; it was apparently taken by the Rupenid prince T'oros I in 1113–1114. Situated some 50 kilometers (c. 31 mi.) south of the original Rupenid base at Vahga in the mountains, it gave better access to the plain, and it seems to have been the prince's chief residence from the time of Mleh (1169–1175). While at this time it lacked a bishop, there was an archbishop by 1197, and after the fall of Hromgla (1292) Sis became the seat of the catholicos of the Armenian Orthodox Church. The coronation of King Leon I of Armenia took place at Tarsos (mod. Tarsus, Turkey), but later ceremonies were held at Sis (Leon invested his intended heir there in 1211), and it became the regular seat of the royal court.

The ruined fortress, high on an isolated mountaintop above the town, is still impressive, but the town itself was never walled. The royal palace and ecclesiastical complex on the slopes of the citadel had some protection but were exposed to serious attacks. From the later thirteenth century Mamlūk raids repeatedly sacked the town; in 1266 the army of Sultan Baybars I burned the cathedral and sacked the royal treasury; in 1302 King Het'um II was nearly captured from among fugitives making for the citadel; in 1337 the citadel was itself sacked. Sis remained the capital of the weakened kingdom until its final capture by the Mamlūks in 1375.

–Angus Stewart

Bibliography

The Cilician Kingdom of Armenia, ed. Thomas S. R. Boase (Edinburgh: Scottish Academic Press, 1978).

Edwards, Robert W., *The Fortifications of Armenian Cilicia* (Washington, DC: Dumbarton Oaks, 1987), pp. 233–237.

Hellenkemper, Hansgard, *Burgen der Kreuzritterzeit in der Grafschaft Edessa und im Königreich Kleinarmenien* (Bonn: Habelt, 1976).

Smpad the Constable (1208–1276)

An Armenian historian and legist, elder brother of Het'um I, king of Armenia.

Smpad (also Smbat, Sempad) served his brother loyally and was constable (Arm. *sparapet*) of the Armenian kingdom. In 1247–1250 Het'um sent Smpad on a diplomatic mission to the Mongol khan Güyük, and a letter written by the constable describing his journey survives; intended for his brothers-in-law, King Henry I of Cyprus and John of Ibelin, it was also received by King Louis IX of France. Smpad died fighting against a Mamlūk-inspired Turcoman invasion in 1276.

Smpad was the author of an important chronicle, of which two versions survive, one of them abbreviated and continued to 1331. The early accounts largely follow the chronicles of Matthew of Edessa and Gregory the Priest, but with important additions; for later years he appears to have used a variety of sources, including Frankish and possibly Byzantine works, as well as his own experiences. He also made a translation of the *Assizes of Antioch,* which is the only surviving version of that law code. It was based on a copy sent to him by his relative Simon Mansel, constable of Antioch, and was part of Smpad's attempt to "Frankicize" the customs of the Armenian kingdom. He also commented on or commissioned translations of Byzantine philosophical or theological works.

–Angus Stewart

Bibliography

La Chronique attribuée au Connétable Smbat, trans. Gérard Dédéyan (Paris: Geuthner, 1980).

Der Nersessian, Sirarpie, "The Armenian Chronicle of the Constable Smpad or of the 'Royal Historian'," *Dumbarton Oaks Papers* 13 (1959), 141–168.

Richard, Jean, "La Lettre du connétable Smbat et les rapports entre chrétiens et mongols au milieu du XIIIeme siècle," in *Armenian Studies—Etudes arméniennes: In Memoriam Haig Berberian,* ed. Dickram Kouymjian (Lisboa: Fondaçao Calouste Gulbenkian, 1986), pp. 683–696.

Smyrna Crusade (1344)

A joint crusading operation carried out by the so-called Holy League (Lat. *Sancta Unio*) against the powerful Turcoman ruler of the Aydin emirate, Umur Begh or Umur Pasha (1334–1348), who had his headquarters at Smyrna (mod. İzmir, Turkey), a stronghold on the western Anatolian coast.

The crusade was preached in August–September 1343 by Pope Clement VI and undertaken by a united Western fleet carrying forces of the papacy, the Venetians, the Hospitallers, the Lusignan kingdom of Cyprus, and some other minor Latin rulers of the Aegean region. The operation's main target was Smyrna itself, held since 1317 by the Aydin Turcomans and used since 1326–1329 as their base for piratical operations in the southeastern Mediterranean. The crusade operations of 1343–1344 came as a sequel to an earlier abortive attempt by the Holy League in 1332–1334 to seize the port (autumn–winter 1334). The participants had included the Byzantine emperor Andronikos III Palaiologos and the French king Charles VI of Valois, but its failure had left Umur Begh's position strengthened until the early 1340s.

The crusade of the Holy League venture met with success on 28 October 1344, when a surprise attack by the titular Latin patriarch of Constantinople, Henri of Asti, occupied the port and the lower citadel of the town. Umur Begh's naval prestige thus received a severe blow, and he was then forced to mount attacks by land aimed at recapturing the harbor of Smyrna and dislodging the crusaders from the lower town. During the period of the emir's counteroffensives, the Christians received assistance from a new crusading fleet headed by Humbert II, the dauphin of Viennois, who was officially appointed leader of the crusade by Clement VI. In an attempt to neutralize Umur Begh's efforts to retake Smyrna, Humbert led repeated unsuccessful operations in the Aegean between early 1345 and late 1346, using as his base from mid-1346 the island of Chios, recently captured by the Genoese. It was only in late April–early May 1347 that his forces (chiefly the Hospitallers) scored a victory over a united Turcoman fleet from the emirates of Aydin and Sarukhan near the island of Imbros.

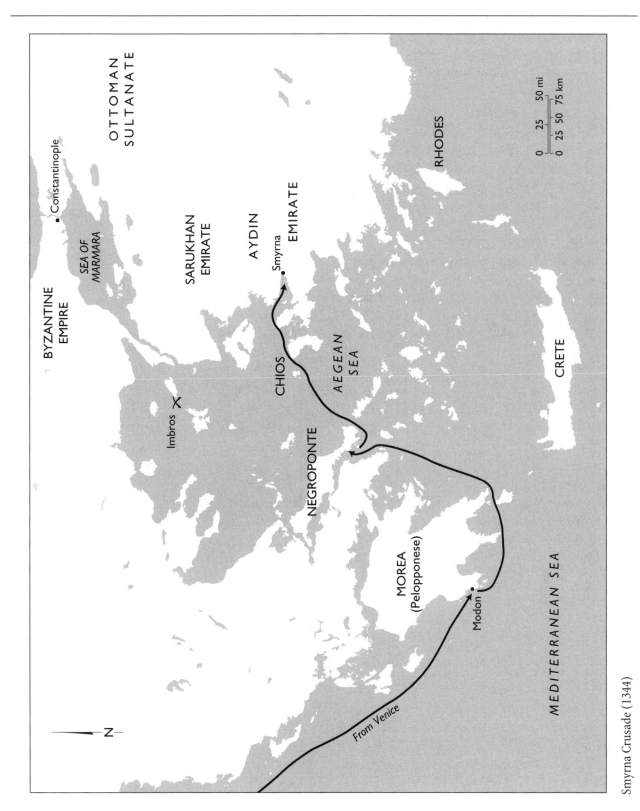

Umur Begh was killed in action (April–May 1348, according to the dating of the contemporary Byzantine historian Nikephoros Gregoras) during one of his raids against lower Smyrna, thus meeting with a hero's death according to his biographer Enveri, the fifteenth-century Ottoman epic historian. Umur's demise occurred just as his former ally, the Byzantine usurper-emperor John VII Kantakouzenos (1347–1354), was on the verge of joining the Holy League, while Clement VI had since 1347 been contemplating a peace treaty with Aydin, having, however, rejected it in February 1348.

Umur's brother and successor, Hizir (Hidir Begh), eventually signed a treaty with the Latins on 18 August 1348. Smyrna remained in Latin hands until its seizure by Timur Lenk (Tamerlane) in the autumn of 1402, following the latter's victory over the Ottomans at the battle of Ankara.

–Alexios G. C. Savvides

Bibliography
Ahrweiler, Hélène, "L' histoire et la géographie de la region de Smyrne entre les deux occupations turques, 1081–1317," *Travaux et mémoires* 1 (1965), 1–204.
Inalcık, Halil, "The Rise of the Turcoman Principalities in Anatolia, Byzantium and Crusades," *Byzantinische Forschungen* 9 (1985), 179–217.
Lemerle, Paul, *L' Emirat d'Aydin, Byzance et l' Occident: Recherches sur "La Geste d'Umur Pacha"* (Paris: Bibliothèque Byzantine, 1957).
Setton, Kenneth, *The Papacy and the Levant, 1204–1571,* vol. 1 (Philadelphia: American Philosophical Society, 1976).
Zachariadou, Elizabeth, *Trade and Crusade: Venetian Crete and the Emirates of Menteshe and Aydin, 1300–1415* (Venice: Institute for Byzantine and Post-Byzantine Studies, 1983).

Solomon bar Simson

A Jewish chronicler, credited with the longest of the three Hebrew narratives of the First Crusade (1096–1099).

Solomon bar Simson names himself as the recorder of the pogrom in one of the villages to which Jews of Cologne (Ger. *Köln*) had fled; it is uncertain whether he was also responsible for editing the whole composition sometime between 1140 and the Second Crusade (1147–1149). The narrative contains sections on the persecutions by the so-called People's Crusades in Speyer, Worms, Mainz (sharing material with the Mainz Anonymous), Cologne, Trier, Metz, and Regensburg, along with an exaggerated account of the diffi-

culties experienced by these crusaders in Hungary. The section on Trier, where most Jews were probably forcibly converted, is especially interesting and probably contemporaneous. The evocative descriptions of Jewish self-martyrdom are arresting, but compelling too is the admonition not to malign those who were baptized against their will.

–Anna Sapir Abulafia

Bibliography
Chazan, Robert, *God, Humanity and History: The Hebrew First Crusade Narratives* (Berkeley: University of California Press, 2000).
Hebräische Berichte über die Judenverfolgungen während der Kreuzzüge, ed. A. Neubauer and H. Stern, trans. S. Baer (Berlin: Simion, 1892).
Hebräische Berichte über die Judenverfolgungen während des ersten Kreuzzugs, ed. Eva Haverkamp (Hannover: Hahn, 2005).
The Jews and the Crusaders: The Hebrew Chronicles of the First and Second Crusade, ed. and trans. Shlomo Eidelberg (Madison: University of Wisconsin Press, 1977).

Song of the Cathar Wars

See Chanson de la croisade albigeoise

Sources

See Arabic Sources, Armenian Sources, Greek Sources, Russian Sources, Syriac Sources, Western Sources

Spanish and Portuguese Literature

The vernacular literatures of the Iberian Peninsula (Castilian, Catalan, and Gallego-Portuguese) show little evidence of crusading as a specific theme. Frequently involved in conflicts with each other and with the Muslims of al-Andalus, the Christian kings of Iberia were not inclined to participate in crusades to the Holy Land, with the notable exceptions of Alfonso X of Castile and James I of Aragon.

Even though modern historians date the beginning of the Iberian *Reconquista* (reconquest) to the eighth century, for a long time the religious aspect of the recovery of lost Christian territory from the Moors (the Muslims of Spain) was not of primary importance to the Christian rulers of the northern peninsula: periods of cultural exchange and mutual influence of the Christian, Jewish, and Islamic religions and cultures (Sp. *convivencia*) often coincided with strife. However, from the beginning of the tenth century, the desire for religious unification and reestablishment of the Visigothic kingdom was articulated by Christian rulers, particularly the kings of León and Castile. For Portugal, the reconquest almost ended in the thirteenth century. The battle of Salado (1340), fought by an alliance of Castilians and Portuguese, produced the final victory for Portugal against the Moors of the peninsula. From that time, Portuguese voyages of exploration along the African coast, bound for Asia, were declared to be crusades, at a time when the crusades to the Holy Land apparently had come to an end. Thus, in the *Crónica dos Feitos da Guiné* by Gomes Eanes de Zurara, Prince Henry the Navigator (d. 1460), who sent out the expeditions to Asia, is characterized as a knight and crusader.

Iberia began to be affected by the idea of crusades from as early as 1095, when Pope Urban II in his call to crusade spoke of the necessity of fighting the Muslims in Spain. Later papal bulls and calls to crusade repeatedly and explicitly equated the Reconquista with the crusades to the East. Crusade ideas are evident in the Latin compilation known as the *Codex Calixtinus,* written after 1140. This ascribes to the fight against the "unbelievers" in Spain the same importance and religious merit as to the struggle to free the Holy Land; a pilgrimage to the Galician shrine of Santiago de Compostela has the same spiritual benefit, not only as a pilgrimage to Rome but also as a crusade to Jerusalem. It can be assumed that the composition of the *Codex Calixtinus* was closely connected to the special interests of the pope and the Cluniac Order, which aimed to give a greater importance to the pilgrimage to Santiago de Compostela by equating it with participation in a crusade to Jerusalem.

For a long time the absence of lyric poetry connected with the reconquest of the Holy Land was regarded as a peculiarity of the literature of the Iberian Peninsula. However, this view was radically altered with the discovery in the second half of the twentieth century of the poem *¿Ay, Jherusalem!* This work, belonging to the genre of lament or complaint (Sp. *planto*), is the only example of a lyric crusade poem in Castilian medieval literature. Its form belongs to the Castilian popular lyrical tradition: a stanza of five lines (two of twelve syllables and three of six syllables), the last line ending in the *estribillo* (refrain) "Iherusalem." The poem probably dates from 1274, and is thus contemporaneous with the Second Council of Lyons; it may also be connected with the compilation of the narrative known as the *Gran Conquista*

de Ultramar. Like the numerous crusade poems known from Old French, Occitan, and Middle High German literature, *¿Ay, Jerusalem!* clearly has a propagandistic purpose, namely, the recruitment of crusaders for the recovery of the city of Jerusalem, lost to the Muslims in 1244. The anonymous author describes in dark colors the cruelties of the Muslims and exalts the courage of the Christians. Besides this vernacular work, a Latin poem on the conquest of Jerusalem by the crusaders in 1099 (found in a manuscript also containing a poem on the Cid and another on Raymond Berengar IV of Barcelona) is also known to have originated in the Benedictine monastery of Ripoll before 1218.

The romance chronicle (*crónica novelesca)* known as *La Gran Conquista de Ultramar,* dating from the late thirteenth century, can be regarded as a unique and extraordinary example of a crusade narrative in the Iberian Peninsula. Based on French originals, it is a compilation that exists in Castilian, Gallego-Portuguese, and Catalan versions. The Castilian version was probably begun at the instigation of King Alfonso X of Castile, although his son and successor Sancho IV may well have been responsible for part of it. It may have served as propaganda for both kings: possible contexts are Alfonso's interest in a crusade to the Holy Land or Sancho's own campaigns against the Muslims of Spain. The core narrative (books 3 and 4) deals with the historical events of the crusades between 1095 and 1271, drawing on the *Estoire d'Eracles* (the French translation of the Latin chronicle of William of Tyre) and the *Chronique d'Ernoul et de Bernard le trésorier.* The other two books present predominantly fictional material concerning the legendary ancestry of Godfrey of Bouillon, the first Frankish ruler of Jerusalem (d. 1100), and the life of Charlemagne, king of the Franks and Holy Roman Emperor (d. 814); this material consists of translations or adaptations of French chansons de geste (epic poems), including some belonging to the Old French Crusade Cycle.

These interferences between history and fiction did not present a problem to the readers of the Middle Ages, for whom the *Gran Conquista* was a historical narrative. This was made clear by James I, king of Aragon (1264–1327), who in a document of 1313/1314 asked his daughter Doña María for a translation of the *Gran Conquista* into Catalan out of historical interest, as he expressed it. In that context it is worth noting that in 1269 there had been an Aragonese crusade to Acre (mod. 'Akko, Israel) led by the bastard sons of James I, Fernando Sánchez and Pedro Fernández. The

Aragonese ambitions with regard to crusading in the fourteenth and fifteenth centuries were connected with the growing interest of merchants from Venice, Genoa, and Aragon in the routes to and ports in the Near East and North Africa. The "revival" and translation of the chronicle into Catalan reinforced this aim. The final version of the *Gran Conquista de Ultramar,* included in the Portuguese *Crónica general* of 1404, is the only example of crusade literature in Gallego-Portuguese; it is remarkable for its explicit connection of the crusades to the Holy Land with the Reconquista in the Iberian Peninsula, which is not found in the original Castilian text, or in the Catalan version.

The popularity of the *Gran Conquista de Ultramar* lasted for a long time. As the only vernacular narrative on the crusades to be produced in Iberia, it had a great importance for the evolution of the Spanish chivalric novel (Sp. *novela de caballerías*), which flourished during the fifteenth and sixteenth centuries, as exemplified by the Castilian *Amadis* by Garci Rodriguez de Montalvo and *Tirant lo Blanc* (first edition 1490) written in Catalan by Joanot Martorell (1414–1468). Even before these works were written, in the time of Sancho IV, or by the mid-fourteenth century at the latest, the *Gran Conquista* had been used as a source for an early *novela de caballerías,* the *Historia de Enrique, fi de Oliva.* It later went on to influence numerous other chivalric novels, up to the composition of *El ingenioso hidalgo Don Quijote de la Mancha* by Miguel de Cervantes Saavedra (1547–1616), who superseded the chivalric novel with his masterpiece, thus initiating the modern novel.

Together with the *Gerusalemme liberata* of the Italian author Torquato Tasso, the *Gran Conquista* even served as a model for Lope de Vega's *La Jerusalén conquistada* (1603), a tragic heroic epic dealing with the Third Crusade (1189–1192) and the deeds and adventures of King Richard the Lionheart of England and King Philip II of France, as well as King Alfonso VIII of Castile, who, at the instigation of Pope Innocent III, mounted a campaign that culminated in victory against the Muslims in the battle of Las Navas de Tolosa in 1212.

At the end of the fifteenth century, in the time of the "Catholic Monarchs," Isabella I of Castile (1451–1504) and Ferdinand II of Aragón (1452–1516), there emerged a clear religious dimension in the political ideas of the final phase of the Reconquista as it was formulated by Pope Sixtus IV in his crusade bull of 1483, which defined the fighting against the Muslims in the Iberian Peninsula as a crusade.

Crusading in this wider sense had already begun to find expression in Castilian literature, as, for example, in the fourteenth century *Libro de Patronio o Conde Lucanor* by Alfonso X's nephew Don Juan Manuel: though its first three books are devoted to worldly ethics inspired by ideas and writings from antiquity and oriental sources as a result of the influence of the *convivencia,* the fourth book propagates militant Christian attitudes toward Muslim and Jewish "unbelievers." In the sections of his *Libro de los Estados* dealing with military science (chapters 76–79), Don Juan Manuel describes the peculiarities of warfare between Christians and Moors in a most realistic way. Another work to be mentioned in this context is one of the most famous poems of medieval Spain: the *Coplas a la muerte de su Padre* by Jorge Manrique (1440–1479), a poem of lament for his father, who had died in battle against the Moors.

The complex situation of the *convivencia* of the three cultures and religions in the Iberian Peninsula, as well as the continuous Reconquista, gave rise to literary testimonies to the encounter of Christians and Muslims in times of peace and war: these can be found in the anonymous fifteenth-century *Romancero,* a collection of poems (Sp. *romances*) in octosyllabic stanzas of diverse length and contents. It is in the *romances históricos* (historical poems) and especially in the *romances fronterizos* (border romances) that the image of the "good" Moor appears and respect for him is manifested, in contrast to the official Christian policies of conversion and expulsion in the later Middle Ages. Examples of the best known *romances* are *Moricos, los mis moricos, Romance del rey moro que perdió Alhama,* and *Romance que dicen Abenámar.* The same positive image of the Moor is present in the *novela morisca* (Moorish novel) of the sixteenth century, for example, the anonymous *Historia del Abencerraje y la Hermosa Jarifa* (1561) and the *Historia de los bandos de Zegríes y Abencerrajes, caballeros moros de Granada* by Ginés Pérez de Hita.

–Elisabeth Schreiner

Bibliography

Asensio, Eugenio, *Poética y realidad en el cancionero peninsular de la Edad Media* (Madrid: Gredos, 1970).

Burns, Robert I., "Mudejar Parallel Societies: Anglophone Historiography and Spanish Context, 1975–2000," in *Christians, Muslims and Jews in Medieval and Early Modern Spain: Interaction and Cultural Change,* ed. Mark D. Meyerson and Edward D. English (Notre Dame: University of Notre Dame Press, 2000), pp. 91–124.

Deyermond, Alan D., *Historia y crítica de la literatura española*, vol. 1: *Edad Media* (Barcelona: Ed. Crítica, 1991).

Fletcher, Richard, *The Quest for El Cid* (London: Century Hutchinson, 1989).

La Gran conquista de Ultramar, 4 vols., ed. Louis Cooper (Bogota: Publicaciones del Instituto Caro y Cuervo, 1979).

Grieve, Patricia E., "Architectural and Biblical Building Blocks: The Poetic Structure of *¿Ay Jherusalem!*" *Forum for Modern Language Studies* 22 (1986), 145–156.

Historia de Abencerraje y la hermosa Jarifa, ed. Francisco López Estrada (Madrid: Catedra, 1985).

Lacarra, María Jesus, and Francisco López Estrada, *Orígenes de la Prosa* (Madrid: Jucar, 1993).

Don Juan Manuel, *El Libro de los Estados,* ed. R. B. Tate and I. R. Macpherson (Oxford: Clarendon, 1974).

———, *Libro de los enxiemplos del Conde Lucanor e de Patronio,* ed. Alfonso I. Sotelo (Madrid: Catedra, 1981).

Rehrmann, Norbert, *Das schwierige Erbe von Sefarad: Juden und Mauren in der spanischen Literatur. Von der Romantik bis zur Mitte des 20. Jahrhunderts* (Frankfurt am Main: Vervuert, 2002).

El Romancero viejo, ed. Mercedes Díaz Roig (Madrid: Catedra, 1997).

Jorge Manrique, *Poesías completas,* ed. Miguel Angel Pérez Priego (Madrid: Espasa-Calpe, 1995).

Salinas, Pedro, *Jorge Manrique o tradición y originalidad* (Barcelona: Peninsula, 1947).

Seniff, Dennis P., *Antología de la literatura hispánica medieval* (Madrid: Gredos, 1992).

Spanische Literaturgeschichte, ed. Hans-Jörg Neuschäfer (Stuttgart: Metzler, 2001).

Stedinger Crusades (1233–1234)

Crusades carried out against the Stedinger, a peasant population living around the rivers Weser and Hunte in northwestern Germany.

In the early Middle Ages the Stedinger settled the land to the west of the Weser near Bremen. Eventually the name also came to include those who settled north and south of the lower Hunte. The Stedinger were subject to the archbishop of Bremen, who governed the land through ministerial knights. The counts of Oldenburg, whose influence extended north of the Hunte, were another dominant power in the region.

In 1204 the Stedinger of the northern regions rebelled against the count of Oldenburg, burning down two of his castles. Soon their compatriots in the south followed them in a well-planned uprising, attacking and driving off the knightly servants of the archbishop, to whom they refused to pay any taxes and tithes thenafter. Weakened by political unrest and internal schism, the archbishops in Bremen were unable to suppress the rebellion for years to come. The Stedinger took advantage of the situation with renewed attacks on several castles in 1212, 1213, and 1214.

The situation changed in 1219 when Gerhard II of Lippe became the new archbishop of Bremen and immediately began to restore archiepiscopal power, demanding that the Stedinger pay taxes and tithes. The Stedinger refused to do so. Gerhard seems to have excommunicated them in 1227 or 1229, and he also decided to use military force to subdue them. In December 1229, together with his brother, Hermann of Lippe, Gerhard attacked the land of the Stedinger with a small army. However, during the ensuing fight on Christmas Day, the archiepiscopal army was defeated and Hermann was killed "for the liberation of the church of Bremen," as Gerhard expressed it when he founded the nunnery of Lilienthal for the salvation of his brother in 1232 [Schmidt, "Zur Geschichte der Stedinger," pp. 58–59].

In March 1230 or 1231 a diocesan synod under the presidency of Gerhard declared the Stedinger to be heretics, accusing them of murdering clerics, burning churches and monasteries, desecrating the Eucharist, carrying out superstitious practices, and rejecting the teachings of the church. Other heretical acts also formed part of the accusations. Clearly Gerhard was preparing the way for a formal crusade against the Stedinger and was only waiting for papal permission to start preaching the crusade. In October 1232 Pope Gregory IX gave his permission after having called for an investigation of the alleged heresy of the Stedinger in July 1231. Frederick II, the Holy Roman Emperor, placed the Stedinger under the ban of the empire.

At first the crusade was preached in the bishoprics of Minden, Lübeck, and Ratzeburg, but only a few local knights seem to have responded to this call. A renewed call for crusaders in early 1233 (this time over a wider area) led to the formation of a crusader army that attacked the Stedinger during the summer. The crusaders had some initial success but were defeated near Hemmelskamp in July. While the crusade was in progress, Gregory IX renewed his call for crusaders, this time promising them a full indulgence for their participation in the fight against the Stedinger. This papal act placed the crusades against the Stedinger on an equal footing with other German crusades against heretics as well as with the crusades to the Holy Land.

In early 1234 the archbishop of Bremen raised a new crusader army that included the duke of Brabant and the counts of Holland, Geldern, Kleve, Jülich, Berg, and Ravensberg as well as several Flemish barons; on 27 May 1234 the crusaders were finally able to defeat the Stedinger in a bloody battle near Altenesch.

A papal attempt in March 1234 to end the conflict through negotiations rather than force had not stopped the crusade. Apparently the Teutonic Order had intervened on behalf of the Stedinger, arguing for more negotiations. Gregory IX seems to have given his legate, William of Modena, the task of reconciling the Stedinger and the archbishop. Either this decision did not reach Gerhard II in time to stop the crusade, or the archbishop simply chose to ignore it.

After the defeat at Altenesch the surviving Stedinger could do nothing but surrender to the demands of the archbishop, and in August 1235 Gregory IX ordered that the excommunication of the once-rebellious Stedinger should be lifted.

–Carsten Selch Jensen

Bibliography
Köhn, Rolf, "Die Verketzung der Stedinger durch die Bremer Fastensynode," *Bremisches Jahrbuch* 57 (1979), 15–85.
———, "Die Teilnehmer an den Kreuzzügen gegen die Stedinger," *Niedersächsisches Jahrbuch für Landesgeschichte* 53 (1981), 139–206.
Krollmann, Christian, "Der Deutsche Orden und die Stedinger," *Altpreußische Forschung* 14 (1937), 1–13.
Schmidt, Heinrich, "Zur Geschichte der Stedinger: Studien über Bauernfreiheit, Herrschaft und Religion an der Unterweser im 13. Jahrhundert," *Bremisches Jahrbuch* 60–61 (1982–1983), 27–94.

Stensby, Treaty of (1238)

A treaty between King Valdemar II of Denmark and the Teutonic Order, concluded on 7 June 1238 in Stensby near Vordingborg on Sjælland, which transferred the northern part of Estonia to the Danish king.

After the abduction of Valdemar II by his vassal Count Henry of Schwerin in May 1223, Danish power in the Baltic region collapsed. Unable to hold their Estonian provinces, the Danes in 1225 transferred authority to the papal legate William of Modena, but the Order of the Sword Brethren soon took possession. Pope Gregory IX repeatedly tried to persuade the Sword Brethren to relinquish the provinces, and in February 1236 he resolved that they were to cede Reval

(mod. Tallinn, Estonia), Jerwia, Harria, and Vironia to the Danish king. Shortly after this, however, the Sword Brethren were annihilated at the battle of Saule, and the remnants of the order were incorporated into the Teutonic Order.

William of Modena was now charged with the task of persuading the Teutonic Order to observe the papal resolution. He met representatives of all parties in Stensby, where the Teutonic Order agreed to hand over Reval, Jerwia, Harria, and Vironia to the Danish king, who then as "penitence" returned Jerwia to the order. Finally, it was agreed that the Danish king was to retain two-thirds and the order one-third of future conquests. The treaty enabled the Danes and the order to collaborate closely in crusades against Novgorod and Pskov over the next four years and laid the legal foundation for continuing Danish rule in North Estonia.

–John H. Lind

See also: Baltic Crusades; Denmark; Estonia, Duchy of
Bibliography
Diplomatarium Danicum, ed. Niels Skyum-Nielsen et al., ser. 1, 7 vols. (København: Munksgaard, 1956–1990), 7:8–11.
Kreem, Juhan, "The Teutonic Order as a Secular Ruler in Livonia: The Privileges and Oath of Reval," in *Crusade and Conversion on the Baltic Frontier, 1150–1500,* ed. Alan V. Murray (Aldershot, UK: Ashgate, 2001), pp. 215–232.
Tarvel, Enn, "Die dänische Ostseepolitik im 11.–13. Jahrhundert," in *Studien zur Archäologie des Ostseeraumes von der Eisenzeit zum Mittelalter: Festschrift für Michael Müller-Wille,* ed. Anke Wesse (Neumünster: Wachholtz, 1998), pp. 53–59.

Stephen of Blois (d. 1102)

One of the leaders of the First Crusade (1096–1099), who died during the Crusade of 1101.

Stephen (more correctly Stephen-Henry) was born around 1045, a son of Thibaud III, count of Blois and Champagne, whom he succeeded in 1089. It is commonly believed that Stephen was persuaded to take his crusading vows by his wife Adela (d. 1137), daughter of William the Conqueror. While on crusade he wrote three letters to his wife, two of which survive; he emerges from these as an enthusiastic and insightful crusader.

Stephen traveled east with his brother-in-law Robert Curthose, duke of Normandy, and with Robert II, count of Flanders. During the siege of Antioch (mod. Antakya,

Turkey), however, Stephen deserted from the crusade army (2 June 1098) and returned to France; he became an object of contempt for abandoning his vows and was continually reproached by his wife.

To restore his reputation Stephen joined the Crusade of 1101, traveling out with other northern French nobles, who joined with a force of Lombards in Asia Minor. When they were defeated at the battle of Mersivan in August 1101, Stephen returned to Constantinople (mod. İstanbul, Turkey) and eventually sailed to Antioch, where the survivors of the crusade were regrouping. After marching south to Jerusalem, Stephen fought bravely against the Fāṭimids alongside King Baldwin I at the second battle of Ramla on 17 May 1102 and is widely believed to have died in the fighting, although James Brundage argued in 1960 that there is evidence that Stephen may have been captured and executed at Ascalon (mod. Tel Ashqelon, Israel) on 19 May 1102. His third son, Stephen (d. 1154), became king of England in 1135.

–Alec Mulinder

Bibliography
Brundage, James A., "An Errant Crusader: Stephen of Blois," *Traditio* 16 (1960), 380–395.
Krey, August C., *The First Crusade: The Accounts of Eye-Witnesses and Participants* (Princeton: Princeton University Press, 1921).
Pryor, John, "Stephen of Blois: Sensitive New Age Crusader or Victim of History?" in *Arts: Journal of the Sydney University Arts Association* 20 (1998), 26–74.

Stephen, Patriarch of Jerusalem (d. 1130)

Latin patriarch of Jerusalem (1128–1130) who strengthened the Latin Church in Outremer but quarreled with his kinsman King Baldwin II of Jerusalem.

Stephen had been a knight and viscount in Chartres, but later he entered the church and became abbot of St. John in Chartres. He was elected patriarch while visiting the Holy Land in 1128.

Stephen created a new Latin diocese at Sebastea and organized the fledgling Knights Templar. He also tried to reassert Daibert of Pisa's demands concerning the patriarchate's possessions in Jerusalem and also claimed the city of Jaffa (mod. Tel Aviv-Yafo, Israel), thereby causing a breach with the king that lasted until Stephen's death.

–Deborah Gerish

Bibliography
Hamilton, Bernard, *The Latin Church in the Crusader States: The Secular Church* (London: Variorum, 1980).
Mayer, Hans Eberhard, *Bistümer, Klöster und Stifte im Königreich Jerusalem* (Stuttgart: Hiersemann, 1977).

Stephen of the Perche (d. 1205)

Participant in the Fourth Crusade (1202–1204) and subsequently a baron of the Latin Empire of Constantinople as duke of Philadelphia.

The second, or more probably, the third son of Rotrou III (d. 1191), count of the Perche, and Matilda, daughter of Thibaud IV, count of Blois (1107–1152), Stephen built a career for himself in the service of King Richard I of England in the 1190s. He was preparing to join the Fourth Crusade when the premature and unexpected death of his brother Count Geoffrey III placed the command of the Percheron forces in his hands. King John of England stood surety for a loan to Stephen, and in June 1202 Stephen made numerous religious benefactions that reveal the extensive resources at his disposal.

Stephen must then have made his way to Venice with the rest of the crusaders, but he fell ill and did not set sail for Zara (mod. Zadar, Croatia) in October 1202. He may have been injured when his transport ship, the *Viola*, sank shortly after embarkation, but he may equally have feigned sickness because he disagreed with the diversion of the expedition. The latter is implied by criticism made by the chronicler Geoffrey of Villehardouin, who claims that Stephen deserted from the army. Stephen then spent some time in Apulia before making his way to Syria in the spring of 1203.

It is possible that Stephen felt his crusading obligations had thus been honored, for in the winter of 1204–1205 he arrived in Constantinople (mod. İstanbul, Turkey). He brought to the new Latin emperor, Baldwin I, reinforcements from Outremer and the services of himself and his cousin, Reginald of Montmirail. He was granted the duchy of Philadelphia in Asia Minor, an area that was outside the emperor's actual control but that gave Stephen scope to create his own territory. In Easter week of 1205 he was fighting with the emperor's forces before Adrianople (mod. Edirne, Turkey) and lost his life in the engagement against the Bulgars.

–Kathleen Thompson

Bibliography

Lock, Peter, *The Franks in the Aegean, 1204–1500* (London: Longman, 1995).

Thompson, Kathleen, "Family Tradition and the Crusading Impulse: The Rotrou Counts of the Perche," *Medieval Prosopography* 19 (1998), 1–33.

Suerbeer

See Albert Suerbeer

Al-Sulamī (1039–1106)

'Alī ibn Ṭāhir al-Sulamī is one of the most important Muslim sources for the period of the First Crusade (1096–1099).

He was a Shāfi'ite teacher and scholar at the Great Mosque in Damascus who in 1105 dictated a series of public lectures calling the Muslims to *jihād* (holy war). Only parts of the original manuscript from which he dictated, entitled *Kitāb al-Jihād* (*Book of the Holy War*), have survived. The manuscript has been partially edited, with a French translation, by Emmanuel Sivan. Al-Sulamī's text is vital to modern understanding of the crusades, representing one of the earliest extant calls to the jihād from the period. However, the impact of his work at the time seems to have been limited. Only later in the twelfth century did calls to the jihād begin to have significant effect.

–*Niall Christie*

Bibliography

Christie, Niall, and Deborah Gerish, "Parallel Preachings: Urban II and al-Sulamī," *Al-Masāq: Islam and the Medieval Mediterranean* 15 (2003), 139–148.

Eliséeff, Nikita, "The Reaction of the Syrian Muslims after the Foundation of the First Latin Kingdom of Jerusalem," in *Crusaders and Muslims in Twelfth-Century Syria*, ed. Maya Shatzmiller (Leiden: Brill, 1993), pp. 162–172.

Hillenbrand, Carole, *The Crusades: Islamic Perspectives* (Edinburgh: Edinburgh University Press, 1999).

Sivan, Emmanuel, "La genèse de la contre-croisade: Un traité damasquin du début du XIIe siècle," *Journal Asiatique* 254 (1966), 197–224.

Süleyman I the Magnificent (d. 1566)

Ottoman sultan (1520–1566), the son of Sultan Selim I. Under Süleyman, known to Europeans as "the Magnificent" and in Turkish as *Kanuni* (the lawgiver), the Ottoman Empire expanded to its effective territorial limits in both east and west, although to the south the Ottomans were unable to contain the Portuguese in the Red Sea and the Persian Gulf. Ottoman law was codified, and the empire came to play a major role in international politics. For later Ottomans, the reign of Süleyman was a golden age.

Much of Süleyman's reign was spent campaigning against Hungary. In 1521 he took Belgrade, and on his second campaign, he routed the Hungarians at Mohács (August 1526) and entered Buda (mod. Budapest). King Louis II was killed in battle, and the Hungarian throne left vacant. At this point Süleyman withdrew, due to a serious revolt in Anatolia. A succession dispute erupted, with the Hungarian Estates electing John Szapolyai, while the Habsburg archduke Ferdinand of Austria (brother-in-law of Louis) had himself crowned. Süleyman backed Szapolyai, and Ferdinand occupied Buda. In 1529 Süleyman marched on Hungary, retook Buda, and laid siege to Vienna. In 1530 Ferdinand besieged Buda and took western Hungary. In 1533 an agreement was made whereby Hungary was divided between Ferdinand and Szapolyai and their lands remained Ottoman tributaries. After a renewed period of fighting in Hungary, a five-year truce was eventually concluded in 1547.

In the eastern Mediterranean region, Süleyman expelled the Hospitallers from the island of Rhodes (mod. Rodos, Greece), which fell to the Ottomans in 1522. In the west, he faced the Spanish fleet. In 1535 the Spanish king and Holy Roman Emperor Charles V led a successful campaign against Tunis. When war broke out with Venice in 1536, Süleyman entered into an alliance with Charles's enemy, King Francis I of France. There were several further French-Ottoman alliances, the Ottoman fleet even wintering at Toulon in 1543. Venice lost most of her Aegean islands and, as part of the Holy League with Pope Paul III, Charles V, and Ferdinand of Austria, suffered a major defeat at Prevesa in 1538. According to the peace concluded in 1540, Venice lost various islands including Naxos, Santorini, Paros, and Andros, as well as Monemvasia and Nauplion. Further successful Ottoman campaigns in the Mediterranean in the 1550s under Piyale Paşa were followed by the siege of Malta (1565) and the capture of Chios from the Genoese (1566).

In the east Süleyman campaigned against the Safavids of Persia. Ottoman forces took Bitlis (1533), Tabriz (1534), and Baghdad (1534), and Iraq became an Ottoman possession. Despite further warfare against the Safavids, no major conquests were made, and what was to become the permanent frontier between the two states was set by the Treaty of Amasya (1555). In 1553 Süleyman executed his son Mustafa for apparently plotting to take the throne. Bayezid, another son of Süleyman, revolted in 1558 but was defeated near Konya (1559) and fled to Persia. After negotiations with the Safavid ruler Shah Tahmasb, Bayezid was killed in 1562. In 1566 Süleyman set off against Hungary for what was to be his last campaign. He died at the siege of Szigetvár.

–Kate Fleet

Bibliography

Hungarian-Ottoman Military and Diplomatic Relations in the Age of Süleyman the Magnificent, ed. Géza Dávid and Pál Fodor (Budapest: Department of Turkish Studies, Eötvös Loránd University, 1994).

Imber, Colin, *The Ottoman Empire 1300–1481* (Istanbul: Isis, 1990).

Soliman le magnifique et son temps, ed. Gilles Veinstein (Paris: Documentation française, 1993).

Süleyman II and his Times, ed. Halil İnalcık and Cemal Kafadar (Istanbul: Isis, 1993).

Süleyman the Magnificent and his Age: The Ottoman Empire in the Early Modern World, ed. Metin Kunt and Christine Woodhead (London: Longman, 1995).

Sulṭān Shāh

Saljūq ruler of Aleppo (1114–1118).

Sulṭtān Shāh was a son of a previous ruler of Aleppo, Riḍwān (d. 1113). He came to the throne at the age of six when his elder brother Alp Arslān ibn Riḍwān was murdered on the orders of one of his officers, Lu'Lu', in September 1114. Lu'Lu' functioned as regent and the real ruler of Aleppo; however, he was unpopular because of his inability to mount an effective resistance to the incursions of the Franks of Antioch and because of his exactions to pay for the army.

Lu'Lu' was murdered by some of Sulṭān Shāh's *mamlūks* (slave soldiers) in May 1117. After a summer of confusion, some of the populace of Aleppo called in the Artūqid ruler Īlghāzī, lord of Mardin, who seized control of the city. Sulṭān Shāh, the last Saljūq ruler of Aleppo, was deposed, but remarkably, seems to have been spared by the new Artūqid regime.

–Alan V. Murray

Bibliography

El-Azhari, Taef, *The Saljūqs of Syria during the Crusades, 463–549 A.H./1070–1154 A.D.* (Berlin: Schwarz, 1997).

Sunnī Islam

The majority, or "orthodox," form of Islam.

Sunnīs (Arab. *ahl al-sunna,* "people of the *sunna*") are so called because they follow the *sunna* (customary practice), that is, the customary sayings and actions of the Prophet Muḥammad. The *sunna* supplements the Qur'ān, clarifying points of law and theology that might otherwise be open to misinterpretation, and is derived from the *ḥadīth* (report) literature, which records the words and actions of the earliest members of the Muslim *umma* (community).

In the early days of Islam use was made of customary practices traceable back to the Prophet, his companions, and their successors. However, in the eighth century the influential jurist al-Shāfi'ī (d. 820) insisted that the term *sunna* should be used to refer only to the customary practice of the Prophet (Arab. *sunnat al-Nabī*). In his view, this *sunna* of the Prophet was the second most important *aṣl* (source) of Islamic jurisprudence, after the Qur'ān, a view that despite some initial difficulties became more widely established during the ninth century.

During the period of the crusades the majority of Muslims living in the Near and Middle East, whether Arabs, Turks, or Kurds, were Sunnīs. Even in Fāṭimid Egypt, where the rulers were Shī'ites, the majority of the populace remained Sunnīs. The Sunnī community was ruled, in theory at least, by the caliph in Baghdad, or after 1261 in Cairo, but for much of the period power actually lay in the hands of the caliph's immediate subordinates and local rulers, such as the Great Saljūq, Zangid, and Ayyūbid sultans. Few caliphs were successfully able to assert their own personal authority. In the meantime their subordinates frequently presented themselves as acting on the behalf of Islam and the caliphate.

–Niall Christie

Bibliography

Hodgson, Marshall G. S., *The Venture of Islam: Conscience and History in a World Civilization,* 3 vols. (Chicago: University of Chicago Press, 1974).

Holt, Peter M., *The Age of the Crusades* (London: Longman, 1986).

Kamali, Mohammad Hashim, *Principles of Islamic Jurisprudence* (Selangor Darul Ehsan, Malaysia: Pelanduk, 1989).

Rippin, Andrew, *Muslims: Their Religious Beliefs and Practices,* 2d ed. (London: Routledge, 2001).

Rosenthal, E. I. J., *Political Thought in Medieval Islam: An Introductory Outline* (Cambridge: Cambridge University Press, 1958).

Watt, W. Montgomery, *Islamic Philosophy and Theology* (Edinburgh: Edinburgh University Press, 1962).

Sweden

The kingdom of Sweden was the last of the Scandinavian countries to become firmly Christianized. Sweden was finally incorporated into the Latin Church with the foundation of the Danish archbishopric of Lund in 1104, although it was only in 1164 that a separate organization for the Swedish church was created with the establishment of a new archbishopric at Uppsala.

This delay explains why the first association of Sweden with the crusade movement was in fact as a target, when, in 1123 or 1124, Niels Svensen, king of Denmark, and Sigurd Jorsalfar, the seasoned crusader king of Norway, planned a joint operation against the alleged pagan population in the peripheral region of Småland. It also explains why we know of no Swedish participation in the First Crusade (1096–1099), launched only a few decades before. In fact, unlike kings in Denmark and Norway, no Swedish king ever went on crusade to the Holy Land or, it seems, made plans to do so. However, some of the later crusades were preached in Sweden (the earliest documentary evidence dates from 1213), while testaments, mainly from the thirteenth century, indicate that individual Swedish aristocrats did make crusading vows to go to the Holy Land and Livonia.

Crusades against Estonia and Finland

Sweden's participation in the crusading movement was directed against the eastern Baltic region. The principal target was Finland, although initially Sweden was active in other directions, too. Thus, in the 1170s the Swedes were involved in the crusades being planned to support Fulco, whom Pope Alexander III had appointed bishop among the Estonians. The chronicler Henry of Livonia relates that in 1197 a Swedish *jarl* (earl) planned a campaign together with Germans and Gotlanders against the pagan Curonians but ended up in Estonia after being thrown off course by a storm. Henry also reports that King Johan Sverkersson (1216–1222) led an expedition to western Estonia soon after the Danish conquest of the region of Reval (mod. Tallinn, Estonia) in 1219. The Swedes established themselves in a coastal fortress at Leal (mod. Lihula, Estonia) and attempted to convert the inhabitants, but a year later they were defeated and driven out by the pagan Oeselians.

The Swedes were more successful in Finland, which was incorporated into the Swedish realm over a period of 150 years from around 1150. According to a historiographical tradition founded by the Swedish historian and poet Erik

Gustaf Geijer (1783–1847), this occurred as a result of three successive crusades. The "First" Swedish Crusade is known only from the thirteenth-century life of the Swedish king and saint Erik Jedvardsson (d. 1160): according to this source, in 1155/1157 Erik and a bishop named Henry are supposed to have led a crusade to the southwestern area of Finland around Turku (Sw. Åbo). King Erik returned to Sweden only to be killed soon after, while the bishop stayed on in Finland, later to be martyred and venerated as Finland's patron saint. That the Swedes did in fact establish themselves in the region is confirmed by a papal bull from 1171/1172. It repeats Swedish complaints that the Finns promised to observe the Christian faith whenever they were threatened by an enemy army but denied the faith and persecuted the priests when the army retreated. Therefore, the pope urged the Swedes to force the Finns to observe the Christian creed. At this stage a missionary bishopric for the Finns was established, later to be located at Turku.

The "Second" Swedish Crusade is connected with the later *jarl* and founder of a new dynasty, Birger Magnusson, who in 1238 or 1239 attacked the Tavastians, a people settled to the east of the Finns proper. By this time the Tavastians must to a certain extent have been subjected to the Swedish church, because in December 1237 Pope Gregory IX quoted an alleged uprising among the Tavastians as a reason for requiring the archbishop of Uppsala to preach a crusade against them. The actual crusade, which must have taken place in 1238/1239, is only known from the so-called *Erik Chronicle* (Sw. *Erikskrönikan*), a Swedish rhymed chronicle written in the 1320s. As a result Tavastia was conquered and the inhabitants forced to accept Christianity. The crusade allowed the Swedes to colonize the coastal region along the Gulf of Finland south of Tavastia, subsequently known as Nyland (New Land). Here it may have replaced earlier Danish settlements.

This crusade to Tavastia was immediately followed by a crusade directed further to the east in 1240, when Birger Magnusson attempted to entrench himself on the river Neva together with a number of bishops and Finns, Tavastians, and perhaps even Norwegians. This was part of the crusades against Russia called for by Pope Gregory IX, but it ended in defeat, when the Swedes were taken by surprise by the Novgorodians under Prince Alexander Yaroslavich (Nevskii).

Crusades against Karelia and Novgorod

From this time the Swedish rulers kept their eyes firmly fixed on the trade routes that linked the Gulf of Finland and Lake

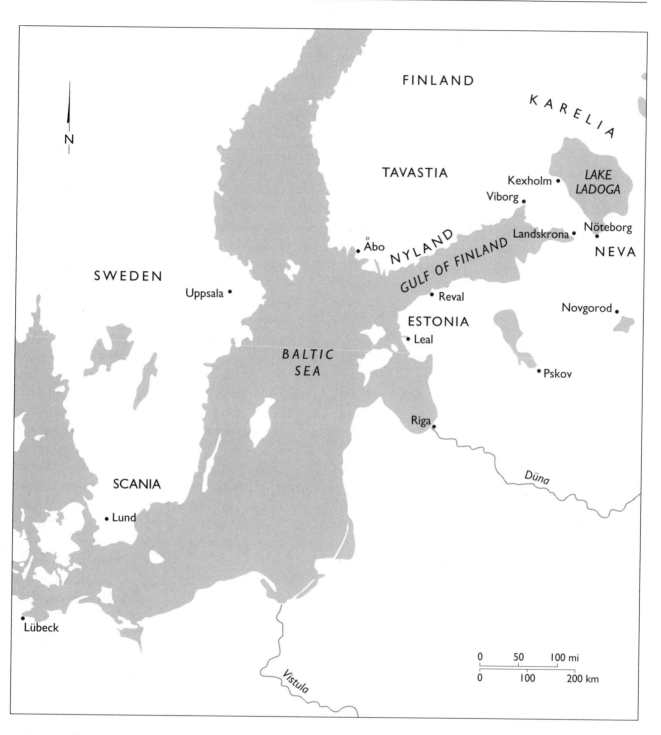

Main areas of Swedish crusading activity in the Baltic Region

Ladoga, and after a short-lived alliance against the Mongols between the papacy and Russian princes during the pontificate of Innocent IV, Sweden once more started planning crusades toward the east.

In 1257 Pope Alexander IV issued a new bull proclaiming a crusade against the Russians, and at the request of King Valdemar Birgersson (1250–1275), he urged the Swedish bishops to preach a crusade against the Karelians, who were then under the rule of Novgorod. That signaled the beginning of a succession of Swedish attacks on Novgorodian Karelia that in their totality have been labeled the "Third" Swedish Crusade. From the 1280s the Swedes began to impose restrictions on trade with Novgorod in order to weaken their enemy, and in 1293 they began to build the fortress of Viborg (mod. Vyborg, Russia), blocking the western outlet of the river Vuoksi that linked Lake Ladoga and the Gulf of Finland. The next year they attempted unsuccessfully to take and hold Kexsholm (mod. Priozërsk, Russia), a strong place in the center of Karelia, situated at the Ladoga end of the Vuoksi.

The most dangerous move for Novgorod, however, was the attempt by the Swedes, with the assistance of engineers from Rome, to establish a fortress with the proud name of Landskrona ("Crown of the Land") at the Neva delta. That too failed, when Novgorodians, helped by forces from central Russia, arrived the following year and managed to annihilate the garrison and demolish the fortress.

To judge by the dramatic account in the *Erik Chronicle*, there can be no doubt that the Swedes saw themselves as fighting paganism on behalf of Christianity. Yet they also met with opposition from Orthodox Russians as well as potential western allies. Had the Swedes succeeded in achieving their goal, they would have been able to control a large part of the all-important trade between Novgorod and western Europe. The Swedish restrictions on trade with Novgorod, however, angered the Hanseatic towns. In 1295 the Swedes tried to mollify the merchants by intimating that the war they fought was a holy war and that the pagan Karelians had now been pacified and converted, while Viborg had been built "to the honour of God and the Virgin" [*Sverges Traktater*, 15 vols., ed. Olof S. Rydberg et al. (Stockholm: Norstedt & Söner, 1877–1934), 1: 310]. This, they tried to persuade the merchants, would also benefit them. The merchants were not convinced, and in 1300 they asked the king of Germany, Albrecht of Habsburg, to pressure the king of Sweden, Birger Magnusson, into abolishing the restrictions.

In 1301 the Novgorodians invited the city of Lübeck to collaborate against the Swedes, and in 1302 the Danish king, Erik VI Menved, who had previously guaranteed the Hanseatic merchants free access to Novgorod through his lands, concluded a treaty with Novgorod. It was clear that major agents of the Latin West gave priority to the interests of trade over Sweden's crusading efforts, probably on the correct assumption that Swedish policy was also to a large extent guided by economic interests. The war with Novgorod continued in desultory fashion until 1323, when hostilities were ended by the Treaty of Nöteborg (Russ. *Orekhovets*), signed at the fortress the Novgorodians had built in 1322 on an island that blocked the entrance to Lake Ladoga from the Neva.

A contributing factor to Sweden's inability to strike efficiently against Novgorod after 1301 was the fratricidal war between King Birger Magnusson and his two brothers, dukes Erik and Valdemar. This conflict ended when the king left his brothers to starve to death in prison in 1318, but he was then expelled by the brothers' supporters, who in 1319 elected Duke Erik's infant son, Magnus II (1319–1363), as new king of Sweden. The same year Magnus also inherited the Norwegian throne. Until Magnus's majority, the aristocracy ruled Sweden through a regency, but even later the young king remained strongly under the influence of the aristocracy, not least the circle around the mystic (and later saint) Birgitta Birgersdottir, who was also tutor to the young queen, Blanche of Namur.

During the regency and the first years of Magnus's personal rule, Swedish attention was directed toward Denmark, at this time without a king. In 1332 the Swedes were able to exploit the situation to purchase Scania, the Danish territory on the southern Swedish mainland. After 1340, when Denmark again had a king, Valdemar IV Atterdag, Magnus II had to fight Denmark in order to safeguard his hold on Scania. For this, however, he was strongly criticized by the ever-more-vociferous Birgitta Birgersdottir. In her visions or revelations, Birgitta claimed to be the mouthpiece of both the Virgin Mary and Christ: several revelations were addressed directly or indirectly to King Magnus, who, instead of waging war against his fellow Christians, was supposed to turn against the pagans in the east. To some extent the Swedes were already active in that region as part of their anti-Danish policy. When Valdemar IV Atterdag ascended the Danish throne, he hardly controlled any part of the realm. His best asset was the duchy of Estonia, which he planned to sell to the Teutonic Order. However, the Swedes were themselves eager to take over the duchy; even if they did not actually incite the uprising that broke out in April 1343 among the Estonians, they at least supported it, and even after the sale to the order went through in 1346, King Magnus still prepared to lay claim to the duchy.

By this time King Magnus was already at work preparing his crusade against Novgorod as urged by Birgitta Birgersdottir. In a number of revelations she gave specific directions: the king, accompanied by priests and monks who could refute the errors of the pagans and infidels, should first attempt to convince them by peaceful means; only as a last resort should he take to the sword. These directions form the background for the course of events related in the Novgorod Chronicles. According to these, King Magnus started his crusade in 1347 by inviting the Novgorodians to a theological debate that should decide whose faith was best. Each party was to accept the result and then unite in the faith agreed upon as best. If the Novgorodians did not consent to this, King Magnus would attack them. Baffled by this approach, the Novgorodians refused to enter such a debate, referring the king to the patriarch of Constantinople. Consequently, King Magnus immediately pressed on with his attack and managed to capture the island fortress of Nöteborg. At once he began to baptize the pagan Ingrians and prepared to do the same among the Karelians. When winter set in, however, the Novgorodians were able to attack Nöteborg over the ice and force the Swedes to surrender the fortress. Having toured Estonia and Livonia, soliciting support from the local aristocracy, King Magnus made another attack from Estonia in 1350 but was forced to withdraw. The bulls in support of the crusade issued by Pope Clement VI in March 1351 came too late because King Magnus was already negotiating a peace recognizing the status quo.

The defeat in the Birgittine crusade to all intents and purposes ended Sweden's participation in the crusading movement, although one later Swedish ruler managed to procure yet another crusading bull against the Russians. For Magnus II, his dynasty, and his kingdom, the defeat also proved a turning point. Whereas Denmark regained its former strength with amazing speed, King Magnus was deposed by the aristocracy in 1363. Sweden was ruled by the dukes of Mecklenburg for a brief spell until they too were expelled with the help of the Danish queen Margaret I. As a result Sweden became part of the Danish-led union of the crowns of Denmark, Sweden, and Norway (the Kalmar Union).

Kings and Queens of Sweden (in the period of the crusades)

Erik Jedvardsson	1153–1160
Magnus Henriksson	1160–1161
Karl Sverkersson	1161–1167
Knut Eriksson	1167–1196
Sverker II Karlsson	1196–1208
Erik Knutsson	1208–1216
Johan Sverkersson	1216–1222
Erik Eriksson	1222–1229
Knut Långe	1229–1234
Erik Eriksson (again)	1234–1250
Valdemar Birgersson	1250–1275
Birger Magnusson (de facto ruler)	1250–1266
Magnus I Ladulås Birgersson	1275–1290
Birger Magnusson	1290–1319
Magnus II Eriksson (also Norway to 1344)	1319–1363
Albrekt of Mecklenburg	1364–1389
Margaret (also Denmark)	1389–1412
Erik of Pomerania (also Denmark as Erik VII)	1412–1439
Christopher (also Denmark)	1441–1448
Karl Knutsson Bonde	1448–1457
Christian I (also Denmark to 1481)	1457–1464
Karl Knutsson Bonde (again)	1464–1465
Christian I (again)	1465–1467
Karl Knutsson Bonde (again)	1467–1470
Sten Sture the Elder (regent)	1471–1497
Hans (also Denmark 1483–1513)	1497–1501
Sten Sture the Elder (regent, again)	1501–1504
Svante Nilsson (regent)	1504–1511
Sten Sture the Younger (regent)	1512–1520
Christian II (also Denmark 1513–1523)	1520–1521

During the later fifteenth century part of the Swedish aristocracy wanted to leave the union and repeatedly managed to have its own candidate elected as king or regent. Whenever that happened, the Danish kings attempted to reclaim Sweden for the union, as happened during the regencies of Sten Sture the Elder (1471–1497 and 1501–1503). In 1493 the union king Hans (1481–1513), offering Danish support against Lithuania in return for Russian help to regain Sweden, formed an alliance with the Muscovite grand prince Ivan III (1462–1505), who had by then incorporated Novgorod into the ever-expanding Muscovite state. In 1495 Ivan followed up by attacking Finland on three fronts. This gave Sten Sture the opportunity to procure a last crusading bull against the Russians, which Pope Alexander VI duly provided in 1496. Ironically, the papacy was at the same time trying to involve the Muscovite grand prince in its planned crusades against the Ottoman Turks. Although the Russians were ousted, the papal bull did not help Sten Sture. In 1497 he was defeated by the Danes and had to accept Hans as the King of Sweden.

Conclusions

The importance of the crusades for Sweden is clear from the fact that the acquisition of Finland was almost entirely the result of its participation in the Baltic Crusades. However, in contrast to the Germans, who dominated Livonia and Prussia, the Swedes never endeavored to dominate the local population. A division of the population in Finland into a privileged upper class and a suppressed lower class along ethnic lines similar to the division between *Deutsch* (German) and *Undeutsch* (non-German) in Livonia never occurred.

There are few traces of influence of the crusades in Sweden itself. A convent of the Order of St. John was established in Eskilstuna in 1185. Later, in 1262, a commandery of the Teutonic Order, the only one in Scandinavia, was established at Årsta as a result of the testament of Karl Ulfsson, son of *jarl* Ulf Fase (d. 1248). Karl had decided to join the Teutonic Order after fighting on the losing side against Birger Magnusson in 1251. He was killed in 1260 by the Lithuanians in the battle of Durben. The only other Swede known to have joined the order was St. Birgitta's brother, Israel Birgersson.

More importantly, it was a crusader king, Erik Jedvardsson, who became Sweden's patron saint. His cult was instituted by his son Knut Eriksson in 1167, but it was only during the Kalmar Union that it began to prosper, when the saint came to represent Swedish resistance to Danish domination. This dual function as anti-Danish national saint and crusader saint made him extremely useful to Sten Sture in his battle for independence against the Danish-Russian alliance in 1495–1497.

–*John H. Lind*

See also: Baltic Crusades; Finland; Karelia

Bibliography

Korpela, Jukka, "'The Russian Threat against Finland' in the Western Sources before the Peace of Nöteborg (1323)," *Scandinavian Journal of History* 22 (1997), 161–172.

Lind, John H., "Early Russian-Swedish Rivalry: The Battle on the Neva in 1240 and Birger Magnusson's Second Crusade to Tavastia," *Scandinavian Journal of History* 16 (1991), 269–295.

————, "The Russian-Swedish Border according to the Peace Treaty of Nöteborg (Orekhovets-Pähkinälinna) and the Political Status of the Northern Part of Fennoscandia," *Mediaeval Scandinavia* 13 (2000), 100–117.

————, "The Russian Testament of King Magnus Eriksson—a Hagiographic Text?" in *Medieval Spirituality in Scandinavia and Europe: A Collection of Essays in Honour of Tore Nyberg*, ed. Lars Bisgaard, Carsten Selch Jensen, Kurt Villads Jensen, and John Lind (Odense: Odense University Press, 2000), pp. 195–212.

————, "Consequences of the Baltic Crusades in Target Areas: The Case of Karelia," in *Crusade and Conversion on the Baltic Frontier, 1150–1500*, ed. Alan V. Murray (Aldershot, UK: Ashgate, 2001), pp. 133–149.

Lindkvist, Thomas, "Crusades and Crusading Ideology in the Political History of Sweden, 1140–1500," in *Crusade and Conversion on the Baltic Frontier, 1150–1500*, ed. Alan V. Murray (Aldershot, UK: Ashgate, 2001), pp. 119–130.

Lindkvist, Thomas, and Maria Sjöberg, *Det svenska samhället, 800–1720: Klerkernas och adelns tid* (Lund: Studentlitteratur, 2003).

Nilsson, Bertil, *Sveriges kyrkohistoria*, vol. 1: *Missionstid och tidig medeltid* (Stockholm: Verbum, 1998).

Pernler, Sven-Erik, *Sveriges kyrkohistoria*, vol. 2: *Hög- och senmedeltid* (Stockholm: Verbum, 1999).

Sword Brethren

The first military order in the Baltic region, founded in Livonia in 1202 on the model of the Templars and absorbed into the Teutonic Order in 1237. The order's original Latin name was the *Fratres Milicie Christi de Livonia* ("Brethren of the Knighthood of Christ of Livonia"); the more usual modern name Sword Brethren or Sword Brothers (Ger. *Schwertbrüder*) corresponds to the Middle High German designation *Swertbrûdere*, which derives from the knights' insignia of a sword beneath a red cross, which they wore on their white mantles.

According to the chronicler Henry of Livonia, the initiative for the new order came from the Cistercian Theoderic, a veteran in the Livonian mission. However, its establishment is often attributed to the newly ordained bishop of Livonia, Albert von Buxhövden (1199–1229), under whose obedience the order was placed. The foundation has to be seen against the background of the disastrous lack of military resources that had cost the life of the previous bishop,

Berthold of Loccum (1197–1198). A permanent army in the region to supplement the unpredictable arrival of seasonal crusaders and garrison the castles must have been seen as necessary in order to control the newly converted and conquered territory. In 1204 both Bishop Albert and Pope Innocent III gave their approval of the order. The same year it began to establish itself in its first convent in Riga under its first master, Winno (1204–1209).

Organization

The Sword Brethren lived according to the Rule of the Templars. They consisted of three classes: knight brethren, priests, and service brethren. A general assembly of the knight brethren was in principle the highest decision-making body, but in practice the master, elected for life by the assembly, was in charge of the order, with an authority comparable to that of the abbot of a Cistercian monastery. Under him served a vice-master who also deputized for him in his absence. A marshal took care of the order's military affairs and led it in battle, while a treasurer was in charge of finances. Provincial masters were placed in charge of new castle convents, each of which included a priest and a number of knight brethren, service brethren, and mercenaries. Advocates served as local administrators on the order's estates and acted as its link to the local population. Also associated with the order were a number of secular vassals who were enfeoffed with lands on its territory. They were mainly recruited from immigrant German nobles, but also, at least in some cases, from among the native nobility.

Even in its heyday, that is from around 1227 to 1236, the order probably had only some 110 knight brethren and perhaps 1,200 service brethren; with approximately 400 knights and soldiers supplied by its secular vassals, the order could at best field an army of some 1,800 men, in addition to local Livonian auxiliaries [Benninghoven, *Der Orden der Schwertbrüder,* pp. 223–224, 407–408]. During that time the order had a convent in Riga, convent castles in Ascheraden (mod. Aizkraukle, Latvia), Fellin (mod. Vijandi, Estonia), Reval (mod. Tallinn, Estonia), Segewold (mod. Sigula, Latvia), and Wenden (mod. Cēsis, Latvia), and also lesser strongholds in Adsel (mod. Gaujiena, Latvia), Wolmar (mod. Valmiera, Latvia), and Oberpahlen (mod. Pōltsamaa, Estonia).

Early History: Establishment of the Order

The Sword Brethren had their first experience of local warfare in the winter of 1204–1205, when they joined the

Member of the Order of the Sword Brethren. Woodcut from Sebastian Münster, *Cosmographia*, 1550. (Courtesy Alan Murray)

Semgallians in an ambush of a Lithuanian force returning from a raid into Estonia. In the following years the order soon proved its worth in battle, not least when it defeated a rebellion of the Livonians, centered on the fortress of Holm (1206).

Despite the obedience it owed to the bishop of Riga, the order was soon able to act on its own initiative, and throughout its short lifespan it continuously struggled to achieve independence from the church of Riga. It was important for the order to secure an independent territorial power base and financial resources, and it claimed part of the territory that was being conquered in conjunction with the forces of the bishop and the seasonal crusaders. This claim soon led to a conflict with Bishop Albert in respect of the division of the conquests and the terms on which the order held its territory, convents, and castles. In this struggle the balance of power constantly shifted, as seasonal crusaders left Livonia and Bishop Albert had to leave for Germany to recruit new crusaders, as occurred approximately every second year.

When Albert returned from Germany in 1207, the Sword Brethren demanded the right to retain a third of all future conquests. This initiative on the part of the order may well have resulted from a stay in Riga of the Danish archbishop of Lund in 1206–1207. The order may have seen a possibility of playing the Danish primate off against Bishop Albert by threatening to acknowledge the primacy of the archbishopric of Lund. Under pressure, Albert reluctantly agreed to assign new territory to the order, but in the case of the lands already conquered he tried to exclude the order from the core region along the river Düna. This was probably not a wise move, since as a result the Sword Brethren now looked north toward Estonia. Soon the order was able to establish its second convent and castle, Segewold, close to the Livish stronghold of Treiden (mod. Turaida, Latvia). A third convent was founded around the same time in Nussburg at Wenden deep in Lettish territory. These foundations enabled the order to push on into Estonian territory in 1208 independently of Bishop Albert. It suffered a momentary setback in 1209, when Master Winno was killed in an internal power struggle, but with the election of Volkwin (1209–1237) as its second master, the order quickly managed to reestablish stability in its leadership.

In the continued struggle for supremacy, both parties appealed to Pope Innocent III, who in October 1210 decreed that in the future the order was to retain one-third of conquered territory. In July 1212 the Sword Brethren received imperial confirmation of this privilege and were also promised free possession of the Estonian provinces of Ugaunia and Sakkala. This was undoubtedly a victory for the order and may be seen as the beginning of its state in Livonia. Bishop Albert received some compensation, when (probably in 1211) the pope authorized his ordination of new bishops in Livonia and soon after refused the order's request to have the same right in its own territory (1212). However, Innocent III compensated for this in 1213 by confirming the order's possession of Sakkala and Ugaunia and also authorizing Anders Sunesen, archbishop of Lund, to ordain bishops in these provinces. Albert of Buxhövden's decision to ordain Theoderic as bishop of Estonia (1211) can only be seen as an attempt to curb the order's designs in Estonia. Yet the advantage gained was soon lost, when Innocent III in 1213 decreed that Theoderic henceforth was to be subject only to the pope or his legate to the region, who happened to be Anders Sunesen.

The final effort to subdue the pagan Estonians began in 1215, initially with the order as its driving force. Having defeated the Estonians at Fellin in 1217, the order now dominated both the northern part of Livonia and a large part of Estonia. The threat this posed to the position of Bishop Albert prompted him to appeal in person to King Valdemar II of Denmark for help in 1218. The king obliged by sending a large fleet to Estonia the following year. Despite initial difficulties, the Danes managed to conquer the remaining northern provinces of Estonia in the summer of 1219, with the exception of the island of Ösel (mod. Saaremaa, Estonia).

The Danish crusade may have come as a surprise to the order, and in 1220 a diplomatic crisis arose when the order raided Harria. The Danes declared that, according to an agreement with the Livonian church, all of Estonia belonged to them and asked the order to hand over the hostages it had taken. Master Volkwin complied and subsequently decided to enter into an agreement with the Danes, which formally divided Estonia between them: the Danes kept the northern provinces, including the still unconquered island of Ösel, while the order received the southern provinces. In this way the order presumably hoped to avoid handing two-thirds of its conquest over to the church in accordance with the ruling of 1210. There was, however, a certain division of opinion within the order as to the wisdom of this, and later in the year it did decide to allot the church its two-thirds. Yet faced with an alliance between the order and the Danes and a Danish blockade of crusader ships embarking from Lübeck, Bishop Albert in March 1221 found himself forced to recognize Danish overlordship not only in Estonia but also in Livonia. This opened new possibilities for the order to throw off its obedience to the bishop and replace it with a link to the distant Danish king and church.

Order Domination

The scene was now set for a complete Danish takeover in the Baltic region, although this domination was to prove short-lived. After the Danes had gained a foothold on Ösel and established a stone fortress there, Valdemar II left Estonia in 1222; according to Henry of Livonia, he gave up the royal rights in Sakkala and Ugaunia to the order and spiritual rights to Bishop Albert in return for their perpetual fealty. Soon afterward, however, an uprising broke out on Ösel, and the Christian forces were unable to hold the fortress. In the following winter, the Osilians joined mainland Estonians in defeating local Danish forces before unleashing a successful attack on Fellin in January 1223. The order was taken by complete surprise and suffered heavy losses as stronghold after stronghold fell, until only the castle in Reval remained in Christian hands.

To make matters worse, Valdemar II and his eldest son were kidnapped in May 1223 by one of his vassals. They remained prisoners for two years, while the Danish Empire collapsed. To survive in Estonia, the order now had to rely on help from the Livonian church. The situation began to stabilize with the recapture of Fellin by the combined forces of the order and Livonian bishops, and the return of Bishop Albert from one of his recruitment tours with a substantial crusader army. By the end of 1224 the insurgents had to surrender. For the order, however, the events of 1223–1224 meant that the balance of power had changed significantly in favor of Bishop Albert and the Livonian church. With the Danes neutralized, the order had to agree to a new division of Estonia with the bishops, so that the order retained little more than one-third of the territory.

Hoping to perpetuate his ascendancy over the order, Bishop Albert in 1224 asked Pope Honorius III to dispatch a legate to the region to settle the territorial organization of Livonia on the current basis. This, however, proved to be a miscalculation on Albert's part. When the legate, William of Modena, arrived in 1225 he had no intention of favoring the Livonian church. When Albert's brother, Bishop Hermann of Leal (mod. Lihula, Estonia), who was now also lord of Dorpat (mod. Tartu, Estonia), together with local vassals seized some of the Danish possessions, William ordered these and the remaining Danish possessions to be transferred to himself as the pope's representative.

Many of William's other initiatives were designed to strengthen both the city of Riga and the Sword Brethren, and it was Bishop Albert and his colleagues who were disadvantaged. Now the city was allowed to gather crusaders under its banner, and it was also entitled to one-third of future conquests so that the church, originally allocated two-thirds of conquests, was left with only one-third. At the same time the order received a number of privileges and exemptions for its church in Riga (the Church of St. George). This allowed the Sword Brethren to play a far greater role in the internal life of Riga, where they could now compete for the favors of visiting and established merchants. William

also allowed the Sword Brethren to accept seasonal crusaders into their forces. This was important because many crusaders preferred to fight along with the order rather than the bishop.

These changes made the city of Riga the natural ally in the order's continued rivalry with the bishops, and in 1226 the order and city formalized their collaboration in an alliance of mutual assistance, whereby brethren became "true" citizens of Riga, while members of the upper strata of burgesses could join the order as *confratres* (lay associates).

When William of Modena left later in 1226, the territories he had held were transferred to his deputy and vice-legate, Master John. However, when the population of Vironia revolted again, John could only quell the uprising with the help of the Sword Brethren, who then went on to expel the remaining Danes from Reval. When John in turn left the region in 1227, he handed over all his territories to the order, so that it now controlled Revalia, Harria, Jerwia, and Vironia. To strengthen the legitimacy of its possession of the former Danish provinces, the order acquired a letter of protection from Henry (VII), king of Germany, in July 1228. Despite a devastating defeat in 1223 as a result of William of Modena's first legatine mission, the Sword Brethren had emerged as the leading power in Livonia.

Between Pope and Papal Legate

A new chapter in the order's history began when the Cistercian Baldwin of Aulne arrived in Livonia in 1230 as vice-legate charged with resolving the conflict that had arisen over the succession to the bishopric of Riga after the death of Bishop Albert in 1229. Soon, however, Baldwin began to involve himself in wider Livonian affairs. He came into conflict with the Sword Brethren over the former Danish provinces, which he claimed the order held illegally; with reference to William of Modena's earlier ruling, Baldwin demanded that they should be transferred to him. Faced with resistance from the local powers, Baldwin left for the Curia, where, in January 1232, he managed to have himself appointed as bishop of Semgallia (a title created for the occasion) and full legate with far-reaching authority. During the summer of 1233, Baldwin returned with a crusader army with which to bolster his demands. An army was sent to Estonia, where the Sword Brethren were ordered to surrender their territories and castles.

The order was divided over how to react to Baldwin's demands. Master Volkwin was in favor of yielding to Baldwin, but was temporarily deposed and imprisoned. The interim leadership decided to fight the legatine army, which in the ensuing battle in September 1233 was annihilated on the Domberg in Reval. The order speedily dispatched a delegation to the Curia in order to defend its action against the pope's legate. It succeeded to the extent that in February 1234 Pope Gregory IX decided to recall Baldwin and replace him as legate by William of Modena, who soon persuaded the pope to annul all of Baldwin's initiatives. But at the Curia Baldwin persuaded the pope in November 1234 to summon all his adversaries to answer a formidable list of charges. The order was accused of having summoned heretic Russians and local pagans to fight against the bishop and church of Leal, a charge that could have made the order itself a target of crusades.

In a trial at Viterbo during the spring of 1236, the order was largely exonerated. However, the king of Denmark had also begun to lobby for the return of the former Danish provinces. On this point Gregory IX supported the Danes and ordered Revalia, Jerwia, Vironia, and Harria to be given back to the Danish king. To comply would seriously have reduced the power base of the Sword Brethren, and it is doubtful whether they were prepared to do so. In the event, the order did not survive long enough for this to become evident.

Defeat and Unification with the Teutonic Order

During the 1230s the Sword Brethren had begun to direct their attention toward Lithuania, now seen as the greatest threat to Christianity in the Baltic region. This was a sentiment shared by the Russians of Pskov, with whom the order now often allied itself. In the summer of 1236, a substantial number of crusaders had arrived in Riga eager for action. Perhaps against its better judgment, the order was persuaded to organize a raid into Lithuanian territory involving both local forces and Pskovians. At a place called Saule (perhaps mod. Siauliai, Lithuania), the Christian forces suffered a crushing defeat on 22 September 1236. Probably only a tenth of the Christian force survived, and among the casualties were Master Volkwin and at least 49 knight brethren. The existence of the order was not immediately threatened. It still held its castles and had a substantial number of vassals, particularly in the northern parts of Estonia. But it was hardly in a position to raise another army for separate actions, and in the south the order had to fear Lithuanian retaliations.

Consequently, the order had to speed up negotiations that were already in progress concerning a merger with the Teutonic Order. With its bargaining power now reduced by military defeat, the representatives of the order had no choice but to accept the terms of a separate agreement reached between Hermann von Salza, grand master of the Teutonic Order, and Gregory IX to restore the former Danish provinces to Denmark. In May 1237 Pope Gregory announced the incorporation of the Sword Brethren into the Teutonic Order in four letters to the relevant parties: the order, Hermann von Salza, William of Modena, and the bishops of Riga, Dorpat, and Ösel. Later in the summer the Teutonic Order in Marburg grudgingly accepted the unification, although this was only carried out in practical terms by the end of 1237, after the arrival of the first contingent of Teutonic Knights in Livonia.

Conclusions

Despite its short lifespan, it was the Order of the Sword Brethren that introduced the military religious order as an institution to the Baltic Crusades. Much more than the seasonal crusaders, it was able to fight and keep fighting according to a chosen strategy. Without its introduction, Christianity might not have survived in Livonia, and it was a sign of its initial success that it was taken as a model for the likewise short-lived Knights of Dobrin. Both orders, however, suffered from the lack of a European network of estates and houses outside their main region of activity that could provide them with financial resources and a secure basis of recruitment. In that sense it was logical that both were absorbed by the Teutonic Order.

–John Lind

Bibliography

Benninghoven, Friedrich, *Der Orden der Schwertbrüder* (Köln: Böhlau, 1965).

———, "Zur Rolle des Schwertbrüderordens und des Deutschen Ordens im Gefüge Alt-Livlands," *Zeitschrift für Ostforschung* 41 (1992), 161–185.

Ekdahl, Sven, "Die Rolle der Ritterorden bei der Christianisierung der Liven und Letten," in *Gli Inizi del Cristianesimo in Livonia-Lettonia: Atti del Colloquio internazionale di storia ecclesiastica in occasione dell'VIII centenario della Chiesa in Livonia (1186—1986), Roma, 24–25 giugno 1986*, ed. Michele Maccarrone (Città del Vaticano: Libreria Editrice Vaticana, 1989), pp. 203–243.

Elm, Kaspar, "Die *Ordines militares*. Ein Ordenszötus zwischen Einheit und Vielfalt," in *The Crusades and the Military Orders: Expanding the Frontiers of Medieval Latin*

Christianity, ed. Zsolt Hunyadi and József Laszlovszky (Budapest: Department of Medieval Studies, Central European University, 2001), pp. 351–377.

Forey, Alan, *The Military Orders: From the Twelfth to the Early Fourteenth Centuries* (London: Macmillan, 1992).

Hellmann, Manfred, "Der Deutsche Orden im politischen Gefüge Altlivlands," *Zeitschrift für Ostforschung* 40 (1991), 481–499.

Jähnig, Bernhart, "Zisterzienser und Ritterorden zwischen geistlicher und weltlicher Macht in Livland und Preußen zu Beginn der Missionszeit," in *Die Ritterorden zwischen geistlicher und weltlicher Macht im Mittelalter,* ed. Zenon Hubert Nowak (Toruń: Wydawnictwo Uniwersytetu Mikołaja Kopernika, 1990), pp. 70–86.

Lind, John H., "The Order of the Sword-Brethren and Finland. Sources and Traditions," in *Vergangenheit und Gegenwart der Ritterorden. Die Rezeption der Idee und die Wirklichkeit,* ed. Zenon Hubert Nowak and Roman Czaja (Toruń: Wydawnictwo Uniwersytetu Mikołaja Kopernika, 2001), pp. 159–164.

Mugurēvics, Evalds, "Die militärische Tätigkeit des Schwertbrüderordens (1201–1236)," in *Das Kriegswesen der Ritterorden im Mittelalter,* ed. Zenon Hubert Nowak (Toruń: Wydawnictwo Uniwersytetu Mikołaja Kopernika, 1991), pp. 125–132.

Nielsen, Torben K., "The Missionary Man: Archbishop Anders Sunesen and the Baltic Crusade, 1206–21," in *Crusade and Conversion on the Baltic Frontier, 1150–1500,* ed. Alan V. Murray (Aldershot, UK: Ashgate, 2001), pp. 95–117.

Rebane, P. Peter, "Denmark, the Papacy and the Christianization of Estonia," in *Gli Inizi del Cristianesimo in Livonia-Lettonia: Atti del Colloquio internazionale di storia ecclesiastica in occasione dell'VIII centenario della Chiesa in Livonia (1186—1986), Roma, 24–25 giugno 1986,* ed. Michele Maccarrone (Città del Vaticano: Libreria Editrice Vaticana, 1989), pp. 171–201.

Selart, Anti, "Confessional Conflict and Political Co-operation: Livonia and Russia in the Thirteenth Century," in *Crusade and Conversion on the Baltic Frontier, 1150–1500,* ed. Alan V. Murray (Aldershot, UK: Ashgate, 2001), pp. 151–176.

Tarvel, Enn, "Livländische Chroniken des 13. Jahrhunderts als Quelle für die Geschichte des Schwertbrüderordens und Livlands," in *Werkstatt des Historikers der mittelalterlichen Ritterorden,* ed. Zenon Hubert Nowak (Toruń: Wydawnictwo Uniwersytetu Mikołaja Kopernika, 1987), pp. 175–185

Sword, Order of the

The Order of the Sword was an order of chivalry founded by King Peter I of Cyprus (1359–1369). With its motto, *C'est pour loiauté maintenir* (To maintain loyalty) it clearly imi-tated other fourteenth-century chivalric orders from western Europe.

According to the contemporary author Guillaume de Machaut, its foundation dated from before Peter's accession, but Machaut's story of its origins is open to doubt. There is no indication that membership of the order was conferred on Cypriot nobles, and in creating his order, Peter was evidently recognizing the need to appeal to Western knights and Western knightly values if he was to gain support in waging war on the Muslims. Not much is known about the function of the order, but by the fifteenth century it would seem that Cypriot kings were investing aristocratic visitors from the West with membership as a way of honoring them at little expense to themselves.

–Peter W. Edbury

Bibliography

Boulton, D'Arcy Jonathan Dacre, *The Knights of the Crown: The Monarchical Orders of Knighthood in Later Medieval Europe, 1325–1520* (Woodbridge, UK: Boydell, 1987).

Guillaume de Machaut: The Capture of Alexandria, trans. Janet Shirley, intro. and notes Peter W. Edbury (Aldershot, UK: Ashgate, 2001).

Symeon II of Jerusalem

Greek Orthodox patriarch of Jerusalem at the time of the First Crusade (1096–1099).

Symeon II assumed office sometime after 1088; he is first mentioned as a participant at a synod in Constantinople (mod. İstanbul, Turkey) in 1094–1095. As the crusaders arrived in northern Syria and laid siege to Antioch (mod. Antakya, Turkey) in October 1097, Symeon was forced to leave Jerusalem by the Artūqid governor of the city. He went into exile to Cyprus, from where he made contact with the crusader army. Two letters to Western Christianity written perhaps at the end of 1097 and the beginning of 1099 in Symeon's name were probably drawn up by the crusaders. They nevertheless reflect Symeon's relationship to the crusaders at this time, who acknowledged him as rightful patriarch of Jerusalem.

During the siege of Jerusalem (June–July 1099), Symeon sent diplomatic gifts to the crusader lords in preparation for his return to office. According to the chronicler Albert of Aachen, this return was prevented only by Symeon's death on Cyprus. However, according to the first version of the chronicle of Fulcher of Chartres, the crusaders allowed him to remain in office pending the pope's decision about the policies to be pursued with regard to the church in Palestine. When the papal legate Daibert of Pisa arrived, the decision was taken to establish a Latin Church, and Daibert was invested as patriarch of Jerusalem. It remains unclear whether Symeon II died in summer 1099 on Cyprus or lived on as patriarch in exile. The assumption of office by his successor as Greek Orthodox patriarch did not take place until 1106/1107.

–Johannes Pahlitzsch

See also: Jerusalem, Greek Orthodox Patriarchate of

Bibliography
Pahlitzsch, Johannes, "Symeon II. und die Errichtung der lateinischen Kirche von Jerusalem durch die Kreuzfahrer," in *Militia Sancti Sepulcri: Idea e Istituzioni,* ed. Kaspar Elm and Cosimo Damiano Fonseca (Città del Vaticano: Ordine Equestre del Santo Sepolcro di Gerusalemme. Scientifica Commissio pro Historia Ordinis, 1998), pp. 341–360.

———, *Graeci und Suriani im Palästina der Kreuzfahrerzeit: Beiträge und Quellen zur Geschichte des griechisch-orthodoxen Patriarchats von Jerusalem* (Berlin: Duncker & Humblot, 2001).

Plank, Peter, "Patriarch Symeon II. von Jerusalem und der erste Kreuzzug," *Ostkirchliche Studien* 43 (1994), pp. 277–327.

Syriac Sources

Classical Syriac, originally the Aramaic dialect of Edessa (mod. Şanlıurfa, Turkey) and adjacent regions of Mesopotamia, was a language widely used by Christians of the Near and Middle East during late antiquity and the early years of Muslim rule. Syriac lost its universal status gradually during the following centuries, being largely replaced by Arabic for everyday use. But it remained a sacred and venerated liturgical language in all the churches in the Syrian tradition: the Maronites, the Melkites, the Syrian Orthodox (Jacobites), and the Church of the East (Nestorians). During the age of the crusades, mainly scholars of the Syrian Orthodox Church and the Church of the East wrote nonliturgical texts in Syriac.

There is no work in Syriac exclusively devoted to the crusades or to Frankish rule in the Levant, and none of the extant narrative works originated in the states of Outremer. The most important narrative sources are three great world chronicles by Syrian Orthodox authors. Besides these works, lesser narratives, as well as fragments of correspon-

dence, coins, and inscriptions, deserve interest. Of special note are colophons, that is, scribes' notes in manuscripts on the date of their completion, which often contain historical information and comments. Important legal sources are also part of the heritage. Some of the thirteenth- and early fourteenth-century poetry of the Church of the East comments on historical events, expressing experiences of Christians under Mongol rule and describing religious changes in the region. Analysis of comments about historical and cultural matters in the theological literature of all the churches in the Syriac tradition during the time of the crusades is a desideratum.

Considering that the authors of the three Syriac universal chronicles were born in areas under Muslim rule, they appear extraordinarily well informed about the Franks, especially in comparison with the sketchy Latin reports about Syrian Christians in Outremer, let alone in the cities of the Middle East. This is partly explained by the fact that the writers took temporary residence in and traveled through territories occupied by the Franks. Two of them held the highest positions in the ecclesiastical hierarchy and thus were representatives of their communities to the Christian and Muslim authorities: Michael I the Great (1126–1199), patriarch of Antioch, and Gregory Bar Ebroyo (1226–1286), the *maphrian* (primate) of the eastern part of the Syrian Orthodox Church. The author of the third, the *Anonymous Syriac Chronicle,* is unknown; he was probably a member of the higher clergy who died after 1237. Of the three universal chronicles, only the history of the world by Bar Ebroyo is preserved in its entirety. The maphrian Gregory III (d. 1307), who was Bar Ebroyo's own brother (and originally named Barsaumo), was one of the first to continue the chronicle of Bar Ebroyo.

Because of their different scope and perspective, the three chronicles complement one another. Source criticism has identified occasional misinformation and lack of detailed knowledge, for example, about the courts, social life, and economy of the Latins in Outremer. Yet it also values these works as the sole witnesses for some matters regarding the Franks, especially in eastern Anatolia and the northern states of Outremer, for which Latin sources are poor. Above all they are irreplaceable for the study of policies toward the Eastern Christian subjects of the Latins and for their perception of the crusades and Outremer, although this information is refracted through the viewpoint of clerics from outside the Frankish principalities. It is clear that the highly educated chroniclers felt equal to and even slightly superior to the culture of the Frankish conquerors. They have a tendency to portray actions of Greek Orthodox clerics in a negative light. Mostly they appear rather detached and remain distant observers, and none of them is particularly partial to the Latins. In this respect they differ from the Syrian subjects of the Franks, who took up more definite positions either for or against their particular government. Typically of a people with little interest in military action, the chroniclers do not share the ideas of warrior heroism or holy war, either of crusaders or Muslims, although they are aware of the Latins' understanding of themselves as fighting on behalf of Christianity as a whole. Instead they judge each representative of secular rule by his ability to maintain peace and security, and especially by the effects of his government on their own church. Michael the Great and the Anonymous Chronicler criticize the lack of unity of the Latins at the time that they were losing ground to the Muslims in the second half of the twelfth century. They also reveal the slow deterioration of relations between indigenous Christians and the Muslim populace throughout the Middle East. Information about intellectual and cultural life as well as about mutual cultural contacts need further investigation.

The same holds true for the lesser sources. Colophons, fragments of historical narrative, and correspondence contain information about details of Latin rule in Jerusalem and its religious landscape. Other texts provide a rare witness to regret on the part of the Syrian Christians about the loss of the city to the Muslims in 1187 and again in 1244. Recently discovered Syriac and Arabic inscriptions in the context of art made by Christians, seals with names in Syriac letters, and other material give an idea of the normality of cultural exchange between the different Christian denominations, as well as between the religions in the Middle East at that time. Medieval inscriptions, for example, on graves and in churches, prove the existence of Syriac-speaking Christians of different denominations throughout the Middle East, along the Silk Road to China, and in the south of India.

A few years before the final loss of the last Frankish strongholds in Outremer and the Mongols' adoption of Islam, mutual diplomatic contacts intensified. The Mongol Ilkhan sent a confidant of Yahballaha III (1244–1317), catholicos of the Church of the East, as ambassador to the Christian powers of Europe to seek support for the Ilkhan's plan to conquer Syria and Jerusalem. The ambassador, Mar Bar Sauma, who like the catholicos was of Öngüt origin, met Byzantine and Western representatives with great openness and naively explored their cities, prepared to admire and entirely unconcerned with the long history of religious dispute. His report survives in a Syriac summary translation and gives an insight into the political constellations and sentiments of the time.

–Dorothea Weltecke

Bibliography

Anonymi Auctoris chronicon ad annum Christi 1234 pertinens, ed. and trans. Jean–Baptiste Chabot, Albert Abouna, and Jean-Maurice Fiey, 4 vols. (Louvain: Peeters, 1952–1974).

Assemani, Josephus S., *Bibliotheca Orientalis Clementino-Vaticana,* 4 vols. (Roma: Sacra Congregatio de propaganda fide, 1719–1728).

Baumstark, Anton, *Geschichte der syrischen Literatur mit Ausschluß der christlich-palästinensischen Texte* (Bonn: Marcus, 1922).

Chronique de Michel le Syrien. Patriarche Jacobite d'Antioche (1166–1199), ed. and trans. Jean–Baptiste Chabot, 5 vols. (Paris: Leroux, 1899–1924).

The Chronography of Gregory Abû'l Faraj, the son of Aaron, the Hebrew physician, commonly known as Bar Hebraeus, trans. Ernest A. W. Budge (Oxford: Oxford University Press, 1932).

"The First and Second Crusades from an Anonymous Syriac Chronicle," ed. and trans. A. S. Tritton and Hamilton A. R. Gibb, *Journal of the Royal Asiatic Society* 92 (1933), 69–102, 273–306.

Gregorii Barhebraei Chronicon ecclesiasticum, ed. and trans. Jean Baptiste Abbeloos and Thomas J. Lamy, 3 vols. (Louvain: Peeters, 1872–1877).

Gregorii Barhebraei Chronicon syriacum, ed. Paul Bedjan (Paris: Maisonneuve, 1890).

Histoire de Mar Jabalaha, de trois autres patriarches, d'une prêtre et de deux laïques nestoriens, ed. Paul Bedjan (Paris: Harrassowitz, 1895).

Kaufhold, Hubert, "Zur syrischen Kirchengeschichte des 12. Jahrhunderts. Neue Quellen über Theodoros bar Wahbûn," *Oriens Christianus* 74 (1990), 115–151.

Lüders, Anneliese, *Die Kreuzzüge im Urteil syrischer und armenischer Quellen* (Berlin: Akademie-Verlag, 1964).

The Monks of Kûblâi Khân, Emperor of China, trans. E. A. Wallis Budge (London: Religious Tract, Society 1928).

Moosa, Matti, "The Crusades: An Eastern Perspective, with Emphasis on Syriac Sources," *Muslim World* 93 (2003), 249–289.

Palmer, Andrew, "The History of the Syrian Orthodox in Jerusalem, Part Two: Queen Melisende and the Jacobite Estates," *Oriens Christianus* 76 (1992), 74–94.

Syrian Orthodox Church

The Syrian Orthodox Church was one of the Eastern churches the crusaders came into contact with when they arrived in the Near East. To Westerners, the Syrian Orthodox Church and community have often been known as Jacobites. The official English name of the church today (since 2000) is the Syriac Orthodox Church.

Origins

The dogmatic position of the Syrian Orthodox Church was (and is) that of the theological tradition of Severus, patriarch of Antioch (d. 538), who opposed the Christological dogma promulgated by the Council of Chalcedon (451). The Syrian Orthodox Church rejected the Monophysite Christology of Eutyches (d. after 454). It venerated Christ as truly man and truly God, the divine and the human neither being separated nor mixed. But, as the Aristotelian term *nature* could not be conceived in the plural, Christ's nature was thought of as single (i.e., verbal monophysitism, or miaphysitism).

The Latin sources usually refer to the Syrian Orthodox as "Jacobites." This name refers to Jacob Baradaeus (d. 578), who was instrumental in organizing the miaphysite resistance against the Chalcedonian imperial church in the decades following the expulsion of Patriarch Severus in the year 518. In the middle of the sixth century, a separate, non-Chalcedonian hierarchy was created with an independent patriarch of Antioch (mod. Antakya, Turkey), who, however, never resided in that city. Originating in the context of an inner-miaphysite schism, to distinguish Jacob's adherents from those of Paul of Beth Ukkome (d. 581), the name Jacobites later came to be used by outsiders to designate miaphysite Christians in Asia Minor, Syria, Palestine, and Egypt.

By the time of the crusades, a second meaning had developed: The term "Jacobite" was used to designate the Syrian Orthodox to differentiate them from the Chalcedonian (Greek Orthodox) Christians of Syria and Palestine; these were called "Syrians" in Arabic and Latin, or "Melkites" and "Greeks" by the non-Chalcedonians. Often the term was used in a pejorative sense. By contrast, the combination of the term "orthodox" with "Syriac" was already in use by the church itself during the time of the crusades. Syriac, the classical Aramaic dialect of the school of Edessa (mod. Şanlıurfa, Turkey), was always the language of the theology and liturgy of the church, and in many of its communities Aramaic dialects were spoken.

Church Organization and Hierarchy

In the twelfth and thirteenth centuries, the area called the "West" in Syriac sources, that is from Cappadocia in the north as far as Arabia in the south, was under the ecclesiastical jurisdiction of the Syrian Orthodox patriarch of Antioch, and bordered on the Coptic patriarchate of Alexandria. The Syrian Orthodox and Coptic patriarchates recognized each other's full authority as Orthodox sister churches. From 726 this was also usually the case with the Armenian Orthodox (Apostolic) Church. What was called the "East," that is Mesopotamia, Assyria, Azerbaijan, and Iraq, was under the authority of the metropolitan of Tagrit (mod. Tikrit, Iraq), called the *maphrian,* who resided in the monastery of Mor Mattai near Mosul. During this time he always was a cleric from the "West" and acted as primate.

The Frankish states of Outremer included the Syrian Orthodox archdioceses of Edessa, Samosata (mod. Samsat, Turkey), Manbij, Tarsos (mod. Tarsus, Turkey), Antioch, and Jerusalem, and many bishoprics, such as Acre (mod. 'Akko, Israel), Tripoli (mod. Trâblous, Lebanon), Cyprus, Marash (mod. Kahramanmaraş, Turkey), Raban, Kesoun (mod. Kaysun, Turkey), and Saruj (mod. Suruç, Turkey). The new political borders cut into the Syrian Orthodox administrative structures; for example, the important archdiocese of Melitene (mod. Malatya, Turkey) was split between the rule of the Dānishmendid emirate and the Frankish county of Edessa. The communities in the Middle and Far East remained beyond Frankish rule.

The Syrian Orthodox communities played an active part in church politics along with the secular clergy: they proposed candidates for the bishoprics and opposed others successfully. Their elites, who were mainly occupied as physicians, scribes, courtiers, and merchants throughout the Middle East, supported the infrastructure of the church financially. The Syrian Orthodox are not normally considered to have held feudal estates of substantial size. The existence of estates is, however, detectable, especially in the north. Cenobites and anchorites, whose life was deeply rooted in the early Christian Syriac spirituality, were another important factor.

The patriarch usually sought formal recognition from the Frankish authorities, as he did with the Muslim governors in the area of his jurisdiction. During the twelfth century, the patriarchs were based mostly in Upper Mesopotamia and Syria. They resided partly in monasteries in Frankish territory and partly in Muslim areas. The monastery of Mor

Barsaumo on the northern frontier in the archdiocese of Melitene was one of the favorite places. Insecurity in the Middle East on the one hand, and protection by the Rupenid dynasty on the other, made the kingdom of Armenia in Cilicia a favorite place of residence, notably at Hromgla (mod. Rumkale, Turkey) and Sis (mod. Kozan, Turkey) in the thirteenth century. The official residence of the patriarch remained beyond the borders of Outremer, first in Amida (mod. Diyarbakır, Turkey), and from 1166 in Mardin.

Ecclesiastical integration of the entire area of patriarchal jurisdiction was increasingly difficult. The hostility of secular powers and general insecurity were problems that the Syrian Orthodox authorities could do little about. Both the Mesopotamian and Cilician residences were occupied simultaneously during cases of schism, which occurred three times between 1180 and 1261 (1180–1193, 1199–1220, and 1253–1261), and as a result the regions drifted further apart. In 1292 a more serious schism in the Syrian Orthodox "West" began, which lasted until 1493. Several patriarchs, however, won the support of the greater part of the suffragans and the communities. They used their spiritual authority and central administrative position to improve the situation of the church according to Christian principles. Two of them, Michael I the Great (1166–1199) and Ignatius III David (1222–1252), are especially remembered as great patriarchs of that period, praised for their piety and their wisdom, their reform measures, and their generous support of the material infrastructure of the church.

Syrian Orthodox Life in Outremer and Beyond

The Syriac narrative sources paint rather a bleak picture, underlining the hardship caused by war, bandits, and encroachments on the Syrian Orthodox Church and communities. They name numerous churches destroyed by or lost to the Muslims. Syrian Orthodox refugees were swept into Frankish territory after the conquest of Edessa in 1146 and again during the swift and deadly advance of the Mongols. A slow deterioration in relations between the Syrian Orthodox and the Muslim population can be detected. Neither Muslims nor Franks sufficiently protected the Syrian Orthodox population, and on occasion even turned violently against them. Authorities on both sides did not hesitate to put pressure on Syrian Orthodox prelates for their own ends. To find explanations for their experiences and their losses, the communities turned toward their own religious and ethical conduct. Their introspection resulted in the harsh moral self-criticism reflected in the historical works of the time.

The reports in these works, however, have to be put into perspective. Scholars have even raised doubts as to the actual severity of the crisis. The situation under Muslim rule was often stable enough to allow for the construction of new churches, monasteries, and representative ecclesiastical buildings. The originality of twelfth-century artists is increasingly attracting scholarly interest. It is obvious that for literature and science this also was a period of consolidation as well as of new departures. The classical Syriac language was studied with renewed effort and used as a language of scholarship. The libraries and schools in the cathedrals and monasteries were actively sponsored by the higher clergy, and the entire traditions of church and community were gathered in encyclopedic works. At the same time, Syrian Orthodox scholars took notice of the latest developments in the philosophical and medical schools of the Middle East, shared by Muslims and Eastern Christians alike. Works by authors such as Dionysius bar Salibi or Bar Ebroyo (Bar Hebraeus) have remained standard points of reference in exegesis, theology, and legal decisions for the church and community to the present day.

A synthesis of Syrian Orthodox life in Outremer is a desideratum. In the city of Jerusalem the community had the representative monastery and church of St. Mary Magdalene, which also served as the residence of the metropolitan of Jerusalem. It was lost to the Muslims after the reconquest by Saladin in 1187. For its maintenance, the church possessed villages protected by Queen Melisende (d. 1161), while Patriarch Michael I regained a chapel in the Church of the Holy Sepulchre during his visit in 1169. The writings of James of Vitry suggest that the community of Acre was rather neglected at the beginning of the thirteenth century. However, an active scriptorium can be detected there, and a bishop was probably present throughout the time in question. In thirteenth-century Tripoli, an Eastern (Nestorian) rhetor named Jacob attracted several young men to undertake studies in medicine and rhetoric; it remains to be seen whether Tripoli was also an intellectual center for the Syrian Orthodox. The city of Antioch certainly was such a center in the thirteenth century, and Greek and Syriac as well as secular sciences were studied. Several churches and monasteries were maintained by the Syrian Orthodox in Antioch and environs, among them a Church of Our Lady and a new church of Mor Barsaumo, consecrated in 1156. In the mid-thirteenth century, Ignatius III David even built a new patriarchal residence in Antioch.

The clerical hierarchy provided not only the religious infrastructure but also the framework for the cultural and social cohesion of the communities, and acted as political representatives in dealings with the Franks. In the county of Edessa, they also became involved in the Frankish administration and even in military activities to some extent. However, on several occasions the Franks are known to have intervened directly in the government of the church. Their interference undermined the central administration of the patriarch and consequently prolonged conflicts between him and the suffragans. In Cilicia, the Syrian Orthodox communities shared in the cultural and economic upswing of thirteenth-century Cilicia, and the patriarch occasionally joined the Armenian catholicos on diplomatic missions concerning the kingdom.

Some scholars consider relations between Franks and Syrian Orthodox in Outremer to have been cordial. This certainly holds true for some individual personal relationships, such as that between Patriarch Michael I and the Latin patriarch of Antioch, Aimery of Limoges (d. 1193). Yet neither the Latin nor the Syriac sources justify this as a general assessment. The Latin sources on the whole appear rather detached and incompetent in their reports on the Syrian Orthodox, exhibiting little interest in this section of their subject population. As the Syrian Orthodox were considered to be heretics, their hierarchy on the whole was left intact. The discriminatory poll tax that they had been required to pay under Muslim rule was lifted.

In theological terms, a mutual pragmatic recognition seems to have taken place, making practical cooperation on all levels easier: At a council held in Jerusalem in 1141, dogmatic differences were not perceived as being as serious as the Franks had previously believed. Friendly encounters, joint religious practices, and also theological disputations took place. Some Franks in the north venerated the Syrian Orthodox saint Mor Barsaumo, and they occasionally accepted the service of Syrian Orthodox priests in extraordinary situations, for example, in the cases of prisoners of war outside Outremer. The Syrian Orthodox were also able to improve their position by the circumstance that the Frankish governments were largely unsympathetic to the Greek Orthodox church. Their interpretation of what the Latin Church understood as achievements of a union in the time of patriarch Ignatius III David is, however, controversial.

As with the other powers in the Middle East under which their flock was dispersed, the Syrian Orthodox authorities had to seek a modus vivendi with the secular and religious hierarchy of the Frankish principalities. They also made ample use of the possibility of establishing themselves in Antioch. Bar Ebroyo reported that it became a custom to ritually enthrone the Syrian Orthodox patriarch after his election on St. Peter's chair in the Latin-held cathedral of Antioch. Nevertheless, they avoided becoming too close to the Franks, and preferred to reside under Armenian protection. The complicated relations between Syrian Orthodox subjects and Frankish lords, the motives and interests of prelates, dignitaries, and populace, respectively, require differentiated and nuanced treatment.

–Dorothea Weltecke

Bibliography

Balicka-Witakowski, Ewa, Sebastian Brock, David G. K. Taylor, and Witold Witakowski, *The Hidden Pearl: The Syrian Orthodox Church and its Ancient Aramaic Heritage*, vol. II (Rome: TransWorld Film Italia, 2001).

Baumstark, Anton, *Geschichte der syrischen Literatur mit Ausschluß der christlich-palästinensischen Texte* (Bonn: Marcus, Weber und Ahn, 1922).

Brincken, Anna-Dorothee von den, *Die "Nationes Christianorum Orientalium" im Verständnis der lateinischen Historiographie von der Mitte des 12. bis in die zweite Hälfte des 14. Jahrhunderts* (Köln: Böhlau, 1973).

Brock, Sebastian, *Syriac Studies: A Classified Bibliography, 1960–1990* (Kaslik: Université Saint-Esprit de Kaslik, 1996).

Fiey, Jean-Maurice, *Pour un Oriens Christianus Novus: Répertoire des diocèses syriaques orientaux et occidentaux* (Stuttgart: Steiner, 1993).

Hamilton, Bernard, *The Latin Church in the Crusader States: The Secular Church* (London: Variorum, 1980).

History of Syriac Literature and Sciences (Kitab al-Lulu al-Manthur fi Tarikh al-Ulum wa al-Adab al Suryaniyya) by Ignatius Aphram Barsaum (1887–1957), ed. Matti Moosa (Pueblo: Passeggiata, 2000).

Kawerau, Peter, *Die jakobitische Kirche im Zeitalter der syrischen Renaissance: Idee und Wirklichkeit* (Berlin: Akademie Verlag, 1960).

Leroy, Jules, *Les manuscrits syriaques à peintures*, 2 vols. (Paris: Geuthner, 1964).

Moosa, Matti, "The Crusades: An Eastern Perspective, With Emphasis on Syriac Sources," *Muslim World* 93 (2003), 249–289.

Prawer, Joshua, "Social Classes in the Crusader States, the Minorities," in *A History of the Crusades*, ed. Kenneth M. Setton et al., 2d ed., 6 vols. (Madison: University of Wisconsin Press, 1969–1989), 5:59–116.

Richard, Jean, *La papauté et les missions d'Orient au Moyen Age (XIIIe-XIVe siècles)*, 2d ed. (Rome: Ecole française de Rome, 1998).

Segal, Judah B., *Edessa: The Blessed City* (Oxford: Clarendon, 1970).

Ter-Minassiantz, Erwand, *Die armenische Kirche in ihren Beziehungen zu den syrischen Kirchen bis zum Ende des 13. Jahrhunderts* (Leipzig: Hinrichs, 1904).

Weltecke, Dorothea, "Contacts between Syriac Orthodox and Latin Military Orders," in *East and West in the Crusader States. Context—Contacts—Confrontations, III: Acta of the Congress Held at Hernen Castle in September 2000*, ed. Krijnie Ciggaar and Herman Teule (Leuven: Peeters, 2003), pp. 53–77.

Syria

See Outremer

Syriac Orthodox Church

See Syrian Orthodox Church

T

Table of Honor
See Ehrentisch

Tallinn
See Reval

Tamar (d. 1213)

Queen of the kingdom of Georgia (1184–1213); co-regent in 1178, and successor to her father, King Giorgi III, six years later. Tamar's reign is usually acknowledged as the Golden Age of Georgia.

On Tamar's accession, powerful lords took advantage of the passing of the king to reassert themselves. She was forced to agree to a second coronation that emphasized the role of noble families in investing her with the royal power. Royal officials from nonnoble families were dismissed, and the nobility then demanded the establishment of the *karavi*, a political body with legislative and judicial power. Nobles were also actively involved in choosing a husband for the young queen. On their decision, Tamar married the Russian Prince Yuri Bogolubskii, the son of Grand Duke Andrei Bogolyubskii of Suzdal', in 1185, but the marriage was dissolved because of Yuri's debauchery and intrigues. Tamar later married Prince David Soslan, a member of the Ossetian branch of the Bagration dynasty (1189). In 1189–1191, Yuri allied himself with certain Georgian nobles and organized two unsuccessful revolts.

Despite internal dissent, Georgia remained a powerful kingdom and enjoyed major successes in its foreign policy. In 1193–1194, the Georgian army expanded its operations into Armenia and southwestern Transcaucasia. In 1195, a large Muslim coalition was crushed in the battle at Shamkhor. In 1203, Tamar achieved another triumphant victory when the sultan of Rūm was crushed at Basiani. The Georgians annexed Ani, Arran, and Duin in 1201–1203, and, in 1209 captured the emirate of Kars, while the mighty Armen-Shahs, the emirs of Erzurum and Erzincan, and the north Caucasian tribes became vassals of the kingdom. In 1204, Tamar actively supported the Greek nobleman Alexios Komnenos in establishing the Empire of Trebizond. The Georgians then carried war into Azerbaijan and advanced as far as Ardabil and Tabriz (1208) and to Qazvin and Khoy in northern Persia (1210). She died in 1213; her burial place remains unknown. She was succeeded by her son Lasha-Giorgi.

–Alexander Mikaberidze

Bibliography

Allen, William, *A History of the Georgian People: From the Beginning down to the Russian Conquest in the Nineteenth Century* (New York: Barnes & Noble, 1971).

Metreveli, Roin, *Tamari* (Tbilisi: Metsniereba, 1992).

Toumanoff, Cyril, "On the Relationship between the Founder of the Empire of Trebizond and the Georgian Queen Thamar," *Speculum* 15 (1940), 299–312.

Vasiliev, Alexander, "The Foundation of the Empire of Trebizond (1204–1222)," *Speculum* 11 (1936), 3–37.

Tancred (d. 1112)

Prince of Galilee (1099–1101) and regent of the principality of Antioch (1101–1103 and 1104–1112).

Capture of Tarsos by Tancred during the First Crusade. Illustration from the *Roman de Godefroi de Bouillon*, MS Paris, Bibliothèque nationale de France, fr.22495, fo. 32v. (1337). (Giraudon/Art Resource)

Tancred was born around 1076, a scion of the Norman dynasty of Hauteville in southern Italy. His parents were Odo "the Good Marquis" and Emma, a daughter of Robert Guiscard, duke of Apulia and Calabria.

In 1096 Tancred joined his maternal uncle, Bohemund of Taranto, in taking part in the First Crusade (1096–1099) and very soon distinguished himself as one of its chieftains, especially in the fighting at Nicaea (mod. İznik, Turkey) and Dorylaion (near mod. Eskişehir, Turkey), to the point that his uncle gave him the command of a company of knights. He then penetrated into Cilicia, where he clashed with Baldwin of Boulogne, brother of Godfrey of Bouillon, over the possession of Tarsos (mod. Tarsus, Turkey). Tancred rejoined the main armies at Antioch (mod. Antakya,

Turkey), where he played a significant role in the siege and the conquest of the city. After the establishment of Bohemund's principality at Antioch (1098), Tancred continued toward Jerusalem, joining first Raymond of Saint-Gilles and then Godfrey of Bouillon. Tancred became one of the most important chiefs of Godfrey's army; in June 1099 he conquered Bethlehem on Godfrey's behalf and, having joined him at the siege of Jerusalem, he commanded raids to obtain materials for building siege machines and ladders. During the conquest of the Holy City (15 July 1099), he seized the mosques of the Temple Mount and claimed the lordship of the area.

After the establishment of Frankish rule in Jerusalem, Tancred went northward and conquered Tiberias (mod.

Teverya, Israel), Nazareth (mod. Nazerat, Israel), Mount Tabor, and other places in Galilee. He was enfeoffed with these territories by Godfrey of Bouillon. Tancred took the title of prince of Galilee, and by campaigning in the areas of the Golan and the Terre de Suète, he enlarged his principality into the northern Transjordan. In 1100 he commanded the land forces at the siege of Haifa (mod. Hefa, Israel), hoping to secure an outlet for his principality on the Mediterranean. Supported by Daibert of Pisa, the new patriarch of Jerusalem, he took advantage of Godfrey's death (18 July 1100) to establish his men in Haifa castle. However, these ambitions were checked by Baldwin of Boulogne, Godfrey's brother, who came from Edessa to become the first Latin king of Jerusalem and appointed Tancred's rival Geldemar Carpinel as lord of Haifa. The clash between Tancred and King Baldwin I, who had been rivals since their march through Cilicia, was cut short as a result of the capture of Bohemund by the Dānishmendid Turks in 1101: Tancred was appointed regent in Antioch and relinquished his Galilean principality to the king.

As regent of Antioch Tancred distinguished himself both militarily, fighting against the Armenians of Cilicia and the Byzantines, who were based in the port of Laodikeia (mod. Al-Lādhiqīyah, Syria), as well as against the Turkish lords of Aleppo and elsewhere in northern Syria, and also as an administrator. After Bohemund's release in 1103, Tancred became regent of Edessa during the captivity of Count Baldwin II (of Bourcq). Called to Antioch upon Bohemund's departure to the West in 1104, he became its effective ruler until his death. According to his uncle's wish, in 1107 he married Cecilia, who was the daughter of King Philip I of France and Bertrada of Montfort and who was then in her childhood.

During the next few years Tancred's rule in Antioch was uncontested. His combined military and diplomatic talents enabled him to enlarge the principality to the south by annexing Laodikeia, Jabala, and Margat, which connected it with the county of Tripoli, and by establishing a protectorate over Muslim Aleppo. In the dispute over the succession to the county of Tripoli, he supported William-Jordan, cousin of Raymond of Saint-Gilles, in his claims against Bertrand, who was backed by King Baldwin I. In 1108 Baldwin restored Tancred's title of prince of Galilee and returned to him the ownership of the Temple area of Jerusalem, though the foundation of the abbey of the Temple of the Lord prevented Tancred from exercising any effective authority there.

Tancred's main activity was concentrated in northern Syria, where the rising power of Mawdūd, emir of Mosul, threatened both Antioch and Edessa. Due to the failure of Mawdūd's attack against the Frankish states in 1111, Tancred's power reached its zenith. He died in the fall of 1112, aged thirty-six years.

Tancred's personality was complex. A young adventurer, belonging to a cadet branch of his family, he achieved a brilliant career in the crusade and the Latin East. His military and diplomatic skills and immense energy, which were highlighted by his chronicler and admirer Radulph of Caen, were counterbalanced by his hard, self-seeking, faithless, and unscrupulous character; he was unpopular even among his own men. Yet his achievements and prestige became the basis for the growth of his romantic image, to the point that he became a popular hero through the centuries, particularly among the romanticists of the nineteenth century.

–*Aryeh Grabois*

Bibliography

Murray, Alan V., *The Crusader Kingdom of Jerusalem: A Dynastic History, 1099–1125* (Oxford: Prosopographica et Genealogica, 2000).

Mutafian, Claude, "L'enjeu cilicien et les prétensions normandes (1097–1137)," in *Autour de la Première Croisade: Actes du Colloque de la Society for the Study of the Crusades and the Latin East (Clermont-Ferrand, 22–25 juin 1995)*, ed. Michel Balard (Paris: Editions de la Sorbonne, 1996), pp. 453–463.

Nicholson, Robert L., *Tancred: A Study of His Career and Work in Their Relation to the First Crusade and the Establishment of the Latin States in Syria and Palestine* (Chicago: University of Chicago Press, 1940).

Rheinheimer, Martin, *Das Kreuzfahrerfürstentum Galiläa* (Frankfurt am Main: Lang, 1990).

Runciman, Steven, *A History of the Crusades*, vols. 1–2 (Cambridge: Cambridge University Press, 1953).

Tannenberg, Battle of (1410)

A major battle between the Teutonic Order in Prussia and the united armies of Lithuania and Poland during the Great War of 1409–1411.

During a period of truce (8 October 1409–4 July 1410) both sides prepared for a new conflict, and peace-keeping efforts by the kings of Hungary and Bohemia proved futile. Władysław II Jagiełło (Lith. *Jogaila*), king of Poland, and his cousin Vytautas, grand duke of Lithuania, devised an exceptional strategy to join forces in northern Poland in June 1410 and then march through Prussia toward Marienburg (mod. Malbork, Poland), the seat of Ulrich von Jungingen, grand master of the order.

On 15 July 1410 the Polish-Lithuanian army was engaged in battle by the Teutonic Knights in fields around the villages of Tannenberg (mod. Stębark), Grünfelde (mod. Grunwald), and Ludwigsdorf (mod. Łodwigowo) in the commandery of Osterode (mod. Ostróda). It is impossible to determine how many soldiers were involved, but the order may have had 12,000–15,000 men at its disposal, including 3,700 mercenaries mainly from Silesia and smaller detachments from the duchies of Pomerania-Stettin and Oels (Silesia), as well as some knightly pilgrims from western Europe. The Lithuanian and Polish troops were considerably superior in numbers and included Russians, Tatars, Moldavians, and mercenaries, mainly from Bohemia.

The marches and dispositions of the armies and the exact site or sites of the battlefield(s) are still disputed. Tannenberg was the last village the order's army passed through, hence the battle's German name. The Poles refer to the battle of Grunwald, indicating that Polish forces marched up and fought near Grünfelde. The Lithuanian name is Žalgiris, a translation of the name Grunwald.

The battle began late in the morning, Władysław and Vytautas waiting until the sun dazzled the enemy. Then Vytautas charged the order's left flank. The order's warriors seemed to have won, as part of the Lithuanian army withdrew after heavy fighting, harried by an undisciplined pursuit. This was, however, only a feigned flight, which caused the knights' formation to become disordered, whereupon strong Polish forces attacked from the side and broke the order's left flank; this was one of the battle's decisive moments. The order's right flank was at that time involved in fighting other Polish forces, and so when fortune seemed to favor the enemy, Ulrich von Jungingen attacked the Polish center with his third division, consisting of heavy cavalry and until then held in reserve. Three times he and his men rode the *Kehre* (that is, passing through the enemy lines and turning back again), but they were outnumbered, and most were killed or taken prisoner, and a general flight ensued. At sunset the order's wagon laager was taken by storm.

According to Polish sources, casualties were especially high among the Lithuanians and the order's army, whereas ethnic Polish losses were rather low. The Teutonic Order suffered the loss of its grand master, all its higher officers, more than 200 knight brethren, and thousands of other men. Over the next three days the defeated army's colors were collected from the battlefield and taken to the Polish and Lithuanian capitals. A peace treaty was concluded at Thorn (mod. Toruń) on 1 February 1411.

This decisive defeat ended the eastward expansion of the Teutonic Order, and Prussia lost its position as the most powerful country in east central Europe to Lithuania and Poland. Because of its symbolic character, the victory has always played an important role in the political and cultural life of these two nations.

–*Sven Ekdahl*

Bibliography

Ekdahl, Sven, "Die Flucht der Litauer in der Schlacht bei Tannenberg," *Zeitschrift für Ostforschung* 12 (1963), 11–19.

———, *Die "Banderia Prutenorum" des Jan Długosz—eine Quelle zur Schlacht bei Tannenberg 1410* (Göttingen: Vandenhoeck &Ruprecht, 1976).

———, *Die Schlacht bei Tannenberg 1410: Quellenkritische Untersuchungen*, 2 vols. (Berlin: Duncker & Humblot, 1982–).

———, "Tannenberg/Grunwald—ein politisches Symbol in Deutschland und Polen," *Journal of Baltic Studies* 22 (1991), 271–324.

Urban, William L., *Tannenberg and After* (Chicago: Lithuanian Research and Studies Center, 1999).

———, *The Teutonic Knights: A Military History* (London: Greenhill, 2003).

Tannhäuser

A German lyric poet, not historically documented, but thought to have been active in the mid–thirteenth century, two of whose songs may belong in the context of crusade.

The Manesse Codex (MS Heidelberg, Universitätsbibliothek, cpg.848) from around 1350, which has the largest collection of his songs, pictures Tannhäuser in the mantle of a knight of the Teutonic Order. His erotic and political lyrics show a strong tendency to parody the forms and themes of earlier courtly poetry.

The song "Wol ime, der nu beizen sol" ("Happy the man who goes hunting") gives an ironic account of a Mediterranean voyage: unlike the knight who can hunt and disport himself in Apulia, he is tossed on the sea in a ship with tattered sails and broken rudder, buffeted by winds from all round the compass, subsisting on ship's biscuit, salt meat, and stale wine. "May wave and ocean swell be purgatory for my sin!" [*Kreuzzugsdichtung,* ed. Müller, 71, strophe IV,

The poet Tannhäuser in the robes of a Teutonic Knight. *Manesse* manuscript (MS Heidelberg, Universitätsbibliothek, germ.848), c. 1305–1340. (Archivo Iconograpfico, S.A./Corbis)

lines 5–7]. Only sporadic phrases evoke the vocabulary of pilgrimage or crusade: "I left the land for God's sake" (V, 15); "I'd have been shipwrecked on Crete but that God saved me" (III, 3–4). A penitent's song attributed to Tannhäuser in MS Jena, Universitätsbibliothek, E1.f.101, dating from around 1330, describes the decision, on a "joyful day" (I, 1), to renounce the world and seek salvation through penance, though it has no specific features of crusading lyric.

–*Jeffrey Ashcroft*

Bibliography

Kischkel, Heinz, *Tannhäusers heimliche Trauer: Über die Bedingungen von Rationalität und Subjektivität im Mittelalter* (Tübingen: Niemeyer, 1998).

Kreuzzugsdichtung, ed. Ulrich Müller (Tübingen: Niemeyer, 1979).

Tannhäuser: Die lyrischen Gedichte, ed. Helmut Lomnitzer and Ulrich Müller (Göppingen: Kümmerle, 1973).

Thomas, John Wesley, *Tannhäuser: Poet and Legend* (Chapel Hill: University of North Carolina Press, 1974).

Tarsos

One of the principal cities of ancient Cilicia, Tarsos (mod. Tarsus, Turkey) retained its prestige in the medieval world through its association with the apostle Paul and its proximity to the Cilician Gates, the premier mountain pass between Cilicia and Anatolia.

Conquered by the Muslims in 637, Tarsos was part of the Syrian frontier with Byzantium. Emperor Nikephoros II Phokas conquered the city for the Byzantines in 965, but the catastrophic defeat of the Byzantine army by the Turks at Mantzikert in 1071 effectively isolated Tarsos from Constantinople. Initially conquered by Tancred in the course of the First Crusade (1096–1099), the city changed hands frequently among the Byzantines, the Franks of Antioch, and the Armenian Rupenid dynasty. With Adana, the town formed part of the dower of Cecilia, sister of Baldwin I of Jerusalem, after she married Roger, regent of Antioch. In 1172 the Armenians conquered the city for a final time, and it remained in their hands until it was seized by the Mamlūks sometime after 1337.

Circumstantial evidence from the twelfth and thirteenth centuries suggests that the city was thinly inhabited. The silting up of its harbor slowly redirected trade toward Ayas (mod. Yumurtalık, Turkey) and other ports in Cilicia. The Church of St. Paul, once the Latin cathedral, survives as the Kilisse Camii, and parts of two other medieval churches also survive.

–*Christopher MacEvitt*

Bibliography

The Cilician Kingdom of Armenia, ed. Thomas S. R. Boase (Edinburgh: Scottish Academic Press, 1978).

Tartu

See Dorpat

Tartūs

See Tortosa (Syria)

Tasso, Torquato (1544–1595)

An Italian poet, whose epic poem *Gerusalemme liberata*, set against the background of the siege and capture of Jerusalem on the First Crusade (1096–1099), was first published in its complete form in 1581.

To the events of the crusade, sometimes altered for dramatic effect, Tasso added episodes and characters such as the pagan sorceress Armida, who has a thwarted romance with the Christian knight Rinaldo, the tragic love story of the crusader Tancred and the pagan female warrior Clorinda, whom he unwittingly kills, and the unresolved love of Erminia, princess of Antioch, again for Tancred. Tasso wrote at a time of renewed Christian-Muslim engagement: his father Bernardo took part in Emperor Charles V's expedition against Tunis, but his specific interest in the crusades may have been stimulated by the publication of histories of the crusades by Robert of Rheims (1533) and William of Tyre (1549). Indeed Tasso's patron, Duke Alfonso of Ferrara, is known to have had a copy of Robert's *Historia Iherosolimitana* in his library.

Gerusalemme liberata was widely read in Tasso's lifetime, and numerous later editions and translations influenced the popular image of the crusades. The first full English translation, by Edward Fairfax, was published in 1600, and there seems to have been a copy of the poem in most libraries; a later translation by John Hoole (1763) ran to ten editions in fifty years. The combination of the subject matter and Tasso's own eventful and rather tragic life, culminating in his confinement in the hospital of St. Anna in Ferrara after angrily denouncing his patron the duke, appealed to and influenced fellow writers such as John Milton, John Keats, Walter Scott, and William Wordsworth, as well as

Rinaldo Under the Spell of Armida, from Torquato Tasso's poem *Gerusalemme liberata,* by Giambattista Tiepolo (1696–1770). (Erich Lessing/Art Resource)

artists from Anthony Van Dyck to Nicolas Poussin and Ferdinand Delacroix. *Gerusalemme liberata* also inspired nearly 100 operas by composers as diverse as Claudio Monteverdi, Georg Friedrich Händel, Franz Joseph Haydn, and Antonin Dvořák. Some later, particularly nineteenth-century, historians of the crusades seem to have had some difficulty in disentangling the accounts given by contemporary chroniclers of the First Crusade from events as told by Tasso.

–Elizabeth Siberry

Bibliography
Brand, Charles, *Torquato Tasso: A Study of the Poet and of His Contribution to English Literature* (Cambridge: Cambridge University Press, 1965).
Siberry, Elizabeth, "Tasso and the Crusades: History of a Legacy," *Journal of Medieval History* 19 (1993), 163–169.
Tasso, Torquato, *Gerusalemme liberata,* ed. F. Chiapelli (Milano: Rusconi, 1982).
———, *Jerusalem Delivered,* ed. and trans. A. M. Esolen (Baltimore: Johns Hopkins University Press, 2000).

Tatikios

The most famous of the Turcopoles, christianized ex-Turkish mercenaries in Byzantine service during the period of the crusades.

Tatikios was chiefly active in the last two decades of the eleventh and the beginning of the twelfth centuries, mainly in the service of the Byzantine emperor Alexios I Komnenos, who rewarded him with various high offices for his services against Normans, Saljūqs of Rūm, Pechenegs, Cumans, and crusaders.

During the First Crusade (1096–1099), Tatikios played an instrumental role in the surrender of Nicaea (mod. İznik, Turkey) by the Saljūqs to the Byzantines (June 1097) as well as in the ensuing Byzantine-crusader negotiations. In early 1098, however, in the course of the joint Byzantine-crusader operations against Antioch (mod. Antakya, Turkey), the Norman Bohemund of Tarento succeeded in persuading Tatikios to flee to Cyprus on the grounds that his life and the lives of his soldiers were in imminent danger. Bohemund claimed that Alexios I had secretly made contact with a Muslim army coming to the relief of Antioch, and that on hearing of this the enraged crusaders would naturally seek revenge on the treasonous imperial agent. Tatikios is last heard of in Cyprus between 1099 and 1103 as *periphanes-*

tate kephale (deputy admiral) of the Byzantine navy, defeating a Pisan fleet off the shores of Rhodes (mod. Rodos, Greece) that was on its way to assist Bohemund (I), now prince of Antioch.

–Alexios G. C. Savvides

See also: First Crusade (1096–1099)
Bibliography
France, John, "The Departure of Tatikios from the Crusading Army," *Bulletin of the Institute of Historical Research* 44 (1971), 137–147.
Harris, Jonathan, *Byzantium and the Crusades* (London: Hambledon & London, 2003).
Lilie, Ralph-Johannes, *Byzantium and the Crusader States, 1096–1204* (Oxford: Clarendon, 1993).
Savvides, Alexios G. C., "Taticius the Turcople," *Journal of Oriental and African Studies* 3–4 (1991–1992), 235–238.
Skoulatos, Basile, *Les personages byzantins de l'Alexiade* (Louvain: Nauwelaerts, 1980).

Taxation

See Finance of Crusades

Templar of Tyre

See Gestes des Chiprois

Temple, Order of the

The Order of the Temple was a military religious order founded around 1119 in the Latin kingdom of Jerusalem. It was dissolved by Pope Clement V at the Council of Vienne in 1312. The order took its name from its headquarters in the al-Aqṣā mosque at the southern end of the Temple platform in the city of Jerusalem, which the crusaders believed to be the site of the Temple of Solomon (Lat. *Templum Salomonis*).

In January 1129 at the Council of Troyes, the order received a Latin Rule; subsequently, further sections were added in French in the 1160s, in the early 1180s, and between 1257 and 1267. In 1139 Pope Innocent II issued the bull *Omne datum optimum,* which took the order directly under papal protection and granted it a range of basic privileges. Members could be knights or sergeants, to which the bull added a smaller group of priests. Knights wore white mantles with a red cross, and sergeants a black tunic with a red cross and a black or brown mantle, a distinction mainly

Templar castle of Baghras in Cilician Armenia; it served as the northern Templar headquarters. (Courtesy Alfred Andrea)

based on previous social status. In addition, seculars could become associates for set periods without joining the order for life.

Origins

The origins of the order remain obscure, since they were not recorded by contemporaries. However, during the first generation of Frankish settlement in Outremer after the First Crusade (1096–1099), there was little aid for pilgrims visiting the holy places. This circumstance seems to have inspired Hugh of Payns (from Champagne) and Godfrey of Saint-Omer (from Flanders), together with a small group of other knights resident in the Holy Land, to devote themselves to the protection of pilgrims. This duty was formalized by taking vows before the patriarch of Jerusalem and was probably recognized by the Latin Church in the East at the Council of Nablus in 1120. The knights may have sought to complement the care facilities offered by the Order of the Hospital, and they may have once occupied the Hospitallers'

site in the Muristan in Jerusalem. This would have placed them close to the Augustinian Canons of the Holy Sepulchre, with whom they appear to have been associated. Both King Baldwin II of Jerusalem and Warmund of Picquigny, the Latin patriarch, encouraged their efforts, and they received benefices on the Temple platform. They seem to have taken up residence in the "Temple of Solomon" in the mid-1120s, when it was vacated by the king, who moved across the city to the citadel.

In 1127 Hugh of Payns and some of his companions traveled to the West as part of the drive by Baldwin II to stimulate interest in the crusader states, and, specifically, to complete the negotiations that would lead to the marriage of Fulk V, count of Anjou, to Melisende, the king's eldest daughter. This journey enabled Hugh both to present his case for papal recognition at Troyes and to recruit new members and crusaders for the East. A letter to the brethren remaining in the Holy Land written by a certain "Hugo Peccator" ("Hugh the Sinner," possibly Hugh of Payns himself) at this time suggests that some of them were losing confidence in their mission, but this seems to have been forgotten in the rapid expansion that followed the granting of the Rule in 1129. Nevertheless, the problems discussed in the letter do serve to emphasize the novelty of the concept of a military religious order, and to a degree the letter reflects doubts about the legitimacy of such an order in the wider ecclesiastical community. These doubts were countered in part by the willingness of Bernard of Clairvaux to support the order, first by making a substantial contribution to the shaping of the Rule, and second by responding to Hugh's request to write a treatise in support of the order. The treatise, *De laude novae militiae*, praised the Templars as both monks and knights, for, quite uniquely, they performed both functions.

Functions

Although the original founders had been primarily motivated by the charitable desire to protect pilgrims on the road from Jaffa (mod. Tel Aviv-Yafo, Israel) to Jerusalem, as the order gained popularity it was able to accumulate sufficient resources in the West to finance a greatly enlarged role in Outremer. This role included garrisoning castles, supplying troops for Frankish armies, and providing military and logistical support for visiting crusaders. By the late 1130s, the Templars had been given responsibility for the defense of the castle of Baghras in the Amanus Mountains north of Antioch (mod. Antakya, Turkey). In the kingdom of Jerusalem, they may have taken over the castle of Toron des Chevaliers, on the road between Ramla and Jerusalem, in the early 1140s; certainly they held Gaza in the south by 1149–1150. By the 1160s, together with an increasingly militarized order of the Hospital, they had become an integral part of the defense of Outremer, providing a disciplined force of around 600 knights and 2,000 sergeants.

From time to time, the Templars used turcopoles or hired mercenaries to supplement their forces. At different periods they held at least fifty castles and fortified places, ranging from modest enclosures intended to provide temporary refuge for pilgrims on the routes between Jaffa and Jerusalem, and between Jerusalem and the river Jordan, to spectacular castles conceived and built on a scale seldom contemplated in the West. Vitally important in the twelfth century was their supply depot at La Fève, where roads converged from Tiberias, Jerusalem, Acre, and Bethsan. This may have had its beginnings in the 1140s; a generation later it had been established as a formidable enclosure protected by a huge ditch. By this time, it was important for the Templars to maintain such a base in the center of the kingdom because the Frankish territories, carved out by opportunism and necessity in the early stages of the conquest, were increasingly developing definable frontier zones, and the defense of these passed more and more into the hands of the military orders. Thus the castle at Jacob's Ford, situated at an important crossing point on the river Jordan, north of the Sea of Galilee (Lake Tiberias), which survived less than a year in 1178–1179, was closely linked to the Templar sphere of influence around Saphet in northern Galilee.

In addition to their responsibilities in the north and south, the Templars were granted extensive rights in the county of Tripoli, including a substantial part of the city of Tortosa (mod. Tartūs, Syria) on the coast and the castle of Chastel Blanc (Safita) inland, enabling them to maintain east-west communication in a state that was particularly vulnerable to attack because of its small size. In the thirteenth century, the order's wealth, together with the declining power of the kings and the secular aristocracy, made it even more important. Its role was symbolized by two castles: the great sea-castle of Château Pèlerin (Athlit), built between 1217 and 1221 next to the road between Haifa and Caesarea, which was intended to replace the order's much smaller fort at nearby Destroit; and Saphet (mod. Zefat, Israel), largely reconstructed between 1240 and 1243, an inland castle situated on a volcanic outcrop 800 meters (c. 2,600 ft.) above Galilee and overlooking the route between Acre and Damascus. The Templars also became heavily involved in the Reconquista in Iberia; among the grants made to them were a number of important castles in Aragon and Portugal. The expertise gained from their various activities was utilized by Western rulers, especially the popes and the kings of France and England, who employed the Templars in their administrations as well as using them as bankers, envoys, and guarantors of treaties.

Structure and International Organization

As a unique organization, the order had no obvious monastic model to imitate, so initially its structure was ill-defined. However, the sections of the Rule added in the 1160s show that by this time a hierarchy had been established: the master of the order acted in concert with a chapter of high officials, usually made up of those resident in the East; in the West, provincial commanders governed specific regions. By the late twelfth century, there was a "master on this side of

Templar castle at Ponferrada, Spain, built between 1218 and 1282 to protect pilgrims on the road to Santiago. Much of what remains today is post-Templar. (Courtesy Alfred Andrea)

the sea" in overall charge of the Western lands; around 1250 this post was retitled "visitor" and divided in two, a recognition of the basic difference between France, England, and Germany, on the one hand, and Iberia, on the other.

Financing the order's heavy responsibilities was never easy, but it was possible because of the growth of Western resources. According to the Rule, in the 1160s there were already provinces of Francia, England, Poitou, Aragon, Portugal, Apulia, and Hungary. The Western structure continued to develop, and new provinces were established in the thirteenth century. The most important of these were in Cyprus and in Aquitaine, Normandy, and the Auvergne. The emergence of a grand preceptor of Italy, with powers over provincial commanders in Lombardy, Tuscany, the Papal States, and Sardinia, reflected the need to enlarge the organization in the peninsula. Within these provinces, local preceptories were established, often clustered in groups around the main house of the region. Some performed specialist

functions, such as horse-breeding; others were set up in uncolonized territories that the order aimed to develop. In Paris and London, large houses were founded by the mid–twelfth century; both of these became financial as well as administrative centers. From the time of King Philip II of France, the treasurer of the Temple in Paris had become a central figure in Capetian demesne administration, acting both as a royal auditor and financial adviser and as head of what became the Templar bank. All the main houses and many of the other preceptories had their own churches, which often acted as centers of cults based on relics acquired by the order in the East.

Throughout the order's history, Francia (the region north of the Loire) and Languedoc always produced the greatest share of Templar resources, a proportion of which was sent to the East through payments called responsions. However, in the second half of the thirteenth century, following the conquest of the kingdom of Sicily by Charles I of Anjou, the younger brother of Louis IX of France, Italian preceptories grew in relative importance, especially those situated on the southern Adriatic coast, where exports of food, equipment, and horses through the ports helped to prop up the ailing lands in Outremer. Some of these supplies were carried on the order's own ships, although the number of ships they possessed is not known.

In Iberia, the Templars were even more directly concerned with the conflict with Islam. In 1130 Raymond Berengar III, count of Barcelona, granted them his frontier castle of Grañena, although they were evidently not expected to garrison and equip it with their own personnel at this time. In 1143 Raymond Berengar IV ceded them five major castles, including Monzon and Chalamera, as well as the further castle of Corbins, not yet in his possession, and a fifth of lands captured from the Saracens in the future. The wording of the charter shows a clear intention to encourage the order to commit more men and resources to the region. Six years before, he had agreed with the master, Robert of Craon, that the order should send ten knights to Aragon, presumably to act as a nucleus of a new Templar province. This request is reminiscent of the methods of expansion used by contemporary monastic orders, such as the Cistercians. As the frontier moved south, the Templars received more castles, notably Miravet on the Ebro River. However, although Alfonso I of Aragon had shown intense interest in the idea of a military order as early as the 1120s, the first known castle granted to the order was in Portugal at Soure on the river Mondego, given by Queen Teresa in 1128. In 1147, following the capture of Lisbon, the Templars received Cera on the river Tomar, which later developed into their main house in Portugal.

The order never established houses in eastern Europe on an equivalent scale to the West, but the inclusion of Hungary in the list of provinces of the 1160s shows that its rulers were well aware of contemporary developments. Hungary lay across the land routes used by crusaders to the East, and the Croatian extension of the kingdom incorporated Dalmatian ports with Eastern connections. From 1219 there are regular references to the master of Hungary and Slavonia. To the north, in the fragmented kingdom of Poland, recorded donations are mainly from the thirteenth century, when the aim seems to have been to use the Templars (like other monastic orders) as colonizers, especially on the borders with Germany in Silesia, Pomerania, and Greater Poland, where their estates acted as a buffer against German

expansionism. In Germany itself, the first donations date from the time of the Second Crusade (1147–1149), but the order never developed on any scale from this initial foothold, partly because of its uneasy relations with the Staufen rulers, who favored first the Hospitallers and then, in the thirteenth century, the Teutonic Knights. Generally the Templars of Central Europe were not intended as fighting forces; on the one occasion when they were involved in a major battle, at Liegnitz against the Mongols in 1241, their contribution was mainly in the form of peasant dependents, for there were only six knights present.

The Order in the Thirteenth Century

Although the disasters that struck Outremer at Hattin in 1187 and subsequently did not enhance the Templars' reputation, they nevertheless continued to perform their military and financial functions as far as was possible in the changed circumstances. By the 1230s, however, the flow of donations characteristic of the formative years of successful monastic orders began to falter, and by 1250 the order was no longer as fashionable as it had been a century before. The problems arising from this decline differed according to region. On the one hand, in Aragon thirteenth-century expansion left the order stranded, with most of its strongholds now a considerable distance behind the frontier; there were only three preceptories in Valencia. In Outremer, on the other hand, the rise of the Mamlūks in the 1260s rapidly escalated into a crisis for the Franks. Fighting to preserve a shrinking landed base, dogged by the internal rivalries of the Franks (to which the Templars made a significant contribution), and committed to apparently endless defense spending, the order was caught in a situation from which ultimately there was no escape.

When the Franks were driven out of Palestine in 1291, the military orders inevitably came under scrutiny, since their presence had failed to prevent the loss of Outremer despite their heavy consumption of resources. Plans for reform, which had been circulating since the Second Council of Lyons in 1274, were now energetically promoted; the most common idea was the creation of an order uniting the Templars and the Hospitallers, perhaps under a new master appointed from outside their ranks. In practice, nothing came of these ideas, and during the 1290s the Templars continued to organize attacks on the Syrian and Egyptian coasts, even briefly establishing themselves on the island of Ruad (mod. Arwād, Syria), off their old base at Tortosa. Their gar-

Templars burned at the stake. Anonymous chronicle. From *The Creation of the World until 1384,* translated by Bernard Guy. (Erich Lessing/Art Resource)

rison there was wiped out in 1302 and thereafter their closest bases to the Holy Land were on Cyprus.

The Trial of the Templars (1307–1312)

This new situation certainly made the military orders vulnerable, at least in the eyes of those who believed that they could not be effective without fundamental changes in structure and outlook, but not even the most radical reformers predicted the events of October and November 1307. On 13 October, the Templars in France were suddenly arrested by the officials of King Philip IV, nominally acting on the orders of William of Paris, papal inquisitor in France. Accused of

denying Christ, worshipping idols, and promoting institutionalized sodomy, the great majority confessed to one or more of the charges within six weeks of the arrests. The master, James of Molay, repeated his own confession before a public assembly of university theologians and leading ecclesiastics. Pope Clement V, who had not been forewarned, tried to prize control from the French Crown by taking over the proceedings; on 22 November 1307, he issued the bull *Pastoralis preeminentiae,* ordering a general arrest of the Templars in the name of the papacy. This began a series of trials in England, Spain, Germany, Italy, and Cyprus in addition to those already instituted in France and territories within the French sphere of influence, such as the kingdom of Navarre.

Encouraged by the papal intervention, the leaders of the order withdrew their confessions at Christmas 1307, and the following February Clement V suspended the proceedings. In an effort to force Clement to change his mind, the French Crown attempted to marshal academic and popular opinion by posing a series of questions to the masters of theology at Paris. It circulated anti-Templar and antipapal propaganda and called a general assembly of the French Estates for May 1308. This appeal to wider opinion met with mixed success, but the pope was finally obliged to meet the king at Poitiers in June, where he was virtually imprisoned by French troops. Following powerful speeches by two government ministers, William of Plaisians and Gilles Aycelin, archbishop of Narbonne, a face-saving formula was eventually found. A group of seventy-two carefully selected Templars was brought before the pope and the cardinals, where they repeated their previous confessions. Then, in the bull *Faciens misericordiam* (12 August 1308), Clement instituted two inquiries: a papal commission to investigate the order as a whole, and a series of episcopal hearings into the guilt or innocence of individual Templars within the bishops' own dioceses. In a second bull, *Regnans in coelis,* issued on the same date, the pope announced that a general council would meet at Vienne in October 1310, where the agenda would cover the three themes of the Templars, church reform, and plans for a new crusade.

In practice, the inquiries that followed took much longer than the pope had anticipated. This was partly because the Templars mounted an unexpectedly determined and coherent defense before the papal commission in the spring of 1310. But in addition, the pace of the episcopal inquiries was uneven; not all of them were accomplished with the dispatch of the Clermont hearings under Bishop Aubert Aycelin, completed in only five days in June 1309. The papal commission met in Paris between November 1309 and June 1311 in a series of three sessions. It was made up of eight members, chaired by Gilles Aycelin, although in fact one of the nominees did not sit. Apart from Gilles Aycelin, who was a long-standing servant of the king, three were French prelates, and one of the others was drawn from a background likely to ensure that he was pro-French. However, once in session, the commission proved to be far more impartial than this arrangement suggests, and slowly the Templars, now assembled in Paris in far greater numbers than before,

began to find their voice. By April 1310, nearly 600 of them had pledged themselves to the defense of the order, although the master, James of Molay, contributed little, continuing to insist that he would present his case before the pope once the opportunity arose.

The defense was led by two lawyer-priests: Peter of Bologna, a former procurator of the order at the papal court, and Reginald of Provins, preceptor of Orléans. They castigated the proceedings as illegal and arbitrary, declared that the Templars had only confessed because of torture and threats of force, and claimed that the king and the pope had been deliberately misled by malicious and venal informers. So effective was this defense that the French government was driven to halt it by outside intervention. In May 1310, Philip of Marigny, archbishop of Sens, and brother of the king's finance minister, Enguerrand, condemned Templars from his province as relapsed heretics; they were handed over to the secular authorities and burnt to death. At the same time, the two leading defenders were prevented from making any further appearances before the commission, which was now fed a succession of witnesses apparently so terrified by the news of the executions that they could be guaranteed to confess. However, only a minority of these are listed among the defenders of the previous April, so it is by no means certain that the defense would have collapsed had not the French government been able to exploit its position as jailer.

The Council of Vienne began a year later, in October 1311. Opinions had been sought from leading members of the church on the matters to be discussed, and reports on the Templars had been gathered from the various inquiries. The fathers, however, were not convinced by the evidence and voted to allow the Templars to present their case, a decision apparently taken literally by seven Templars who suddenly appeared at the council, claiming to represent a further 1,500 brethren still at large in the region. But the French Crown had no intention of allowing such an outcome. After secret discussions with Philip's representatives in February 1312, reinforced by the appearance of the king and his entourage the following month, the pope agreed to dissolve the order and grant its property to the Hospitallers. Although the bull *Vox in excelso* (2 March 1312) did not condemn the order, it did declare that it was impossible for it to continue and that its property should still be deployed in aid of the Holy Land in accordance with the wishes of the original donors. Another bull, *Ad providam* (2 May 1312), established that the Templars themselves should be considered on

Masters of the Order of the Temple

Hugh of Payns	1119–c. 1136
Robert of Craon	c. 1136–1149
Everard of Les Barres	1149–1152
Bernard of Tremelay	1153
Andrew of Montbard	1154–1156
Bertrand of Blancfort	1156–1169
Philip of Nablus	1169–1171
Odo of Saint-Amand	1171–1179
Arnold of Torroja	1181–1184
Gerard of Ridefort	1185–1189
Robert of Sablé	1191–1192/1193
Gilbert Erail	1194–1200
Philip of Plessis	1201–1209
William of Chartres	1210–1218/1219
Peter of Montaigu	1219–1230/1232
Armand of Périgord	c. 1232–1244/1246
William of Sonnac	c. 1247–1250
Reynald of Vichiers	1250–1256
Thomas Bérard	1256–1273
William of Beaujeu	1273–1291
Thibaud Gaudin	1291–1292
James of Molay	1292–1306

an individual basis, with the imposition of appropriate penances for the guilty. Monastic vows remained valid, and provision for unconvicted Templars was to be made, either in the form of pensions, as was frequently done in Aragon and Roussillon, or by acceptance into existing religious orders, such as the Cistercians, as in England.

Dissolution of the Order (1312–1318)

The dissolution of the order brought its own problems. The French Crown continued to press the Hospitallers for reparations, both for expenses incurred and debts claimed; the Hospitallers were obliged to pay 200,000 *livres tournois* (pounds of the standard of Tours) in 1313 and another 60,000 soon after. Closure was not achieved until 1318, when the order paid out a further sum of 50,000 livres tournois. In England, grants of former Templar property to royal supporters were not easily regained; some were still outstanding in 1338 when the Hospitallers surveyed their lands in England. In Aragon and Portugal, where there had been little belief in the guilt of the Templars, neither King James II nor King Dinis would accept the creation of a potentially over-

mighty order, which the Hospitaller absorption of the Templar lands might bring, and lengthy and complicated negotiations with the papacy followed. Clement V remained stubborn, but under John XXII compromises were reached.

In 1316 the Aragonese were allowed to use the Templar property to establish the Order of Montesa in Valencia, although the Hospitallers were to have the lands in the other territories of the Aragonese Crown. In Portugal no action had been taken against the Templars, and in 1319 the king was granted the right to create the new Order of Christ. In Cyprus the Templars had supported the coup of Amaury of Lusignan, lord of Tyre, against his brother King Henry II in 1306; when the king returned in 1310, it was not likely he would make much effort to help the Templars, even though the trial proceedings on the island had produced nothing to suggest that the knights had any cognizance of the accusations made by the French government. This did mean, however, that the transfer of lands was effected more easily than elsewhere, partly because of good relations between the king and the Hospitallers. Few individual Templars were still alive by the 1350s, although before that time some drew attention to themselves through criminal activities, including piracy, rape, and robbery, while others occasionally turned up in Muslim lands, either in service or in captivity. Most, however, seem to have been able to live on their pensions, which, in regions controlled by the Aragonese Crown, were often quite generous. Others of high social status were protected by their families, especially in Aragon and Germany.

Conclusions

The dissolution of the Templars (an act unprecedented in papal history in the early fourteenth century) after nearly two centuries of fame and power, and achieved after what was seen as a humble and pious beginning, has encouraged deterministic interpretations of its history, for it seems to offer a classic example of the Boethian Wheel of Fortune. However, despite conflict with other institutions, a decline in the level of donations, and some vocal criticism from parties who were themselves often far from disinterested, the order continued to perform important functions. This was acknowledged by Edward II of England and James II of Aragon, both of whom, at least initially, were reluctant participants in the trial. Although the fall of Acre in 1291 had been a tremendous blow, the order was still able to recruit, and there are signs that it was beginning to adapt to the new military setting of naval warfare, which, as the Hospitallers later demonstrated, was becoming the most effective means of crusading combat.

The explanation of the fate of the Templars must therefore be sought less in the nature and state of the order itself than in the motives of the enigmatic ruler of France, Philip the Fair. No consensus has ever been reached about his reasons for initiating the attack against the order. Neither is there agreement about whether it was the king or his advisers who really controlled and determined policy. The prospect of financial gain (even if only in the short term) to a monarchy under immense pressure from unresolved conflicts with England and Flanders, yet without a reliable system of regular taxation to pay for them, must have played a major part, as many contemporaries living outside France did not hesitate to point out. Moreover, Templar property in France does appear to have been more extensive than that of the Hospitallers, even if that was not necessarily true elsewhere.

The king's own religious sensibilities, combined with a strong sense of monarchical obligation, probably deriving from his perception of the reign of his revered grandfather, may have convinced him that the Templars were guilty of heretical crimes and that, once known, toleration would bring down divine wrath upon his people. Before him lay the example of the Jews from whom, in Capetian propaganda, God had withdrawn his favor, replacing them with the French as his chosen people. In these circumstances, the king may have seen the confiscation of Templar wealth as his Christian duty. Nevertheless, in succeeding centuries some were unable to accept the order's demise, and legends about the continued secret existence of linear successors still persist. The manner of the order's end has created a unique historical afterlife of such tenacity that for many, "Templarism" is more real than the known history of the order in the twelfth and thirteenth centuries.

–*Malcolm Barber*

Bibliography

Barber, Malcolm, *The Trial of the Templars* (Cambridge: Cambridge University Press, 1978).
———, *The New Knighthood: A History of the Order of the Temple* (Cambridge: Cambridge University Press, 1994).
Borchardt, Karl, "The Templars in Central Europe," in *The Crusades and the Military Orders: Expanding the Frontiers of Medieval Latin Christianity,* ed. Zsolt Hunyadi and József Laszlovszky (Budapest: Department of Medieval Studies, Central European University, 2001), pp. 233–244.
Bramato, Fulvio, *Storia dell'Ordine dei Templari in Italia,* 2 vols. (Roma: Atanòr, 1991–1994).
Bulst-Thiele, Marie-Luise, *Sacrae Domus Militiae Templi Hierosolymitani Magistri: Untersuchungen zur Geschichte des Templerordens, 1118/9–1314* (Göttingen: Vandenhoeck & Ruprecht, 1974).
Cartulaire général de l'Ordre du Temple, 1119?–1150: Recueil des chartes et des bulles relatives à l'Ordre du Temple, ed. Guigue A.M.J.A. d'Albon (Paris: Champion, 1913).
Demurger, Alain, *Les Templiers: Un chevalerie chrétienne au Moyen Age* (Paris: Seuil, 2005).
Finke, Heinrich, *Papsttum und Untergang des Templerordens,* 2 vols. (Münster: Aschendorffsche Buchhandlung, 1907).
Forey, Alan J., *The Templars in the Corona de Aragón* (London: Oxford University Press, 1973).
———, *The Fall of the Templars in the Crown of Aragon* (Aldershot, UK: Ashgate, 2001).
Nicholson, Helen J., *The Knights Templar: A New History* (Stroud: Alan Sutton, 2001).
Papsturkunden für Templer und Johanniter: Vorarbeiten zum Oriens Pontificus, ed. Rudolf Hiestand, vols. 1–2 (Göttingen: Vandenhoeck & Ruprecht, 1972–1984).
Partner, Peter, *The Murdered Magicians: The Templars and Their Myth* (Oxford: Oxford University Press, 1981).
La Règle du Temple, ed. Henri de Curzon (Paris: Librairie Renouard, 1886).
The Rule of the Templars: The French Text, trans. Judi Upton-Ward (Woodbridge, UK: Boydell, 1992).
Sans i Trave, Josep Maria, *Els Templers catalans: De la rosa a la creu,* 2d ed. (Lleida: Pagès editors, 1999).
Selwood, Dominic, *Knights of the Cloister: Templars and Hospitallers in Central-Southern Occitania, c. 1100–c. 1300* (Woodbridge, UK: Boydell, 1999).
The Templars: Selected Sources, trans. Malcolm Barber and Keith Bate (Manchester: Manchester University Press, 2002).

Terre de Suète

The Terre de Suète was the name applied by the Franks of Outremer to the region east of Lake Tiberias (Sea of Galilee), deriving from the Arabic *al-Sawād* ("the black"), which referred to its dark basalt soil. The core of the region was the fertile, corn-producing area known as the Hauran (mod. southwestern Syria), but the Terre de Suète was regarded as extending into the Jaulan (Golan) to the north and beyond the river Yarmuk to the south.

The region was inhabited predominantly by settled Muslim Arabs, with minorities of Syrian Christians and Bedouin. In the period 1105–1126, the Franks of Jerusalem made strenuous efforts to wrest control of the region from the atabegs of Damascus, without being able to annex it permanently, and during this time an accommodation was reached (which came to be repeatedly renewed by treaty up to the time of Saladin) recognizing the Terre de Suète as a condominium under the joint sovereignty of Damascus and the kingdom of Jerusalem. Each party took a third of its produce and revenues, the remainder being left to its inhabitants. The area north of the river Yarmuk remained largely demilitarized, although for most of the twelfth century the Franks maintained an important strongpoint south of the river at the cave fortress of Cave de Suète (mod. Habis Jaldak).

–*Alan V. Murray*

Bibliography

Dédéyan, Gérard, "Un émir arménien du Hawrân entre la principauté turque de Damas et le royaume latin de Jérusalem (1147)," in *Dei Gesta per Francos: Etudes sur les croisades dédiées à Jean Richard / Crusade Studies in Honour of Jean Richard,* ed. Michel Balard, Benjamin Z. Kedar, and Jonathan Riley-Smith (Aldershot, UK: Ashgate, 2001), pp. 179–186.

Mayer, Hans Eberhard, *Die Kreuzfahrerherrschaft Montréal (Šōbak): Jordanien im 12. Jahrhundert* (Wiesbaden: Harrassowitz, 1990).

Prawer, Joshua, *The Latin Kingdom of Jerusalem: European Colonialism in the Middle Ages* (London: Weidenfeld and Nicolson, 1972).

Rheinheimer, Martin, *Das Kreuzfahrerfürstentum Galiläa* (Frankfurt am Main: Lang, 1990).

Teutonic Order

The Teutonic Order (Ger. *Deutscher Orden*), also known as the Teutonic Knights, was one of the three great international military religious orders, alongside the orders of the Temple and the Hospital of St. John. It possessed houses and administrative structures in the Mediterranean countries, but it was mainly based in the Holy Roman Empire, from which most of its members were recruited.

The Origins of the German Hospital at Acre

The origins of the order date back to the foundation of a field hospital by German crusaders at the siege of Acre (mod. 'Akko, Israel) around the year 1190 during the Third Crusade (1189–1192). When the siege ended in July 1191, the hospital was transferred into the city, where it found a site close to the Gate of St. Nicholas. In September 1190 Sibrand, the master of the German hospital, was granted the hospital of the Armenians in Acre by Guy of Lusignan, king of Jerusalem.

Though this donation was never realized, the document recording it is the first relating to the order's early history. Today there is a consensus that there was no personal or material connection with an older German hospital in Jerusalem that was incorporated by the Hospitallers in 1143. Yet one remaining problem concerning the hospital's early history is presented by an account of its foundation given in a text known as the *Narratio de primordiis ordinis Theutonici.* Here two men named Konrad and Burchard are claimed as its founders and first masters: the account states that they had come to Jerusalem in the company of Duke Frederick V of Swabia, the younger son of Emperor Frederick I Barbarossa, and that they took over a temporary hospital from citizens of Bremen and Lübeck. However, these two (described as chaplain and chamberlain of the duke) were probably inserted into the story to stress the close relationship between the early order and the Staufen emperors, which lasted until the middle of the thirteenth century. Sibrand is most likely to have been the real founder of the hospital.

Sibrand's successors Gerhard (1192), Heinrich (1193/ 1194), and perhaps Ulrich (1195) were probably priests, since Heinrich is referred to as a prior. Already during the time of Sibrand, a fraternity had been formed at the hospital, which was recognized and taken under papal protection by Clement III in February 1191. This fraternity received another papal privilege in December 1196 from Celestine III, who freed the brethren from the payment of the tithe from newly cultivated lands and gave them the rights to elect their own master and to bury people who were not members of the community. King Guy and his successor Henry of Champagne donated lands in Acre, Tyre (mod. Soûr, Lebanon), and Jaffa (mod. Tel Aviv-Yafo, Israel) along with additional rights in the kingdom of Jerusalem.

The Formation of the Military Order

A new development was probably initiated by the Holy Roman Emperor Henry VI, who was planning a crusade when he died in Sicily in 1197. A first German contingent had already reached the Holy Land by this time, and when its leaders discussed the situation, together with the higher clergy of the Frankish states, in March 1198, they decided to ask the pope to allow the brethren to engage in warfare against the pagans. This request was granted by Innocent III in February 1199, who gave to the fraternity the Rule of the Hospitallers for their charitable tasks and the Rule of the Templars for their military activities. This was proba-

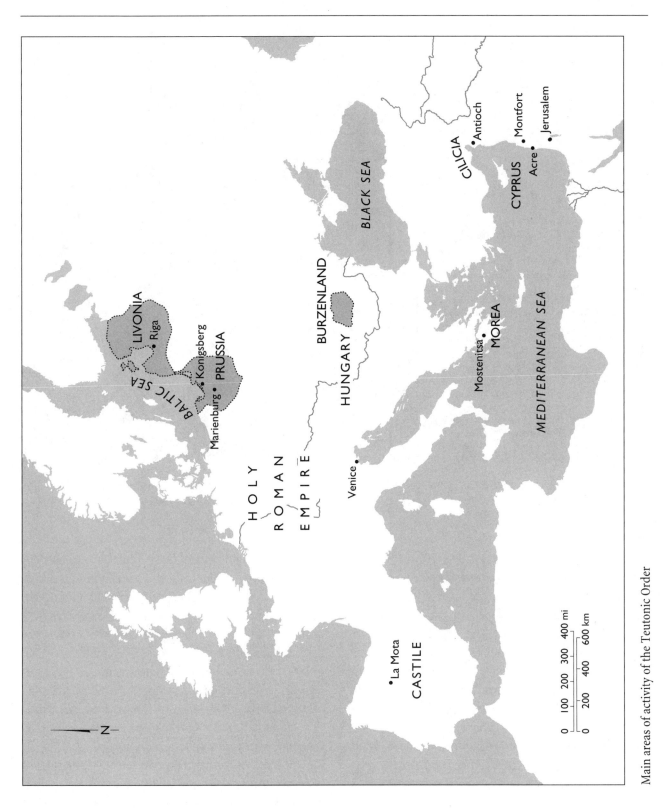

Main areas of activity of the Teutonic Order

CYPRUS
CILICIA
Antioch
Montfort
Jerusalem
Acre
BLACK SEA
BURZENLAND
HUNGARY
MEDITERRANEAN SEA
MOREA
Mostenitsa
LIVONIA
Riga
Konigsberg
PRUSSIA
Marienburg
BALTIC SEA
HOLY
ROMAN
EMPIRE
Venice
CASTILE
La Mota

N

0   100   200   300   400 mi
0   200   400   600 km

Ruins of Montfort, headquarters of the Teutonic Order in the kingdom of Jerusalem. (Courtesy Alfred Andrea)

bly only a provisional regulation, since the brethren soon (at least after 1209) started to formulate their own customs (Lat. *consuetudines*). In 1244 Pope Innocent IV gave them permission to adapt some of their regulations in the light of the current problems of the order. This led to a final revision of the statutes, divided into a rule, laws, and customs, to which only some laws of the later grand masters were added. After 1199, the order consisted of knight brethren and priests, but there were also half-brethren (Ger. *Halbbrüder* or *Graumäntler*) of nonnoble origin who took full vows, (half-)sisters, and friends of the order (Lat. *familiares*). The order took over the white mantle of the Templars but with a black cross, while half-brethren were dressed in grey.

The order was basically oligarchic. It was led by a master, who from the time of Hermann von Salza was termed "grand master," literally "high master" (Ger. *Hochmeister*), probably to distinguish him from the "land masters" (Ger.

Landmeister) of Prussia and Livonia. The master depended on the council of the most senior brethren and on the yearly chapters general (the assemblies of brethren in the East). Later, the chapters general met only rarely and were formed by the representatives of the order's bailiwicks (Ger. *Balleien*) and houses.

Soon other officials were introduced. The earliest known high dignitaries (Ger. *Grossgebietiger*) were in 1208 the grand commander (Lat. *praeceptor*, Ger. *Grosskomtur*), the marshal (Lat. *marescalcus*, Ger. *Marschall*), and the hospitaller (Lat. *custos infirmorum*, Ger. *Spittler*). The grand commander was the lieutenant of the master, responsible for provisioning and finance; the marshal had mainly military tasks, while the hospitaller was the director of the order's main hospital. In 1228 a draper (Ger. *Trappier*) is mentioned for the first time; after 1240 there was a treasurer (Ger. *Tressler*), while the castellan of the order's castle at Montfort near Acre, constructed in the 1220s, became equally important.

These offices were modeled on to the statutes of the Hospitallers. Unlike the earlier case of the Hospitallers, the militarization of the fraternity at the German hospital in Acre obviously met no resistance, though its first European donations were only concerned with hospitals. In May 1197 Emperor Henry VI donated the hospital of St. Thomas in Barletta, and donations of hospitals in Halle, Bolzano, and Friesach followed between 1200 and 1203. By 1209 the order had also acquired property in Tripoli, Antioch, Cilicia, Cyprus, and Greece, although not all donations were realized. Houses were founded in Italy, Germany, Spain, and France, which were subordinated to local commanders. A bailiwick as an administrative unit of several houses under a land commander (Ger. *Landkomtur*) is first mentioned for Sicily in 1212, and a German land commander in 1218. Other bailiwicks were soon instituted in Cilicia, Romania (i.e., Greece), Apulia, and Austria, then in Lombardy and Spain. When in 1236 the German land commander became the superior of another regional land commander, this was the beginning of the office of the German master (Ger. *Deutschmeister*), which, together with the later institutions of land masters of Prussia and Livonia, formed the highest level of the regional administration of the order.

Little is known of the first masters Heinrich (or Hermann) Walpot, Otto von Kerpen, and Heinrich Bart, but the fourth master, Hermann von Salza (1209/1210–1239), was very successful. He became one of the counselors of Emperor Frederick II, and at the same time managed to develop a close relationship with popes Honorius III and Gregory IX. Honorius III granted no less than 113 privileges to the Teutonic Knights, who in 1221 also received all the rights of the other military orders, thus finally becoming an international order of the church. Hermann was involved in Frederick's crusade of 1228–1229, and he also successfully mediated the Treaty of San Germano (1230) between Frederick and Gregory IX.

The Order's Policies in the Thirteenth Century and Its Acquisitions in Hungary, the Holy Land, and the Baltic Region

As well as with the Holy Land, Hermann's policies were concerned with eastern central Europe, first with southeastern Hungary (until 1225), and then with Prussia. In 1211, King Andrew II of Hungary, who was married to a German princess, gave the Teutonic Knights the region of Burzenland (mod. Tara Bîrsei, Romania) close to the territories of the

heathen Cumans (Lat. *terra Borza nomine ultra silvas versus Cumanos*) in order to organize the defense of the area, to find (German) settlers, and to bring about the Christianization of the Cumans. A first contingent of the order arrived in 1212, but soon serious problems arose, since the queen was murdered in 1213 and the section of the Hungarian nobility that opposed the order's engagement gained in influence. Thus the Teutonic Knights were driven out in 1218 and (after a short reinstatement in 1222) once again, this time finally, in 1225. Perhaps the order had attracted German settlers from the areas newly populated by the king's predecessors, and probably it went too far in its efforts to gain political and ecclesiastical autonomy.

In the Holy Land, Hermann strengthened his position by his successful participation in the Fifth Crusade (1217–1221). Using a donation of 6,000 marks of silver by Duke Leopold VI of Austria, in 1220 he acquired the possessions of Otto and Beatrix of Henneberg (the heirs of Joscelin III of Courtenay): the so-called Seigneurie de Joscelin, mainly the barony of Toron with the castles of Banyas and Châteauneuf. This acquisition enabled him to start building the order's main castle, Montfort, situated east of Acre, though Toron itself was never conquered from the Muslims. More property was acquired from the lords of Caesarea and Beirut after 1244. Lands purchased east of Beirut (1257/1261) were soon lost, but the order managed to establish its own small territory around Montfort until the Mamlūks devastated its surroundings in 1266 and finally took the castle in 1271. The Teutonic Knights became nearly as important for the weakened states of Outremer as the Templars and Hospitallers.

When Emperor Frederick II came to the Holy Land in 1228, having been excommunicated by Gregory IX, he was supported only by the Teutonic Knights. They were also involved in the military conflicts over the regency for the nominal king of Jerusalem, Frederick's son Conrad IV. In the 1250s, the order, having large properties in Cilicia (Lesser Armenia), favored an alliance with the Mongols, like the crusade leader King Louis IX of France, while the Templars and Hospitallers opted for a military response. Together with the other military orders, the Teutonic Knights remained in Acre probably until 1291, though in 1290 Grand Master Burchard von Schwanden, who had gathered about 40 knight brethren and 400 crusaders to defend the Christian territories, resigned and left the order.

In the second half of the thirteenth century, the order was

weakened by internal quarrels. After the deaths of Hermann von Salza (1239) and Konrad von Thüringen (1240), the brethren elected Gerhard von Malberg, who distanced himself from the emperor, was invested by Innocent IV with a ring, and took an oath of fidelity to the pope. When he came to the Holy Land, he was criticized for his financial policies and finally forced to resign early in 1244. During the intensified conflict between papacy and empire, the order was no longer able to maintain its neutral position, and different factions formed. Gerhard's successor, Heinrich von Hohenlohe, had to travel to Rome to explain the order's position, while Frederick II confiscated the order's property in the kingdom of Sicily, only to return it on his deathbed (1250).

Meanwhile the order had established itself in the eastern Baltic region, in Prussia and Livonia. From 1230 onward following a call by Duke Conrad of Mazovia and helped by crusader contingents, the order succeeded in conquering the Kulmerland (the territory of mod. Chełmno, Poland) and the area east of the river Vistula from Thorn (mod. Toruń, Poland) in the south as far as the Baltic coast in the north. Castles were built and towns were founded with the help of German settlers mainly from northern Germany and Silesia. When in Livonia the Sword Brethren, a military order founded by the bishop of Riga, suffered a heavy defeat by the Lithuanians at Saule, in 1237 the surviving Sword Brethren were incorporated into the Teutonic Order following an order by Pope Gregory IX. In contrast to Prussia, where the order succeeded in establishing an "order state" (Ger. *Ordensland*), government in Livonia was shared with other powers: the bishop (later archbishop) of Riga, the bishops of Ösel-Wiek, Curonia, and Dorpat (mod. Tartu, Estonia), the town of Riga, and even the (secular) knights of the territories of Harria and Vironia in North Estonia, which the order bought from the Danish king Valdemar IV in 1346. But the order now became responsible for Livonia's defense, also in the conflicts with the Russian principalities of Pskov and Novgorod. After the order's defeat at the battle of Lake Peipus by the prince of Novgorod, in April 1242 the Prussians rose against the Christian mission.

Thus from 1242 to 1249 the order had to face a serious rebellion by the native Prussians (helped by the duke of Pomerelia), which only ended after mediation by a papal legate. Then, in the short interval before the outbreak of a second rebellion in 1260, there emerged the first signs of tensions between the order's headquarters in Palestine and its distant branches. About 1251, the Grand Commander Eber-

hard von Sayn was sent to Prussia and Livonia as land master to reorganize the order's structures there. He stressed that the order's headquarters were in the Holy Land and that the brethren were not allowed to promulgate new regulations without the consent of master and chapter. The land masters had to submit written reports every year and to come to the central convent every three years. In the Holy Land, an important faction within the order sought to ensure that the master remained in the East. Thus in the time of Master Anno von Sangerhausen (1256–1273), statutes were passed according to which the master had to ask for permission of the chapter to return to the West.

Even after Montfort was lost in 1271, large sums of money were spent in extending the order's properties around Acre. At the same time, the Prussian branch had to defend its lordship against the rebellious native Prussians, and it was only in 1283 that all heathen territories in Prussia were brought under the order's control. Since men and money were needed in both Prussia and Palestine, opposing factions soon quarreled about the order's future policies. After the resignation of Burchard von Schwanden, who adhered to the Palestine faction, in 1291 Konrad von Feuchtwangen, a member of the Baltic faction, was elected. When Acre was lost to the Mamlūks, the order's headquarters were moved to Venice. This new site was of course an important starting point for crusading activities, but it was also closer to the Baltic region than was, for example, Cyprus, and Konrad clearly cared little about the situation in the Holy Land. This changed again with the next master, Gottfried von Hohenlohe (1297–1303), but the Palestine faction lost ground when it became clear that there would be no new crusade to the Holy Land in the near future. Finally, in 1309 Grand Master Siegfried von Feuchtwangen transferred the order's headquarters to Marienburg (mod. Malbork, Poland) in Prussia.

The Grand Masters in Prussia and the Order's Role in Late Medieval Christianity

Siegfried von Feuchtwangen's successor, Karl von Trier (elected 1311), also faced serious internal resistance; he was deposed in Prussia in 1317, reinstated at a chapter general in Erfurt 1318, and thereafter resided in his home town of Trier, where he died in 1324. Yet the decision of 1309 had a lasting impact. Far away from strong secular authorities such as the king of France, who had brought down the Templars, the Teutonic Order succeeded in building up its own territory in the Baltic region, based on a German settlement that

Teutonic Knights kneel to be blessed in a battle against the Russians, as imagined in the film *Alexander Nevsky,* directed by Sergei Eisenstein (1938). (Mosfilm/The Kobal Collection)

had already started in around 1230 and that became more intensive after 1283, but also on a loyal native Prussian nobility that helped to organize the order's lordship over the original inhabitants.

It was in the time of Grand Master Werner von Orseln (1324–1330) that the later medieval structures took shape. The grand masters were supported financially by some of the Prussian commanderies and advocacies (Ger. *Vogteien*), while the high dignitaries were based in other commanderies: the marshal in Königsberg (mod. Kaliningrad, Russia), the hospitaller in Elbing (mod. Elbląg, Poland), and the draper in Christburg (mod. Dzierzgón, Poland), while the grand commander and treasurer remained in Marienburg.

After the final conquest of Prussia in 1283, the order turned against the still heathen Lithuanians, with the help of crusading contingents from all over Christian Europe. It was only the Polish-Lithuanian union of 1386 and the baptism of the Lithuanian ruler Jogaila (Pol. *Jagiełło*) that called the order's policies into question and led to a series of conflicts, all of which were lost by the order. The first major defeat was that of Tannenberg (Grunwald) in July 1410, in which Grand Master Ulrich von Jungingen and about 300 knight brethren died. The immense indemnities that had to be paid to Poland and Lithuania caused internal conflicts, and the *Ordensland* was widely devastated, as it was in the following wars. Finally, after the Thirteen Years' War (1454–1466), in which the Prussian estates (towns and knights) subjected themselves to Polish authority, the order lost two-thirds of its Prussian territories.

From the fourteenth century onward, the order concentrated its activities on the eastern Baltic area, but it also remained an international military order with houses in different parts of the Mediterranean regions. It received large donations in Castile from the 1220s (in La Mota near Valladolid, in Seville, Córdoba, and in the vicinity of Toledo), having somehow participated in the final phase of the Reconquista (the reconquest of the Iberian Peninsula from the Muslims) after the campaign of Las Navas de Tolosa (1212).

Until the beginning of the fifteenth century, the order's commanderies were mostly governed by German knight brethren, but in 1453 La Mota had a Spanish commander, Juan de la Mota. The order's Spanish properties were lost during the Thirteen Years' War, when it tried to sell rights and possessions outside La Mota. The situation was similar in southern Italy, where the order's first donations by Emperor Henry VI (Barletta and La Magione in Palermo) were expanded up to the beginning of the fourteenth century; in 1260 Pope Alexander IV donated the Church of St. Leonard in Siponto (Apulia). Due to the financial problems of the proctor general at the Roman Curia—who was for some time after 1466 administrator of Apulia—and the behavior of the last land commanders, the bailiwicks in Apulia and Sicily were lost in 1483 and 1492, respectively.

In Frankish Greece, the order had received some lands in the west and south of the Peloponnese since 1209, though its center was in Mostenitsa in the north. But its position there was too weak to organize any effective resistance against the Turkish advance, and between 1397 and 1402 the order had to pay tribute to the Turks. In 1411 it tried to sell the bailiwick of Romania to Venice, but no agreement was reached. When the Byzantines of Mistra conquered the northwest of the Peloponnese between 1422 and 1432, Mostenitsa and other possessions were lost. Only its house in the Venetian possession of Modon in the south remained in the order's hands, until the city was taken by the Turks in 1500.

Throughout the fifteenth century, different efforts were made to renew the order's crusading activities. When Grand Master Konrad von Jungingen for a time won over Grand Duke Vytautas (Ger. *Witold*) of Lithuania and received Samogitia in the Treaty of Sallinwerder in October 1398, he also agreed to join a Lithuanian campaign against the Mongols of the Golden Horde. The army, which received a crusading bull from Pope Boniface IX, consisted of Lithuanians, Poles, rebellious Mongols, and about 300 men from Prussia, some knight brethren, and the commander of Ragnit, Marquard von Salzbach. When the army was heavily defeated near the Vorskla, a tributary of the Dnepr, in spring 1399, the alliance broke down, and the whole affair came to nothing.

After its defeat at Tannenberg, the order faced repeated criticism that it was not following its original aims and would not act against the Mongols and Turks. When Sigismund of Luxembourg, king of Hungary, asked for the order's help against the Turks, Grand Master Paul von Rusdorf agreed in 1429 to send out a contingent of six brethren led by Nicolaus von Redwitz, probably accompanied by Prussian craftsmen and soldiers. Sigismund gave them lands around Severin on the Danube where they were supposed to organize the defense of the border region near the area where the order had tried to establish itself 200 years earlier. Though in May 1430 the proctor general at the papal court was informed that the order had done well in Hungary, by 1432 the situation had deteriorated. The brethren were prevented by the Hungarian nobility from fortifying their castles, and they received no help when attacked by the Turks in the summer of 1432. Some of the order's castles were lost, and many of its men must have died. Under very poor conditions, the brethren managed to hold out in three castles until 1434, but then the grand master decided to withdraw his halfhearted support.

After 1466 the order was involved in two Polish campaigns against the Turks. When in 1485 the Ottomans devastated Wallachia, the order's contingent was too small to offer any substantial help and was sent back, but in 1497 Grand Master Hans von Tiefen came with some of the order's officials, about 1,500 mounted men and their attendants, in all probably about 4,000 men. When they reached Lemberg (mod. L'viv, Ukraine), the grand master fell seriously ill, and he died on 25 August. The order's dignitaries brought his body back to Prussia, but many of his men subsequently died in the heavy defeat suffered at the hands of the Turks.

While the position of the grand master and the central officials in Prussia was weakened by the defeats at the hands of Poland and Lithuania, the German and Livonian branches of the order gained substantial degrees of independence. Thus the German master Eberhard von Saunsheim opposed the peace treaty with Poland in 1435, while the Livonian brethren succeeded in securing a far-reaching autonomy from the early 1430s: at first, the grand master could choose the master of Livonia from two candidates presented to him by the Livonian brethren, but after 1466 he only had the option to confirm the future Livonian masters. These conducted their own foreign policy toward the principality of Muscovy, and in 1501 and 1502, respectively, Wolter von Plettenberg achieved two impressive victories against large Muscovite contingents at the Seritsa and Lake Smolina, which substantially contributed to the continued existence until 1561 of the Livonian "confederation" of the bishoprics, the order, the town of Riga, and the knighthood of Harria and Vironia. Meanwhile, the German masters became princes of the Holy Roman Empire in their own right in 1494 and concentrated on building up their own territory in the region of the Neckar.

After the death of Hans von Tiefen in 1497, the order decided to change its policies. With Friedrich von Sachsen (1498–1510) and Albrecht von Brandenburg-Bayreuth (1511–1525), two princes of the Holy Roman Empire were elected as grand masters, in an effort to reform the order and to intensify support from Germany. Neither was very successful, though the Prussian conflict became more and more international. When Albrecht lost another war against Poland in 1519–1521 (the so-called *Reiterkrieg*), he returned to the empire, where he made contact with the leaders of the Protestant Reformation. Martin Luther suggested the secularization of the order and its territories, and thus after some negotiations Albrecht received Prussia as a fief dependent on the kingdom of Poland in April 1525.

The Order's Survival into the Modern Period

Yet this was not the end of the order's history. The Livonian branch was secularized in 1561 under military pressure from Muscovy during events similar to those in Prussia, the last Livonian Master Gotthard Kettler becoming duke of Courland. The German branch survived attacks during the Peasants' War of 1525 and was reformed by the German master Walter von Cronberg, who became administrator of the grand mastership in December 1527. He and his successors tried in vain to recover the order's Prussian and Livonian territories.

In the sixteenth and seventeenth centuries, the order became closely associated with the Habsburg dynasty. When at the diet of Regensburg in 1576 Emperor Maximilian II proposed that the order should take over and defend one of the castles on the borders of Hungary (with support from the empire), Grand Master Heinrich von Bobenhausen (1572–1585/1590) opposed the plan, still hoping to regain Prussia. The situation changed when one of the Habsburg princes, Maximilian, was received into the order and soon (1585)

became coadjutor (i.e., lieutenant) of the aging grand master. After Bobenhausen resigned in 1590 and Maximilian became grand master (until 1618), he also took over the administration of Styria for the young archduke Ferdinand II. In this situation, the chapter general at Mergentheim decided to support the defense of Styria against the Turks with men and money (about thirty knights with seventy servants). The grand master continued with campaigns in Hungary and Croatia from 1595 to 1597, though he was not very successful. One of the knights of the order present in Maximilian's campaigns was the later grand master Johann Eustach von Westernach (1625–1627), who in 1627 again proposed to the chapter general that the order should reconquer Prussia or take over one of the castles in Hungary. Neither scheme came to fruition, probably because of the consequences of the Thirty Years' War (1618–1648) in Germany, but at least the coadjutor for Grand Master Johann Kaspar von Ampringen and later Grand Master Ludwig Anton von Pfalz-Neuburg fought in the defense of Vienna in 1683 and in the campaigns against the Turks until 1687.

When Napoleon seized the order's properties and its territory around Mergentheim in 1809–1810, Grand Master Anton Victor of Austria (1804–1835) was thrown back on the Austrian houses of the order. Thus the Teutonic Order under its grand and German master (Ger. *Hoch- und Deutschmeister*) became an order of the Austrian Empire. Finally, in 1923, the knightly branch of the Teutonic Knights was dissolved. Today the order consists of priests and sisters who are mainly engaged in charitable activities.

–Jürgen Sarnowsky

See also: Baltic Crusades; Burzenland; Castles: The Baltic Region
Bibliography
800 Jahre Deutscher Orden. Ausstellung des Germanischen Nationalmuseums Nürnberg, ed. Gerhard Bott and Udo Arnold (Gütersloh: Bertelsmann, 1990).
Acht Jahrhunderte Deutscher Orden, ed. Klemens Wieser (Bad Godesberg: Wissenschaftliches Archiv, 1967).
Die Berichte der Generalprokuratoren des Deutschen Ordens an der Kurie, 6 vols., ed. Kurt Forstreuter and Hans Koeppen (Göttingen: Vandenhoeck & Ruprecht, 1961–1976).
Boockmann, Hartmut, *Der Deutsche Orden: Zwölf Kapitel aus seiner Geschichte*, 4th ed. (München: Beck, 1994).
Burleigh, Michael, *Prussian Society and the German Order: An Aristocratic Society in Crisis, c. 1410–1466* (Cambridge: Cambridge University Press, 1984).
Christiansen, Eric, *The Northern Crusades: The Baltic and the Catholic Frontier, 1100–1525* (London: Macmillan, 1980).

Favreau, Marie-Luise, *Studien zur Frühgeschichte des Deutschen Ordens* (Stuttgart: Klett, 1974).

Forstreuter, Kurt, *Der Deutsche Orden am Mittelmeer* (Bonn: Wissenschaftliches Archiv, 1967).

Die Hochmeister des Deutschen Ordens, 1190–1994, ed. Udo Arnold (Marburg: Elwert, 1998).

Kluger, Helmuth, *Hochmeister Hermann von Salza und Kaiser Friedrich II* (Marburg: Elwert, 1987).

Maschke, Erich, *Domus hospitalis Theutonicorum: Europäische Verbindungslinien der Deutschordensgeschichte* (Bonn-Godesberg: Wissenschaftliches Archiv, 1970).

The Military Orders: Fighting for the Faith and Caring for the Sick, ed. Malcolm Barber (Aldershot, UK: Variorum, 1994).

Militzer, Klaus, *Die Entstehung der Deutschordensballeien im Deutschen Reich,* 2d ed. (Marburg: Elwert, 1981).

———, *Von Akkon zur Marienburg: Verfassung, Verwaltung und Sozialstruktur des Deutschen Ordens, 1190–1309* (Marburg: Elwert, 1999).

Milthaler, Frank, *Die Großgebietiger des Deutschen Ordens bis 1440* (Königsberg: Ost-Europa-Verlag, 1940).

Die Statuten des Deutschen Ordens nach den ältesten Handschriften, ed. Max Perlbach (Halle an der Saale: Niemeyer, 1890).

Tabulae ordinis Theutonici, ed. Ernst Strehlke (Berlin: Weidmann, 1869).

Tumler, Marian, *Der Deutsche Orden im Werden, Wachsen und Wirken bis 1400 mit einem Abriß der Geschichte des Ordens von 1400 bis zur neuesten Zeit* (Wien: Panorama, 1955).

Urban, William, *The Teutonic Knights: A Military History* (London: Greenhill, 2003).

Zimmermann, Harald, *Der Deutsche Orden in Siebenbürgen: Ein diplomatische Untersuchung* (Köln: Böhlau, 2000).

Teutonic Order: Literature

The literature of the Teutonic Order (Ger. *Deutschordensliteratur*) is a term used by scholars to describe works written in German that were produced in or associated with the order.

Modern scholarship has largely refuted the once held belief that there was a calculated and programmatic attempt by the leadership to produce a body of literature specifically for the use and education of the order. However, there is no doubt that the order did commission some writing and that other works became widely disseminated throughout its commanderies and were closely associated with it. The order was an obvious focus for the development of vernacular translations of scriptural and devotional texts: its lay members were not literate in the traditional sense, in that they could probably not read Latin, but many undoubtedly fell into the growing category of educated laymen who could read German and who were increasingly demanding access to scriptures in the vernacular. In addition, the order needed suitable texts that could be read aloud during mealtimes, as required by its statutes, and that would be accessible to its lay members and would contribute toward strengthening its ethos.

The body of work usually regarded as belonging to the literature of the Teutonic Order falls into three main categories: Bible translations, devotional literature, and chronicles and accounts of the order's history. The majority of the most significant works were written during the final years of the thirteenth century and the first decades of the fourteenth, a period that coincides with the order's relocation to Prussia after the fall of Acre (mod. 'Akko, Israel) in the Holy Land in 1291. This chronology has led many scholars to accept that the nurturing of literature did form a conscious part, albeit not to quite the extent that early commentators suggested, of the order's attempts to revive morale, to set the interpretation of the early campaigns in Prussia securely within the context of the early crusading tradition, and to reestablish itself as a legitimate vehicle for crusading activity during the pivotal years after the loss of the Holy Land.

Bible Translations

The earliest works associated with the order are translations of the Bible, of which the earliest dates from 1254 and the latest from around 1345. The writing of Bible translations in the late thirteenth and particularly the fourteenth century corresponds to a general increase in demand by lay people for accessible scriptural texts, and it can be assumed that this demand was particularly acute in the Teutonic Order, given the nature of its membership. The beginning of the fourteenth century saw a marked increase in the number of biblical texts that were translated into the vernacular and used in the order, to the extent that it has been suggested that the order planned a complete translation of the Bible by the time of Grand Master Luder von Braunschweig (1330–1335). This view is no longer tenable, but there is no doubt that the order acted as patron in commissioning some translations and popularizing and disseminating others, within the context of a desire to give knight brethren access to the scriptures.

The earliest Bible translation linked with the order is the vernacular translation of the Book of Judith, written in 1254.

The author of *Judith* is anonymous, and is unlikely to have been a member of the order. His stated priority is to make the scripture available to *illiterati* (those who could not understand Latin), and the vernacular text has obvious thematic relevance for the order. It begins with an exhortation, based on Joseph's rejection of Pharoah's wife (Gen. 39:7), to reject secular love in favor of spiritual values. The allegorical tale of Judith's killing of Holofernes held the interest of the order throughout the Middle Ages, and a prose translation was written in 1479 by the knight brother Jörg Stuler. *Hester,* completed shortly after *Judith,* around 1255–1260, is attributed by Karl Helm and Walther Ziesemer to a priest in the order, although there is no direct evidence for this. The link lies more in the evident relevance for the order of a vernacular translation of inspirational scriptural texts of this nature. Like *Judith,* the heroine of *Hester* also saves her people from their persecutors. At the end of the poem, the author compares Hester with the Virgin Mary and her husband with Christ, and their struggle is presented as a model for the wars of the order.

The first named author of biblical translations who is associated with the order is Heinrich von Hesler, who wrote the *Evangelium Nicodemi* (1304–1305), the *Apokalypse* (1309), and the *Erlösung*. Evidence for linking him with the order is based on the content of his work and its dissemination through the order's libraries, but there is no direct evidence to suggest either that he was a member or that the order was his patron. The *Evangelium Nicodemi* is an account of events related in the Gospels and the legends of Veronica, Tiberius, and Vespasian. *Erlösung* survives only in fragments and is an account of God's dealings with the devil and his mercy to man. Hesler's longest work is the *Apokalypse,* a translation and interpretation of the Revelation of St. John according to the traditional medieval commentaries.

Das Buch der Makkabäer, a translation of the Books of the Maccabees by an unidentified author writing around 1330, has been attributed to Luder von Braunschweig; in the sole surviving manuscript (MS Stuttgart, Württembergische Landesbibliothek, HB.XIII poet.germ.11), his coat of arms immediately precedes the poet's introduction. Although authorship cannot be definitely established, and there are no references in the text linking it with the order, this connection with a grand master reflects the importance of the typological exploitation of the Maccabees for the legitimization of the order. The Maccabees are used repeatedly as models in the two chronicles written during the same period, those of Peter von Dusburg and Nicolaus von Jeroschin, and

it is not implausible to suggest that this, at least, did form part of an explicit strategy of self-justification through the use of biblical typology.

The translation of the Book of Daniel, completed around 1331 at the request of Luder von Braunschweig by an unknown cleric and dedicated to the Teutonic Knights, is one of three Bible translations that can be directly attributed to the order. Daniel's trials at the hands of the infidel are a popular motif in crusading literature and particularly relevant for the order. The author of *Daniel* also touches on contemporary issues: the *translatio imperii* (the Holy Roman Empire's claim to be the divinely ordained successor to the Roman Empire, with its implicit challenge to the papacy) and criticism of worldliness within the church.

The other translations that can be directly linked with the order are *Von den siben Ingesigeln* by Tilo von Kulm and *Hiob*. Like *Daniel, Von den siben Ingesigeln* was written in 1331 in honor of Luder von Braunschweig. It is an account of God's dealings with man from the Creation to the Last Judgment, but also a critique of contemporary corruption in the church and a treatise on the nature of secular and spiritual authority. *Hiob,* a paraphrase of the Book of Job completed in 1338, was primarily a devotional tool for the knight brethren, but it also eulogizes Grand Master Dietrich von Altenburg (1335–1341) as a perfect model for the brethren and Christian warriors. Finally, the *Historien der alden E,* by an unknown author, is a digest of Old Testament stories completed between 1338 and 1345 and is also commonly associated with the order. However, it contains no direct reference to the order, nor was its author apparently aware of the earlier translations, in spite of the shared subject matter; in this case assumed links with the order are based on language and dissemination.

Devotional Works

The second group of works associated with the order is devotional in nature. The earliest extant work is *Der Sünden Widerstreit,* a spiritual, allegorical poem about the struggle between virtue and evil. It was written in 1275 by an unidentified priest, for a lay audience whom he describes in the text as being not particularly enthusiastic about religion. The theme is moral renewal, and the author contrasts the secular values of the lay knight with those of the *militia Christi* (knighthood of Christ). He does not identify the order in the text, but the poem has always been linked with it because of its subject matter and distribution.

The next surviving work in this genre is the *Legende der heiligen Martina*, completed in 1293 by Hugo von Langenstein, a priest of the order, who may have been commissioned to write this poem as part of his duties. The story of the aristocratic St. Martina's war against the heathen, involving her capture, torture, and execution, is presented as a prefiguration of the militia Christi and is calculated to engage the sympathy of the lay crusaders who fought alongside the order; the text was extracted from a Latin source with the purpose of interesting a new audience.

The poem *Marienleben* was written during the first decade of the fourteenth century by the Carthusian monk Philip, and was dedicated by him to the order in recognition of its particular veneration of the Virgin Mary. Thereafter it appears to have been disseminated widely through the order's libraries. It had the widest distribution and greatest impact of any medieval German poem. The Virgin was regarded as the patron of the order, and her cult also features prominently in the chronicle of Nicolaus von Jeroschin as a counterbalance to the secular knight's pursuit of *minne* (secular courtly love).

The order played a similar role in the dissemination of two collections of lives of the saints, the *Passional* and the *Väterbuch*. The *Väterbuch* is a translation of the lives of the Fathers of the Church, written in the final third of the thirteenth century by a priest whose identity and patron are not known. He praises the *Marienritter* (Knights of Mary) in the text and, like the author of *Der Sünden Widerstreit*, contrasts the worldly values of profane knighthood with the spiritual values of the true Christian knight. The author of the *Väterbuch* also wrote the *Passional*, a rhymed account of the lives of the saints, intended for the edification of a lay audience. This work was also widely distributed by the order over a short period of time; over 80 percent of the extant manuscripts were completed before the middle of the fourteenth century. Marked similarities between the manuscripts lend weight to the theory that many were reproduced under the supervision of, and for the use of the order. Two further works, a life of St. Barbara attributed to Luder von Braunschweig and a life of St. Adalbert attributed to Nicolaus von Jeroschin, have not survived.

Historiography

The final and most significant group of works comprises the historical accounts of the order's wars and campaigns. Chronicles were written throughout the course of the Baltic Crusades. The earliest, dating from shortly after 1290, is the *Livonian Rhymed Chronicle* (Ger. *Livländische Reimchronik*), which is generally accepted as having been written by an anonymous knight brother. It deals with the crusade in Livonia from the end of the twelfth century until the conquest of Semgallia in 1290. The next work, the Latin *Chronicon Terrae Prussiae* of Peter von Dusburg, was written at the instigation of Grand Master Werner von Orseln (1324–1330); it deals with the history of the order from its origins until 1330 and is the main source for its early history. In contrast to the *Livonian Rhymed Chronicle*, which focuses primarily on warfare, Dusburg uses the concept of the militia Christi of earlier crusading chronicles and sermons to interpret and shape his account of the events of the previous 100 years in Prussia. His chronicle was translated into the vernacular within a few years by Nicolaus von Jeroschin, at the request of Luder von Braunschweig, and this version was evidently popular and widely used. Its purpose, like that of the spiritual literature discussed above, was to place the order's historical mission and ethos firmly within the context of crusading ideology and to make this interpretation accessible to the lay members of the order. It too was designed to be read aloud at mealtimes. Its appeal to lay members of the order was undoubtedly heightened by Jeroschin's striking use of everyday motifs and language and his appropriation and reworking of imagery and themes from secular crusading literature.

The next substantial chronicle produced in the order, and the final one during the period of the Baltic Crusades, is that of the herald Wigand von Marburg. It deals with the history of the order from 1293 until 1394, but survives only in fragments and in Latin translation. Its preoccupation with secular values and the physical tools of warfare suggest that the order's identification with the values of the militia Christi, expounded in the spiritual literature and by Dusburg and Jeroschin, had become diluted and compromised.

–*Mary Fischer*

Bibliography

Boockmann, Hartmut, "Geschichtsschreibung des Deutschen Ordens im Mittelalter und Geschichtsschreibung im mittelalterlichen Preußen. Entstehungsbedingungen und Funktionen," in *Literatur und Laienbildung im Spätmittelalter und in der Reformzeit*, ed. Ludger Grenzmann and Karl Stackmann (Stuttgart: Metzler, 1984), pp. 80–93.

Das Buch der Maccabäer in Mitteldeutscher Bearbeitung, ed. Karl Helm (Tübingen: Literarischer Verein in Stuttgart, 1904).

Buschinger, Danielle, "La littérature comme arme de combat de l'Ordre Teutonique," *Jahrbücher der Reineke-Gesellschaft* 7 (1996), 11–22.

Feistner, Edith, "Vom Kampf gegen das 'Andere'. Pruzzen, Litauer und Mongolen in lateinischen und deutschen Texten des Mittelalters," *Zeitschrift für deutsches Altertum und deutsche Literatur* 132 (2003), 281–294.

Fischer, Mary, *"Di himels rote": The Idea of Christian Chivalry in the Chronicles of the Teutonic Knights* (Göppingen: Kümmerle, 1991).

———, "Biblical Heroes and the Uses of Literature: The Teutonic Order in the Late Thirteenth and Early Fourteenth Centuries," in *Crusade and Conversion on the Baltic Frontier, 1150–1500*, ed. Alan V. Murray (Aldershot, UK: Ashgate, 2001), pp. 261–275.

———, "The Books of the Maccabees and the Teutonic Order," *Crusades* 4 (2005), 59–71.

Forey, Alan, "Literacy and Learning in the Military Orders during the Twelfth and Thirteenth Centuries," in *The Military Orders, 2: Welfare and Warfare*, ed. Helen Nicholson (Aldershot, UK: Ashgate, 1998).

Helm, Karl, and Walther Ziesemer, *Die Literatur des Deutschen Ritterordens* (Gießen: Schmitz, 1951).

Teutonic Source

Also known as the *Lisbon Letter*, a Latin eyewitness account of the capture of Lisbon (October 1147). It narrates the only real success of the Second Crusade (1147–1149), when crusaders from the Rhineland participated in a fleet that assisted the king of Portugal, Afonso I Henriques (1128–1185), in taking the city from the Moors.

The source started existence as a letter from a priest named Winand to Archbishop Arnold I of Cologne. Two fellow participants copied the letter and sent versions as their own. The same text was used for entries in the annals of Cologne and Magdeburg, and an unfinished draft appears in a Trier manuscript (MS Trier, Stadtbibliothek, 1974/641).

The source relates the departure of the Cologne contingent in April 1147, its rendezvous with the rest of the fleet off Dartmouth (England), and its voyage to Lisbon. It includes interesting details of siege warfare. The final, successful assault is vividly described, and the original letter finishes abruptly with a doxology. Another version reveals that the crusaders wintered in Lisbon before continuing their journey to Outremer.

–Susan B. Edgington

Bibliography

Edgington, Susan B., "The Lisbon Letter of the Second Crusade," *Historical Research* 69 (1996), 328–339.

———, "Albert of Aachen, St Bernard and the Second Crusade," in *The Second Crusade: Scope and Consequences*, eds. Martin Hoch and Jonathan Phillips (Manchester: Manchester University Press, 2001), pp. 54–70.

Thaddeus of Naples

Author of a contemporary account of the fall of the city of Acre (mod. 'Akko, Israel) to the Mamlūks (April–May 1291).

Magister (Master) Thaddeus wrote his *Hystoria de desolacione civitatis Acconensis* in Messina in Italy in December 1291. He was not present at the siege of Acre, but he used eyewitness accounts. He claimed to have lived in Outremer, and his account was critical of merchants operating there who, he said, collaborated with the Christians' enemies. His style is highly rhetorical, but conveys the drama of events and some scraps of topographical detail. Like the anonymous *Excidium Acconis*, Thaddeus's *Hystoria* has been little used by historians. The edition by Comte Riant (1873) has been superseded by one edited by Huygens based on all the extant manuscripts (five complete and one fragmentary), of which the best is MS London, British Library, Add.22800.

–Susan B. Edgington

Bibliography

Thaddeus of Naples, "Hystoria de desolacione civitatis Acconensis," in *Excidium Acconis*, ed. Robert B. C. Huygens (Turnhout: Brepols, 2004).

Thebes

A city in central Greece (mod. Thiva, Greece), under Frankish rule from 1205 to 1311.

Thebes was an ancient city that was founded, according to tradition, by Kadmos in 1313 B.C. Later it became the reputed place of burial of St. Luke the Evangelist. Despite devastation by the Goths in 397 and destruction by an earthquake in 551, the city underwent a revival in the Middle Ages. From the ninth century it was the base of the *strategos* (governor) of the Byzantine theme of Hellas and established itself as the center of Byzantine silk manufacture. In 1146 the Normans of Sicily sacked it: many native silk workers were taken to Sicily, and the monopoly of the Theban silk manufacture was broken.

In 1205 Thebes was captured by the forces of Boniface of Montferrat and subsequently granted to Otho of La Roche to form part of the lordship of Athens and Thebes. In the mid–thirteenth century, the marriage of Bela of Saint-Omer with Bonne of La Roche brought half the lordship of the city to the Saint-Omer family, which put in hand considerable building works in the city. Certainly before 1311 all those Franks who held land in Boeotia seem to have maintained residences in the city. In 1311 it passed into the control of the mercenary Catalan Company, which also seized power in Athens. To prevent the seizure of the city by Walter II of Brienne in 1332, the Catalans destroyed most of the second city of the duchy of Athens and Thebes. The city fell to the Turks in 1450.

Very little of medieval Thebes has survived. The two major earthquakes of 1853 and 1893, and the depredations of modern development, destroyed what the Catalans did not slight in 1332. Of the city's walls only three towers survive, and of the magnificent palace built here by Nicholas II of Saint-Omer with moneys derived from his wife, Maria of Antioch, there is nothing to be seen. Thebes also contained a cathedral and many Latin churches.

–Peter Lock

See also: Athens, Duchy and Lordship of
Bibliography
Lock, Peter, *The Franks in the Aegean* (London: Longman, 1995).

Miller, William, *The Latins in the Levant* (London: Murray, 1908).

Symeonoglou, Sarantis, *The Topography of Thebes from the Bronze Age to Modern Times* (Princeton, NJ: Princeton University Press, 1985).

Theodore I Laskaris (d. 1222)

Despot and first emperor of Nicaea (1204–1222) after the overthrow of the Byzantine Empire by the Fourth Crusade (1202–1204).

While still a member of the Byzantine aristocracy, Theodore married Anna, second daughter of Emperor Alexios III Angelos (1199). After the Latin conquest of Constantinople in 1204, he fled with his wife and children to Nicaea (mod. İznik, Turkey), where he was acknowledged by the locals as their ruler as early as fall 1204. First using the title of despot, he was crowned as "emperor of the Romans" in

1208, shortly after the election of the first patriarch of Constantinople in exile. Theodore seems to have shown an interest in the negotiations between representatives of the Greek Orthodox and the Latin churches, and in 1214 he took an active role in the talks that took place in the Nicaean Empire. He was unsuccessful in most of his military encounters with the Franks of the newly established Latin Empire of Constantinople and with the Venetians, but in 1211 he successfully repelled a Turkish invasion.

In the late 1210s, Theodore was able to establish a close relationship with the ruling family of Constantinople by marrying Maria, sister of Emperor Robert, and by planning to marry his own daughter Eudokia to Robert, in spite of fierce opposition by the ecumenical patriarch. He also offered Venice trading privileges, which were to last for five years, in 1219. Theodore seems to have died without a male heir and was buried in the monastery of Hyakinthos in Nicaea. He was succeeded by his son-in-law, John III Vatatzes.

–Aphrodite Papayianni

Bibliography
Brezeanu, Stelian, "Le premier traité économique entre Venise et Nicée," *Revue des études sud-est européennes* 12 (1974), 143–146.

Savvides, Alexios G. C., "Constantine XI Lascaris, Uncrowned and Ephemeral 'Basileus of the Rhomaoi' after the Fall of Constantinople to the Fourth Crusade," *Βυζαντιακά* 7 (1987), 141–174.

Theodore II Laskaris (d. 1258)

Emperor of Nicaea (1254–1258), son of Emperor John III Vatatzes (d. 1254) and Irene, daughter of Emperor Theodore I Laskaris, the founder of the Empire of Nicaea. On his accession to the throne, Theodore adopted his mother's imperial family name.

During Theodore's short reign, the territorial status quo between the Empire of Nicaea and the Latin Empire of Constantinople remained the same, while two imperial marriages, between his daughters and the new tsar of Bulgaria, Constantine Tich, and the heir of the ruler of Epiros, Nikephoros, appeared to consolidate the Nicaean holdings in Europe. Theodore was a distinguished scholar who wrote essays on theological, philosophical, and scientific topics and composed rhetorical works. He also resumed talks with Rome concerning the reunification of the Greek Orthodox and Latin churches. On his death, at the age of thirty six, he was succeeded by his eight-year-old son John IV.

–Aphrodite Papayianni

Bibliography

Dräseke, Johannes, "Theodoros Lascaris," *Byzantinische Zeitschrift* 3 (1894), 498–515.

Lascaris, Theodore, "In Praise of the Great City of Nicaea," in *Nicaea: A Byzantine Capital and its Praises*, ed. Clive Foss (Brookline, MA: Hellenic College Press, 1996), pp. 132–153.

Papadopoulos, Jean, *Théodore II Lascaris* (Paris: Picard, 1908).

Prato, Giancarlo, "Un autografo di Teodoro II Lascaris imperatore di Nicea?," *Jahrbuch der Österreichischen Byzantinistik* 30 (1981), 249–258.

Theodore Angelos Komnenos Doukas (d. 1253/1254)

Byzantine ruler of Epiros (c. 1215–1230) and emperor of Thessalonica (1224/1227–1230).

Theodore became second ruler of the autonomous Epirot state on the assassination of his half-brother Michael I. In 1217 he defeated and captured Peter of Courtenay, the Latin emperor of Constantinople; by 1224 he had taken Thessalonica (mod. Thessaloniki, Greece) and extinguished its Latin kingdom. With the capture of Adrianople (mod. Edirne, Turkey) in 1225, Theodore emerged as Nicaea's chief rival for the restoration of the Byzantine Empire, an aspiration signaled by his coronation as emperor in Thessalonica (c. 1227). However, his ambitions to conquer Constantinople were crushed by Tsar Ivan Asen II of Bulgaria in March 1230 at Klokotnitcha, where he was captured and blinded.

Released from captivity around 1237, Theodore later incited his nephew, Michael II of Epiros (1231–1268/1271), to attack Nicaea (1252–1253). However, the Nicaean emperor John III Doukas Vatatzes defeated the Epirot troops and apprehended Theodore, who was incarcerated in Nicaea and died soon afterward.

–Alexios G. C. Savvides

See also: Epiros

Bibliography

Bredenkamp, François, *The Byzantine Empire of Thessalonike, 1224–1242* (Thessaloniki: Thessaloniki Municipality History Center, 1996).

Karpozelos, Apostolos, *The Ecclesiastical Controversy between the Kingdom of Nicaea and the Principality of Epiros, 1217–1233* (Thessaloniki: Byzantine Research Centre, 1973).

Nicol, Donald M., *The Despotate of Epiros* (Oxford: Blackwell, 1957).

Stavridou-Zaphraka, Alkmene, *Νίκαια και Ήπειρος τον 13ο αιώνα* (Thessaloniki: Vanias, 1990).

Varzos, Konstantinos, *Η γενεαλογία των Κομνηνών* , vol. 2 (Thessaloniki: Byzantine Research Centre, 1984).

Theodore Balsamon

Canonist and Greek Orthodox patriarch of Antioch (1183–c. 1204).

Theodore Balsamon was born in Constantinople (mod. İstanbul, Turkey) between 1130 and 1140. He was ordained as a deacon, probably in the 1160s, and by 1179 he had become the leading official of the patriarchal bureaucracy in Constantinople. He was commissioned by Emperor Manuel I Komnenos and Patriarch Michael III of Constantinople with the task of writing commentaries on the *nomokanon* (compilation of imperial laws and ecclesiastical regulations concerning the church) and on the canons of the apostles, the ecumenical and local synods, and the church fathers. The first edition of these commentaries was completed before September 1180; the second edition, dedicated to Patriarch George II Xiphilinos, before February 1195.

Probably in autumn 1183, Balsamon was nominated Greek patriarch of Antioch (mod. Antakya, Turkey). Like most of his predecessors in the twelfth century, he had to stay in Constantinople, because the patriarchal throne of Antioch was occupied by a Latin. As the most important canonist of the Byzantine church, Balsamon was strictly anti-Latin and a champion of canonical and liturgical standardization.

–Klaus-Peter Todt

Bibliography

Gallagher, Clarence, *Church Law and Church Order in Rome and Byzantium: A Comparative Study* (Aldershot, UK: Ashgate, 2002).

Pitsakes, Konstantinos, " Η εκσταση της εξουσίας ενος υπερορίου πατριάρχη: ο πατριάρχης Αντιοχείας στην Κωνσταντινούπολη," in *Byzantium in the 12th Century: Canon Law, State and Society*, ed. Nicolas Oikonomides (Athens: Hetaireia Byzantinon kai Metabyzantinon Meleton, 1991), pp. 91–139.

Stevens, Gerardus Petrus, *De Theodoro Balsamone. Analysis*

operum ac mentis iuridicae (Roma: Libreria Editrice della Pontificia Università Lateranense, 1969).

Tiftixoglu, Viktor, "Zur Genese der Kommentare des Theodoros Balsamon. Mit einem Exkurs über die unbekannten Kommentare des Sinaiticus gr. 1117," in *Byzantium in the 12th Century: Canon Law, State and Society*, ed. Nicolas Oikonomides (Athens: Hetaireia Byzantinon kai Metabyzantinon Meleton, 1991), pp. 483–532.

Thessalonica

A Frankish kingdom established by the Montferrat dynasty after the Fourth Crusade (1202–1204) in Macedonia, with its capital at Thessalonica (mod. Thessaloniki, Greece), which survived for only two decades until it was overrun by the Greeks of Epiros in 1224.

The creation of a separate kingdom around Thessalonica, the second city of the Byzantine Empire, was not envisaged in the pact of 1204 by which the crusaders at Constantinople made arrangements for the future governance of their conquests on Byzantine territory. According to the chronicler Geoffrey of Villehardouin, the unsuccessful candidate in the election of a Latin emperor was to receive "all the land across the strait toward Turkey and also the Isle of Greece" [Villehardouin, *La Conquête de Constantinople*, ed. Edmond Faral, 2d ed., 2 vols. (Paris: Les Belles Lettres, 1961), 2:64]. The election of Baldwin of Flanders as emperor meant that Boniface of Montferrat should have received these lands; however, Boniface persuaded both Baldwin and the Venetians to exchange "the land . . . toward Turkey" (that is, Byzantine Anatolia) for Thessalonica and its environs, thus ensuring a contiguous block of territory. Boniface continued to call himself marquis and was never crowned king of Thessalonica, although he was well placed to capitalize upon his possessions: he had occupied the city, conquered territories as far as Thessaly and central Greece, and married Maria (Margaret) of Hungary, widow of the Byzantine emperor Isaac II Angelos.

Relations between Boniface and Emperor Baldwin were at first strained. However, the threat posed to both Constantinople and Thessalonica by the Bulgaro-Vlach coalition under Kalojan (Johannitsa), as well as Baldwin's death at their hands in late 1205, made reconciliation both urgent and possible. The new emperor, Henry, married Boniface's daughter Agnes, and Boniface paid homage to him. In September 1207 Boniface was killed in battle by the Bulgarians,

leaving an infant son, Demetrius, under the regency of his widow Margaret and a council of Lombard lords. The latter sought to replace Demetrius with his older half-brother William VI, marquis of Montferrat. However, Emperor Henry moved on Thessalonica in December 1208 and secured the coronation of Demetrius as the first (and, as it happened, last) ruling king of Thessalonica (9 January 1209). Henry's actions were endorsed by Pope Innocent III, who recognized Demetrius as king in March 1209 and took him under papal protection.

The emperor and his brother Eustace busied themselves with occupying the Maritsa Valley and securing control of the Via Egnatia around Thessalonica, but in the summer of 1210 the Epirot Greeks attacked the kingdom. Although Henry responded swiftly and saved the city, land was lost in Thessaly and the capital effectively cut off from the rest of the kingdom in Greece. The death of Henry in 1216, and the failure of his successor, Peter of Courtenay, to open up a route to Thessalonica from Durazzo (mod. Durrës, Albania), left the kingdom struggling for its existence. In 1221 the loss of Serres and Platamonas meant that there was no safe land route between Thessalonica and Constantinople, and in December 1224 the city surrendered to the Epirot Greeks. A crusade mounted by William VI of Montferrat failed to achieve anything, and Demetrius was forced to flee to Italy. The kingdom of Thessalonica was effectively at an end.

Frankish claims to Thessalonica persisted through the thirteenth century. Demetrius passed his claim to Frederick II, the Holy Roman Emperor, and in 1266 the exiled Latin Emperor of Constantinople, Baldwin II, granted title to the kingdom to Hugh IV of Burgundy. The Montferrat claim to the city ended with the marriage of Yolande of Monferrat to Andronikos II Palaiologos in 1284; a later Burgundian claim was heard of no more after it was sold to Philip of Taranto in 1331.

–Peter Lock

See also: Boniface I of Montferrat (d. 1207); Demetrius of Thessalonica (1206–1230)

Bibliography

Laiou, Angeliki E., *Constantinople and the Latins: The Foreign Policy of Andronicus II, 1282–1328* (Cambridge: Harvard University Press, 1972).

Lock, Peter, *The Franks in the Aegean* (London: Longman, 1995).

Tafrali, Oreste, *Thessalonique des Origines au XIV siècle* (Paris: Leroux, 1919).

Vacalopoulos, Apostolos E., *A History of Thessaloniki* (Thessaloniki: Institute of Balkan Studies, 1972).

Thibaud IV of Champagne (1201–1253)

Count of Champagne (1201–1253) and king of Navarre (1234–1253), leader of the Crusade of 1239–1241, and author of several French crusade songs.

Thibaud was born posthumously, the son of Thibaud III, count of Champagne, and Blanche, daughter of Sancho VI, king of Navarre. From his father, Thibaud IV inherited Champagne, a large and prosperous northern French county known for its fairs and courtly culture. From his mother he inherited a claim to the throne of the Iberian kingdom of Navarre, which he made good in 1234. It was in that year that Pope Gregory IX preached a crusade to the Holy Land. The counts of Champagne had a long tradition of responding to such appeals. Thibaud's father was preparing to depart on the Fourth Crusade (1202–1204) when he died in 1201. Thibaud's grandfather (Henry I) went on crusade to the Holy Land three times, and between 1192 and 1197 ruled the kingdom of Jerusalem. Thibaud himself had participated in the Albigensian Crusade (1209–1229), where at the siege of Avignon in 1226 he was rumored to have poisoned King Louis VIII of France.

Whether out of allegiance to this dynastic imperative, or the need, on the eve of yet another rebellion against the French Crown, to acquire the papal protection afforded by crusader status, Thibaud took the cross in the fall of 1235. He spent four times as long preparing for the crusade as he did fighting it. The pope delayed the expedition by trying to convince Thibaud and others to fulfill their vows in Frankish Greece. Nevertheless, Thibaud set off for the Holy Land in the spring of 1239, after overseeing a mass execution of alleged heretics in Champagne.

At a council of war held in Acre (mod. 'Akko, Israel) in November 1239, the leading figures of the crusade elected Thibaud commander and swore to obey him for the duration of the campaign. Some of these crusaders were his social and political equals, despite not wearing crowns; some had been at war with him through much of the 1230s. Thibaud proved incapable of imposing discipline upon the army. Marching south to fortify Ascalon (mod. Tel Ashqelon, Israel), the crusade split in two when Amalric of Montfort and Henry of Bar, ignoring Thibaud's command to remain with the host, went off to raid around Gaza. The raiders promptly fell into an Egyptian ambush, which killed or captured most of them. In the wake of this military catastrophe, Thibaud turned to diplomacy.

In treaties with al-Ṣāliḥ Ismāʿīl, the ruler of Damascus, and al-Nāṣir Dāwūd, the prince of Kerak, Thibaud won substantial territorial concessions for the kingdom of Jerusalem: the hinterland of Sidon (mod. Saïda, Lebanon), several northern fortresses, and in eastern Galilee, the restoration of the kingdom's former border at the river Jordan. When Thibaud sailed home in September 1240, the kingdom of Jerusalem encompassed more territory than at any time since 1187. Yet he departed under a cloud of suspicion just the same, resented by some for his military failings and by others for his willingness to engage in diplomacy with Muslim powers.

Thibaud is best known today as the most accomplished lyric poet of thirteenth-century France. Among his surviving works are three crusade songs (Fr. *chansons de croisade*) that praise those valiant knights who, for the sake of honor in this world and paradise in the next, go forth to restore Christ's patrimony in the Holy Land.

–*Michael Lower*

Bibliography

Jackson, Peter, "The Crusades of 1239–41 and their Aftermath," *Bulletin of the School of Oriental and African Studies* 50 (1987), 32–62.

Jordan, William Chester, "The Representation of the Crusades in the Songs Attributed to Thibaud, Count Palatine of Champagne," *Journal of Medieval History* 25 (1999), 27–34.

Lower, Michael, "The Burning at Mont-Aimé: Thibaut IV of Champagne's Preparations for the Barons' Crusade," *Journal of Medieval History* 29 (2003), 95–108.

———, *The Barons' Crusade: A Call to Arms and Its Consequences* (Philadelphia: University of Pennsylvania Press, 2005).

Thibaud Gaudin (d. 1292)

Master of the Templars (1291–1292).

Thibaud belonged to a family from the Ile-de-France that supplied several members of the order in the thirteenth century. Thibaud's early career is unknown. In 1260 he and several other Templars (including the future Master William of Beaujeu, who probably supported his career) were captured by the Muslims during an ill-planned raid in northern Galilee and released upon payment of ransom. Thibaud served as the Templars' commander of Acre (mod. 'Akko, Israel) from 1270 to 1271/1273 and probably as their turcopolier (1277) before he was sent to France (1279). After his return to Acre, he became commander of Outremer

(1283–1291), and after the death of William of Beaujeu, during the siege of Acre by the Mamlūks (1291), he was elected master of the order. He fled from Acre via Sidon to Cyprus, allegedly having managed to rescue the order's treasure and relics. He traveled to Armenia in 1292 but died on 16 April of that year. He was succeeded by James of Molay. His name is repeatedly mentioned in depositions made during the trial of the Templars.

–Jochen Burgtorf

Bibliography
Barber, Malcolm C., *The New Knighthood: A History of the Order of the Temple* (Cambridge: Cambridge University Press, 1994).

Thierry of Alsace (d. 1168)

Count of Flanders (1128–1168) and participant in four separate expeditions to Outremer.

Thierry was born shortly after 1095 at Bitche in Alsace, a son of Thierry II, duke of Upper Lotharingia, and Gertrude, daughter of Count Robert I of Flanders. In 1128 he emerged as the victorious claimant to the county of Flanders from the civil war that had broken out on the murder of Count Charles the Good (1127). After the death of his first wife, Swanehilde (1133), Thierry married Sibyl, a daughter of Fulk V of Anjou, who by this time had become king of Jerusalem as husband of Queen Melisende.

In 1139 Thierry went to the Holy Land and participated in an expedition beyond the river Jordan, returning to Flanders before Christmas. He attended the meeting at Vézelay (31 March 1146) in preparation for the Second Crusade (1147–1149) and traveled to the East with the army of King Louis VII of France. He was present at the council of crusade leaders on 24 June 1148 that decided on the campaign against Muslim Damascus. During the siege of the city he declared he would hold the town as a fief from his brother-in-law King Baldwin III, but this was opposed by the barons of the kingdom of Jerusalem. This disagreement may have contributed to the abandonment of the siege. He returned home in the spring of 1149.

In 1157 Thierry came to Outremer for the third time, accompanied by the Countess Sibyl and 400 knights, and took part in the siege of Shaizar (mod. Shayzar, Syria). King Baldwin III of Jerusalem had evidently promised the town to Thierry, but Reynald of Châtillon, prince of Antioch, disputed this decision and the siege was suspended. At Christ-mas 1157 Thierry was at the siege of Harenc (mod. Ḥarim, Syria), which was captured early in February 1158, and the same year he took part in a victorious battle against Nūr al-Dīn near Lake Tiberias (15 July 1158). In August 1159 the count was back in Flanders, while Sibyl remained in Palestine at the abbey of St. Lazarus at Bethany.

In 1164 Thierry came to Outremer for the last time but did not take part in military operations. Sibyl died during this visit (1165), and Thierry returned, reaching Flanders shortly after Christmas 1165. He died at Gravelines on 17 January 1168.

–Jan Anckaer

Bibliography
Coppieters-De Stochove, Hubert, "Voyages de Thierry d'Alsace en Orient," *Bulletijn der Maatschappij van Geschied- en Oudheidkunde te Gent* 16 (1908), 159–163.
De Hemptinne, Thérèse, and Michel Parisse, "Thierry d'Alsace, comte de Flandre: Biographie et actes," *Annales de l'Est*, ser. 5, 43 (1991), 83–113.
Hechelhammer, Bodo, "Die Kreuzfahrerin: Sibylle von Anjou, Gräfin von Flandern (*1110, †1165)," in *Die Kreuzzüge: Kein Krieg ist heilig*, ed. Hans-Jürgen Kotzur, Winfried Wilhelmy, and Brigitte Klein (Mainz: Von Zabern, 2004), pp. 229–233.

Third Crusade (1189–1192)

Initiated in response to Saladin's defeat of the forces of the kingdom of Jerusalem at the battle of Hattin (4 July 1187) and his subsequent capture of the city of Jerusalem (2 October 1187), this campaign did not recapture the Holy City, but did reestablish the kingdom of Jerusalem in much reduced form and laid the basis for its continued existence for another century. It is arguably the best-known crusade to modern readers after the First Crusade, because of the involvement of Saladin and of King Richard I of England. Nevertheless the Third Crusade has received less modern critical analysis than others, perhaps because of the complexity of the campaigns and of the extensive primary sources that have survived.

Origins

At Hattin the Muslims captured Guy of Lusignan, king of Jerusalem, and many leading nobles, along with the True Cross, the sacred symbol of the kingdom. This defeat left very few able-bodied warriors for the defense of Christian Palestine. Saladin went on to capture the important port of

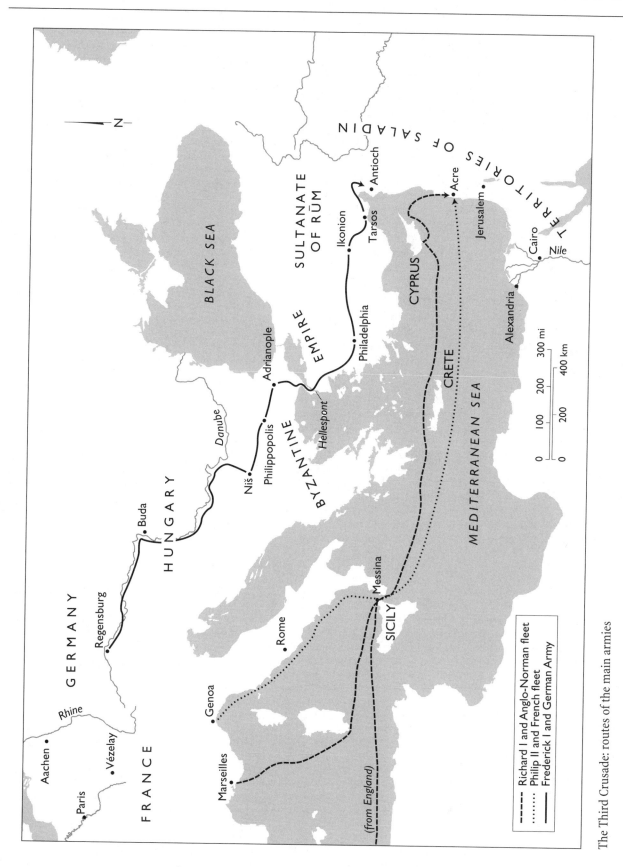

The Third Crusade: routes of the main armies

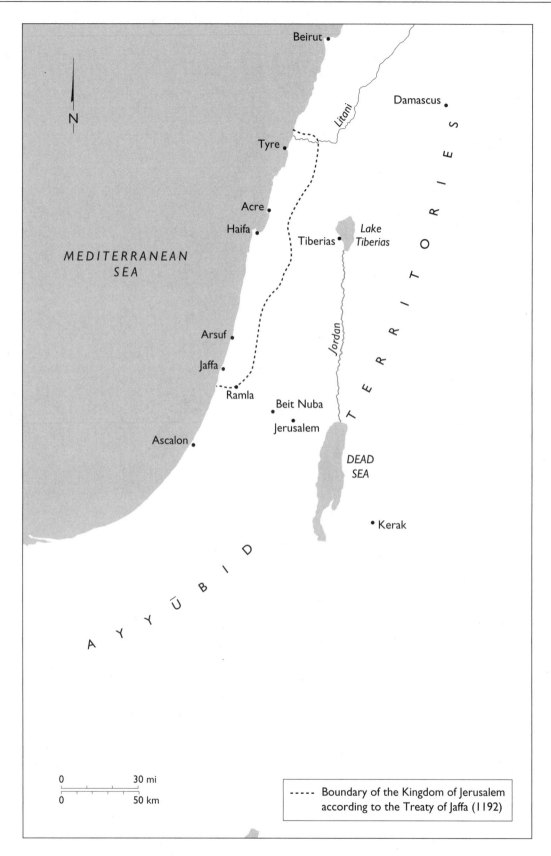

The Third Crusade in Palestine

Acre (mod. 'Akko, Israel), as well as Beirut, Sidon (mod. Saïda, Lebanon), Ascalon (mod. Tel Ashqelon, Israel), and Jerusalem itself. He failed to take the coastal city of Tyre (mod. Soûr, Lebanon), which was defended by Conrad, marquis of Montferrat, who had recently arrived by ship on pilgrimage; his naval attacks were repelled by ships from the powerful Italian maritime cities of Genoa and Pisa. With fortresses such as Kerak and Montréal in Transjordan and Saphet and Belvoir in Galilee also resisting, Saladin went on to make other conquests in Palestine, and in late spring 1188 moved north, campaigning against the Frankish states of Tripoli and Antioch.

Saladin released King Guy from prison in May 1188, on condition that he should return to the West. Instead Guy went to the island of Ruad (mod. Arwād, Syria) opposite Tortosa to meet Queen Sibyl, and they proceeded to Antioch (mod. Antakya, Turkey), where they assembled an army. Crusaders were already beginning to arrive in the East.

The Beginnings of the Crusade

The news of the disaster at Hattin and the fall of Jerusalem was transmitted to the West in letters written by various individuals and groups, such as Patriarch Eraclius of Jerusalem, the Genoese consuls, and the grand commander of the Order of the Temple. Pope Urban III died shortly after hearing the news of the disaster at Hattin. His successor, Gregory VIII, issued a crusading bull entitled *Audita tremendi,* describing the terrible events in the East and urging all Christians to take up arms and go to help their fellow religionists. They would receive certain benefits, such as release from penance imposed for all sins for which they had made proper confession. Archbishop Joscius of Tyre traveled to the West to seek aid and was given papal permission to preach the crusade north of the Alps. In January 1188, he succeeded in negotiating a peace settlement between Philip II of France and Henry II of England, in which both kings agreed to take the cross and lead a joint expedition to the East. They planned to set out at Easter 1189, but a renewed outbreak of war delayed their departure.

Other individuals and groups set out in the meantime. Geoffrey of Lusignan, elder brother of King Guy of Jerusalem, reached the East in the second half of 1188 or early 1189; King William II of Sicily sent a fleet of 50 ships under his admiral Margarit. By August 1189 Guy had (according to one contemporary writer) a force of around 9,000, including 700 knights, and the support of the Pisans, whose ships gave him valuable sea power. With this army he began to besiege the port of Acre. If the city could be recaptured, it could act as the base for a counterattack on Saladin in Palestine. But the Marquis Conrad, who still held Tyre, refused aid.

The First Stage of the Crusade: The Siege of Acre

Other crusaders flocked to join the siege of Acre during the autumn of 1189, including 50 ships from Denmark, Frisia, Flanders, and England, carrying 12,000 warriors (according to contemporary writers). Landgrave Ludwig III of Thuringia was appointed leader of the crusading army, and in September 1189 he persuaded Conrad to come from Tyre to Acre to assist the siege. In March 1190 the barons of the kingdom and the crusaders succeeded in working out a peace settlement between the marquis and King Guy: Conrad would hold Tyre, Beirut, and Sidon (when the latter two cities were recaptured from Saladin) and assist Guy as king.

Saladin had moved his army to Acre soon after the siege had begun, and he effectively surrounded the besieging Christian army. He was not able to prevent the crusaders from receiving reinforcements by sea, but neither were they able to prevent Muslim vessels from entering the port of Acre. Saladin's naval forces held the advantage until the end of March 1190, when the marquis's ships, based at Tyre, returned to the crusader camp at Acre with supplies. The Muslims in Acre sent out their ships to challenge the crusaders, but were defeated. Christian control of the sea made it difficult for Saladin to supply Acre by ship, but sufficient ships slipped through the crusader blockade to enable the defense to continue. Sometimes these vessels were disguised as Christian ships, flying banners with crosses and carrying pigs on the decks. Swimmers were also used to carry supplies and information between Saladin's army and the defenders of Acre.

Neither the crusaders nor Saladin could gain the advantage. The crusaders lacked the forces to make a decisive assault and to drive back Saladin's surrounding army, while Saladin experienced problems in keeping his army together for the duration of the long campaign. In the late summer of 1190, many small groups of crusaders arrived at Acre from France, Italy, and England, including Count Henry of Champagne and Archbishop Baldwin of Canterbury. Count Henry was elected leader of the crusade in place of Landgrave Ludwig, who had had to leave the crusade because of ill health.

The political situation was complicated by the death of

Taking of Acre and return of Philip II, king of France. Illustration from *Le Miroir Historial* (*The Mirror of History*), by Vincent de Beauvais (1190–1264). (The Art Archive/Museé Condé Chantilly/dagli Orti)

Queen Sibyl and her two daughters, Alice and Maria, in early autumn 1190. Guy of Lusignan, who had ruled as Sibyl's consort, now had no right to the title of king. The heir to the throne was Sibyl's sister Isabella, but her husband, Humphrey IV of Toron, did not want to be king. Conrad approached the leaders of the crusade with the proposal that Isabella's marriage be nullified, and she be married to him instead; he would then provide effective military leadership for the crusade, with supplies brought in through Tyre, and strong naval support. Despite vehement opposition from Archbishop Baldwin, acting in place of Patriarch Eraclius (who was ill), and Isabella's own reluctance, and although the marquis already had two wives (in Montferrat and Constantinople), the nobles of the kingdom and the leaders of the crusade agreed to Conrad's scheme. Isabella was married to the marquis, who then retired to Tyre rather than remaining at Acre to lead the siege.

The Crusades of the Kings

The Holy Roman Emperor, Frederick I Barbarossa, held an assembly at Metz in March 1188 to make preparations for the crusade, and set out in May 1189. He traveled overland, down the river Danube, crossing the Hellespont and marching across Asia Minor. This was a shorter route from Germany than the sea route via the North Sea, and Frederick lacked the ships to transport his whole force by sea. The emperor was accompanied by his son Frederick V, duke of Swabia, and left his son Henry (later Emperor Henry VI) as regent in Germany. Frederick Barbarossa's arrival was eagerly awaited by the crusaders, for the forces he was bringing, for his military experience, and for his authority as emperor of the West. He defeated the forces of the sultan of Rūm, but on 10 June 1190 he was drowned in the river Selef in Cilicia. The remnants of his army reached Antioch late in June, where many abandoned the crusade. A small force, led by Frederick of Swabia, continued to Tripoli (mod. Trâblous, Lebanon), where Marquis Conrad, the duke's kinsman, met them and escorted them to Acre. The duke began renewed assaults on the city, but the city was still holding out when he died in January 1191 from plague.

The kings of England and France were still expected at the siege. Henry II of England had died on 6 July 1189. His son and successor, Richard (the Lionheart), count of Poitou, had been one of the first to take the cross in the West, and was anxious to set out on his crusade. While Richard's speed in setting out on crusade soon after he was crowned king of England indicates that he was genuinely devoted to the crusading cause, he was also bound by family and feudal obligations. Queen Sibyl of Jerusalem and her sister Isabella were related to Richard: the royal family of Jerusalem was descended from Count Fulk V of Anjou (d. 1143), who was Richard's great-grandfather. The family of King Guy were Richard's vassals, as Lusignan was in Richard's county of Poitou. As his cousin and his vassal were in need of his aid, it was Richard's duty to go to their assistance.

King Philip II of France also crusaded partly from family obligations. His father, Louis VII, had taken part in the Second Crusade (1147–1149) with his then queen, Eleanor of Aquitaine, who later became Richard's mother. Many of the nobles of the kingdom of Jerusalem were members of French families, vassals of Philip.

Richard and Philip agreed to travel together and to share any booty they won. They set out in July 1190 and traveled overland across France, taking ship from Marseilles (Richard) and Genoa (Philip) to Sicily. The island was an obvious meeting point, as it was centrally located in the Mediterranean, it could supply the fleets with food for the voyage, and King William II of Sicily was dedicated to the crusade and was also married to Richard's younger sister Joanna. William's death in November 1189 changed the situation, as his successor, Tancred, was not well disposed toward the king of England and refused to surrender Joanna's dowry, which Richard wanted to help finance his crusade.

Philip had engaged Genoese ships to carry his force; Richard had assembled a fleet of English ships, which sailed via the Strait of Gibraltar to meet the king at Sicily in September. Some crusaders, such as the archbishop of Canterbury, continued directly to the Holy Land; the rest waited for Richard. After the arrival of the two kings, skirmishing broke out between crusaders and Sicilians, culminating in open warfare. On 4 October 1190, Richard captured the city of Messina. Eventually he agreed on peace terms with King Tancred, who surrendered Joanna's dowry. As it was now too late in the year to continue to the East, the crusaders wintered in Sicily and proceeded in early April.

While Philip sailed directly to the Holy Land, Richard and his fleet landed on Cyprus, whose self-professed emperor, Isaac Doukas Komnenos, took some of the crusaders prisoner. Richard counterattacked and conquered the island, which came to prove a valuable source of supply for the crusade and a useful haven for crusaders on their way to and from the Holy Land. It is possible that Richard had deliberately set out to conquer it for this reason.

Richard finally reached Acre early in June 1191. The Muslim defenders of the city were suing for peace; although King Philip agreed to the terms, Richard refused, as the defenders wished to take all their possessions with them, which would leave no booty for the crusaders. After further assaults, part of the wall of Acre was undermined and collapsed. On 12 July 1191 the defenders surrendered, in exchange for life and limb only. The peace terms included the return of the True Cross lost at the battle of Hattin, the payment of a sum of money, and the return of Christian captives; the Muslims gave hostages as a guarantee. They evacuated the city, and the crusaders entered, but many were furious when Philip and Richard took all the property within the city as their own booty and divided it between themselves, rather than allowing it to be divided between all the crusaders who had taken part in the siege.

The conflicting claims of King Guy and Marquis Conrad were settled: Guy would hold the kingdom of Jerusalem until his death, and Conrad would succeed him. Philip of France then departed for the West, although the crusade was far from over. Various explanations were given for his sudden departure, including claims that he was worried by news that his young son Louis was sick, or that he was afraid that Richard of England was trying to poison him. Other French crusaders remained under the overall command of Hugh III, duke of Burgundy. Richard, claiming that Saladin had not fulfilled the terms of the treaty of surrender, had most of the Muslim hostages executed and then set out on the next stage of the crusade: the recapture of Jerusalem.

The Second Stage of the Crusade: The Campaign for Jerusalem

King Richard advanced cautiously, having decided that the army should march down the coast to Jaffa (mod. Tel Aviv-Yafo, Israel) and then move inland toward Jerusalem by the most direct route. This would enable him to keep his army supplied by sea for most of the journey, making use of the ships that he had brought from England, as well as those of Pisa and Genoa. The army set out late in August and marched along the coast road, harassed by Saladin's army, which marched on its left, until 7 September 1191, when a skirmish at Arsuf became a major engagement. The Muslims withdrew, and the Christians remained in control of the field. Saladin then destroyed most of the fortresses in Palestine, so that they could not be repossessed and defended by the crusaders. At Jaffa, Richard set about repairing the city's fortifications and other neighboring fortresses on the road to Jerusalem.

Negotiations between the crusaders and Saladin had been in train for many months. Marquis Conrad was in negotiation with Saladin, while Richard himself had contacted Saladin almost as soon as he entered the kingdom. During the period at Jaffa, negotiations between Richard and Saladin reached an advanced stage, but broke down because neither side trusted the other.

In late November the crusaders moved toward Jerusalem, reaching the town of Ramla. The army spent Christmas 1191 in this area, divided between various fortresses on the Jerusalem road. But early in January 1192, on the advice of the Templars, the Hospitallers, and the barons of Outremer, the leaders of the crusade decided to withdraw to Ascalon and refortify that city. As Ascalon controlled the road from Egypt, this move would prevent Saladin bringing up reinforcements and supplies from there. Yet this decision was a serious blow to the crusaders' morale, and during the long march back through the cold, wet winter weather the French contingent left the main army and split up. At Ascalon, King Richard supervised the refortification of the city, and the crusaders ravaged the Muslim-held countryside. The various factions among the crusaders now broke into open dispute: supporters of the marquis against supporters of King Guy, the "French" against the "Normans" or "English," and the Genoese against the Pisans. In addition, Richard received news from England that the government he had left in his absence was in disarray. Realizing that he would have to return home, Richard sought a settlement as a matter of urgency. The leaders of the army chose the Marquis Conrad as king of Jerusalem, but late in April 1192 he was murdered by two members of the Isma'ili Assassin sect. The French then chose Count Henry of Champagne, nephew of both Philip of France and Richard of England, as king. Richard agreed to this settlement, and Henry married Conrad's widow Isabella, the heiress of the kingdom. Although they were acknowledged as rulers of the kingdom, the pair were not actually crowned. Guy, the former king, purchased the island of Cyprus from the Templars, who had bought it from Richard.

The crusaders continued to ravage the land in order to undermine Saladin's hold on it, but their ultimate aim was the reconquest of Jerusalem. The leaders were aware that as soon as the city was captured the crusade would break up and most of the warriors would return to the West, and so they preferred to delay an attack until they had recovered as much territory as possible and thus laid the basis for retaining the kingdom. Yet the crusaders were running out of funds and could not stay much longer in the East. In June 1192 it was decided to make another advance on Jerusalem. The army advanced as far as Beit Nūbā, around 20 kilometers (13 mi.) from the Holy City. Debate continued within the army: the Franks and the military orders argued that the city could not be held if it were captured at this juncture, while King Richard argued that their supply lines were too long and that in summer there would be too little water in the countryside around Jerusalem to support the besiegers. He preferred to make an attack on Egypt, using ships to support his land army. The eventual decision was to withdraw to Ascalon.

After this second withdrawal, the crusade effectively broke up. Many crusaders went home. Richard withdrew to Acre, from where he launched an attack on Beirut. His plans to return to the West were interrupted by the news that Saladin had attacked Jaffa. The town fell, but the citadel was saved by Richard's arrival with his ships from Acre. Richard's forces drove back Saladin's army, which was none too willing to fight (5 August). Clearly neither side was in a position to fight any longer.

The Treaty of Jaffa (1192)

The two sides negotiated a three-year truce, the Treaty of Jaffa (2 September 1192), which effectively ended the crusade. The important strongholds of Ascalon, Gaza, and Darum were returned to Saladin, but their fortifications were to be demolished. The Franks retained Jaffa; both Christians and Muslims would have free passage through each other's lands; Christian pilgrims could visit the Holy Sepulchre in Jerusalem without paying tolls; and trade could be exercised freely. The treaty effectively acknowledged the continuing existence of the kingdom of Jerusalem, albeit in a much reduced state. After this treaty was made, many of the pilgrims visited Jerusalem to see the holy sites. Richard sent Hubert Walter, bishop of Salisbury, as his representative, but did not visit the city himself. The crusaders left the Holy Land in autumn 1192.

Conclusions

The crusade was undermined from the beginning by disputes between the leaders. The rivalry between King Guy of Jerusalem and Conrad of Montferrat developed early in the undertaking. Conrad had taken the initiative in trying to encourage powerful lords in the West to assist the Holy Land: without his efforts in 1187–1188, the whole of the kingdom would have been lost to Saladin. As a renowned warrior who was related to the king of France and Emperor Frederick I, Conrad may have intended to use Tyre as a base from which to reconquer the kingdom of Jerusalem and make himself king. Philip II of France and the Genoese supported Conrad's claim to the throne of Jerusalem, while Richard of England and the Pisans supported Guy's claim. The dispute was only resolved by Conrad's death and Guy's replacement by Henry of Champagne.

The Italian city republics also brought their rivalries to the Holy Land. Genoa and Pisa had lost their trading rights in the Byzantine Empire and were anxious to ensure their rights in Outremer by winning concessions from the rival claimants to the kingdom of Jerusalem in return for their support. Philip of France and Richard of England also brought their rivalry to the Holy Land. Although Richard was Philip's vassal for his lands in France (Normandy, Anjou, and Aquitaine), he seems to have taken the lead in military affairs, to Philip's annoyance. The French accused Richard of arranging the assassination of Marquis Conrad, and by June 1192, according to the contemporary writer Ambroise, King Richard and Hugh III of Burgundy, the chosen leader of the French contingent, were singing insulting songs about each other.

The crusading army was also divided over strategy. Richard preferred to advance cautiously, establishing a base and securing his rear and supply lines before proceeding. By summer 1192, he had decided that the best strategy was to attack Egypt rather than Jerusalem, which could not be held securely against a well-organized, well-supplied enemy. This strategy was supported by many of the Franks, but many in the crusading army wanted to attack Jerusalem and regarded the diversion to Ascalon and the policy of raiding into Muslim territory as a distraction from the crusade's true purpose. The argument over strategy eventually led to the disintegration of the army in the summer of 1192. In effect, the crusade ended in stalemate, with neither side able to inflict final defeat on the other, and both sides divided, demoralized, and short of resources.

–Helen J. Nicholson

Bibliography

Cardini, Franco, "Gli italiani e la crociata di Federico," *Bullettino dell'Istituto italiano per il Medio Evo e Archivio Muratoriano* 96 (1990), 261–281.

Edbury, Peter W., "The Templars in Cyprus," in *The Military Orders: Fighting for the Faith and Caring for the Sick,* ed. Malcolm Barber (Aldershot, UK: Variorum, 1994), pp. 189–195.

Eickhoff, Ekkehard, *Friedrich Barbarossa im Orient: Kreuzzug und Tod Friedrichs I.* (Tübingen: Wasmuth, 1977).

Flahiff, George B., "Deus non vult: A Critic of the Third Crusade," *Mediaeval Studies* 9 (1947), 162–188.

Gibb, Hamilton A. R., "The Rise of Saladin: 1169–1189," in *A History of the Crusades,* ed. Kenneth M. Setton et al., 6 vols., 2d ed. (Madison: University of Wisconsin Press, 1969–1989), 1:562–589.

Gillingham, John, "Roger of Howden on Crusade," in *Medieval Historical Writing in the Christian and Islamic Worlds,* ed. D. O. Morgan (London: School of Oriental and African Studies, University of London, 1982), pp. 60–75.

———, "Richard I and the Science of War in the Middle Ages," in *War and Government in the Middle Ages: Essays in Honour of J. O. Prestwich,* ed. John Gillingham and J. C. Holt (Woodbridge, UK: Boydell, 1984), pp. 78–91.

———, *Richard Coeur de Lion: Kingship, Chivalry and War in the Twelfth Century* (London: Hambledon, 1994).

———, *Richard I* (New Haven: Yale University Press, 1999).

Hiestand, Rudolf, "Precipua tocius christianismi columpna: Barbarossa und der Kreuzzug," in *Friedrich Barbarossa: Handlungsspielräume und Wirkungsweisen des staufischen Kaisers,* ed. Alfred Haverkamp (Sigmaringen: Thorbecke, 1992), pp. 51–108.

Jacoby, David, "Conrad, Marquis of Montferrat, and the Kingdom of Jerusalem (1187–1192)," in *Atti del Congresso Internazionale "Dai feudi monferrini e dal Piemonte ai nuovi mondi oltre gli Oceani" Alessandria, 2–6 aprile 1990,* ed. Laura Bolletto (Alessandria: Accademia degli Immobili, 1993), pp. 187–238.

Johnson, Edgar N., "The Crusades of Frederick Barbarossa and Henry VI," in *A History of the Crusades,* ed. Kenneth M. Setton et al., 6 vols., 2d ed. (Madison: University of Wisconsin Press, 1969–1989), 2:86–122.

Lyons, Malcolm C., and D. E. P. Jackson, *Saladin: The Politics of the Holy War* (Cambridge: Cambridge University Press, 1982).

Markowski, Michael, "Richard Lionheart: Bad King, Bad Crusader?" *Journal of Medieval History* 23 (1997), 351–365.

Mayer, Hans Eberhard, *The Crusades,* 2d ed., trans. John Gillingham (Oxford: Oxford University Press, 1988).

Möhring, Hannes, *Saladin und der Dritte Kreuzzug: Aiyubidische Strategie und Diplomatie im Vergleich vornehmlich der arabischen mit den lateinischen Quellen* (Wiesbaden: Steiner, 1980).

Nicholson, Helen J., "Women on the Third Crusade," *Journal of Medieval History* 23 (1997), 335–349.

Painter, Sidney, "The Third Crusade: Richard the Lionhearted and Philip Augustus," in *A History of the Crusades,* ed. Kenneth M. Setton et al., 6 vols., 2d ed. (Madison: University of Wisconsin Press, 1969–1989), 2: 44–85.

Pringle, R. Denys, "King Richard I and the Walls of Ascalon," in *Palestine Exploration Quarterly* 116 (1984), 133–147.

Richard, Jean, "Philippe Auguste, la croisade et le royaume," in *La France de Philippe Auguste: Le temps des mutations,* ed. Robert-Henri Bautier (Paris: Editions du C.N.R.S., 1982), pp. 411–424.

———, "1187: Point de depart pour une nouvelle forme de croisade," in *The Horns of Hattin,* ed. Benjamin Z. Kedar (Jerusalem: Yad Izhak Ben-Zvi Institute, 1992), pp. 250–260.

Rogers, Randall, *Latin Siege Warfare in the Twelfth Century* (Oxford: Clarendon, 1992).

St. Thomas of Acre, Order of

A small English military order founded during the Third Crusade (1189–1192) and named after the martyred Thomas Becket, archbishop of Canterbury.

Twelfth- and thirteenth-century sources credit the order's foundation variously to one William, chaplain to Ralph of Diceto; to Hubert Walter, archbishop of Canterbury; or to King Richard I of England; it is possible that all three men were involved. The Order of St. Thomas of Acre originally consisted of a chapel served by Augustinian canons. It performed charitable and devotional duties, including hospital and ransom work, before being militarized by Peter of Roches, bishop of Winchester, probably in 1228. In 1236 Pope Gregory IX instructed it to follow the Rule of the Teutonic Order, with which St. Thomas had been associated since at least 1192, and to carry out both military and hospitaller functions.

The order was never large or powerful enough to play a significant role in the affairs of Outremer; it is mentioned only occasionally by contemporary chroniclers. Despite this, the knights of St. Thomas seem to have acquitted themselves well enough in battle and at times became embroiled in the political squabbles of the Latin East. Although the order had possessions throughout western Europe, most of its holdings were concentrated in England and Ireland, and they were few in number compared to those of the other military orders. It fought a constant but losing battle for resources for much of its existence, partly because Englishmen who wished to join or support a military order usually turned to the Hospitallers or Templars.

After the fall of Acre (mod. 'Akko, Israel) to the Mamlūks in 1291 the Order of St. Thomas retreated to Cyprus and established its headquarters there. In the early fourteenth century tensions apparently arose between the military brethren in the East and the members of the order in England, for whom hospitaller activities were paramount. Ultimately the English chapter appears to have won out. The last mention of a militant officer of St. Thomas in Cyprus occurs in 1367; thereafter its military function seems to have been abandoned entirely, and the order concentrated on charitable and devotional activities in England for most of the next two centuries. The order became increasingly associated with the Mercers' Company of London, reverted to following the Rule of St. Augustine, and in the early sixteenth century even operated a grammar school in London. In October 1538 it was dissolved on the order of King Henry VIII of England. Its property was confiscated by the Crown, and the Mercers' Company purchased it for £969. Its archive was ultimately split into three parts, which are now in the Mercers' Company (London), the British Library, and the Public Record Office.

–Paul Crawford

Bibliography
Forey, Alan J., "The Military Order of St Thomas of Acre," *English Historical Review* 92 (1977), 481–503.
———, *The Military Orders from the Twelfth to the Early Fourteenth Centuries* (London: Macmillan, 1992).
Watney, John. *Some Account of the Hospital of St. Thomas of Acon, in the Cheap, London, and of the Plate of the Mercers' Company* (London: Blades, East and Blades, 1892).

Thoros

See T'oros

Tiberias

Tiberias (mod. Teverya, Israel) was a major town in the kingdom of Jerusalem, the capital of the lordship of Tiberias.

Situated on the western shore of the Sea of Galilee (Lake Tiberias), Tiberias was occupied by Tancred and his followers after the arrival of the First Crusade (1096–1099) in Palestine. It became the center of the lordship of Tiberias (sometimes known as the principality of Galilee) and the seat of a Latin bishop who was a suffragan of the archbishop of Nazareth. The population included a substantial Jewish community. The town's walls were in a poor state of repair at the time of the Frankish conquest, but had been improved by 1113. A citadel, erected or fortified on an earlier site at some point during the twelfth century, was situated on the lake shore, occupying an area of some 70 by 50 meters (230 by 165 ft.).

The citadel was surrendered to Saladin in the aftermath of the battle of Hattin in 1187 by Eschiva, lady of Tiberias, who accepted a safe conduct for herself and her men. In 1190 Saladin had the fortifications destroyed. The town was restored to Frankish rule in 1241, and the citadel may have been rebuilt by Odo of Montbéliard, who held the lordship at that time. However, the town was captured by the Ayyūbids on 17 June 1247.

–Alan V. Murray

Bibliography
Prawer, Joshua, *The Latin Kingdom of Jerusalem; European Colonialism in the Middle Ages* (London: Weidenfeld and Nicolson, 1972).
Razi, Zvi, and Eliot Braun, "The Lost Crusader Castle of Tiberias," in *The Horns of Hattin,* ed. Benjamin Z. Kedar (Jerusalem: Yad Izhak Ben-Zvi Institute, 1992), pp. 216–227.

Rheinheimer, Martin, *Das Kreuzfahrerfürstentum Galiläa* (Frankfurt am Main: Lang, 1990).

Stepansky, Yosef, "The Crusader Castle of Tiberias," *Crusades* 3 (2004), 179–181.

Tiberias, Lordship of

The lordship of Tiberias, also known as the principality of Galilee, was one of the major lordships of the kingdom of Jerusalem during the crusader period.

The lordship's origins are to be found during the immediate aftermath of the First Crusade (1096–1099): in 1099 the Norman Tancred conquered much of Galilee and took the title of prince of Galilee. Under Muslim rule the town of Tiberias (mod. Teverya, Israel) had been the capital of Jund al-Urdunn (that is, "province of the Jordan"). Tancred fortified the northern part of the city; the other parts, including the famous thermal baths, had been devastated after the flight of its Muslim inhabitants and the murder of its Jewish ones. In 1100 Tancred extended his authority eastward across the Jordan into the Sawād region (Fr. *Terre de Suète*) and the Golan Heights, becoming suzerain of its Arab lord, who was known as the Fat Peasant.

After Tancred's departure to Antioch (1101), King Baldwin I of Jerusalem appointed Hugh of Fauquembergues as lord of Tiberias. Hugh dedicated his efforts to the eastern sector of the lordship, facing constant attacks from Damascus. As a defensive measure he built two castles: Toron, near the sources of the Jordan, and El-ʿAl, on a hill east of the Sea of Galilee (Lake Tiberias). Hugh was killed during one of these battles in 1105. As his successor Baldwin appointed an experienced warrior, Gervase of Bazoches, who was captured and killed by Ṭughtigin, *atabeg* of Damascus, in 1108. Thereupon the king appointed Tancred as titular prince, but the lordship was administered by royal officers until 1113, when it was bestowed on Joscelin I of Courtenay, who had come from Edessa after a conflict with its ruler, Baldwin II (of Bourcq). Joscelin dedicated his efforts to the consolidation of the lordship, increasing the number of vassals. Some of them were established in the sumptuous castle of Tiberias, while others were entrusted with lordships of villages. Joscelin built a small castle on a hill northeast of Lake Tiberias at Qasr Bardawil in order to control access to the heart of his lordship. Joscelin attempted to extend his authority into northern Transjor-dan, but with little success.

Upon the election of Baldwin of Bourcq as king of Jerusalem, Joscelin was made count of Edessa by the new king and left Galilee. In 1119 Baldwin II appointed William of Bures, who founded a dynasty at Tiberias. He played a significant role in the affairs of the kingdom. In 1123, during the king's captivity, he became constable of the kingdom and led the attacks that resulted in the conquest of Muslim-held Tyre (mod. Soûr, Lebanon); in 1128 Baldwin II sent him to France to find a suitable husband for Melisende, the heiress to the kingdom. By 1140 William of Bures was succeeded by his son, also called William, and later by his second son, Elinand.

Elinand's rule in Tiberias was characterized by his faithful cooperation with Queen Melisende and her husband Fulk. After the building of the castle of Belvoir in 1136, which was given to the Hospitallers, Elinand carried out a reorganization of the lands of his vassals in the area. In 1144 he helped Melisende to establish her joint rule with her son, Baldwin III, and in 1148 he took part in the unsuccessful expedition of the Second Crusade (1147–1149) against Damascus. Elinand's prestige in the Latin East grew, and as one of the most powerful princes of the kingdom, he increased it by his own marriage to Ermengarde of Ibelin and by that of his sister Agnes to Gerard, lord of Sidon. Under Elinand's rule, the city of Tiberias grew and became a prosperous center of the realm. Its agricultural products (especially fruits) were shipped through Haifa (mod. Hefa, Israel) and Acre (mod. ʿAkko, Israel) to western Europe and became a significant source of revenue for the principality. His sole daughter and heiress, Eschiva, was married to Walter of Saint-Omer (who may have been a grandson of Hugh of Fauquembergues). She bore four sons, who were still children at the premature death of Walter (by 1170).

As princess of Galilee and lady of Tiberias, related to the Ibelin and Sidon families and on friendly terms with the counts of Tripoli, Eschiva became a patron of cultural activities in Outremer. However, the campaigns of the Muslim leader Nūr al-Dīn were a real danger to the principality, and according to feudal custom Eschiva could not govern the fief on her own. In 1173 she married Raymond III, count of Tripoli, who thus became the most important baron of the kingdom of Jerusalem. In 1174, after the death of King Amalric I, Raymond served as regent of the kingdom of Jerusalem; under Baldwin IV he became the leader of those barons who supported a policy of compromise with the Muslims. Raymond and Eschiva established good terms with Saladin, who spared Tiberias during his incursions into Galilee. His stepsons were not associated with their administration, though they grew to maturity. In 1179 Eschiva's eldest son, Hugh, was taken captive by the Muslims near Beaufort and was ransomed by his mother for 55,000 dinars. While Raymond spent most of his time either at the royal court or with the army, Eschiva dedicated her energy to the government of Tiberias, ordering the vassals to respect the truce concluded by Raymond with Saladin. During Saladin's invasion in 1187 she held Tiberias in her husband's absence until the aftermath of the battle of Hattin (4 July 1187), when she surrendered the city to Saladin, who allowed her to leave with her household to Tripoli. Raymond died there in the same year.

The history of the principality or lordship of Tiberias ends after the collapse of the kingdom at the battle of Hattin. Eschiva's sons settled in Acre, hoping for a reconquest of Galilee. After the failure of one such attempt in 1197, Hugh of Tiberias, who had married Margaret, daughter of Balian of Ibelin and Maria Komnene, tried to organize another expedition. However, in 1204 he left Acre and took service with Baldwin of Flanders, the Latin emperor of Constantinople. Hugh's brother William settled in Cyprus as titular prince of Galilee, holding one of the four main baronies of the kingdom of Cyprus. The third brother, Otto, left Acre in 1201 and settled in Cilicia, where he took service at the court of Leon I of Armenia. The youngest brother, Ralph of Tiberias, who was held in high repute for his legal training, remained in the kingdom of Jerusalem. He served the new ruler, Henry of Champagne, at Acre, and upon Henry's death (1197) he was proposed by his brother Hugh as a husband for Henry's widow, Queen Isabella I. The barons rejected his candidature on the ground that he was a younger son and therefore unsuited to her royal dignity. Instead, they chose the king of Cyprus, Aimery of Lusignan. Ralph agreed to serve his rival, advising him on legal questions. However, when he was suspected of a plot against the king, Ralph left the court and settled in Tripoli. There he compiled his main contribution to Frankish society, the draft of the *Livre au Roi,* an introduction to the *Assizes of Jerusalem.*

–*Aryeh Grabois*

See also: Galilee; Jerusalem, (Latin) Kingdom of
Bibliography
Baldwin, Marshall W., *Raymond III of Tripolis and the Fall of Jerusalem* (Princeton: Princeton University Press, 1936).

Boase, Thomas S. R., *Castles and Churches of the Crusading Kingdom* (Oxford: Oxford University Press, 1967).
Du Cange, Charles du Fresne, *Les familles d'Outremer,* ed. Emmanuel-Guillaume Rey (Paris: Ministre de l'Instruction Publique, 1869).
Mayer, Hans Eberhard, "The Crusader Principality of Galilee between Saint-Omer and Bures-sur-Yvette," in *Itinéraires d'Orient: Hommages à Claude Cahen,* ed. Raoul Curiel and Rika Gyselen (Bures-sur-Yvette: Groupe pour l'Etude de la Civilisation du Moyen-Orient, 1994), pp. 157–166.
Murray, Alan V., *The Crusader Kingdom of Jerusalem: A Dynastic History, 1099–1125* (Oxford: Prosopographica et Genealogica, 2000).
Prawer, Joshua, "La noblesse et le régime féodal du royaume latin de Jérusalem," *Le Moyen Age* 65 (1959), 41–74.
———, *The Latin Kingdom of Jerusalem: European Colonialism in the Middle Ages* (London: Weidenfeld and Nicolson, 1972).
———, *Crusader Institutions* (Oxford: Clarendon, 1980).
Rheinheimer, Martin, *Das Kreuzfahrerfürstentum Galiläa* (Frankfurt am Main: Lang, 1990).

Toison d'Or
See Golden Fleece, Order of

Toron des Chevaliers

A Templar castle built on a low hill in the Judaean foothills adjacent to 'Amwas (in mod. West Bank) at the point where the road from Jaffa (mod. Tel Aviv-Yafo, Israel) to Jerusalem was met by one from Ascalon (mod. Tel Ashqelon, Israel).

The foundation of Toron des Chevaliers between 1137 and 1141 is attributed by the *Chronica Aldephonsi imperatoris* to Rodrigo González, count of Toledo, who was apparently serving with the Templars at the time. Like the castles of Ibelin, Blanchegarde, and Bethegibelin, its purpose was to protect the southern parts of the kingdom of Jerusalem from Muslim raiding from Ascalon, and to serve as a nucleus for Frankish settlement. In 1169–1171, the Jewish traveler Benjamin of Tudela refers to it in Spanish as Toron de los Caballeros (Tower of the Knights).

Archaeological remains confirm that this name, from which the Arabic name Latrun was subsequently derived, referred to a large tower, or donjon, that stood at the center of the castle, within a rectangular enclosure filled with vaulted buildings, including a chapel. Enclosing this was a larger polygonal enceinte, containing stables and other buildings.

It seems likely that the Templars held an extensive estate in the area, including 'Amwas (Lat. *Emmaus*) and Chastel Hernaut (Lat. *Castellum Arnaldi*), though information about it is sparse. They surrendered Toron and Gaza to the Ayyūbid prince al-'Ādil in September 1187 in return for the release of their master, Gerard of Ridefort, and in December 1191 Saladin ordered its destruction. Although it was returned to the Christians between 1229 and 1244, there is no evidence that the order ever rebuilt it.

–*Denys Pringle*

Bibliography
Folda, Jaroslav, *The Art of the Crusaders in the Holy Land, 1098–1187* (Cambridge: Cambridge University Press, 1995).
Pringle, Denys, *The Churches of the Crusader Kingdom of Jerusalem: A Corpus,* 2 (Cambridge: Cambridge University Press, 1993).
———, *Secular Buildings in the Crusader Kingdom of Jerusalem* (Cambridge: Cambridge University Press, 1997).
———, "Templar Castles between Jaffa and Jerusalem," in *The Military Orders,* vol. 2. *Welfare and Warfare,* ed. Helen Nicholson (Aldershot, UK: Ashgate, 1998), pp. 89–109.

T'oros I, Rupenid (d. 1129)

Armenian prince, of the Rupenid family, foremost chieftain in northern Cilicia (Lesser Armenia).

In 1100 T'oros succeeded his father Constantine to territories in the Taurus Mountains, centered on the castle of Vahga (mod. Feke Kalesi, Turkey). T'oros tried not to get involved in the conflict between the Byzantines and the Franks of Antioch over control of the Cilician plain, but he was able to extend his rule by capturing the city of Anazarba. He based himself there, refortifying it and building a church. Despite the occupation of Anazarba, and his revenge-killing of some Greek castellans at Herakleia (mod. Ereğli, Turkey), he maintained good relations with the Byzantines. He sought to do the same with the Franks, who were dispossessing other Armenian barons: he contributed troops to assist Roger of Antioch's successful siege of Azaz in 1118. He was able to consolidate control of his lands and was succeeded by his brother Leon.

–*Angus Stewart*

Bibliography
Der Nersessian, Sirarpie, "The Kingdom of Cilician Armenia," in *A History of the Crusades,* ed. Kenneth M. Setton et al., 2d ed., 6 vols. (Madison: University of Wisconsin Press, 1969–1989), 2:630–659.

T'oros II, Rupenid (d. 1168)

Armenian prince of the Rupenid family, ruler of much of Cilicia (Lesser Armenia).

In 1137 T'oros was captured with his father, Leon, by the Byzantine emperor John II Komnenos and imprisoned in Constantinople (mod. İstanbul, Turkey). He was able to escape in 1145, and by 1148 he had regained the family's old centers. Exploiting the concentration of the Franks and the Muslims on the former county of Edessa, T'oros was able to expand his realm, occupying Mamistra (mod. Misis, Turkey). This provoked a Byzantine intervention: one Byzantine army was defeated in 1152, but T'oros was forced to submit to Emperor Manuel I Komnenos in 1158. Relations remained good, despite conflict following the murder of T'oros's brother, Stephen, in 1162.

T'oros sought friendship with the Franks: he married the daughter of Simon of Raban and allied with Reynald of Châtillon, prince of Antioch; he participated in the campaign to relieve Harenc (mod. Ḥarim, Syria) in 1164, withdrawing before the disastrous battle but then obtaining the release of Bohemund III of Antioch.

–*Angus Stewart*

Bibliography
Der Nersessian, Sirarpie, "The Kingdom of Cilician Armenia," in *A History of the Crusades,* ed. Kenneth M. Setton et al., 2d ed., 6 vols. (Madison: University of Wisconsin Press, 1969–1989), 2:630–659.

T'oros of Edessa (d. 1098)

T'oros, a Chalcedonian Armenian, ruled the city of Edessa (mod. Şanlıurfa, Turkey), nominally on behalf of the Byzantine Empire, in the period after the Turkish invasions of Upper Mesopotamia in the late twelfth century, holding the titles of *doux* and *kouropalates.*

In 1095, however, T'oros was forced to accept the presence of a Turkish garrison in the citadel of Edessa. After their expulsion, he strengthened the fortifications and maintained a strong armed force, although he became unpopular because of his heavy taxation of the local population. In 1098 he requested the assistance of Baldwin of Boulogne, who had arrived with the armies of the First Crusade (1096–1099) and was then campaigning in the Upper Euphrates Valley. Though contemporary accounts are contradictory, T'oros probably offered Baldwin a share in the government of Edessa and may even have adopted him as his son and heir.

After an unsuccessful campaign to Samosata, Baldwin returned to Edessa, where dissident Armenians in the city overthrew T'oros. He was murdered while trying to escape, having been warned of the plot by Baldwin, whose role in the affair is unclear.

–Rosemary Morris

Bibliography

Beaumont, André Alden, Jr., "Albert of Aachen and the County of Edessa," in *The Crusades and Other Historical Essays Presented to Dana C. Munro,* ed. Louis J. Paetow (New York: Crofts, 1928), pp. 101–138.

Forse, James H., "Armenians and the First Crusade," *Journal of Medieval History* 17 (1991), 13–22.

Laurent, J., "Des Grecs au croisés: Etude sur l'histoire d'Edesse entre 1071 et 1098," *Byzantion* 1 (1924), 367–449.

Tortosa (Spain)

Town in the northeast of the Iberian Peninsula, situated on the river Ebro.

The ancient Iberian Dertosa was an important trading emporium under Muslim rule. Its control was imperative to secure the Ebro region politically and economically. During the first half of the twelfth century, Christian forces under the counts of Barcelona repeatedly attempted to conquer the town. The ultimately successful campaign of 1148 was heavily influenced by crusading ideals, repeatedly depicted as part of a general struggle against Islam, and strongly supported by the papacy. Count Raymond Berengar IV assembled an army comprised of Catalan, Aragonese, Genoese, and Occitan forces, aided by military orders and by Anglo-Flemish crusaders on their way to the Holy Land in the course of the Second Crusade (1147–1149). After a seven-month siege, Tortosa surrendered on 30 December 1148. Many of the conquerors remained in Tortosa, cohabiting with the local Jewish and Muslim population, thus forming a multicultural and multiconfessional urban society that in some ways resembled that of the towns in the Latin East.

–Nikolas Jaspert

Bibliography

Jaspert, Nikolas, "'Capta est Dertosa, clavis Christianorum': Tortosa and the Crusades," in *The Second Crusade. Scope and Consequences,* ed. Jonathan Phillips and Martin Hoch (Manchester, UK: Manchester University Press, 2001), pp. 90–110.

Virgili i Colet, Antoni, "'. . . Ad detrimentum Yspaniae . . .'. La cruzada de Turtūša y la feudalización de la región de Tortosa (1148–1200)," in *L'incastellamento,* ed. Miquel Barceló and Pierre Toubert (Rome: Ecole Française de Rome, 1998), pp. 99–121.

Tortosa (Syria)

Tortosa (mod. Tartūs, Syria) was a small port town at the northern end of the county of Tripoli.

The town was acquired by the Order of the Temple, probably in the 1150s. It was surrounded by walls (which have now largely disappeared) and contained a twelfth-century cathedral, now a museum. This is one of the most perfect surviving examples of Frankish ecclesiastical architecture in a simple early gothic style with a pointed barrel-vaulted roof. At the northwest corner of the city, the Templars built a castle. The twelfth-century donjon was strengthened (probably between 1202 and 1212) by the addition of shooting galleries and a bailey surrounded by ditches and a double curtain wall with rectangular interval towers. The inner walls rose to the height of 25 meters (82 ft.) and were equipped with vaulted galleries and arrow slits at two different levels. In the interior there were a chapter house and chapel with ribbed vaulting, now incorporated into the houses of the town. The Templars held Tortosa until 3 August 1291, when it was finally abandoned, two months after the fall of Acre to the Mamlūks. The Templars held the small offshore island of Ruad (mod. Arwād, Syria) for the next ten years.

–Hugh Kennedy

Bibliography

Burns, Ross, *The Monuments of Syria* (London: Tauris, 1992).

Kennedy, Hugh, *Crusader Castles* (Cambridge: Cambridge University Press, 1994).

Toulouse

The city and county of Toulouse in southern France were home to Raymond IV of Saint-Gilles (1093–1105), one of the richest and most respected leaders of the First Crusade, yet only a century later Toulouse and its hinterland were the target of a crusade launched against the Cathar sect.

The city of Toulouse, located on a sharp bend of the river Garonne, grew exceedingly rich in the eleventh century as a port and crossing point for regional trade. Its wealth also came from pilgrims from northern France and elsewhere, who rested in the city before continuing their journeys to the shrine of St. James at Santiago de Compostela in northwestern Spain.

Links between Toulouse and Spain were strengthened by the involvement of the Cluniac monks of Saint-Sernin in the wars against the Moorish kingdoms of Spain. Count Raymond IV participated in such campaigns. Pope Urban II visited Toulouse during his tour of southern and central France in the fall of 1095, and he consecrated the rebuilt abbey church of Saint-Sernin, which included a relic of St. James. Raymond probably met with Urban at that time and committed his support to Urban's expedition to the Holy Land, weeks before the Council of Clermont. The First (1096–1099) and Second (1147–1149) crusades furthered the reputations of Count Raymond IV and Count Alphonse-Jordan (1112–1148) as devout *milites Christi* ("knights of Christ") and conquerors of the county of Tripoli in Outremer. Their protracted absences encouraged the people of Toulouse to establish an elected consulate (Fr. *consulat*) to govern the courts and markets of the growing city, and the autonomy of the consulate became a significant marker of Toulousan identity after the middle of the twelfth century.

The fame linking Toulouse and the crusades suffered a reversal at the end of the twelfth century, however. The growth of the sect of the Cathars in the region was blamed on the tolerance shown by Count Raymond VI (1195–1222). After the murder of the papal legate Peter of Castelnau in the region in January 1209, a crusade was called against Raymond and the Cathars he purportedly protected. Many Toulousans initially supported the crusade, because they too envisioned Catharism as a threat to religious and social order. Yet once the crusaders came to be perceived as being more interested in conquering wealthy towns than in destroying heresy, Toulouse became the center of resistance, a shift evident in the Occitan *Chanson de la Croisade albigeoise* begun by William of Tudela. The leader of the crusade, Simon of Montfort, was killed outside its walls in 1218, but the crusade dragged on until the Treaty of Paris was drawn up between Count Raymond VII (1222–1249) and King Louis IX of France in 1229. The treaty required Raymond's daughter Jeanne to marry Louis's brother Alphonse, which brought Toulouse within the influence of the Capetian dynasty.

–*Christopher K. Gardner*

Bibliography
Dossat, Yves, "L'Université de Toulouse, Raymond VII, les Capitouls et le Roi," in *Les Universités du Languedoc au XIIIe siècle,* ed. Marie-Humbert Vicaire (Toulouse: Privat, 1970), pp. 58–91.
Dubled, Henri, "Les Comtes de Toulouse et la Provence (990–1274)," in *Mélanges Roger Aubenas: Recueil de mémoires et travaux publiés par la Société d'histoire du droit et des institutions des anciens pays de droit écrit* (Montpellier: Presses de Savoie, 1974), pp. 259–280.
Macé, Laurent, *Les Comtes de Toulouse et leur entourage, XIIe–XIIIe siècles—rivalités, alliances et jeux de pouvoir* (Toulouse: Privat, 2000).
Mundy, John H., *Society and Government at Toulouse in the Age of the Cathars* (Toronto: Pontifical Institute of Mediaeval Studies, 1997).
Paterson, Linda M., *The World of the Troubadours, Medieval Occitan Society, c. 1100–c.1300* (Cambridge: Cambridge University Press, 1993).
Wolff, Philippe, *Histoire de Toulouse* (Toulouse: Privat, 1958).

Tractatus de locis et statu sancte terre Ierosolimitane

A Latin treatise that systematically describes the kingdom of Jerusalem in the years before the battle of Hattin (1187).

The anonymous author situates the *terra Ierosolimitana* ("land of Jerusalem") at the world's center and goes on to describe the adjacent countries. He then presents the Christian groups inhabiting the land (Franks, Greeks, Syrians, Armenians, Georgians, Jacobites, and Nestorians), remarking on their military worth, external appearance, dogmatic tenets, and alphabet. A lengthy passage on the Templars is followed by a brief one on the Hospitallers. The structure of the Latin Church is surveyed in detail, and the country's most prominent holy places are listed. Sections on mountains, fauna, and fruit trees are followed by a passage on the names by which main towns were known in different periods. Next, the author turns to the kingdom's governance, mentions the king's coronation oath, lists the ten most important barons, and spells out that each must follow the king into battle with a specified number of knights. The treatise concludes with the characterization of the non-Christian groups living in the country: Jews, Samaritans, Assassins, and Bedouins.

The treatise was probably written after 1168 and before 1187 by a visitor from Europe. It was utilized by Thietmar, James of Vitry, and Burchard of Mount Zion.

–*Benjamin Kedar*

Bibliography
Kedar, Benjamin Z., "The *Tractatus de locis et statu sancte terre Ierosolimitane,*" in *The Crusades and Their Sources: Essays Presented to Bernard Hamilton,* ed. John France and William G. Zajac (Aldershot, UK: Ashgate, 1998), pp. 111–133.

Thomas, Georg M., "Ein Tractat über das heilige Land und den dritten Kreuzzug," *Sitzungssberichte der Königlich Bayerischen Akademie der Wissenschaften zu München: Philosophisch-philologische Classe*, 2 (1865), 141–160.

Transjordan

Transjordan (Fr. *Oultrejourdain*) is a modern designation for one of the main lordships of the kingdom of Jerusalem, situated to the east and south of the Dead Sea and covering the biblical lands of Moab and Edom (Idumaea).

The Franks first penetrated this region in the year after the conquest of Palestine by the First Crusade (1096–1099), when King Baldwin I of Jerusalem led an expedition to reconnoiter the area south of the Dead Sea in November–December 1100. Further reconnaissances and raids followed, but a permanent Frankish presence was only established in 1115–1116, when the king constructed the castle of Montréal (Lat. *Mons Regalis*) at Shaubak in Edom. Under Baldwin I the entire region remained part of the royal demense, but Baldwin II formed Moab and Edom into a lordship for Roman of Le Puy, whom, however, he later dispossessed for rebellion (probably before 1126). Roman's successor, the royal butler Pagan, constructed a larger castle in 1142 at the town of Kerak (mod. Karak, Jordan) in Moab, east of the Dead Sea, which became the new capital of the lordship.

After the death of the third lord, Maurice (c. 1153), the territory reverted to the royal demesne until 1161, when Baldwin III gave it to Philip of Nablus in exchange for the latter's fiefs in Samaria, and added to it the lands to the south as far as Aila at the head of the Gulf of 'Aqaba. When Philip joined the Order of the Temple (c. 1166), he was succeeded first by Walter III Brisebarre (husband of his elder daughter Helena), and in 1174 by Miles of Plancy (husband of his younger daughter Stephanie), who, however, was murdered later the same year, possibly at the instigation of the Brisebarre family. The lordship was kept vacant until 1177, when Baldwin IV gave Stephanie in marriage to Reynald of Châtillon, who received Transjordan together with the neighboring fief of Hebron.

Transjordan ranked as one of the four major lordships of the kingdom of Jerusalem, owing the service of forty knights to the king. Nevertheless, the number of resident Franks was small, probably consisting mainly of garrisons and their families. There were few Latin churches and no Latin monasteries. A metropolitan see was established in 1168; although its title derived from the ruined city of Petra, the archbish-

ops resided in Kerak. The settled population of the lordship consisted predominantly of Syrian Christians with smaller numbers of Muslims, concentrated in the two fertile regions around Kerak and Montréal, which produced an abundance of wheat, olives, wine, sugar cane, fruit, salt, and other products. In addition to their two major fortresses, the Franks held smaller castles at Taphila, situated midway between Kerak and Montréal, and at Le Vaux Moïse (mod. Wādī Mūsā, Jordan), Celle (or Sela), and Hormoz, all to the south of Montréal. This chain of strong points gave the Franks possession of most of the main water supplies as far as the Syrian desert for a distance of over 100 kilometers (c. 60 mi.) south of Kerak, and for most of the twelfth century, the lordship not only protected the kingdom from attack from the southwest, but also controlled the main trade route from Muslim Syria to Egypt and the Ḥijaz. Muslim traders were obliged to pay tolls to obtain passage (which constituted an important part of the lordship's income), while Muslim armies moving between Syria and Egypt were impeded by having taken a more difficult route to the east of the Transjordanian castles.

By 1161 Frankish Transjordan stretched from the river Zerqa (a tributary of the Jordan) in the north to the Red Sea in the south. Although separated from the rest of the lordship by some 90 kilometers (c. 55 mi.) of uninhabited territory, the southern strong points of Aila and the Ile de Graye (Pharoah's Island) in the Gulf of 'Aqaba controlled the main road from Egypt across the Sinai peninsula to Arabia. From these bases the Franks could prey on pilgrims going to Mecca as well as traders, and even impede the movement of Muslim armies. Aila therefore posed a significant threat to the empire of Saladin after his conquest of Egypt (1169). He besieged and captured it in December 1170 and invaded Edom in 1171 and Moab in 1173. However, in late 1181 Reynald of Châtillon retaliated with an audacious raid that bypassed Aila and struck deep into Arabia; in the winter of 1182–1183 he transported ships from Kerak to the Red Sea, which blockaded the Ile de Graye and preyed on Muslim shipping until they were defeated by a fleet organized by Saladin's brother al-'Ādil. Two subsequent sieges of Kerak by Saladin were repulsed by Frankish relieving armies (1183, 1184), but Saladin's great victory at Hattin (July 1187), at which Reynald was captured and executed, left Transjordan exposed. Kerak capitulated in late 1188 and Montréal in the spring of 1189.

The Franks cherished hopes of recovering Transjordan well into the thirteenth century, and claims to the lordship

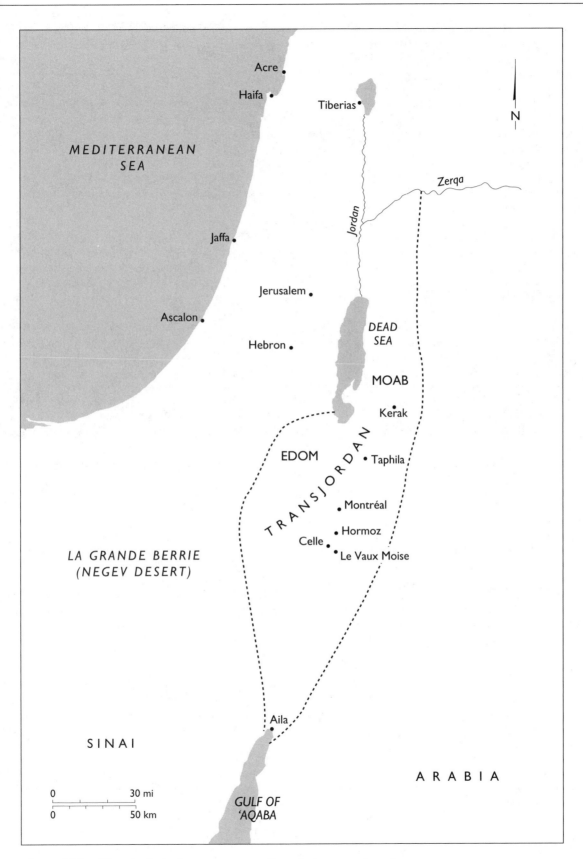

The Lordship of Transjordan at its greatest extent (boundaries approximate)

Castle of Montreal in Transjordan, built by King Baldwin I of Jerusalem in 1115, which fell to Saladin in 1188. (Erich Lessing/Art Resource)

passed to the family of the lords of Toron. However, Saladin's Ayyūbid heirs had too great an appreciation of the region's strategic significance to risk it again passing under Frankish control, as it formed the vital link between the Ayyūbid possessions in Syria and Egypt. Thus when the sultan al-Kāmil offered to surrender Saladin's conquests in Palestine as the price for the withdrawal of the Fifth Crusade from Egypt (1219), he specifically excluded Kerak and Montréal from any concessions. Transjordan was also excluded from the territories he conceded by treaty to Emperor Frederick II in 1229.

–Alan V. Murray

Bibliography
Deschamps, Paul, *Les Châteaux des croisés en Terre Sainte*, vol. 2: *La défense du royaume du Jérusalem* (Paris: Geuthner, 1939).
Hamilton, Bernard, *The Leper King and His Heirs: Baldwin IV and the Crusader Kingdom of Jerusalem* (Cambridge: Cambridge University Press, 2000).
Mayer, Hans Eberhard, *Die Kreuzfahrerherrschaft Montréal (Šōbak): Jordanien im 12. Jahrhundert* (Wiesbaden: Harrassowitz, 1990).
Prawer, Joshua, *The Latin Kingdom of Jerusalem: European Colonialism in the Middle Ages* (London: Weidenfeld and Nicolson, 1972).

Trebizond, Empire of

An empire on the northern coast of the Black Sea (Gr. *Pontos*), with its capital at the thriving city of Trebizond (mod. Trabzon, Turkey) from 1204 until 1461. Although its foundation was not a direct consequence of the capture of Constantinope (mod. İstanbul, Turkey) by the Fourth Crusade in 1204 (as was the case with the Empire of Nicaea and the despotate of Epiros), the Empire of Trebizond is often considered as one of the three main successor states of the Byzantine Empire following the Latin conquest.

The empire was founded when two grandsons of the last Komnenian emperor of Byzantium, Andronikos I (d. 1185), namely the *Megalokomnenoi* ("Great Komnenoi") Alexios I (1204–1222) and David (d. 1212/1213), seized Trebizond from its Byzantine duke, Nikephoros Palaiologos, with the help of their aunt Tamar, queen of Georgia, in March or early April 1204.

For most of its history the new state was cut off from the main Byzantine centers at Nicaea (mod. İznik, Turkey) and Constantinople and was restricted to a narrow strip of land along the southeast Pontic littoral. Its main coastal centers were Kerasous (mod. Giresun, Turkey), Oinaion (mod. Ünye), Amisos (mod. Samsun), and Sinope (mod. Sinop). Its chief inland centers were Bayberdon (mod. Bayburt), Neocaesarea (mod. Niksar), Amaseia (mod. Amasya), and Payrae (mod. Bafra), while its two celebrated monastic centers were those of Soumela and Vazelon.

Although not directly involved in the crusades, the empire holds a particular place in Anatolian affairs in the late Middle Ages, with its twenty-one rulers claiming the imperial Byzantine title until 1280/1282 and thereafter the title of basileus and autokrator (both reflecting Byzantine imperial usage) of all the East, the Iberians (i.e., Georgians), and Perateia.

The empire's initial years were consumed in fratricidal strife with the rival empire of Nicaea and in attempts to ward off attacks from the Saljūqs of Rūm, who took Sinope in 1214 but failed twice before Trebizond itself (1205/1206 and 1222/1223). For much of the remainder of the century, the empire was in a state of vassalage to the Rūm sultanate and (from 1243) to the Ilkhanids. However, with the decline of the sultanate, the empire was frequently attacked by Turcomans, especially the Ak-Koyunlu (White Sheep) confederacy, from the 1340s onward, and in the late fourteenth and early fifteenth centuries, the Grand Komnenoi pursued a consistent policy of marriage alliances with Georgian and Turcoman dynasties. Alexios II (1297–1330), Michael (1344–1349), and Alexios III (1349–1390) were also forced to grant commercial privileges to the Genoese and Venetians. However, the most menacing adversary was the Ottoman sultanate. John IV Kaloioannes (1429–1458/1460) was forced to acknowledge Ottoman suzerainty in 1456, and after a long Ottoman siege by land and sea, the last Trebizondine ruler, David I (1458/1460–1461), was forced to capitulate on 15 August 1461 and surrender his capital to Sultan Mehmed II. The execution of David and his male descendants in 1463 shattered any future attempts to restore the Grand Komnenian Empire.

–*Alexios G. C. Savvides*

See also: Byzantine Empire

Bibliography

Bryer, Anthony, *The Empire of Trebizond and the Pontos* (London: Variorum, 1980).

———, *People and Settlement in Anatolia and the Caucasus, 800–1900* (London: Variorum, 1988).

Bryer, Anthony, and David Winfield, *The Byzantine Monuments and Topography of the Pontos*, 2 vols. (Washington, DC: Dumbarton Oaks Research Library and Collection, 1985).

Janssens, Emile, *Trébizonde en Colchide* (Bruxelles: Presses Universitaires de Bruxelles, 1969).

Karpov, Sergei, *L'Impero di Trebisonda, Venezia, Genoa e Roma, 1204–1461: Rapporti politici, diplomatici e commerciali* (Roma: Il Veltro, 1986).

———, Средневековий Понт (Lewiston, NY: Mellen, 2001).

Lampsides, Odysseus, *Δημοσιεύματα περί τον ελληνικόν Πόντον τους Έλληνας Ποντίους* (Athinai: Epitrope Pontiakon Meleton, 1982).

Lymperopoulos, Vassileios, *Ο βυζαντινός Πόντος: Η αυτοκρατορία της Τραπεζούντας, 1204–1461* (Athinai: Demiourgia, 1999).

Savvides, Alexios G. C., *Βυζαντινά στασιαστικά και αυτονομιστικά κινήματα στα Δωδεκάνησα και στη Μικρά Ασία , 1189–1240* (Athinai: Domos, 1987).

———, *Οι Μεγάλοι Κομνηνοί της Τραπεζούντας και του Πόντου , 1204–1461* (Athinai: Epitrope Pontiakon Meleton, 2005).

Savvides, Alexios G. C., and Stelios Lampakes, *Γενική Βιβλιογραφία περί του βυζαντινού Πόντου και του κράτους των Μεγάλων Κομνηνών της Τραπεζούντας* (Athinai: Domos, 1992).

Shukurov, Rustam, Великие Комнины и восток, 1204–1461 (Sankt-Peterburg: Aleteya, 2001).

Treiden, Battle (1211)

A battle between crusaders and pagan Estonians fought in the course of the conquest of Livonia at the castle of Treiden (mod. Turaida, Latvia).

During the spring of 1211 the Estonians made a series of raids into the Christian-held areas of Ymera, northern Lettgallia, and the lower reaches of the river Aa (mod. Gauaja, Latvia). In the course of this fighting a force of up to 3,000–4,000 Estonians from the areas of Ösel, Wiek, and

Revele mounted a campaign against the castle of Treiden on the north bank of the Aa, which was held by baptized Livs. The Estonian forces assembled by land and waterways and besieged the castle until the arrival of reinforcements, consisting of members of the Order of the Sword Brethren and German crusaders from Riga.

The Estonians defended their position on a hill until they declared that they were ready to surrender and accept baptism. At night, however, they tried to escape in their ships. The crusaders then built a wooden bridge over the Aa and prevented the ships from leaving. The Estonians were forced to abandon their ships; they retreated the following night, suffering heavy losses and relinquishing a large amount of booty to the crusaders. The source for the battle is the chronicle of Henry of Livonia.

–Anti Selart

Bibliography
Benninghoven, Friedrich, *Der Orden der Schwertbrüder* (Köln: Böhlau, 1965).
Urban, William, *The Baltic Crusade* (Chicago: Lithuanian Research and Studies Center, 1994).

Trencavel, Family

A noble family in southern France that was dispossessed in the course of the Albigensian Crusade (1209–1229) and its aftermath.

The Trencavels traced their origins to the tenth century, when Bernard was viscount of Albi around 918. In 1068 Raymond-Bernard Trencavel married Ermengarde, the daughter of the count of Carcassonne. Their son, Bernard Aton IV, became viscount of Carcassonne, Béziers, Albi, Razès, Nîmes, and Agde. Thus, during the eleventh century, by judicious marriages the family built itself a power base in eastern Languedoc with Béziers as the core of its lands. The Trencavels often divided the family possessions among sons; after the death of Bernard Aton IV, his domains were divided, with Roger (1130–1150) receiving Carcassonne, Albi, and the Razès, Raymond (1130–1167) receiving Béziers and Agde, and Bernard Aton (1130–1163) receiving Nîmes. Raymond inherited Carcassonne, Albi, and Razès when Roger died, and his grandson, Raymond-Roger II, became viscount at the age of nine, in 1194.

By 1179 the family had become vassals of the kings of Aragon. Despite this, when the crusaders entered Langue-doc, the Trencavel town of Béziers was sacked by the crusaders, and its inhabitants were massacred (1209). Raymond-Roger II was expropriated by Simon of Montfort when Carcassonne surrendered, and he died in prison. He was unfortunate in that the crusaders were unable to attack the county of Toulouse immediately, because Raymond VI of Toulouse had submitted to the leaders of the crusade and done public penance for his defiance of the pope and his complicity in the death of the pope's legate, Peter of Castelnau. Raymond-Roger was more vulnerable because his viscounty of Carcassonne contained many heretics, including numbers of Cathar sympathizers among the landowning nobility. In these circumstances it was easy for the crusaders to turn their energies against Raymond-Roger.

Raymond-Roger II's son Raymond Trencavel was born in 1207 and spent his youth in exile in Barcelona. On the withdrawal of Amalric of Montfort from Carcassonne in January 1224, Raymond Trencavel was installed as viscount, but in the summer of 1226 he was driven out by King Louis VIII of France. During the revolt of 1242 he regained control of Carcassonne but was rapidly swept aside by the royal forces. In August 1246 he came to terms with King Louis IX. He relinquished his claim to the Trencavel titles and lands in exchange for the grant of a small estate, and he followed Louis to the Holy Land. In 1332 his granddaughter was living at Cesseras, near Minerve. Thereafter the family disappeared.

–Michael D. Costen

Bibliography
Costen, Michael, *The Cathars and the Albigensian Crusade* (Manchester, UK: Manchester University Press, 1997).
Graham-Leigh, Elaine, "Morts suspectes et justice papale: Innocent III, les Trencavel et la réputation de l'église," in *La Croisade Albigeoise: Actes du Colloque du Centre d'Etudes Cathares, Carcassonne, 4, 5 et 6 octobre 2002*, ed. Marie-Paul Gimenez (Balma: Centre d'Etudes Cathares, 2004), pp. 219–233.

Trinitarian Order

The Order of the Most Holy Trinity and of the Redemption of Captives (Lat. *Fratres Ordinis sanctae Trinitatis et redemptionis captivorum*), generally known as the Trinitarian Order, was a redemptionist religious order founded by St. John of Matha (1154–1213) at the end of the twelfth century. It was the first church institution whose main purpose was the redemption of Christian captives from the Muslims, by means of ransom, charity, and mercy. The Rule of the order was devised by John of Matha but was modified over time. According to monastic tradition, the hermit St. Felix of Valois was the cofounder of the order and was instrumental in establishing its first house in the desert of Cerfroid, some 80 kilometers (50 mi.) northeast of Paris. John based his Rule on his own monastic experiences in Cerfroid, which was soon joined by two other communities at Bourg-la-Reine and Planels. The Rule was approved by Pope Innocent III in the bull *Operante Divine dispositionis* (17 December 1198), and a modified version of it was confirmed by Pope Urban VI in 1267.

The distinctive element of the white Trinitarian habit was a red and blue cross. By the 1250s some fifty Trinitarian monasteries had been founded in France, Italy, Portugal, Ireland, Scotland, and England. Soon the Trinitarians also dedicated themselves to the various services of mercy, hospitality, care of the poor and sick (Lat. *cura hospitum et pauperum*), education, and even preaching. The Rule required every Trinitarian community to devote a third of its income for the purpose of ransoming, which also was the main object of fundraising. The friars took vows of chastity, poverty, and obedience. During journeys they were allowed to ride a donkey.

The general chapter of the order was held every year at Pentecost. The monastery of St. Mathurin located near the Sorbonne in Paris became its main house. By the end of the Middle Ages, there were some 150 houses within twelve provinces throughout Europe. The order received numerous endowments from the various Iberian rulers, notably King Peter I of Aragon (d. 1213) and his son James I the Conqueror (d. 1234), and maintained close relations with the Iberian monarchies to the end of the Reconquista (the reconquest of the Iberian Peninsula from the Muslims).

The initial character of the order was the dedication to redemption of Christian captives, mainly crusaders or those taken by Muslim pirates on the Mediterranean Sea. The total number of rescued captives is hard to estimate, but can be counted in the thousands. The redemption missions to the North African coast, mainly undertaken by Spanish friars, were organized and carried out with the financial support (from alms and specific donations) of the order's other provinces, as well as of the local magnates and knights. The redemption missions were sometimes connected with trading activity (e.g., in textiles and jewelry), organized at the request of Spanish or North African rulers. Their contacts with the Muslim world allowed the Trinitarians to develop theological and apologetic studies of Islam. They were involved in redemptionist activities until the middle of the nineteenth century. For example, friars of the Polish-Lithuanian province organized eighteen great redemption missions in 1688–1782 to the Crimea, the Golden Horde, and Turkey and succeeded in ransoming over 500 Christians. Another important element of Trinitarian activity was the maintenance of hospitals for the poor and sick, established since the very beginning of the order, for example, at Marseilles, Arles, Saint-Gilles, Lérida (Lleida), Toledo, and Burgos. The hospitals could also be used to accommodate freed captives.

Political, economic, and religious changes between the late fifteenth century and the mid–sixteenth century brought about a period of decline for the Trinitarians. All of their houses in England, Scotland, and Ireland, as well as some of those in Germany, were suppressed as a consequence of the Protestant Reformation. A move toward reform could be observed after the Council of Trent, when the Spanish, Portuguese, and French houses issued new, reformed provincial statutes. The new revised versions were published as *Regula et statuta* in 1586 at Douai. According to this book of statutes there were 154 monasteries distributed in provinces: Ile de France (12), Champagne (11), Picardy (14), Normandy (14), Languedoc (14), Provence (10), Aragon (26), Portugal (5), Old Castile (15), and New Castile and Andalusia (21), as well as so-called *domus antiquae* (former houses) in the provinces of England (6) and Scotland (6), which by that time had been suppressed.

A strong and vital reform movement among the Trinitarians, known later as the Recollection (Lat. *Reformatorium*), was led by the zealous John Baptist of the Conception (1561–1613). It resulted in the establishment of the Spanish Discalced Trinitarians, soon followed by the French Discalced Trinitarians (1622). The Discalced (barefooted) Trinitarian reform movement followed the example of the Discalced Carmelites and symbolized the Christian virtues of poverty and chastity. Pope Clement VIII in his letter *Ad militantes ecclesiae* (20 August 1599) recognized this new observance officially as the Congregation of the Reformed and Discalced Brothers (Lat. *Congregatio fratrum reformatorum et discaleatorum*). By the time of the death of John Baptist, as many as eighteen convents had joined his reform movement, which also flourished in the Habsburg territories and the Polish-Lithuanian Commonwealth. The suppression of religious communities in 1782–1783 by Joseph II of Austria, followed by the French Revolution (1789) and Spanish and Portuguese suppressions in the 1830s, brought about the near total destruction of the order. After the dissolution of the surviving Polish monasteries in the 1860s, the Trinitarians were restricted to Rome, where the monastery of the Spanish friars survived (S. Carlino alle Quattro Fontane). The restoration of the order began at the end of the nineteenth century in France, Spain, Italy, and Austria and resulted in the unification of the discalced and calced branches in 1900.

–*Rafal Witkowski*

Bibliography

Cipollone, Giulio, "Les Trinitaires: Fondation du XIIe siècle pour les captifs et pour les pauvres," in *Fondations et oeuvres charitables*, ed. Jean Dufour and Henri Platelle (Paris: CTHS, 1999), pp. 75–87.

Grimaldi-Hierholz, Rosaline, *L'Ordre des Trinitaires: Histoire et spiritualité* (Paris: Le Sarment-Fayard, 1994).

Gross, Joseph J., *The Trinitarian Apostolate of Ransom-Activity and Mercy Work during the Order's First Centuries* (Rome: Trinitarian Historical Institute, 1982).

Marchionni, Isaia, *Note sulla storia delle origini dell'Ordine della SS. Trinità* (Roma: Arti Grafiche dei Fiorentini, 1973).

Pujana, Juan, *La Orden de la Santísima Trinidad* (Madrid: Universidad Pontificia de Salamanca: Fundación Universitaria Española, 1993).

Tripoli, City of

The capital (mod. Trâblous, Lebanon) of the Frankish county of Tripoli.

Before the First Crusade (1096–1099), the city of Tripoli, by then reduced to the peninsular part of the present city (al-Mina), was ruled by the *qāḍī* (magistrate) Fakhr al-Mulk ibn ʿAmmār, who had made himself independent of the Fāṭimids. He was able to hold Raymond of Saint-Gilles, count of Toulouse, at bay during the siege of Arqah (February–May 1099), but Raymond returned in 1102 and started a siege by constructing the castle of Mont-Pèlerin (Arab. *Qalʿat Sanjil*) above the city. Tripoli capitulated to Raymond's son Bertrand and his allies on 12 July 1109, suffering a certain amount of pillaging, in which the great library of the *qāḍī* was destroyed.

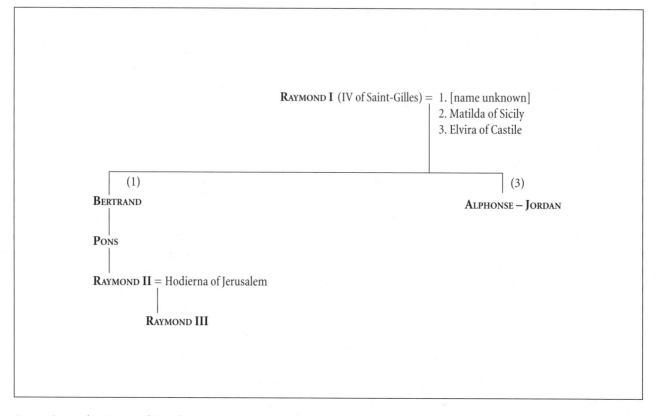

Succession to the County of Tripoli

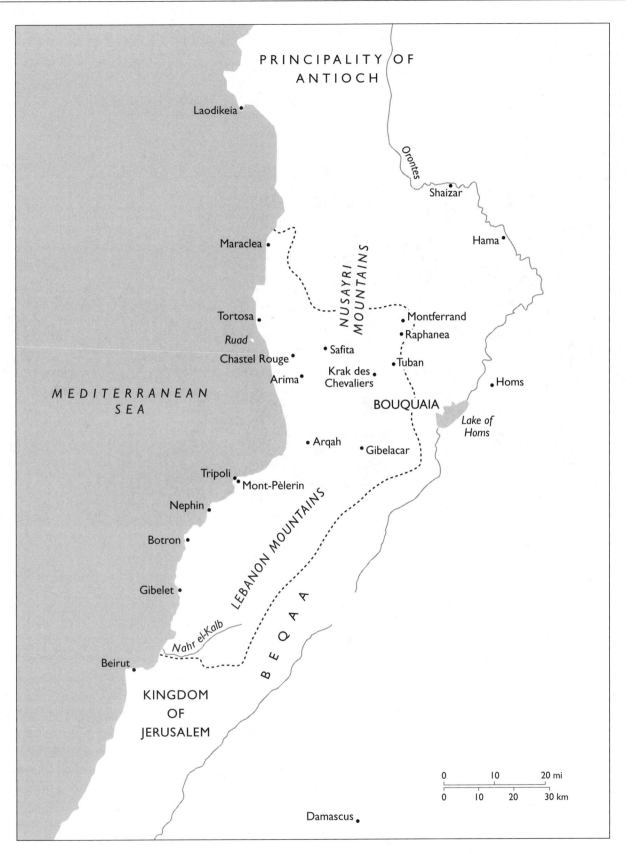

The County of Tripoli in the earlier twelfth century

Castle at Tripoli, c. 1920. (Library of Congress)

As capital of the county of the same name, Tripoli attracted inhabitants originating from southern France and Italy who joined a primarily Christian local population. A Latin diocese was founded that combined the former sees of Botrys, Arqah, and Orthosias, and was directly subject to the patriarchate of Antioch (mod. Antakya, Turkey). The cathedral of St. Mary was destroyed by an earthquake in 1171 but was soon rebuilt. Several Latin religious institutions were established, both around Mont-Pèlerin and in the older town.

The principal industry was silk weaving, which produced renowned fabrics known as *camelines.* The port had good communications with inland Syria and attracted merchants from Pisa, Venice, Amalfi, and Marseilles, all of whom estab-lished *fondes* (markets) there. Genoa was promised a third of the city at the time of the conquest, but this undertaking was never fully kept. The city was governed by a viscount, who presided over the burgesses' court (Fr. *Cour des Bourgeois*). A medical school, which became famous in the thirteenth century, attracted many Syrian clerics, and the city became an important point of contact between the different churches. It was a cantor of the Latin cathedral, Philip, who translated the *Secretum Secretorum,* attributed to Aristotle, from Arabic at the request of his bishop.

From 1278 onward, the city increasingly suffered from factional strife. In 1282 the Templars tried to seize the town with the help of the lord of Gibelet, and in 1288, after the death of Count Bohemund VII, knights and burgesses who

Counts of Tripoli

Raymond I (of Saint-Gilles)	1102–1105
Bertrand	1109–1112
Pons	1112–1137
Raymond II	1137–1152
Raymond III	1152–1187
Bohemund IV of Antioch	1187–1233
Bohemund V	1233–1252
Bohemund VI	1252–1275
Bohemund VII	1275–1287
Lucy	1287–1289

were hostile to the new regent of the county rebelled and formed a commune, choosing as their mayor Bartholomew Embriaco of Gibelet, who appealed to the Genoese for help. A settlement was negotiated with the new countess, Lucy, which confirmed the liberties of the commune and the autonomy of an enlarged Genoese quarter. However, certain Franks convinced the Mamlūk sultan Qalāwūn of the potential threat posed to Egypt by a Genoese base in Tripoli, and in violation of the truce then in force, the Mamlūks seized Mont-Pèlerin and besieged the city. Despite assistance from Acre and Cyprus, Tripoli fell on 26 April 1289, and those inhabitants who had not been able to flee were massacred. The city was razed to the ground, and a new town established around Mont-Pèlerin.

–Jean Richard

Bibliography

Antweiler, Wolfgang, *Das Bistum Tripolis im 12. und 13. Jahrhundert* (Düsseldorf: Droste, 1991).

Richard, Jean, "Le chartrier de Sainte-Marie Latine et l'établissement de Raymond de Saint-Gilles à Mont-Pèlerin," in *Mélanges d'histoire dédiés à la mémoire de Louis Halphen* (Paris: Presses Universitaires de France, 1951), 605–612.

———, *Le comté de Tripoli sous la dynastie toulousaine (1102–1187)*, 2d ed. (Paris: Geuthner, 2000).

Salame-Sarkis, Hassan, *Contribution à l'histoire de Tripoli et de sa région* (Paris: Geuthner, 1980).

Tripoli, County of

The fourth and last of the Frankish states founded in Outremer by the First Crusade (1096–1099). It survived to the late thirteenth century.

The county of Tripoli came into existence when Raymond of Saint-Gilles, count of Toulouse, having seized Tortosa (mod. Tartūs, Lebanon) in 1102, attempted to conquer the surrounding country with his southern French followers, with the city of Tripoli as his principal objective. Raymond attacked Homs (1103), occupied Raphanea (mod. Rafanỳah, Syria) and Gibelet (mod. Jubail, Lebanon) in 1104, and invested Tripoli (mod. Trâblous, Lebanon) by constructing the castle of Mont-Pèlerin ("Mount Pilgrim") outside the city.

History to 1187

On the death of Raymond of Saint-Gilles (1105), his cousin William-Jordan, count of Cerdagne, took possession of his conquests, while Raymond's younger son, Alphonse-Jordan, was sent back to Toulouse. William-Jordan had taken Arqah (1108 or 1109) when Raymond's elder son, Bertrand, arrived in Tortosa to claim his father's inheritance. King Baldwin I of Jerusalem imposed a settlement dividing the county between the two cousins, but William-Jordan died, whereupon Bertrand seized Arqah, and Tancred of Antioch, who had supported William-Jordan, occupied the rest of his share. Meanwhile Bertrand had captured the city of Tripoli (1109) and pushed his frontier as far as the mountains that dominated the upper Orontes Valley. After Bertrand's death, his son Pons placed himself under the protection of Tancred, who ceded to him Tortosa, Chastel Blanc (Safitha), and Krak des Chevaliers (Ḥisn al-Akrād). Thus by 1113 the unity of the county was established.

Bertrand was succeeded by his descendants Pons (1112–1137), Raymond II (1137–1152), and Raymond III (1152–1187), without incident other than the unexpected arrival (1148) of the count of Toulouse, Alphonse-Jordan. The latter may have envisaged claiming the county for his own illegitimate son Bertrand, but soon died in a manner regarded as suspicious; Bertrand seized the castle of Arima, and Raymond II was obliged to appeal to Nūr al-Dīn, who recaptured the castle. The childless Raymond III intended that the county should pass to his godson Raymond, son of Bohemund III of Antioch, although he reserved the rights of the counts of Toulouse. Nevertheless, Bohemund III appointed his second son Bohemund (IV) as heir in Tripoli. After a war against his nephew Raymond-Rupen, Bohemund of Tripoli gained control of Antioch (1219), and thereafter Tripoli was ruled by successive princes of Antioch, who, however, maintained the separate character of the county, notably with regard to its legal customs, the usages of its chancery, and the appointment of its chief officers.

The political status of the county was a complex issue. Raymond of Saint-Gilles had benefited from the support of the Byzantine emperor, and Bertrand also received Byzantine subsidies and supplies, and apparently agreed to support the emperor when he tried to establish a coalition against Tancred, but Pons did not continue such policies. In 1137 Raymond II went to Antioch to do homage to Emperor John II Komnenos, but by this time the county's ties with Byzantium had become much looser. Raymond III even led a punitive expedition against Cyprus when Manuel I Komnenos broke a promise of marriage made to his sister Melisende. Pons had done homage to the prince of Antioch when he received the north of the county from him, but this vassalage does not seem to have had further consequences. By contrast, Bertrand had done homage to the king of Jerusalem at the time of the capture of the city of Tripoli; he and his successors often took part in the military operations of the kings of Jerusalem, and King Amalric governed the county during the captivity of Raymond III (1164–1174), although it was always stipulated that Tripoli was not part of the kingdom.

At first the county expanded swiftly at the expense of its Muslim neighbors. The early counts apparently even intended to conquer Homs and Hama, and sometimes these towns did pay tribute. Yet it took a considerable effort to conquer Raphanea, which was taken only in 1126 by Pons after he had built the castle of Montferrand to control it, and both places were lost by 1137. Other castles (such as Tuban) dominated the plain of Homs, known to the Franks as the Bouquée (Arab. *Buqaia*). Raymond II even claimed fishing rights in the Lake of Homs. A series of defeats, however, demonstrated the limits of the counts' power: a Damascene raid reached Mont-Pèlerin in 1137 (the same year that Montferrand capitulated to Zangī); Nūr al-Dīn seized Tortosa in 1152 and in 1167 exploited the captivity of Raymond III to take Arima, Chastel Blanc, and Gibelcar (Jebel 'Akkar), albeit only temporarily. Thereafter the counts increasingly turned to the military orders to rebuild and garrison castles. In 1144 the Hospitallers received Krak des Chevaliers, Felis, and Lak (Tell Kalakh), which guarded the approaches to the valley of the Nahr al-Kabir; they received Chastel-Rouge in 1177, Tuban in 1180, and Eixserc in 1183. The Templars were given Tortosa in 1152 and Chastel Blanc in 1167. From that time, it was the orders who held the frontier facing Homs,

Hama, and the mountain massif where Ismā'īlīs of the Bāṭinīya sect (better known as the Assassins) had built up a domain bristling with fortresses, of which at least one, La Coïble (al-Khawabi), had been captured from the Franks. The knights of the orders feared assassination by these fanatics much less than the secular rulers did: the Assassins' victims included Bohemund IV's eldest son Raymond (1213), but the orders were able to exact a tribute from the Ismā'īlīs.

History, 1187–1289

The fall of the kingdom of Jerusalem in 1187 occurred at a time when Count Raymond III's relations with the king, Guy of Lusignan, were strained. Although present at the defeat of Hattin, Raymond managed to return to his county and died not long afterward. In 1188 Saladin's army invaded the county but failed to take Krak des Chevaliers, Chastel Blanc, or Arima, and made only a demonstration at the city of Tripoli, which was protected by a fleet sent by the king of Sicily. A complete collapse of Frankish positions in the county was thus prevented. Hostilities with the Ayyūbid rulers remained sporadic, and primarily involved the military orders. Yet some Frankish raids went deep into Muslim territory, and the Mamlūk sultan Baybars I used one such as a pretext to punish the Christian inhabitants of Qara, supposedly for collusion with Frankish raiders from Gibelcar. The situation changed with the arrival of the Mongols in Syria and their alliance with Bohemund VI of Antioch-Tripoli. In 1261 Baybars invaded the county, capturing Tuban, Arqah, Halba, and Coliath and thus reaching the coastal plain. The Mamlūks also seized Krak des Chevaliers, Chastel Blanc, and Gibelcar, and forced the counts to share the revenues of the plain of Tripoli. A treaty concluded in 1281 delimited the size of the count's domain, which included Tripoli, Nephin, Botron, Gibelet, Arqah, and fifty-one villages, and established a condominium in the mountains. Bohemund V married Luciana of Segni, a relative of Pope Innocent IV. Her brother Paul of Conti became bishop of Tripoli and attracted a number of "Roman" clerics and laymen who became members of the count's entourage. During the reign of Bohemund VI, a conflict broke out between the count and the lord of Gibelet, who had fought against him during the War of St. Sabas. In the course of hostilities, Bohemund was wounded by Bertrand of Gibelet, who was subsequently killed by peasants. Eventually a settlement was imposed by the master of the Temple, who set up a commission to mediate between the count and the barons (1258). Another conflict broke out between the count and the Gibelet family on the occasion of the marriage of a brother of the lord of Gibelet to the heiress of a rich lord whom Bohemund VI had intended for another suitor. The ensuing struggle pitted the Templars and Paul of Conti against the count and his vassals: the Templars' house in Tripoli and the cathedral were besieged, and many "Romans" were massacred, while the Templars attacked the count at Botron and inflicted two defeats upon him (1278–1279). When eventually it seemed that peace might be restored, the master of the Temple and Guy of Gibelet tried to take Tripoli by surprise. Guy was obliged to submit, and was imprisoned and left to die of starvation. His heir placed himself under the sultan's protection.

On the death of Count Bohemund VII (1287), a fresh conflict erupted because of his mother's decision to confer the regency on Bartholomew Mansel, bishop of Tortosa. The count's vassals rejected this choice and refused to accept Bohemund's sister Lucy as countess unless she removed the cause of their grievances. A commune was established at Tripoli under the leadership of Bartholomew Embriaco, lord of Gibelet, and sought an alliance with Genoa. Lucy, who had found refuge at Nephin under the protection of the Hospitallers, was installed as countess after accepting the terms of the Genoese, but enemies of the Republic provoked an intervention by the sultan Qalāwūn, who seized Tripoli by surprise on 26 April 1289, massacring its inhabitants. The lordship of Gibelet was permitted to survive as an iqṭāʿ (grant of revenues) belonging to Qalāwūn's empire. Only in 1303, after the withdrawal of the Mongols from Syria, did the last of the Embriaci set fire to his castle and abandon the lordship.

Government and Institutions

Raymond of Saint-Gilles and his successors retained direct lordship over a number of towns (Tripoli, Raphanea, Arqah, Mont-Pèlerin, Montferrand, and others) and villages. They granted the rest of the county as fiefs to lords who largely came from Languedoc and Provence: the Porcelet family in Artussa; the Montolieu in Chastel Rouge; the Puylaurens in Gibelcar, Felis, and Lac; the Meynes in Maraclea and Tortosa; the d'Agout and d'Aurel families in Botron. Gibelet was a special case: in return for naval help rendered to Counts Raymond I and Bertrand, the city was given to the Genoese, who installed the Embriaci family as lords. The Embriaci became integrated into the Tripolitan nobility, as did one

Pleban, a wealthy Pisan, who married the heiress to Botron. When the count had occasion to grant castles to the military orders, he was obliged to indemnify the owners of these fiefs. Fiefs were subject to an evaluation expressed as caballarie, that is, the number of knights a lord had to contribute to the comital army. In the twelfth century the total number of knights available to the count through enfeoffment was around 300, a figure considerably smaller than those of the other Frankish states.

The accession of the Antiochene dynasty in Tripoli does not seem to have caused any conflict between the new counts of Poitevin extraction and their vassals, who largely originated from the southern French lands of the Saint-Gilles family; indeed, on his accession Bohemund IV made a point of marrying into the Gibelet family. Yet serious disputes did arise, often as a consequence of the right claimed by the counts to authorize the marriages of heiresses to fiefs. When Raynouard of Nephin married the heiress to the fief of Gibelcar without the count's consent, Bohemund IV seized his fief. A coalition immediately formed to oppose the count and attacked Tripoli, but Bohemund prevailed, and Raynouard had to surrender Nephin and Gibelcar to him (1205). Bohemund was careful not to commit himself to the cause of Emperor Frederick II when the latter came into conflict with the Ibelin family in the kingdom of Jerusalem; yet neither did he compromise himself with the Ibelins, for fear of antagonizing the powerful Porcelet family, who were allied with the Barlais family, the Ibelins' chief adversaries.

The Latin Church

Raymond of Saint-Gilles had intended to create endowments in his future county for the religious institutions of the Holy Land and his own country of origin. The canons of St. Ruf in Avignon were offered the church of Artussa when it was restored to Christian worship, as well as a church in Tripoli. Around the castle of Mont-Pèlerin, Raymond established priories dependent on the churches of the Holy Sepulchre, St. Mary of the Latins, and Bethlehem (and later Mount Zion), as well as on the Hospital of St. John, endowing them with landed properties in the neighboring region. Hospitals for pilgrims founded by the early counts at Mont-Pèlerin and Raphanea were handed over to the Hospitallers by Count Pons in 1126. The Hospitallers especially were richly endowed at the time when their activities were purely charitable, but from 1144, as the order became militarized, they acquired an extensive dominion based on the possession of several castles, as did the Templars. During the thirteenth century, both orders were frequently involved in political disputes, as, for example, when the Templars backed the party hostile to Count Bohemund VI. A Cistercian monastery was founded in Belmont near Tripoli (1157) and another at St. Sergius near Gibelet (1231); we also know of a nunnery dedicated to St. Mary Magdalene in Tripoli. Religious life also included the veneration of the sanctuary of Our Lady at Tortosa; it was visited by numerous pilgrims, including the chronicler Joinville, and the son of Bohemund IV was praying there when he was murdered. We know less of parochial life, although it is clear that many Latin churches existed in the city of Tripoli, which had a large population belonging to the Roman rite.

Before the capture of Tripoli, Raymond of Saint-Gilles had appointed a bishop for the city, who administered the united former dioceses of Tripoli, Arqah, Orthosias (Artussa), and Botron. A second bishop was appointed at Tortosa for the former dioceses of Arados, Antarados, and Maraclea, and a third at Gibelet. All three bishoprics, which were probably in existence by 1110, were part of the ecclesiastical province of Tyre (mod. Soûr, Lebanon), which had traditionally belonged to the patriarchate of Antioch (mod. Antakya, Turkey). They thus depended directly on Antioch as long as Tyre remained in Muslim hands. After the capture of Tyre by the Franks in 1124, an archbishop was appointed by the patriarch of Jerusalem, and thereafter the see and its southern bishoprics were treated as part of the Jerusalem patriarchate. The Tripolitan bishoprics, however, continued to be dependent on Antioch, as did a fourth bishopric, that of Raphanea (1126), which belonged to the see of Apamea.

The Native Communities

The non-Latin Christian communities prospered in the days of Frankish rule, as is demonstrated by the architectural and artistic activity of the Lebanese churches. Arabic-speaking Melkites of the Greek Orthodox rite as well as Western (Monophysite) and Eastern (Nestorian) Syrians each had their own clergy and episcopal hierarchy. The Greek Orthodox Church, however, was most probably subject to the same restrictions as in the kingdom of Jerusalem: it was regarded as an integral part of the Latin Church, and in each diocese the Greek bishop had to make submission (at least formally) to the Latin bishop, although he had sole authority over the clergy and congregations of the Greek rite. Syrian Monophysites were numerous, particularly on the coast, and

according to the Syrian chronicler Bar Hebraeus, they and the less numerous Nestorians were on friendly terms with the Latins. The Latins themselves were not ignorant of Arabic culture: it was a cantor of the cathedral of Tripoli, Philip, who in the mid-thirteenth century translated from Arabic the *Secretum Secretorum,* attributed to Aristotle.

The particular ecclesiastical characteristic of the county was the presence of the Maronite Church. The Syriac-speaking Maronite community had its own patriarchate, episcopal hierarchy, and priests; the life of the church, however, was centered on the monasteries, where the archbishops and bishops normally resided. The precise doctrines of the Maronites have been much discussed, but it seems that at least part of the church adhered to monotheletism (a doctrine that recognized one will and two natures in Christ); this seems to have been the understanding of the Latin Church, which in the twelfth century conducted negotiations with the Maronite hierarchy with the aim of reaching doctrinal agreement. An accord was proclaimed in 1182, thanks to the efforts of Aimery of Limoges, Latin patriarch of Antioch, and at the Fourth Lateran Council (1215), the Maronite patriarch Jeremiah received from Pope Innocent III a bull confirming his dignity and authority as head of the Maronite archbishops and bishops. Some conflicts among the Maronites have been ascribed to opposition to the union of the churches, but it is difficult to establish the extent of ecclesiastical quarrels. The election of the patriarch Jeremiah in 1283 was carried out in the presence of the lord of Gibelet and an envoy from Rome, and apparently coincided with a schism in which he was opposed by a rival patriarch, Luke of Beniharan, who was backed by the leaders of the Besharri region.

The Maronites (and probably other Christians) of the Lebanese mountains provided the counts of Tripoli and their vassals with auxiliary soldiers, especially archers. It was customary in all of the Frankish states of Outremer to employ "Syrian" recruits, yet in this particular region we also know of the existence of lordships held by local headmen or chieftains (known in Arabic as *ra'is* or *muqaddam*). While recognizing the authority of Frankish lords, these leaders administered villages, presided over courts of justice, maintained order, and also on occasion raised troops. This did not rule out the possibility of conflicts among the chieftains or collusion with the Muslims: Count Pons was the victim of an act of treachery in 1137, which his son punished by confiscating the lands of the culprits. The Franks had similar relations with non-Maronite local chieftains, whether Muslim,

Druze, or Nuṣayri, including the Ismāīʿīlis who occupied the frontier areas to the north.

Economy

Frankish society in the county does not seem to have involved rural colonization: villages maintained their traditional structure, under their *raʾis* and other notables, while paying traditional dues to the counts or Frankish lords. In the towns, by contrast, Frankish burgesses mingled with a population of Eastern origin that included some wealthy merchant families; the Saïs family who advanced Guy of Lusignan the money he paid for the acquisition of Cyprus may have been one of these. These Syrian burgesses enjoyed personal freedom and came under the authority of their own *raʾis*. In Tripoli and Raphanea (and probably elsewhere), the Frankish burgesses were answerable to a court consisting of jurors chosen from among their own numbers and presided over by a viscount.

The county had considerable agricultural resources. The flow of the rivers permitted abundant irrigation, which particularly benefited sugarcane plantations, while olive cultivation produced sufficient quantities of oil to supply soap factories. Industrial activity was also important. According to Burchard of Mount Zion, there were some 4,000 weavers in Tripoli, and Louis IX of France is known to have commissioned John of Joinville to bring back fabrics from the city. These products contributed to a flow of commerce that also involved merchandise originating from inland Syria: according to the Arab geographer al-Idrīsī, Tortosa was the port for Homs, and Tripoli that for Damascus. Even states of war did not interrupt these relations, and merchants from Montpellier, Genoa, and Pisa enjoyed trading rights in the towns of the county, although Genoa, originally promised a third of the city of Tripoli, was obliged to be content with the possession of Gibelet, which it made over to the Embriaci; in the late thirteenth century the republic was still trying to obtain a street in Tripoli that it claimed it had been granted by one of the counts. The Pisans had a more favored status until they fell out with Bohemund IV.

The county of Tripoli seems to have enjoyed real prosperity under both comital dynasties, in no small part thanks to its geographical situation, which enabled it to escape the worst effects of the conquest of the Frankish states by Saladin in 1187–1188. The multi-ethnic structure of the Latin East may well have been more pronounced there than in the other states, and in the twelfth century the county had a certain individuality owing to the predominance of southern French elements in its nobility, although this characteristic gradually faded. But the county of Tripoli never possessed a power comparable to the neighboring states of Antioch and Jerusalem.

–*Jean Richard*

Bibliography
Deschamps, Paul, *Le Crac des Chevaliers* (Paris: Geuthner, 1934).
———, *La défense du comté de Tripoli et de la principauté d'Antioche* (Paris: Geuthner, 1973).
Irwin, Robert, "The Mamlūk Conquest of the County of Tripoli," in *Crusade and Settlement: Papers Read at the First Conference of the Society for the Study of the Crusades and the Latin East,* ed. Peter W. Edbury (Cardiff, UK: University College Cardiff Press, 1985), pp. 246–250.
Nordiguian, Levon, and Jean-Claude Voisin, *Châteaux et églises du Moyen Age au Liban* (Beirut: Terre du Liban, 1999).
Richard, Jean, "Le comté de Tripoli dans les chartes du fonds des Porcellet," *Bibliothèque de l'Ecole des Chartes* 130 (1972), 341–382.
———, "Les comtes de Tripoli et leurs vassaux sous la dynastie antiochénienne," in *Crusade and Settlement: Papers Read to the First Conference of the Society for the Study of the Crusades and the Latin East,* ed. Peter W. Edbury (Cardiff, UK: University College at Cardiff Press, 1985), pp. 213–224.
———, "Affrontement ou confrontation? Les contacts entre deux mondes au pays de Tripoli au temps des croisades," *Chronos: Revue d'histoire de l'Université de Balamand* 2 (1999), 7–28.
———, *Le comté de Tripoli sous la dynastie toulousaine (1102–1187),* 2d ed. (Paris: Geuthner, 2000).
Riley-Smith, Jonathan S. C., "The Templars and the Castle of Tortosa," *English Historical Review* 84 (1969), 278–288.
Salibi, Kamal, "The Maronite Church in the Middle Ages," *Oriens Christianus* 42 (1958), 92–104.

Troyes, Council (1129)

A church council, held at Troyes in Champagne in January 1129 (not 1128, as often cited in earlier works), that was a pivotal moment in the early history of the Order of the Temple.

The assembly marked the church's formal approval of a rule (regulations for the observance of a religious life) for this group of knights, which had formed in the Holy Land in 1120 with the aim of protecting pilgrims to Jerusalem. Although initial recruitment had been slight, King Baldwin II of Jerusalem saw the knights as making an important contribution to the defense of his lands, and in 1125/1126 he wrote to Bernard, abbot of Clairvaux, to try to secure his endorsement for the Templars. In 1127 their leader, the Champenois knight Hugh of Payns, toured the West to seek backing for the order and also to recruit men for a planned crusade against Damascus, and he successfully solicited grants of land and money in Champagne, Flanders, and Anjou.

In 1129 the papal legate Matthew of Albano presided over a council where Hugh set out the basic precepts for his men. Hugh proposed a community that attended the offices of the choir (or recited a set number of Paternosters), wore plain clothing, was celibate, but was also active in the outside world and had horses and servants. The order was to be governed by a master, under the jurisdiction of the patriarch of Jerusalem. The churchmen present dissected Hugh's proposals, and, with the guiding hand of Bernard of Clairvaux, a rule of seventy-two clauses was drafted. This approval for the new order enabled it to attract substantial support over the next few years and laid the foundations for its long-term existence.

–*Jonathan Phillips*

Bibliography

Barber, Malcolm, *The New Knighthood: A History of the Order of the Temple* (Cambridge: Cambridge University Press, 1994).

Hiestand, Rudolf, "Kardinalbischof Matthäus von Albano, das Konzil von Troyes und die Entstehung des Templerordens," *Zeitschrift für Kirchengeschichte* 99 (1988), 295–323.

Templar castle of Baghras in Cilician Armenia; it served as the northern Templar headquarters. (Courtesy Alfred Andrea)

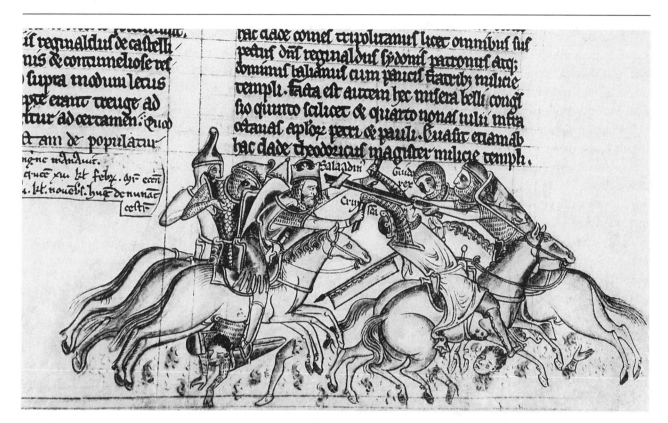

Capture of the True Cross by Saladin at the battle of Hattin (1187). Illustration from a manuscript of Matthew Paris, *Chronica Majora* (c. 1250). (TopFoto.co.uk)

Truce of God

See Peace and Truce of God

True Cross

The cross on which Christ died was a major impulse of the crusade movement, a symbol of the Frankish states of Outremer, and an important element of devotion to the Holy Land.

According to Eusebius of Caesarea (d. 339), the Roman emperor Constantine the Great chose the cross as his military insignia and standard following a vision, and Cyril of Jerusalem (d. c. 386) was the first to relate that the True Cross itself had been discovered. This event, which must have occurred before the middle of the fourth century and which two generations later was ascribed to St. Helena (d. 329), stimulated devotion to the True Cross both in Palestine and in the Latin West. When the Persians conquered Jerusalem in 614, the relic was abducted, but Emperor Heraclius (d. 641) recovered it in the course of a counteroffensive in 628. When Jerusalem fell to the Muslim Arabs (c. 637) the relic was sent to Constantinople for safety. These occurrences only intensified the cult of the True Cross: from the seventh century onward, the Exaltation of the Cross (Lat. *Exaltatio sanctae Crucis*) was celebrated liturgically in both Eastern and Western Christendom; the Discovery of the Cross (Lat. *Inventio sanctae Crucis*) was also commemorated in some areas, and hymns or poems reinforced popular devotion. Particles of the True Cross formed part of processions and other liturgical acts, particularly in Rome and Constantinople, and relics of the True Cross were also carried into battle even before the First Crusade (1096–1099), both in Byzantium and in Christian Spain. Thus, it is not surprising that participants in the First Crusade carried relics of the True Cross to the East, just as crusaders from Germany and Flanders did when they made their way to the Holy Land in the course of the so-called Second Crusade (1147–1149).

The conquest of Jerusalem by the Christians in 1099 substantially promoted the cult of the True Cross. In the summer of that year, a fragment of the cross came to light, which was entrusted to the Latin patriarch and the chapter of the Church of the Holy Sepulchre. This relic had supposedly been hidden in the seventh century before the Muslims took the town, and the major part was sent to Constantinople; it now became the symbol and liturgical focal point of the kingdom of Jerusalem. In the principality of Antioch, a separate particle was taken into battle as a palladium, only to be lost in battle at the Field of Blood on 28 June 1119. The Jerusalem relic, however, continued to serve liturgical, political, and military functions. It was kept in the Church of the Holy Sepulchre, where it was an object of devotion for pilgrims and was watched over by the canons of the church. The patriarch and his chapter sometimes presented particles of the Cross to prominent visitors or sent *staurotheques* (reliquaries in the form of a double cross, which held a part of the original wood of the Cross) to the West, especially to priories of their own order.

The main Jerusalem relic, the "wood of the Lord" (Lat. *lignum Domini*), played a central part in the religious life of the kingdom during celebrations and processions; on occasions it also left the Holy City, most notably during military crises. It first served as battle insignia at the victory of Ascalon of 1099, and subsequently was taken on military expeditions no less than thirty-one times. It also accompanied the army on the ill-fated march to Hattin, where it was seized by the Muslims on 4 July 1187. In spite of diplomatic efforts to recover it, the Jerusalem relic remained lost. However, devotion to the True Cross remained strong, and fragments of it continued to be used, among other things, to emphasize crusade preaching. The flow of reliquaries from Constantinople to the West persisted and reached its climax as a result of the town's sack and pillage in 1204.

–Nikolas Jaspert

Bibliography
Folda, Jaroslav, *The Art of the Crusaders in the Holy Land, 1098–1187* (Cambridge: Cambridge University Press, 1995).
Frolow, Anatole, *La relique de la Vraie Croix: Recherches sur le développement d'un culte* (Paris: Institut français d'études byzantines, 1961).
———, *Les reliquaires de la Vraie Croix* (Paris: Institut français d'études byzantines, 1965).
Gerish, Deborah, "The True Cross and the Kings of Jerusalem," *Haskins Society Journal* 8 (1996), 137–155.
Jaspert, Nikolas, "Vergegenwärtigungen Jerusalems in Architektur und Reliquienkult," in *Jerusalem im Hoch- und Spätmittelalter: Konflikte und Konfliktbewältigung—Vorstellungen und Vergegenwärtigungen,* ed. Dieter Bauer, Klaus Herbers, and Nikolas Jaspert (Frankfurt am Main: Campus, 2001), pp. 219–270.
Klein, Holger A., *Byzanz, der Westen und das "wahre" Kreuz: Die Geschichte einer Reliquie und ihrer künstlerischen Fassung in Byzanz und im Abendland* (Wiesbaden: Reichert, 2004).
Ligato, Giuseppe, "The Political Meanings of the Relics of the Holy Cross among the Crusaders and in the Latin Kingdom of Jerusalem: An Example of 1185," in *Autour de la Première Croisade: Actes du Colloque de la Society for the Study of the Crusades and the Latin East, Clermont-Ferrand, 22–25 juin 1995* (Paris: Publications de la Sorbonne, 1996), pp. 315–330.
Murray, Alan V., "'Mighty against the Enemies of Christ': The Relic of the True Cross in the Armies of the Kingdom of Jerusalem," in *The Crusades and Their Sources: Essays Presented to Bernard Hamilton,* ed. John France and William Zajac (Aldershot, UK: Ashgate, 1998) pp. 217–238.

Tudebode

See Peter Tudebode

Ṭughtigin (d. 1128)

Ẓāhir al-Dīn Ṭughtigin was *atabeg* and regent for Duqāq, king of Damascus (1093–1104), and thereafter effectively independent lord of Damascus and its dominions (1105–1128).

In his youth, Ṭughtigin was in the service of Alp Arslān, the Great Saljūq sultan (d. 1072), and later joined the administration of Alp Arslān's son Tutush I, the ruler of the Saljūq kingdom of Syria. In 1093 Tutush appointed Ṭughtigin as atabeg for his heir, Duqāq, and married him to Duqāq's mother, Ṣafwat, after divorcing her. After the death of Tutush (1095), Ṭughtigin was de facto ruler of Damascus and southern Syria in his capacities of atabeg and commander of the army, under the nominal rule of Duqāq, who died in June 1104 at a relatively young age. Ṭughtigin then recognized Duqāq's son, Tutush II, as ruler. After three months he replaced him with Duqāq's brother Artāsh, who, however, soon fled to Frankish territory.

Ṭughtigin was now the unchallenged ruler of the realm. He continued to rule Damascus until 1115 without any change of title, declaring loyalty to the Saljūq sultan

Muḥammad in Persia. The sultan did not recognize him as ruler, but was too preoccupied with civil wars to intervene. The Saljūqid king of Aleppo, Riḍwān, was unable to claim Damascus, as he was occupied in warfare with the Franks of Antioch. Throughout his long career, Ṭughtigin was acutely pragmatic, aiming only to secure power for himself and for his son Būrī, who was a well-trained candidate married to Zumurrud, the sister of Duqāq. Ṭughtigin repeatedly shifted his alliances between the Turcoman lords of Iraq, the sultan, the Franks, and even the Fāṭimids in order to survive.

Between 1095 and the fall of Antioch (mod. Antakya, Turkey) to the crusaders in 1099, Ṭughtigin fought alongside his lord Duqāq against the latter's brother Riḍwān of Aleppo. Until the death of Duqāq, Ṭughtigin did not show serious hostility toward the new Frankish states in Jerusalem or Edessa. He participated with a limited force in the ill-fated campaign of Karbughā at Antioch in 1098 and failed to defend the Damascene city of Haifa (mod. Hefa, Israel), which fell to the Franks in 1100. Ṭughtigin focused instead on consolidating his grip on Upper Mesopotamia, the lifeline for new Turcoman recruits. He turned down an Egyptian request to cooperate against the Franks in 1103, as he feared the large Egyptian army and the consequences for Damascus if it was successful.

From 1105 to 1108, the Frankish lords of Tiberias tried to build forts on the Jaulan heights, threatening the vital trade route between Damascus and the port of Tyre (mod. Soûr, Lebanon). After much fighting in which two lords, Hugh of Fauquembergues and Gervase of Bazoches, were killed, Ṭughtigin and King Baldwin I of Jerusalem in 1108 agreed on a truce and a division of the revenues from the border area of al-Sāwad (Terre de Suète). The capture of the Fāṭimid port of Sidon (mod. Saïda, Lebanon) by Baldwin I (1110) put more economic pressure on Damascus. In consequence Ṭughtigin made an alliance with Mawdūd, lord of Mosul, and also responded to a Fāṭimid appeal to save Tyre from the Franks of Jerusalem. In 1112 Ṭughtigin sent troops under his capable son Būrī, who relieved the city, thus securing the last coastal outlet for Damascene trade, and improving relations with Fāṭimid Egypt.

The high point of Ṭughtigin's political career occurred in 1113, when Baldwin I invaded Damascene territory and Mawdūd of Mosul responded to Ṭughtigin's request for help. On 28 June 1113 the armies of Ṭughtigin and Mawdūd defeated the Franks at al-Sinnabrāh in Galilee and plundered northern Palestine as far as the coast for months. However,

Ṭughtigin feared that Mawdūd's success might endanger his own position and ended the campaign. After they returned to Damascus, Mawdūd was murdered by Assassins hired by Ṭughtigin (September 1113). Ṭughtigin then concluded a truce with King Baldwin, and proceeded to form a great alliance that included his son-in-law Īlghāzī and Roger, prince of Antioch. Deterred by this alliance and in order to secure nominal authority over southern Syria, Sultan Muḥammad confirmed Ṭughtigin's political status in Damascus in November 1115, granting him the title *amīr* (prince, emir) and giving his family the right of inheritance.

In 1116 Ṭughtigin allied with Aq-Sunqūr al-Bursuqī, the new lord of Mosul, and both rulers defeated an invading army led by Pons, count of Tripoli. The last major victory for Ṭughtigin came about in alliance with Īlghāzī, now lord of Aleppo, in defending their lands against the Franks of Antioch. In June 1119 the allies inflicted a major defeat on the Antiochenes, known as the *Ager Sanguinis*, in which Prince Roger was killed and his army largely destroyed. Yet Ṭughtigin never capitalized on the victory, as he feared the revenge of Baldwin II of Jerusalem and could not keep his army of seasonally mustered Turcomans together. When the Franks of Jerusalem finally captured Tyre in 1124, Damascus was weakened and came under renewed attacks from Jerusalem for the rest of Ṭughtigin's rule. In 1128 Ṭughtigin died after two years of illness, appointing his son Būrī as sucessor.

–*Taef El-Azhari*

Bibliography

Al-Zanki, Jamal, "The Emirate of Damascus in the Early Crusading Period, 1095–1154" (Ph.D. diss., University of St. Andrews, 1989).

El-Azhari, Taef, *The Saljūqs of Syria during the Crusades, 463–549 A.H./1070–1154 A.D.* (Berlin: Schwarz, 1997).

Mouton, Jean-Michel, *Damas et sa principauté sous les Saljoukides et les Bourides, 1076–1154* (Le Caire: Institut Français d'Archéologie Orientale, 1994).

Mustafa, Shaker, "Tughtakin, Ras al-Usra al-Buriyya," *Journal of the Faculty of Arts, Kuwait University* 1 (1972), 35–97.

Tūrān Shāh (d. 1250)

Tūrān Shāh ibn al-Ṣāliḥ Najm al-Dīn Ayyūb (royal title al-Muʿaẓẓam) was the last Ayyūbid sultan of Egypt (March–May 1250).

He was one of four sons of Sultan al-Ṣāliḥ, and he acted

as his father's deputy at Hisn Kayfa and other dominions of Diyar Bakr until al-Ṣāliḥ's death. Al-Ṣāliḥ constantly turned down his commanders' advice to recall Tūrān Shāh to his father's court in Egypt; neither did he nominate him (or anyone else) as successor to the Ayyūbid sultanate during his final illness, even though the army of the first Crusade of Louis IX of France (1248–1254) had occupied the eastern part of the Nile Delta.

When al-Ṣāliḥ died (November 1249), his widow Shajar al-Durr, with the help of two commanders, concealed his death from the army and the locals, fearing a collapse in morale in the struggle against the crusaders. Shajar al-Durr dispatched an embassy to Hisn Kayfa to summon Tūrān Shāh to Cairo to assume the sultanate. Tūrān Shāh came with a small force via Damascus to Egypt, where he took power in early March, with the full support of his father's widow and the commanders of the *mamlūk* troops (military slaves). In April 1250 King Louix IX was defeated in the Delta, although Tūrān Shāh made little personal contribution to the Ayyūbid victory. He showed ingratitude to his fathers' commanders, replacing some of them with his Iraqi companions, and further isolated himself by threatening and even killing them while drunk. Encouraged by Shajar al-Durr, the *mamlūk* commanders, led by Baybars and Aqtay, murdered Tūrān Shāh in a brutal fashion (May 1250). This coup marked the inception of the Mamlūk sultanate in Egypt, and King Louis was allowed to leave Egypt for Palestine in the same month.

–Taef El-Azhari

Bibliography

Ayalon, David, *Eunuchs, Caliphs and Sultans: A Study of Power Relationships* (Jerusalem: Hebrew University, 1999).

Humphreys, R. Stephen, *From Saladin to the Mongols: The Ayyubids of Damascus (1192–1260)* (Albany: State University of New York Press, 1977).

Turbessel

Turbessel, known in Arabic as Tall Bāshir (mod. Tellbaşar Kalesı, Turkey), was a castle and town in northern Syria in the valley of the Sājūr, a tributary of the Euphrates. During the Frankish period Turbessel was one of the most important strongholds of the county of Edessa and was the seat of its greatest lordship from 1101 to 1113.

The castle is sited on a high, steep mound (partly artificial), about 350 meters (c. 1,150 ft.) long; in the crusader period the town was also defended by a wall. It was a minor Byzantine center after its reconquest from the Muslims by Emperor Nikephoros I in 962, and it was repopulated by Armenians. It was captured by the Saljūq sultan Malik Shāh in 1086, but during the First Crusade (1096–1099) it was taken by Baldwin of Boulogne in 1097 with local support. On his departure for Edessa (February 1098) Baldwin gave it to a local Armenian lord, Fer; and then, with Ravendel, to Godfrey of Bouillon, who based himself there in the summer of 1098. In 1101 Baldwin II of Edessa granted it to his cousin Joscelin I of Courtenay as the main seat of a fief covering all of the lands of the county of Edessa west of the Euphrates.

Turbessel was a base for raids into Muslim territory and became very wealthy, so much so that Baldwin confiscated it from Joscelin in 1113. Thereafter it formed part of the count's own domain, and after Joscelin succeeded to the county (1119) when Baldwin became king of Jerusalem, the counts tended to live there rather than in Edessa. Turbessel was probably also the usual residence of the Latin archbishops whose nominal see was at the smaller town of Duluk further to the north.

Turbessel's strategic position also attracted raids: it was briefly besieged by the army of Mawdūd of Mosul in 1111; the region was raided by the Artūqid ruler Īlghāzī in 1120; it was threatened by the Byzantine emperor John II Komnenos in 1142. After the capture of Count Joscelin II by the Turks in 1150, Turbessel was defended by his wife, Beatrix, against the Saljūq sultan Ma'sūd and Nūr al-Dīn. Beatrix sold the castle to the Byzantine emperor, who sent a garrison to occupy it, but in July 1151 it surrendered to Nūr al-Dīn's general Hassan al-Manbijī. It remained in the hands of followers of the Zangids until a brief occupation by the Saljūq sultan 'Izz al-Dīn Kay-Kāwūs in 1218, after which it belonged to Ayyūbid princes.

The town flourished until the Mongol invasion of Hülegü in 1260. It may have been briefly given to the Armenian king, Het'um I, but by 1263–1264 it was held by the Mamlūk sultan Baybars I, who demolished the castle. An Arab geographer writing at this time, Ibn Shaddād, describes Turbessel as having been rich and fertile but as being by then depopulated apart from a group of Turcoman nomads; it still possessed a Mamlūk governor, and some of the dependent villages remained settled. The town was sacked by the army of the Turkic conqueror Timur in 1400, after which the Mamlūks no longer maintained a garrison there.

–Angus Stewart

Bibliography
Cahen, Claude, *La Syrie du Nord à l'époque des croisades et la principauté franque d'Antioche* (Paris: Geuthner, 1940).
Hellenkemper, Hansgard, *Burgen der Kreuzritterzeit in der Grafschaft Edessa und im Königreich Kleinarmenien* (Bonn: Habelt, 1976).

Turcomans

Turcomans, or Türkmen, was the name given principally to the Oghuz (Ghuzz) Turks when they entered the Islamic world from their homeland to the northeast of the Caspian Sea in the course of the eleventh century.

The term is most likely to mean "*the* Turks," and to have been used for Turkish immigrants who had accepted Islam. The Turks in question were those who had accompanied the Saljūq clan of the Oghuz into Persia from the beginning of the eleventh century. As unarmored horsemen armed with composite bows and curved swords, they provided the Saljūqs with the numbers to conquer an empire, but as sheepherding nomads, they moved through the mountains to the south of the Caspian Sea in search of pasture, resisting Saljūq control as they pressed ahead into Mesopotamia, Anatolia, and Syria as *ghāzīs* (warriors for Islam) to create their own principalities. They failed at Damascus and Jerusalem, but the Dānishmendid dynasty and others established themselves in highland Anatolia, and the Artūqids in Diyar Bakr, becoming more heavily armed and armored in the Saljūq fashion.

The westward spread of these nomads across the uplands of northern Persia and Anatolia introduced a major new element into the population and the economy of the highland zone. In Anatolia (Asia Minor) it began the process of Turkification and Islamization of the majority of the population by the end of the Middle Ages, but whether this resulted from repopulation or conversion is difficult to say. Turcomans often made up an important element of the Muslim military forces that confronted the Franks of Outremer, serving not only their own leaders but frequently also joining armies led by Saljūq commanders. However, they were usually less amenable to discipline than the Saljūqs' own household troops.

By the end of the twelfth century, the Turcoman principalities of Anatolia were in retreat before the Saljūq sultanate of Rūm and the Ayyūbids, but farther east the Turcomans of Khurasan had defeated the Great Saljūqs, before the whole region fell to the Khwārazm-Shāh and the Mongols. Turcoman expansion, however, continued, until by the end of Mongol rule in the fourteenth century, a rash of new Turcoman principalities appeared in Anatolia, notably the Ottomans, the Aydin dynasty at İzmir (Smyrna), and the Karaman at Konya (Ikonion). By the fifteenth century, the Turcoman Kara Koyunlu ("Black Sheep") in eastern Anatolia, followed by the Ak Koyunlu ("White Sheep") in Diyar Bakr, had conquered a vast but ephemeral empire in Iraq and Persia. All fell victim to the Ottomans and the Ṣafawids of Persia.

–Michael Brett

Bibliography
Bosworth, Clifford Edmund, "The Political and Dynastic History of the Iranian World (A.D. 1000–1217)," in *The Cambridge History of Iran,* vol. 5: *The Saljuq and Mongol Periods,* ed. J. A. Boyle (Cambridge: Cambridge University Press, 1968), pp. 1–202.
———, *The New Islamic Dynasties* (Edinburgh: Edinburgh University Press, 1996).
Cahen, Claude, *Pre-Ottoman Turkey: A General Survey of the Material and Spiritual Culture and History, c. 1071–1330* (London: Sidgwick and Jackson, 1968).
İnalcık, Halil, *The Ottoman Empire: The Classical Period, 1300–1600* (London: Weidenfeld and Nicolson, 1973).
Nicolle, David, *The Armies of Islam, 7th–11th Centuries* (London: Osprey, 1982).

Turcopoles

Turcopoles or Turcoples (Gr. *Tourkopouloi,* Lat. *Turcopoli* or *Turcopolieri*) were Christianized mercenaries of Turkish origin in the service of Byzantine and Frankish armies in the Balkans and the Near and Middle East in the period of the crusades, especially from the late eleventh century onward.

Turcopoles were found fighting for the Franks of Outremer against the Muslims (twelfth–thirteenth centuries), for Byzantium against the Catalan invaders in Greece, on the latter's side against the eastern empire (fourteenth century), as well as in Cyprus and Rhodes in the course of the Latin dominations there (late twelfth to early sixteenth centuries). Western sources such as Raymond of Aguilers and Albert of Aachen present them mainly as offspring of mixed marriages between Turkish (either Saljūq or Turcoman) fathers (archaically referred to as Persians by the Byzantines) and Christian (Anatolian Greek) mothers.

Initially encountered in late eleventh-century Byzantine

sources as *Tourkopouloi*, they were active in imperial service chiefly in the thirteenth and fourteenth centuries, according to the Byzantine historians Pachymeres and Gregoras. They played a significant role in the Byzantine-Frankish war of 1263–1264 in the Peloponnese, while in the late thirteenth century the Turcopole descendants of Kay-Kāwūs II, Saljūq sultan of Rūm (1246–1257), were installed in imperial lands in central and northwest Macedonia, in the area of the river Axios (Vardar). In the early fourteenth century, several of them were settled in western Thrace, following their participation in Catalan raids against Byzantium.

In Frankish states of Outremer, Cyprus, and Greece, Turcopoles were employed in imitation of the Byzantine *Tourkopouloi*. Several twelfth- and thirteenth-century Western sources mention them as troops in the service of various Frankish rulers or of the military orders. After 1204 the Latin Empire of Constantinople received Turcopole reinforcements against the Bulgarian Asenids. In Cyprus, from 1192 the Lusignan rulers distributed fiefs among Turcopole mounted troops under the command of an officer known as the Grand Turcopolier, and from that time Latin sources refer to them mainly as light-armed archers who served in the capacity of police forces. The Hospitaller Knights effected the conquest of Rhodes (1306–1309/1310) with the help of light-armed horsemen called *Turcopolieri* or *Turcupelleri*, who were then used extensively by the order to patrol the island's coasts.

–Alexios G. C. Savvides

See also: Warfare: Outremer

Bibliography

Diament, Henri, "Can Toponomastics Explain the Origins of the Crusader French Lexemes Poulain and Turcople," *Names: Journal of American Name Society* 25 (1977), 183–204.

Moravcsik, Gyula, *Byzantinoturcica*, 2d ed., 2 vols. (Leiden: Brill, 1983).

Richard, Jean, "Les turcoples au service des royaumes de Jérusalem et de Chypre: Musulmans convertis ou chrétiens orientaux?," *Revue des études islamiques* 54 (1986), 259–270.

Savvides, Alexios G. C., "Morea and Islam, 8th–15th Centuries: A Survey," *Journal of Oriental and African Studies* 2 (1990), 47–75.

———, "Late Byzantine and Western Historiographers on Turkish Mercenaries in Greek and Latin Armies: the Turcoples/ Tourkopouloi," in *The Making of Byzantine History: Studies Dedicated to D. M. Nicol*, ed. Roderick Beaton and Charlotte Roueché (Aldershot, UK: Variorum, 1993), 122–136.

Turks

Turks is a name that refers to any group speaking a language from the Turkic subfamily of the Ural-Altaic language family. The original home of these groups was in Central Asia, where there was a Turkic empire during the sixth century. During the period of the crusades, large areas of the Muslim world were under Turkish rule, and the period of the later crusades saw the unification of the region under the Ottoman Turkish dynasty.

When the crusades began, the Saljūqs represented the most important Turkish dynasty in the Near and Middle East. They were a family of Ghuzz (or Oghuz) Turks who had filtered into the Islamic world in the tenth century; by the eleventh they had come to rule an empire covering most of the region from Syria and Anatolia in the west to Khurasan in the east. However, the division of territory among different princes led to the break-up of the Saljūq domains, and by the thirteenth century only one branch of the family held power, in the sultanate of Rūm, with its capital at Ikonion (mod. Konya, Turkey).

Several smaller Turkish dynasties rose to fill the power vacuum left by the Saljūq decline. One of these, the Dānishmendids, ruled central and northeastern Anatolia in the late eleventh and twelfth centuries. The Artūqids ruled in northern Iraq and Syria during much of the same period, and prevented the Franks from taking Aleppo in 1119. They were in part superseded by the Zangids, who conquered Egypt before both they and some of the remaining Artūqids lost power to the Ayyūbids, a dynasty that was Kurdish in origin but that nonetheless retained Turkish features. The Khwārazm-Shahs ruled in Central Asia and Persia from the late eleventh until the early thirteenth century, when they were defeated by the Mongols.

In addition, nomadic Turkic groups, usually called Turcomans (Türkmen), inhabited much of the Middle and Near East. Some of these groups followed regional urban rulers, while others paid allegiance only to their own chiefs. Different groups fought for both Muslim and Christian powers. At the time of the First Crusade (1096–1099), the Kipchak confederation occupied the steppes of southern Russia (i.e., mod. Ukraine), and large numbers of the Mamlūks were originally slaves taken from their numbers. Some Kipchaks also fought for the Franks or Byzantines. During the fourteenth century, two large Turcoman confederations, the Kara Koyunlu (Black Sheep) and Ak Koyunlu (White Sheep), fought for preeminence in Iraq and Persia.

The age of the later crusades saw the rise of the Ottoman Empire. Dispute rages on the ultimate origin of the Ottomans, but during the thirteenth century they emerged as a leading *ghāzī* (warriors for Islam) state in the vicinity of Bursa in northwestern Anatolia. By the sixteenth century the Ottomans had united the Balkans, the Near East, and North Africa in an empire with its capital at Constantinople (mod. İstanbul, Turkey). Crusades called against the Ottomans, such as the Nikopolis Crusade (1396) and the Varna Crusade (1444), were unsuccessful, and the empire lasted for several centuries.

–Brian Ulrich

Bibliography

Agadzhanov, Sergei G., *Der Staat der Seldschukiden und Mittelasien im 11–12. Jahrhundert* (Berlin: Schletzer, 1994).

Cahen, Claude, *Pre-Ottoman Turkey: A General Survey of the Material and Spiritual Culture and History, c. 1071–1330* (London: Sidgwick and Jackson, 1968).

Grousset, René, *The Empire of the Steppes: A History of Central Asia* (New Brunswick, NJ: Rutgers University Press, 1970).

Hillenbrand, Carole, *A Muslim Principality in Crusader Times* (Leiden: Nederlands Historisch-Archaeologisch Instituut te Istanbul, 1990).

Holt, Peter M., *The Age of the Crusades: The Near East from the Eleventh Century to 1517* (London: Longman, 1986).

Imber, Colin, *The Ottoman Empire, 1300–1600: The Structure of Power* (London: Palgrave Macmillan, 2002).

İnalcık, Halil, *The Ottoman Empire: The Classical Period, 1300–1600* (London: Weidenfeld and Nicolson, 1973).

Tutush I (1066–1095)

Tutush I ibn Alp Arslān was Saljūq king (Arab. *malik*) of Syria (1078–1095), with the title Taj al-Dawla (Crown of the State), ruling under the overlordship of his brother the Great Saljūq sultan Malik Shāh I (d. 1092).

Tutush was a son of Sultan Alp Arslān (d. 1072), whose armies conquered Syria from the Fāṭimids of Egypt in the years 1070–1075. His appointment as ruler came about after the defeat of Atsiz ibn Uwaq, the Saljūq commander of southern Syria and Palestine, by the Fāṭimids at Cairo (February 1077) and the ensuing rebellions against Saljūq rule in Palestine. At this time Malik Shāh I was busy fighting a civil war in Persia, but wanted to ensure continuing Saljūq rule of Syria and Palestine, and ultimately, a successful invasion of Egypt and the ending of the Fāṭimid Shīʿite caliphate.

Tutush came to Syria in 1078. He executed Atsiz ibn Uwaq and took control of Damascus and most of Palestine, including Jerusalem and the important coastal cities of Jaffa (mod. Yel Aviv-Yafo) and Sidon (mod. Saïda, Lebanon). In his government the young king depended on several Turcoman officers, notably his faithful commander Ẓāhir al-Dīn Ṭughtigin, who acted as his deputy. Tutush did not gain control of all of inland Syria until May 1094, when he finally captured Aleppo. He established a modus vivendi with the ruling dynasties of Tyre (mod. Soûr, Lebanon), the Banū ʿUqail, and of Tripoli (mod. Trâblous, Lebanon), the Banū ʿAmmār. In 1081 Tutush seized Tortosa (mod. Tarṭūs, Syria) from the Fāṭimids, weakening further the Fāṭimid naval presence in Syria.

With most of the Palestinian coast under Tutush's control, the Fāṭimids allied with the ʿUqailids of Aleppo, who refused to submit to Tutush's authority. In June 1083 Damascus came under siege from the Aleppan army, which was defeated by Tutush. The Fāṭimid-Aleppan alliance caused Tutush to change his strategy by seeking good relations with the Fāṭimids of Egypt, although his diplomatic initiatives proved fruitless. In 1086 Sultan Malik Shāh arrived in northern Syria and appointed some of his Turkish commanders as governors in key cities there: Yāghī Siyān at Antioch (mod. Antakya, Turkey) and Aq-Sunqur at Aleppo. As they answered to Malik Shāh in Persia, Tutush's authority and ambition in Syria were restricted. The Fāṭimids continued to press him in Palestine, capturing Sidon, Tyre, and Acre (mod. ʿAkko, Israel).

On the death of Malik Shāh (December 1092), Tutush decided to claim the sultanate, challenging the dead sultan's sons Maḥmūd (the designated heir) and Barkyārūq. He secured the support of all the Turkish leaders of Syria (including Aq-Sunqur) and was about to confront his nephew Barkyārūq in battle at al-Rayy in summer 1093, when Aq-Sunqur and another commander, Buzān, shifted their loyalties to Barkyārūq, forcing Tutush to retire to Damascus. Tutush spent the winter of 1093–1094 in Damascus and in the spring attacked Aleppo, having arranged a marriage between his son Riḍwān and a daughter of Yāghī Siyān of Antioch. In May 1094 he defeated the Aleppan army and had Aq-Sunqur executed. By January 1095 Tutush had gained recognition as sultan from the Abbāsid caliph, and controlled most of Syria, Anatolia, Iraq, and western Persia. However, on 26 February 1095 his forces were defeated by the army of Barkyārūq in a battle at the village of Dashlu, south of the Caspian Sea, where Tutush was killed. He left five sons; two of them, Duqāq and Riḍwān, started a civil war in Syria that continued up to the arrival of the First Crusade (1096–1099).

–Taef El-Azhari

Bibliography

El-Azhari, Taef, *The Saljūqs of Syria during the Crusades, 463–549 A.H./1070–1154 A.D.* (Berlin: Schwarz, 1997).

Mouton, Jean-Michel, *Damas et sa principauté sous les Saljoukides et les Bourides, 1076–1154* (Le Caire: Institut Français d'Archéologie Orientale, 1994).

Tutush II (d. 1105)

Nominal Saljūq ruler of Damascus in June–October 1004.

At the age of one, Tutush was nominated as successor by his father, Duqāq, who died at the end of June 1104. However, real power in Damascus was exercised by Duqāq's *atabeg*, Ẓāhir al-Dīn Ṭughtigin, who after little more than three months replaced the young prince with Duqāq's brother Artāsh ibn Tutush.

–Alan V. Murray

Bibliography

El-Azhari, Taef, *The Saljūqs of Syria during the Crusades, 463–549 A.H./1070–1154 A.D.* (Berlin: Schwarz, 1997).

Tyre

The city of Tyre (mod. Soûr, Lebanon) was one of the most important ports of the kingdom of Jerusalem from the time of its capture by the Franks (1124) up to its final loss to the Mamlūks in 1291.

Tyre was a major entrepôt for the exchange of goods between the Near East and Europe, thanks to its position at the end of roads from Damascus and Aleppo. Its physical location made the city almost impregnable: it was situated on a tongue of land that was defended on the seaward side by a double, and on the landward side by a triple wall. Muslim Tyre owed allegiance to Fāṭimid Egypt at the time of the crusader conquest of Palestine in 1099, and resisted the Franks until 1124, when it was forced to capitulate after a concerted siege by land and sea conducted by the army of the kingdom of Jerusalem and a Venetian fleet, lasting almost four months.

For its help in conquering Tyre, the Republic of Venice received by treaty (the *Pactum Warmundi* of 1123) one-third of the city and its surrounding area as sovereign territory, along with wide-ranging legal privileges and an annuity of 300 bezants from the proceeds of the royal market in the city. The estates in the surrounding area were granted to leading Venetians as fiefs. The non-Venetian section of the city and its surrounding territory became part of the royal demesne, and this was where the commercial activity of the other Western merchants came to be concentrated. In the period up to 1187, only the Pisans maintained a trading dependency in the royal part of the city; from the time of the Third Crusade (1189–1192) onward, they attempted to secure additional privileges. The Genoese and Provençals obtained a privileged toehold in Tyre only after 1187.

The native population played no part in long-distance trade, which was dominated by the Italians. The city itself had important industries, notably silk, produced by highly specialized Syrian weavers (especially in the Venetian Quarter), as well as the manufacture of glass. The coastal plain was fertile, and agriculture there was very productive, thanks to a well-developed system of irrigation (at least in the thirteenth century) and to some extent was geared toward the export of products such as sugarcane, wine, and oil.

In the church hierarchy of the Latin patriarchate of Jerusalem, the archbishop of Tyre was second only to the patriarch. However, only his suffragan bishops within the kingdom of Jerusalem (Acre, Beirut, and Sidon) came under the authority of the patriarchate of Jerusalem; the others belonged to the Latin patriarchate of Antioch (mod. Antakya, Turkey). The cathedral was the burial place of Frederick I Barbarossa, Holy Roman Emperor (1190) and of other prominent individuals. Documents refer to several parish churches, as well as to churches inside the Italian trade quarters (whose legal status was frequently contested between the Italian communes and the archbishop), and those belonging to other bishops, military and monastic orders, and canons.

After the defeat of the army of Jerusalem by Saladin at Hattin (3–4 July 1187), Tyre became the most important base of military operations for the Franks of Outremer and crusaders from the West. Thanks to the assistance of the Italians, especially Pisan and Genoese fleets, it was able to repel two Muslim sieges. From July 1187 the defense of the city was directed by Conrad, marquis of Montferrat, who proceeded to make it into a power base of his own in opposition to Guy of Lusignan, king of Jerusalem. The following year Conrad refused Guy entry to Tyre after his release from captivity by Saladin, and in 1190 the king ceded the city to him. On the death of Guy's wife, Queen Sibyl (3 November 1190), Conrad married her sister Isabella, who was the heiress to the kingdom, and claimed the government for himself. In the spring of 1192 Conrad was recognized as future ruler of the kingdom, but shortly before his coronation he was murdered by the Assassins (28 April 1192); he was buried in the cathedral of Tyre.

From this time Tyre replaced Jerusalem as the coronation venue for the kings of Jerusalem. Its financial importance for the Crown began to overtake that of Acre (mod. 'Akko, Israel), where, although it was the more important metropolis, many of the royal prerogatives could no longer be exploited or had been surrendered to the Italian and Provençal cities. Thus, from the reign of Henry of Champagne (1192–1197) onward, the monarchy revoked many of the privileges that had been conceded in Tyre to the Italian cities.

When Emperor Frederick II came to the Holy Land in 1228–1229 as regent for his son Conrad (king of Jerusalem after the death of his mother Isabella of Brienne), he was able to assert his claims to Tyre, and secured Frankish rule through his treaty with the Ayyūbid sultan al-Kāmil. After Frederick's departure (May 1229), Tyre became a stronghold of the pro-Staufen party in the kingdom and the residence of the imperial *bailli* (regent) Richard Filangieri until his expulsion in 1243. Thereafter it was governed by Balian of Ibelin and from 1246 by Philip of Montfort (d. 1283), to whom King Henry I of Cyprus assigned the guardianship (Lat. *custodia*) of the city. Philip invested a great deal of money in improving the city's defenses, which had suffered considerable damage from an earthquake in 1203/1204.

During the War of St. Sabas (1257–1258), Philip allied himself with Genoa against Venice. The expulsion of the Genoese from Acre by the Venetians led him to confiscate all Venetian possessions in Tyre and expel the Venetians from the city. The Genoese who had been driven out of Acre settled in Tyre, which became the seat of the Genoese colonial administration for all of Syria and Palestine. Philip's treaty with the Genoese in 1264 and its precise description of their position, rights, and responsibilities shows his hope of a revival of international trade from their presence in Tyre and with it an increase of his own income. His son and successor John reestablished peace with Venice in 1277, restoring the rights and property the Venetians had previously held in Tyre, and granting reparations for loss of income and funds to reconstruct buildings in the Venetian Quarter.

In 1269 John of Monfort married Margaret of Lusignan, sister of King Hugh III of Cyprus I of Jerusalem, thus securing the position of his family in Tyre. The city now became Hugh's most important base on the mainland, although this did not save Tyre from Mamlūk expansion. After the city was threatened by Mamlūk raids in 1266 and 1269, John of Montfort was forced to enter into a treaty with Sultan Baybars I in 1270–1271 over the division, administration, and financial use of the territory around Tyre. In 1285 John's widow Margaret agreed to a ten-year truce with Sultan Qalawūn, by which she relinquished half of her revenues and promised never to rebuild the defenses of the city. This armistice secured for the sultan the most profitable lands in the lordship. After the fall of Acre (1291), the nobility and wealthier inhabitants fled to Cyprus, and when Mamlūk troops occupied Tyre on 19 May, the remaining inhabitants were either killed or sold into slavery. The city was completely destroyed on the orders of the sultan; it had no significance in the Mamlūk and Ottoman periods.

–*Marie-Luise Favreau-Lilie*

Bibliography

Chéhab, Maurice H., *Tyr à l'époque des croisades*, 2 vols. (Paris: Maisonneuve, 1975–1979).

Favreau-Lilie, Marie-Luise, "Die italienischen Kirchen im Heiligen Land," *Studi Veneziani*, n.s., 13 (1987), 15–101.

———, *Die Italiener im Heiligen Land vom ersten Kreuzzug bis zum Tode Heinrichs von Champagne* (Amsterdam: Hakkert, 1989).

———, "Durchreisende und Zuwanderer. Zur Rolle der Italiener in den Kreuzfahrerstaaten," in *Die Kreuzfahrerstaaten als multikulturelle Gesellschaft*, ed. Hans Eberhard Mayer (München: Oldenbourg, 1997), pp. 69–86.

———, "Der Fernhandel und die Auswanderung der Italiener ins Heilige Land," in *Venedig und die Weltwirtschaft*, ed. Wolfgang von Stromer (Stuttgart: Thorbecke, 1999), pp. 203–233.

———, "Multikulturelle Gesellschaft oder Persecuting Society? Franken und Einheimische im Königreich Jerusalem," in *Jerusalem im Hoch- und Spätmittelalter: Konflikte und Konfliktbewältigung—Vorstellungen und Vergegenwärtigungen*, ed. Dieter Bauer, Klaus Herbers, and Nikolas Jaspert (Frankfurt am Main: Campus, 2001), pp. 55–93.

Lucas, Leopold, *Geschichte der Stadt Tyrus zur Zeit der Kreuzzüge* (Marburg: Hamel, 1895).

Mayer, Hans Eberhard, "On the Beginnings of the Commune of Tyre," *Traditio* 94 (1968), 160–189.

Prawer, Joshua, *Crusader Institutions* (Oxford: Oxford University Press, 1980).

Tzachas

See Chaka

U

Ugaunia

Ugaunia (Est. *Ugandi*) was a province of medieval Livonia corresponding to the southeastern part of modern Estonia. Its main centers were Odenpäh (mod. Otepää) and Dorpat (mod. Tartu). During the Baltic Crusades, Ugaunia was one of the first Estonian provinces to confront the crusaders.

The chronicler Henry of Livonia claims that Lettgallian tribes had suffered greatly under the Ugaunians, who had also robbed merchants from the Baltic island of Gotland. The first crusader raid to Ugaunia was undertaken in 1208, when Odenpäh was burned. In the following years, Ugaunia was raided often by crusaders, Lettgallians, and Russians. The Ugaunians were, however, able to organize counterraids. By 1216 the people of the province had been baptized and the crusaders had started to fortify themselves in Odenpäh, but they were temporarily driven out by Estonian tribes allied with Russians from Pskov, who also had claims over the province.

Another serious drawback in the development of German government in the province was an Estonian uprising in 1223–1224 that was also supported by neighboring Russian principalities. After the final subjection of the province by crusader forces from Riga (1224), Ugaunia formed the core possession of the bishops of Dorpat.

–Juhan Kreem

Bibliography

Mäesalu, Ain, "Die Burg Otepää als ein Zentrum in Südostestland im 11.–14. Jh," in *Castella Maris Baltici*, vol. 1, ed. Knud Drake (Stockholm: Almqvist & Wiksell, 1993), pp. 143–148.

Tarvel, Enn, "Sakala ja Ugandi kihelkonnad," *Keel ja Kirjandus* (1968), pp. 586–596.

Tvauri, Andres, *Muinas-Tartu Prehistoric Tartu* (Tartu: Tartu Ülikool, 2001).

Ulrich von Jungingen (d. 1410)

Grand master of the Teutonic Order (1407–1410) who died in the battle of Tannenberg.

Ulrich was born around 1360 into a knightly family from Swabia, and later joined the order along with his elder brother Konrad. From 1383, Ulrich held different offices in Prussia before becoming the order's marshal in 1404. After the death of Konrad, who had been grand master, Ulrich became his successor, on 26 June 1407. One of his main tasks was the permanent pacification of the province of Samogitia, which had been granted to the order in 1398 by the Treaty of Sallinwerder. The order could not, however, secure its lordship, and in 1409 Vytautas, the grand duke of Lithuania, supported a Samogitian uprising. Because Poland refused to guarantee a truce while the order was fighting its Lithuanian opponents, Ulrich decided on an attack on Poland.

This plan seemed at first to be a convincing one, but it turned out to be a fatal mistake. In late summer 1409, the order started a successful attack against Poland that led to a nine-month truce. When hostilities were resumed, King Władysław II of Poland had allied with Vytautas, whereas Sigismund, king of Hungary, and Wenzel, king of Bohemia, did not provide the help that Ulrich had hoped for. On 15 July 1410, the order's army clashed with the united Polish-

Lithuanian forces near the villages of Tannenberg and Grunwald. After a fierce battle, the order suffered the most dramatic defeat in its history. Ulrich and more than 200 knight brethren died in combat. His body was later recovered from the battlefield and buried in St. Anne's chapel at the castle of Marienburg (mod. Malbork, Poland). Because of his decision for war, Ulrich has often been labeled as a hothead, but modern historians have developed a more balanced view of Ulrich's character.

–Axel Ehlers

Bibliography

Ekdahl, Sven, "Ulrich von Jungingen," in *Die Hochmeister des Deutschen Ordens, 1190–1994*, ed. Udo Arnold (Marburg: Elwert, 1998), pp. 106–114.

Urban, William, *Tannenberg and After: Lithuania, Poland, and the Teutonic Order in Search of Immortality* (Chicago: Lithuanian Research and Studies Center, 1999).

Unur (d. 1149)

Mu'in al-Dīn Unur, *atabeg* of Damascus (1138–1149). Unur was originally a Turcoman *mamlūk* (slave soldier) of Ṭughtigin, atabeg of Damascus (d. 1128). He came to power in a coup in April 1138, and until his death was atabeg and army commander (Arab. *isfahsālār*) under three successive rulers ("kings"): Maḥmūd ibn Būrī (d. 1139), Muḥammad ibn Būrī (d. 1140), and Ābaq ibn Muḥammad.

Up to 1146–1147, Unur's policies were characterized by resistance to Zangī, atabeg of Mosul, and cooperation with the Franks of the kingdom of Jerusalem. When Maḥmūd ibn Būrī was murdered in June, probably at the instigation of Zangī, Unur managed to keep Damascus secure by smoothly transferring the government to Muḥammad ibn Būrī. The latter died during a seven-month siege of the city by Zangī (1139–1140), and Unur installed Muḥammad's young son Ābaq as the new sovereign. Unur obtained help from King Fulk of Jerusalem, offering him 20,000 dinars per month during the campaign and the surrender of the strategic town of Banyas. Zangī abandoned the siege at the approach of the Frankish army. The alliance between Damascus and Jerusalem lasted until 1147. In that year, Unur gave his daughter in marriage to Nūr al-Dīn, Zangī's son and successor, which led to an improvement in relations between the two rulers.

Later in the year, Queen Melisende of Jerusalem abandoned the long-standing alliance with Damascus and supported a rebellion against Unur by one of his vassals in Bosra. Unur joined with Nūr al-Dīn, and their combined forces inflicted a heavy defeat on the Franks during the summer; Unur prevented the Turcoman troops from pursuing the defeated Franks. On 24 July 1148 Unur successfully defended his city against the siege mounted by the combined armies of the kingdom of Jerusalem and the Second Crusade (1147–1149), having obtained military assistance from Mosul and Aleppo for help. He welcomed the truce for two years proposed in May 1149 by the kingdom of Jerusalem, which enabled him to continue his policy of keeping the balance of power between the Franks and the Turkish powers in the north. Unur died on 28 August 1149, and Damascus suffered long economic warfare by Nūr al-Dīn until it was forced to surrender to him in 1154.

–Taef El-Azhari

Bibliography

El-Azhari, Taef, *The Saljūqs of Syria during the Crusades, 463–549 A.H./1070–1154 A.D.* (Berlin: Schwarz, 1997).

Mouton, Jean-Michel, *Damas et sa principauté sous les Saljoukides et les Bourides, 1076–1154* (Le Caire: Institut Francais d'Archéologie Orientale, 1994).

Urban II (d. 1099)

Pope (1088–1099), who can be considered as the initiator of the crusade movement through his promulgation of the expedition that came to be known as the First Crusade (1096–1099).

Originally named Odo of Châtillon, the future pope was born in the diocese of Soissons around the year 1035, a member of the aristocracy of Champagne. Odo was educated at the cathedral school of Rheims and became a canon and eventually archdeacon at Rheims. In 1067/1070 he entered the monastery of Cluny, where he became prior under Abbot Hugh. In about 1080 Pope Gregory VII appointed Odo as cardinal bishop of Ostia, a signal honor that indicates the great esteem in which he was by then held in the church. During the crisis of Gregory's last years, he entrusted Odo with a legatine mission to Germany, where he shored up support for the reformed papacy in the south. After the death of Gregory's successor, Victor III (September 1087), the papacy seemed in greater distress than ever, with Rome firmly in the hands of the imperialist antipope, Clement III (Guibert, archbishop of Ravenna). Odo was elected pope at Terracina south of Rome on 12 March 1088, choosing the papal name

The arrival of Pope Urban II in France, from the *Roman de Godefroi de Bouillon,* 1337. (Giraudon/Art Resource)

Urban; this was most likely out of veneration for his distant predecessor Urban I (222–230), familiar to him on the basis of decretals forged under his name in the ninth-century canonical collection known as the *Pseudo-Isidorian Decretals,* but the name could also be understood as an indication that he considered himself the bishop of the Eternal City.

Urban's beginnings were very difficult indeed. He could not enter Rome until 1093, after Clement III had withdrawn to the north of Italy. The situation in southern Italy, where Norman princes struggled against each other, the Byzantines, and non-Normans, was politically and ecclesiastically confused. The issue of whether bishops and churches were to follow Greek or Latin rites was nearly insoluble, and the experiences gained in that struggle as well as during the *Reconquista* (the reconquest of Iberia from the Muslims) probably formed the background to one of his later rulings regarding the Holy Land. As reported by Paschal II at the Council of Benevento (1113), in response to an appeal regarding the archbishopric of Tyre, Urban II determined at

the Council of Clermont that ecclesiastical and political boundaries in Outremer should coincide, a decision that Paschal upheld.

Even during the early years of his pontificate, Urban never hesitated in his efforts to reform the church and elevate the Christian morals of both clergy and laity, particularly of the former, enjoining celibacy, ensuring canonical elections to church offices, prohibiting simony in connection with ordinations, and excluding lay influence in general from matters ecclesiastical. He convened three major councils while in southern Italy: Melfi (1089), Benevento (1091), and Troia (1093). The canons (decisions) of these councils were included in contemporary canonical collections and thus preserved. A decree from Melfi prohibited lay investiture of bishops and abbots. Like the letters and privileges of the pontiff, many of his conciliar and juridical decisions were of fundamental importance for the burgeoning new religious movements, foremost among them eremitical foundations and the canons regular. It is no exaggeration to state that it was Urban II who rescued the eleventh-century church reform and endowed the measures of Gregory VII with permanent validity. Urban's successes were also in part a result of administrative changes at the Curia, in particular the reorganization of papal finances under a chamberlain on the pattern established at Cluny. He secured support from Roman churches by further expanding the college of cardinals and granting all ranks of cardinals participation in the government of the church.

Urban's return to Rome in late 1093 marked the second phase of his pontificate, a rebuilding of papal authority throughout the Latin Church. Even with the invaluable assistance in the north of Countess Matilda of Tuscany and her troops, who defended Urban against Emperor Henry IV, and in the south of the Normans, Urban was never able to defeat Clement III, who had withdrawn to his archbishopric of Ravenna, but he proved himself a master of diplomacy. Willing to grant concessions and dispensations, he managed to secure the recognition of his pontificate in France and Spain as well as in England, ecclesiastically isolating the German monarchy. Since Henry IV refused to renounce the traditional right of investiture and to abandon Clement III, no compromise was possible there. Urban II even expanded the prohibition of lay investiture to a prohibition of fealty or homage by clerics to laymen. He gained the unstinting support of Count Roger I of Sicily, whom he granted special privileges regarding legations (1098), in a document that was to become the basis of the Sicilian monarchy. He carefully avoided a complete rupture with King Philip I of France despite that king's marital problems. In Spain Urban furthered the Reconquista and reorganized the church by establishing Bernard, the Cluniac archbishop of Toledo, as primate and settling quarrels over episcopal ranking among old and newly Christian towns. In 1095 he granted a solemn papal privilege to King Peter I of Aragon.

Urban's journey to France in 1095–1096 along an itinerary that touched many important regions, though not the area under the authority of Philip I, could be described as a triumphal return to his homeland. Beginning with the Council of Piacenza in northern Italy (March 1095), the journey was punctuated by several important councils, which Urban used to publicize reforming legislation and to give pastoral encouragement, as well as to settle disputes: Clermont (1095), and Tours and Nîmes (1096). His later councils at the Lateran in Rome (1097), Bari (1098), and St. Peter's in Rome (1099) continued the traditions established since the beginning of his pontificate and probably repromulgated and expanded the legislation best known from the councils of Piacenza and Clermont. The Council of Bari was one of his largest councils, but no decrees issued there have survived. However, it is known as a forum for the exchange of views held by the Latin and the Greek church; Anselm of Canterbury, who was in exile at the time, gave an address defending the Latin tradition of the double procession of the Holy Spirit, that is, the belief that the Holy Spirit proceeds from the Father "and from the Son" (Lat. *filioque*).

Urban's most famous council is that of Clermont in Auvergne (18–28 November 1095). It is forever associated with the crusades because two of its recorded regulations became the juristic foundation of the crusading movement. Urban announced a remission of all penance for all those who went to Jerusalem for the sake of liberating the church without any desire for personal gain. He placed the goods and property of all who participated under the protection of the Peace and Truce of God, that is, he protected them from any kind of seizure or infringement until the owners had returned from the East. As a third component, he issued a call to arms in a public speech at the conclusion of the council. The immediate motivation was an appeal to Urban as the leader of the Latin West by emissaries of Alexios I Komnenos, the Byzantine emperor, for military aid against the Turks, an appeal that arrived prior to the Council of Piacenza in March 1095. But Urban's request at Clermont was not formulated as a response to the emperor's appeal. He asked for aid for the Christian churches in the East and mentioned Jerusalem, but geography made an alliance between Alexios and Urban II a precondition of the crusade, and Constantinople the only possible point of departure for an army on the way to the Holy Land. Thus, assisting Constantinople and assisting the Eastern Christians and Jerusalem must be seen as a single objective.

The reconquests of Spain and southern Italy (especially Sicily) were examples that certainly must have come to mind. At Clermont Urban is not known to have mentioned Byzantium or the rapprochement between Latin and Greek Christians, but it is conceivable that he may have hoped to create better conditions for future negotiations. Urban's appeal brought forth an immediate response from those assembled to hear it and rapidly gained adherents throughout the West. Adhemar of Monteil, bishop of Le Puy, was appointed as leader of the expedition on 27 November, and its departure was fixed for August 1096, after the harvest.

Chroniclers tell unanimously of crosses worn by those who were to participate.

After Clermont, Urban continued to drum up support for the crusade through his travels and letters. During the winter of 1098–1099, he appointed Daibert, archbishop of Pisa, as legate for the new territories that the crusaders had conquered. However, Urban's death on 29 July 1099 at Rome meant that he did not hear of the culmination of the expedition he had proclaimed, the capture of Jerusalem on 15 July 1099.

—Uta-Renate Blumenthal

Bibliography

Becker, Alfons, *Papst Urban II. (1088–1099),* 2 vols. (Stuttgart: Hiersemann, 1964–1988).

———, "Le Voyage d'Urbain II en France," in *Le Concile de Clermont de 1095 et l'appel à la croisade,* ed. André Vauchez (Rome: Ecole française de Rome, 1997), pp. 127–140.

Le Concile de Clermont de 1095 et l'appel à la croisade: Actes du Colloque Universitaire International de Clermont-Ferrand (23–25 juin 1995), ed. André Vauchez (Rome: l'Ecole française de Rome, 1997).

Cowdrey, H. E. John, "Pope Urban II's Preaching of the First Crusade," *History* 55 (1970), 177–188.

———, "Pope Urban II and the Idea of Crusade," in *Le Concile de Clermont de 1095 et l'appel à la croisade,* ed. André Vauchez (Rome: Ecole française de Rome, 1997), pp. 721–742.

Erdmann, Carl, *The Origin of the Idea of Crusade* (Princeton, NJ: Princeton University Press, 1977).

Somerville, Robert, "The Council of Clermont (1095), and Latin Christian Society," *Archivum Historiae Pontificiae* 12 (1974), 55–90.

———, *Papacy, Councils and Canon Law in the 11th–12th Centuries* (London: Variorum, 1990).

Urban IV (d. 1264)

Pope (1261–1264).

Jacques (James) Pantaléon, as he was originally known, was born toward the end of the twelfth century (perhaps in 1185) as the son of a shoemaker at Troyes. After attending the cathedral school of Notre-Dame-aux-Nonnains in Troyes, he studied canon law in Paris and became a canon of Laon in 1223. Around 1242 he was appointed archdean of Campine (Liège) and three years later attended the First Council of Lyons. Pope Innocent IV, probably recognizing his diplomatic qualities on this occasion, sent him as legate to Poland, Prussia, and Pomerania in 1247. During this legation he held a synod at Breslau (mod. Wroskaw, Poland) in 1248, where he restored the ecclesiastical discipline of the clergy and mediated a peace between the Teutonic Order and its rebellious Prussian vassals.

Three years later Innocent IV sent Pantaléon to Germany (1251), where his task was to strengthen the position of William of Holland, the papal candidate for the throne, against King Conrad IV. Elected bishop of Verdun in 1253, Pantaléon was appointed by Pope Alexander IV as Latin patriarch of Jerusalem on 9 April 1255 and as legate to the kingdom of Jerusalem on 7 December of the same year. After his arrival at Acre (mod. 'Akko, Israel) in June 1256, Pantaléon was confronted with the so-called War of St. Sabas between the Venetians and the Genoese for economic hegemony over Acre, a conflict that developed into a general civil war in the kingdom of Jerusalem. His attempts to negotiate a peace between the conflicting parties failed during the following years. As a consequence Thomas Agni, bishop of Bethlehem, was appointed as legate by the pope in 1259. Probably because he rejected this appointment, Pantaléon returned to the papal court at Viterbo in late 1260 or early 1261.

After the death of Alexander IV (25 May 1261), a conclave, composed of only eight cardinals, surprisingly elected Pantaléon as pope on 29 August 1261, probably as a compromise candidate. He was consecrated on 4 September and assumed the name Urban IV. Urban strengthened his position in the church by nominating fourteen new cardinals, among them several Frenchmen.

The main task of the newly elected pontiff was a solution to the problem of the succession to the kingdom of Sicily, as he was determined to end the rule of the Staufen dynasty in southern Italy. The possibility of an intervention by King Henry III of England in favor of the papacy, a project favored by Urban's predecessor, became increasingly improbable. From 1258 onward, Manfred, the Staufen king of Sicily, was able to stabilize his rule and extend his influence into central and northern Italy. Although Manfred tried to come to an agreement with the pope in 1262, Urban never took the offers of the king into serious consideration. Instead, the pope started negotiations (as early as 1261) with the royal family of France, and despite some initial reservations on the part of King Louis IX, Urban offered the Sicilian crown in 1262 to Louis's younger brother Charles, the ambitious count of Provence and Anjou. The result of these negotiations was a treaty (17 June 1263), by which Charles of Anjou was invested with the kingdom of Sicily, in return for an annual tribute of 10,000 ounces of gold, a lump sum of 50,000 marks sterling, and explicit agreement not to accept any imperial dignity. However, as a consequence of the election of Charles as senator of Rome in summer 1263 and the military pressure of Manfred, Urban was forced to accept some modifications of the draft treaty in favor of the French prince. Although the pope's death on 2 October 1264 (probably at Deruta between Orvieto and Perugia) prevented him from seeing the downfall of the hated Staufen dynasty, the final conquest of southern Italy by Charles I of Anjou in 1265–1266 was mainly the result of Urban's diplomatic abilities.

The Sicilian question also overshadowed the other problems of Urban's pontificate. He initially supported the efforts of Baldwin II, titular Latin emperor of Constantinople, who since 1262 had been attempting to organize a military campaign for the reconquest of his lost capital. However, the pope changed his mind completely when he got wind of an alliance between Baldwin II and Manfred of Sicily. The Latin emperor supported the Staufen case at the court of Louis IX in 1263 and tried to undermine the negotiations of Urban with Charles of Anjou. After initial hesitation, the pope intensified relations with Baldwin's mortal enemy, the Byzantine emperor Michael VIII Palaiologos, and sent envoys to Constantinople in summer 1263 to negotiate the union between the Latin and Greek churches. Because of his sudden death, these negotiations came to a standstill and were then broken off by his successor Clement IV.

In the kingdom of Jerusalem, Urban especially favored the Order of the Holy Sepulchre, perhaps with the purpose giving it a future central role in the administration of Outremer. In 1263 or 1264 he received also an envoy from the Mongol Īlkhan of Persia, Hülegü, who proposed a united action by Latins and Mongols against the Mamlūks. The pope's death meant that this project, too, was not pursued.

Despite the brevity of his pontificate, Urban IV can be considered as one of the most important popes in history. As the first French pope of the thirteenth century, he prepared the ground for the close alliance between the French Crown and the papacy, which had as a short-term consequence the establishment of the Angevin dynasty in southern Italy and as a long-term effect the so-called Babylonian Captivity of the papacy under the influence of the French monarchy during the fourteenth century, with all its dramatic consequences.

–Andreas Kiesewetter

Bibliography

Berg, Beverly, "Manfred of Sicily and Urban IV. Negotiations of 1262," *Mediaeval Studies* 55 (1993), 111–136.

Bresc-Bautier, Geneviève, "Bulles d'Urbain IV en faveur de l'ordre du Saint-Sépulcre (1261–1264)," *Mélanges d'archéologie et d'histoire de l'Ecole française de Rome* 85 (1973), 283–310.

Hamilton, Bernard, *The Latin Church in the Crusader States: The Secular Church* (London: Variorum, 1980).

Hampe, Karl, *Urban IV und Manfred, 1261–1264* (Heidelberg: Winter, 1909).

Jackson, Peter, "The Crisis in the Holy Land in 1260," *English Historical Review* 95 (1980), 481–503.

Jordan, Edouard, *Les origines de la domination angevine en Italie* (Paris: Picard, 1909).

Lupprian, Karl-Ernst, *Die Beziehungen der Päpste zu islamischen und mongolischen Herrschern im 13. Jahrhundert anhand ihres Briefwechsels* (Città del Vaticano: Biblioteca Apostolica Vaticana, 1981).

Pásztor, Edith, *Onus apostolicae sedis: Curia romana e cardinalato nei secoli XI–XV* (Roma: Sintesi Informazione, 1999).

Roberg, Burkhard, *Die Union zwischen der griechischen und lateinischen Kirche auf dem II. Konzil von Lyon (1274)* (Bonn: Röhrscheid, 1964).

Sievert, Wilhelm, "Das Vorleben des Papstes Urban IV," *Römische Quartalschrift für christliche Altertumskunde und für Kirchengeschichte* 10 (1896), 451–505; 12 (1898), 127–161.

Souplet, Maxime, *Jacques de Troyes, le "pacificateur," évêque de Verdun (1247) 1253–1255, pape Urbain IV, 1261–1264* (Verdun: n.p., 1954).

Sternfeld, Richard, *Karl von Anjou als Graf der Provence (1245–1265)* (Berlin: Gaertner, 1888).

Waley, Daniel, *The Papal State in the Thirteenth Century* (London: Macmillan, 1961).

Usāma ibn Munqidh (1095–1188)

Usāma ibn Munqidh was a remarkably long-lived warrior, political adventurer, and poet, who wrote the *Kitāb al-I'tibār* (*Book of Examples*), a memoir that drew on incidents in his action-packed life in order to provide moral guidance for his descendants.

Usāma was born on 25 June 1095. His father, a member of the Banū Munqidh clan who ruled over the city of Shaizar (mod. Shayzar, Syria), renounced his inheritance in favor of his youngest brother. Most of Usāma's kinsmen were killed in an earthquake that struck Shaizar in 1157 at the time of a circumcision feast. Successively Usāma sought service with Muÿin al-Dīn Unur in Damascus, with Ibn Salār in Egypt, and with Nūr al-Dīn in Damascus. In the 1160s he spent time in Ḥisn Kayfā before retiring to Damascus, where he died on 6 November 1188 at the age of ninety-three. Usāma's account of his political intrigues is somewhat disingenuous and elliptical. He finally ended up in Damascus as a pensionary of Saladin, who is reported to have been a great admirer of Usāma's poetry. During his early career in Unur's Damascus, Usāma went on frequent embassies to the kingdom of Jerusalem, and it emerges from the various vivid anecdotes in the I'tibār that he fraternized with the Frankish aristocracy, hunting with them, and enjoying their hospitality. It is clear that he found much to ridicule as well as much to admire in such matters as Frankish medicine and justice. Together with Ibn Jubayr's account of his journey through Palestine, Usāma's I'tibār provides the most vivid and revealing account of the Latin kingdom seen through Muslim eyes. However, Usāma wrote a great many other books, and in his own lifetime he was chiefly famous as a poet. Some of his writings, such as his books on women and on dreams, have not survived, but historians still have not paid sufficient attention to the historical materials to be found in such texts as the Kitāb al-'Aṣā, his anthology of stories about sticks.

–Robert Irwin

Bibliography

Christie, Niall, "Just a Bunch of Dirty Stories? Women in the 'Memoirs' of Usamah ibn Munqidh," in Eastward Bound: Travel and Travellers, 1050–1550, ed. Rosamund Allen (Manchester, UK: Manchester University Press, 2004), pp. 71–87.

Cobb, Paul M., "Usāma Ibn Munqidh's Book of the Staff: Autobiographical and Historical Excerpts," Al-Masāq: Islam and the Medieval Mediterranean 17 (2005), 109–123.

Derenbourg, Hartwig, Ousâma ibn Mounkidh: Un emir syrien au premier siècle des croisades (1095–1188), 2 vols. (Paris: Leroux, 1889).

Irwin, Robert, "Usamah ibn Munqidh, an Arab Syrian Gentleman at the Time of the Crusades Reconsidered," in The Crusades and Their Sources: Essays Presented to Bernard Hamilton, ed. John France and William Zajac (Aldershot, UK: Ashgate, 1998), pp. 71–87.

Memoirs of an Arab-Syrian Gentleman, or An Arab Knight in the Crusades. Memoirs of Usāmah ibn Munqidh ("Kitāb al-I'tibār"), trans. Philip K. Hitti (New York: Columbia University Press, 1927).

Morray, D. W., The Genius of Usāmah ibn Munqidh: Aspects of "Kitāb al-I'tibār" by Usāmah ibn Munqidh (Durham, UK: University of Durham Centre for Middle Eastern and Islamic Studies, 1987).

Usāma ibn Munqidh, Kitāb al-I'tibār, ed. Ḥasan Zayn (Beirut: Dār al-Fikr al-Ḥadīth, 1988).

Üxküll

Üxküll (mod. Ikšķile, Latvia) was a site on the river Düna some 28 kilometers (17 mi.) upstream from Riga. It became the earliest center of missionary activity in medieval Livonia.

The first known missionary in Livonia, an Augustinian canon from Segeberg named Meinhard (d. 1196), settled there with some German merchants in the 1180s, erecting a church on the site of an older stone building, and began to preach Christianity to the Livic inhabitants. In about 1185, Meinhard had a castle built at Üxküll by masons from Gotland, the first stone fortress in Livonia. Together with another castle on the island of Holme, Üxküll was important in securing commerce on the waterway between Russia and the West. In 1186 Meinhard was named bishop of Üxküll by Hartwig II, archbishop of Hamburg-Bremen.

The bishopric remained at Üxküll until it was moved downstream to the newly established town of Riga by Bishop Albert of Buxhövden in 1201, probably because of better connections overseas. Üxküll was subsequently enfeoffed to members of the German nobility in Livonia. The castle itself remained small and was ruined in the seventeenth century.

–Juhan Kreem

Bibliography

Graudonis, Janis, "Archäologische Forschungen in Uexküll," Zeitschrift für Ostforschung 44 (1995), 475–508.

Studien über die Anfänge der Mission in Livland, ed. Manfred Hellmann (Sigmaringen: Thorbecke, 1989).

Tuulse, Armin, Die Burgen in Estland und Lettland (Dorpat: Estnischer Verlag, 1942).

V

Vadum Jacob
See Jacob's Ford

Valdemar I of Denmark (1131–1182)

King of Denmark (1157–1182), whose military expeditions against the pagan Wends established Denmark as a major sea power in the Baltic.

Valdemar, known to posterity as "the Great" (Dan. *den Store*), was the son of Knud Lavard, duke of Schleswig, and Ingeborg, daughter of Mstislav, prince of Kiev; he was named after his maternal great-grandfather, Vladimir II Monomakh, prince of Kiev.

Born only a week after his father's murder in 1131, Valdemar was brought up by a Danish nobleman, one of whose sons was later the archbishop of Lund, Absalon. Following years of civil war, which opened Denmark to attacks from the pagan Wendish tribes on the southwestern shore of the Baltic Sea, Valdemar became sole ruler of Denmark in 1157. The chronicler Saxo Grammaticus recounts almost yearly crusading expeditions led by Valdemar and Absalon against the Wends in cooperation and competition with Henry the Lion, duke of Saxony. These culminated in the conquest of the pagan island of Rügen in 1168 and the submission of this region to the Danish church. After 1170 Danish crusading efforts were directed further east, against Pomerania. Valdemar was the founder of Antvorskov, the first hospital of the Order of St. John in Scandinavia, although the precise date of the foundation is unknown.

Valdemar died in 1182. A lead plate on his grave tells of a king devoted to conquering and converting the Wends. He was married to a Russian princess, Sophia of Minsk (d. 1198). Of his seven children, two legitimate sons, Knud VI (d. 1202) and Valdemar II (d. 1241), became kings of Denmark.

–*Torben K. Nielsen*

Bibliography
Christiansen, Eric, *The Northern Crusades,* 2d ed. (London: Penguin, 1997).

Jensen, Kurt Villads, "The Blue Baltic Border of Denmark in the High Middle Ages: Danes, Wends and Saxo Grammaticus," in *Medieval Frontiers: Concepts and Practices,* ed. David Abulafia and Nora Berend (Aldershot, UK: Ashgate, 2002), pp. 173–193.

Lind, John H., Carsten Selch Jensen, Kurt Villads Jensen, and Ane L. Bysted, *Danske korstog—Krig og mission i Østersøen* (København: Høst og Søn, 2004).

Valdemar II of Denmark (d. 1241)

Valdemar II Sejr (the Victorious) was king of Denmark (1202–1241) in succession to his brother Knud VI.

Valdemar was born around 1168, the second son of King Valdemar I and Sophia of Minsk. In 1201 the city of Lübeck, the most important port on the Baltic Sea, submitted to Valdemar after a period of Danish expansion in northern Germany, partly due to Valdemar's efforts in the area as duke of Schleswig in the 1190s. By the beginning of the thirteenth century Denmark under Valdemar was a naval superpower, since all of the southwestern shores of the Baltic Sea as far as Prussia had yielded to Danish rule.

Despite a remark in the chronicle of Henry of Livonia, it is doubtful whether Valdemar took part in an abortive crusade against the island of Ösel (mod. Saaremaa, Estonia) in 1206, as other sources report him to have been militarily engaged in Germany at the same time. However, following crusades to Livonia in 1217 undertaken by Valdemar's vassal Count Albert of Orlamünde, Bishop Albert of Riga asked for support from Valdemar in 1218. The ensuing agreements secured (at least temporarily) Danish royal recognition of Albert of Riga. In the summer of 1219 a royal Danish army conquered the northern parts of Estonia, where Valdemar swiftly introduced a Danish administration.

To secure his position against Danish claims, Albert appealed to Pope Honorius III, who confirmed the bishop's right to Estonia and the Livonian provinces of Selonia and Semgallia. However, in 1221, following a Danish blockade of Lübeck lasting over a year, Albert of Riga was forced to accept Valdemar's lordship over Estonia and Livonia as well as Valdemar's bestowal of land on the Order of the Sword Brethren. In 1222 Valdemar conquered Ösel in a campaign joined by Albert of Riga and the Sword Brethren, and negotiations between the three parties led to a division of Estonia. Valdemar still claimed overlordship over the whole country, but retained direct rule only over the northern provinces. He ceded the central and southern provinces to the Sword Brethren, and granted spiritual rights there to the bishop of Riga. He gave up his claims to Livonia proper.

The Estonians of Ösel had not been fully subjected and soon revolted against Danish rule. The rebellion spread to the mainland, with the result that all the Danish conquests in Estonia were lost with the exception of the town of Reval (mod. Tallinn). At the same time Valdemar was taken hostage by one of his northern German vassals, Count Henry of Schwerin (May 1223). This incident effectively halted Danish expansionist politics. Although Valdemar was released from captivity after payment of a large ransom (1225), his defeat by the forces of Lübeck and its allies at the battle of Bornhöved (1227) marked the end of Danish supremacy in the Baltic region. Valdemar worked hard to regain power in Estonia, and the Christian powers in the Baltic region finally agreed on a division of Estonia in the Treaty of Stensby (1238). A royal cadastral work from the 1230s gives details of the Danish administration of Estonia.

Valdemar's two marriages, to Dagmar (Margaret) of Bohemia (1205) and Berengaria of Portugal (1212), reflect the level of international recognition accorded to the Danish king at the beginning of the thirteenth century.

–*Torben K. Nielsen*

Bibliography

Christiansen, Eric, *The Northern Crusades*, 2d ed. (London: Penguin, 1997).

Jensen, Carsten Selch, "Valdemar Sejr, korstogsbevægelsen og den pavelige reformpolitik i 1200-tallets første halvdel," *Historisk Tidsskrift* 102 (2002), 23–54.

Lind, John H., Carsten Selch Jensen, Kurt Villads Jensen, and Ane L. Bysted, *Danske korstog—Krig og mission i Østersøen* (København: Høst og Søn, 2004).

Rebane, P. Peter, "Denmark and the Baltic Crusade, 1150–1227" (Ph.D. diss., Michigan State University, 1969).

La Valette, Jean de (1495–1568)

Grand master of the Order of the Hospital (1557–1568).

Born in Quercy in Gascony on 4 February 1495, La Valette joined the *langue* (Hospitaller province) of Provence in 1515. Hardly anything else is known of his childhood or his early years within the order, except that he was on Rhodes during the Ottoman siege of 1522. In 1546 he was elected governor of Hospitaller Tripoli (mod. Tarābulus, Libya) in North Africa, serving until 1549. The style of his governorship here was a foretaste of his later magistracy, dictated by sound Christian moral values, a deep sense of commitment to hospitaller and military ideals, firm allegiance to orthodoxy, and an inborn enmity toward the infidel. In 1548, he convinced the Hospital's chapter general of the advantages of transferring the convent to Tripoli. The project failed to materialize because the North African fortress fell to the Ottomans in August 1551.

Six years later La Valette was elected as forty-eighth grand master of the order (21 August 1557). Apparently reluctant to retain Malta, he repeatedly sought unsuccessfully a better place for the convent, first on Corsica and then again at Tripoli. It was the Ottoman siege of 1565, the major event of his magistracy, that ultimately made the order's stay on Malta permanent and determined the building of the new fortress city, Valletta, which still bears his name today. He died on 21 August 1568.

–*Victor Mallia-Milanes*

See also: Hospital, Order of the; Malta

Bibliography

Mallia-Milanes, Victor, "Frà Jean de la Valette 1495–1568: A Reappraisal," in *The Maltese Cross*, ed. T. Cortis (Malta: Malta University Publishers, 1969), pp. 117–129.

Varna Crusade (1444)

The last great land-based crusade against the Ottoman Empire, which ended in the defeat of a Balkan Christian coalition by the Turks near the city of Varna (in mod. Bulgaria).

The Varna Crusade came about in response to Ottoman advances in the Balkans, notably the occupation of Serbia (1439) and the siege of Belgrade (1440). In 1443, for the first time after the disastrous Nikopolis Crusade (1396), Hungary initiated an ambitious offensive campaign against the Ottoman Empire, encouraged by Pope Eugenius IV and his legate Cardinal Giuliano Cesarini. A Hungarian army of some 35,000 troops, led by the famous general John Hunyadi (Hung. *Hunyadi János*), was accompanied by Cesarini, the Serbian despot George Branković, and King Vladislav I (king of Poland as Władysław III), who had been elected as king of Hungary in expectation of significant Polish support against the Turks. The army left Buda on 22 July 1443, crossed the Serbian border by mid-October, and occupied Sofia by December. Having gained some other minor victories, it returned home in January after learning that Sultan Murad II had crossed the Bosporus, and celebrated a spectacular triumphal march in Buda.

Faced with a revolt by the Karamanids in Anatolia in spring 1444, the sultan was unwilling to face war on two fronts, and offered favorable peace conditions to Hungary: peace for ten years, the surrender of Serbia and Bosnia, the liberation of the sons of Branković, and 100,000 gold florins. The extravagant peace terms confused the political parties in Hungary; before the sultan's offer in April the Hungarian diet had voted for war, and the king had taken a solemn oath to carry it out. The war was also supported by the legate Cesarini, who envisaged the union of the Roman Catholic and Greek Orthodox churches and the relief of Constantinople, and by the Polish court party in Buda, though it was rejected by Poland.

The period between April and September is very controversial, and has been clarified only recently. Despot Branković accepted the sultan's conditions, and offered John Hunyadi his own immense possessions in Hungary in exchange for his support of a future peace treaty. Hunyadi seems to have accepted Branković's offer, which meant that Hungary was preparing for war and negotiating peace terms at the same time. A tentative peace treaty was concluded by the Hungarians at Adrianople (mod. Edirne, Turkey) on 15 June, and the sultan left Europe on 12 July to lead his troops against his adversaries in Anatolia. In this precarious situation, the Hungarians tried to win both peace and war. On 4 August at Szeged, King Vladislav declared invalid any former or future treaties made with the infidels, with the approval of Cesarini. Meanwhile the Hungarian-Ottoman peace treaty was ratified on 15 August in Várad (mod. Oradea, Romania) by the king, John Hunyadi, and Branković, only a few miles from the forward outposts of the royal army. A papal-Venetian fleet sailed to blockade the Dardanelles, but the Hungarian-Ottoman diplomatic activity disturbed the European Christian coalition and the efficacy of the blockade, causing delay and depriving the campaign of the necessary surprise effect. The unity of the coalition was now in tatters. Despot Branković was satisfied to have at least regained northern Serbia together with its capital (22 August); he not only failed to join the coming war, but even tried to hinder it.

The Christian coalition army amounted to some 20,000 men, considerably fewer than the previous year. It consisted mostly of Hungarians, along with Polish and Bohemian mercenaries and some 2,000–3,000 Wallachian light cavalry led by Vlad Dracul; the absence of any Serbian and Albanian auxiliary troops should have been a warning signal. The army left Orşova on 20 September, intending to strike at the Ottoman capital of Adrianople. The Christians marched along the Danube route via Vidin (26 September) and Nikopolis (16 October), and turned southeast via Novi Pazar and Shumen, capturing and plundering all these cities. Due to bad reconnaissance, they did not know that the sultan had already crossed the Bosporus with an overwhelming (perhaps double) numerical superiority.

The Christians met the sultan at the city of Varna on 9 November, on terrain unfavorable for them, between the lake of Devna and the sea coast. Despite John Hunyadi's military talent, the Christians were defeated as a result of poor cooperation among the multinational coalition forces. Hunyadi initially gained the upper hand on both wings by the overwhelming attack of his heavy cavalry. The sultan considered a retreat, but at the next decisive moment King Vladislav attacked the Turkish elite janissary units with his Polish troops. This ruined the Christian tactics, and resulted in the death of the king and the papal legate. The Christian battle order dissolved, and the cavalry left in panic-stricken flight, including John Hunyadi, who escaped to Wallachia. Both sides suffered heavy losses, above all among the Christian infantry units that attempted to defend their camp

The Varna Crusade (1444)

behind wagons in a manner similar to that of the Hussite troops of Bohemia.

The Hungarian and papal war parties had been correct in their assessment that 1444 presented the best opportunity in a long time to wear down Ottoman power by force of arms. This crusade, however, proved to be the last spectacular failure of traditional crusading strategy: sweeping the Ottomans out of Europe in a single campaign, in the absence of political unity among the fragmented and partly conquered Balkan states, proved to be impossible, and the Christians were unable to make full use of the favorable peace conditions. Much more could have been achieved by accepting the peace terms than by launching a campaign into an unstable region. As had been done by King Sigismund after the defeat of the Nikopolis Crusade in 1396, the Hungarian kings again adopted a deliberate defensive strategy (particularly under King Matthias Corvinus, son of John Hunyadi) up to the final collapse of the Hungarian defense system in 1521 and of the medieval kingdom of Hungary itself in 1526.

–László Veszprémy

Bibliography

Babinger, Franz, "Von Amurath zu Amurath. Vor- und Nachspiel der Schlacht bei Varna 1444," *Oriens* 3 (1950), 229–265.

Cvetkova, Bistra, *La Bataille mémorable des peuples: Le sud-est européen et la conquête ottomane* (Sofia: Sofia Press, 1971).

Engel, Pál, "János Hunyadi: The Decisive Years of his Career, 1440–1444," in *From Hunyadi to Rákoczi: War and Society in Medieval and Early Modern Hungary*, ed. János M. Bak and Béla K. Király (Boulder, CO: Atlantic, 1982), pp. 103–123.

———, "János Hunyadi and the Peace of Szeged," *Acta Orientalia Academiae Scientiarum Hungaricae* 47 (1994), 241–257.

Halecki, Oscar, *The Crusade of Varna: A Discussion of Controversial Problems* (New York: Polish Institute of Arts and Sciences in America, 1943).

Imber, Colin, *The Crusade of Varna, 1443–45* (Aldershot, UK: Ashgate, 2006).

Papp, Sándor, "Der ungarisch-türkische Friedensvertrag im Jahre 1444," *Chronica: Annual of the Institute of History, University of Szeged* 1 (2001), 67–78.

Setton, Kenneth M., *The Papacy and the Levant, 1204–1571*, vol. 2: *The Fifteenth Century* (Philadelphia: American Philosophical Society, 1978).

Venice

With the exception of the papacy, no polity in Europe was as frequently and consistently engaged in crusading as the republic of Venice. Unlike elsewhere in the medieval world, Venetians tended to approach crusading from a communal perspective. In other words, although they individually took crusading vows, the decision to go on crusade was usually a corporate one. In part this was due to the necessities of producing large war fleets in a republican commune, but it was also a reflection of the Venetians' highly developed self-identity. Despite centuries of crusading, modern accounts have tended to write the Venetians (indeed, all Italians) out of crusade histories.

Venice joined the First Crusade (1096–1099) as a state enterprise, although belatedly, either because of the infirmity of Doge Vitale Falier (1084–1096) or a skepticism that he may have shared with his royal counterparts in England, France, and Germany. When the Venetians assembled to choose a new doge on Falier's death, they turned to Vitale Michiel (1096–1101), a proponent of the crusade. Michiel immediately sent word to the towns on the Dalmatian coast to prepare for a great enterprise to free the Holy Land. In the Venetian lagoon, shipwrights began work on war galleys, while merchant vessels were pressed into service as supply transports. In the spring of 1099, Venice was at last ready: an armada of some 200 major vessels was prepared for war—the largest single contribution to the First Crusade. The fleet left in July 1099, commanded by the doge himself, and with some 9,000 Venetian crusaders on board. In June 1100 they landed at Jaffa (mod. Tel Aviv-yafo, Israel), recently conquered by the crusade. Godfrey of Bouillon was eager to extend Christian control to other port cities and agreed with Michiel to launch an attack on Acre (mod. 'Akko, Israel). However, Godfrey's subsequent death scuttled that plan. Instead, Michiel helped Tancred capture Haifa, which fell on 20 August 1100. Doge Ordelafo Falier (1101–1118) took command of another crusade fleet, sailing to Sidon, which was captured in 1110 with the help of King Sigurd of Norway. King Baldwin I of Jerusalem rewarded the republic with a street and a marketplace in Acre.

After the crushing defeat of the Franks of Antioch by the Turks at the *Ager Sanguinis* in 1119, the king and patriarch of Jerusalem requested assistance from Pope Calixtus II, who, preoccupied with the Investiture Controversy, passed the request on to Venice. In 1120 Doge Domenico Michiel (1118–1129) made an impassioned appeal to the people, who consented to a new crusade. Michiel suspended all overseas commerce while the Venetians prepared a fleet of approximately 120 major vessels. With the doge in com-

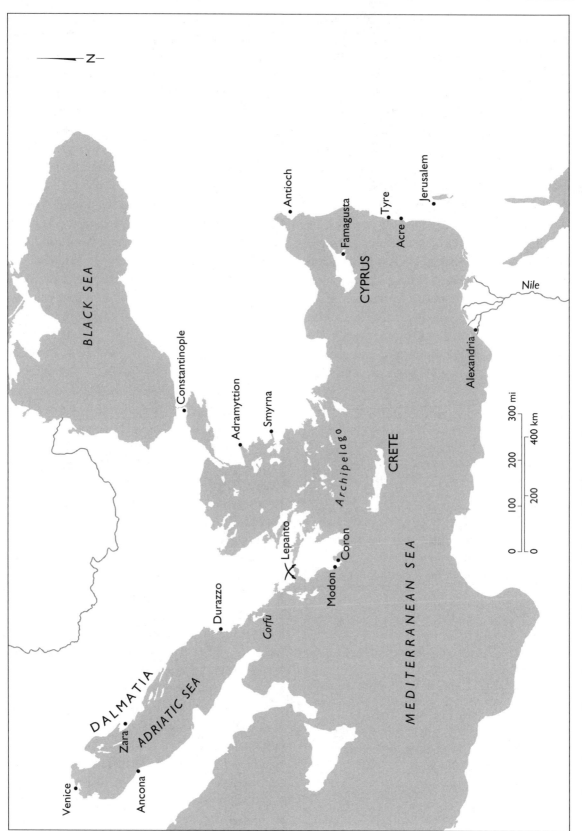

Areas of Venetian crusading and commercial activity in the period of the crusades

Within the map:

N

BLACK SEA

Antioch

Jerusalem

Tyre

Famagusta

Acre

CYPRUS

Constantinople

Nile

Adramyttion

Smyrna

Alexandria

Archipelago

CRETE

300 mi

400 km

200

200

100

0

0

Lepanto

Coron

Modon

MEDITERRANEAN SEA

Durazzo

Corfu

DALMATIA

ADRIATIC SEA

Zara

Venice

Ancona

mand, it set sail on 8 August 1122, carrying more than 15,000 Venetian crusaders. During the winter, it tried without success to capture Corfu in retaliation for John II Komnenos's refusal to renew Venetian trading privileges in the Byzantine Empire. The Venetian fleet arrived at Acre in May 1123, where it destroyed the Fāṭimid navy. The following year, the Venetians joined with the Franks to capture the coastal city of Tyre (mod. Soûr, Lebanon), which fell in July 1124. The Venetians were granted one-third of Tyre as well as a street, bakery, bath, and church in every city in the kingdom of Jerusalem. More than sixty years later, Doge Orio Mastropiero sent a large crusade fleet to join the Third Crusade (1189–1192), which took part in the siege of Acre.

Given a century of Venetian involvement in the crusades, it is not too surprising that Pope Innocent III turned to Venice for support when he proclaimed the Fourth Crusade (1202–1204) in 1198. The aged and blind Doge Enrico Dandolo (1192–1205) was inclined to support the crusade, but he pointed out to the pope that Venetian merchants were already paying a heavy price for the good of Christendom because of the ban on trade with Muslims. The pope responded by allowing the Venetians to trade in nonstrategic goods with Egypt. The failure of the Frankish crusaders to meet their commitments forced Dandolo to balance the good of the crusade against the enormous financial losses of the commune. The diversion of the crusade to Zara (mod. Zadar, Croatia) solved several problems, getting the expedition under way, providing a place to winter, and in part compensating the Venetians for their losses. But the attack on Zara, which was under papal protection, convinced Innocent that Dandolo and the Venetians had hijacked the crusade for their own purposes. He excommunicated all of the Venetian crusaders, although this was kept secret from the rank-and-file, including the Venetians.

There was no direct Venetian involvement in the decision to divert the Fourth Crusade to Constantinople (mod. İstanbul, Turkey) to support the claims of the Byzantine pretender Alexios Angelos. Dandolo went along with the deal negotiated by the Frankish barons, although it posed significant risks to Venice's profitable position in Byzantium. The crusade's original goal, Egypt, was much more favorable from the Venetian perspective, since the low level of business that Venetian traders did there risked little, while the possible gains were great. The exhaustion of the crusade's provisions, however, made the trip to Egypt impossible; only the diversion to Constantinople offered the opportunity to repair the crusade sufficiently so that it could repay its debts to Venice and embark on its mission.

The conquest of Constantinople in 1204 would one day be a boon to Venice, but at the time the communal government viewed the fall of Byzantium with great trepidation. In theory, Dandolo had won three-eighths of the empire, yet the Venetians did not at first act to claim much of it. They moved quickly to secure those areas that were crucial to safeguarding shipping (such as Dyrrachion, Corfu, Coron, and Modon) and only gradually extended their control over the entire eastern shore of the Adriatic Sea. The Venetians showed little interest in Crete (which Dandolo had purchased from Boniface of Montferrat) until the Genoese moved to capture it; the island, which remained in Venetian hands until 1691, became the centerpiece of the republic's maritime empire. Over time, Venice also extended control over other nearby islands, including Negroponte (Euboea). Elsewhere in the Aegean, the Venetian government gave permission to individual Venetians to capture islands at their own expense.

Despite the disappointing results of the Fourth Crusade, Innocent still urged Venetians to take part in the Fifth Crusade (1217–1221). Buoyed up by a ten-year truce with Genoa, a Venetian fleet transported King Andrew II of Hungary and his armies to Outremer. Vessels from Venice and Crete participated in the siege of Damietta in Egypt in 1219, suspending high ladders from their masts just as they had done at Constantinople in 1204. The following year, Doge Pietro Ziani (1205–1229) sent a fleet of 14 galleys to join the crusade.

Venetians in the Latin East were not immune to the factional strife and violence that afflicted the region in the thirteenth century. The worst outbreak was in Acre, where a street fight over a house that belonged to the monastery of St. Sabas escalated into a war between Venice and Genoa. The War of St. Sabas finally ended in June 1258 when the Venetians defeated the Genoese and demolished their quarter in Acre.

After the fall of Outremer in 1291, the Venetians took their share of blame for rivalries that pitted Christian against Christian. The military orders were also blamed, as were the popes, who had increasingly been more interested in using crusades to advance political interests at home rather than the good of Christendom in the East. Venetians, who had long been committed to crusades against Muslims, had little patience for domestic crusades. When Pope Martin IV

Bronze horses from the fourth century B.C., seized from Constantinople in 1204 and later mounted on the Cathedral of St. Mark, Venice. (Mimmo Jodice/Corbis)

proclaimed a crusade against the king of Aragon in 1284, the communal government refused to allow it to be preached in Venetian lands. Martin responded by putting Venice under interdict, although it was lifted by Martin's successor the following year.

Venice's support for crusades against Muslims found an eloquent voice in the writings of the Venetian nobleman Marino Sanudo Torsello. In 1321 he presented to Pope John XXII and King Charles IV of France his *Liber secretorum fidelium crucis,* which laid out plans and advice for the reconquest of Outremer. In his various writings, Sanudo sharply criticized the popes for diverting crusade energy to fight their Ghibelline enemies at home. He argued for an economic blockade of Egypt before a general invasion. With Egypt as a base, the Holy Land could then be restored.

Sanudo's ideas did not fall on deaf ears; there was a real desire throughout the West to organize a large crusade to check Turkish expansion. When Pope John XXII called a new crusade to deal with the Turks, Philip VI of France took up the cause, sending word to Venice that he wanted to contract ships and provisions to transport his crusade army. The following year, the Venetians agreed to provide a large crusade

fleet, provided that the arrangement was confirmed by the pope and that there would be no attack on Christians. In addition, the Venetians promised to join the crusade themselves and to immediately launch war galleys to engage Turkish pirates. But the enterprise was delayed by other events, including the death of the pope. Nevertheless, the Venetians sent galleys to capture Turkish vessels in the Aegean. Together with the Byzantines and Hospitallers, the Venetian crusaders defeated the Turks at Adramyttion in 1334. The French, though, never did show up. Distracted by the English threat, they dropped the idea, and Pope Benedict XII finally canceled the crusade in 1336.

In 1342 Pope Clement VI authorized the crusade indulgence for Venetians who would join with the king of Cyprus and the Hospitallers in a war against the Turks. A fleet was quickly assembled and sailed to Smyrna (mod. İzmir, Turkey) on the coast of Asia Minor, which the crusaders captured. Despite these minor successes, Turkish power continued to grow, closing off and isolating Constantinople. When Pope Boniface IX called a crusade to aid the great city in 1399, the Venetians sent a fleet that, together with crusaders from Genoa, Rhodes, Lesbos, and France, broke through the Turkish blockade and pillaged coastal territories.

After the fall of Constantinople in 1453, several crusades were called to recapture it. The most ambitious was that of Pope Pius II, finalized at the Council of Mantua in 1459. Of all the European states that promised troops for the enterprise, Venice alone kept its promise by declaring war on the Turks. Doge Cristoforo Moro (1462–1471) took the cross himself and led the Venetian crusade fleet to Ancona to rendezvous with the pope and the promised armies. However, the armies failed to materialize, and Pius died shortly before the Venetians arrived. The crusade came to nothing, except that Venice was now at war with the Ottomans, who wrested the island of Negroponte from the republic. Despite the setback, Venetians still responded favorably when Pope Sixtus IV proclaimed a new crusade against the Turks in 1471. A large Venetian fleet joined with papal and Neapolitan vessels to deal damaging blows to Antalya and Smyrna.

By 1500 the Venetians had paid dearly for their support of crusades, losing additional territories in the East (although picking up control of Cyprus by inheritance). Venetians had come to believe that the incessant crusade talk in Europe was little more than that. This feeling was amplified in 1508 when the pope formed the League of Cambrai. The league's stated purpose was to launch a crusade against the Turks, but in reality it was the result of an agreement to destroy Venice. Thus, when Pope Leo X and other European powers began planning a grand crusade to sweep the Muslims out of the Mediterranean (which took on a new urgency after the Ottoman conquest of Syria and Egypt in 1517), Venice promised to take part only when it was clear that something other than paper was being generated. In fact, that is all that was generated. Despite this caution, the Venetians would still be stung by failed crusade promises. In 1537 Venice and the papacy planned a large crusade to recapture Constantinople. Emperor Charles V joined the following year, promising to send substantial forces. The Venetian-papal fleet was launched, but it was quickly defeated by the Turks. Charles then backed out of the crusade, leaving Venice to fight alone, which cost Venetians their last holdings in the Peloponnese and 300,000 ducats to make peace. Throughout the remainder of the sixteenth and seventeenth centuries, Venetians continued their crusading tradition. Their most famous engagement was at the battle of Lepanto in 1571, when, in league with papal and Spanish forces, they destroyed the Ottoman fleet.

–*Thomas F. Madden*

Bibliography

Jacoby, David, "The Venetian Privileges in the Latin Kingdom of Jerusalem: Twelfth and Thirteenth-Century Interpretations and Implementation," in *Montjoie: Studies in Crusade History in Honour of Hans Eberhard Mayer,* ed. Benjamin Z. Kedar, Jonathan Riley-Smith, and Rudolf Hiestand (Aldershot, UK: Ashgate, 1997), pp. 155–175.

Madden, Thomas F., *Enrico Dandolo and the Rise of Venice* (Baltimore: Johns Hopkins University Press, 2003).

Nicol, Donald M., *Byzantium and Venice: A Study in Diplomatic and Cultural Relations* (Cambridge: Cambridge University Press, 1988).

Prawer, Joshua, *Crusader Institutions* (Oxford: Oxford University Press, 1980).

Queller, Donald E., and Irene B. Katele, "Venice and the Conquest of the Latin Kingdom of Jerusalem," *Studi Veneziani,* n.s., 12 (1986), 15–43.

Queller, Donald E., and Thomas F. Madden, *The Fourth Crusade: The Conquest of Constantinople,* 2d ed. (Philadelphia: University of Pennsylvania Press, 1997).

Riley-Smith, Jonathan, "The Venetian Crusade of 1122–1124," in *I comuni italiani nel regno crociato di Gerusalemme,* ed. Gabriella Airaldi and Benjamin Z. Kedar (Genova: Università di Genova, 1986), pp. 337–350.

Robbert, Louise Buenger, "Venetian Participation in the Crusade of Damietta," *Studi Veneziani,* n.s., 30 (1995), 15–33.

Setton, Kenneth M., *The Papacy and the Levant,* 4 vols. (Philadelphia: American Philosophical Society, 1976–1984).

Thiriet, Freddy, *La Romanie vénitienne au Moyen Age: Le developpement et l'exploitation du domaine colonial vénitien (XIIe-XVe siècles)* (Paris: Boccard, 1959).

Venice, Treaty of (1201)

The Treaty of Venice was a contract, entered into by Doge Enrico Dandolo and the Venetian Republic on one side, and Baldwin IX of Flanders, Thibaud III of Champagne, and Hugh of Saint-Pol on the other, to provide transport for the army of the Fourth Crusade (1202–1204). The treaty, which was confirmed by Pope Innocent III, committed the Venetians to providing sufficient vessels and provisions for 4,500 knights, 4,500 horses, 9,000 squires, 20,000 infantry, and all of their equipment. The vessels were to remain in the service of the crusade for one year, beginning 29 June 1202. The crusaders were to pay the Venetians 85,000 silver marks of Cologne.

The terms of this treaty would ultimately be responsible for the Fourth Crusade's tragic diversions: only one-third of the projected number of crusaders arrived in Venice, making it impossible to reimburse the Venetians fully for their enormous expenses. The resulting poverty of the army led the crusade first to Zara (mod. Zadar, Croatia) and then to Constantinople (mod. İstanbul, Turkey) in an attempt to secure the funds necessary to meet the terms of the treaty. In August 1203 the newly crowned Emperor Alexios IV Angelos paid the crusaders for their services, thus closing the books on the troubled treaty. Yet by that time the crusade was already entangled in a thicket of Byzantine politics that would later lead to the conquest of Constantinople in April 1204.

–*Thomas F. Madden*

Bibliography

Madden, Thomas F., *Enrico Dandolo and the Rise of Venice* (Baltimore: Johns Hopkins University Press, 2003).

Queller, Donald E., and Thomas F. Madden, *The Fourth Crusade: The Conquest of Constantinople,* 2d ed. (Philadelphia: University of Pennsylvania Press, 1997).

Urkunden zur älteren Handels- und Staatsgeschichte der Republik Venedig, ed. G. L. F. Tafel and G. M. Thomas, 3 vols. (Wien: Kaiserlich-königliche Hof- und Staatsdruckerei, 1856–1857), 1: 362–373.

Venetian Crusade of 1122–1124

See Crusade of 1122–1124

Viborg

Viborg (mod. Vyborg, Russia) was a Swedish fortress, founded in 1293 during the so-called Third Swedish Crusade against Karelia.

The fortress was located on an island in the western estuary of the river Vuoksi that linked Lake Ladoga and the Gulf of Finland. An attempt to gain control over the eastern estuary into Lake Ladoga at Kexholm a year later failed. A further attempt in 1300 to control the Neva link between Lake Ladoga and the Baltic Sea by founding the fortress of Landskrona likewise failed, and so Viborg remained the cornerstone in Sweden's defense against Russia and in future crusades toward the east. On numerous occasions Novgorod and later Moscow tried to take Viborg, always in vain. The Russians came closest to achieving this during the war in 1495–1497, which was also the last occasion when a Swedish ruler obtained a crusading bull from the pope against the Russians.

–*John H. Lind*

See also: Baltic Crusades; Karelia; Novgorod; Sweden
Bibliography
Lind, John H., "Consequences of the Baltic Crusades in Target Areas: The Case of Karelia," in *Crusade and Conversion on the Baltic Frontier, 1150–1500,* ed. Alan V. Murray (Aldershot, UK: Ashgate, 2001), pp. 133–149.

Vienne, Council of (1311–1312)

A church council held at the town of Vienne in the Dauphiné (16 October 1311–4 May 1312).

The main topics discussed in the course of the council were the fate of the Order of the Temple, the renewal of the crusade, and the reform of the church. Although impressive delegations from Aragon, England, Sicily, Portugal, Castile, Cyprus, and France attended, most Christian rulers stayed away; only the dauphin of Viennois, John II, came to the opening session. The number of prelates present (between 144 and 170) was relatively small in comparison with the average ecclesiastical participation in thirteenth-century councils; furthermore, the committee system established in the council reduced its general sessions to three.

At the opening session Pope Clement V reported on the different stages in the prosecution of the Templars and alluded in general terms to the project of the crusade and to the difficult situation of the church. Though during the first sessions of the council most prelates advocated giving the Templars the chance to defend their order against the charge of heresy, Capetian pressure prevailed. On 3 April 1312 a great majority of prelates voted for the immediate abolition of the order by apostolic mandate. Without pronouncing a guilty verdict on the order as a whole, the constitution *Vox in excelso* decreed the abolition of the Order of the Temple because of the many flaws of its members, which had become evident during the five-year trial. Clement V appointed special commissioners to carry out the conciliar decisions throughout Christendom. Provincial councils were to decide the fate of the Templars. Those who were found innocent or who had submitted to the church were to be given a pension, drawn on the property of the order, in accordance with their respective status. Those who relapsed or remained impenitent were to be treated with the full rigor of canon law. All fugitives were ordered to appear before the relevant provincial council within one year, failing which they were to be declared heretics. The property of the order, probably a main factor in the arrest of the Templars by King Philip the Fair of France, was assigned to the Order of the Hospital on the grounds of the latter's efforts in the defense of Christendom.

Apart from the trial of the Templars, it was the business of a new crusade that received the highest priority in the deliberations. On 3 April 1312 Clement proclaimed a new *passagium generale* (major crusade expedition) overseas, its expense to be covered by the ecclesiastical establishment and its management to be entrusted to Philip IV the Fair. Philip took the cross in 1313, together with his three sons, his son-in-law Edward II of England, and many nobles, but the crusade never materialized.

In the field of church reform, the council objected to the infringement on ecclesiastical privileges by royal agents and to their readiness to condone crimes committed against the church. The prelates also accused the exempt orders (i.e., monastic orders subject only to the papacy) of encroaching on the rights of the secular clergy and eventually succeeded in restricting their prerogatives. Neither revolutionary nor conservative, on the whole the Council of Vienne maintained the doctrinaire path established by former ecumenical councils.

–*Sophia Menache*

Bibliography
Boyle, Leonard E., "A Committee Stage at the Council of Vienne," in *Studia in Honorem Eminentissimi Cardinalis Alphonsi M. Stickler,* ed. Rosalius Josephus Castillo Lara (Roma: Libreria Ateneo Salesiano, 1992), pp. 25–35.

Lecler, Joseph, "Vienne," in *Histoire des conciles oecuméniques,* 8, ed. Gervais Dumeige (Paris: Orante, 1964).

Müller, Ewald, *Das Konzil von Vienne (1311–1312), seine Quellen und seine Geschichte* (Münster: Aschendorff, 1934).

Wetzel, Lilian, *Le concile de Vienne, 1311–1312, et l'abolition de l'Ordre du Temple* (Paris: Dervy, 1993).

Villehardouin

See Geoffrey of Villehardouin (the Marshal)

Villehardouin Family

A noble French family from the area of Troyes in Champagne. In the wake of the Fourth Crusade (1202–1204), a branch of the Villehardouin family came to rule the Frankish principality of Achaia in southern Greece from 1209 to 1278.

The first known lord of Villehardouin was Vilain of Arxilleres, who had died by 1170, when the family is mentioned in the sources for the first time. His second son was Geoffrey (d. 1218), later chronicler of the Fourth Crusade, who became marshal of Champagne in 1185 and as such represented the count of Champagne on a number of diplomatic missions, including negotiations at Venice in 1201 to arrange transport of the crusading army to Egypt. As a member of the inner councils of the Fourth Crusade, Geoffrey provides insights into the organization and decision-making processes of the expedition. By 1208 he had been given the title of marshal of Romania, and he stayed in Greece until his death in 1218.

The chronicler's nephew Geoffrey I of Villehardouin established the family as princes of Achaia by substantially subduing the Morea in the years after 1209. He brought his wife from Champagne to Greece in 1210. In 1217 he arranged the marriage of his son, the future Geoffrey II (1228–1246), to Agnes of Courtenay, daughter of the Latin emperor of Constantinople. Geoffrey II succeeded as prince in 1228 and substantially established the hegemony of Achaia in Frankish Greece by the time of his death, without heirs, in 1246.

Geoffrey II's brother William, who had been born in Kalamata in 1210 and was recorded as fluent in Greek, followed him. William completed the conquest of the Morea by capturing Monemvasia and the district of Skorta, but he was forced to cede lands around Mistra in 1261 following his defeat at the battle of Pelagonia and subsequent captivity in Constantinople. In the face of Greek opposition from Mistra, he sought help from Charles I of Anjou, king of Naples. By the Treaty of Viterbo (1267), William became a vassal of Charles. He betrothed his daughter and heiress, Isabella, to Charles's son Philip; their children were to inherit the principality, and in the event of no heirs being born, the principality was to revert to the Angevin kings of Naples. The marriage took place at Trani in 1271. In 1277 Philip of Anjou died. The marriage was childless, and so when Prince William himself died on 1 May 1278, the principality passed to the Angevins of Naples.

In France the lands of Villehardouin passed to the heirs of Geoffrey, the marshal of Romania. His son Erard (1175/1180–1226) was mentioned as lord of Villehardouin as early as 1213. Erard's son William became marshal of Champagne in 1231 but was never referred to as lord of Villehardouin. He died in 1246.

–Peter Lock

See also: Achaia

Bibliography

Ilieva, Aneta, *Frankish Morea (1205–1262)* (Athens: Basilopoulos, 1991).

Lock, Peter, *The Franks in the Aegean* (London: Longman, 1995).

Longnon, Jean, *Recherches sur la vie de Geoffrey de Villehardouin suivies du catalogue des actes des Villehardouins* (Paris: Honoré Chapman, 1939).

Miller, William, *The Latins in the Levant* (London: Murray, 1908).

Morris, Colin, "Geoffrey de Villhardouin and the Conquest of Constantinople," *History* 53 (1968), 24–34.

Petit, Ernest, "Les Sires de Villehardouins," *Mémoires de la Société académique de l'Aube* 76 (1912), 11–80.

Setton, Kenneth, *The Papacy and the Levant,* vol. 1 (Philadelphia: American Philosophical Society, 1976).

Villiers de L'Isle Adam, Philippe (1464–1534)

Grand master of the Order of the Hospital of St. John of Jerusalem (1521–1534).

Born in Beauvais in France, Villiers de L'Isle Adam occupied various posts in the order (captain-general of the galleys, seneschal of Rhodes, grand hospitaller, and grand prior of France) before being elected grand master on 22 January 1521. Less than sixteen months later, the second

Ottoman siege of Rhodes (mod. Rodos, Greece) had begun. On 18 December the grand master surrendered to the Turks, and on 1 January 1523, along with the rest of the convent, the order's archives, and a few thousand inhabitants of Rhodes, he was allowed to leave the island in safety, proceeding to Rome via Crete and Sicily. On the death of Pope Adrian VI (November 1523), he and his knights were entrusted with guarding the conclave that elected Clement VII. Established temporarily at Viterbo, they spent eight years without a home, experiencing plague, war, famine, religious schism, and near institutional collapse. On 23 March 1530, they were granted the islands of Malta and Gozo and the North African fortress city of Tripoli (mod. Tarābulus, Libya) by Charles V, Holy Roman Emperor and king of Spain.

On Malta, Villiers de L'Isle Adam chose to reside in Fort St. Angelo, the medieval castle overlooking the Grand Harbour where the order's fleet anchored for the next 268 years. He died on 21 August 1534. By then he had summoned a general chapter, in an endeavor to restore the order's confidence, raise its morale, and reassess the value of its European estates. Through his initial legislation, he also set the tone and style of Hospitaller government for Malta.

–*Victor Mallia-Milanes*

See also: Hospital, Order of the
Bibliography
Setton, Kenneth M., *The Papacy and the Levant 1204–1571*, 4 vols. (Philadelphia: American Philosophical Society, 1976–1984).
Schermerhorn, Elizabeth W., *Malta of the Knights* (Kingswood, UK: Heinemann, 1929).

Vincent of Kraków

See Wincenty Kadłubek

Vironia

Vironia (mod. Virumaa, Estonia; Ger. *Wierland*) was a province of medieval Livonia on the southern coast of the Gulf of Finland, roughly situated between the rivers Loop, Valgejõgi, and Narva.

In 1217 German crusaders from Riga raided Vironia for the first time, but in the following years the province was subjected by the Danes from Reval, although the Germans persisted in their claims. It was only the Treaty of Stensby (1238) that definitively placed the province under the rule of the king of Denmark.

Most of the land in Vironia was enfeoffed to the vassals of the king. According to the land register known as the *Liber Census Daniae,* the most powerful among the new magnates was Dietrich von Kievel; some native Estonians also appear among the lesser vassals. During the Danish period, the two main urban centers of Vironia were Wesenberg (mod. Rakvere, Estonia), at the foot of a royal castle, and the economically more important town of Narva on the eastern frontier. In 1346, along with the rest of Danish Estonia, Vironia was sold to the Teutonic Order.

Bailiwicks of the order were established in Wesenberg and Narva, and during the fifteenth century the order erected the new castles of Tolsburg on the coast and Neuschloß on the northern shore of Lake Peipus, where the river Narva exits the lake. In 1558 the Russians were able to quickly conquer most of Vironia. Along with the rest of Estonia, it came under Swedish rule in the 1580s.

–*Juhan Kreem*

Bibliography
Johansen, Paul, *Die Estlandliste des Liber Census Daniae* (Kopenhagen: Hagerup, 1933).
Koguteos Virumaa, ed. Kalju Saaber (Tallinn: Lääne-Viru Maavalitsus, Ida-Viru Maavalitsus, 1996).

Votia

Votia (Ger. *Watland*, Russ. *Vodskaya zemlya*) was the land situated between the river Narva, the southern shore of the Gulf of Finland, and the Izhorian plateau. The native population, related to the northeastern Estonians, were the Votians (Russ. *Vod'* or *Vozhane*). The authentic native names are Vad'jalaizet or Vatjalane. The Votians are first mentioned in written sources from the second half of the eleventh century, when their land was incorporated into the Novgorodian state. The first invasion via Votia into Novgorodian territory by Estonians subject to the Order of the Sword Brethren occurred in the winter of 1221–1222.

In the first half of the thirteenth century, the Votians were mostly pagans. Their nobles resented the growing power of the Novgorodian rulers; by the end of the 1230s Roman Catholic preaching among the Votians and other Finnic peoples of the Novgorodian state resulted in a number of Votian noblemen promising to embrace the Latin faith, hoping that the Livonians would help free them from Novgorodian rule. In the winter of 1240–1241, the Teutonic Knights from Livonia and the Estonian vassals of the Danish crown occupied Votia and built a fortress at Kopor'e in concert with the Votian social elite. According to an agreement between the order and the bishop of Ösel (13 April 1241), the bishop was to have ecclesiastical authority over any newly conquered lands, while temporal power would belong to the Livonian order. Late in 1241 the order and its allies were expelled from Novgorodian territory by Prince Alexander Yaroslavich, who destroyed the fortress and hanged the Votian traitors.

Archaeological evidence suggests that after these events the Russian Orthodox church made a more active attempt to convert the Finnic peoples to Christianity. At the same time, Roman Catholic attempts at conversion continued. Around 1257 Frederick of Gaseldorf was ordained as bishop of Kopor'e (or Karelia). The new bishopric, which was to depend on the archbishopric of Riga, was meant to be established during a new offensive that was planned for the end of the 1260s. These plans failed and were not renewed after the signing of the Russian-Livonian treaty of 1270.

–Evgeniya L. Nazarova

Bibliography

Gadzyatskii, Sergei S., "Водская и Ижорская земли Новгородского государства," Исторические записки 6 (1940), 100–148.

Nazarova, Evgeniya L., "The Crusades against Votians and Izhorians in the Thirteenth Century," in *Crusade and Conversion on the Baltic Frontier, 1150–1500,* ed. Alan V. Murray (Aldershot, UK: Ashgate, 2001), pp. 177–195.

Ryabinin, Evgenii A., "Водь," in Финны в Европе, VI-XV века, ed. Anatolii N. Kirpichnikov and Evgenii A. Ryabinin, 2 vols. (Moskva: Nauka, 1990), 2:15–31.

Vow

The crusade vow was the means that transformed an individual's inner conversion and intention to participate in an armed expedition in defense of the Holy Land or Christendom against Muslims, pagans, heretics, or other enemies of the church into a penitentially and legally binding obligation.

Development and Implications of the Crusading Vow

Retrospectively described by chroniclers and scholars as the fusion of holy war with the Jerusalem pilgrimage, the First Crusade (1096–1099) appealed to the knightly classes as a form of arduous yet temporary renunciation of the world close in penitential efficacy to the permanent adoption of the monastic life, which was unavailable to those committed to a life of temporal warfare. At the same time, although Pope Urban II seems to have intended to recruit knights to serve the Byzantine emperor against the Muslims, it was the pope's focus on the popular pilgrimage site of Jerusalem as the ultimate goal of service in the *militia Christi* (knighthood of Christ) that led many noncombatants to join the crusade.

The terminology, ritual, and spiritual imagery of the new expeditions to the Holy Land remained tightly tied to the concept of pilgrimage. Legally and spiritually, crusaders were viewed as pilgrims. From the Council of Clermont (1095) onward, crusaders usually had crosses sewn on their clothing as an outward sign of the obligations inherent in their vows. Yet a distinctive liturgical rite for bestowing the crusader's cross was slow to develop; when it did, it was modeled closely on existing ceremonies used to mark an individual's solemn vow of pilgrimage through the blessing and bestowal of the pilgrim's distinctive insignia, the staff and scrip (wallet), before his or her departure. Some individuals received their tokens from a priest or chaplain in a relatively private atmosphere, while others took their crosses and vows in the rather more public setting of a clerical or secular court or during the revivalism that characterized the galvanizing sermons preached by local clergymen or crusade recruiters. Moreover, the term *crucesignatus* (one signed with the cross) gradually began to supplement the term *peregrinus* (pilgrim) as a title for individuals who had taken the crusade vow only during the twelfth century. The full or partial remission of the penance enjoined for confessed sins (known as the indulgence) granted to crusaders also remained mentally linked to the full remission believed to be earned by an unarmed pilgrimage to Jerusalem and the partial remissions granted to those journeying to other holy sites.

Not until the period of the late twelfth to late thirteenth centuries was the theory of the crusade vow fully developed in canon law and the privileges and rules governing the vow's obligations and the legal enforcement of them systematically defined and elaborated. For, as in the case of a vow of pilgrimage, the crusader's vow placed him in a category of persons temporarily granted privileges and responsibilities normally reserved for secular ecclesiastics or those who had taken the vows of poverty, chastity, and obedience required for entry in a religious order. Such privileges and responsibilities included the adoption of distinctive clothing or habit and varying degrees of dietary and sexual abstinence. In fact, the crusade was often viewed as an ideal preparation or substitution for entry into monastic life.

The crusade vow and the penalty of excommunication for failing to fulfill it (or for doing so in a dilatory fashion) enabled the mustering of organized military campaigns, and the obligations and privileges attached to its adoption evolved over time, as did the categories of persons considered capable of taking it. From the First Crusade onward, attempts were made to prevent unfree serfs, minors, secular clergymen, and monks and nuns sworn to obedience and stability in the cloister from making the crusade vow without their superior's permission. Married persons were also urged not to take the cross without their spouse's consent. Other groups considered to present logistical burdens or temptation to crusading armies were periodically discouraged from taking the cross or from fulfilling their crusade vow by personally participating in a military expedition, including young single women, the poor or physically debilitated, the aged and very young, and those lacking both military skill and the funds necessary to subsidize contingents of trained fighters. For this very reason, until the pontificate of Innocent III (1198–1216), individuals were urged to confess their sins and be vetted by a clergyman for suitability before taking the cross. However, limited numbers of some categories of noncombatants were considered potentially valuable to the crusader host, including clergymen necessary for moral leadership and provision of the sacraments, experienced albeit aged fighters, merchants, artisans, laundresses, and farmers.

Confessors and ecclesiastical and secular courts in regions with a long tradition of penitential pilgrimages also imposed the crusade vow upon those guilty of serious crimes or notorious sins, including violence against ecclesiastics, murder, arson, sacrilege, sorcery, illegal trading with Muslim powers, heresy, and clerical incontinence or pluralism. Such a penance or judicial penalty was viewed by many as an honorable or attractive alternative to humiliating public penances, heavy fines, mutilation, or the death penalty. Increasingly, deceased individuals' heirs were considered liable to fulfill crusading vows assumed both voluntarily and involuntarily, whether in person or through the provision of a substitute or donation. Although in principle the crusade was meant to enable perpetrators to expiate their sins and earn spiritual benefits for their victims while temporarily shielding them from vengeance, reformers complained that the Holy Land had become a dumping ground for moral undesirables, who, removed from the strictures of their kin, culture, and native laws, earned God's ire by their recidivist turpitude.

Privileges Attached to the Crusading Vow

As the privileges attached to the crusading vow were increasingly defined, elaborated, and enforced, many assumed the cross in order to obtain the temporal and spiritual benefits it provided. In addition to the various indulgences offered to those participating in the crusading movement, *crucesignati* shared in the spiritual credit generated by prayers and liturgies organized for the crusades. As pilgrims, they were allowed to deal with excommunicates and receive the sacraments in regions under interdict. They could sometimes choose their own confessors, who like crusade preachers were often granted the ability to absolve *crucesignati* from excommunication and other irregularities normally requiring an arduous journey to Rome. Reformers complained that the cynical used these concessions to escape the penitential jurisdiction of their local parish priests and bishops, to circumvent the arduous penances or excommunications imposed upon them for sins or crimes, and to avoid making restitution to their victims.

From the First Crusade onward, crusaders were also promised papal protection of their persons, property, and households until their return or certain evidence of their death, a privilege enforced by the power of excommunication and interdict wielded by local prelates. However, surviving petitions and court records show that these spiritual penalties were disregarded by many eager to wreak revenge upon the crusader's vulnerable family or encroach upon undefended lands by violence or lawsuits. Some crusaders obtained individualized papal letters of protection; popes threatened to punish prelates who failed to shield crusaders and called upon secular rulers to stop encroachments by force if necessary.

Crusaders also enjoyed certain legal and financial privileges that evolved over time. Enumerated, extended, and clarified in papal letters written in response to specific cases, they received one of their most elaborated and authoritative descriptions in Innocent III's bull *Ad liberandam* (1215), which became a crucial authority cited by canon lawyers who continually redefined crusaders' privileges and the institutions of the crusading movement. To enable clergymen to personally participate in various expeditions, ecclesiastical crusaders were exempted from the income taxes levied on diocesan and regular churches for the crusade. Those with benefices were freed from the usual residence requirements and were allowed to either mortgage or continue receiving the incomes attached to them for up to three years, provided that they remained on crusade and appointed a vicar to minister in their absence if pastoral responsibilities were attached to their office. By 1145, if their lords or relatives were unable or unwilling to lend them money, laypersons were allowed to sell or mortgage inalienable lands to raise funds for their journey and were also granted a moratorium on paying interest on debts contracted before, and in some instances, after they took the cross, until their return.

Later popes attempted to extend these financial privileges to include freedom from payments on the principal of debts and exemption from all taxes and tolls, as well as from levies instituted for the crusade such as the Saladin Tithe (1188). Prelates were called upon to enforce these privileges with excommunication and interdict, and secular rulers were urged to force Jews in their lands to remit interest on crusaders' debts and make restitution of any interest already charged. Crusaders soon found, however, that creditors were reluctant to lend them money unless they waived their privileges, and some secular and ecclesiastical magnates proved notoriously reluctant to restrict the incomes of the Jewish and Christian moneylenders to whom they lent protection in return for lucrative taxation. Secular rulers also proved loath to exempt crusaders from feudal duties (including military service), taxation, and tallages, particularly in times of war or when a significant percentage of the population took the cross.

As pilgrims, crusaders were also entitled to expedite or delay legal proceedings initiated after they took the cross and to enjoy freedom from all lawsuits concerning possessions held peacefully and without dispute before taking the crusade vow. As temporary religious, they could also opt for trial in ecclesiastical courts. As with clerical immunity from prosecution in secular courts, this privilege became the object of much jurisdictional wrangling between secular rulers and the papacy and local ecclesiastics, resulting finally in compositions that specified that in cases arising after individuals took the cross, they could be tried in church courts except in instances involving property or serious crimes, which fell under feudal and royal law. These compositions redressed rulers' concerns regarding lawlessness, defaulting on loans, and the abuse of legal privileges by those who, like Gerald of Wales, became *crucesignati* in order to gain advantage in ongoing lawsuits. By the thirteenth century, popes sought to restrict abuses by stressing that those who took the crusade vow in prison forfeited any special legal privileges, while appointing crusade preachers and legates to supplement local prelates as official protectors of crusaders' rights. Innocent III extended many of these rights to those involved in crusades other than those destined for the Holy Land, including the crusade against heretics in southern France, and enshrined them in *Ad liberandam,* which became the basis for crusading bulls' declarations of crusaders' privileges and obligations throughout the thirteenth century.

Dispensation from and Redemption of Crusading Vows

From the 1190s onward, immense developments took place in the definition of the precise nature of the duties attached to the crusade vow and the possibility of dispensations from it. A dispensation meant the relaxation of the original terms of the vow because of unavoidable circumstances preventing its fulfillment, such as grave or permanent disability, illness, poverty, public necessity such as the safety of the realm, or old age. Dispensations could include fulfilling one's pilgrimage through a hired substitute, the commutation of its obligations into an alternative pilgrimage goal or charitable work, and its redemption through a donation of the funds that would otherwise have been spent in personally fulfilling the vow to a crusade or another charitable cause. Boundaries between redemptions of the full crusading vow and voluntary donations to the crusading effort rewarded by partial indulgences could be easily blurred, particularly when groups of impoverished crusaders banded together to subsidize one fighter as a substitute.

During the period when individuals were required to seek the permission of their spouse and temporal and spiritual superiors before taking the vow, and were theoretically examined for their ability to fulfill its obligations before being allowed to take it, dispensations were granted only under strict circumstances. Although bishops possessed the ability to dispense from pilgrimage vows, popes attempted to reserve the ability to absolve individuals from the crusade vow to themselves and their delegates, who were ideally meant to weigh the particulars of each case and prescribe fitting penitential alternatives. Typically, up until and throughout the pontificate of Innocent III, a combination of poverty and infirmity was necessary to justify redeeming the crusade vow. Those unable to fight in person or provide aid to the crusading army through providing sacramental services, spiritual exhortation, military advice, or contingents of fighters could redeem or commute their vows, and those whose absence on crusade would prove dangerous to their lands or realm could delay their fulfillment.

These general guidelines partly reflected the attempts of secular rulers to rid crusading armies of noncombatants and convert the desire of pious noncombatants for personal participation in the crusade enterprise into monetary subsidy of trained fighters. The priorities of noblemen often responsible for organizing crusade contingents thus often conflicted with the desire of many poor noncombatants to personally participate in expeditions. And even though some popes often wanted to enable the participation of as many penitents as possible and believed that all physically capable of fulfilling their vows ought to make the journey, they were also responsible for ensuring the military viability of crusade expeditions. From the First Crusade onward, attempts were made to discourage monks, women, the poor, the weak, and the elderly from taking the cross, until Innocent III called for crusade preachers to give the vow to whoever desired it without first examining their ability to fulfill it or requiring permission from their spouse or superiors. Many historians have seen in this declaration a prescient attempt to hijack the crusade vow and use it to secure support for papal crusade policy or deliberately convert the devotion of the faithful into the financial subsidy of professional fighters. In fact, Innocent III seems to have followed reformers from Peter the Chanter's school in Paris who saw the crusade vow as the means of signifying and institutionalizing the penitential fervor required of the home and foreign fronts for the crusades' success. He appears to have intended that alms gathered during crusade preaching and processions and the institution of a clerical income tax would subsidize the financially insolvent but hardy poor. To this end, he deferred the examination and dispensation of crusaders until just before the crusading expedition departed, when those who could not be subsidized or were unfit to participate could commute, redeem, or delay their vows.

By the time of the Fourth Lateran Council (1215), however, Innocent had come under pressure from military leaders who worried about being burdened with the poor and militarily useless. *Ad liberandam* made no mention of indiscriminate signing, and soon weak or poor individuals were urged to and, by the mid-thirteenth century, often forced to redeem their vows by donating money to the crusade. Commutations followed a similar pattern, from the voluntary commutation of goals from the Holy Land to the antiheretical crusade and vice versa under Innocent III, to attempts by Gregory IX and Innocent IV to force individuals to transfer their vows for the Holy Land to aid for the Latin Empire of Constantinople and the papal struggle against Emperor Frederick II. Gradually, despite continuing manifestations of populist enthusiasm for personal participation, the vast majority of vows made during preaching tours, which were increasingly organized by members of the mendicant orders, were almost immediately redeemed for money granted to those organizing crusade contingents to subsidize trained *milites* and professional soldiers.

Terms for the Fulfillment of Crusading Vows

In this and other instances, policies were not merely mandated in a top-down fashion by the papacy, but were formed as the result of a dialogue between the pope, legates and crusade preachers, local clergymen, the military leaders of the crusade, and *crucesignati* of all stripes. This is particularly true in the case of the discussion of precisely what kind and what length of service was considered necessary to fulfill the crusade vow. Although many crusaders considered their vows completed when they had attained their pilgrimage goal of the Holy Sepulchre in Jerusalem, once the vow became severed from the journey to Jerusalem, the period of military service considered necessary to fulfill one's vow became the subject of debate. Popes occasionally set a period of one to three years for crusades to the Holy Land in papal bulls, although the term needed to gain the plenary indulgence was often left unspecified. In the case of the Albigensian Crusade (1209–1229), Innocent III delegated the decision to the men he appointed to organize the crusade in France, who specified the forty-day period typical of the military service owed by vassals to their lord as the minimum needed to earn the plenary indulgence. Departure dates and locations were often set in bulls outlining the organization of a crusade, and papally appointed preachers responsible for organizing crusading contingents in a certain diocese or region were often urged to ensure that a sufficient army materialized by threatening to excommunicate those who did not leave in a timely fashion from the appointed ports. However, dates and departure points often became the subject for negotiation, as local crusaders experienced trouble in finding funding or settling disputes. For example, many of the common crusaders in the Fifth Crusade (1217–1221) complained that while delays had been granted to the noblemen expected to lead local contingents, they were being threatened with excommunication if they failed to depart at the date set by the Fourth Lateran council, despite the fact that the funding meant to subsidize them had been granted to these same noblemen, who refused to disburse it. Some became so frustrated that they simply tore off their crosses and refused to fulfill their vows. Similarly, crusaders often considered their vow fulfilled and left the army once their funding ran out or once a significant military or devotional objective had been obtained.

During the Third Crusade (1189–1192), Richard I of England refused to proceed directly to Jerusalem, for fear that his army would dissolve before the outlying regions necessary to protect the city had been taken. During the Fifth Crusade, the papal legate Pelagius attempted to stem the flood of crusaders planning to depart after the capture of Damietta (1219) before crucial reinforcements arrived, by threatening to excommunicate anyone who left without obtaining a letter of permission from him. Letters were also sent to recruiting centers in Europe broadcasting the legatine excommunication of those who had deserted the army prematurely or had failed to join the army in Egypt, demanding that they be forced to return to fulfill their vows. These events illustrate that, in the end, the conditions for the fulfillment of the crusade vow remained open to debate, even during a period that saw great advancements in the institutionalization of the crusading movement.

–*Jessalynn Bird*

Bibliography

Bird, Jessalynn, "Innocent III, Peter the Chanter's Circle, and the Crusade Indulgence: Theory, Implementation, and Aftermath," in *Innocenzo III: Urbs et Orbis,* ed. Andrea Sommerlechner, 2 vols. (Roma: Istituto storico italiano per il Medio Evo, 2002), 1:504–524.

Brundage, James A., "'Crucesignari': The Rite for Taking the Cross in England," *Traditio* 22 (1966), 289–310.

———, "The Votive Obligations of Crusaders: The Development of a Canonistic Doctrine," *Traditio* 24 (1968), 77–118.

———, *Canon Law and the Crusader* (Madison: University of Wisconsin Press, 1969).

———, "Crusaders and Jurists: The Legal Consequences of Crusader Status," in *Le Concile de Clermont de 1095 et l'appel à la croisade, Clermont-Ferrand, June, 1995* (Rome: Ecole française de Rome, 1997), pp. 141–154.

———, "Immortalizing the Crusades: Law and Institutions," in *Montjoie: Studies in Crusade History in Honour of Hans Eberhard Mayer,* ed. Benjamin Z. Kedar, Jonathan Riley-Smith, and Rudolf Hiestand (Aldershot, UK: Variorum, 1997), pp. 251–260.

Evans, Michael R., "Commutation of Crusade Vows: Some Examples from the English Midlands," in *From Clermont to Jerusalem: The Crusades and Crusader Societies, 1095–1500,* ed. Alan V. Murray (Turnhout: Brepols, 1998), pp. 219–229.

Markowski, Mark, "Crucesignatus: Its Origin and Early Usage," *Journal of Medieval History* 10 (1984), 157–165.

Pennington, Kenneth, "The Rite of Taking the Cross in the Twelfth Century," *Traditio* 30 (1974), 429–435.

Purcell, Maureen, *Papal Crusading Policy: The Chief Instruments of Papal Crusading Policy and the Crusade to the Holy Land from the Final Loss of Jerusalem to the Fall of Acre, 1244–1291* (Leiden: Brill, 1975).

Riley-Smith, Jonathan, *The First Crusaders, 1095–1131* (Cambridge: Cambridge University Press, 1997).

Siberry, Elizabeth, *Criticism of Crusading: 1095–1274* (Oxford: Oxford University Press, 1985).

Tyerman, Christopher, *England and the Crusades, 1095–1588* (Chicago: University of Chicago Press, 1988).

———, *The Invention of the Crusades* (Toronto: University of Toronto Press, 1998).

Vytautas (d. 1430)

Grand duke of Lithuania (1392–1430), who broke the power of the Teutonic Order and brought medieval Lithuania to the peak of its might.

Vytautas (Germ., Pol. *Witold*, Russ. *Vitovt*) was born around 1350, the son of Kęstutis, duke of Trakai, and Birutė of Palanga. He was meant to succeed his father in Trakai and to co-rule the grand duchy of Lithuania with Jogaila, the son of Grand Duke Algirdas. But after Algirdas died, the Teutonic Order provoked a conflict between Kęstutis and Jogaila. In 1382 Kęstutis was murdered, but Vytautas managed to escape to Prussia. There he persuaded the Teutonic Order to wage war against Jogaila in his favor. In 1384 Vytautas was received into the Roman Catholic Church (taking the baptismal name Wigand) and granted the order the strategic western Lithuanian territory of Samogitia, which lay between the order's possessions in Prussia and Livonia. But soon Jogaila offered him peace, and Vytautas returned to Lithuania, receiving Grodno and later, Lutsk. Vytautas converted to the Orthodox form of Christianity, but when Jogaila was baptized into the Roman Catholic faith on becoming king of Poland (1386), Vytautas also converted back to Catholicism (with the new name Alexander). However, as Jogaila failed to keep his promise to return Trakai, Vytautas fled to Prussia again in 1390 and fought against Jogaila with the help of the Teutonic Order until peace was concluded. In 1392 Jogaila was forced to recognize Vytautas as grand duke of Lithuania.

In 1398 Vytautas granted Samogitia to the Teutonic Order again, in the hope of gaining a respite from its attacks. He also tried to exploit the idea of the crusade by applying its ideology to his own war against the Mongols of the Golden Horde, but his crusade ended in defeat at Vorskla (1399). Then Vytautas organized a Samogitian rebellion (1401). The struggle was complicated by wars in Rus', and in 1404 Vytautas had to give up his claims on Samogitia once more, but in 1409 he organized a new rebellion and finally succeeded in liberating Samogitia. Next year Vytautas and Jogaila marched on Prussia, and at the battle of Tannenberg (15 July 1410) they inflicted on the Teutonic Order its greatest ever defeat. In 1411 the order conceded Samogitia to Vytautas for his lifetime, although he sought a permanent recognition of his possession, claiming that Samogitia was "our heritage and patrimony . . . which is and always was one and the same with the land of Lithuania due to the same language and the same people" [*Codex epistolaris Vitoldi, magni ducis Lithuaniae, 1376–1430,* ed. Antoni Prochaska (Cracoviae: Academia Literarum, 1882), p. 467].

As the dispute over Samogitia continued, Vytautas and Jogaila strengthened the Lithuanian-Polish alliance, formalizing it through the Union of Horodlo (1413); they imposed Christianity on Samogitia (1413) and established a diocese there.

Vytautas also gave support to the Hussites and was elected king of Bohemia (1421–1423), thus preventing Emperor Sigismund from providing active support for the Teutonic Order. In 1422 Vytautas and Jogaila attacked Prussia again and forced the final recognition of Samogitia as a Lithuanian possession. Thereafter Vytautas's relationship with the order improved, as he sought to rid Lithuania of Polish suzerainty. In 1429 Emperor Sigismund offered to have Vytautas crowned as king of Lithuania, but this overture was undermined by the Polish nobility. Vytautas died on 27 October 1430. He was succeeded by Švitrigaila, brother of Jogaila.

Vytautas was married twice: to Anna (d. 1418), then to Juliana, both of Lithuanian origin. His daughter from the first marriage, Sofia, married Grand Duke Vasilii I of Moscow.

–*Tomas Baranauskas*

Bibliography

Koncius, Joseph B., *Vytautas the Great, Grand Duke of Lithuania* (Miami: Franklin, 1964).

Pfitzner, Josef, *Großfürst Witold von Litauen als Staatsmann* (Brünn: Rohrer, 1930).

Urban, William, *Tannenberg and After: Lithuania, Poland, and the Teutonic Order in Search of Immortality,* 3d ed. (Chicago: Lithuanian Research and Studies Center, 2003).

W

Waldemar

See Valdemar

Walter the Chancellor

The author of a Latin text known as the *Bella Antiochena,* which deals with the "Antiochene Wars," that is, the campaigns fought against the Turks by the Franks of the principality of Antioch between 1115 and 1119.

Walter is known only through two references to himself made in his work; he is not recorded in any charter or witness list, although he was chancellor of Antioch between about 1114 and about 1122. Thus when he records that "the chancellor" was consulted by Roger, prince of Antioch, on the eve of the battle of the *Ager Sanguinis* (Field of Blood) in 1119, this is a reference to his own part in the events he narrates. That Walter was educated as a cleric is a safe assumption, which is borne out by his use of biblical and liturgical allusions, and also by his explicit intent to demonstrate the workings of divine will. His work comprises two books: the first recounts the Antiochenes' triumphant campaign against Bursuq of Hamadan in 1115; the second their disastrous defeat at the hands of Īlghāzī of Aleppo in 1119. Although Walter exploits the contrast between initial success and defeat in book 2, nothing in book 1 foreshadows the later reverses: it was apparently originally intended to stand alone as a record of a great victory.

As an eyewitness, Walter left an invaluable account. He probably accompanied Roger on the 1115 campaign and was almost certainly present when Roger was killed at the *Ager Sanguinis*. He was probably among those taken prisoner afterward: he says that his vivid description of the torments of the Christian captives derives from his own eyewitness experience.

–Susan B. Edgington

Bibliography
Asbridge, Thomas, *The Creation of the Principality of Antioch, 1098–1130* (Woodbridge, UK: Boydell, 2000).

Cahen, Claude, *La Syrie du Nord à l'époque des croisades et la principauté franque d'Antioche* (Paris: Geuthner, 1940).

Galterii Cancellarii Bella Antiochena, ed. Heinrich Hagenmeyer (Innsbruck: Wagner'sche Universitäts-Buchhandlung, 1896).

Walter the Chancellor's The Antiochene Wars: A Translation and Commentary, trans. Thomas Asbridge and Susan B. Edgington (Aldershot, UK: Ashgate, 1999).

Walter Mahomet

A nobleman in the kingdom of Jerusalem, who is attested as lord or castellan of Hebron between 1107/1108 and 1115. He is known to have accompanied King Baldwin I on a military expedition to the north in 1111. Nothing is known of his origins, although his name may indicate that, unusually for a member of the ruling class of the kingdom, he may have been a converted Muslim.

–Alan V. Murray

Bibliography
Mayer, Hans Eberhard, "Die Herrschaftsbildung in Hebron," *Zeitschrift des Deutschen Palästinavereins* 101 (1985), 64–82.

Murray, Alan V., *The Crusader Kingdom of Jerusalem: A Dynastic History, 1099–1125* (Oxford: Prosopographica et Genealogica, 2000).

Walter Sans-Avoir (d. 1096)

A military commander in one of the contingents of the so-called People's Crusades of 1096. Although Walter's surname has sometimes been translated into English as "the Penniless," it more probably derives from the village of Boissy-Sans-Avoir, west of Paris.

In the spring of 1096 Walter and his uncle (also called Walter) were inspired by the preaching of Peter the Hermit, but rather than following him, they departed with a separate band of crusaders via Cologne and Hungary, arriving (the first contingent of the People's Crusades to do so) in Constantinople (mod. İstanbul, Turkey) in July 1096. They crossed the Bosporus into Bithynia along with Peter the Hermit's main army and crusader groups from northern Italy (6 August 1096), and this combined force based itself at the fortress of Kibotos on the Sea of Marmara to await the arrival of further armies. Walter seems to have been recognized as military commander among the French crusaders during Peter's absence in Constantinople, but he was unable to prevent crusader incursions into the territory of Qilij Arslān I, sultan of Rūm, who annihilated a German-Lombard force that had seized a castle called Xerigordon. Walter was killed when, against his counsel, the remaining crusaders at Kibotos marched out to confront the approaching Turkish forces and were rapidly ambushed and routed (October 1096).

–Alan V. Murray

Bibliography

Murray, Alan V., "Walther Duke of Teck: The Invention of a German Hero of the First Crusade," *Medieval Prosopography* 19 (1998), 35–54.

Runciman, Steven, *A History of the Crusades,* vol. 1 (Cambridge: Cambridge University Press, 1951).

Walther von der Vogelweide

The greatest medieval German lyric poet and first exponent of German political poetry, active in the period 1190–1230. A clerically educated professional singer, he was the first nonchivalric German poet of crusade.

Walther composed four songs of recruitment and religious motivation and some twenty topical verses commenting on crusading issues within the broader context of imperial and papal politics. He had many patrons, including King Philip, the emperors Otto IV and Frederick II, Landgrave Hermann of Thuringia, the Austrian dukes Frederick and Leopold VI, and Wolfger, bishop of Passau and patriarch of Aquileia, as well as lesser magnates, such as Diether of Katzenellenbogen. Frederick II conferred an unspecified fief on him around the year 1220.

Walther's four crusading songs cannot be firmly dated. *Owe, waz eren sich ellendet von tiuschen landen* ("Alas, how honor flees the German lands") [*Walther von der Vogelweide,* ed. Cormeau, L 13, 5–32] is an eschatological summons to penance. In *Vil süeze waere minne* ("Most sweet true love," L 76, 22–78, 23), a meditation on divine love and redemptive sacrifice, each stanza ends with an appeal to liberate Jerusalem. The song's metrical form resembles Latin hymns. Both of these songs speak in the collective first-person plural. *Nu alrest lebe ich mir werde* ("Now at last my life has worth," L 14, 38–16, 35), also known as the *Palästinalied* (Palestine Song), voices the pilgrim's first-person singular celebration of treading in the earthly footsteps of Christ, visiting the scenes of Nativity, Passion, Resurrection, and anticipating Judgment and God's adjudication that Christians are rightful heirs of his earthly kingdom. Walther's melody for this song survives, based on Latin hymn types. *Owe, war sint verswunden alliu miniu jar* ("Alas, where has my whole life vanished," L 124, 1–125, 10) contains a personal lament for his exclusion, as "needy man" (III, 11), from the rewards of the chivalric crusader. He depicts the courtly world suddenly stricken with disaster, pleads for penitence, and beseeches the knighthood to seize the offer of redemption, "the dear journey overseas" (III, 15). The catalyst of spiritual crisis is "stern letters from Rome" (II, 9). The song has traditionally been linked with the excommunication of Emperor Frederick II in 1228, despite Walther's polemics since 1201 against papal abuse of spiritual sanctions against German kings.

In his political satires, Walther comments frequently on crusading issues. He castigates Duke Leopold V and Duke Frederick I of Austria for holding King Richard the Lionheart to ransom after his return from crusade; urges Emperor Otto IV to lead a crusade after his imperial coronation in 1209; lampoons Pope Innocent III for the crusade tax of 1213; and praises Leopold VI of Austria for crusading in 1219. Repeatedly he urges Frederick II to fulfill his crusading vow, though he defends him from critics in Germany and Rome, and he reminds the archangels that even they have left the heathen unscathed.

–Jeffrey Ashcroft

Bibliography

Ashcroft, Jeffrey, "Die Anfänge von Walthers politischer Lyrik," in *Minnesang in Österreich,* ed. Helmut Birkhan (Wien: Halosar, 1983), pp. 1–24.

Nix, Matthias, "Der Kreuzzugsaufruf Walthers im Ottenton und der Kreuzzugsplan Kaiser Ottos IV," *Germanisch-Romanische Monatsschrift,* n.s., 34 (1984), 278–294.

Ranawake, Silvia, "Untersuchungen zur Frage der lyrischen Gattungen am Beispiel von Walthers Kreuzzugsdichtung," in *Lied im deutschen Mittelalter,* ed. Cyril Edwards, Ernst Hellgardt, and Norbert C. Ott (Tübingen: Niemeyer, 1996), pp. 67–80.

Walther von der Vogelweide: Leich, Lieder, Sangsprüche, ed. Christoph Cormeau (Berlin: de Gruyter, 1996).

Wentzlaff-Eggebert, Friedrich Wilhelm, *Kreuzzugsdichtung des Mittelalters* (Berlin: De Gruyter, 1960).

Warfare: The Baltic Crusades

In nineteenth- and twentieth-century literature on the history of war, warfare in the Baltic region at the time of the crusades is mentioned only marginally, because the Christianization and subjection of the pagan Finno-Ugrian and Baltic tribes to the south and east of the Baltic Sea between the twelfth and fourteenth centuries largely occurred without the kind of highlights that lend themselves to the writing of grand narrative. Decisive battles were rare, and warfare mostly consisted of expeditions for the purposes of looting and devastation. During the last few decades, however, this type of warfare has attracted increasing attention not only from scholars in Germany and the modern countries in what once were the target areas of crusading, but also from English-speaking historians. The best known aspect of the Baltic Crusades is the century-long war against the Lithuanians, which ended in 1410 with the disastrous defeat of the Teutonic Order at Tannenberg (also known in Polish as *Grunwald* and Lithuanian as *Žalgiris*). That battle can be seen as the final point of the crusading era in the Baltic region.

Not only heathens but also the Greek Orthodox Christians of Russia, regarded as "schismatics" by the Roman Catholic (Latin) Church, were targets for the crusades. One main theater of war in this respect was the inner part of the Gulf of Finland, where the Swedes fought with the Novgorodian state for control of important trade routes. The Livonian branch of the Teutonic Order also tried to expand its territory at the expense of Novgorod but had to give up this undertaking after a defeat in 1242.

Except for the Lithuanians, the heathen tribes in the Baltic had not yet begun any process of nation building, which is one important reason why the early and successful expansion of the numerically much inferior Christians was possible. The crusaders profited from the rivalry and hostility between the tribes, using the old technique of divide and rule to secure victory and expand. Through alliances with some tribes, others could be fought and defeated. Thereafter the allies were often ready to accept Christian protection and domination and to convert to the new faith. Within the sphere of influence of the military religious orders, Christianity mostly spread by force, by means of the so-called mission of the sword (Ger. *Schwertmission*).

Any peaceful coexistence of the heathen tribes in the Baltic region before the arrival of the crusaders was the exception rather than the rule. Just as modern anthropology has ascertained that the descriptions of the idyllic life of the indigenous peoples on the Pacific islands given by Margaret Mead in her book *Coming of Age in Samoa* (1928) are highly exaggerated, a reading of the chronicle of the thirteenth-century writer Henry of Livonia provides proof that similar romantic ideas about the heathen tribes in the eastern Baltic do not correspond to reality. Equally, it would be a mistake to think that the Christians in the Baltic region were always united. There were numerous tensions and conflicts between the military orders and the bishop (after 1250 archbishop) of Riga; in 1233 there was even a fierce battle between the Order of the Sword Brethren and papal troops in Reval (mod. Tallinn, Estonia), in which the former were victorious.

Recorded history in the Baltic region mostly derives from the victors; only the Greek Orthodox Christians of Russia had a written culture like that of the Latin West from the beginning of the crusade period. The pagan tribes in Finland, Livonia, and Prussia left no written records. In Lithuania diplomatic correspondence gradually developed, but there were no early Lithuanian chronicles; the first appeared only at the beginning of the sixteenth century, written in Belorussian. For that reason research is heavily dependent on Russian annals and chronicles and, above all, the many important chronicles from the crusader states of Livonia and Prussia: the *Chronicle* of Henry of Livonia, the *Livonian Rhymed Chronicle,* and chronicles by Peter von Dusburg, Nicolaus von Jeroschin, Hermann von Wartberge, Wigand von Marburg, Johann von Posilge, and others. There are also several extensive editions of charters, letters, and different sorts of accounts. The most important records of the Teutonic Order in Prussia (most of them still unedited) are now kept in the Geheimes Staatsarchiv Preußischer Kulturbesitz in Berlin. Unfortunately, no equivalent records of the Livonian branch of the order have survived.

Crusaders battle Russians in the film *Alexander Nevsky*, directed by Sergei Eisenstein (1938). (Bettmann/Corbis)

Besides written sources, archaeological sites and artifacts give evidence of warfare at the time of the Baltic Crusades. There are hundreds of remains of pagan hill forts and other defensive structures, which are now being thoroughly investigated and sometimes reconstructed by archaeologists. The advance of settlement and colonization is exemplified by the many imposing, strong castles of the military orders, notably the main castle of the Teutonic Order, Marienburg (mod. Malbork, Poland) in Prussia.

Pagan Arms, Armor, and Warfare

If battle could not be avoided, pagan warriors fought on foot at long range with bows, slings, and javelins and man-to-man with spears, swords, long and broad battle knives, axes, and clubs. As speed and surprise were decisive for the success of an attack, body protection was relatively light.

However, when heathen warriors are described in the chronicles as being unarmed (Lat. *inermes*), this merely means that they were not ironclad; that is, they had no armor corresponding to that of the Western knights. Besides their weapons they may at least have had shields and helmets and probably also had other body protection of leather and metal. There was no uniformity in equipment but, rather, regional differences in the vast area from Finland in the north to Prussia in the south.

Eastern elements sometimes played an important role, as can be demonstrated in the case of the open conical "Prussian" helmet that originated in Byzantium and Russia and was equipped with mail aventails (flaps) on the sides and at the rear or with aventails consisting of small rectangular plates fixed together on leather. This type of helmet was adopted from the Prussians by the Teutonic Order and became very popular, being worn not only by the indigenous auxiliary troops. A similar helmet, called *pekilhube* in the inventories of the order (the origin of the later German *Pickelhaube,* literally "spiked bonnet"), was also borrowed from the Prussians by the Teutonic Knights. A type of equestrian shield, or pavise, of Baltic origin was the so-called Prussian or Lithuanian shield (Lat. *scutum Pruthenicum* or *clipeus Litwanicus*), which became popular even in western Europe. It was rather small, ranging in size from 30 to 50 centimeters in width and 60 to 70 centimeters in height. Another example of transfer from East to West was the light Lithuanian lance called the *sulice.* According to the Polish chronicler Jan Długosz, such lances could be seen among the weapons of the Teutonic Order's troops at Tannenberg.

The heathen armies in the Baltic region were levies of peasants under the command of a small elite of nobles, who could be regarded as professional warriors. Each village had an elder, villages formed districts, and districts formed provinces, governed by councils of district elders. It was possible to decide in advance the numbers required by the territorial levy (in Livonia called *malewa*) and to coordinate plans.

Swift expeditions with surprise attacks, designed to plunder and devastate enemy territory, were characteristic of such tribal warfare. The small but tenacious and hardy indigenous horses (Ger. *Schweike,* from a Baltic word for "healthy") served as fast and reliable warhorses, saddle horses, packhorses, and draft horses for carts and sledges. When enemy settlements were reached, fixed quarters (called *maia* by Henry of Livonia, and *sowalk* by Hermann von Wartberge) were set up, and groups of men spread out for looting. Booty consisted largely of captives, horses and livestock, weapons, textiles, furs, and metals and was gathered in the *maia;* it was then important either to continue the campaign elsewhere or to withdraw quickly in order to avoid counterattack by the local levy. The defeated men were in most cases killed, whereas the women and children were taken along with the expedition as captives. On occasion no one was spared. People and animals that could not be taken away were killed, and houses and stores were burned. As the principal purpose of warfare was plundering and devastation, not the acquisition of land, battles and sieges were avoided. Places of refuge existed in the form of forts built of timber and earth, or sometimes of loose stones from the fields (without mortar), and surrounded by ditches and palisades. Sites were chosen with the criterion of providing

refuge: preferably hills, islands, or locations near a river or lake. When the alarm was given, villagers took refuge in their forts along with their animals and belongings or retreated to hiding places in surrounding forests and bogs.

Enemy territories and settlements that were selected to be ravaged were often surrounded by vast forests and swamps. Besides such natural obstacles, the attacking levy often had to face artificially erected barriers or barricades (in the German chronicles called *hagen*) made of felled trees, branches, bushes, and thicket. These were constructed at strategic sites and were carefully maintained by the local population as protection for their territories or villages. Such obstacles could delay an attack and make it possible for guards to give the alarm. Raids mostly took place in summer or early autumn, but sometimes also in winter when weather conditions were favorable. They could be short or could last for many weeks, and often covered hundreds of kilometers.

Christian Arms, Armor, and Military Innovations

The confrontation of the heathen levies with the crusaders and the armies of the military orders (the Sword Brethren, the Teutonic Order, and the short-lived Knights of Dobrin) was a clash between two different worlds: one of a fundamentally archaic structure, the other representing the peak of military progress of the time. The development of chivalry and warfare in Latin Europe had profited from the experiences of Christian knights during the crusades to the Holy Land. Horses were not simply a means of transport; large horses were systematically bred and trained to carry a saddle with an armored knight, who fought the enemy with his lance and sword. The knight of the thirteenth century was protected by a coat of mail (known as a hauberk) consisting of small iron or steel rings and by a pot helmet or (from the end of the century) a great helm, as well as a shield. The great helm was an irreplaceable attribute of chivalry in the West, but in Livonia and Prussia it never became popular among the knights during the campaigns because it was heavy, limited the range of sight, and made breathing difficult. The Teutonic Knights surmounted their great helms with crests in the shape of a circle with a black cross or with white pennons also with a cross. From the second half of the fourteenth century the more practical basinets with mail aventails were worn even by the highest dignitaries of the order. Also kettle-hats (iron caps with brims) were often used by the Teutonic Knights as well as by knights of lesser status.

After the mid-fourteenth century the very popular and

common mail hauberk was slowly being replaced by new body and limb defenses (various types of lamellar and scale plates) and, from the end of the century, by full plate armor. At an earlier stage plates were made in the form of a "poncho" consisting of rows of iron plates arranged vertically or horizontally and riveted to leather or thick cloth. There is also evidence of a combination of the two types of armor, the mail hauberk being worn under the plates. Thus, a horse had to carry a knight weighing up to 150 kilograms (c. 330 lb.) or even more. On the battlefield under normal conditions such heavy cavalry was able to crush even numerically superior heathen armies. Only in forests, in boggy terrain, or in places with poor visibility was it possible for light cavalry and infantry to defend themselves successfully and win victories. The surviving inventories of the Teutonic Order in Prussia give much information about the knights' arms and armor stored in the castles.

Because Christian campaigns had to deal with the difficult terrain of forests and bogs, the Teutonic Knights often did without armor and coverings for the horses and straps for their breast and croup. The saddles had to be simple, without superfluous heads and straps, since both horse and equipment needed to be streamlined to avoid being caught in the scrub.

There were many innovations in Christian military techniques in the Baltic region. One such important development was the erection of permanent fortresses in stone or brick: the manufacture of bricks and mortar was unknown in the eastern Baltic lands until the crusader conquest. The military orders undoubtedly took over and practiced the heathen techniques of erecting fortifications made of wood and mounds of earth, but they also built networks of castles in suitable sites all over the Baltic region. These, together with the fortified larger towns, constituted the backbone of the new Christian states: it was practically impossible for heathen forces to take them by storm.

When the crossbow was introduced to the Baltic region (in the thirteenth century at the latest), the Christians had an effective long-range weapon that proved superior to the javelins, slings, and bows of their opponents and could be used in battle as well as in sieges and the defense of fortifications. The heathen tribes and their Russian neighbors in Novgorod, Polotsk, Smolensk, and Pskov dreaded the crossbow; up to this time they knew only the traditional bow, which was less effective. There was an extensive production of crossbows in the order's workshops (Ger. *Schnitzhaus*, pl.

Schnitzhäuser), probably on a scale that was unparalleled elsewhere in Europe. To be sure, the longbows of the English archers were more powerful than crossbows of wood and horn, although not more so than the steel crossbows introduced at the end of the fifteenth century; they also had faster rates of fire, as did the composite bows of the Turks and Mongols. The Teutonic Order became increasingly aware of this, as can be seen in the chronicle of Johann von Posilge, in which the effectiveness of the English longbow is praised. However, it was used only in the Baltic region on occasions when English crusaders came to Prussia. Thus, the crossbow remained the most important long-distance hand weapon in the Baltic until it was slowly replaced by firearms from the fifteenth century onward.

Also unknown to the peoples in the Baltic region were the heavy siege weapons, such as catapults and trebuchets, battering rams, and siege towers, which were also introduced by the crusaders. In the second half of the fourteenth century the use of gunpowder was effectively demonstrated, first by the Christians and then, two decades later, by the Lithuanians, who were eager and sufficiently skillful to adopt the new techniques.

The combination of these new developments made it possible for Christian garrisons to withstand long sieges, provided they had sufficient supplies of food, weapons, and crossbow bolts. Conquered territories were secured systematically with new fortresses that served different purposes. One such purpose was to enable new military operations into enemy territory. For that reason the breeding of large horses was established on the order's estates (Ger. *Vorwerke*), and stud farms were protected by castles. The warhorses of the order were mostly rendered infertile by sterilization or (less commonly) by castration in order to prevent them from being used for breeding in case they were caught by the enemy; for this reason they were called "monk horses" (Ger. *Mönchhengste*). Mares were not used as warhorses.

The large horses were bred not only by the military orders but also in the Livonian and Prussian bishoprics and on the estates of the German and (in Estonia) Danish nobles. Around 1400 there were almost 14,000 horses in the Prussian castles, on the breeding farms, and on the estates, of which 7,200 belonged to the breed of large military horses. In addition there were the warhorses and saddle horses of the brethren, estimated at 2,250, and the horses belonging to the bishoprics and cities and some 4,700 nobles who were obliged to perform military service. These were the so-called

freemen (Ger. *Freie*). The figures for Livonia are more difficult to estimate because of the lack of sources, but they were
probably about half of the totals just mentioned.

Christian Military Service and Warfare

According to the Charter of Kulm (Ger. *Kulmer Handfeste*)
of 1233, those nobles who held more than forty hides of land
(672 hectares, or about 1,680 acres) from the Teutonic Order
were to serve with heavy armor on a covered horse (Lat. *dex-
trarius opertus*); in this case the horse was specified as having to be a stallion, and at least two further horsemen were
required as escorts. This form of service was called *Ross-
dienst* (stallion service). Those with ten to forty hides had to
perform one or more of the less expensive services known
as *Platendienst* (plate service), with plate armor or light
weapons. In this form of service the horse was sterilized or
castrated; castrated horses were certainly easier to handle on
the march and in camp.

With the increasing importance of the crossbow as a
long-range weapon, armor became heavier and plate service developed into service on a warhorse, which was about
three to four times as expensive as the horses of the indigenous peoples. Around 1400 plate cost one-fifth of the price
of a good warhorse. The native light auxiliary troops who
made up a large proportion of the Christian forces fought on
foot with their native weapons, using their smaller horses
primarily as a means of transport.

Around 1400 there were some 700 knight brethren, sergeants, and priests of the Teutonic Order in Prussia and some
250 in Livonia. In Prussia the army, including the forces of
the bishoprics and the towns, numbered well in excess of
10,000 men. This number did not include those serving in the
baggage train, troops held reserve, seasonal crusaders, or
mercenaries. The army of the Livonian branch of the order
may have been about half as large as the Prussian.

In many respects the crusaders and military orders
adopted the forms of warfare practiced by their heathen
adversaries. They undertook swift expeditions and assaults
in order to weaken and demoralize the enemy. Looting,
killing, and taking prisoners were also important aims,
whereas conversion often seems to have been of only secondary interest. Sometimes the pagans could save their lives
if they agreed to accept the Christian faith, but mostly the
men were killed and the captured women and children were
brought as prisoners to Prussia or Livonia, where they were
ransomed or sold, used in prisoner exchanges, or employed

as slaves or settlers. It was a great advantage for the order to
have access to this reserve of heathen human labor when
Europe was struck by demographic crisis in the fourteenth
century and the influx of settlers from the west gradually
ceased. According to the theologian Thomas Aquinas, Christians could not be enslaved, but heathens could be. This was
one of the reasons why the order refused to accept the Christianization of Lithuania (1387) and ignored the prohibitions
on military expeditions into Lithuania by Wenceslas IV, king
of Bohemia, in 1394 and Pope Boniface IX in 1403.

Besides brief attacks there were also longer campaigns,
which could last several weeks. In all cases good planning
was a precondition for the success of the undertaking. The
provision of sufficient fodder for the horses and other supplies was part of this. In winter food for the troops and hay
and oats for the horses had to be transported on packhorses
or sledges; in summer the stages of the march had to be
planned so as to give the horses the opportunity to graze. If
necessary, provisions and fodder were also transported on
packhorses, as the terrain made the use of carts difficult. The
indigenous horses were well suited for this. Depots for provisions and fodder were placed along the line of march. If,
when the army arrived, these were found to have been captured or destroyed by the enemy, the situation often became
so acute that it was a matter of life or death. Because of the
many lakes, rivers, and swamps in the wild frontier countryside (Ger. *Wildnis*), expeditions were very dependent on
the weather: too much rain in summer made the terrain just
as difficult to travel through as when the winter was too mild,
too hard, or very snowy. A cold but not too snowy winter
provided the best conditions: waterways and bogs froze
over, thereby helping rather than hindering the progress of
horses and sledges. Tracks in the snow also made it easier
to find settlements and hiding places in the district that was
to be ravaged. Thus the winter *reyse* ("campaign" or "journey") of the Teutonic Order from Prussia against the Lithuanians was the order's campaign par excellence. The excellent
logistics and organization of the order functioned well in
winter, whereas the more lightly armed heathens on their
smaller horses preferred expeditions in summer.

In summer the Teutonic Knights in Prussia transported
parts of the army and supplies along waterways when this
was possible, whereas the mounted army had to force its way
through the dreaded wilderness area east of Sambia, called
Grauden. The chronicles tell of the hardships endured by the
men and horses during these marches. In 1427 the marshal

of the order remarked that there were no waterways from Livonia into Lithuania, so that campaigns in that direction could only be carried out with the indigenous small, shaggy horses. Both sides used spies and scouts (Lat. *speculatores*). Often barricades of felled trees had to be cleared or bypassed. Sometimes trees along the planned route of march were marked by axes before the expedition started, to enable it to find the way easily and avoid obstacles and pass the wilderness more quickly.

One hundred descriptions of campaign routes from the two last decades of the fourteenth century have been preserved in the archives of the Teutonic Order: these are the so-called *Wegeberichte*, which originated from scouts and guides (Ger. *Leitsleute*) in the region. These valuable sources were compiled and revised by local knight brethren or servants of the order and sent to the marshal, who was also commander of Königsberg (mod. Kaliningrad, Russia). They served as an important resource in the planning and execution of expeditions from Prussia to Lithuania. They give details of distances, Lithuanian settlements, suitable places for depots and camps, the condition of the terrain, roads, and paths as well as of natural or artificial obstacles to be overcome. They also carefully note where water and, in summer, grass for the horses could be found. Besides their importance for military history these sources are valuable for Lithuanian linguistic research.

When the targeted settlements were reached, a camp was built and groups of knights and armed men spread out to loot and kill. The Sword Brethren and the Teutonic Knights thus used the same tactics that the indigenous peoples had practiced for hundreds of years before they were confronted with Christianity. In order not to be surprised by a counterattack of the local levy, the army did not stay long at the same place but soon moved to another district, where the same procedure was repeated. Some days or weeks later the campaign ended, and the army marched back to Prussia or Livonia with its prisoners of war, captured horses, and other booty.

Small groups of irregulars were used by the Teutonic Order in the wilderness, where they ravaged and killed settlers on their own initiative. These were the dreaded *latrunculi* ("robbers" or "bandits"), who were called *struter* in the contemporary sources of the order. The order wanted to keep the wilderness intact as a broad natural defensive barrier, especially against the Lithuanians.

The indigenous peoples in the target countries defended themselves by various means: by defending their own castles and other fortifications, by besieging those of the Christians, and by attacks, ambushes, feigned retreats, and the destruction of the crusaders' depots of provisions and fodder. The Lithuanians especially also undertook long expeditions into the lands of the order, killing, plundering, and taking prisoners, who, according to the chroniclers of the order, were enslaved. It was a vicious circle that was broken mainly by the battle of Tannenberg in 1410.

There were also types of expeditions other than the raids mentioned above: fortresses and castles had to be erected, and enemy fortresses had to be besieged and destroyed. Fortifications in the wilderness were built in summer for preference, when the waterways could be used for transporting building materials. If possible, heavy equipment for sieges was also carried by boat; otherwise these war machines had to be constructed before the enemy's fortresses. Defensive measures in the event of an attack required the levy (or parts of it) to be mobilized and mustered at places of strategic importance near the frontier. The levy not only consisted of the knight brethren of the order and German, Danish (in Estonia), and indigenous nobles but also included armed men from the bishoprics and towns.

Compared to expeditions for plundering and devastation, pitched battles were rather rare. In these cases the knight brethren and crusader heavy cavalry took their place in the middle of the formation, with the indigenous auxiliaries and other troops on the wings to the right and the left. Many of the battles were won by the Christian armies, but in a significant number the pagans or Russians were victorious. The heathen Estonians were defeated at Treiden (1211), Fellin (1217), and Lyndanise (1219), whereas the Sword Brethren were defeated by the Lithuanians at Saule in 1236. The Livonian branch of the Teutonic Order was defeated by the Novgorodians at Lake Peipus in 1242 and by the Lithuanians of Samogitia at Schoden in 1259 and at Durben in 1260. Well-known battles of the Teutonic Order in Prussia include the victories over the Lithuanians at Strebe (1348) and at Rudau (1370) and the defeat at Tannenberg at the hands of the Lithuanians and Poles in 1410. The Novgorodians had already halted Swedish expansion at the inner part of the Gulf of Finland through a victory at the river Neva in 1240.

A constant strategic goal of the Teutonic Order was to conquer the western Lithuanian land of Samogitia (Lith. *Žemaitija*) in order to achieve a territorial connection between the two branches of the order in Livonia and Prussia. Military operations were therefore often coordinated. The warlike Samogitians were never subjugated by the order, but in the peace treaty between Grand Master Konrad von Jungingen and the Lithuanian grand duke Vytautas at Sallinwerder in 1398, Samogitia was awarded to the order. However, this acquisition only brought disaster, because an uprising in Samogitia in 1409 launched the chain of events that ended one year later with the defeat at Tannenberg.

Mutual Influences and Adaptation

For the military orders it was always a struggle to maintain their advantage through continual improvements in techniques, equipment, and horsepower. The element of surprise was short-lived. Innovations are notorious for the speed with which they spread, and it was always only a question of time before the Christians' opponents became familiar with them and thus able to use them in turn. In the first half of the fourteenth century stone or brick fortresses were increasingly replacing wood and earth constructions in Lithuania, while heavy siege weapons were also known to the heathens by this time. The first reliable report of the use of firearms (Ger. *Lotbüchsen*) by the Teutonic Order occurs in a chronicle describing a siege in 1362. Two decades later, bombards were used by the Lithuanians against the fortresses of the order. The possession of large warhorses and knightly armament was not confined to the Christians in the long term, since capture or purchase made it possible for the heathens to overcome this disadvantage to some extent. After the defeat at Tannenberg, the Teutonic Order's lawyers accused the Poles of having disregarded the old prohibitions on supplying warhorses and knightly weapons to the heathens (as they still called the Lithuanians) and other nonbelievers and of having taught them Christian techniques of warfare. These accusations suggest that by this time the heathen armies were in no way inferior in equipment to those of the Christians. Even if they are regarded as harsh anti-Polish propaganda, they reveal the truth that times had changed and that the opponents of the military orders had made good many of their former deficiencies.

Christian warfare in the Baltic region also adapted to the particular conditions existing there and thus differed significantly from knightly warfare in western Europe. The enslavement of women and children had deep roots in Baltic tradition. The Christian knights took over the Prussian helmet and shield, the light Lithuanian lance, the use of small indigenous horses, and heathen building techniques. Other indications of adaptation to regional and local conditions are the sterilization or castration of warhorses, the "streamlined" equipment of the horsemen, and the relinquishing of horse armor. More than elsewhere warfare was dependent on weather, because of the nature of the wild countryside, with its dense forests, rivers, and swamps. Warfare in winter was therefore common in the Baltic but unusual in western Europe. This feature was undoubtedly an additional exotic enticement for crusaders from the west.

The Crusaders

Among the crusaders who participated in the campaigns of the order in the thirteenth and fourteenth centuries were kings, dukes, counts, and many renowned nobles. Werner Paravicini has listed more than 300 expeditions from Livonia and Prussia against Lithuania between 1305 and 1409 [Paravicini, *Die Preußenreisen*, 2:20–45].

It was a very expensive undertaking to travel to Livonia or Prussia, and only those with a solid financial background could afford it. Among the most famous expeditions were the crusade of King Ottokar II of Bohemia in 1255, when Königsberg was founded, and the campaign in the summer of 1390, when the Lithuanian capital of Vilnius was besieged by an army that included Henry Bolingbroke, earl of Derby (the future King Henry IV of England). He brought with him English longbowmen, who proved very effective in fighting.

Very often crusaders from western Europe took part in these martial enterprises not only out of religious devotion and an eagerness to convert heathen peoples but also for other reasons, including desire for adventure, the search for fame and honor, and material advantage: these various motives frequently overlapped. Despite all its harshness and cruelty the crusade was regarded like a kind of chivalric romance: this conception was manifested in the late Middle Ages in the Teutonic Order's renowned Table of Honor (Ger. *Ehrentisch*), knightly dubbings, feasts, and hunts during the military campaigns to Lithuania. However, the continuing importance of indulgences in inducing crusaders to risk their lives in the fight against the heathen demonstrates that they were not motivated only by secular concerns.

Conclusions

The Teutonic Order strove to unite its territories in Livonia and Prussia by the conquest and subjection of the western Lithuanian territory of Samogitia, but this strategic goal was never reached. Instead, the Polish-Lithuanian Union of

1385 and the Christianization of Lithuania in 1387 changed the political map of Europe. Two decades later the defeat at Tannenberg in 1410 marked the end of the order's forays against the "heathens." Prussia had lost much of its might and influence, and the question now was of the survival of the order's territories. Instead of carrying out raids, the Teutonic Knights had to defend themselves against enemies both within and beyond their borders. The greatest threat to Prussia came from rebellious towns and nobles and from the Poles; the threat to Livonia came from the Russians. War in the region took on the forms that prevailed in the rest of Europe: mercenaries replaced crusaders, firearms increased in importance, and sieges with artillery became a matter of routine. Crusaders and knightly warfare now belonged to the past.

–Sven Ekdahl

Bibliography

Benninghoven, Friedrich, "Probleme der Zahl und Standortverteilung der livländischen Streitkräfte im ausgehenden Mittelalter," *Zeitschrift für Ostforschung* 12 (1963), 601–622.

———, *Der Orden der Schwertbrüder* (Köln: Böhlau, 1965).

———, "Zur Technik spätmittelalterlicher Feldzüge im Ostbaltikum," *Zeitschrift für Ostforschung* 19 (1970), 631–651.

———, "Die Burgen als Grundpfeiler des spätmittelalterlichen Wehrwesens im preußisch-livländischen Deutschordensstaat," in *Die Burgen im deutschen Sprachraum: Ihre rechts- und verfassungsgeschichtliche Bedeutung,* ed. Hans Patze (Sigmaringen: Thorbecke, 1976), pp. 565–601.

Chodyński, Antoni Romuald, "The Preparations for War Expeditions to Lithuania and Samogitia According to the Chronicle by Wigand of Marburg," in *Fasciculi Archaeologiae Historicae,* XV, ed. Tadeusz Poklewski-Koziełł (Łódź: Wydawnictwo Polskiej Akademii Nauk, 2002), pp. 39–46.

Ekdahl, Sven, "Die Flucht der Litauer in der Schlacht bei Tannenberg," *Zeitschrift für Ostforschung* 12 (1963), 11–19.

———, "Über die Kriegsdienste der Freien im Kulmerland zu Anfang des 15. Jahrhunderts," *Preußenland* 2 (1964), 1–14.

———, *Die Banderia Prutenorum des Jan Długosz—eine Quelle zur Schlacht bei Tannenberg 1410: Untersuchungen zu Aufbau, Entstehung und Quellenwert der Handschrift* (Göttingen: Vandenhoeck & Ruprecht, 1976).

———, *Die Schlacht bei Tannenberg 1410: Quellenkritische Untersuchungen,* vol. 1: *Einführung und Quellenlage* (Berlin: Duncker & Humblot, 1982).

———, "Das Pferd und seine Rolle im Kriegswesen des Deutschen Ordens," in *Das Kriegswesen der Ritterorden im Mittelalter,* ed. Zenon Hubert Nowak (Toruń: Uniwersytet Mikołaja Kopernika, 1991), pp. 29–47.

———, "Die Armbrust im Deutschordensland Preußen zu Beginn des 15. Jahrhunderts," in *Fasciculi Archaeologiae Historicae,* V, ed. Andrzej Nadolski (Łódź: Wydawnictwo Polskiej Akademii Nauk, 1992), pp. 17–48.

———, "The Treatment of Prisoners of War during the Fighting between the Teutonic Order and Lithuania," in *The Military Orders,* 1: *Fighting for the Faith and Caring for the Sick,* ed. Malcolm Barber (Aldershot, UK: Variorum, 1994), pp. 263–269.

———, "Horses and Crossbows: Two Important Warfare Advantages of the Teutonic Order in Prussia," in *The Military Orders,* 2: *Welfare and Warfare,* ed. Helen Nicholson (Aldershot, UK: Ashgate, 1998), pp. 119–151.

———, "The Strategic Organization of the Commanderies of the Teutonic Order in Prussia and Livonia," in *La Commanderie: Institution des ordres militaires dans l'Occident médiéval,* ed. Anthony Luttrell and Léon Pressouyre (Paris: Comité des travaux historiques et scientifiques, 2002), pp. 219–242.

Kasekamp, Andres, "Characteristics of Warfare in the Times of Henry of Livonia and Balthasar Russow," *Lituanus* 36 (1990), 27–38.

Nicolle, David, *Lake Peipus, 1242* (London: Osprey, 1996).

Nikžentaitis, Alvydas, "Changes in the Organisation and Tactics of the Lithuanian Army in the 13th, 14th and the First Half of the 15th Century," in *Fasciculi Archaeologiae Historicae,* VII, ed. Tadeusz Poklewski (Łódź: Instytut Archeologii I Etnologii PAN, Warszawa, 1994), pp. 45–53.

———, "Prisoners of War in Lithuania and the Teutonic Order State, 1288–1409," in *Der Deutsche Orden in der Zeit der Kalmarer Union, 1397–1521,* ed. Zenon Hubert Nowak and Roman Czaja (Toruń: Wydawnictwo Uniwersytetu Mikołaja Kopernika, 1999), pp. 193–208.

Nowakowski, Andrzej, "Some Remarks about Weapons Stored in the Arsenals of the Teutonic Order's Castles in Prussia by the End of the 14th and Early 15th Centuries," in *Das Kriegswesen der Ritterorden im Mittelalter,* ed. Zenon Hubert Nowak (Toruń: Uniwersytet Mikołaja Kopernika, 1991), pp. 75–88.

———, *Arms and Armour in the Medieval Teutonic Order's State in Prussia* (Łódź: Oficyna Naukowa MS, 1994).

Paravicini, Werner, *Die Preußenreisen des europäischen Adels,* 1–2 (Sigmaringen: Jan Thorbecke, 1989–1995).

Rünger, Fritz, "Herkunft, Rassezugehörigkeit, Züchtung und Haltung der Ritterpferde des Deutschen Ordens: Ein Beitrag zur Geschichte der ostpreußischen Pferdezucht und der deutschen Pferdezucht im Mittelalter," *Zeitschrift für Tierzüchtung und Züchtungsbiologie einschließlich Tierernährung* 2 (1923), 264–308.

Urban, William L., "The Organization of the Defence of the Livonian Frontier in the Thirteenth Century," *Speculum* 48 (1973), 525–532.

———, *The Baltic Crusade,* 2d ed. (Chicago: Lithuanian Research and Studies Center, 1994).

———, *The Prussian Crusade,* 2d ed. (Chicago: Lithuanian Research and Studies Center, 2000).

———, *Tannenberg and After: Lithuania, Poland, and the Teutonic Order in Search of Immortality,* rev. ed. (Chicago: Lithuanian Research and Studies Center, 2003).

———, *The Teutonic Knights: A Military History* (London: Greenhill, 2003).

———, *The Livonian Crusade,* 2d ed. (Chicago: Lithuanian Research and Studies Center, 2004).

Warfare: Byzantium and Frankish Greece

The crusader armies that conquered large parts of the Byzantine Empire at the start of the thirteenth century found themselves facing forces that were much closer to themselves in terms of tactics and equipment than were the Muslim armies they faced in the Holy Land. Yet Byzantine armies were by no means identical to those of western Europe. The type of terrain in which the crusaders campaigned was, however, familiar, at least to those who came from or had served in Mediterranean regions such as southern Italy. The Frankish states established around the Aegean in the wake of the Fourth Crusade (1202–1204) also existed in a state of almost permanent war, their foes including not only Byzantine Greeks, but also Bulgarians, occasionally Serbs, and of course the Muslim Turks who gradually took control of the Anatolian coast of the Aegean Sea. During the second half of the fourteenth century and after, the Ottoman Turks went even further, conquering the Balkans and what remained of Byzantine northern and central Greece, thus reaching the land frontiers of the now much reduced Frankish principalities in later medieval Greece.

The social and military organization of the short-lived Latin Empire of Constantinople and of the small Frankish principalities in Greece were practically identical to those of southern France and of the feudal (rather than urban-republican) states of thirteenth-century Italy. The only important difference was that the Frankish principalities in Greece soon enlisted local troops whose military traditions were those of the Byzantine world. Most of these men served as light cavalry or light infantry. Such similarities made it almost inevitable that, as far as the Franks in Greece were concerned, warfare was conducted in much the same manner as was seen in, for example, Italy. Offensive operations largely consisted of raiding and ravaging enemy territory to inflict as much economic damage as possible, or to take or recapture a fortified place. The latter ranged from isolated castles to small but strategically significant coastal towns. After the first rush of conquest in the early thirteenth century, the Frankish states on former Byzantine territory were usually on the defensive. The initiative had largely gone to the various rival Byzantine successor states, when these were not fighting each other. Major offensive operations by Frankish or crusade armies were almost always in the form of attacks from farther afield, most notably from southern Italy. Some of the latter were quite ambitious, but most ended in failure. This caused surprise and embarrassment in western Europe, which, with some justification, considered itself to be superior to the declining Byzantine world in military and economic terms.

Byzantine success in containing and, to a large extent, expelling the Franks is something of a paradox, for during these same centuries the Byzantine states suffered repeated and eventually complete defeat at the hands of the Muslim Turks. The Byzantine Greeks also suffered significant setbacks at the hands of their fellow Orthodox Christian (Bulgarian and Serb) neighbors in the Balkans. So how did the Greeks defeat the Latins?

Traditional Byzantine defensive strategy had failed against the Saljūq Turks in the eleventh century because these new invaders occupied the hills as well as the central plains. There is also evidence that Byzantine military morale had declined and that the old systems of defensive guerrilla warfare, or "shadow warfare," were not attempted until too late. Once the richest western part of Anatolia had been regained by the Komnenian emperors in the early twelfth century, however, it was secured by a broad band of depopulated no-man's-land with a series of impressive fortresses to the rear. The Byzantines had held on to the northern coastal strip along the Black Sea, and this area, though apparently narrow and vulnerable, was protected by densely forested mountains where raiders could be ambushed. It could also be reinforced by sea. Everywhere a first line of defense was provided by garrisons and local militias backed up by mobile central forces, a system that worked well until the second half of the thirteenth century. But then the Frankish occupation of Constantinople and much of the Byzantine heartland seriously weakened the ability of central armies to support the often rundown frontier forces.

After the Greeks of the Empire of Nicaea regained Constantinople from the Franks in 1261, they remained more concerned about western European invasions and consequently concentrated the better part of their forces in the Balkans, thus further weakening the eastern frontier, which increasingly relied on static defenses to plug the valleys against Turkish raiders. Meanwhile the success of relatively lightly equipped cavalry and infantry archers in defending places like Albania against Western heavy cavalry from southern Italy in the late thirteenth century suggests that the Byzantine army was not as enfeebled as sometimes thought. It apparently relied on guerrilla tactics, cutting enemy communications with the coast, then isolating and blocking enemy forces inland. A similar strategy was used against the Frankish states in southern Greece. Its ultimate failure against similar Serbian forces in the fourteenth century, and even more dramatically against Ottoman Turkish forces, probably reflected the greater economic, manpower, and moral resources of these enemies.

Western European prejudice concerning the supposedly superior strategy but inferior fighting skills of the average twelfth–fourteenth century Byzantine soldier may, in fact, have been based on reality, since the Komnenian emperors certainly tried to train their own heavy cavalry along Western knightly lines. In the event, this Western-style cavalry failed dismally against the Turks but may have been more effective against Western invaders.

Several sources provide interesting details about Byzantine tactics during this period. Attempts to fight the Turks in their own manner, with light cavalry horse-archers, failed and the Byzantines reverted to ambushing their enemies in mountainous or close country. Nevertheless they still made great use of archery. On one occasion a Byzantine force lit many campfires at night to make its numbers appear larger, then ambushed its disconcerted foes as the latter withdrew through a narrow mountain pass. Even against Frankish forces, the Byzantines used their armored cavalry to hold high ground while their light cavalry harassed the enemy in the valleys. Here they again used the ruse of lighting multiple fires, but also moved herds of cattle around to look like additional cavalry from a distance.

Otherwise Byzantine cavalry tactics remained very traditional. Cavalry still used the *syntagma* (a close formation) within a formation known as a *parataxis,* whose precise meaning is obscure, as had been the case since at least the tenth century. The *taxis* was probably one of three usual divisions. These divisions may have formed part of what the early thirteenth-century crusader observer Geoffrey of Villehardouin described as a *bataille* ("battalion," or "division"), with archers and crossbowmen ahead of the cavalry, and infantry sergeants bringing up the rear. A battle line was theoretically formed of *allagia* (regiments or squadrons) divided according to ethnic origin or combat role.

At the battle of Peritheorion (1345) during a Byzantine civil war, some of the Byzantine cavalry, probably consisting of relatively heavily armored troops, were placed on the defensive left, with allied Turkish horse-archers placed on the offensive right, while the best troops, both infantry and cavalry, held the center. Somewhat earlier a Byzantine army had drawn up in five *syntaxeis* (divisions) with Alan cavalry (refugees originally from the northern Caucasus) and Turcopole archers in the vanguard. Cavalry was still the dominant arm, though the *pezoi* (infantry) had an important role to play. These were often given classical titles, as, for example, the *hoplitai* (armored infantry) and *psiloi* (infantry archers).

By the fourteenth century, Byzantine armies were usually small, and this accords well with the assertion by the Italian-educated Prince Theodore Palaiologos that, if a force was caught by surprise, it should not waste time trying to form divisions. Instead it should gather into one large formation. Even so, the baggage animals and squires must remain at some distance to the rear where the squires could also catch riderless horses and hold any prisoners. Other interesting observations made by this Byzantine prince were that natural obstacles such as rivers and passes should be defended from a slight distance, rather than too close, and that some of the enemy should be permitted to cross such obstacles before being attacked, presumably before they had time to reform. Cavalry should not be divided into too small companies; the best should be in the vanguard with a division of inferior cavalry remaining a crossbow shot behind them. A third division should be to the left of the second, since this was where the enemy was most likely to launch a flank attack. The third division would also be able to hit the foe in the flank if the latter broke through the Byzantines' own front line. If, however, the commander had sufficient infantry archers, crossbowmen, and spearmen, these, rather than the third cavalry division, should be on the left flank. In reality, however, such theories probably reflected northern Italian military practice as much as that of the fourteenth-century Byzantine world.

–David Nicolle

Bibliography

Bartusis, Mark C., *The Late Byzantine Army: Arms and Society, 1204–1453* (Philadelphia: University of Pennsylvania Press, 1992).

Bon, Antoine, *La Morée franque*, 2 vols. (Paris: Boccard, 1969).

Ducellier, Alain, *La Façade maritime de l'Albanie au Moyen Age: Durazzo et Valone du XIe au XVe siècle* (Thessaloniki: Institute for Balkan Studies, 1981).

Geanakoplos, Deno J., "Greco-Latin Relations on the Eve of the Byzantine Restoration: The Battle of Pelagonia—1259," *Dumbarton Oaks Papers* 7 (1953), 99–141.

———, *The Emperor Michael Palaeologus and the West, 1258–1282* (Cambridge: Harvard University Press, 1959).

Heath, Ian, *Byzantine Armies, 1118–1461 AD* (London: Osprey, 1995).

Jacoby, David, *Studies on the Crusader States and on Venetian Expansion* (Aldershot, UK: Ashgate, 1989).

Latins and Greeks in the Eastern Mediterranean after 1204, ed. Benjamin Arbel, Bernard Hamilton, and David Jacoby (London: Cass, 1989).

Luttrell, Anthony, *Latin Greece: The Hospitallers and the Crusades, 1291–1400* (London: Variorum, 1982).

Nicol, Donald M., *The Last Centuries of Byzantium 1261–1453* (London: Hart-Davis, 1972).

Nicolle, David, *Knight of Outremer, 1187–1344* (London: Osprey, 1996).

———, *Knight Hospitaller (2), 1306–1565* (Oxford: Osprey, 2001).

Warfare: Iberia

Until the tenth century, the army of the Christian kingdom of Asturias seems to have maintained some Visigothic military traditions, while also reflecting Muslim influence from al-Andalus. Nevertheless, a different army developed as the Christians pushed southward into Muslim-held territory. Towns as well as noblemen played a major role in both León and Castile, with urban cavalry and infantry both existing by the tenth century. In eleventh-century Castile, the powerful magnates (Sp. *ricos hombres*) fought for their king, and many had their own *masnada* (military retinue). A lesser aristocracy (Sp. *infanzones*) consisted of warriors like the famous Rodrigo Díaz de Vivar, better known as El Cid. Urban militias were divided into *caballería* (cavalry) and *peonía* (infantry), the former including *caballeros villanos* (nonnoble cavalry). Soldiers from north of the Pyrenees played some role in the Spanish *Reconquista* (reconquest of the Iberian Peninsula from the Muslims), but the Christian states of northern Iberia received limited help from outsiders after the mid-twelfth century.

Recruitment and Military Service

A western European feudal structure of military obligation was never fully implemented in the Iberian Peninsula. Instead poorer *peones* (the nonnoble, or peasant, strata of society) paid taxes and fought as infantry; richer but still nonnoble *caballeros villanos* served as cavalry and were generally excused taxation; while many Muslim troops who served in Christian armies were listed as nonnoble *cavallers* (horsemen). Even in the early fourteenth century, the garrison of Mahon in Mallorca included so-called Turks, presumably remnants of the Muslim population. The *almogavers* (lightly equipped troops, from the Arabic *al-mughāwar*, "raiders") clearly included both Christians and Muslims recruited from autonomous nonfeudal mountain pastoralists.

The small northern kingdom of Navarre had limited manpower, and perhaps as a result the late fourteenth-century local military elite (Sp. *mesnaderos*) included Muslim soldiers from around Tudela, each serving in person with an armed retinue for forty days a year. Castile became the most powerful state in the Iberian Peninsula, and despite the fact that the military religious orders provided a permanent army to defend Castile's advancing frontier, urban militias played an increasingly vital role from the early twelfth century onward. Here again many Muslims transferred their loyalty to Christian kings. Portugal was the least influenced by French military systems among the Christian Iberian states. Nevertheless, a new military elite emerged, and by the thirteenth and fourteenth centuries most Portuguese troops were drawn from the military orders, the towns, the king's own feudal following, and mercenaries paid through taxes. Richer farmers or peasants still had an obligation to serve as *cavaleiros-vilãos* (nonnoble cavalry, comparable to the Spanish *caballeros villanos*).

Andalusian Muslims were of very mixed origins; they included descendants of the original Muslim conquerors, of more recent Muslim immigrants, and of Iberian Christian or Jewish families that had converted to Islam. All played some military role, as did an indigenous aristocracy of Mozarabs (Arabized Christians), usually in regions where central authority was weak. The early eleventh century probably saw the peak of Berber recruitment in al-Andalus, but when Muslim Iberia fragmented into tiny states known as the Taifa kingdoms, most of the latter were too small to maintain large armies. Their recruitment patterns also tended to reflect the origins of their dynasties, being variously Arab, Berber,

"Slav" (i.e., descended from European slaves), or merely Andalusian.

There was a second Taifa period after the collapse of the North African Almoravid domination in the twelfth century, during which most Andalusian troops were apparently mercenaries. A third Taifa period following the collapse of Almohad domination was stifled by the Christian conquest of all Andalusia except the state of Granada. During this period, Andalusian military systems had more in common with those of Christian northern Iberia than those of Muslim North Africa. The army of Granada initially consisted of the ruler's clan and its political clients, while refugees fleeing Christian conquest and Berbers from Morocco provided additional troops. In later years, large numbers of religiously motivated volunteers, including North Africans, continued to play a major role, while a bodyguard of Christian renegades plus *mamlūks* (slave soldiers) drawn from Christian captives formed an elite light cavalry regiment.

The army of the Almoravids who ruled half of the Iberian Peninsula in the eleventh century was initially recruited from a Berber tribal confederation. Yet as the Almoravid Empire grew, so its army became more varied, including slave-recruited black African troops alongside an elite of Christian Iberian captives and mercenaries. The army of the subsequent Almohad rulers was initially a Moroccan rather than a Saharan tribal levy. Nevertheless, it again included slave-recruited Africans, Christian prisoners of war, and a guard of Christian mercenaries.

Military Organization

Military organization in Christian Iberia differed considerably from that farther north, while the states of northern Iberia also differed from one another. Asturias and Galicia retained strong Visigothic traditions; León and Castile were superficially influenced by military developments in France, and Aragon and Catalonia were deeply influenced by France.

Two basic characteristics, however, distinguished the military organization of twelfth–thirteenth century Christian Iberia. The first was a looser command structure and inferior discipline when compared to Muslim forces from al-Andalus. The second was the extent of conquered land handed over to the military orders as the Christian frontier pushed southward. Meanwhile the old Pyrenean heartland of Aragon had never been fully feudalized, and by the thirteenth century the kingdom was dominated by its cities. Most soldiers were now apparently paid professionals,

largely recruited from urban militias. Castles were held by officers of the king or his leading barons, while the latter also had their own professional armies. The newly conquered south was organized along similar lines, though the rugged mountains around Valencia were divided into military zones, often dominated by a free Christian and Muslim peasantry. Many of these mountaineers were led by their own Muslim military elites, some of whom controlled castles as late as 1276.

In Castile and León, the traditional term *apellido* still meant a defensive operation, usually involving urban forces, while the *fonsadera* (the duty of taking part in offensive operations) had generally been commuted for a money payment. The French term *hueste* appeared in the thirteenth century, meaning a major expedition. By the fourteenth century, a *hueste* necessitated urban militias assembling according to their *collación* (quarter) under a *juez* (town leader) appointed by the Crown. Among the most effective Castilian frontier forces, however, were *almugavers* comparable to the *almogavers* of Aragon. Until the fourteenth century, Portugal remained traditional in its military organization, the only consistent command position being that of *alférez môr* (army commander). Extensive changes came in the wake of English and French involvement in Iberian affairs in the late fourteenth century, and the Portuguese military system was overhauled in 1382, the *alférez môr* being replaced by a more typical constable and marshal on western European lines.

A link between military obligation and the possession of land seems to have been more characteristic of al-Andalus than elsewhere in the medieval Islamic world. Nevertheless, fortresses and fortified towns formed the framework of Andalusian military organization. In other respects the Umayyad rulers of Córdoba adopted the military systems of the 'Abbāsid caliphate to the east. By the tenth century, the provincial armies, supported by elite units in the capital, were regulated by a government department (Arab. *diwān*) divided into three sections dealing, respectively, with mercenaries around Córdoba, provincial-territorial troops, and short-term volunteers. The highly regularized command structure was again similar to that of the 'Abbāsid army. In the late tenth century, the ineffectiveness of such forces convinced the military dictator al-Manṣūr to instigate ruthless reforms. Yet some Andalusian *jund* cavalry evolved into a provincial elite, maintained by *iqṭā'* (grants of revenue), organized into squadrons, and operating alongside a rag-tag army of largely infantry volunteers.

The organization of the Umayyad Andalusian frontier had been based upon large military provinces, each facing a Christian state. "Popular" military organizations, such as the urban *futūwa* (religiously motivated confraternity) or *ahdath* (urban militia) only developed in response to the massive Christian conquests of the late eleventh and twelfth centuries, although the militia of Córdoba did play a role in the emergence of a small Taifa state when Umayyad authority collapsed. Two types of Taifa state emerged in the eleventh century: relatively large ones in sparsely populated regions, usually close to the Christian frontier, and smaller statelets in the urbanized south. Most reflected the old *jund* (territorial military divisions), and their tiny armies generally used existing military systems. In later years the organization of indigenous rather than North African forces in al-Andalus had features in common with the Christian territories. Nevertheless, Andalusian society was not as differentiated along class lines as was the case in the Christian north. Instead it consisted of extended family networks and alliances. As a result, ordinary soldiers often garrisoned a castle held by a leader to whom they were related through shared or imaginary tribal origins. In Granada, however, this military structure was overhauled in the mid-fourteenth century, resulting in separate Andalusian and North African Berber armies under their own leaders. Theoretically an *amir* (senior officer) led 5,000 men, a middle-ranking *qa'id* 1,000, while the junior-officer ranks of *naqib* led 200, an *'arif* led 40 and a *nazir* led 8, but it is unknown how far this classical Islamic ideal was reflected in reality.

Strategy and Tactics

Until the eleventh century, Christian Iberian warfare was modeled upon that of Islamic Andalusia, with raiding by light cavalry being the main form of offensive operation. At that time the high plains of La Mancha and Extramadura were not the cereal-growing regions that they are in modern times. Instead they were dominated by sheep ranching, raiding, and rustling. Meanwhile Christians and Muslims both made great efforts to control the passes through the sequence of mountain ranges that straddle the Iberian Peninsula.

Ecological factors continued to play a part in the strategy of the Christian states during the twelfth to fourteenth centuries. For example, control of winter and summer pastures was economically important for frontier communities on both sides, resulting in small-scale but sometimes far ranging campaigns. Offensive warfare largely consisted of such raiding, plus larger campaigns of conquest. Major operations usually took place in the dry summer and autumn, the Christian reconquest largely being channeled via the main bridges and passes. As a result, such choke points were defended by castles or fortified towns. Smaller raids took place at almost any time of year, the main concern being to keep escape routes open. The main problem with such a strategy was that it could leave an army's own urban base vulnerable to an enemy counter-raid.

An early fourteenth-century book on military affairs by the Castilian prince Don Juan Manuel emphasized the significance of fortresses as bases for attack and as centers of resistance, but also indicated that the old raiding strategy still had a major part to play. Juan Manuel also emphasized the importance of sowing dissension within enemy ranks, adopting good defensive positions while moving through enemy territory, and using special large lanterns when marching at night. These preoccupations seem to stem from Islamic rather than western European military traditions.

The main thrust of Muslim operations in Iberia was against enemy fortresses and the towns from which Christian armies launched their raids. By and large the Muslim armies of North Africa and al-Andalus relied on superior mobility when compared to the Christians and habitually sent raiders far ahead of their main line of march. In later centuries, of course, the rump state of Granada relied on counter-raiding rather than full-scale invasions of its powerful Christian neighbors.

Most troop types seen in early medieval Christian Iberia were the same as those of al-Andalus, largely consisting of light cavalry armed with javelins and infantry using long spears. The little that is known of Christian Iberian battlefield tactics during this period indicates that cavalry still used the tactic of repeated charges and withdrawals (Sp. *turnafuye*) that, once employed by Roman horsemen, had been continued by Arab cavalry, who knew it as *karr wa farr*. Paradoxically, western European heavy cavalry proved ineffective in the Near East because of their Muslim foes' increasing ability to use their own relative lightness and notably superior maneuverability to evade such crusader cavalry charges. Nevertheless, heavily armored cavalry modeled upon the even heavier Western knightly horsemen became more widespread in Iberia, at least until the late thirteenth century. There then seems to have been a reversal, with the majority of fourteenth-century Spanish cavalry being lightly armored skirmishers fighting *a la jineta* (riding on the relatively light horse subsequently known in English as a jennet) as opposed to heavy cavalry fighting *a la brida* (riding a heavier horse, using a *bridón,* "snaffle," and a deeper saddle and with a straight-legged riding position). Clearly they were under military influence from Granada or North Africa.

As the frontiers of al-Andalus collapsed in the eleventh and twelfth centuries, there was a growth in the importance of small monastery-like *ribāṭs:* this term perhaps originally meant a group of religiously motivated frontier or coastal defenders, but now also referred to the small fortification in which they served. From such positions religiously motivated volunteers conducted small-scale counter-raids. Despite their Arabic name of *al-Murābiṭūn* ("those organized into *ribāṭs*"), the early Almoravid armies of the western Sahara and Morocco did not emerge from the same circumstances. During the eleventh century, they were largely infantry, including many camel-riding mounted infantry, whose animals were at first said to have terrified Spanish cavalry horses. In battle, North African and Andalusian armies traditionally relied on an infantry phalanx; cavalry made repeated charges and withdrawals, while also being expected to overthrow an exhausted enemy. The early Almoravids, who had few cavalry, introduced significant changes by relying on absolute discipline, neither advancing nor retreating but expecting their enemies to break against their own static formations.

During the late twelfth and thirteenth centuries, an elite of Muslim Andalusian cavalrymen were equipped much like their Christian opponents, perhaps because traditional military systems were failing and Andalusians now tried to adopt Christian cavalry styles. These even included the couched lance, as well as the deep saddle and a long-legged riding position. In the mid-fourteenth century, however, the horsemen of Granada abandoned Western fashions and largely adopted Berber-style weapons and harness, including lighter swords, leather shields, and heavy javelins. The only major difference between the armies of Granada and those of Morocco was that the former continued to make considerable use of crossbows, both on foot and on horseback.

–*David Nicolle*

Bibliography

Bishko, Charles J., "The Castilian as Plainsman: The Medieval Ranching Frontier in La Mancha and Extramadura," in *The New World Looks at its History,* ed. Archibald Lewis and Thomas McGunn (Austin: University of Texas Press, 1963), pp. 46–69.

De Hoffmeyer, Ada Bruhn, *Arms and Armour in Spain,* 2 vols. (Madrid: Instituto de Estudios sobre Armas Antiguas, Consejo Superior de Investigaciones Científicas, Patronato Menéndez y Pelayo, 1972–1982).

De Moraes Farias, Paulo Fernando, "The Almoravids: Some Questions Concerning the Character of the Movement during its Periods of Closest Contact with the Western Sudan," *Bulletin de l'Institut Fondamental d'Afrique Noir,* ser. B, 29 (1967), 794–878.

Huici Miranda, Ambrosio, *Las grandes batallas de la Reconquista durante los invasiones africanas* (Madrid: Istituto de Estudios Africanos, 1956).

Powers, James F., "The Origins and Development of Municipal Military Service in the Leonese and Castilian Reconquest, 800–1250," *Traditio* 26 (1970), 91–111.

———, "Two Warrior-Kings and their Municipal Militias: The Townsman-Soldier in Law and Life," in *The World of Alfonso the Learned and James the Conqueror,* ed. Robert Ignatius Burns (Princeton: Princeton University Press, 1985), pp. 95–129.

Prescott, William H., *The Art of War in Spain: The Conquest of Granada, 1481–1492,* ed. and intro. Albert D. McJoynt (London: Greenhill, 1995).

Sánchez-Albornoz, C., "El Ejército y la guerra en al reino asturleonés, 718–1037," in *Ordinamenti militari in Occidente nell'Alto Medioevo: Settimane di Studio del Centro Italiano di Studi sull'Alto Medioevo,* vol. 15 (Spoleto: Presso la sede del Centro, 1968), pp. 299–335.

Soler del Campo, Alvaro, "Sistemas de combate en la iconografia mozarabe y andalusi altomedieval," *Boletin de la Associación Española de Orientalistas* 22 (1986) 61–87.

———, *La Evolución del armamento medieval en el reino castellano-leonés y al-Andalus (siglos XII–XIV)* (Madrid: Coleccion Adalid, 1993).

Warfare: Injuries

Fighting in the course of crusade expeditions and in the states established by them in the Near East, Greece, and the Baltic region meant that many thousands died from weapon injuries in battle.

By comparing mortality among clergy and knights in the course of the Fifth Crusade (1217–1221), James Powell has suggested that roughly 14 percent of knights died from weapon injuries during the campaign [James M. Powell, *Anatomy of a Crusade, 1213–1221* (Philadelphia: University of Pennsylvania, 1986), pp. 169–171]. We would expect the figure to be much higher for the poor foot soldiers, who would have been able to afford little armor or medical care for wounds.

Past excavation of battlefields from medieval Europe has demonstrated what parts of the body were most likely to suffer injuries. The vulnerable areas were the left side of the head, the forearms, and the right lower leg. This is thought to be due to the right-handedness of most soldiers, the stance taken while fighting, and the protective armor worn. Rather surprisingly, evidence of healing on the bones shows that it was common to survive many of the blows sustained in such battles. The study of accounts of battles in the crusader chronicles suggests that the most lethal weapon employed by Frankish troops was the lance. This is because it could be guided by a horseman right up until it hit the target, while its weight and speed meant that it carried significant energy, and the tip could penetrate mail. The most common injuries were from arrows and crossbow bolts. A widespread practice of the time was to shower an opposing army with arrows, and many accounts tell of individuals being hit by a significant number. However, the inability to correct their course after release, coupled with their light weight, meant that arrows were much less likely to kill a soldier in armor than a lance thrust.

In close-quarter fighting other weapons were more widely used, such as the sword, mace, and war hammer. Those wounds most likely to be fatal were penetrating wounds to the abdomen, chest, and skull and amputation of a limb. The Frankish castle at Jacob's Ford in Galilee was besieged in 1179 by Saladin's forces, and many of the Frankish garrison died when it was captured. Excavation of their skeletal remains has shown evidence for multiple sword and arrow wounds and has demonstrated the effectiveness of mail as protective armor. In contrast to injuries from hand-to-hand fighting in a pitched battle, siege warfare led to other types of wounds as well. Greek fire (an oil-based flammable composition) was employed to set siege engines alight, and many soldiers using siege towers and battering rams suffered burns. Engineers undermining city walls with tunnels were at risk from crush injuries if the tunnels collapsed unexpectedly.

Excavation of the port city of Caesarea (mod. Har Qesari, Israel) has shown a very different pattern with regards to the trauma sustained by the population there. Virtually no weapon injuries were present in the crusader-period inhabitants, while a significant proportion did sustain fractures from falls and other accidental causes. It seems that the location of a community, the strength of its defenses, and the professional activities undertaken by the inhabitants were closely associated with the likelihood of sustaining weapon injuries at the time of the crusades. However, participation in a crusade army was clearly associated with a significant risk of sustaining wounds that may have led to disfigurement, disability, or death.

–Piers D. Mitchell

Bibliography

Ingelmark, Bo E., "The Skeletons," in *Armour from the Battle of Visby, 1361,* ed. Bengt Thordman et al., 2 vols. (Stockholm: Kungl. Vitterhets Historie och Antikvitets Akademien, 1939–1940), 1:149–209.

Mitchell, Piers D., *Medicine in the Crusades: Warfare, Wounds and the Medieval Surgeon* (Cambridge: Cambridge University Press, 2004).

Mitchell, Piers D., Yossi Nagar, and Ronnie Ellenblum, "Weapon Injuries in the Twelfth Century Crusader Garrison of Vadum Iacob Castle, Galilee," *International Journal of Osteoarchaeology* 15 (2005).

Warfare: Muslim Armies

The crusades to the Near East, Egypt, and the Balkans encountered a variety of Muslim armies between the late eleventh and the fifteenth centuries. The earliest crusades were confronted by the Great Saljūq Empire and its dependencies (covering Persia, Iraq, and Syria), the Saljūq sultanate of Rūm in Anatolia, and the Fāṭimid caliphate in Egypt. Later the main enemies were the Ayyūbids in Syria and Egypt (the later twelfth and earlier thirteenth centuries), the Mamlūk sultanate in Egypt, Palestine, and Syria (thirteenth century and later), and the Ottoman Empire (fourteenth–sixteenth centuries).

Recruitment

Military recruitment in the Islamic world during the period of the crusades reflected established traditions until the coming of the Mongols in the thirteenth century. Most eastern Muslim states recruited multi-ethnic armies, which included local volunteers as well as large numbers of soldiers of slave origin called *mamlūks* or *ghulāms*. Even the Saljūq Turks turned to such traditional methods as their authority spread across most of the Middle and Near East. Paradoxically, however, it seems that many of the first so-called Turks who erupted into Byzantine Anatolia around 1025 were actually Persians, Daylamis, or Kurds. Non-Turks, including Armenians and Arabs, also played an important role in the armies of several Saljūq successor states in eleventh-century Syria and Iraq. Meanwhile, by the end of the eleventh century, some of the Christian Greek and Armenian military elites of Anatolia had also been Turkified through intermarriage. The Khwārazm-Shāhs, who took over Transoxania and eastern Persia following the decline of the Saljūqs, recruited numerous troops of slave origin, though their garrisons also included freeborn Turkish and Persian professional soldiers. Traditional Islamic military recruitment reappeared in Mongol Persia and Iraq during the fourteenth century, but was more characteristic of the post-Mongol successor states.

The most significant military development in the heartlands of Islamic civilization was a continuing professionalization of most armies, because the skills demanded of a soldier were now so high that the old militias and tribal forces could not compete. This trend prevailed despite the fact that, after the fragmentation of the Great Saljūq sultanate, many of the states involved were remarkably small and could only maintain small armies. Most rulers could only afford a small *'askar* (bodyguard of slave-recruited *mamlūks*), which formed the core of a larger force of provincial soldiers, mostly Turks or Kurds plus a few Arabs. *Ahdath* (urban militias) played a minor role in some cities, while, further south, Bedouin Arab tribes continued to dominate the semi-desert and desert regions.

Saladin and his Ayyūbid successors built a large and powerful military system in Egypt, Syria, and northern Iraq, making use of existing Zangid-Turkish and Fāṭimid-Egyptian structures. Though Saladin was himself of Kurdish origin, the role of Kurds in Ayyūbid armies has been greatly exaggerated, and the *ḥalqa*, "elite," of Saladin's army were slave-recruited Turks. Thereafter *mamlūks* continued to form the elites of subsequent Ayyūbid forces. Among the more exotic troops in Saladin's army were ex-Fāṭimid infantry of black African slave origin, but these proved unreliable and were soon disbanded. The same applied to most of the ex-Fāṭimid Armenian soldiers. Many North Africans were recruited by the Ayyūbid navy, while large numbers of renegade European warriors served Saladin and his successors after Saladin's reconquest of most of Outremer.

The army of Mamlūk Egypt was essentially the same as that of the preceding Ayyūbid dynasty, except that *mamlūks* now formed the ruling caste, as well as forming the military elite. Under the Baḥrī, or first "dynasty" of Mamlūk sultans, the majority were of Turkish origin, but

in the late fourteenth century larger numbers of Circassians, Russians, Greeks, and western Europeans were enlisted. Meanwhile, freeborn troops had a far lower status in the Mamlūk army.

The Saljūqs of Rūm who ruled central Anatolia attempted to model their army on that of the Great Saljūqs of Iraq and Persia. At first their military forces consisted of Turcoman tribesmen around an elite of slave-recruited *ghulāms* that included many Greek prisoners of war, but by the later twelfth and early thirteenth centuries, the bulk of the professional cavalry were probably freeborn Turks. Other characteristics of the army of the Saljūqs of Rūm were its assimilation of existing Byzantine, Armenian, and Georgian military elites, and the use of professional mercenaries (at the height of the sultanate's prosperity). Rūm and the subsequent Turkish principalities (*beyliks*) also encouraged urban Islamic brotherhoods as a source of religiously motivated volunteers.

Like the other western *beyliks*, the Ottomans attracted military and civil refugees from the Mongol occupation of central Anatolia. Nevertheless, the earliest Ottoman armies were entirely traditional, consisting of a majority of Turcoman tribal cavalry, perhaps a tiny elite recruited from slaves or prisoners, and a few ill-trained infantry. By 1338 the Ottoman ruler already had a small force of ex-prisoner or slave-recruited soldiers, and although these were not as yet known as such, the famous janissary (Turk. *yeni çeri*) infantry may have developed out of this earlier formation. The janissaries also differed from previous slave-recruited formations because they eventually came to be drawn from "enslaved" members of the Ottoman sultan's own non-Muslim population.

Organization

Traditional systems of military organization characterized the Islamic world until the Mongol invasions. Military ranks remained much the same as they had been for centuries. The Great Saljūq sultanate was theoretically divided into twenty-four military zones, each commanded by an officer whose Turkish or Persian title reflected the culture of his district. Each had to raise, train, equip, and lead a specified number of local troops. However, this idealized system proved inadequate, and the sultan soon created a palace-based army loyal to himself. The inadequacy of traditional structures also led to a great extension of the *iqtā'* system of allocations of revenue. Although this system was largely destroyed by the invading Mongols, it was partially recreated by the Ilkhans (the Muslim Mongol rulers of Persia) and their successors.

The success of the Ayyūbids, Mamlūks, and Ottomans in expelling the Franks of Outremer and defeating later crusading expeditions was not a result of superior numbers but reflected superior organization, logistical support, discipline, and tactics. Such sophistication could even be seen in the small forces of some city-states, such as that of twelfth-century Damascus. This force was divided into five sections, according to the origins of the soldiers or their specific role. The militia, though primarily defensive, sometimes took part in offensive campaigns. The *mutaṭawwi'a* (religious volunteers) also formed a permanent though part-time force. There were three senior military ranks: the *isfahsalār* (commander) who was often the ruler himself, the *ra'īs* (head of the militia), and the *shiḥna* (head of internal security forces). Many grants of *iqṭā'* appear to have become hereditary and were largely reserved for the ruler's *'askar* of regular cavalry. This force was in turn divided into *ṭulb* (platoons), whose weapons were normally held in the ruler's own *zardkhānah* (arsenal).

Cavalry was now the dominant arm, but Egypt, the primary center of Ayyūbid power, was seriously short of pasture. Consequently the Egyptian army relied on small numbers of exceptionally well-trained and equipped horsemen, with larger mounted forces being stationed in Syria. In Egypt the Ayyūbids also inherited the sophisticated Fāṭimid *Dīwān al-Jaysh* (ministry of war).

The elite of the Ayyūbid army was the *jandariyah*, which largely consisted of regiments of *mamlūks*, while the bulk of the army consisted of the professional but non-elite *ḥalqa*. Infantry remained essential for siege warfare but mostly consisted of mercenaries and volunteer auxiliaries. On campaign, Ayyūbid tactical units were not necessarily the same as the administrative formations, and they varied considerably, often overlapping or being created in response to circumstances. These included a *yazak* (advance guard) selected from the best cavalry and the *jālīsh*, which appears to have been a cavalry vanguard carrying banners. The term *qufl* (literally "fortress") may have referred to soldiers sent to secure the main routes; the term *ḥārafisha* ("rabble") seems to have referred to guerrillas operating inside enemy territory, while the *liṣūṣ* were light cavalry sent to attack enemy supplies or caravans. Ayyūbid logistical organization was even more sophisticated and was based upon an *atlab al-mīra* (supply train) commanded by a senior officer. There

was also a recognized military market (Arab. *sūq al-'askar*) of civilian, specialized merchants.

The army of the Mamlūk sultanate was a development of that of the preceding Ayyūbid dynasty and consisted of three main elements. The most important were the Royal Mamlūks (Arab. *mustakhdamūn*), while the *khāṣṣakīya* formed an elite bodyguard within the Royal Mamlūks. Lower in status were the *mamlūks* of senior officers, and thirdly there was the *ḥalqa*, the freeborn cavalry. However, the status of the *ḥalqa* steadily declined and, within Egypt, had little military value by the end of the fourteenth century.

The Mamlūk army's ranking structure was equally elaborate. Until the late thirteenth century, the most senior officer was the *nā'ib al-salṭana* (viceroy of Egypt), but later the *atābak al-'asākir* ("father-leader of soldiers") was considered senior. The *amīr silah* (master of arms) was in overall charge of government arsenals, the *ra'īs nawbat al-nawāb* commanded the Royal Mamlūks, the *ustadar* was in charge of *mamlūk* pay, and the *dawadar al-kabīr* selected which members of the *ḥalqa* went on campaign. Other officers were in charge of government stables, arsenals, garrisons, and so on. Ordinary officer ranks were based upon the number of soldiers the man maintained as his own retinue rather than the number he commanded on campaign. Provincial forces remained vital for the Mamlūk state, each *qirāṭ* (military district) theoretically supplying 1,000 soldiers. Syria was by far the most important region outside Egypt. Its army commander was called the *'atābak 'amīr kabīr* and was directly responsible to the sultan in Cairo. Syria itself was divided into small *mamlaka* (districts), each with a local administration with an officer called *nā'ib al-salṭana* in charge of local military forces.

The army of the Saljūqs of Rūm was divided into two parts: an "Old" or traditional force and a "New" army. The "Old Army" mainly consisted of Turcoman tribesmen and the ruler's *mamlūks*, plus the *havashvi* (armed retainers) of *iqṭā'* holders and urban governors. The "New Army" was essentially a mercenary force under the ruler's immediate control. Following the Mongol conquest of Anatolia, these elite forces were replaced by Turcoman tribesmen whose loyalty was gained by giving them grants of freehold land rather than grants of revenue, while urban militias known as *igdish* were responsible for maintaining security under their own *igdishbashis*. The little beyliks that then emerged had small military forces under the command of the local ruler. Many of the *ghāzīs* ("fighters for the Faith") who typified this period formed religious brotherhoods (Arab. *futūwa*) characterized by a very egalitarian spirit.

The Ottoman Turks absorbed a variety of military traditions, of which that of the Mamlūks was most important. At the start of the fourteenth century, the Ottomans' Turcoman tribal forces were led by their own chiefs, whose loyalty was based upon traditional Turco-Mongol rather than Islamic concepts. But by the late fourteenth century the Ottoman army consisted of two parts. The freeborne *timarli* (holders of estates) were mostly *sipahi* (cavalry), while the *maasli* (troops recruited from slaves or prisoners-of-war) received salaries from the government. Irregulars and auxiliaries formed an unrecognized third part of the Ottoman army. At the very heart of the later fourteenth-century Ottoman army were the elite *silahdar* ("guardians of the ruler's weapons") who formed one of six Palace cavalry regiments. Quite when the two janissary cavalry regiments were established is unclear, though another elite janissary unit, the *solak* (infantry bodyguard), certainly existed from an early date. The janissary infantry were part of the Ottoman sultan's *birun* ("outer service") and consisted of a single *ocak* ("hearth"), a corps commanded by the *Yeniçeri Agasi*. This *ocak* was divided into *orta* (companies), each commanded by a *Çorbaci basi* ("soup chief"). Ottoman provincial forces were divided into European and Asian armies, those in the Balkans consisting of three *uc* (frontier marches), which had, in fact, existed even before the Ottomans crossed into Europe. By the late fourteenth century, the fast expanding Ottoman Empire was divided into *sanjaq* (provinces), each of which fielded a specified number of cavalrymen. The *timarli* of these provinces were grouped into *alay* (regiments) under *alay bey* (officers), who were in turn led by the *sanjaq bey* (provincial governor). Several *sanjaq beys* were commanded by the *beylerbeyi* of the wider *eyalet* (military province).

–David Nicolle

See also: Arms and Armor; Iqṭā'; Warfare: Iberia; Warfare: Mamlūk; Outremer; Siege Warfare

Bibliography
Ayalon, David, "Studies in the Structure of the Mamluk Army, I: The Army Stationed in Egypt," *Bulletin of the School of Oriental and African Studies* 15 (1953), 203–228.

———, "Studies in the Structure of the Mamluk Army, II: The Halqa," *Bulletin of the School of Oriental and African Studies* 15 (1953), 448–476.

———, "Studies in the Structure of the Mamluk Army, III: Holders of Offices Connected with the Army," *Bulletin of the School of Oriental and African Studies* 16 (1954), 57–90.

Bombaci, Alessio, "The Army of the Saljuqs of Rum," *Istituto orientale di Napoli, Annali*, n.s., 38 (1978), 343–369.

Elbeheiry, Salah, *Les Institutions d'Egypte au Temps des Ayyubides* (Lille: Service de Reproduction des Theses, 1972).

Jandora, John W., *The March from Medina* (Clifton: Kingston, 1990).

Kennedy, Hugh, *The Armies of the Caliphs* (London: Routledge, 2001).

Nicolle, David, *Armies of the Muslim Conquest* (London: Osprey, 1993).

———, *Armies of the Caliphates, 862–1098* (Oxford: Osprey, 1998).

Warfare: Outremer

Palestine and Syria were the scene of constant warfare from the inception of Frankish rule at the beginning of the twelfth century up to its final overthrow by the Mamlūks in 1291.

Western and Eastern Warfare

In the period of the crusades western European state structures were weak and depended on subsistence agriculture. Standing armies, except for the small personal followings gathered around kings and lords, could not be afforded. The rich equipped themselves and their retainers with horses, armor, and swords and lances. This military elite was well trained to fight on horse or foot. Some were nobles; others, simply bully-boys for whom a military career offered prospects. They were housed in and around fortified residences, castles, which they defended for their masters, whose rule they imposed upon the peasantry.

At the end of the eleventh century military capacity was vested in the aristocracy and their retainers. Any large army was a gathering of retinues of lords. This elite was accompanied to war by foot soldiers, humbler men prepared to take the risks of war, among whom were sergeants, who held petty lands of lords in return for military service. Infantry were mostly spearmen and archers, sometimes supplemented by mercenaries, who became increasingly popular in the twelfth century, and by crossbowmen. Mobility gave cavalry the initiative in war, but they were not necessarily the decisive arm. Climate, geography, and topography in western Europe often favored infantry. At the battle of Hastings (1066) solid ranks of English foot soldiers massed on a hill held off the Norman cavalry for a long time. Armies in Europe had almost no light horsemen. By the late twelfth century *sergeants à cheval* (mounted sergeants) were fairly common and were clearly less well equipped than knights, but they did not represent a different kind of cavalry and fought in much the same way. At the battle of Bouvines (1214) the Flemish knights scorned the French sergeants who charged them like knights. Europe lacks vast plains where ponies can be easily grazed, so the focus of horse raising was on stall-feeding larger animals.

Tactically, commanders knew that infantry and cavalry needed to be deployed in close-ordered units so that men could support one another in battle. But large armies were occasional bodies that were so expensive to maintain that they were dispersed as soon as possible; thus, they were relatively incoherent. This partly explains the reluctance of commanders to risk battle. Even sieges raised organizational problems. The need for hand-to-hand fighting favored the besieged, and protracted operations meant that besiegers needed equipment and regular supply. Therefore, the staple of war was ravaging to destroy the enemy's economic base.

Cities, with flourishing money economies, dominated the Near and Middle East. The Great Saljūq sultanate and the Fāṭimid caliphate of Egypt were centralized, and their rulers depended on ministries (Arab. *diwāns*) that collected and spent revenues centrally. The *Sisāyat-nāma* (*Book of Government*), by the Saljūq vizier Niẓām al-Mulk, records much about the support of armies in Syria at the end of the eleventh century. Standing forces were larger than in the West but represented only the cores of armies that, as in Europe, were ad hoc gatherings. Saladin created an unusually strong regular core, but even he had difficulty keeping the remainder of his forces together. In 1250 the Circassian and Turkish *mamlūks* (slave soldiers) in Egypt slew his descendant Turān-Shāh, and set up the Mamlūk sultanate, which created a standing army. The Mamlūk regime was able to fight off the Mongol onslaught and in 1291 captured Acre (mod. 'Akko, Israel), extinguishing the Frankish states of Outremer.

Infantry can be isolated and cut off from water in the arid lands of the Near and Middle East. However, these provided large areas of grazing for light horses. Light cavalry were easily available and useful, though heavily equipped cavalry became more important in the course of the twelfth century. Saladin's *ghulāms* (horsemen using the bow and close-quarter weapons) were never as heavily equipped as the best of the crusader knights, but they were not very different. Among the light cavalry of the East, Turkish horse-archers

direct from the steppes were preeminent. At the battle of Dorylaion (1097) the anonymous knight who wrote the *Gesta Francorum* was impressed by the swirls of Turkish horsemen who surrounded the crusaders. Armenians, Syrians, and North Africans also provided light cavalry, while infantry were relegated to a subsidiary role. Tactically, Islamic commanders used mounted archers to shake the resolve of an enemy and thin their ranks, destroying isolated individuals or groups to open gaps in enemy formations. Victory against any resolute enemy depended on charging home, but the Muslim style of war, in contrast to that of the West, allowed for considerable maneuver in the approach to battle.

The Crusades to the East in the Twelfth and Thirteenth Centuries

The First Crusade (1096–1099) was a collection of five major armies and many lesser forces run by a committee of leaders. Divided command dogged all crusades. On the Second Crusade (1147–1149) King Louis VII of France and King Conrad III of Germany did not meet until the German army had been defeated in Asia Minor. On the Third Crusade (1189–1192) King Richard I of England and King Philip II of France bickered, and after Philip's departure Richard quarreled with other leaders. The republic of Venice commandeered the Fourth Crusade (1202–1204). On the Fifth Crusade (1217–1221) crusaders came and went so frequently that military decisions were made by the papal legate Pelagius of Albano. Only the crusade of Louis IX of France to the East (1248–1254) had a single leader. The problem was that crusader leaders were reluctant to accept subordination to any single person. This did not improve the coherence of crusading armies.

In the case of the First Crusade, good leadership, good luck, and the divisions of its enemies enabled it to survive long enough to become an efficient fighting force. The siege of Nicaea (mod. İznik, Turkey) from 14 May to 19 June 1097 placed no special strains on the collective leadership, though the scale of the fortifications astounded the Westerners. An ill-judged Turkish relief effort on 16 May was repelled easily because the lightly armed enemy attacked in a confined space. The sheer number of the crusaders, about 50,000–60,000 strong, enabled them to brush aside the Turks of Asia Minor at Dorylaion on 1 July. During the siege of Antioch (mod. Antakya, Turkey), lasting from 21 October 1097 to 3 June 1098, they slowly extended their siege in an effort to

Crusaders and Turks in battle during the First Crusade. (Bettmann/Corbis)

strangle the city. With the aid of a fleet and of food from the Byzantines on Cyprus and the Armenians in the mountains, they managed to supply their army, though in early 1098 they almost starved to death. In battle they learned the value of solidity of formation, of guarding their flanks, and of establishing a rear guard against the Turkish tactics of encirclement. On 2 February 1098, under threat from a Muslim army from Aleppo, they chose as sole commander Bohemund of Taranto, who led a successful ambush of the enemy army.

After the capture of Antioch Bohemund claimed the city. This caused dissension among the leaders, and eventually a relatively small army of about 12,000 marched south and captured Jerusalem from the Fāṭimids of Egypt in July 1099. The Fāṭimids had been taken by surprise because they had initially regarded the crusaders as potential allies against the Saljūq Turks. They concentrated a great force at Ascalon (mod. Tel Ashqelon, Israel) in August 1099: the crusaders marched toward them, adopting a formation in which each squadron of cavalry was protected by footmen. This complex formation was only possible because they had become a disciplined force, and this contributed to their triumph in the battle.

No later crusade, except that of Louis IX of France, stayed together long enough to achieve this kind of coherence. On the Second Crusade Louis VII's vanguard abandoned the main force, leaving it open to Turkish attack in the mountains of southern Anatolia, while the crusading fleet attacked the city of Lisbon in the Iberian Peninsula, delaying its arrival in the Holy Land. Crusades to the eastern Mediterranean remained wedded to Western methods of war throughout their relatively short lives.

The Strategic Situation of the Franks of Outremer

Because there was no "land bridge" to Europe, the condition of survival for the Frankish settlers in Outremer was the naval supremacy of the Italian cities. Their fleets helped supply the First Crusade. Egypt, the only Islamic naval power in the Mediterranean, offered some resistance, but this weakened as Egypt suffered factional struggles in the twelfth century. The Italian cities received privileged quarters in the Frankish cities to serve as bases for trade. This stimulated their maritime power and helped sustain their naval supremacy, which was enhanced when Richard I of England conquered Cyprus in 1191. The only serious Muslim challenge before the rise of the Ottoman Turks was mounted unsuccessfully by Saladin. This acquiescence in Western naval supremacy was not due to technical factors, because the Islamic world enjoyed a flourishing trade with the Far East. Perhaps this promoted a lack of interest in trade with Europe. Moreover, the Europeans interfered very little with the Islamic trade routes across the southern Mediterranean. Above all, Islamic forces defeated the Franks on land, negating the need to revive naval power.

The most important military problem of the Franks was that they were few in number. By the mid-twelfth century the kingdom of Jerusalem contained about 120,000 Westerners [Prawer, *Crusader Institutions,* pp. 102–104, 380–381], and perhaps the same number lived in the other Frankish principalities of Outremer. It has been suggested that castles were an adaptation to this circumstance and that they copied the art of stone fortification from Byzantium and the Islamic states. In fact castles were the consequence of the seigneurial structure of Frankish society, and stone was used because numerous ruins provided supplies of readily available building materials. Most were not especially formidable. Fortified cities anchored the Frankish states just as they anchored the Islamic states. However, the growing power of the Islamic states stimulated the Franks to produce the first concentric

Attack on the city of Tyre. From the *History of Alexander the Great,* fifteenth century. MS Paris, Musée du Petit Palais, Dutuit 456, fo. 58 v. (Réunion des Musées Nationaux/Art Resource)

castle: Belvoir, overlooking the Jordan Valley, was built in a single campaign in 1168–1170. There is little doubt that Jacob's Ford, under construction between October 1178 and March 1179, would have been built in the same style had Saladin not overwhelmed it before completion. This represented a formidable adaptation of castle design to the circumstances of war in the East.

Siege warfare was vital to the Franks in the twelfth century because they needed to capture the well-fortified Levantine ports. Siege warfare demanded machinery, but the Westerners enjoyed no technical advantages over the Islamic world and, indeed, never mastered the use of oil-based fire projectors, collectively called Greek fire. What is striking about crusader sieges is their persistence and organization. The Franks of the kingdom of Jerusalem prepared carefully, with a Venetian alliance, for the attack on Tyre (mod. Soûr, Lebanon) in 1124. Once the siege had begun, the Frankish army had to dig fortifications against a relief force as well as create a strong camp from which machines and attacks could be launched against the city. A similarly massive preparation brought the long siege of Ascalon (January–August 1153) to a successful conclusion.

Frankish Tactics

The key tactical adaptations of the Franks to the conditions of war in the East were readiness for battle and the employment of the massed cavalry charge as a battle-winning tactic. The Franks were a minority whose existence depended on a psychological supremacy. The Arab writer Usāma ibn Munqidh refers to their caution, but overall their hallmark was aggression. In 1119 Prince Roger of Antioch and his army were trapped when the larger army of the Artūqid emir Īlghāzī infiltrated the mountains and passes around the plain in which he had encamped on his way to relieve the siege of Atharib, but Roger chose the option of attack. In 1149 Raymond, prince of Antioch, challenged the power of

Nūr al-Dīn, only to go down to total defeat at Fons Muratus. At the springs of Cresson on 1 May 1187 about 140 Templars and Hospitallers attacked 7,000 of their enemies. These were defeats, but King Baldwin IV of Jerusalem took the enormous risk of confronting Saladin in 1177 and won at Mont Gisard.

The Franks were constantly at war and so gained experience in fighting together. As a result the armies of Outremer were more disciplined and coherent than those of the West. This meant that the Franks were ready for battle. In the face of a mobile enemy their cohesiveness enabled them to employ their magnificent warhorses in what Muslim sources call their "famous charge." This sudden, disciplined onslaught had to be timed precisely if it was to be successful, as at Marj al-Suffar on 25 January 1126. In Europe cavalry was not disciplined enough to risk a mass charge, a tactic that only evolved there in the thirteenth century. Another indication of the Franks' discipline was the fighting march. Frankish forces in certain circumstances refused to confront their enemies when they met them in the field but, instead, formed into columns of march that fought off the enemy in a kind of mobile siege. This could only have been achieved by disciplined and coherent forces.

Frankish Armies

Another remarkable military development was the establishment of military orders that provided regular forces to support the Frankish states. The Order of the Temple was originally founded to protect pilgrims on the dangerous roads of Palestine, but it quickly developed into a small army with enormous resources in the West, and the Order of the Hospital followed a rather similar evolution from its original purpose of caring for poor pilgrims. Each order could probably field about 300 knight brethren, but their wealth enabled them to hire mercenaries and foot soldiers in addition. They formed the nucleus of a standing army, and the Rule of the Templars lays down careful rules for the conduct of their forces in almost all circumstances, in much the same way as does a modern military manual. The discipline of the orders should not be exaggerated, but by the standards of the age it was remarkable.

The Franks were few, but the army of the Latin kingdom of Jerusalem, which was defeated at Hattin on 3–4 July 1187, contained about 1,300 knights and 12,000–15,000 others. By comparison, France and the German Empire mustered only about 15,000 between them at Bouvines in

1214. How was such a great force raised? At its core were 1,200–1,300 knights raised by the nobility and the military orders. Pilgrims could be pressed into service in an emergency: The chronicler William of Tyre says that pilgrims who fought at the siege of Ascalon in 1153 were paid. We know that Western knights sometimes came to the East to do service with the king or with one of the religious orders. In addition, mercenaries were employed. In 1183 a special tax was levied throughout the kingdom in order to raise mounted men and infantry. King Guy used all possible resources to hire paid men for the army of 1187.

Among the 12,000–15,000 "others" in the Frankish army at Hattin were many horsemen described as turcopoles (light horsemen), who were perhaps more numerous than the knights. The identity of the turcopoles has raised much controversy. Early chroniclers say that they were the children of Christian-Turkish marriages, but this applies to Byzantine turcopoles. In Outremer the turcopoles were light cavalry, used as mounted archers, in reconnaissance, and to carry messages. Richard I of England used them to ambush a supply caravan. The use of such an arm represents a substantial modification of Frankish fighting methods, though the turcopoles never seem to have been numerous enough to play the major role of the light cavalry in Muslim armies in battle. This still leaves the question of where they and large numbers of infantry came from. Good evidence suggests that the Franks could raise 5,000 Frankish sergeants, but this may be an underestimate. It has recently been shown that Frankish settlement in the Latin kingdom was intimately associated with Eastern Christian settlement, and this must lead us to suspect that in 1187 this population provided infantry, perhaps with the stimulus of the money that we know King Guy was liberally paying out. This might explain where the huge numbers of turcopoles and foot soldiers came from. Moreover, from early times the Franks had employed Armenians, Maronites, and Syrians as soldiers. Such native Christians, long used to contact with the Franks and attracted into military service by pay, probably made up a sizable proportion of Frankish forces and may well have been a very large element in the army of 1187. The readiness of the Franks to enlist such people represented a considerable adaptation of European military methods.

The kingdom of Jerusalem was destroyed at the battle of Hattin. We have relatively little reliable information about why King Guy gave battle or about the course of events

Frankish knights before a fortified city. From a twelfth-century fresco in the former Templar church in Cressac, France. (The Art Archive/Templar Chapel Cressac/Dagli Orti)

because our sources are poisoned by partiality, obscurity, and ignorance. This confusion should not be allowed to obscure the fact that Guy's army held together through two days of constant attack by an enemy vastly superior in numbers and that even at the last it kept its baggage train and attempted to erect a fortress-camp. But Guy failed to realize just how heavily outnumbered he was; Saladin had enough troops, perhaps as many as 30,000 in all, to surround and harass the Franks, while standing his main force off, protecting them from a charge. Considering that much of the Christian army had been hastily recruited, it was no small achievement that the Franks fought on for two days, and this underlines the skillful adaptation to Eastern

conditions that the Franks had achieved in their years in the Holy Land.

The kingdom of Jerusalem continued to exist until 1291, but after the failure of the Third Crusade it was always heavily dependent upon outside aid. The military culture of this period was dominated by the need to defend a few well-fortified cities, notably Acre, Tripoli (mod. Trâblous, Lebanon), and Antioch, and some remarkable castles, notably Margat (mod. Marqab, Syria), Krak des Chevaliers (mod. Ḥisn al-Akrād, Syria), Château Pèlerin (mod. ‘Atlit, Israel), and Arsuf. They could no longer challenge the Muslim powers in open battle and so sought to extend their influence by raids, consolidated by new fortresses and agreements with neighbors. At La Forbie in 1244 the forces of the kingdom were decimated, but on this occasion they were really only ancillaries to a quarrel between Muslim powers.

Conclusions

The Franks of Outremer in the twelfth century substantially adapted their style of warfare to regional conditions. Outnumbered, they developed an aggressive style of war that depended on a readiness to face their Muslim enemies in battle to a degree unknown in the West. They depended on a high degree of cohesion and discipline, and this enabled them to introduce their great tactical innovation: the mass cavalry charge. They raised infantry and cavalry through landed obligation and by payment, as in the contemporary West. The military orders provided regular troops to supplement the secular armies. The skills of Eastern Christians supplemented their forces. In siege warfare their persistence, discipline, and organization gave them success. Castles were a consequence of their social and political structure, but the rise of powerful enemies led them to develop a radically new design, the concentric castle. In an age when technological innovation was very limited, these were major adaptations of Western fighting methods to the conditions of warfare in the Near and Middle East.

–John France

Bibliography

Edbury, Peter, "Warfare in the Latin East," in Medieval Warfare: A History, ed. Maurice Keen (Oxford: Oxford University Press, 1999), pp. 89–112.

France, John, Victory in the East: A Military History of the First Crusade (Cambridge: Cambridge University Press, 1994).

———, Western Warfare in the Age of the Crusades, 1000–1300 (London: UCL, 1999).

———, "Crusading Warfare," in Palgrave Advances in the Crusades, ed. Helen Nicholson (Basingstoke, UK: Palgrave Macmillan, 2005), pp. 58–80.

Harari, Yitzak, "The Military Role of the Frankish Turcopoles," Mediterranean History Review 12 (1997), 75–116.

Hillenbrand, Carole, The Crusades: Islamic Perspectives (Edinburgh: Edinburgh University Press, 1999).

Housley, Norman, The Later Crusades, 1274–1580 (Oxford: Oxford University Press, 1992).

———, "European Warfare c. 1200–1320," in Medieval Warfare: A History, ed. Maurice Keen (Oxford: Oxford University Press, 1999), pp. 113–135.

Kedar, Benjamin K., "The Battle of Hattin Revisited," in The Horns of Hattin, ed. Benjamin Z. Kedar (Jerusalem: Yad Izhak Ben-Zvi Institute, 1992), pp. 190–207.

Kennedy, Hugh, Crusader Castles (Cambridge: Cambridge University Press, 1994).

Marshal, Christopher, Warfare in the Latin East, 1192–1291 (Cambridge: Cambridge University Press, 1992).

The Oxford Illustrated History of the Crusades, ed. Jonathan Riley-Smith (Oxford: Oxford University Press, 1995).

Prawer, Joshua, Crusader Institutions (Oxford: Oxford University Press, 1980).

Pryor, John, Geography, Technology and War: Studies in the Maritime History of the Mediterranean, 649–1571 (Cambridge: Cambridge University Press, 1992).

Rogers, Randall, Latin Siege Warfare in the Twelfth Century (Oxford: Oxford University Press, 1992).

Smail, Raymond C., Crusading Warfare, 1097–1193, 2d ed., ed. Christopher Marshal (Cambridge: Cambridge University Press, 1995).

Warfare: Prisoners
See Captivity

Warmund of Picquigny (d. 1128)
Latin patriarch of Jerusalem (1118–1128) during the reign of King Baldwin II of Jerusalem.

Nothing is known about Warmund's early career apart from his origins in northern France. Baldwin II nominated him as patriarch shortly after his own accession in spring 1118. Together, Warmund and Baldwin II summoned the Council of Nablus (1120), which promulgated the first canons consciously designed to meet the needs of the Latin Church in Palestine. During the king's captivity in 1123–1124, Warmund negotiated a treaty with the republic of Venice (the Pactum Warmundi) that added a wealthy port to the kingdom through a successful joint siege of Tyre (mod. Soûr, Lebanon). Warmund did little to further church organization, but he was not above exploiting his spiritual position, particularly his control over the True Cross, to intervene in political and military issues.

In 1120, Warmund initially refused to carry the relic on a campaign to the north because he and many magnates disapproved of the king's regency of Antioch and consequent absences from the kingdom. Warmund rarely allowed Baldwin II to carry the cross into battle after this incident, although the patriarch took it to the siege of Tyre and allowed royal regents access to it during the king's captivity.

–Deborah Gerish

Bibliography

Gerish, Deborah, "The True Cross and the Kings of Jerusalem," *Haskins Society Journal* 8 (1996), 137–155.

Hamilton, Bernard, *The Latin Church in the Crusader States: The Secular Church* (London: Variorum, 1980).

Mayer, Hans Eberhard, *Bistümer, Klöster und Stifte im Königreich Jerusalem* (Stuttgart: Hiersemann, 1977).

———, "The Concordat of Nablus," *Journal of Ecclesiastical History* 33 (1982), 531–543.

Wenden

Wenden (mod. Cēsis, Latvia) was one of the main castles of the Teutonic Order in Livonia.

First mentioned in 1210, the castle was evidently built by the Order of the Sword Brethren on the site of a hill fort. After passing into the possession of the Teutonic Order, it underwent considerable enlargement into a conventual building. By the fifteenth century, because of its central position in the territories of the order in Livonia, Wenden became the place where the chapter of the order was held. After the destruction of the order's castle in Riga in 1484, it became the administrative center of the master of the Livonian branch of the order. In 1577 Wenden was captured by Russians, and later by the Poles.

–Juhan Kreem

Bibliography

Apala, Zigurda, "Archäologische Zeugnisse aus der Burg Cesis/Wenden zur Zeit des Livländischen Krieges," in *Wolter von Plettenberg und das mittelalterliche Livland,* ed. Norbert Angermann and Ilgvars Misans (Lüneburg: Nordostdeutsches Kulturwerk, 2002), pp. 199–228.

Neitmann, Klaus, "Riga und Wenden als Residenzen des livländischen Landmeisters im 15. Jahrhundert," in *Stadt und Orden: Das Verhältnis des Deutschen Ordens zu den Städten in Livland, Preußen und in Deutschen Reich,* ed. Udo Arnold (Marburg: Elwert, 1993), pp. 59–93.

Tuulse, Armin, *Die Burgen in Estland und Lettland* (Dorpat: Estnischer Verlag, 1942).

Wenden, Treaty (1501)

A treaty between Lithuania and Livonia, directed against Muscovy.

Fearing an attack by the Russian principality of Muscovy, Grand Duke Alexander of Lithuania concluded a ten-year treaty with the Teutonic Order and the bishops of Livonia. Both parties were obliged to support the other against Muscovy, to attack the Russians simultaneously, and to divide any conquered territories. Each party could only initiate war or make peace with the agreement of the other party. Provision was also made for the future regulation of the border between Lithuania and Livonia. Finally, if Poland were to attack Prussia, peace would be made with Muscovy.

The treaty was ratified on 15 May in Vilnius, the Lithuanian capital, and on 21 June in Wenden (mod. Cēsis, Latvia) in Livonia. Alexander's brother John Albert, king of Poland, died on 17 June, whereupon Alexander claimed the Polish throne; this meant that in fact Livonia was left alone in the war against the Russians in 1501–1502.

–Anti Selart

Bibliography

Kentmann, Ruth, "Livland im russisch-litauischen Konflikt: Die Grundlegung seiner Neutralitätspolitik, 1494–1514," *Beiträge zur Kunde Estlands* 14 (1929), 85–160.

Wendish Crusade (1147)

The name traditionally given to the expeditions, that developed as part of the Second Crusade (1147–1149), mounted by German, Danish, and Polish armies against the pagan Slavic tribes (known as Wends in the Germanic languages), living between Poland and Saxony in the regions bounded by the rivers Oder and Elbe.

Antecedents and Origins

The Wendish Crusade was not the first attempt by neighboring Christian powers to convert and dominate the Wends. In fact some, although by no means all, of the Wendish tribes had already been Christianized after coming under the administration of the system of marches set up on the frontiers of the early German kingdom (the so-called Nordmark, the March of the Billungs, and other marches), but they had risen against German supremacy in 983 and resumed paganism. Later attempts to reintroduce Christianity, usually by indigenous Christian princes, met with new pagan insurrections in 1018 and 1066, leading to the abandonment of bishoprics that had been established at Oldenburg in Holstein, Havelberg, and Brandenburg. This in itself provided a perfect foundation for future crusades. In 1108 Adelgoz, archbishop of Magdeburg, had already thought of applying the idea of crusading against the Wends, calling upon the seasoned crusader Count Robert II of Flanders and other rulers to join the Danish and German kings.

Together they were to follow the example of those who had freed Jerusalem by freeing what the archbishop called "our Jerusalem" from defilation by local pagans. This would be an occasion to "save their souls" and, if they wished, "acquire the best land in which to live" [*Urkundenbuch des Erzstifts Magdeburg,* vol. 1, ed. Friedrich Israël and Walter Möllenberg (Magdeburg: Landesgeschichtliche Forschungsstelle für die Provinz Sachsen und für Anhalt, 1937), pp. 249–252]. It is worth noting that, in contrast to the Wendish Crusade of 1147, the archbishop did not envisage converting the Wends but contemplated only (in a similar fashion to the First Crusade) defending Christianity. This "crusade" probably did not come off, but the double promise of remission of sins and acquisition of land may well have been an important stimulus for those who in 1146–1147 advocated a Wendish crusade as an alternative to a crusade to the Holy Land.

Soon after the Magdeburg initiative, Bolesław III of Poland (1102–1138) began to put the Wends under pressure from the east when he started a drawn-out conquest of Pomerania, culminating in the capture of Stettin (mod. Szczecin, Poland) in 1121. Although this campaign was described as a missionary war by the contemporary writer known as Gallus Anonymus, the Poles failed to convert the Pomeranians. Bolesław therefore invited Bishop Otto of Bamberg, former chaplain at the Polish court, to undertake a mission to the region in 1124–1125. This led at least to the nominal conversion of the Pomeranians. At this point, however, Germany, under Lothar of Supplingenburg (first as duke of Saxony and from 1125 as king), began a more active policy toward the Wends. Lothar supported the Pomeranian prince Vartislav (who had been one of Otto's earliest converts) in his attempt to regain independence from Poland, by enfeoffing him with the pagan lands west of Pomerania. With Lothar's support Vartislav in 1127 invited Otto of Bamberg to undertake a second mission. This brought Vartislav, Otto, and indirectly Lothar into conflict not only with Bolesław but also his ally, King Niels Svensen of Denmark, who laid claim to the pagan-inhabited island of Rügen. Lothar, however, managed to weaken Niels by installing Niels's nephew Knud Lavard as prince of the pagan Abodrites. The murder of Knud in 1131 and the ensuing civil war in Denmark together with internal pressures on Lothar, however, gave paganism in the region a breathing space.

It was not only in the north that Lothar activated German policy toward the Wends. While still duke of Saxony, he had installed Albert the Bear, a nobleman of the Ascanian dynasty, in the march of Lusatia. However, on becoming king, Lothar wished to avoid having too powerful a vassal and refused to bestow the duchy of Saxony on Albert. Instead, he installed a member of the Welf dynasty, Henry the Proud of Bavaria, who was succeeded in 1143 by his son Henry the Lion. Supported in turn by the archbishops of Magdeburg and Hamburg-Bremen in their attempts to regain their former influence among the Wends, the Ascanians and Welfs thereafter competed in seeking to extend their rule into the former Wendish marches, often in changing alliances with successive kings and emperors. In the 1130s Albert had already managed to establish himself beyond the Elbe in Havelland, where he began to settle colonists from the west, and by the 1140s he had taken the title margrave of Brandenburg, although the territory was as yet unconquered.

Preaching and Recruitment

This was the situation when Bernard, abbot of Clairvaux, began preaching in Germany in 1146, following the proclamation of the Second Crusade by Pope Eugenius III. King Conrad III and many German nobles decided to go to the Holy Land, but a number of aristocrats, primarily Saxons, and churchmen such as Bishop Anselm of Havelberg thought that a crusade nearer to home was called for: they argued that if many crusaders left for Outremer, Christianity at home would be exposed to attacks from pagan Wends east of the Elbe. Such a threat was scarcely real: when the chronicler Helmold of Bosau and the author of the *Annales Palidenses* described events from a distance of a generation, they were only able to point to some Wendish raids against the fairly distant Danes. Nevertheless, at a diet in Frankfurt am Main on 13 March 1147 Bernard accepted this view. He managed to construe the crusade as a war of defense by arguing that the devil, fearing the impending salvation of Israel, had incited the wicked pagans, who now "with evil intent lie in wait." Therefore, in order to keep the "road to Jerusalem" open, the "enemies of the cross of Christ," across the Elbe, had to be attacked [Bernardus abbas Claravallensis, "Epistolae," in *Patrologiae Cursus Completus: Series Latina,* ed. Jacques-Paul Migne, 225 vols. (Paris: Migne, 1844–1865), 182, no. 457]. Consequently, Bernard promised those who took the cross against the Wends the same privileges as those who departed for the Holy Land.

A delegation from the diet, which included Anselm of Havelberg, was sent to Pope Eugenius, who responded on 11

April by issuing the bull *Divini dispensatione*. The pope officially proclaimed the crusade against the Wends and appointed Anselm as legate to it. Eugenius explicitly confirmed Bernard's promised remission of sins but also made a point of threatening with excommunication those who agreed to take money or other benefits for allowing the Wends to remain infidels.

Bernard was even more outspoken in a letter he circulated soon after the diet to rulers in order to rally crusaders. There he forbade them in any circumstances to come to terms with the pagans, until "either the religion or the nation be wiped out (Lat. *aut ritus ipse, aut natio deleatur*)" [Bernardus abbas Claravallensis, "Epistolae," no. 457]. This stipulation and other passages in the letter have been the subject of intense debate as to Bernard's exact intentions. Did Bernard envisage the outright extermination of the pagan Wends unless they converted to Christianity, as argued by Hans-Dieter Kahl? Or was the choice, as Friedrich Lotter suggests, not between baptism or death but between voluntary baptism with preserved independence on the one hand and coerced destruction of communal bonds and traditions under foreign Christian rule on the other?

In any case, it does seem that Bernard changed his view on how to treat pagans during his preaching of the Second Crusade. In a letter from the autumn of 1146, touching on why Jews under Christian rule should not be destroyed, Bernard made a point of stating that "if the pagans were similarly subjugated to us then, in my opinion, we should wait for them [to convert] rather than seek them out with swords." Then, however, as an afterthought, he continued, "but as they have now begun to attack us, it is necessary that those of us who do not carry a sword in vain repel them with force" [Bernardus abbas Claravallensis, "Epistolae," no. 363]. This may suggest that Bernard thought the situation of the Christians on the Elbe to be desperate. At any rate, in connection with the Wendish Crusade, conversion of pagans came to play a role it had not done during earlier crusades. In that respect it seems that Bernard and the pope deliberately wished to widen the scope of crusading so that all pagans could be targeted.

Course of the Crusade

According to Bernard of Clairvaux, the crusaders were to muster on 29 June 1147 in Magdeburg. It took, however, another month before they were ready. By then the forthcoming crusade had already forced Count Adolf of Holstein to abandon the agreement with the Abodrite prince, Niklot, that had allowed him to reestablish the town of Lübeck, restore churches, and even establish a monastery. Not wishing to wait for the crusaders to strike, Niklot took the offensive by attacking Lübeck and ravaging the surrounding country.

When the crusaders were finally ready, at least four armies moved against the Wends: two from Saxony (a northern and a southern one), one from Poland, and one from Denmark. According to the *Annales Magdeburgenses*, a Polish army also joined the Orthodox Russians in an attack on the pagan Prussians. Since the pope had targeted the crusade not only against Wends but also "other pagans" in the north, this campaign would qualify as the first crusade against the Prussians.

The northern Saxon army under Archbishop Adalbero of Bremen, Conrad of Zähringen, and Henry the Lion was the first to depart, moving against Niklot's Abodrites. When they laid siege to his stronghold, Dobin, they were joined by the Danes, who had arrived by sea. A Wendish attack on the Danish fleet, however, forced it to retreat. The Saxons, disregarding the papal ban, then made peace, in return for a Wendish promise to convert. Soon afterward Count Adolf reestablished his pact with Niklot, who remained a pagan.

The southern Saxon army, led by Bishop Anselm of Havelberg and Albert the Bear, moved toward Pomerania, probably cooperating with the Poles. Part of the army laid siege to Demmin on the river Peene but gave up in September and returned home. Another part invested Stettin. The people of Stettin demonstrated their Christian faith by displaying crosses on the walls, and through their bishop, Adalbert, they rebuked the crusaders for wishing to conquer the land instead of strengthening the faith by preaching. Having lost many knights without taking the town, the crusaders finally decided to make peace with the Pomeranian prince, Ratibor, and return home. Next year Ratibor appeared in Havelberg in order to profess his Christian faith as he had received it from Otto of Bamberg. In choosing to target Stettin, Albert the Bear and the archbishopric of Magdeburg probably hoped to achieve precisely what they had failed to accomplish through Otto's mission in 1128: to bring Pomerania under their influence.

Consequences

The poor results of the Wendish Crusade (one pagan temple is recorded to have been destroyed) led to severe criticism from several quarters. Helmold of Bosau, with hindsight, explained the crusaders' lame performance by their disinclination to devastate the land they saw as future possessions. Yet even if the crusade accomplished little, it did begin a kind of permanent crusade against the Wends throughout the remainder of the twelfth century, perhaps still based on the bull *Divini dispensatione.* Step by step, the Wends were converted and subjugated to foreign rule. In 1157 Albert the Bear finally managed to make good his title as margrave of Brandenburg by capturing the town of Brandenburg itself. Soon afterward Henry the Lion intensified his activity among the Wends, partly in collaboration and partly in competition with a rejuvenated Denmark under Valdemar I the Great. During the 1160s most of the Wends along the Baltic coast between the Oder and Elbe were brought under either Saxon or Danish rule, culminating in the Danish conquest of the important temple-fortress at Arkona. When Henry the Lion fell out with Emperor Frederick I Barbarossa in 1180, the Danes managed to take political control over most of the region as a basis for their further crusades into, and temporary domination of, the Baltic region.

The Saxon-Danish expansion was accompanied by colonization by peasants from northern Germany, Holland, and Frisia, similar to that which Albert the Bear had begun in his territory in the 1130s. This gave rise to a layer of indigenous Germanized princes, who managed to stay in power as vassals, while Wendish peasant villages managed to coexist with German settlements for several centuries. By the end of the twelfth century churches and monasteries had been established in all former pagan regions and linked to one or other of the surrounding archbishoprics. Only the Pomeranian church, now centered in Kammin (mod. Kamień Pomorski, Poland), managed to remain exempt.

–*John H. Lind*

See also: Abodrites; Polabians; Second Crusade (1147–1149)

Bibliography

Constable, Giles, "The Place of the Magdeburg Charter of 1107/08 in the History of Eastern Germany and of the Crusades," in *Vita Religiosa im Mittelalter: Festschrift für Kaspar Elm zum 70. Geburtstag,* ed. Franz J. Felten and Nikolas Jaspert (Berlin: Duncker & Humblot, 1999), pp. 238–299.

Gaethke, Hans-Otto, *Herzog Heinrich der Löwe und die Slawen nordöstlich der unteren Elbe* (Frankfurt am Main: Lang, 1999).

Guth, Klaus, "The Pomeranian Missionary Journeys of Otto I of Bamberg and the Crusade Movement of the Eleventh to Twelfth Centuries," in *The Second Crusade and the Cistercians,* ed. Michael Gervers (New York: St. Martin's, 1992), pp. 13–23.

Hill, Thomas, "Von der Konfrontation zur Assimilation: Das Ende der Slawen in Ostholstein, Lauenburg und Lübeck vom 12. bis zum 15. Jahrhundert," in *Slawen und Deutsche um südlichen Ostseeraum vom 11. bis zum 16. Jahrhundert,* ed. Michael Müller-Wille, Dietrich Meier, and Henning Unverhau (Neumünster: Wachholtz, 1995), pp. 79–104.

Jensen, Kurt Villads, "Denmark and the Second Crusade: The Formation of a Crusader State?" in *The Second Crusade: Scope and Consequences,* ed. Jonathan Phillips and Martin Hoch (Manchester, UK: Manchester University Press, 2001), pp. 164–179.

Kahl, Hans-Dietrich, "Wie kam es 1147 zum 'Wendenkreuzzug'?" in *Europa Slavica—Europa Orientalis: Festschrift für Herbert Ludat zum 70. Geburtstag,* ed. Klaus-Detlev Grothusen and Klaus Zernack (Berlin: Duncker & Humblot, 1980), pp. 286–296.

———, "Die weltweite Bereinigung der 'Heidenfrage'—ein übersehenes Kriegsziel des Zweiten Kreuzzuges," *Spannungen und Widersprüche, Gedächtnisschrift für František Graus* (Sigmaringen: Thorbecke, 1992), pp. 63–89.

Lotter, Friedrich, *Die Konzeption des Wendenkreuzzugs: Ideengeschichtliche, kirchenrechtliche und historischpolitische Voraussetzungen der Missionierung von Elb- und Ostseeslawen um die Mitte des 12. Jahrhunderts* (Sigmaringen: Thorbecke, 1977).

———, "The Crusading Idea and the Conquest of the Region East of the Elbe," in *Medieval Frontier Societies,* ed. Robert Bartlett and Angus McKay (Oxford: Oxford University Press, 1989), pp. 267–306.

Lübke, Christian, "Die Beziehungen zwischen Elb- und Ostseeslawen und Dänen vom 9. bis zum 12. Jahrhundert: Eine andere Option elbslawischer Geschichte?" in *Zwischen Reric und Bornhöved,* ed. Ole Harck and Christian Lübke (Stuttgart: Steiner, 2001), pp. 23–36.

Neumeister, Peter, "Die slawische Ostseeküste im Spannungsfeld der Nachbarmächte (bis 1227/1239)," in *Zwischen Reric und Bornhöved,* ed. Ole Harck and Christian Lübke (Stuttgart: Steiner, 2001), pp. 37–55.

Szacherska, Stella Maria, "The Political Role of the Danish Monasteries in Pomerania, 1171–1223," *Mediaeval Scandinavia* 10 (1977), 122–155.

Taylor, Pegatha, "Moral Agency in Crusade and Colonization: Anselm of Havelberg and the Wendish Crusade of 1147," *International History Review* 22 (2000), 757–784.

Werner von Orseln (d. 1330)

Grand master of the Teutonic Order (1324–1330).

Werner was probably born between 1285 and 1290, and

originated from the family of the bailiffs of Ursel in Hesse. He is first mentioned as a brother of the order while serving as commander of Ragnit (mod. Neman, Russia) in Prussia in 1312. Three years later he had become grand commander. When Grand Master Karl von Trier was deposed in 1317, Werner supported him against the opposition in Prussia. After Karl's death, Werner was elected grand master (6 July 1324). One of his opponents, Friedrich von Wildenberg, became grand commander, thus creating a balance between the factions. Werner attempted to restore and increase spiritual life and discipline.

During Wener's mastership the priest brother Peter von Dusburg wrote the *Cronicon Terrae Prussiae*, the first extensive narrative of the order's history in Prussia, possibly aiming, among other purposes, at stirring new vigor among the brethren. Werner also welcomed the first international guests who participated in the order's campaigns. His attempts to impose discipline seem to have caused his murder at Marienburg (mod. Malbork, Poland) on 18 November 1330. According to Peter von Dusburg, the murderer, Brother Johannes von Endorf, wanted to take revenge for having been rebuked harshly by the master.

–Axel Ehlers

See also: Baltic Crusades; Teutonic Order
Bibliography
Conrad, Klaus, "Werner von Orseln," in *Die Hochmeister des Deutschen Ordens, 1190–1994*, ed. Udo Arnold (Marburg: Elwert, 1998), pp. 60–65.
Urban, William, *The Samogitian Crusade* (Chicago: Lithuanian Research and Studies Center, 1989).

Wesenberg, Battle of (1268)

A battle fought between Livonians and Russians near Wesenberg (mod. Rakvere, Estonia), a fortress in the district of Vironia in northeastern Estonia, which at the time belonged to the Danish Crown.

Wesenberg had been a target of the Novgorodians in their attempts to ward off a new crusade against Russia. In 1267 the Novgorodians besieged the fortress unsuccessfully and retreated with losses. They then prepared for another attack, mustering a large army from the Novgorodian state and elsewhere in northeast Russia. They also signed a treaty with the archbishop of Riga, the bishop of Dorpat (mod. Tartu, Estonia), and the Livonian master of the Teutonic Order, which forbade their interference in the war between the Russians and the Estonian vassals of the Danish king.

On 23 January 1268 the Russian troops entered Vironia, but unexpectedly came upon a combined army of the Livonian rulers who had broken the treaty. The battle took place on 18 February, by the river Kegol about 8 kilometers (5 mi.) from Wesenberg. The Russians managed to drive the Livonians back to Wesenberg, but in the evening the Livonians attacked their enemies' baggage train and thus drew the Russian forces off. Fighting ceased in the darkness, and as both armies had suffered heavy losses, the action was not begun anew the next morning. The Russians retired, and the Livonians did not have sufficient forces to pursue them. Alexander, bishop of Dorpat, Mikhail, the mayor of Novgorod, and many Russian noblemen were killed in the battle.

–Evgeniya L. Nazarova

See also: Baltic Crusades
Bibliography
Matuzova, Vera I., and Evgeniya L. Nazarova, Крестоносты и Русь: Конец XII в. – 1270. Тексты, переводы, комментарии (Moskva: Indrik, 2002).
Selart, Anti, "Confessional and Political Co-operation: Livonia and Russia in the Thirteenth Century," in *Crusade and Conversion on the Baltic Frontier, 1150–1500*, ed. Alan V. Murray (Aldershot, UK: Ashgate, 2001), pp. 151–176.

Western Sources

At the time of the inception of the crusade movement, Latin was the near-universal language of reading and writing throughout western Europe. Latin was thus the dominant medium of primary sources until the end of the Middle Ages, although from the late twelfth century, such texts also began to be written in the main vernacular languages, notably French and German. The linguistic character of narrative, documentary, and other sources thus stood in marked contrast to that of imaginative, that is nonfactual, literature with crusade themes, in which the predominant linguistic vehicles were French, Occitan (Provençal), Middle English, Middle High German, Middle Dutch, and other vernaculars. The number of individual sources potentially relevant to the various aspects of crusading is simply too vast to allow an exhaustive treatment in the scope of an encyclopedia. This entry, therefore, concentrates on the most important and accessible sources specifically devoted to crusade expeditions and associated settlement.

Principal Genres

It is usual to divide primary sources into different generic categories. Narrative sources of the crusades can be understood as comprising prose (or very rarely, verse) accounts of the crusading expeditions and settlement in the countries of the Near East, Greece, and the Baltic region. There survive a great number of chronicles, histories, and biographies specifically devoted to such themes, often composed by eyewitnesses, whose testimony is usually to be preferred to that of those more removed from the events they describe in space or time. However, the number of narrative accounts relevant to the crusades is vast and goes far beyond works with specific crusading themes. Particularly in the twelfth and thirteenth centuries, the crusades were regarded as so important that they were treated in a vast range of works, and so important information can often be obtained from texts not specifically devoted to crusading or settlement, such as universal histories (histories of the world from the Creation up to the writer's time) or annals of particular cities or regions.

The success of the First Crusade encouraged the writing of histories that were more elaborate and engaging than previous chronicles. Moreover, participants who wrote histories of the First Crusade were conscious that they were describing an unprecedented event, and the writers in western Europe who took up their stories emphasized the importance of divine intervention in ensuring success. This interpretation of events was to present difficulties to those who wanted to record later expeditions, since all of them fell short of expectations. Thus there is considerable variation in coverage and quality among Western sources for the different crusades. Furthermore, before the end of the twelfth century, a single writer dominated the field: William of Tyre, whose *Chronicon,* written in Outremer using a wealth of earlier materials, displaced its exemplars and formed the basis of secondary history writing on the crusades through the Middle Ages, Renaissance, and Enlightenment, only being challenged in the nineteenth century. The critical study of Western sources began with Heinrich von Sybel (1817–1895), a pupil of the great historian Leopold von Ranke (1795–1886). Sybel's *History of the Crusades* appeared in 1841. Thereafter, critical editions of many Western sources began to appear, notably those produced by Heinrich Hagenmeyer between 1877 and 1913. Many of the Western texts edited for the series *Recueil des historiens des croisades* (1841–1906) have now been superseded by better editions.

Documentary sources include charters, diplomas, letters, privileges, and similar texts. The most common form of documentary source in the Middle Ages was the charter, which was essentially the written record of a legal transaction, such as the sale or gift of property, or concession of rights. Since charters were important to document such property and rights, the majority of those that survive derive from versions or copies originally held by the recipients of such transactions rather than the issuers or donors. Charters survive in various forms: originals, contemporary copies, confirmations (often issued by higher authorities), and authenticated copies (usually known by the Latin terms *vidimus* or *inspeximus*) made by notaries or other officials. Particularly where the recipients were ecclesiastical institutions, such as religious orders or individual monasteries or bishoprics, a common practice was to compile cartularies: these were collections of individual charters and other documents copied into manuscript volumes or parchment rolls, to provide a consolidated record of the recipient's property and rights.

A significant number of charters have come down to us that were issued by departing or potential crusaders, recording acts intended to raise funds for their journeys or to make pious donations for the benefit of their souls or those of their families. Such documents provide valuable information about the financing of crusades, but also about the motivation and state of mind of crusaders, as well as family traditions of crusading. Charters, which have a greater immediacy, and also record more prosiac information than narrative sources, are also fundamental to the study of the histories and societies of the states founded by the crusades in Outremer, Greece, and the Baltic region. Particularly valuable in this context are the extensive collections of charters relating to military orders such as the Hospitallers and other ecclesiastical institutions based in the Holy Land, such as the Church of the Holy Sepulchre in Jerusalem.

Letters can also be considered as belonging to the category of documentary sources. These include diplomatic correspondence as well as private communications, such as letters sent home by individual crusaders. Many of these have not survived in their original form, but have been transmitted as quotations or reports embedded in narrative sources. Other types of letters had a more public relevance and, in some cases, a legal status. This applies particularly to papal letters dealing with the crusades (often known as bulls). These were the means used by the papacy to proclaim and regulate crusades: they generally set out the cause and aims of a new crusade and specified the various spiritual and temporal privileges to be gained by crusaders. Another type of letter with a specific, crusading-related content was the appeal for military assistance sent by monarchs and ecclesiastical leaders in Outremer, directed to popes and Western rulers. Such appeals became more frequent with the major Muslim military encroachments on the Frankish states by Nūr al-Dīn and Saladin in the second half of the twelfth century

Treaties and contracts also give important information on the organization, course, and outcomes of many individual crusades. Important examples are the Treaty of Adrianople (1190), which regulated relations between Byzantium and Frederick I Barbarossa during the Third Crusade; the Treaty of Venice (1201), the fateful agreement between the Venetian Republic and the leaders of the Fourth Crusade that determined the terms for the transport and provisioning of the expedition to the East; and the Treaty of Christburg (1269), which ended the first great rebellion of the native Prussians against the rule of the Teutonic Order.

Apart from these main categories, there are numerous other types of sources relating to the crusade movement, Outremer, Frankish Greece, and the Baltic lands. These include crusade sermons, law codes, genealogies, financial records, the rules and customs of military orders, and inscriptions. Although most narrative sources specifically devoted to the crusades are available in good editions and, in most cases, translations into English or other modern European languages, documentary and other sources are much less accessible, particularly for the later Middle Ages, where as many are dispersed among different archives and still remain to be edited.

The First Crusade (1096–1099) and the Crusade of 1101

Three participants wrote about their experiences in the course of the expedition that culminated in the capture of Jerusalem in 1099: the anonymous author of the *Gesta Francorum,* Raymond of Aguilers, and Fulcher of Chartres. All three were clerics writing in Latin, but each accompanied a different contingent of the crusade, and so there are differences of perspective. However, they are to some extent interdependent, Raymond and Fulcher having apparently used the *Gesta Francorum.* This last work was also reproduced with some variations by Peter Tudebode and the *Historia Belli Sacri,* both of which preserve scraps of original information. The *Gesta Francorum* was more thoroughly rewrit-

ten by three authors, all French Benedictine monks, early in the twelfth century. Guibert of Nogent retitled his work *Dei Gesta per Francos,* a change that expresses his didactic purpose; book 7 contains valuable information unique to Guibert. Baldric of Dol's alterations to the *Gesta* were mostly stylistic. He was the chief source for the account of the expeditions of 1096 and 1101 given by the Anglo-Norman monk Orderic Vitalis, who added details from oral sources and biographical detail about Norman participants in the expeditions. Robert, a monk of Rheims, was both the least adventurous adapter and the most influential; his text was widely copied. The original Latin version exists today in more than 120 manuscripts, and at least four German translations were made in the later Middle Ages. Robert's influence may be discerned in texts as disparate as the works of Henry of Huntingdon and Gilo of Paris.

Four other chroniclers also wrote accounts of the First Crusade early in the twelfth century. Ekkehard of Aura was a participant in the Crusade of 1101, traveling with an army from German territory. The Genoese annalist Caffaro also sailed to Outremer in 1101, and his *Annals,* as the work of a layman, record interesting detail. Radulph of Caen, who arrived in Outremer in 1108, wrote the *Gesta Tancredi,* which, as its title suggests, celebrated the exploits of Tancred, later prince of Galilee and regent of Antioch. This work is extant in a single manuscript, written in very idiosyncratic Latin. However, the longest and most detailed account of the First Crusade and of the first twenty years of settlement in Syria and Palestine was written by Albert of Aachen, a cleric from the German Rhineland. Since Albert never traveled to Outremer, there has been much discussion of his sources and veracity. Nevertheless, he has proved himself indispensable to later historians, from William of Tyre in the twelfth century to Steven Runciman in the twentieth. One virtue of Albert's *Historia Iherosolimitana* is that he presents a version of the instigation and preaching of the crusade that was evidently current in his region and features the charismatic preacher Peter the Hermit. Albert gives the fullest account of the so-called People's Crusade of 1096, including the massacres of the Jews in the Rhineland cities. Later he centers his story on Godfrey of Bouillon and his brother Baldwin. Thus his focus is quite different from and independent of the eyewitness accounts.

There are two vernacular accounts of the First Crusade that have been thought to incorporate authentic and original material, but both must be dismissed: that contained in the *Chronicle of Zimmern* has been shown to be a sixteenth-century fabrication, while the Old French *Chanson d'Antioche* was composed in the last quarter of the twelfth century and any authentic material cannot be distinguished from later additions with any security.

There is a small but significant corpus of letters sent by participants of the crusade to recipients in the West. Some of these can be regarded as essentially diplomatic correspondence, such as the famous Laodikeia Letter sent by the leaders of the crusade to the pope in September or October 1099. Others, such as those written by Anselm of Ribemont and Stephen of Blois, have a more private character. However, all are important for their information on the atmosphere in the crusade army and events and conditions in the course of the march.

Outremer (1098–1291)

Fulcher of Chartres was not an eyewitness to the culminating events of the First Crusade because he was with Baldwin of Boulogne in Edessa. However, when Baldwin became king of Jerusalem in 1100, Fulcher was at his side, and for the next twenty-seven years he wrote the best-informed account of the Frankish settlement of Outremer. Albert of Aachen provides supplementary and sometimes contradictory detail for the years to 1119, based apparently on the testimony of returning travelers. Quite independently, the official known as Walter the Chancellor wrote the *Bella Antiochena*, a history of the wars fought by the principality of Antioch against the Turks of northern Syria between 1114 and 1122.

The texts of Fulcher and Walter were used by William of Tyre, the outstanding chronicler of life in the Latin East in the twelfth century. In addition to his surviving *Chronicon,* which deals with the history of Palestine and Syria from the reign of the Byzantine emperor Heraclius up to 1184, he is also known to have written another work, now lost, which was a history of the Islamic world up to his own day. For the *Chronicon*'s account of the period before his own lifetime, William was dependent on other writers, but after the late 1120s he provides a well-informed account of the affairs of the kingdom of Jerusalem. His influential history was translated into French and attracted continuators, whose accounts are important for the end of the first kingdom of Jerusalem (1099–1187) and the thirteenth century. The "Latin Continuation" is generally thought to give a sober and reliable account of events. An interrelated group of continuations in Old French were written in France and are usually known as the *Eracles,* while the *Chronique d'Ernoul* was written in Outremer and at some time attached to the French translation of William. Events leading up to the battle of Hattin (1187) and Saladin's subsequent conquests are described in a short but detailed work known as the *Libellus de expugnatione Terrae Sanctae per Saladinum expeditione,* and in two narratives by the theologian Peter of Blois, the *Passio Reginaldi* and the *Conquestio de dilatione vie Ierosolimitane,* as well as in other works of more general character. Insights into the topography and society of the Holy Land can be gained from the travel accounts of pilgrims such as John of Würzburg, Saewulf, and Nikulás of Munkethverá.

For the thirteenth century, there is a notable corpus of legal texts, written in Old French and collectively known as the *Assizes of Jerusalem* (Fr. *Assises de Jérusalem*), while the genealogical compilation called *Lignages d'Outremer* (first version from around 1268/1270), gives important genealogical and prosopographical information on the nobility of Outremer and Cyprus, although its accuracy can often be questioned for the earlier twelfth century.

Regarding the end of Frankish settlement with the fall of Acre in 1291, there is only one eyewitness account: the *Gestes des Chiprois,* written by the "Templar of Tyre," who was not in fact a Templar, though as secretary to the master of the order he was well placed to describe events. Marino Sanudo the Elder based his account on the *Gestes.* Two works accused the garrison of Acre of cowardice, and even treachery, but the author of neither was present during the siege: the anonymous author of *De excidio urbis Acconis,* and Thaddeus of Naples who called his account *Hystoria de desolacione civitatis Acconensis.*

The conquest of much of Syria and Palestine by Saladin in 1187 and the final loss of Outremer in 1291 meant that a large number of the archives of these countries were lost. There survive a considerable number of documents of the kings of Jerusalem, the princes of Antioch, and the counts of Tripoli. However, there are only a handful of documents from the county of Edessa, while the only baronial archive to survive was that of the lordship of Joscelin III of Courtenay (the so-called *seigneurie de Joscelin*), which was taken over by the Teutonic Order when it acquired the lordship from Joscelin's heirs in 1220. The vast majority of the documents and letters that survive relate to the military orders or the other main ecclesiastical institutions: the Hospitallers, the Templars, and the Teutonic Order; the Church of the Holy Sepulchre; and the abbey of Our Lady of Jehosaphat in

Jerusalem. A large number of the documents relating to Outremer are not yet available in full-text editions, and the historian is still dependent on the calendar of documents in digest form provided by Reinhold Röhricht in his *Regesta Regni Hierosolymitani* (1893–1904).

The Second Crusade (1147–1149)

The success of the First Crusade engendered a large number of histories; the failure of the Second ensured it would be less well recorded. For the expedition to Outremer, there are three main narrative sources: Odo of Deuil's *De Ludovici VII profectione in Orientem,* Suger's *Life of Louis VII,* and Otto of Freising's *Gesta Friderici,* which is a good example of how historians did not like to write about failure. From the point of view of the Franks of Outremer, William of Tyre is important, less for narrative content, since the Second Crusade happened during the period of his absence from the Levant, but because he took pains to seek out information that might help to explain the expedition's failure. An interesting development in Second Crusade studies is a new understanding of the crusade as an advance on three fronts: against the Turks in the Levant, against the pagan Slavs in northern Europe, and against the Moors in the Iberian Peninsula. The last campaign is recounted in the work known as *De expugnatione Lyxbonensi* and in the "Teutonic Source," now more generally known as the "Lisbon Letter." These two texts are largely in agreement as to the events of the campaign in Portugal, though the *De expugnatione* incorporates theological discussion. The expedition against the Slavic tribes to the east of the river Elbe has also been established as part of the papal master plan, and so the only chronicle to describe this in detail, by Helmold of Bosau, should be added.

The Third Crusade (1189–1192)

The part played by King Richard I of England in the Third Crusade, as well as its comparative, if qualified, success, ensured that it would be celebrated in historical narrative. An important source is the *Itinerarium peregrinorum et Gesta Regis Ricardi.* This has some disputed relationship with the "Latin Continuation" of William of Tyre. Ambroise, who claimed to be an eyewitness of many of the events he described, wrote a long poem in Old French. Anglo-Norman writers who were well informed about some part of the crusade are Roger of Howden, who traveled with the fleet to Outremer, returning in 1191; Richard of Devizes, whose informant traveled with the royal party as far as Sicily; Ralph

de Diceto, whose chaplain went on the expedition and provided him with information; Ralph of Coggeshall, who names his informants; and William of Newburgh, whose account is well-informed and who may have used the "Latin Continuation." Only one source takes the French perspective: the *Gesta Philippi Augusti* of Rigord, while several German chroniclers recorded the exploits of Emperor Frederick I until his death in Asia Minor. The best known of these accounts is the *Historia de expeditione Friderici imperatoris,* whose author is unknown but traditionally called Ansbert. The voyage of a Danish-Norwegian fleet, which arrived much later than the other contingents, is described in the *Historia de profectione Danorum in Hierosolymam,* composed by a monk of the Norwegian monastery of Tønsberg. A short text known as the *Narratio de primordiis ordinis Theutonici* gives an account of the foundation of the German hospital at Acre (1190), the institution that was converted into the Teutonic Order eight years later.

The Fourth Crusade (1202–1204) and Frankish Greece

Geoffrey of Villehardouin's *Conquête de Constantinople* has long overshadowed all other works: the author was at the center of the events and recorded them in engrossing detail. His authoritative and "top-down" account has its counterpart in Robert of Clari's view (with the same title) from the ranks of poorer knights: it is partial and unreliable but occasionally gives information, particularly about attitudes, that serves to correct Villehardouin. The *Devastatio Constantinopolitana,* thought to be the work of a participant from the Rhineland, complements these two sources: it conveys accurate data, but also the disillusionment of the poorer crusaders. Three sources celebrated the triumphal return of their heroes with relics that were seen as proof of divine favor: Gunther of Pairis, whose work reads as an apologia for his patron Abbot Martin; the Anonymous of Halberstadt's defense of his bishop, Conrad; the Anonymous of Soissons's account of the translation of relics to his church. These three accounts are relevant to the study of mentalities relating to the Fourth Crusade. Finally, the *Gesta Innocentii III* is an uncritical biography of the pope, but preserves innumerable details that would otherwise be lost.

There are fewer narrative accounts of the subsequent Latin settlement in the Empire of Constantinople and Frankish Greece. Villehardouin's account is continued for the reign of Emperor Henry by his court chronicler, Henry of Valenciennes. For the Frankish states of central and southern Greece in the thirteenth and fourteenth centuries, the key text is the *Chronicle of the Morea,* which exists in French, Aragonese, and Italian versions, as well as Greek. The *Assizes of Romania* (Fr. *Assises de Romanie*) represent the legal customs of the Frankish states.

The Albigensian Crusade (1209–1219)

There are three works specifically devoted to the crusade against the Cathars of southern France. Peter of Les Vaux-de-Cernay was a nephew of the bishop of Carcassonne and witnessed many of the events he describes in his *Historia Albigensis.* Peter wrote (in Latin) from the point of view of the crusading knights, and the narrative effectively ends with the death of his hero, Simon of Montfort, in 1218. The vernacular *Chanson de la Croisade albigeoise* had two authors: the first, William of Tudela, supported the papacy and the French campaign, though not without some reservations; the second, anonymous writer was wholeheartedly opposed to the crusade and the intervention of the northerners. As an entertainment intended for a lay audience, the poem is very different in tone from Peter's *Historia,* but where the two narratives cover the same ground they are in substantial agreement. The major difference relates to Simon of Montfort, whom the anonymous poet depicts as villain rather than hero. The third source is the *Chronica* of William of Puylaurens, who was a southerner and also notary for the Inquisition. He covers events more briefly as part of a chronicle of the years 1146–1272.

The Baltic Crusades

Much of the early Danish involvement in the Baltic region is described by the chronicler Saxo Grammaticus, but by far the most important source for the early crusades to Livonia is the chronicle of the German priest Henry of Livonia.

Most of the other narrative sources dealing with the Baltic Crusades were the work of authors associated with the Teutonic Order, and written in High German or Low German: the *Livonian Rhymed Chronicle* (Ger. *Livländische Reimchronik*), the *Ältere Hochmeisterchronik,* and the chronicles of Nicolaus von Jeroschin, Hermann von Wartberge, Wigand von Marburg, Johann von Posilge, and Bartolomäus Hönecke; the main Latin narrative after Henry of Livonia is the chronicle of Peter von Dusburg, a priest of the order. There are also various unique types of source relating to the military campaigns of the Teutonic Knights. These include the records of payments to mercenaries (the *Soldbuch*) as well as some 100 different so-called *Litauische Wegeberichte,*

descriptions of routes to be taken by campaigns against Lithuania, compiled on the basis of information provided by scouts and other local informants. There are extensive edited collections of documents for both Prussia and Livonia, as well as a large number of archival sources, only partly published, in the collections of the Geheimes Staatsarchiv Preußischer Kulturbesitz in Berlin.

Crusades to the Levant in the Later Middle Ages

The popular expeditions of the later Middle Ages, such as the Children's Crusade (1212), and the First and Second Shepherds' Crusades (1251 and 1320), which were largely composed of the poor and uneducated, did not produce specific records. They are described in some narrative sources, although the information these yield is often sketchy and elliptical. Oliver of Paderborn's *Historia Damiatana* is the most important account of the Fifth Crusade (1217–1221); it may be supplemented by the letters of James of Vitry and the universal chronicle of Alberic of Troisfontaines (who also gives information on the Fourth Crusade and the Albigensian Crusade).

The Crusade to the East of Louis IX of France (1248–1254) is described in John of Joinville's life of the king, *Livre de saintes paroles et des bons faiz nostre saint roy Looÿs.* Joinville accompanied Louis to the East, and his narrative is both well informed and vividly readable. However, he did not join the king's crusade to Tunis (1270), and his account of this expedition is much less detailed. Guillaume de Machaut's verse history, *La Prise d'Alixandre,* is the main source for the capture of the city of Alexandria in Egypt by King Peter I of Cyprus in 1365. Important information on the Mahdia Crusade (1390) and the Crusade of Nikopolis (1396) is given by chivalric biographies in French of two of the major participants: Jean Cabaret d'Orville's life of Louis of Bourbon (the *Chronique du bon Loys de Bourbon*) and the anonymous *Livre des Fais* describing the career of Jean II Le Meingre, Marshal Boucicaut (which also describes the marshal's expeditions to Prussia in 1384 and 1385).

Finally, mention should be made of a new genre that came into being after the loss of Syria and Palestine to the Mamlūks, which culminated in the fall of Acre in 1291. This genre consisted of treatises or memoranda setting out projects or strategies relating to the recovery of the Holy Land (Lat. *de recuperatione Terrae Sanctae*) which is often used as a generic name for them. From the late thirteenth century, a large number of such works were produced and circulated, varying considerably in their practicality and influence. Some of the best-known examples were composed by Fidenzio of Padua, Marino Sanudo Torsello, Philippe de Mézières, Bertandon de la Broquière, Ramon Llull, and Pierre Dubois.

-Susan Edgington
Alan V. Murray

Bibliography
For specific bibliography see entries on individual sources.

Major Source Collections
Cartulaire du chapitre du Saint-Sépulcre de Sépulcre de Jérusalem, ed. Geneviève Bresc-Bautier (Paris: Académie des Inscriptions et Belles-Lettres, 1984).

Cartulaire général de l'Ordre des Hospitaliers de S. Jean de Jérusalem, 1100–1310, ed. Joseph Delaville Le Roulx, 4 vols. (Paris: Leroux, 1894–1906).

Cartulaire général de l'Ordre du Temple 1119?–1150: Recueil des chartes et des bulles relatives à l'Ordre du Temple, ed. Guigue A. M. J. A. d'Albon (Paris: Champion, 1913).

Chartes de Terre Sainte provenant de l'abbaye de N.-D. de Josaphat, ed. Henri-François Delaborde (Paris: Ecoles Françaises d'Athènes et de Rome, 1880).

Corpus inscriptionum crucesignatorum Terrae Sanctae, 1099–1291, ed. Sabino De Sandoli (Jerusalem: Franciscan Printing Press, 1974).

Delaville Le Roulx, Joseph, "Chartes de Terre-Sainte," *Revue de l'Orient latin* 11 (1905–1908), 181–191.

Epistulae et chartae ad historiam primi belli sacrae spectantes: Die Kreuzzugsbriefe aus den Jahren 1088–1100, ed. Heinrich Hagenmeyer (Innsbruck: Wagner, 1901).

Jerusalem Pilgrimage (1099–1185), ed. John Wilkinson, Joyce Hill, and W. F. Ryan (London: Hakluyt Society, 1988).

Liv-, Esth- und Curländisches Urkundenbuch nebst Regesten, ed. Friedrich G. von Bunge et al., 15 vols. (Reval: Kluge und Ströhm, 1853–1914).

Marsy, Comte de, "Fragment d'un cartulaire de l'ordre de Saint-Lazare en Terre-Sainte," *Archives de l'Orient latin* 2 (1884), 121–157.

Monumenta Germaniae Historica: Die Urkunden der deutschen Könige und Kaiser (München: Monumenta Germaniae Historica, 1879–).

Monumenta Germaniae Historica: Scriptores (Hannover: Hahn, 1826–).

Monumenta Germaniae Historica: Scriptores rerum Germanicarum in usum scholarum separatim editi (Hannover: Hahn, 1871–).

Monumenta Germaniae Historica: Scriptores rerum Germanicarum, nova series (Hannover: Hahn, 1922).

Preußisches Urkundenbuch, ed. Rudolf Philippi, August Seraphim, Max Hein, Erich Maschke, Hans Koeppen, and Klaus Conrad, 6 vols. (Marburg: Elwert, 1882–2000).

Quinti Belli Sacri scriptores minores, ed. Reinhold Röhricht (Geneva: Fick, 1879).

Recueil des historiens des croisades: Historiens occidentaux, 5 vols. (Paris: Académie des Inscriptions et Belles-Lettres, 1844–1895).

Regesta Regni Hierosolymitani ed. Reinhold Röhricht, (Innsbruck: Wagner, 1893), and *Additamentum* (Innsbruck: Wagner, 1904) .

Scriptores Rerum Prussicarum: Die Geschichtsquellen der preußischen Vorzeit bis zum Untergange der Ordensherrschaft, vols. 1–5, ed. Theodor Hirsch, Max Toeppen, and Ernst Strehlke (Leipzig: Hirzel, 1861–1874); vol. 6, ed. Walther Hubatsch and Udo Arnold (Frankfurt am Main: Minerva, 1968).

Tabulae ordinis Theutonici, ed. Ernst Strehlke (Berlin: Weidmann, 1869).

Testimonia minora de quinto bello sacro, ed. Reinhold Röhricht (Geneva: Fick, 1882).

Collections of Translated Sources
Brundage, James A., *The Crusades: A Documentary Survey* (Milwaukee: Marquette University Press, 1962).

Christian Society and the Crusades, 1198–1229, ed. Edward Peters (Philadelphia: University of Pennsylvania Press, 1971).

Chronicles of the Crusades, ed. Elizabeth Hallam (London: Weidenfeld, 1989).

The Crusades: A Reader, ed. S. J. Allen and Emilie Amt (Peterborough, Ontario: Broadview, 2003).

Documents on the Later Crusades, 1274–1580, ed. Norman Housley (Basingstoke, UK: Macmillan, 1996).

The First Crusade: The Chronicle of Fulcher of Chartres and Other Source Materials, trans. Edward Peters, 2d ed. (Philadelphia: University of Pennsylvania Press, 1998).

Richard, Jean, *Au-delà de la Perse et de l'Arménie: L'Orient latin et la découverte de l'Asie intérieure. Quelques textes inégalement connus aux origines de l'alliance entre Francs et Mongols (1145–1262)* (Turnhout: Brepols, 2005).

Riley-Smith, Jonathan, and Louise Riley-Smith, *The Crusades: Idea and Reality, 1095–1274* (London: Arnold, 1981).

Slack, Corliss, *Crusade Charters, 1138–1270* (Tempe: Arizona Center for Medieval and Renaissance Studies, 2001).

The Templars: Selected Sources, ed. Malcolm Barber and Keith Bate (Manchester: Manchester University Press, 2002).

The World of El Cid: Chronicles of the Spanish Reconquest, trans. Simon Barton and Richard Fletcher (Manchester, UK: Manchester University Press, 2000).

Studies
Andrea, Alfred, "Essay on Primary Sources," in *The Fourth Crusade: The Conquest of Constantinople,* ed. Donald E. Queller and Thomas F. Madden, 2d ed. (Philadelphia: University of Pennsylvania Press, 1997), pp. 299–313.

Aurell, Martin, "Les sources de la Croisade albigeoise: Bilan et problématiques," in *La Croisade Albigeoise,* ed. Michel Roquebert (Carcassonne: Centre d'Etudes Cathares, 2004), pp. 21–38.

Conrad, Klaus, "Erfahrungen bei der Bearbeitung des Preußischen Urkundenbuches," in *Stand, Aufgaben und Perspektiven territorialer Urkundenbücher im östlichen Mitteleuropa,* ed. Winfried Irgang and Norbert Kersken (Marburg: Herder-Institut, 1998), pp. 23–28.

Constable, Giles, "The Second Crusade as Seen by Contemporaries," *Traditio* 9 (1953), 213–279.

———, "Medieval Charters as a Source For the History of the Crusades," in *Crusade and Settlement: Papers Read at the First Conference of the Society for the Study of the Crusades and the Latin East and presented to R. C. Smail,* ed. Peter W. Edbury (Cardiff: University College Cardiff Press, 1985), pp. 73–89.

———, "The Historiography of the Crusades," in *The Crusades from the Perspective of Byzantium and the Muslim World,* ed. Angeliki E. Laiou and Roy Parviz Mottahedeh (Washington, DC: Dumbarton Oaks, 2001), pp. 1–22.

Hiestand, Rudolf, "Zum Problem des Templerzentrlarchivs," *Archivalische Zeitschrift* 76 (1980), 17–38.

Leopold, Antony, *How to Recover the Holy Land: The Crusade Proposals of the Late Thirteenth and Early Fourteenth Centuries* (Aldershot, UK: Ashgate, 2000).

Mayer, Hans Eberhard, *Varia Antiochena: Studien zum Kreuzfahrerfürstentum Antiochia im 12. und 13. Jahrhundert* (Hannover: Hahn, 1993).

———, *Die Kanzlei der lateinischen Könige von Jerusalem,* MGH Schriften, 2 vols. (Hannover: Hahn, 1996).

Neitmann, Klaus, "Geschichte und Zukunft des Liv-, est- und kurländischen Urkundenbuches," in *Stand, Aufgaben und Perspektiven territorialer Urkundenbücher im östlichen Mitteleuropa,* ed. Winfried Irgang and Norbert Kersken (Marburg: Herder-Institut, 1998), pp. 107–121.

Pringle, Denys, "Crusader Inscriptions from Southern Lebanon," *Crusades* 3 (2004), 131–151.

Riley-Smith, Jonathan, *The First Crusade and the Idea of Crusading* (London: Athlone, 1986).

Smalley, Barbara, *Historians in the Middle Ages* (London: Thames and Hudson, 1974).

Sybel, Heinrich von, *The History and Literature of the Crusades* (London: Routledge, 1881).

Wagner, Kay, "Les sources de l'historiographie occidentale de la croisade albigeoise entre 1209 et 1328," in *La Croisade Albigeoise,* ed. Michel Roquebert (Carcassonne: Centre d'Etudes Cathares, 2004), pp. 39–54.

Wetheman (d. c. 1170)

Founder of a lay confraternity in the city of Roskilde in Denmark formed around 1150 in order to fight against the heathen Wends.

Wetheman probably belonged to the Danish aristocracy; he was one of the leading figures in the crusades organized in the Baltic region by King Valdemar I of Denmark and Absalon, bishop of Roskilde (1158–1178) and later archbishop of Lund (1178–1201). Wetheman and his confraternity are known only from the chronicle of Saxo Grammaticus (written around 1200), which seems to give a paraphrase of the statutes of the confraternity from a now lost written source.

All of the members of the confraternity were equal. If they lacked funds, the citizens of Roskilde could share their expenses in return for half of the booty, and the confraternity had the right to take a man's ship, without his approval, in return for an eighth of the booty. Contrary to usual practice and customary law in the area, Christian captives discovered among the Wends were to be given clothes and sent back to their homes. Before battle, the members confessed their sins as if they were on the threshold of death. The ascetic behavior on campaign expected by the statutes gave the wars of the confraternity an almost penitential character, which, taken together with the other religious and charitable elements, places them within the general context of crusading ideology.

Early twelfth-century parallels to this organization are known from Spain, for example, the confraternities of Belchite and Monreal.

–*Janus Møller Jensen*

See also: Baltic Crusades; Denmark
Bibliography
Jensen, Janus Møller, "Denmark and the Holy War: A Redefinition of a Traditional Pattern of Conflict in the Baltic in the Twelfth Century," in *Scandinavia and Europe, 800–1350: Contact, Conflict and Coexistence,* ed. Jon Adams and Kathy Holman (Turnhout: Brepols, 2004), pp. 219–236.

Wigand von Marburg (d. c. 1410)

A chronicler and herald in the Teutonic Order.

Wigand served under Grand Master Konrad von Wallenrod (1391–1393) and is mentioned in the accounts of the order as having received a payment in 1409. He is chiefly known as the author of a rhymed German chronicle that described the history of the order in Prussia from 1293 until 1394.

The original text of Wigand's chronicle, whose length has been variously estimated at between 16,500 and 25,000 lines, survives only as short fragments; its content has been preserved in a Latin translation written at the instigation of the Polish historian Jan Długosz in 1464. The most important sources for Wigand's chronicle were the *Chronicon Olivense* and Hermann von Wartberge's *Chronicon Livoniae*. It was written to be read aloud to lay crusaders from Germany and elsewhere in the West at the high table at the order's castle of Marienburg (mod. Malbork, Poland) as the ceremonial high point of their participation in the Baltic Crusades. The subject of the chronicle is therefore warfare and the celebration of the achievements of warriors, both Christian and pagan, in contrast to the predominantly spiritual concerns of the earlier chronicles of the order.

–Mary Fischer

See also: Teutonic Order; Teutonic Order: Literature
Bibliography
Wigand von Marburg, "Reimchronik," ed. Thomas Hirsch, in *Scriptores Rerum Prussicarum: Die Geschichtsquellen der preußischen Vorzeit bis zum Untergange der Ordensherrschaft*, ed. Theodor Hirsch, Max Toeppen, and Ernst Strehlke, 5 vols. (Leipzig: Hirzel, 1861–1874), 2:429–662; 4:1–8.

William VI of Montferrat (d. 1225)

Marquis of Montferrat (1207–1225) and claimant to the kingdom of Thessalonica.

Son of Boniface I, marquis of Montferrat, and his first wife Helena del Bosco, William was left to administer his father's lands after Boniface left Lombardy as one of the leaders of the Fourth Crusade (1202–1204); Boniface subsequently founded a principality in Thessaly and central Greece, after the crusader capture of Constantinople (mod. İstanbul, Turkey) in 1204. William was thus well experienced in government and warfare by the time of his father's death (1207), and in subsequent years many of Boniface's Lombard followers were keen to see William installed as king of Thessalonica (mod. Thessaloniki, Greece) in the place of the young and inexperienced Demetrius, Boniface's son by his second wife, Margaret of Hungary.

By 1222 the Greek successor state of Epiros had conquered large parts of Demetrius's kingdom, cutting off Thessalonica from Constantinople, and Demetrius himself fled to the West to seek help. Pope Honorius III was now prepared to sanction a crusade under William's leadership for the defense of the Latin Church in Thessalonica. The crusade was proclaimed on 13 May 1223 and preached in Italy

and southern France. Participants were promised an indulgence, and their goods were placed under the protection of the papacy, while a ban was put on the export of horses, weapons, and food to the lands of Theodore Doukas, despot of Epiros. William pledged his own lands to the Emperor Frederick II for 9,000 marks, while further finance was provided by the papacy. The plan for the crusade as it assembled in spring 1224 was for a naval expedition, led by William, Demetrius, and the papal legate, Bishop Nicholas of Reggio, to be coordinated with a land attack from Constantinople by Robert, the Latin emperor. However, William suffered a prolonged illness, and he was not able to sail from Brindisi until 1225. By the time the army arrived in Thessaly, the Frankish garrison of Thessalonica had surrendered to Epirote forces. A dysentery epidemic claimed the lives of many crusaders, including William, and the army broke up. Demetrius returned to Italy and sought refuge at the court of Frederick II. William was succeeded by his son Boniface II (1225–1253), who was able to restore the fortunes of the marquisate.

–Alan V. Murray

Bibliography
Gallina, Mario, "Fra Occidente e Oriente: La 'crociata' aleramica per Tessalonica," in *Piemonte medievale: Forme del potere e della società. Studi per Giovanni Tabacco* (Torino: Einaudi, 1985), pp. 65–83.
Lock, Peter, *The Franks in the Aegean* (London: Longman, 1995).

William IX of Aquitaine (1071–1126)

Count of Poitou and duke of Aquitaine (1086–1126), and one of the leaders of the Crusade of 1101.

At the age of fifteen, William succeeded to a vast inheritance stretching from the Loire to the Pyrenees and from the Auvergne to the Atlantic. As such, he was one of the two or three most powerful princes in the France of his day, and marriage ties linked his family with the royal houses of England, France (he was the grandfather of Eleanor of Aquitaine), and Aragon. As the author of ten or eleven short compositions in Occitan that stand as the oldest surviving vernacular poems in the tradition of courtly love, he is regarded today as one of the famous poets ("William the Troubadour") of medieval literary history. Having failed to take part in the First Crusade (1096–1099), for reasons not fully understood, William had a leading part in the organization and execution of the abortive Crusade of 1101 from its very outset.

The principal source of information on William, Orderic Vitalis, tells how he helped recruit the Aquitanian contingent in the crusader army as well as leading the march overland through Hungary to Constantinople. William also figured prominently in a confused confrontation with the Byzantine emperor Alexios Komnenos after the crusaders had crossed into Asia Minor. He commanded the Aquitanian army in the decisive battle of Herakleia (mod. Ereğli, Turkey) in southeastern Anatolia in late August or early September 1101. In this battle, the Turkish army of the Saljūq sultan Qilij Arslān I routed the crusaders and brought the campaign to a premature end. William and a handful of his men managed to elude the victors, hid in the surrounding countryside, and eventually reached safety in Tarsos (mod. Tarsus, Turkey) and Antioch (mod. Antakya, Turkey). After visiting Jerusalem, William returned home in 1102. Orderic Vitalis, as well as other contemporary historians, most notably Albert of Aachen, Ekkehard of Aura, Fulcher of Chartres, and Matthew of Edessa, leave no doubt that William's narrow escape from death at Herakleia was a harrowing experience that left him deeply shaken.

William remained in his French domains for almost twenty years, but in 1119–1120 he joined Alfonso I, king of Aragon, in a campaign against the Almoravid rulers of southern Spain. He fought at the major victory gained by the Christians at Cutanda near Zaragoza (17 June 1120). William's second son, Raymond of Poitiers, succeeded to the principality of Antioch through marriage to Constance, daughter of Prince Bohemund II.

–George T. Beech

Bibliography

Beech, George T., "The Ventures of the Dukes of Aquitaine into Spain and the Crusader East in the Early Twelfth Century," *Haskins Society Journal* 5 (1993), 61–75.
———, "The Crusade of 1101," in *A History of the Crusades*, ed. Kenneth M. Setton et al., 6 vols., 2d ed. (Madison: University of Wisconsin Press, 1969–1989), 1: 343–367.

William of Beaujeu (d. 1291)

The last master of the Order of the Temple (1273–1291) on the Palestinian mainland.

William was born around 1230, the fourth son of Guichard of Beaujeu, lord of Montpensier, and had joined the Templars

Order by 1253. He was in the East by 1261, and had become preceptor of Tripoli by 1271, and master of Apulia by 1272. He retained close ties with Charles I of Anjou, king of Sicily, to whom he was related, until Charles's death in 1285.

William was elected master in 1273 and spent nearly two years traveling through France, England, and Spain, recruiting men and collecting funds, before attending the Second Council of Lyons in May 1274. He returned to the Holy Land in September 1275, and from that time on he was identified with the claim of Charles of Anjou to the kingship of Jerusalem in opposition to Hugh III of Cyprus. This stance contributed significantly to the political divisions within Outremer but also ensured Charles's continued material support, much needed at this time.

William's partisan role certainly contributed to his lack of credibility in the years 1289 to 1291, when his warnings of impending Mamlūk attacks, derived from spies in the Egyptian army, were ignored. William was killed during the siege of Acre (mod. 'Akko, Israel) by the Mamlūks on 18 May 1291.

–Malcolm Barber

Bibliography

Bulst-Thiele, Marie-Luise, *Sacrae Domus Militiae Templi Hierosolymitani Magistri: Untersuchungen zur Geschichte des Templerordens, 1118/9–1314* (Göttingen: Vandenhoeck & Ruprecht, 1974).

William of Châteauneuf (d. 1258)

Master of the Hospitallers (1242–1258).

Originally from France, William of Châteauneuf had joined the order in Outremer by 1233, when he witnessed the agreement between the Hospitallers, the Templars, and the citizens of Marseilles concerning the military orders' rights in the port of Marseilles. He became marshal of the central convent (1241) and was elected master after the death of Peter of Vieillebride (1242).

William was captured at the battle of Forbie (17 October 1244) and spent the following six years in an Egyptian prison, with John of Ronay serving as vice master in the interim until King Louis IX of France procured his release in 1250, paying a notable ransom. William admitted the priors and brethren of St. James in Acre (mod. 'Akko, Israel) into the Hospitallers' confraternity (1253/1254), and during his mastership the building activities in the order's compound in Acre continued. In 1255 substantial portions of the archdiocese of Nazareth came under the administration of the Hospitallers.

William also reached important agreements concerning disputed rights and possessions with John of Ibelin and Bohemund VI of Antioch-Tripoli (1256/1257). He died in 1258 during the final phase of the War of St. Sabas and was succeeded by Hugh Revel, whose career he had supported since 1250.

–Jochen Burgtorf

Bibliography

Riley-Smith, Jonathan, *The Knights of St. John in Jerusalem and Cyprus, c. 1050–1310* (London: Macmillan, 1967).

William-Jordan of Cerdagne (d. 1109)

Count of the district of Cerdagne in the eastern Pyrenees and claimant to the inheritance of Raymond of Saint-Gilles in Outremer.

A cousin of Raymond, William-Jordan accompanied him on the First Crusade (1096–1099) and remained with him in the East. After Raymond died while engaged in the siege of Tripoli (mod. Trâblous, Lebanon) in 1105, his younger son Alphonse-Jordan was sent back to succeed to the Saint-Gilles lands in the West. William-Jordan was accepted as successor to Raymond's nascent county in the East, although he did not use the title "count of Tripoli." His tenure was challenged by Raymond's elder son, Bertrand, who arrived at Tortosa (mod. Tartūs, Syria) with a large force in 1109. William-Jordan abandoned the siege of Tripoli to Bertrand's men and appealed to Tancred, regent of Antioch, agreeing to become his vassal in return for support. A settlement imposed by King Baldwin I of Jerusalem awarded Tortosa and Arqah to William-Jordan and the remaining domains to Bertrand. Shortly afterward William-Jordan was killed. Though the precise circumstances are unclear, the obvious beneficiary was Bertrand, who succeeded to Raymond's undivided eastern inheritance.

–Alan V. Murray

Bibliography

Richard, Jean, *Le Comté de Tripoli sous la dynastie toulousaine (1102–1187)* (Paris: Geuthner, 1945).

William Longsword (d. 1177)

First husband of Sibyl, sister to King Baldwin IV of Jerusalem, and father of the infant king Baldwin V (1183–1186).

The eldest son of William V "the Old," marquis of Montferrat, and Judith of Austria, William Lungaspada (Longsword) was chosen in 1176 by Baldwin IV and the High Court of the kingdom of Jerusalem as husband for Sibyl, the king's elder sister and heir, most probably on account of his family's ties with Frederick I Barbarossa, Holy Roman Emperor, from whom the kingdom hoped to receive assistance.

On his marriage (November 1176), William was invested with the county of Jaffa (mod. Tel Aviv-Yafo, Israel) and Ascalon (mod. Tel Ashqelon, Israel). He was the obvious candidate to be regent of the kingdom in the event of the leper Baldwin IV becoming incapable of exercising government, and eventually to become king himself. However, William fell ill and died in June 1177. The following winter Sibyl gave birth to a posthumous son, Baldwin V, who was crowned co-king with Baldwin IV in 1183, and succeeded as sole ruler in 1185, but died the following year.

–Alan V. Murray

Bibliography

Hamilton, Bernard, *The Leper King and his Heirs: Baldwin IV and the Crusader Kingdom of Jerusalem* (Cambridge: Cambridge University Press, 2000).

William of Machaut

See Guillaume de Machaut

William of Malmesbury (d. c. 1143)

A Benedictine monk at the abbey of Malmesbury in England and author of the *Gesta Regum Anglorum*, completed in early 1126. This substantial work in five books covers the history of England to 1125, but also includes much continental material, including a history of the First Crusade (1096–1099) and its aftermath to 1102; that history occupies most of book 4 (chapters 343–384), making it as long as some independent crusading chronicles.

Although substantially a summary of the chronicle of Fulcher of Chartres, with occasional reference to the anonymous *Gesta Francorum*, William's work offers much independent and unique information: a detailed report of Pope Urban II's speech at Clermont, summaries of lost descriptions of seventh-century Rome and of relics at Constantinople, biographical information about Godfrey of Bouillon, Bohemund I of Antioch, Robert Curthose, and Raymond of

Saint-Gilles, and a variety of snippets probably gained from returned soldiers. William, who was impressed and worried by the expansion of Islam, interprets the crusade as a pan-European defensive war and as a great knightly exercise, rather than as a penitential pilgrimage. His account is characterized by the skillful use of rhetoric to heighten drama and clarify motivation, often using parallels and reminiscences from Greco-Roman antiquity.

–*Rodney M. Thomson*

Bibliography

Thomson, Rodney M., "William of Malmesbury, Historian of the Crusade," *Reading Medieval Studies* 23 (1997), 121–134.

———, *William of Malmesbury,* 2d ed. (Woodbridge, UK: Boydell, 2003).

William of Malmesbury, *Gesta Regum Anglorum,* 2 vols, ed. and trans. R. A. B. Mynors, Rodney M. Thomson, and Michael Winterbottom (Oxford: Clarendon, 1998–1999).

William of Modena (d. 1251)

A papal legate and diplomat, active in the Christian conquests of Prussia and Livonia.

William was probably born around 1180 in Piedmont. He served as papal vice-chancellor (1219/1220–1222), bishop of Modena (1222–1233/1234), and cardinal-bishop of Sabina (1244–1251).

William first acted as papal legate for Livonia in 1225–1226, where he reached a temporary solution to the territorial disputes between Danish and German crusaders. After serving as a diplomat in Pomerania and Silesia (1229–1230), he returned to Livonia as legate in 1234–1235 and reorganized the structure of the Livonian bishoprics. He also mediated a settlement between Conrad, duke of Mazovia, and the Teutonic Order over the tenure of the lands formerly held by the Knights of Dobrin. In 1236–1238 he arranged the restitution of North Estonia to the king of Denmark, and subsequently (1239–1242) he was in Prussia where he regulated relations between Bishop Christian and the Teutonic Order and established the Prussian diocesan organization that was recognized by the pope in 1243.

In 1244 William was again named as legate for Prussia but actually stayed in Lyons. In 1246 he was appointed as legate for Norway and Sweden; he crowned Haakon IV Haakonsson as king of Norway in 1247, and on his way back from Sweden to Lyons he took part in the coronation of William of Holland as king of Germany. William of Modena played an important role in the politics of the crusade regions of Livonia and Prussia, where he was able to successfully resolve complex political conflicts. He was often appointed legate at the request of local powers and could usually rely on them in his activities; his regulations often favored the Teutonic Order. He also assisted the expansion of the Dominican Order in the Baltic region.

–*Anti Selart*

Bibliography

Donner, Gustav Adolf, *Kardinal Wilhelm von Sabina, Bischof von Modena, 1222–1234: Päpstlicher Legat in den nordischen Ländern († 1251)* (Helsingfors: Societas Scientiarum Fennica, 1929).

Pitz, Ernst, *Papstreskript und Kaiserreskript im Mittelalter* (Tübingen: Niemeyer, 1971).

William of Puylaurens

A cleric and author of a chronicle dealing with the history of the struggle against the Cathar heresy in southern France.

William was born around 1201 in the region of Toulouse, and around 1228 he is found in the entourage of Fulk of Marseilles, bishop of Toulouse. By 1237 he had become vicar of Puylaurens; from 1237 he served Fulk's successor, Raymond de Fauga, and from 1241 was chaplain to Raymond VII, count of Toulouse. William's chronicle, which was completed between 1273 and 1276, covers the period from around 1145 to 1275, dealing with the preaching missions against the Cathars, the Albigensian Crusade (1209–1229), and the work of the Inquisition in the archbishopric of Narbonne and the dioceses of Albi, Rodez, Cahors, and Agen, as well as related events in Aragon and Provence. Three chapters also give an account of the crusades of Louis IX of France to Egypt (1248–1254) and Tunis (1270–1272). William died around the year 1276.

–*Alan V. Murray*

Bibliography

The Chronicle of William of Puylaurens: The Albigensian Crusade and Its Aftermath, trans. W. A. Sibly and M. D. Sibly (Woodbridge, UK: Boydell, 2003).

Dossat, Yves, "La 'Chronique' de Guillaume de Puylaurens," *Annales de Bretagne et des Pays de l'Ouest* 87 (1980), 259–266.

Guillaume de Puylaurens, *Chronique (Chronica magistri Guillelmi de Podio Laurentii),* ed. and trans. Jean Duvernoy (Paris: C.N.R.S., 1976).

William the Troubadour

See William IX of Aquitaine

William of Tyre (d. 1186)

William II, Latin archbishop of Tyre (mod. Soûr, Lebanon), author of a chronicle that is the main narrative source for the history of twelfth-century Outremer.

William was born in Jerusalem to Frankish parents of the burgess class. His early life was illuminated by the discovery of an autobiographical chapter of his chronicle (published by Robert Huygens in 1962), which reveals that (after probably attending the Holy Sepulchre school) William went to the West and studied arts, theology, and canon and civil law at the universities of Paris, Orléans, and Bologna over a period of twenty years, returning to the kingdom of Jerusalem in 1165. His education and ability enabled William, unusually for a Frank born in Outremer, to rise to high ecclesiastical office in a church that was dominated by immigrants from the West. As archdeacon of Tyre (1167–1175), he undertook an embassy to Constantinople to negotiate an alliance against Egypt with the Byzantine emperor Manuel I Komnenos (1168) and was appointed by King Amalric of Jerusalem as tutor to his young son, the future Baldwin IV (1170). During the regency of Raymond III of Tripoli (1174–1176), William was made chancellor of the kingdom (1174–1185) and archbishop of Tyre (1175–1186). After Baldwin's accession he undertook a further diplomatic mission to Constantinople (1179–1180); on his return he was an unsuccessful candidate for the office of patriarch of Jerusalem, which was given to Eraclius, archbishop of Caesarea. William died on 29 September 1186.

William knew Latin, French, Italian, and possibly Greek. His knowledge of Arabic and Persian, often confidently assumed by earlier commentators, is less certain. He wrote two important narrative histories. The first was a history of the Muslim world, which he refers to as the *Historia de gestis orientalium principum* (or variants thereof), and which has not survived. The second is known as the *Historia rerum in partibus transmarinis gestarum* or simply *Chronicon,* conceived as a propagandistic history in twenty-three books dealing with Christian rule in the Holy Land from the time of the Byzantine emperor Heraclius (610–641) up to William's own time. The *Chronicon* was commissioned in 1167 by King Amalric, who provided William with important source materials. Although much of it was written by the

Siege of Antioch from *Estoire d'Outremer,* by William of Tyre. (Art Resource)

1180s, it is evidently incomplete, and the narrative breaks off with the year 1184.

In addition to a great number of archival sources, William made use of earlier Latin narratives, particularly the first six books of the *Historia Iherosolimitana* of Albert of Aachen for the First Crusade (1096–1099). He also drew on Christian Arab writers such as Eutychius, Melkite patriarch of Alexandria. For the period after 1127, the *Chronicon* is the most important extant source on Outremer. Since William died before the defeat of the Franks of Jerusalem at the battle of Hattin (1187), he was not affected by the hindsight that characterized many of the authors writing after the disaster, although he clearly was troubled by the threat to Outremer presented by the increasing unity of the Muslim world under Saladin. As someone close to the royal family and the machinery of government, William was excellently informed about political affairs, but the discretion expected of someone in high office meant that he often chose to reveal far less than he knew of important events. As chancellor and archbishop, he was also an interested party in the politics of his own time; he was sympathetic to his patron Raymond III of Tripoli, and ambivalent toward Byzantium, but ill-disposed to his rival Eraclius, Reynald of Châtillon, and to the military orders, especially the Templars.

In the early thirteenth century the *Chronicon* was translated into Old French. This version, known as the *Eracles*, gained a wide circulation, and many manuscripts continue William's narrative into the thirteenth century. By the fifteenth century translations had been made into Castilian, Italian, and (by William Caxton) Middle English. The first printed edition appeared at Basel in 1549.

–*Alan V. Murray*

Bibliography

Davis, Ralph H. C., "William of Tyre," in *Relations Between East and West in the Middle Ages,* ed. Derek Baker (Edinburgh: Edinburgh University Press, 1973), pp. 64–76.

Edbury, Peter W., and John Gordon Rowe, *William of Tyre: Historian of the Latin East* (Cambridge: Cambridge University Press, 1988).

Folda, Jaroslav, "Manuscripts of the History of Outremer by William of Tyre: A Handlist," *Scriptorium* 27 (1973), 90–95.

Guillaume de Tyr, *Chronique,* ed. Robert B. C. Huygens, Corpus Christianorum, Continuatio Mediaevalis, 63–63A, 2 vols. (Turnhout: Brepols, 1986).

Hamilton, Bernard, "William of Tyre and the Byzantine Empire," in *Porphyrogenita: Essays on the History and Literature of Byzantium and the Latin East in Honour of Julian Chrysostomides,* ed. Charalambos Dendrinos, Jonathan Harris, Eirene Harvalia-Crook, and Judith Herrin (Aldershot, UK: Ashgate, 2003), pp. 219–233.

Hiestand, Rudolf, "Zum Leben und zur Laufbahn Wilhelms von Tyrus," *Deutsches Archiv für Erforschung des Mittelalters* 34 (1978), 345–380.

"Historia rerum in partibus transmarinis gestarum edita a venerabili Willermo Tyrensi archiepiscopo," in *Recueil des Historiens des Croisades: Historiens Occidentaux,* 5 vols. (Paris: Académie des Inscriptions et Belles-Lettres, 1844–1895), 1–2.

A History of Deeds Done beyond the Sea by William Archbishop of Tyre, trans. E. A. Babcock and A. C. Krey, 2 vols. (New York: Columbia University Press, 1943).

Huygens, Robert B. C., "Guillaume de Tyr étudiant: Un chapître (XIX,12) de son Histoire retrouvé," *Latomus* 21 (1962), 811–829.

———, "La tradition manuscrite de Guillaume de Tyr," *Studi medievali* ser. 3, 5 (1964), 281–373.

———, "Editing William of Tyre," *Sacris Eruditi* 27 (1984), 461–473.

Mayer, Hans Eberhard, "Zum Tode von Wilhelm von Tyrus," *Archiv für Diplomatik* 5–6 (1959–1960), 182–201.

———, "Guillaume de Tyr à l'école," *Mémoires de l'Académie des sciences, arts et belles-lettres de Dijon* 117 (1985–1986), 257–265.

Möhring, Hannes, "Zu der Geschichte der orientalischen Herrscher des Wilhelm von Tyrus: Die Frage der Quellenabhängigkeiten," *Mittellateinisches Jahrbuch* 19 (1984), 170–183.

Murray, Alan V., "William of Tyre and the Origin of the Turks: On the Sources of the *Gesta Orientalium Principum,*" in *Dei Gesta per Francos: Etudes sur les croisades dédiés à Jean Richard / Crusade Studies in Honour of Jean Richard,* ed. Michel Balard, Benjamin Z. Kedar, and Jonathan Riley-Smith (Aldershot, UK: Ashgate, 2001), pp. 217–229.

Vessey, D. W. T. C., "William of Tyre and the Art of Historiography," *Mediaeval Studies* 35 (1973), 433–455.

William of Villaret (d. 1305)

Master of the Hospitallers (1296–1305).

William came from a Provençal noble family, several of whose members are known to have joined the Order of the Hospital.

By 1269 William was draper of the order's central convent and was delegated to France to administer the vacant priory of Saint-Gilles (1270/1271–1296), although he repeatedly ignored his obligation to travel to Outremer to report on his priory's status. Pope Gregory X appointed him administrator of the Venaissin in 1274 (the post was renewed by Nicolas III in 1278 and by Martin IV in 1282). In 1295 William and Boniface of Calamandrana, grand preceptor of all Hospitallers in the West, presented Pope Boniface VIII with complaints concerning the conduct in the office of the master, Odo of Pins, and after Odo's death (1296) William was elected master in absentia. His failure to relocate to the order's new headquarters in Cyprus, and his plan to hold a general chapter in Avignon, provoked the opposition of the central convent (1299).

William was forced to move to Cyprus (1300), and in the following years a series of statutes was issued curbing the master's influence (1300–1304). William died on 9 June 1305 and was succeeded by his nephew Fulk of Villaret.

–*Jochen Burgtorf*

Bibliography

Guillaume de Villaret: Des Hospitaliers de Saint-Jean de Jérusalem, de Chypres et de Rhodes hier aux Chevaliers de Malte aujourd'hui (Paris: Conseil International de la Langue Française, 1985).

Riley-Smith, Jonathan, *The Knights of St. John in Jerusalem and Cyprus, c. 1050–1310* (London: Macmillan, 1967).

Winand

See Teutonic Source

Wincenty Kadłubek (d. 1223)

Bishop of Kraków (1208–1218) and chronicler who narrated the events of the Polish crusades against Pomeranians, Prussians, and Sudovians.

Wincenty (Vincent) was born in Poland around 1150 at Kargów near Stopnica or at Karnów near Opatów. His erudition and literary skill were acquired during studies probably in Italy or France, or both, and he returned to Poland between 1183 and 1189 to be ordained a priest. As a canon of the cathedral of Kraków, he became prominent at the court of Kazimierz II Sprawiedliwy (the Just). After 1194 he became a provost at the collegiate Church of Our Lady in Sandomierz and chaplain to Kazimierz's widow Helena. It is likely that he started his work on the *Chronica Polonorum* at this time.

In 1208 the cathedral chapter of Kraków elected Wincenty as bishop (the first to be canonically elected). He was consecrated by Henryk Kietlicz, archbishop of Gniezno, on 24 May. Wincenty supported his metropolitan in the reform of the Polish church and took part in the Fourth Lateran Council (1215). However, he did not take an active role in the political events of the country, possibly due to his personal convictions or because of his long association with his patron Kazimierz II and his family. Wincenty's episcopate ended in 1218 when his supplication to be relieved of his duties was accepted by Pope Honorius III. Subsequently, Wincenty entered the Cistercian convent in Jędrzejów and completed work on his *Chronica*. In 1223 he was reappointed to the see of Kraków, but he died on 8 March 1223 before he could leave Jędrzejów to resume his duties as bishop.

The *Chronica Polonorum* was the second work, after the *Gesta* of Gallus Anonymus, to chronicle the early history of Poland and its rulers (both mythical and historical). The first three books of the *Chronica* were written in the form of a dialogue between Archbishop Jan of Gniezno (1148–1165) and Bishop Mateusz of Kraków (1143/1144–1166), while the fourth was written as a narrative. All were based on oral tradition, the *Gesta* of Gallus Anonymus, and Wincenty's own experiences. The chronicle contains accounts of several Polish expeditions against pagans: by Bolesław III Krzywousty (Wrymouth) in 1109 against the Pomeranians; by Bolesław IV Kędzierzawy (the Curly) to Prussia in 1147 and 1166; and by Kazimierz II Sprawiedliwy in 1191–1192 against the Sudovians.

The language of the *Chronica* suggests the influence of Bernard, abbot of Clairvaux. For example, it cautioned that the Prussians were more dangerous to the soul than the body, and were not simply pagans but followers of Saladin, idolaters, and enemies of the Holy Faith. It also criticizes Bolesław IV for accepting tribute from the Prussians instead of converting them, a practice forbidden by Bernard of Clairvaux. This failure is used to explain Bolesław's failure to subjugate the Prussians. The *Chronica* advocates the use of force in the conversion of souls alienated from God, following the Augustinian interpretation of the Parable of the Great Supper (Luke 14:15–24).

–Darius von Guttner Sporzyński

Bibliography

Górecki, Piotr, *Economy, Society, and Lordship in Medieval Poland, 1100–1250* (New York: Holmes and Meie, 1992).

Grodecki, Roman, "Polska wobec idei wypraw krzyżowych," *Przegląd Współczesny* 2 (1923), 103–116.

Hagiografia Polska, ed. Romuald Gustaw, 2 vols. (Poznań: Księgarnia św. Wojciecha), 2:522–540.

Hammer, Jacob, "Remarks on the Sources and Textual History of Geoffrey of Monmouth's *Historia Regum Britanniae,* with an Excursus on the *Chronica Polonorum* of Wincenty Kadlubek (Magister Vincentius)," *Bulletin of the Polish Institute of Arts and Sciences in America* 2 (1943–1944), 501–564.

"Magistri Vincentii dicti Kadłubek Chronica Polonorum," ed. M. Plezia, in *Monumenta Poloniae Historica,* n.s., vol. 11 (Kraków: Polska Akademia Umiejętności, 1994).

Mistrz Wincenty Kadłubek, *Magistrii Vincentii Chronicon Polonorum,* ed. and trans. Brygida Kürbis (Wrocław: Zakład Narodowy im. Ossolińskich, 1992).

Winrich von Kniprode (d. 1382)

Grand master of the Teutonic Order (1352–1382); perhaps the most influential grand master in the fourteenth century as far as his policies toward the Prussian estates, Lithuania, and the Hanseatic League were concerned. His reign was considered to have been the golden age of the Teutonic Order in Prussia.

Born in the Rhineland about 1310, Winrich made his career in Prussia, as commander at Danzig (mod. Gdańsk, Poland) and Balga, then marshal and grand commander of the order. He was elected grand master after the resignation of Heinrich Dusemer and was the first grand master to be officially honored by the estates. He reorganized the campaigns against the heathen Lithuanians, supported by knights from Western Europe. In 1362, Kaunas was conquered and destroyed, and the order erected fortresses north of the river Nemunas, but military and political success was limited. In 1370, the Lithuanian princes Algirdas and Kęstutis even successfully attacked Sambia, only to be driven back by an army headed by the grand master himself. When Algirdas died and Jogaila became prince of Vilnius in 1377, Winrich's plan to strengthen his position by supporting Jogaila against Kęstutis failed. After the grand master's death (24 June 1382), the conflict with Lithuania was a legacy that weighed heavily on the order's future.

–Jürgen Sarnowsky

See also: Teutonic Order; Teutonic Order: Literature
Bibliography

Conrad, Klaus, "Winrich von Kniprode (6. I. 1352 – 24. VI. 1382)," in *Die Hochmeister des Deutschen Ordens, 1190–1990,* ed. Udo Arnold (Marburg: Elwert, 1998), pp. 84–88.

Hubatsch, Walter, "Winrich von Kniprode, Hochmeister des Deutschen Ordens 1352 bis 1382," *Blätter für deutsche Landesgeschichte* 119 (1983), 15–31.

Władysław II Jagiełło

See Jogaila

Wolfram von Eschenbach

Acknowledged as the greatest narrative poet of the German Middle Ages, much of whose work deals with crusading themes. Wolfram portrays himself in his narrator persona as a professional warrior who is ignorant of books and letters, but for a self-confessed illiterate, he handles Old French sources with confident originality and constructs immense and intricate narrative structures. No documentary evidence of his life survives. His main patron was Landgrave Hermann of Thuringia, crusader and power broker between 1190 and 1215.

Wolfram's Grail romance, *Parzival,* composed in the first decade of the thirteenth century, is set in a fictional world. Its problematics are internal to Christian chivalric society, yet significant details foreshadow the crusades. Parzival's father, Gahmuret, fights for the caliph of Baghdad. His son by the heathen queen Belakane, the piebald Feirefiz, is eventually baptized and sent by his half-brother, the Grail King Parzival, to convert the East; Feirefiz's own son will be Prester John. Through his son Lohengrin, linked in twelfth-century legend with the family of Godfrey of Bouillon, Parzi-

val becomes ancestor of the Christian kings of Jerusalem. The celibate knights who defend the Grail kingdom are called *templeisen,* presumably a calque on "Templars."

War between Christendom and Islam is the dominant theme of *Willehalm,* begun around 1210 and broken off, unfinished, around 1220. Wolfram's source, the Old French epic stories of the warriors Guillaume and Rainouart, he adapts with typical freedom. As in Konrad's *Rolandslied* (c. 1170), the ideological concerns of high medieval German Empire and crusade are injected into the epic tradition of Carolingian holy war. Although Wolfram and his characters frequently invoke events and heroes of the *Rolandslied, Willehalm* is the story of the second Carolingian generation. The age of Charlemagne's and Roland's aggressive expansion of Christian faith and empire is over. The Islamic Empire of Terramer fights back, and Willehalm must defend his marcher county of Provence against overwhelming heathen armies. Crushingly defeated, he seeks reinforcements. While his kinsfolk rally to the cause, King Louis proves a vacillating coward. Though he grudgingly pledges troops, he refuses to lead the army. It is Willehalm, not Louis, who must assume the mantle of Charlemagne. Yet victory is only won by the heroic prowess of Rennewart, the young pagan who, unknown to all, is the lost son of Terramer, but who for his refusal to be baptized has been consigned to menial service in Louis's kitchens. Willehalm recognizes his innate nobility and enlists him in the Christian army.

The catalyst of this conflict between Christians and Muslims is Willehalm's marriage to Giburg, Terramer's daughter, who had freed Willehalm from captivity by her father. Here Wolfram connects an old epic motif with the idealization of marriage as an ethical agency common in courtly fiction around 1200. For Giburg, love for Christ and love for Willehalm are inseparable impulses. Yet Willehalm can only defend his wife and their faith by sacrificing the lives of their Christian and heathen kinsmen. This personal dilemma concretizes a larger ambivalence within the idea and practice of crusade. Willehalm and his army, *die getouften* ("the baptized"), wear the badge of the cross, and death in battle earns the martyr's reward. Yet Giburg reminds them that they and the "heathen" they slaughter are children of one creator. Christian victory is won by the heathen Rennewart, Terramer's son and Giburg's brother. The internecine conflict ends in a welter of blood. Willehalm fears that Rennewart, who disappears in the rout of Terramer's fleeing army, may be the last casualty of a pyrrhic victory. Lamenting the carnage on both sides of the religious divide, he shows mercy toward the defeated enemy.

But it is the narrator Wolfram whose more dispassionate voice articulates the ultimate question: "Is it not a sin to slaughter like cattle those who never heard tell of baptism? I say it is a great sin, for they are all creatures of God's hand" [Wolfram von Eschenbach, *Willehalm*, ed. Heinzle, lines 450, 15–19]. This radical repudiation of crusade might have been partly revoked had Wolfram completed his story. In the source epics, Rennewart reappears, accepts baptism, and marries Alyse, King Louis's daughter, offering new hope of reconciling East and West. Wolfram is not alone in the 1220s in questioning the theological and human justification of crusade, but *Willehalm* remains unique in its time for the cogency with which it challenges the validity of holy war.

–*Jeffrey Ashcroft*

Bibliography

Bertau, Karl, *Wolfram von Eschenbach: Neun Versuche über Subjektivität und Ursprünglichkeit in der Geschichte* (München: Beck, 1983).

Bumke, Joachim, *Wolfram von Eschenbach,* 7th ed. (Stuttgart: Metzler, 1997).

Greenfield, John, and Lydia Miklautsch, *Der 'Willehalm' Wolframs von Eschenbach: Eine Einführung* (Berlin: De Gruyter, 1998).

Jones, Martin H., "Cross and Crusade in Wolfram von Eschenbach's *Willehalm*," in *Literatur – Geschichte – Literaturgeschichte: Beiträge zur mediävistischen Literaturwissenschaft,* ed. Nine Miedama and Rudolf Suntrup (Frankfurt am Main: Lang, 2003), pp. 193–207.

Wolfram von Eschenbach, Willehalm, trans. Marion E. Gibbs and Sidney M. Johnson (Harmondsworth: Penguin, 1984).

Wolfram von Eschenbach, *Willehalm,* ed. Joachim Heinzle (Frankfurt am Main: Deutscher Klassiker Verlag, 1991).

Wolfram's Willehalm: Fifteen Essays, ed. Martin H. Jones and Timothy McFarland (Rochester, NY: Camden House, 2002).

Wolter von Plettenberg (d. 1535)

Master of the Teutonic Order in Livonia (1494–1535).

Wolter von Plettenberg was born in Westphalia around the year 1450. He joined the order in Livonia in about 1464. After holding minor offices, he became marshal of Livonia in 1489 and master in 1494, serving for over forty years. In the face of the expansion of Muscovy, which had subjected Novgorod and Pskov and threatened the eastern frontier of Livonia, Plettenberg attempted to reform the economic basis

of the Livonian military forces and launched a massive campaign to raise funds from the West to pay for mercenaries. He concluded an alliance with Lithuania against Moscow and started hostilities in 1501, which culminated in a battle at Lake Smolino near Pskov in 1502, where the Livonians remained undefeated. A treaty with Muscovy the following year ensured peace until the beginning of the Livonian War in 1558 and brought Plettenberg fame as the last great victorious master of Livonia.

After the Lutheran Reformation, Plettenberg was forced to accept the spread of Protestantism, which remained, however, mostly confined to the towns. The secularization of the order in Prussia by Grand Master Albrecht von Brandenburg put pressure on the Livonian branch, but Plettenberg did not follow the Prussian example. The traditional political structure of the order had survived better in Livonia, and unlike Albrecht, Plettenberg was bound to the institutions of the order through his long career. In 1526 Plettenberg gained the status of a prince of the Holy Roman Empire (Ger. *Reichsfürst*), which further ensured the independence of the Livonian branch from the ambitions of the master of the order in Germany.

–*Juhan Kreem*

Bibliography

Ritterbrüder im Livländischen Zweig des Deutschen Ordens, ed. Lutz Fenske and Klaus Militzer (Köln: Böhlau, 1993).

Wolter von Plettenberg, der größte Ordensmeister Livlands, ed. Norbert Angermann (Lüneburg: Verlag Nordostdeutsches Kulturwerk, 1985).

Wolter von Plettenberg und das mittelalterliche Livland, ed. Norbert Angermann and Ilgvars Misans (Lüneburg: Verlag Nordostdeutsches Kulturwerk, 2001).

Women

The crusade movement was a wide-ranging phenomenon that touched the lives of people all over Europe, crossing social boundaries of wealth, politics, culture, and gender. Three main categories of women were affected by crusading: those who actually accompanied crusade armies, those who helped to maintain and protect the frontier societies that were established in Europe and the Levant, and those who remained in the West to guard the interests of absent kin.

Women and the Sources for Crusading

In the early thirteenth century, the Cistercian monk Thomas

of Froidmont composed an elegy for his elder sister, Margaret of Beverley, celebrating her adventures on crusade. She reputedly fought at the siege of Jerusalem in 1187 wearing a cooking pot on her head for protection, and twice endured capture and slavery at the hands of Muslim enemies. She was ransomed, however, and returned safely to tell her brother about her experiences before entering a convent at Montreuil, where she died in 1215. Thomas's work is unique for its time; it was written as if narrated by Margaret herself, a woman giving a firsthand account of her pilgrimage to the Holy Land. Its exceptional nature was doubtless influenced by the fact that Thomas wrote to emphasize the religious character of his sister's experiences in the Levant rather than to chronicle her deeds in an historical sense.

For the most part, women seldom feature in the surviving sources for crusading. Throughout the twelfth and thirteenth centuries the church and its male clergy dominated education and literature, and there were strong legal and social restrictions on women. This situation resulted in a shortage of written information about them, especially of material presented from a female perspective. In addition to these general conditions, those who wrote histories of the crusades had two further reasons for avoiding the subject of women. First, crusading was by definition a military activity, and warfare was traditionally a male pursuit. Second, women were actively discouraged from taking part in crusade expeditions. Papal appeals and sermons by crusade preachers often specified that women should not accompany armies to the Holy Land unless they had proper permission and guardianship. They could not be banned outright, because the crusade was a form of pilgrimage and open to all repentant Christians. Nonetheless, female crusaders often drew criticism.

Some concerns were based on the logistical problems caused by non-combatants in general: they were "useless mouths" who consumed supplies and slowed the pace of crusader armies. Other fears were more specific to the female sex, especially the fear that the presence of women would tempt crusaders into sexual sin. As pilgrims, crusaders were supposed to refrain from sexual activity, a situation at odds with the reality of life in a medieval army where camp followers abounded. Military setbacks on crusade were often seen as the result of God's displeasure with the crusaders' profligate behavior, and women were blamed accordingly. Despite these views, women of all social levels continued to take the cross. On rare occasions women like Margaret of Beverley even received praise for their bravery, and for their contribution to the holy war.

Women's Motivation

Most of the women mentioned in the sources for crusading are noble, following the established literary and historical traditions of the time. Noblewomen usually followed papal guidelines and accompanied male relatives, which makes it hard to assess the motives of individual women; they were often overshadowed by their male counterparts. Seven women named in the sources for the First Crusade (1096–1099) were the wives of noble crusaders, and of nine women known to have joined the Fifth Crusade (1217–1221), only two may have gone without family [Riley-Smith, *The First Crusaders,* p. 107; Powell, "The Role of Women on the Fifth Crusade," p. 299]. Crusader-queens who accompanied husbands leading major expeditions include Eleanor of Aquitaine, Berengaria of Navarre, Margaret of Provence, and Eleanor of Castile (although her husband, Lord Edward of England, had not yet ascended the throne). Joanna, dowager queen of Sicily, went on the Third Crusade (1189–1192) with her brother, King Richard I of England, but may also have been fulfilling the commitment to the crusade of her dead husband, King William II of Sicily. She used the remainder of her dowry to help finance Richard's expedition. Such important women were usually accompanied by retinues of noble ladies and maidservants, about whom less is known. Family ties and household bonds to crusaders may have influenced women to take the cross, but some managed to make the journey on their own, such as Margaret of Austria, widow of King Béla II of Hungary. Following the death of her husband, she longed to go to Jerusalem, so she sold her dowry and embarked on the German Crusade of 1197–1198 with her own retinue of knights.

Although information about women's motivation is scant, they evidently responded to the same spiritual incentives as men. Medieval women had a pronounced role as patrons of the church, and their involvement in both monastic reform and heretical movements during this period testifies to the sincerity of their religious concerns. Spiritual rewards such as the remission of sins offered to crusaders were attractive to all Christians. Religiously motivated women on the First Crusade included a nun from Trier, and a woman who followed her goose on crusade, believing it to be imbued with the Holy Spirit, although they both attracted criticism from chroniclers for behaving inappropriately.

Pilgrimage was very popular with both men and women, and Jerusalem, the Holy City, represented the pinnacle of such penitential journeys. Hitherto pilgrims had not been supposed to carry arms, but now large numbers of unarmed pilgrims could travel to the Holy Land with an army sanctioned to fight by the pope and destined to succeed by God's will. The advent of crusading thus actually enabled some women to realize their spiritual ambitions and visit the holy places. Sibyl, wife of the serial crusader Thierry of Alsace, count of Flanders, reputedly decided to stay at the convent of Bethany after her first visit to the East, leaving her husband to return home without her. The continued Latin presence in the Holy Land after the success of the First Crusade also made the journey there more achievable for women. Organizations such as the military orders were founded with the intention of aiding and protecting pilgrims, and the settler population provided bonds of kinship with the West. Countess Ermengarde of Brittany acted as regent for her husband, Alan IV, during the First Crusade, and helped to administer the county after he entered a monastery in 1112, despite her own wish to join a convent. She finally took the veil in 1130 at Dijon, but in 1132 her half-brother King Fulk of Jerusalem invited her to visit the Holy Land. Although in her mid-sixties, she took the opportunity to travel to the East, spending some time in Nablus and at the nunnery of St. Anne's in Jerusalem, returning to Brittany before 1135.

Women's Activities on Crusade

Were women attracted by the military aspects of crusading? Romantic and stereotypical images of armed female warriors abound in medieval literature, but it is very unlikely that there were women on crusade who were specifically designated to fight. Medieval women were considered to be unfit to bear arms, which was one of the reasons they were discouraged from crusading. Some eyewitness Muslim sources for the Third Crusade give accounts of Frankish women wearing armor and fighting in battle; one even mentions a female archer at the siege of Acre in 1191, but representations of women warriors were sometimes used to mock the weakness or barbarity of an enemy, and thus cannot always be trusted.

The few examples of Christian women fighting in Western sources were also loaded with gendered symbolism. The chronicler Ambroise recorded how women slit the throats of prisoners taken from a captured galley at Acre in 1190. This was seen as a particularly humiliating death because the women had to use knives instead of swords, prolonging the pain of their dying enemies. During the Fifth Crusade women stood armed guard over the crusader camp and killed the Muslims who fled shamefully from a failed attack on Damietta. In the Baltic region women successfully defended the town of Elbing in 1245 when the garrison of Teutonic Knights was engaged elsewhere, but had to gird themselves with manly armor first. Both on crusade and as settlers defending newly claimed territories, women probably did fight, but only in times of extreme desperation. Chroniclers were keen to emphasize that such fighting only occurred in the absence of suitable male warriors and that women were transcending the natural weakness of their gender by fighting.

Some noblewomen who brought retinues of their own knights on crusade were considered to be feudal lords. Ida, widow of Margrave Leopold II of Austria, was counted among the leaders of the ill-fated Crusade of 1101. Nonetheless, all lords were subject to the acknowledged military leader of the host or contingent in which they traveled, and noblewomen probably had little influence over strategic decisions. Rather than taking an active role, women usually became the casualties of crusader battles: they were regarded as booty by Muslims, Christians, and pagans alike. Ida herself was either killed or captured by the forces of Qilij Arslān I, sultan of Rūm, at Herakleia. Captured women might be ransomed if they were wealthy, but even the most noble risked slavery or even death if they went on crusade.

Less is known about women from the lower classes who took the cross. A passenger list from a crusade ship in 1250 records that 42 of the 342 common people en route to the Holy Land were women, 22 of whom had no male chaperone [Kedar, "The Passenger List of a Crusader Ship, 1250," p. 272]. Such women usually aided crusade armies by performing more mundane duties; on the First Crusade, women were praised for bringing refreshments and encouragement to crusaders at the battle of Dorylaion (1097), and they helped to undermine a tower at Arqah by carrying away rubble in their skirts. At the siege of Acre in 1191, one admirable woman who had been mortally wounded while filling a ditch reputedly begged her husband to use her corpse to continue the work. Women's activities ranged from washing clothes and lice picking to helping provision the crusaders. During the Fifth Crusade both Christian and Muslim women were employed grinding corn, while the women of the camp maintained markets for fish and vegetables, and probably tended to the wounded and sick.

Prostitution was always associated with the presence of lower-class women, and bearing in mind the poverty and hardship that crusader armies sometimes endured, it is not surprising that trade in sex for money or food took place. It was a major concern to crusade leaders and chroniclers because of the perceived link between sin and military failure. At times we are told that crusaders expelled women from the camp to remove sexual temptation, as, for example, at the siege of Antioch in 1098, at Constantinople in 1204, and at Damietta in 1249. Sexual relations with indigenous Muslims and Jews were regarded as being particularly sinful and in some cases leading to divine retribution. Medieval historians were sometimes at pains to obscure any element of sexual crime in crusader successes, emphasizing that the crusaders purified the Holy Places through the wholesale slaughter of men, women, and children.

Sexual activity on crusade also led to an exclusively feminine health issue: pregnancy and all the risks associated with it in the medieval period. The German chronicler Albert of Aachen reported that the harsh conditions of the journey on the First Crusade had led to premature births and mothers abandoning their infants. In a recent study, Sabine Geldsetzer has listed the children known to have been born during crusades or on pilgrimage to the Levant at this time, although these were mostly noble [Geldsetzer, *Frauen auf Kreuzzügen*, pp. 213–215]. There was some recognition that the journey was too dangerous at certain stages of pregnancy; Mabel of Roucy, wife of Hugh II of Le Puiset, went with her husband on the 1107 crusade, but stopped in Apulia to give birth to a son. As the child's health was fragile, he remained there to be brought up by relatives, while Mabel went on to settle in the East. Marie of Champagne, the wife of Count Baldwin IX of Flanders, delayed her departure on the Fourth Crusade (1202–1204) because she was close to childbirth, and afterward died en route to being reunited with her husband. However, Margaret of Provence, the wife of King Louis IX of France, gave birth three times while on her husband's crusade to the East (1248–1254): to John-Tristan (1250), Peter (1251), and Blanche (1253). The chronicler John of Joinville went into considerable detail about her experience giving birth to John-Tristan in Damietta. It was indeed a dramatic situation: her husband had been defeated and imprisoned by the Egyptians, and she was trapped inside the city and terrified of capture. She had to break the traditional confinement of childbed in order to secure the ransom for her husband and organize the surrender of the city.

Despite the restrictions on sexual activity for crusaders, such noble women were seldom criticized for fulfilling what was seen to be their duty, the provision of heirs. Among the lower ranks, however, pregnancy attracted more criticism, as, among the unmarried, it could be evidence of illicit sexual activity. Guibert of Nogent asserted that the crusaders' desperate situation at Antioch in 1098 led them to punish any unmarried pregnant women severely, along with their lovers (or customers).

Crusading and Intermarriage in the Latin East

Despite concerns about the presence of women on crusade expeditions, even the harshest of critics recognized that women were crucial to the establishment of a permanent Christian population on all fronts where religious war was waged. One contemporary, Ralph Niger, reluctantly admitted that relations with women were a necessary evil for repopulating conquered territories, but he asserted that women had no place in armies sent to the East and should only be sent for once the land had been pacified. Women did play an important part in the settlement of conquered lands, but it seems that most female crusaders, like their male counterparts, probably returned home after their pilgrimage vows were fulfilled. In fact, some of the early Frankish rulers of the Levant (including Baldwin I and Baldwin II of Jerusalem) married into the local Armenian Christian population in order to secure new political ties, a policy that extended to include Byzantine marriage alliances in the later twelfth century.

Once a settler society was established, marriage provided diplomatic links between East and West, encouraging new crusade expeditions. Continued warfare created a constant lack of manpower, and in the absence of male heirs, lands and titles often fell to widows and daughters. Delegations were then sent to the West to entice crusaders to the Holy Land with the promise of favorable marriages. Crusaders who married heiresses to the throne of Jerusalem included Fulk V of Anjou, William and Conrad of Monferrat, Guy and Aimery of Lusignan, Henry of Champagne, John of Brienne, and Emperor Frederick II. The more important bridegrooms usually brought with them an entourage of knights on crusade to help secure their new domain, although this could cause friction with the established baronage. Kings and nobles of the Levant also sought wives from western Europe and Byzantium to improve political ties and gain dowries to aid the defense of the Latin East. Bohemund I, prince of Antioch, came to the West on a recruitment drive for a crusade against the Byzantine Empire, a drive that included making a prestigious marriage in 1106 to Cecilia, the daughter of King Philip I of France. Yet the need for cash dowries to fund military activities could also spell the end of political alliances based on marriage. When the dowry from the marriage of King Baldwin I to an Armenian princess failed to materialize, he put her aside and controversially married Adelaide of Sicily, who brought him considerable wealth and military resources. Once he had exhausted Adelaide's resources, he repudiated her in turn, a decision that resulted in a serious political rift with her son, King Roger II of Sicily.

The strong dynastic links between the Latin East and Western Christendom could also cause problems for crusaders. Raymond of Poitiers, prince of Antioch, was famously accused of initiating an affair with his own niece, Eleanor of Aquitaine, during the Second Crusade (1147–1149). This was reputedly because Raymond was bitter at his failure to convince her husband, King Louis VII of France, to provide military support on the grounds of their kinship. Rumors of the affair highlighted negative perceptions about women on crusade, and conveniently sidestepped the political issues. Some contemporaries blamed Eleanor for the failure of the entire expedition. She had encouraged other women to take the cross by her example, leading to dissolute behavior in the crusader camps and ultimately the loss of divine favor.

Women Who Remained in the West

Finally, it is impossible to discuss the impact of the crusade movement without considering those who were left behind: they were affected by the crusades in a number of ways. From the outset the church had pledged to protect the property and families of those who took the cross, but some crusaders left charters including specific provision for their female relatives and other loved ones while they were away. They often gave money or endowments to religious houses for the care of their kin. Gilbert of Aalst founded the nunnery of Merham for his sister Lietgard in 1096 before embarking on the First Crusade. At the same time, the crusader Hugh of Vermandois arranged a marriage for his daughter Elizabeth with Robert, count of Meulan. Crusaders' wives were not kept in chastity belts during their husbands' absence as popular myth supposes, but canonists were concerned about adultery. To avoid this problem, a wife could theoretically prevent her husband from crusading because he would be unable to fulfil his conjugal duty of sexual intercourse.

Crusade preachers often described wives as inhibiting crusaders, but there is little hard evidence to suggest that wives actually stopped their husbands from taking the cross. The chronicler Orderic Vitalis even suggested that after Stephen of Blois deserted the siege of Antioch in 1098 during the First Crusade, his wife Adela used the art of seduction to encourage him to return to the Holy Land in 1101. During both of his absences, Adela was left to continue the administration of the family estates, and there are two extant letters from her husband, in which he gave her news of the expedition and advice for the management of their lands. Female relatives did not always administer the estates of absent crusaders, but certain women were recognized to be capable regents. In particular, Blanche of Castile and Eleanor of Aquitaine filled very high-profile roles in regency governments on behalf of their crusading sons Louis IX of France and Richard I of England, acting with considerable acumen under difficult circumstances.

Women could also support the crusade movement spiritually and financially without taking the cross. Patterns of intermarriage in France have suggested that, far from inhibiting men from taking the cross, certain alliances helped to import traditions of crusading from one family to another. Women may even have encouraged the crusade idea through their participation in the early religious education of their children and by employing chaplains who supported the crusade. In the thirteenth century, Pope Innocent III asked women to pray collectively for the success of crusade expeditions. In some cases, the support of specific holy women was sought. Count Philip of Flanders is known to have written to Hildegard of Bingen, abbess of Rupertsberg, for her advice on the eve of his departure for the Holy Land in 1177. The influential St. Birgitta of Sweden wrote polemics in favor of the Baltic Crusades in the fourteenth century.

With regard to finance, Innocent III encouraged women to donate cash or sponsor a knight instead of going on crusade themselves, in return for the same spiritual benefits as crusaders. This measure was probably designed to address the problem of noncombatants on crusade, but was also an effective way to raise money and at least recognized that women were willing to support crusading. Women could also donate money and endowments to monastic houses that helped to organize cash for crusaders, including the newly established military orders. Crusaders often relied on family relationships, both to raise money for crusade expeditions and to cover debts on their return. Some charters demonstrate that they sold or mortgaged land to female kin, or engaged in transactions where the consent of a female relative was required. At the time of the Fifth Crusade, ten out of fifteen wills in Genoa that left money to support crusading were drawn up by women [Powell, "The Role of Women on the Fifth Crusade," p. 296].

Many men and women who went on crusade were overcome by the arduous journey and its associated dangers, and did not return to their homes at all. Sometimes it was impossible to certify whether crusaders were still alive or not, which meant that women who had remained in the West could not remarry without the risk of committing bigamy. Canonical sources varied from 5 to 100 years as to how long a crusader's wife should wait for her husband's return, and some considered remarriage to be out of the question. Such women lingered in the shadow of widowhood, unable to progress with the normal cycle of life, which usually entailed becoming a dowager, entering a monastery, or a new marriage. Ida of Louvain went to Jerusalem in 1106 in a desperate attempt to find her husband, Baldwin II of Mons, count of Hainaut, who had gone missing in Asia Minor during the First Crusade, but without success.

By the time of the fall of Acre to the Mamlūks in 1291, crusading had become an integral part of medieval society that touched the lives of women all over Europe, whether they took the cross or not. The crusade propagandist Pierre Dubois, writing in 1306–1307, thought that women could be instrumental to the recovery of the lost Holy Land. He asserted that they could be trained in theology and logic, and given as wives to Eastern Christians and Muslims, or educated in the medical care of women's ills, thereby influencing others to convert to Christianity. His vision may not have been realistic, but now that the possibility of a successful military operation to the East was rapidly dwindling, he recognized that women, who had traditionally been excluded from martial activities, might play an alternative role in spreading Christianity. In fact, for good or ill, women had committed themselves together with their families to the holy war throughout the crusading era, and without the network of support they provided, the boundaries of medieval Christendom could not have expanded, nor could a Latin society in the East have flourished for as long as it did.

–Natasha Hodgson

Bibliography

Brundage, James A., "The Crusader's Wife; A Canonistic Quandary," *Studia Gratiana* 12 (1967), 425–441.

———, "The Crusader's Wife Revisited," *Studia Gratiana* 14 (1967), 243–251.

———, "Prostitution, Miscegenation and Sexual Purity in the First Crusade," in *Crusade and Settlement,* ed. Peter Edbury (Cardiff, UK: University College Cardiff Press, 1985), pp. 57–65.

Friedman, Yvonne, "Women in Captivity and Their Ransom during the Crusader Period," in *Cross-Cultural Convergences in the Crusader Period; Essays Presented to Aryeh Grabois on his 65th Birthday,* ed. Michael Goodrich, Sophia Menache, and Sylvia Schein (New York: Lang, 1995), pp. 75–87.

Geldsetzer, Sabine, *Frauen auf Kreuzzügen* (Darmstadt: Wissenschaftliche Buchgesellschaft, 2003).

Gendering the Crusades, ed. Susan B. Edgington and Sarah Lambert (Cardiff, UK: University of Wales Press, 2001).

Hamilton, Bernard, "Women in the Crusader States: The Queens of Jerusalem (1100–1190)," in *Medieval Women,* ed. Derek Baker (Oxford: Blackwell, 1975), pp. 143–174.

———, "King Consorts of Jerusalem and Their Entourages from the West from 1186 to 1250," in *Die Kreuzfahrerstaaten als multikulturelle Gesellschaft,* ed. Hans Eberhard Mayer (München: Oldenbourg, 1997), pp. 13–24. Reprinted in Hamilton, *Crusaders, Cathars and the Holy Places* (Aldershot, UK: Variorum, 1999).

Hay, David, "Gender Bias and Religious Intolerance in Accounts of the 'Massacres' of the First Crusade," in *Tolerance and Intolerance: Social Conflict in the Age of the Crusades,* ed. Michael Gervers and James M. Powell (Syracuse, NY: Syracuse University Press, 2001), pp. 3–10.

Hodgson, Natasha, "Nobility, Women and Historical Narratives of the Crusades and the Latin East," *Al-Masāq: Islam and the Medieval Mediterranean* 17 (2005), 61–85.

Kedar, Benjamin Z., "The Passenger List of a Crusader Ship, 1250: Towards the Popular Element on the Seventh Crusade," *Studi Medievali,* ser. 3, 13 (1972), 269–279.

Maier, Christoph T., "The Roles of Women in the Crusade Movement: A Survey," *Journal of Medieval History* 30 (2004), 61–82.

Mažeika, Rasa, "'Nowhere was the Fragility of Their Sex Apparent': Women Warriors in the Baltic Crusade Chronicles," in *From Clermont to Jerusalem: The Crusades and Crusader Societies,* ed. Alan V. Murray (Turnhout: Brepols, 1998), pp. 229–248.

Nicholson, Helen, "Women on the Third Crusade," *Journal of Medieval History* 23 (1997), 335–349.

Porges, Walter, "The Clergy, the Poor and the Non-Combatants on the First Crusade," *Speculum* 21 (1946), 1–23.

Powell, James M., "The Role of Women on the Fifth Crusade," in *The Horns of Hattin,* ed. Benjamin Z. Kedar (Jerusalem: Yad Izhak Ben-Zvi Institute, 1992), pp. 294–301.

Purcell, Maureen, "Women Crusaders, a Temporary Canonical Aberration?" in *Principalities, Power and Estates: Studies in Medieval and Early Modern Government and Society,* ed. L. O. Frappell (Adelaide: University Union Press, 1979), pp. 57–67.

Riley-Smith, Jonathan, *The First Crusaders (1095–1131)* (Cambridge: Cambridge University Press, 1997).

Woplauken, Battle of (1311)

A battle between the Teutonic Order and the Lithuanians.

In early April 1311 the Lithuanian grand duke Vytenis raided Prussia. The Lithuanians plundered Warmia (Ermland) and withdrew, laden with loot and prisoners. Grand Commander Heinrich von Plötzke (1309–1312) followed the retreating Lithuanians. The armies met on the Wednesday before Easter (7 April 1311) at a place called Woplauken (mod. Wopławki, Poland). The chronicler Peter von Dusburg mistakenly rendered the date as 6 April. Initially the Lithuanians were able to hold out behind wooden barriers, but discouraged by a general assault of the order's full forces, they fled and were pursued by the order's troops. According to the order's chroniclers, most of the Lithuanians were killed. The grand duke, however, escaped. The incident represents one of the few great pitched battles between the order and the Lithuanians. In memory of their victory, the Teutonic Knights founded a Benedictine nunnery at Thorn (mod. Toruń, Poland), which illustrates the importance of the battle for the order.

–*Axel Ehlers*

Bibliography

Urban, William, *The Samogitian Crusade* (Chicago: Lithuanian Research and Studies Center, 1989).

Z

Žalgiris

See Tannenberg, Battle

Zangī (d. 1146)

'Imād al-Dīn Zangī was governor of Mosul and Aleppo, famous for his capture of the city of Edessa (mod. Şanlıurfa, Turkey) from the Franks in 1144.

Zangī was born around 1084, the son of Aq-Sunqūr al-Ḥājib, a Turkish emir in the service of the Great Saljūq sultan Malik-Shāh I. Aq-Sunqūr was appointed governor of Aleppo in 1087, but after Malik-Shāh's death in 1092 he was slain by the sultan's brother Tutush I, whom he had opposed in favor of Malik-Shāh's son Barkyārūq. Zangī was brought up by Karbughā, the governor of Mosul, became an emir, and distinguished himself over the years in the service of the various rulers of the city. In 1123 his efforts were rewarded when he was awarded two governorships in Iraq.

In 1126 Zangī was appointed governor of Baghdad and Iraq. A year later, responding to requests made by envoys from Mosul, Maḥmūd, the Saljūq sultan of Persia and Iraq, appointed Zangī to the governorship of the city. Zangī made his formal entry into Mosul in the autumn of 1127 and soon after also took control of other territories in Iraq and Upper Mesopotamia, including Nisibis (mod. Nusaybin, Turkey) and Harran. He then turned his attention to the city of Aleppo, which was in uproar. The city's governor had made himself unpopular with its people, who had besieged him in the citadel. Zangī sent representatives to the city, then made a formal entry in June 1128. He brought with him the remains of his father, whose memory was very dear to the populace. To further establish his legitimacy he linked himself to his predecessors by marrying the daughter of Riḍwān, one of the earlier Saljūq rulers of Aleppo.

In early 1130 Zangī captured Bahā' al-Dīn Sāwinj, the ruler of Hama (mod. Ḥamāh, Syria), and a son of Tāj al-Mulūk Būrī, the ruler of Damascus. He thus gained possession of Hama itself. He also attempted to take Homs (mod. Ḥimṣ, Syria) but was resisted by its inhabitants. In the same year he raided the Frankish fortress of Atharib. Zangī then conducted a campaign against the Artūqids of Mardin and Ḥisn Kayfa, before spending two years preoccupied by conflict in Iraq. Then, in the spring of 1134, he attacked the Artūqid ruler of Hisn Kayfa, defeating his forces near Amida (mod. Diyarbakır, Turkey) but failing to take the latter. Meanwhile, Zangī had been invited to intervene in Damascus by Shams al-Mulūk Ismā'īl, the son of Būrī, but when he arrived with his army in February 1135, he found that Ismā'īl had been murdered and replaced by his brother Shihāb al-Dīn Maḥmūd. After a number of inconclusive skirmishes with Damascene troops, a message arrived from the 'Abbāsid caliph in Baghdad ordering Zangī to return to Mosul. He was thus able to retreat honorably. He then conducted a campaign against the Franks, taking Atharib, Zerdana, Tell A'di, and Ma'arrat al-Nu'man and repelling an attack by Bertrand, count of Tripoli. He also besieged Homs but was forced to withdraw upon hearing of fresh instability in Iraq. This instability would occupy his attention until 1137.

In December 1135, fearing a renewed assault from Zangī, the ruler of Homs handed it over to the rulers of Damascus. In May 1137 Zangī took troops from Mosul and Aleppo and besieged Homs but was resisted. In July, hearing that the Franks had moved on Hama, he was forced to make peace. The Franks entrenched themselves at Montferrand (mod. Bārīn, Syria), a stronghold to the west of Hama and Homs. Zangī besieged Montferrand, while his troops took Kafartab and Maʿarrat al-Nuʿman from the Franks. Hearing that reinforcements were approaching from Jerusalem and Tripoli, he accepted the capitulation of Montferrand, which he had previously rejected, in August 1137.

Another factor affecting Zangī's decision to accept the capitulation of Montferrand was the arrival at Antioch of the Byzantine emperor John II Komnenos. John's initial intentions had been to try and bring Antioch under his control, and indeed, initially contact between the emperor and Zangī was peaceful, but in 1138 John made an alliance with Prince Raymond of Antioch. In April 1138 the Byzantine emperor took Buzaʿah and then, reinforced by troops from Tripoli, besieged Aleppo for three days. In the face of resistance, the emperor decided to isolate the city. Frankish troops reoccupied Atharib, Maʿarrat al-Nuʿman, and Kafartab, while the emperor besieged Shaizar (mod. Shayzar, Syria). Harassed by Zangī's troops and beset by disagreements with the Franks, the emperor allowed himself to be bought off by the inhabitants of Shaizar and withdrew from the area in May. By the end of October Kafartab, Buzaʿah, and Atharib had been retaken, removing the threat to Aleppo. Meanwhile, in August 1138 Zangī finally took possession of Homs when he married Būrī's widow, Safwat al-Mulk, who brought him the city as her dowry.

In June 1139 Shihāb al-Dīn Mahmūd of Damascus was assassinated and replaced by his brother Jamāl al-Dīn Muhammad. Zangī, who at the time was engaged in a campaign against the Artūqid Timurtash, was incited by Safwat al-Mulk to take vengeance for her son's assassination, with the result that he decided to attack Damascus. Before doing so he attacked Baalbek. The city was taken on 10 October, but the citadel continued to hold out until the twenty-first, when a capitulation agreement was made. However, when the troops of the citadel came out, Zangī reneged on the agreement and had many of them killed, something that only increased hostility toward him elsewhere. Zangī then advanced on Damascus, eventually besieging it in October and November 1139. Jamāl al-Dīn died in March 1140 and was succeeded by his son Mujīr al-Dīn, who was a minor. Acting on his behalf was Muʿīn al-Dīn Unur, an old opponent of Zangī. Unur sought the aid of the Franks, offering to give them the border town of Banyas (mod. Bāniyas, Syria), along with hostages and payment for their expedition. Hearing of this, Zangī withdrew, then reinforced the defenses of Baalbek, which he left in the hands of Najm al-Dīn Ayyūb, the father of Saladin. In June 1140 he returned to Damascus but was forced to retreat in the face of a sortie by the forces of the city. An agreement was made by which Damascus recognized the sovereignty of Zangī, who, having won a moral victory, returned to Mosul.

Zangī spent the next three years subduing rebellions and rivals to the north and east. His efforts caused friction with the Saljūq sultan Masʿūd (1143–1144), but he was able to avoid serious conflict by paying an indemnity. Then, in late spring of 1144, following both the instructions of the sultan and the interests of Mosul, he set out toward Edessa, taking several towns en route. He was engaged in operations against the Artūqids in the Diyar Bakr region when he heard that Count Joscelin II of Edessa, responding to a request for help from the Artūqid Qara Arslan, had left Edessa with a strong force of troops. Seizing the opportunity, Zangī besieged Edessa, taking it by storm on 24 December 1144. Thus the first of the capitals of the Frankish states of Outremer fell back into Muslim hands. Building on his success, Zangī took Saruj (mod. Suruç, Turkey) in January 1145. In March he besieged Bira (mod. Birecik, Turkey) but was forced to abandon the siege in May, when he heard that his deputy in Mosul had been assassinated.

After dealing with plots against his life in Mosul and Edessa, Zangī set out on his last campaign in the spring of 1146. He subdued Timurtash, then attacked Qalaʿat Jaʿbar on the Euphrates. It was during this siege, in September 1146, that Zangī was assassinated by a Frankish slave while he lay in a drunken stupor. He was succeeded at Mosul by his eldest son, Sayf al-Dīn Ghāzī, and at Aleppo by his second son, Nūr al-Dīn Mahmūd.

It is clear that Zangī spent much of his life pursuing military campaigns. The core of his military forces was a permanent body of cavalry, the ʿaskar, consisting of warriors skilled at both close combat and horse archery and composed of a mixture of Turkish mamlūks (slave soldiers) and free Kurdish warriors. The ʿaskar was bulked out by Arab and Turcoman tribal auxiliaries. This core, which was maintained from the income of Zangī's territories, was supplemented by both the ʿaskars of Zangī's subordinates and locally recruited cavalry armed only for close combat. Usually infantry would only be employed if a siege was to be undertaken.

A detailed study of Zangī's career reveals that he was both opportunistic and ruthless, ruling his territory with an iron grip; indeed, he was feared by both his army and his subjects alike. He had far-reaching political ambitions in both the eastern and western Islamic world, and it is worth noting that he spent a significant amount of his career fighting against fellow Muslims. However, he was also an adept politician and skilled military commander, and in the later years of his career he was clearly regarded by some of his Muslim contemporaries as a *mujāhid* (holy warrior), even before the fall of Edessa. The latter achievement significantly enhanced his reputation in this regard, and he received several honorific titles from the 'Abbāsid caliph, stressing his position as a champion of Islam. Had he lived longer, he would probably have taken Damascus and so brought all of Muslim Syria under his control. He might well then have led the united Muslims in the *jihād* (holy war) against the Franks.

–Niall Christie

Bibliography

Elisséeff, Nikita, *Nur ad-Din: Un grand prince musulman de Syrie au temps des croisades,* 3 vols. (Damas: Institut Français de Damas, 1967).

Hillenbrand, Carole, *The Crusades: Islamic Perspectives* (Edinburgh: Edinburgh University Press, 1999).

———, "'Abominable Acts': The Career of Zengi," in *The Second Crusade: Scope and Consequences,* ed. Jonathan Phillips and Martin Hoch (Manchester, UK: Manchester University Press, 2001), pp. 111–132.

Holt, Peter M., *The Age of the Crusades* (London: Longman, 1986).

Sivan, Emmanuel, *L'Islam et la Croisade* (Paris: Maisonneuve, 1968).

Zara

Zara (mod. Zadar, Croatia) was a port on the Dalmatian coast that played an important role in the Fourth Crusade (1202–1204).

Formerly under Venetian control, the city successfully rebelled, with Hungarian aid, in 1180. Venetian attempts to recapture it were unsuccessful and hamstrung by crusading vows taken by the kings of Hungary, Béla III (in 1195/1196) and his son Imre (in 1200), which conferred the protection of the church on their lands, including Zara. The doge of

The Conquest of Zara, 1202, by Andrea Michieli Vicentino (1539–1614). (Scala/Art Resource)

Venice, Enrico Dandolo, became increasingly exasperated with Imre, suspecting that he was cynically exploiting his vow. The problem was brought to the forefront when the Venetians agreed to join the Fourth Crusade in 1201; Pope Innocent III, who still hoped Imre would make good on his vow, warned Dandolo that the crusade could not be used against Hungarian lands.

By late summer 1202, it had become clear that the crusade army camped at Venice was unable to pay the contracted sum for transport. The crusaders accepted an offer made by Dandolo to loan the crusaders the money to pay their passage—if they would sail first to Zara and help recapture it. When the crusade fleet arrived in November 1202, the Zarans insisted that their city was under papal protection, even hanging banners of the cross on the city walls. A letter from Innocent explicitly forbidding an attack on Zara was ignored. The city fell on 24 November 1202.

In response to their disobedience, Innocent excommunicated all of the crusaders. He later absolved the Franks, but not the Venetians, whom he believed had perverted the crusade for their own ends. Dandolo was also eager for an absolution, yet he knew the price would be the restoration of Zara to Imre, and for that reason he had the city demolished in April 1203. The diversion to Zara saved the crusade from collapse and helped stabilize Venice's control of the Adriatic while its military forces were absent, but it also provoked the enduring enmity of the pope against Venice.

–*Thomas F. Madden*

Bibliography
Brunelli, Vitaliano, *Storia della città di Zara,* 2nd ed. (Trieste: Lint, 1974).
Madden, Thomas F., *Enrico Dandolo and the Rise of Venice* (Baltimore: Johns Hopkins University Press, 2003).

Žemaitija

See Samogitia

Zimmern, Chronicle of

A family chronicle written in Early New High German, compiled by Froben Christoph, count of Zimmern (1519–1566). It survives in two manuscripts: a draft version and a fair copy (MSS. Stuttgart, Württembergische Landesbibliothek, Cod.Don.580 and 581). The chronicle includes an account of the First Crusade (1096–1099) that purportedly derives from lost eyewitness traditions. This account gives considerable detail on a large number of named crusaders from Swabia and the Rhineland, who were long thought by scholars to have formed part of the forces led by Peter the Hermit, which were defeated by the Turks in Asia Minor in 1096. In fact, the narrative framework of this section is based largely on the much earlier accounts given by Robert of Rheims and William of Tyre, but almost all of the names of crusaders given are anachronisms or inventions, intended to magnify the German contribution to the crusade and to exalt the ancestry and reputation of the counts of Zimmern and other noble families of sixteenth-century southern Germany.

–*Alan V. Murray*

Bibliography
Die Chronik der Grafen von Zimmern, ed. Hansmartin Decker-Hauff et al., 7 vols. (Konstanz: Thorbecke, 1964–).
Murray, Alan V., "The Chronicle of Zimmern as a Source for the First Crusade," in *The First Crusade: Origins and Impact,* ed. Jonathan P. Phillips (Manchester, UK: Manchester University Press, 1997), pp. 78–106.
———, "Walther Duke of Teck: The Invention of a German Hero of the First Crusade," *Medieval Prosopography* 19 (1998), 35–54.

Texts and Documents

I. A Letter to an Old Crusader

Translated by Kathleen Thompson

In the early twelfth century the focus of Christian expansion in the Iberian Peninsula shifted to the kingdom of Aragon under the energetic leadership of Alfonso I "the Battler" (Sp. *el Batallador*) (1104–1134). The success of his campaigns against the Muslims owed much to the participation of Frankish veterans of the First Crusade (1096–1099). By 1120 Zaragoza and the Ebro valley had been captured with the help of Gaston of Béarn and his half brother, Centulle of Bigorre. After 1123 they were joined by Count Rotrou II of the Perche, who became Alfonso's governor in Tudela until the middle 1130s.

So great was the prestige of these early crusaders in the generation after 1099 that their presence was an important factor in Spanish politics. In this letter its probable sender, Blanche, the daughter of King García IV of Navarre, tries to persuade her great-uncle, Rotrou of the Perche, to come back to the Spanish front after he has returned to northern France. She reminds him of his success against the Muslims, his reputation, and the potential reward in heaven. The letter was subsequently preserved among a collection of exhortatory exemplars in the library of St. Victor of Paris.

To Rotrou, by Grace of God, the distinguished count of the Perche, most beloved lord and uncle, from B, his own dearest niece in both body and spirit. Fight in the earthly army for Christ so that you may be able to obtain a final home among heavenly forces. Obviously I rejoice with you in your glory, which is spread far and wide throughout the world, for the greater it becomes, the more reflected glory I receive. You secured the pagans' land for God's service with his help and grace, and, fighting for God, not the world, you bravely drove from there the infidels and despisers of God. Now I hear that you do not intend to go back to the place where you came from, and I am afraid that you may therefore incur the wrath of the Supreme Judge, for your absence will perhaps encourage the enemy to move against the Christians whom you have so rashly abandoned, and it will enable them to attack those helpless people. Truly the divine scripture declares: "the victory of battle standeth not in the multitude of a host; but strength cometh from heaven." Display wisdom therefore and return to the place you have lightly left. Reach the fulfillment of your life in the place where you spent a good portion of it in the service of God. Out of family affection I would welcome your presence with me, but your spiritual welfare makes me demand it from you as the fruit of good work. If in truth you brought back any silk with you, be kind enough to send it to me to make clothing. Farewell.

Sources

MS Paris, Bibliothèque Nationale de France, lat. 14615, formerly Saint-Victor JJ 23 (Grandrue), fol. 346r–v.

Thompson, Kathleen, "An Old Crusader Is Encouraged Back to the Spanish Front: A Woman's Letter to Count Rotrou of the Perche," *Bulletin of International Medieval Research* 9–10, for 2003–2004 (2005), 40–50.

2. Five Letters Concerning the Second Crusade

Translated by G. A. Loud

These letters, hitherto untranslated, illustrate important aspects of the Second Crusade (1147–1149). Letter A shows clearly that the decision of King Conrad III of Germany to take the cross was made without the knowledge or agreement of the pope.[1] Letters B and C reveal the problems encountered en route, the aims of the crusade leaders, and the very different attitudes toward the Byzantines of the German and French rulers. The last two letters are important evidence for the failure of the siege of Damascus (letter D) and the legacy of bad feelings that were left behind, and the hostility toward Byzantium that resulted from the crusade (letter E). This last letter was part of the attempt to create a new expedition after the crusade's failure.

A. King Conrad III of Germany Writes to Pope Eugenius III from the Diet of Frankfurt to Inform Him of His Plans for the Crusade (March 1147)

Conrad, by the grace of God king of the Romans and always Augustus, to his father in Christ Eugenius, supreme pontiff of the Holy Roman Church, [expressing to him] filial love and due reverence in the Lord.

We have gratefully received the letter from Your Holiness sent with your legate Bishop Theodwin of Santa Rufina, a man who has been received by us with love and honor, and we have carried out the suggestions contained within it with filial and cordial charity. Hence we have with God's assistance taken careful and effective steps for the government of our kingdom, which has been granted to us by God, a matter about which you advised and exhorted us with paternal affection. This was discussed with great attention and thoroughness at a gathering of the princes at Frankfurt, where we held a general court. A lasting peace has been confirmed throughout every part of our kingdom, and our son Henry has been chosen with the unanimous agreement of the princes and the eager acclamation of the whole kingdom as king and as the successor to our scepter. We have ordered that in accordance with divine mercy he should be crowned in the palace at Aachen in the middle of Lent.[2] Indeed, the matter which was of concern to your good self, that we have assumed such a great task, namely, the holy and life-giving cross and the intention of [making] so great and lengthy an expedition, without your knowledge, proceeds from a strong feeling of true love. But the Holy Spirit, which "bloweth where it listeth,"[3] and is accustomed to "coming suddenly,"[4] allowed us to make no delay to take counsel with you or anybody else; and immediately he touched our heart with his wondrous finger, he commanded our absolute obedience without there being any opportunity for delay interposing. Since we understand both from your letter and from the legate that you will come to Gaul, we request, venerable father, and advise you with the utmost respect and thought, that you seek to cross the Rhine so that we can meet together so that we may be able both to discuss and to plan how, with [the help of] God's compassion, the peace of the churches and the ordering of the Christian religion may be augmented with appropriate measures and the well-being of the kingdom that has been granted to us by God, and the enhancement of our honor, may be confirmed through necessary decisions. And since there is very little time available for preparing our journey, we would very much like to have a face-to-face meeting with you at Strasbourg on the sixth day of Easter Week.[5] We commend to your sincerity our envoys, men who are especially prudent and discreet, lovers of the Holy Roman Church and of the kingdom, and who are most dear to us, namely Bishop Bucco of Worms, Bishop Anselm of Havelberg, and Abbot Wibald of Korvey, so that you may hear those things that they say as though [they were] from our own mouth, and you will not refuse to discuss and arrange the affairs of the Holy Roman Church and the kingdom with them in a friendly fashion.

Notes

1. The interpretation of this letter by Jonathan Phillips, "Papacy, Empire and the Second Crusade," in *The Second Crusade: Scope and Consequences,* ed. Jonathan Phillips and Martin Hoch (Manchester, UK: Manchester University Press, 2001), pp. 20–21, is based on a singularly inaccurate translation.
2. The fourth Sunday in Lent would have been 30 March 1147.
3. John 3:8.
4. Mark 13:36.
5. 18 April 1147.
6. 7 March 1148.
7. 10 March 1148.
8. 8 September 1148.

Source

Die Urkunden Konrads III. und seines Sohnes Heinrich, ed. Friedrich Hausmann, MGH Diplomatum Regum et Imperatorum Germaniae 9 (Wien: Monumenta Germaniae Historica, 1969), pp. 332–333, no. 184.

B. King Conrad III of Germany Writes to Abbot Wibald of Korvey Describing His Journey to the East and His Future Plans (January / February 1148)

Conrad, by the grace of God king of the Romans, to the venerable Abbot Wibald of Korvey and Stavelot [wishing him] his grace and all good things.

Since we have had proof of your loyalty toward us and our kingdom shown on many occasions, we do not doubt that you will greatly rejoice now that you hear of the favorable state of our affairs. We therefore bring news to you, our loyal subject. After we had arrived at Nicaea with a numerous and untouched army, we wanted to complete our expedition in good time. So we set off toward Ikonion on the direct route, accompanied by guides to show us the way, and carrying with us as many supplies as we could. But however, after ten days on the road, and with a similar march still left, the supplies began to run short for everyone, particularly for the cavalry, while the Turks unceasingly harried and inflicted death upon the crowd of people on foot, who were unable to keep up. Pitying the fate of the suffering people, who were dying both from famine and from the arrows fired by the enemy, and on the request of all the princes and barons, we led the army away from that wasteland toward the sea, so as to regroup, preferring to keep it unharmed for greater things [in future] rather than to win a bloody victory over the archers. When we arrived at the sea coast and pitched camp, much to our surprise the king of France arrived at our tents in the midst of a great storm, not wanting to wait for better weather in his joy. He was distressed that our army had been worn down by hunger and toil, but showing no little joy in our company. Indeed he and all his princes faithfully and devotedly offered us their service [Lat. *obsequium suum*]. They provided us with money and whatever else they had that we wanted. They then joined forces with us and our princes, although indeed some of our people were left behind, being unable to follow either because of illness or through lack of money, and because of this they became separated from the army. We then went without difficulty as far as St. John [Ephesos], where the saint's tomb is, from which manna is believed to gush forth, and there we celebrated the Lord's Nativity. We stopped there for some days, since both we and many of our men had fallen ill. We wanted to go on when we had recovered our health, but were so ill that we were quite unable to proceed. Hence, after waiting for us as long as they could, the king and his army set off regretfully, but we remained

racked by illness for a considerable time. When our brother the emperor of the Greeks heard of this he was much upset, and he and our most beloved daughter the empress came to us in haste, and generously provided us and our princes with everything that we needed for our journey from his own resources. He brought us back almost by force to his palace in Constantinople, so that we might be speedily restored to health by his doctors. There he showed us greater honor, so we have heard, than had ever been demonstrated to any of our predecessors. We now plan to set off for Jerusalem on Quadragesima Sunday;[6] we shall muster a new army there over Easter and then travel on to Edessa. We ask that you yourself pray, and have your brothers also pray, that God should indeed deign to make our journey a success; and commend us to [the prayers of] all the faithful. We ourselves commend our son to your faithful care.

Source

Die Urkunden Konrads III. und seines Sohnes Heinrich, ed. Friedrich Hausmann, MGH Diplomatum Regum et Imperatorum Germaniae 9 (Wien: Monumenta Germaniae Historica, 1969), pp. 354–355, no. 195.

C. King Louis VII of France Gives News of the Crusade to His Regent, Abbot Suger (March–April 1148)

Louis, by the grace of God king of the French and duke of the Aquitanians, to Suger, venerable abbot of Saint-Denis, greeting and [his] grace. It is our duty to send news of our affairs in the East as quickly as we can to you, who are dear to us. For we know that you have a heartfelt desire to hear about them, and nothing can make us happier than for you to receive good news about us.

After we had departed the frontiers of our kingdom, the Lord favored our journey, and he brought us in good health and unharmed as far as Constantinople, and by divine mercy with our whole army safe and in excellent spirits. There we were joyfully and honorably received by the emperor. After remaining there for a little while to gather the supplies that seemed to be needed, we sailed across the Bosporus and commenced our march through Romania. However, we suffered great damage in these regions, both through the treachery of the emperor and through our own fault, and we were indeed threatened by many and grave perils. For we were spared neither the vicious ambush of robbers nor the serious difficulties of the route, and faced daily battles with the Turks, who with the emperor's permission entered his lands to harry the soldiery of Christ, and who strove with all their might to harm us. Since in many places it was impossible to find food, the people were soon suffering from hunger. And on one particular day divine judgment exacted punishment for our sins, and a number of our barons were killed. For among those who died on the climb into the mountains of Laodikeia the Lesser and in the region round about were our blood relation the count of Warenne, Rainald of Tonnerre, Manasses of Bulles, Walter of Montjay, Everard of Breteuil, and many more, the list of whom will be announced at a more favorable moment than the present, since our grief does not allow us to speak further about them now. We ourselves frequently risked death, but on each occasion were saved by divine grace. We escaped the attacks of the Turks and, protected by the Lord, arrived at Attaleia with our army safe. There we had frequent and prolonged discussions as to the best way to continue our journey, and the general opinion of the bishops and princes was that, since our horses had for a long time been worn down by hunger and the hardships of the journey, and the way forward was beset with great difficulty, we should hurry on to Antioch by ship. We followed their advice, and on the Friday after the middle of Lent[7] we and the majority of our princes arrived safely by sea at the aforesaid city, and it is from there that we have had this letter dispatched to you. As for the rest, all our work is in the hand of God, who, as we trust in him, will not abandon us who have our hopes in him, but will guide his enterprise to a glorious conclusion. For you should most certainly know that we shall either return in glory, or we shall never return at all. It remains therefore for you to think frequently of us, and always commend us most sincerely to the prayers of religious men everywhere. And since our money has been in no small way diminished by many and various expenses, all of which have been entirely necessary to us, you should devote your energy to raising cash, and hasten to send what has been collected to us by trustworthy envoys. We shall not be able to further Christ's business without much expense and great labor. Farewell.

Source

Recueil des Historiens des Gaules et de la France, ed. Léopold Delisle et al., 24 vols (Paris: Palmé, 1840–1904), 15:495–496.

D. King Conrad III of Germany Informs Abbot Wibald of His Imminent Return Home (September 1148)

Conrad, by the grace of God august king of the Romans, to the venerable Abbot Wibald of Korvey [wishing him] his grace and all good things.

Because we know that you very much want to hear from us and to learn how we are prospering, we take this opportunity to tell you first of this. By God's mercy we are in good health, and we have gone on board ship to return on the festival of the Blessed Mary in September,[8] after having accomplished all that God allowed us to do in these regions, and the men of the land permitted.

Let us speak of these men. We arrived by general agreement at Damascus, and we pitched camp by the city gate, albeit with our men facing considerable resistance. There can be no doubt that we came very close to capturing the city. But then certain people whom we had no reason to distrust treacherously alleged that the city was impregnable on that side, and they led us to another position where there was neither water for the army nor could anyone gain entry. Everyone was annoyed, and also upset by this, and we retreated, abandoning the enterprise as a failure. However, they all without exception promised to undertake another expedition against Ascalon, and fixed a place and a day for this. But when we arrived there as had been agreed, we found scarcely anybody else present. After we had waited in vain for the rest to arrive for some eight days, and had been deceived by these people a second time, we consulted our own interests. In short therefore, we shall with God's aid return to you. We render our thanks to you, as you deserve, for the care that you have shown to our son, and for all the loyalty that you have shown us. With regard to other matters, we ask that you continue in the same vein, and all your kindness will be suitably rewarded.

Source

Die Urkunden Konrads III. und seines Sohnes Heinrich, ed. Friedrich Hausmann, MG*H* Diplomatum Regum et Imperatorum Germaniae 9 (Wien: Monumenta Germaniae Historica, 1969), pp. 356–357, no. 197.

E. Abbot Peter of Cluny Writes to King Roger II of Sicily, Offering to Act as Mediator between the King and Conrad III of Germany, and Urging Him to Attack Byzantium in Punishment for the Empire's "Betrayal" of the Second Crusade (c. 1150)

. . . Furthermore, we make known to your royal majesty that we greatly lament the conflicts that are going on between you and the lord king of the Germans (or emperor of the Romans). Both I and many others are strongly of the opinion that this discord is harmful to the Latin kingdoms and to the Christian faith. For we have heard many times and often how your military power has brought benefits to the church of God in the lands of his enemies, that is, those of the Saracens. Moreover, we believe that greater advantages would accrue if you and the aforesaid king were united in a lasting peace and concord. There is also another matter that has long been of concern to us, and to almost all of our fellow countrymen in France, in seeking such a peace for you; namely, the wicked, unheard of, and disgraceful betrayal by the Greeks and their miserable king of our pilgrims, that is, those in the army of God.

I shall speak of what I have in mind. If it should be necessary, insofar as is appropriate for a monk, I would not refuse to perish, if the justice of God would, through the death of one of his servants, revenge that of so many men, both nobles and commoners, indeed the flower of almost the whole of France and Germany, destroyed by wretched treason. Moreover, I can see no Christian prince under heaven through whom this work can be carried out who is better, more suitable, nor more effective than yourself, nor so acceptable to heaven and earth. For, by the grace of God, I say this not in flattery but on account of your outstanding deeds and from the general opinion about you. You are wiser of mind, better endowed with riches, and more practiced in courage than other princes, and furthermore you are physically closer to this place. So therefore, rise up, good prince, to fulfill what not just I with my voice am saying, but what is the wishes both of myself and of everyone else. Rise up to help the people of God, zealously to uphold the law of God like the Maccabees, to revenge so many insults, injuries, and deaths, and such effusion of blood in the army of God, shed so impiously.

I myself am ready, should an opportunity present itself, to go immediately to the aforesaid emperor, along with anybody else I can recruit, to secure the peace of which I spoke above. I shall try with all my strength and all my care to restore and confirm between you and him a peace that is so pleasing to God.

Source

The Letters of Peter the Venerable, ed. Giles Constable, 2 vols. (Cambridge, MA: Harvard University Press, 1967), 2:394–395, no. 162.

3. The Endowment Deed of the Khānqāh al-Ṣalāḥiyya in Jerusalem Founded by Saladin on 17 October 1189

Translated by Johannes Pahlitzsch

After the conquest of Jerusalem in 1187 Saladin started an ambitious building program for the city that had one objective: to restore the Islamic holy sites of old and to re-Islamize the rest of the city through and through. For this purpose, the sultan founded—among other things—three institutions: a *madrasa* (Islamic law school), a *khānqāh,* which designates a Ṣūfī convent, and a hospital. This gave Jerusalem some of the institutions required of an Islamic city: The *madrasa*'s jurisprudents took care of public life in secular and spiritual respects, the ill and the elderly were nursed in the hospital, and the mystically oriented Ṣūfīs led a life entirely devoted to God in their *khānqāh.* All three of them were settled in buildings that had been constructed and used by Latin Christian institutions. The *madrasa* was established in St. Anne's Church, the hospital was probably located in the Church of St. Maria Major, and the Ṣūfīs were assigned the former palace of the Latin patriarch located to the north of the Church of the Holy Sepulchre for their *khānqāh.*

The Khānqāh al-Ṣalāḥiyya was founded on 5 Ramaḍān 585 (17 October 1189). Its endowment deed (Arab. *waqfiyya*), which includes a detailed list of all of the property with which Saladin endowed it, survived in the Ottoman court registers (*sijillāt*) in a confirmation document dating from the sixteenth century. In comparing the *khānqāh*'s real estate with what is known of real estate ownership under Frankish rule, a notable continuity becomes apparent: a considerable part of the property of the patriarch and the canons of the Holy Sepulchre were transferred to the *khānqāh.* However, property previously belonging to other institutions—such as, in this case, land belonging to the Knights Hospitallers—was also integrated into the foundation. The choice of property with which Saladin endowed his foundations was most certainly not arbitrary. As the crusaders had done a century earlier, Saladin seems to have followed a policy of the smoothest possible transition in the administration of real property. Thus, the affiliation of some plots of real estate to their former institutions remained untouched if this fitted in well with the concept of creating a more or less uniform property. On the other hand, old affiliations were dissolved without further ado if this served the same purpose.

Translation[9]

In the name of God, the Merciful, the Compassionate.

This is what the Most Excellent Lord, al-Malik al-Nāṣir [the Victorious King], the Unifier of the Word of the Belief, the Subduer of the Adorers of the Crosses, Ṣalāḥ al-Dunyā wa-l-Dīn [the Righteousness of the World and of the Religion, i.e., Saladin], Sultan of Islam and the Muslims, Revivifier of the Dynasty [or state, dawla] of the Commander of the Believers Abū l-Muẓaffar Yūsuf, Son of the Most Exalted Lord, of the Just King, of the Leader of Kings and Sultans, Abū Saʿīd Ayyūb ibn Shādhī, the Sultan over the Egyptian and Syrian lands,[10] gave, founded, and established as alms. God, may he be exalted, make his kingdom everlasting, commit creation (5) to his protection, uplift his station above the two Simak Stars,[11] fortify his helpers and his army, and grant him abundant graciousnesses. [May he see to it that] his orders are carried out among all peoples and his commands are executed by the one serving him with sword and quill.

[Saladin founded this] in physical health, with stalwart heart, in full possession of his power, in the execution of his precepts regarding the revocation and confirmation of his [orders], steadfast in his opinion, by virtue of his word and his extending powers, with sincere intention and the urgent plea to God, may he be praised and exalted, to accept this from him and [grant] him the beauty of his reward, in the quest for a close bond with [God] and his reward [or "in the quest to be the means of [God's actions] and for the accomplishment with him"] on the day on which God rewards the almsgiver, and the remuneration for the benefactors is not lost.

He [Saladin] endowed the entire house known as the Patriarch's Palace [dār al-baṭrak] and found in the noble Jerusalem, as well as whatever belongs thereto. Belonging to this are the neighboring quarter, namely, a mill called (10) ʿUṣfūr [the sparrow], an oven and a monastery bordering thereon called the New, a large vault called Patriarch's Stable [isṭabl al-baṭrak], and a house that lies to the north of this stall, including the vaults lying thereunder. All this is surrounded by four boundaries. The first, southern boundary runs along the Qubbat al-Qumāma[12] on to the house of Yūsuf

al-Saḥḥāf [the Consumptive][13] and continues on the street called . . ., which leads to the west to the city wall. From this [boundary] opens the entranceway of the house and stall mentioned. The second, eastern boundary leads to the house that is known as that of the priests of the Qumāma.[14] The third, northern boundary runs from below to the street that leads to the house of Pilatus (dār al-Bilāṭ) and further. That is where is located the entranceway to the house mentioned and to the (15) ʿUṣfūr mill. From above, it leads by a house called Fuwayla [small elephant] to a Georgian monastery (dayr kurj) known as al-Tuffāḥa [the apple] and on to the al-Kharājī quarter (?). The fourth, western boundary leads to a certain monastery and a neighboring . . . over the Georgian al-Sanikul monastery (St. Nicholas) to a house called al-Jāmūs [the buffalo].[15]

Further belonging to this are the bath that is known as that of the patriarch, the vault, and the neighboring shops. This is surrounded by four boundaries. The first, southern boundary runs along an alley that leads to the zardkhānāh [i.e., ordnance depot, literally, the place where coats of mail are kept] and onto which the Bāb al-Aqmīn [either "gateway of the chimney" or "gateway of the oven of the bath"] opens. The second, eastern boundary runs along a house that was earlier called that (20) of the Hospitallers [al-isbitār] and now is designated as zardkhānāh. The third, northern boundary runs along the zardkhānāh. The fourth, western boundary runs along the street running there,[16] which is called Sūq al-Zayt. In it are located the entranceways to the bath, to the vault, and to the shops.[17]

To the [endowment] belong also the so-called Patriarch's Pool as well as the quarter bordering above and below.

Outside of the noble Jerusalem belongs to it the pool called Māmillā and the canal in which the water from this pool flows into the inner, so-called Patriarch's Pool.

(25) Moreover, the land of the upper, that is, northern hollow [jūra] belongs to it. It is enclosed by four boundaries. The first, southern boundary runs along the path that leads between [the northern] and the southern jūra to Ṣrnṭa [unidentified place-name]. It ends at the long rock that separates [the northern jūra] from the barren rock bottom that serves as a quarry. The eastern boundary runs along the path that separates [the northern jūra] from the moat. The northern boundary runs along the path that leads to Māmillā and further. The western boundary leads to the low ridge that separates [the northern jūra] from the jūra known as that of Zawīrut [Severus?] ibn Mnklb al-Firanjī.

Moreover, the lower, that is, southern, hollow [*jūra*], which is known as that of the Hospitallers, belongs to it. It is enclosed by four boundaries. The southern one leads along an old wall in which is found (30) an old canal; the eastern boundary runs along the path that leads to the Hebron gate and further; the northern boundary runs along the street to *Ṣrnṭa,* which separates [the southern *jūra*] from the upper *jūra.* The western boundary runs along the street that leads to Jarmīn's Pool [the pool of Germain] and to the Buqʻa and further.

To it also belongs the land known as the Buqʻa. It is enclosed by four boundaries. The southern one leads along a wall that extends from east to west and separates it from fertile estates to which an olive grove belongs, known as that of Salāmah ibn al-Ṣarīṣir [?], further on a piece of land of Ibn Suflāt as well as one known as the land of Ibn Raqiya [?]. Within (35) this boundary lies a piece of land known as pasture of *ʻShbkr* [unidentified name] and belonging to the titles of the Buqʻa. The boundary ends at the estates of Ṭabaliya and consists of an old wall that separates al-ʻUnuq [the Neck] from the estates of Ṭabaliya. The wall mentioned runs along the street that leads from there to Ṭabaliya. The boundary ends at an old wall next to which stands a terebinth and in which a pear tree grows. [This wall] separates the estates of the Buqʻa from those of Bayt Ṣafāfā. The eastern boundary runs along the path to Sūr Bāhir and beyond. The northern boundary runs along the Murabbaʻ al-Nisaʼ [?] and ends at an old street. The western boundary runs along the way to Bayt Ṣafāfā and beyond. (40) To it also belong two pieces of land [within the Buqʻa], a part of one of them being known as the pasture of *ʻShbkr* and the other part as Rās al-Khinnawṣ [Head of the Piglet]. The rest of this [first piece of land] . . . the eastern boundary corresponds [to that] of the Buqʻa and consists of the way that leads to Sūr Bāhir and further. Coming from the north, [the boundary] consists of a small piece of land in the Buqʻa that is called Daqq Maʻāsh [?] and al-Ḥamādiya [?]. Coming from the west, [the boundary] consists of the street and the old canal. The second piece of land is known in part as lowland [or estate] of Abū l-Waqiya and in part as vineyard of Rikār [of Ricard]. The rest of this [second piece of land] consists of two small plots of land, of which one is called al-ʻUnuq and the other Ḍarībat al-Arjām. This [entire second] piece of land is enclosed by four boundaries. The southern boundary is the boundary of the Buqʻa coming from the south and consists of the wall that separates [the Buqʻa] from the estates of Ṭabaliya. The east-

ern boundary runs along the canal mentioned, which separates this piece of land (45) from the first piece of land. The northern boundary of it is known as al-Rikār and the adjacent land. Coming from the west, [the boundary] consists of a street that separates this land from that of Bayt Ṣafāfā.

Everything found within these boundaries, all rights, what is small and what is large, hills, plains, canals, and what is known as [belonging] to it, as well as all that is attributed to it of its rights inside and outside of it, constitutes a fixed and established, inviolable, endless, definite, admissible, valid alms for God's sake, may he be exalted. [All this] is a plea for reward, [an expression of the] desire to please him and to [receive] richly of his gifts. These are the stairs leading to him. By no means shall [all this] be sold. No causes (50) for the transfer [of the property] shall revoke the establishment [of the foundation], which remains existent in its original state. Neither the passage of days and months shall alter it, nor shall the passage of the years and the ages debase it. It shall maintain the provisions [established by the founder] and serve charitable purposes according to its capabilities. It shall [suffer] neither a change nor a substitution, nor shall it ever be abolished or transformed, as long as the heavens and earth exist, until Allāh inherits the earth and those who are on it—verily, he is the best of heirs—according to what [literally: "in the manner that"] will be mentioned here.

The Most Excellent Lord, al-Malik al-Nāṣir, the Unifier of the Word of the Belief, the Subduer of the Adorers of the Crosses, Ṣalāḥ al-Dunyā wa-l-Dīn, this founder, founded, established and made all these marked-off locations imperishable for the venerable *shaykhs* of the Ṣūfis, for all mature men, old, middle-aged, or young, wedded (55) or unwedded, be they Arabs or non-Arabs. He made the upper floor of the above-mentioned building known as Palace of the Patriarch into a hospice (*ribāṭ*) for them and into a dwelling place for the unwedded among well-known Ṣūfis, be they residents of [Jerusalem] or newcomers from remote lands [coming] from *khānqāhs* with their [proper] customs and manners. However, may none join them who is not likewise a Ṣūfi, neither through an advocate nor through one who is in charge [the steward?, *walī amr*]. If someone does this, both the advocate as well as he for whom advocacy has been brought assume the responsibility that each one of them receives for his living only what he needs, without exceeding it and without harming another. [Furthermore, they are responsible] that no one evicts or replaces with another anyone who occupied a place in this house before him and lived in it before the other. When one journeys to (60) any land he wants and returns from his journey to this house, then he shall be permitted to reside therein: If his place is open, then it is to be allocated to him; if someone else occupies this place, then he shall nevertheless be permitted to reside in this house receiving only what he needs for satisfaction and in the same way as the others who live there. When someone dies, however, then [they are likewise responsible] that his right to residence and his other [rights] expire due to his death. And when it [i.e., the right of abode?] is accorded another who has no place to reside in this house, and who urgently requests an abode, then he shall reside [in the house].

Al-Malik al-Nāṣir, the Unifier of the Word of the Belief, the Subduer of the Adorers of the Crosses, Ṣalāḥ al-Dunyā wa-l-Dīn, the founder [muḥabbis] mentioned, has stipulated that the community (65) mentioned (i.e., the Ṣūfī) gather together as a whole every day following the afternoon prayer at this location to recite as much as possible from the illustrious Qur'ān in noble parts of one-thirtieth each, to practice the exercise of dhikr[18] as long as appears good to them, and thereafter to pray for the founder mentioned and all Muslims.

Al-Malik al-Nāṣir Ṣalāḥ al-Dunyā wa-l-Dīn, the founder mentioned, also stipulated that the proceeds from the mentioned goods [jahāt], in accordance with what the lawful steward considers correct, be used according to his discretion and his opinion. All matters of this foundation [waqf] are to be subject to their shaykh, the lawful steward; no other shall speak out on them. Their shaykh, who is one of them, is their steward; the shaykh and steward of this (70) foundation shall transfer the stewardship to someone who both is competent for this office and has the rank of a shaykh, providing he has no son qualified for it. [But] if he has male children, then he shall transfer [the control] and the office of shaykh to the oldest and best of them, without anyone being involved in this [decision]. This provision is in force as long as there are descendants from him. When their line ends and no one else remains from them, then the best of the Ṣūfīs of this place shall be selected. Their shaykh shall be one of them, not one of someone else, and he shall be their steward. He should have the same authority as whoever preceded him. In the case that the encounter with God [wijdān] [of this community] no longer takes place [or "the passion of this community succumb"]—may God protect us from this—

then the revenues of the locations mentioned are to be given to the poor and needy. And if something comes to light from the community mentioned for which he [the steward] must punish and banish [the guilty one], then may he punish and banish [him] from this place. May (75) he return to it only after a journey to the venerable Ḥijāz or elsewhere and [his] betterment as well as his penitence, repentance, and renunciation to God the Exalted.

Al-Malik al-Nāṣir, the founder mentioned, has also ordained that the community mentioned shall gather together with its shaykh on Fridays following sunrise at this place or in the venerable Aqṣā mosque to recite from the noble Qur'ān and thereafter pray for the founder and the Muslims. In the presence of their shaykh [they shall] recite as much as possible from the writings of the Imāms, the Ṣūfī shaykhs, every Friday—may God grant them all well-being. If this is not possible, then may this occur [at least] on some Fridays. May this remain so as long as the world persists.

(80) [Herewith] this foundation was consummated and its stipulations and rules established. It [thus] became through its protection [taḥrīm] of God—may he be praised—an eternally inviolable foundation. This is the all-embracing protection through which he declares inviolable that which is holy to him, forbids profanations of that which is holy to him, designates the unity in his name as inviolable, and preserves the holiness of his prophets, his emissaries, his angels—may God bless them—and his house that God created as a place of refuge for mankind and as security and something that is holy for the belief and its followers. To no one who believes in God and in the Final Days, neither to the shepherd nor to the flock, not on the basis of the strength of his might, the pleasantness of his life, the keenness of his intellect, or the breadth of his interpretation, is it permitted to disband [this foundation], not one of its conditions or rules. It may not be altered, neither concerning its basis or regarding [its] design, exchanged, or impaired by something not befitting the care of [the foundation]. May [no one] strive to attain any of this by any means (85) whatsoever, neither through negligence nor through anything about which God knows, who perceives the treacherous glance and that which is hidden in the heart. He who nevertheless does this or helps therewith harms his soul, robs himself of honor, deviates from the order of his Lord, and violates his prohibition. He rebels against him, disregards his threats, and deserves his curse as well as that of his prophets and emissaries. [This is] a curse that will attach to him its shame in this world and hell

and its fire on the day of the resurrection. God, may he be exalted, demands an accounting from him. He is his avenger, punishing him for his act and repaying him for that which he has done on the day on which every soul is presented with that which it has brought about, good and bad. [Then] he will wish that a great distance lay between [hell] and himself. God himself warns you—by God, he is kind to mankind! He punishes those who do evil and rewards those who do good. He lies in ambush for the evildoers according to his exalted word: "Then if any man changes it after hearing it, the sin shall rest upon (90) those who change it; surely God is All-hearing, All-knowing."[19]

The Most Excellent Lord, al-Malik al-Nāṣir, the Unifier of the Word of the Belief, the Subduer of the Adorers of the Crosses, Ṣalāḥ al-Dunyā wa-l-Dīn, Sultan of Islam and the Muslims, Revivifier of the State of the Commander of the Believers, Killer of the Unbelievers and Dissenters, Abū l-Muẓaffar Yūsuf, the founder already named—may God make his well-being complete and his realm everlasting, eternalize his power and raise his prestige, allow his protection to spread over creation, make his helpers strong and multiply their power—authorizes those righteous witnesses and illustrious lords who place their signature beneath this deed to attest to that to which it refers. They attested to this and this was on the fifth of the venerable Ramaḍān (95) in the year 585 [17 October 1189]. Praise to God, the Lord of the worlds, and may God bless our Lord Muḥammad, his family, and his companions and give them much peace. God is sufficient for us and suffices.

Notes

9. Parenthetical numbers relate to the text of the Arabic edition published in Johannes Pahlitzsch, "The Transformation of Latin Religious Institutions into Islamic Endowments by Saladin in Jerusalem," in *Governing the Holy City: The Interaction of Social Groups in Medieval Jerusalem,* ed. Lorenz Korn and Johannes Pahlitzsch (Wiesbaden: Reichert, 2004), pp. 47–69.

10. For the titles of Saladin and the Ayyūbids, see G. Wiet, "Les inscriptions de Saladin," *Syria* 3 (1922), pp. 307–328; Samuel Miklos Stern, "Two Ayyūbid Decrees from Sinai," in *Documents from Islamic Chanceries,* ed. S. M. Stern (Oxford: Cassirer, 1965), pp. 19–25, reprint in Stern, *Coins and Documents from the Medieval Middle East* (London: Variorum, 1986).

11. That is, Arcturus and Spica.

12. That is, the Church of the Holy Sepulchre.

13. Or al-Ṣaḥḥaf, the bookseller.

14. Probably the convent of the canons of the Holy Sepulchre.

15. The name Jāmūs is testified for the eighth to ninth centuries on pottery lamps from Jerash on which is inscribed "lil-Jāmūs" (for Jāmūs). See A.-J. 'Amr, "More Islamic Inscribed Pottery Lamps from Jordan," *Berytus* 34 (1986), 161–168. I am indebted to Professor Oleg Grabar for this reference.

16. Something seems to be missing here, since *al-shāri'al-maslūk* is in all the other cases followed by *minhu ilā*, "the street that runs somewhere"; cf. lines 12, 14, and 36. Or the phrase might be translated as "the paved street."

17. This is apparently the Street of the Patriarch of the Frankish period, today's Christian Quarter Road. The designation as Sūq al-Zayt is ambiguous, as it suggests an identification with the street known today as Khān al-Zayt that, however, cannot be intended here.

18. A specific mode of prayer that consists of a tireless repetition of an ejaculatory litany; see Louis Gardet, s.v. dhikr, in *Encyclopaedia of Islam,* 10 vols. (Leiden: Brill), 2: 223–227.

19. Qur'ān, Sūra 2:181.

Source

Pahlitzsch, Johannes, "The Transformation of Latin Religious Institutions into Islamic Endowments by Saladin in Jerusalem," in *Governing the Holy City: The Interaction of Social Groups in Medieval Jerusalem,* ed. Lorenz Korn and Johannes Pahlitzsch (Wiesbaden: Reichert, 2004), pp. 47–69.

4. The "Lost" Autobiographical Chapter of William of Tyre's Chronicle (Book XIX.12)

Translated by G. A. Loud and J. W. Cox

This chapter is our main—indeed, almost our only—source for the early career of Archbishop William of Tyre, the principal historian of twelfth-century Outremer. It was omitted from the copies made of William's *History* at a very early stage of its transmission. Only the chapter heading was preserved, and it was believed that its contents had been lost. This chapter was therefore not included in the English translation by Babcock and Krey, published in 1941.[20] It was, however, discovered in a manuscript in the Vatican Library by Robert Huygens, who published it in 1962.[21] It had always been known that William had spent some time at the schools in Europe before his return to the Holy Land around 1165. But it was only with the discovery of the lost chapter that it was realized that he had spent almost twenty years in Europe and that he had attended the classes of most of the leading teachers at the Schools of Paris and Bologna, the two most important intellectual centers of twelfth-century Christendom. Not only does this discovery do much to clarify William's career and intellectual formation, but the text is also important evidence for higher education at a key period during which the nascent universities were developing and gives us almost a who's who of the grammarians, philosophers, theologians, and law teachers of the so-called Twelfth-Century Renaissance. Furthermore, it enables us to be clear as to which parts of the chronicle deal with events when William himself was present in the East, and which must have been based on secondhand evidence, albeit often very detailed and carefully researched.

In the same year [*1165?*] I, William, by God's patience unworthy minister of the holy church of Tyre, author of this history, which I have compiled to leave something of the past to those who come after, after nearly twenty years in which I had most avidly followed in France and Italy the schools of the philosophers and the study of liberal disciplines, as well as the improving dogmatics of the celestial philosophy and the prudence of canon and civil law, returned home to the memory of my father and to my mother—may her soul now receive eternal rest—and was received with embraces. I was born in the holy city of Jerusalem, beloved by God, and was brought up there by my parents. During this middle period, in which I spent my adolescence across the sea in the [various] disciplines and dedicated my days to the study of letters in voluntary poverty, I was taught by the following distinguished doctors in the liberal arts, venerable men worthy of pious record, founts of knowledge, and treasurers of the disciplines. [These were] Master Bernard the Breton, who afterwards returned to the town where he was born and became Bishop of "Cornwall" [Quimper],[22] Master Peter Helias of the Poitevin nation,[23] and Master Ivo from the people and nation of Chartres. All these had for a long time been pupils of that most learned of men Master Theodoric the Elder. The youngest of them, Master Ivo, had also profited from the doctrine of Master Gilbert Porrée, bishop of Poitiers, whom he had heard after Master Theodoric.[24] I heard these alternately, as the pressure of their duties made them available to me or not, for about ten years. I heard others also, albeit not so assiduously, but however more fre-

quently and especially through the means of disputation following the distinguished and praiseworthy Alberic *de Monte*,[25] Master Robert of Melun,[26] Master Mainerius, Master Robert Amiclas and Master Adam of Petit Pont,[27] who seemed to me to be "the greatest luminaries."[28] In theology, I diligently heard for the space of six years a man unrivalled in that field whose surviving work the chorus of the prudent welcome with veneration and study with reverence, a man commendable for his sound doctrine in everything, Master Peter Lombard, afterwards bishop of Paris.[29] I heard most frequently [too] Master Maurice, who later succeeded him in the same bishopric.[30] In civil law at Bologna I had as teachers Don Ugolino di Porta Ravennate and Don Bulgarus, jurists and men of supreme authority.[31] I also often saw, and went to the lectures of, their contemporaries Don Martino and Don Giacomo, men most learned in law; these four seemed as if columns on solid foundations in the Temple of Justice, placed there to sustain it. I also had as a teacher in the exposition of [classical] authors Hilary of Orléans,[32] and in geometry, and especially Euclid, Master William of Soissons, a man of halting speech, but of sharp mind and subtle ingenuity. Memory of all these lives up to the present, and record remains perpetual. Those who elucidate knowledge and make it multiply to those travelling [in search of it], those who teach righteousness to many, shall live in perpetuity and not suffer the waste of oblivion. Their light shall be as of the stars, as in the sermon of Daniel. "Many shall run to and fro, and knowledge shall be increased," and also, "And they that be wise shall shine as the brightness of the firmament; and they that turn many to righteousness as the stars for ever and ever."[33] May the clement and merciful God remember all of them in the reward of the just. Let all of those who mercifully brought me from ignorance to the light of knowledge and righteousness, and who, even to a small extent, raised me by their erudition, deserve eternal reward.

After I returned home by the will of God, Lord William, bishop of Acre,[34] of pious memory, of the nation of the Lombards, a careful and discreet man, who had been translated to that church from the archdeaconate of Tyre, immediately after my arrival and with the generosity of true charity, and with the consent of all his chapter, gave me a benefice, known as a prebend, in his church. Furthermore King Amalric, whose deeds I describe in the present work, seemed to receive my arrival quite welcomingly. Had not a certain person, moved by envy, presented objection to me and turned the royal mind somewhat against me, he would have immediately assigned a whole benefice (as it is called) to me. However, he did not cease to show solicitude for me, and sought an opportunity to direct his prayers among the bishops for a benefice to be promised to me (although I was ignorant of this). He much enjoyed our conversations; and it was at his suggestion, which I freely embraced, that I wrote the volume showing the deeds which happened in the kingdom from [the time of] its liberation from the hand of the enemy. But let us now return to our story.

Notes

20. *A History of Deeds Done beyond the Sea by William Archbishop of Tyre*, trans. Emily A. Babcock and August C. Krey, 2 vols. (New York: Columbia University Press, 1943).

21. Robert B. C. Huygens, "Guillaume de Tyre étudiant: Un chapitre (xix.12) de son 'Histoire' retrouvé," *Latomus* 21 (1962), 811–829.

22. Bernard of Moëlan was bishop of Quimper (in Brittany) from 1159 to 1167.

23. Peter Helias was a famous teacher of grammar who also taught the celebrated English scholar John of Salisbury.

24. Ivo, dean of Chartres cathedral, attested the orthodoxy of Bishop Gilbert Porrée of Poitiers (1142–1154) when the latter was accused of heresy at the Council of Rheims in 1148. See Beryl Smalley, "Master Ivo of Chartres," *English Historical Review* l (1935), 680–686.

25. Those named in the next part of the list, Alberic *de Monte* (Mont-Sainte-Géneviève) and so on, were all teachers in the Schools of Paris.

26. Robert of Melun, despite his name, was an Englishman and was bishop of Hereford from 1163 to 1167.

27. Adam, also known as Adam of Balsham, was another Englishman who taught logic in Paris from 1132 onward, although his teaching was criticized for its complexity by John of Salisbury.

28. Cf. Gen. 1:16.

29. Peter Lombard's *Sentences* (written c. 1150) became the fundamental medieval theology textbook. He was bishop of Paris from 1158 to 1160.

30. Maurice de Sully was bishop of Paris from the autumn of 1160 until his death on 11 September 1196.

31. Ugolino, also known as Ugo Alberici (d. 1168), was famed for his "Disputations." Master Bulgarus wrote glosses (commentaries) on the *Corpus Iuris Civilis* of Justinian. Both were also active as judges, including at the Emperor Frederick Barbarossa's Diet of Roncaglia in 1158.

32. Hilary was yet another Englishman, who taught grammar at Orléans and Angers and at Paris from c. 1145. A number of his letters and poems have also survived. See N. M. Häring, "Hilary of Orléans and His Letter Collection," *Studi Medievali*, ser. 3, 14 (1973), 1088–1122.

33. Dan. 12:3–4.

34. Bishop of Acre c. 1165–1172.

Source

[Translation © G. A. Loud and J. W. Cox (1983)]

Huygens, Robert B. C., "Guillaume de Tyre étudiant: Un chapitre (xix.12) de son "Histoire" retrouvé," *Latomus* 21 (1962), 811–829.

5. German Crusade Songs of the Late Twelfth and Early Thirteenth Centuries

Translated by Jeffrey R. Ashcroft

A. Friedrich von Hausen

Friedrich von Hausen is recorded in charters and chronicles as a ministerial knight with military, legal, and diplomatic functions in the service of Frederick I Barbarossa, Holy Roman Emperor, and his son King Henry VI between 1171 and 1188. He was killed in battle on the Third Crusade, in May 1190. Hausen wrote courtly love songs during the 1180s, and this song of crusading propaganda must date from 1188–1189.

"Min herze und min lip diu wellent scheiden"

My heart and my body want to part company, though they have been together for a long time now. Body is keen to go fight the heathen, but Heart has chosen a woman in preference to all the world. This pains me ever more, that they will not stay with one another. My eyes have caused me much grief. God alone can settle this dispute.

Since, Heart, I cannot dissuade you from leaving me in this unhappy way, I pray God that he may deign to send you somewhere where you will be well received. Alas, how will you fare, poor thing? How can you venture to face such peril alone? Who shall help you bring your cares to an end so loyally as I have done?

I thought I had freed myself of such cares when I took the cross in honor of God. It should by rights have been so, if my own steadfastness had not prevented it. If my heart had given up its foolish will, I should be truly a whole man. Now I realize that it doesn't care how I am to fare in the end.

No one can reproach me with inconstancy if now I hate her whom before I loved. However much I begged and beseeched her, she behaves as if she doesn't understand. It seems to me indeed as if her words behave exactly like the fickle summer weather does in Trier. I'd be a fool if I took her foolish obstinacy seriously. It will not happen again.

Source

Des Minnesangs Frühling, ed. Hugo Moser and Helmut
Tervooren, 36th ed. (Stuttgart: Hirzel, 1977), pp. 81–83.

B. Albrecht von Johansdorf

Albrecht von Johansdorf was a ministerial knight in
the service of the bishops of Passau between 1180 and
1206. His songs of crusade were composed in the context of recruitment either for the Third Crusade
(1189–1192) or for the German Crusade of 1197, in
which Wolfger of Erla, bishop of Passau, played a leading role.

"Guote liute, holt"

Good vassals, claim the wages God our Lord himself pays
out, he who has power over all things. Earn his fee, which lies
waiting for the blessed ones there with all manner of joys
forevermore. Suffer hardship willingly for a while in place of
the death that lasts for ever. God has given you both soul and
body. Give him back your body here on earth, which will
bring the soul eternal life there in heaven.

Love, let me free, you're to leave me without pleasure for
a while. You have robbed me of my senses. If you come by
again once I have completed this crusade for God, then you'll
be welcome once more. But if you will not leave my heart—
and perhaps that's not to be avoided—I shall take you with
me to the Holy Land. Then I shall there appeal to God for half
my reward to go to my dear one.

"Alas," said that woman, "what sorrow love has gifted me.
What pain love inflicts on me. Joyless creature, what will you
do with yourself when he goes away from here, since it was
he who gave you all your happiness. How can I live with the
world and my misery?

"In this situation I would need good counsel if I were to succeed in meeting both demands. It was never so urgent a need:
the moment approaches when he will set out on crusade."

Blessed is that fortunate woman, whose pure womanly
virtue makes her lover take her with him in his heart overseas. Anyone who ever experienced heartfelt love should
praise her purity, since she suffers such pain here at home.
When, alone, she thinks about the danger he is in, she says
"Whether my dearest love is alive or dead, may God care for
him on whose behalf my sweetheart gave up this world."

Source

Des Minnesangs Frühling, ed. Hugo Moser and Helmut
Tervooren, 36th ed. (Stuttgart: Hirzel, 1977), pp. 194–195.

C. Hartmann von Aue

Hartmann von Aue, best known as the first adaptor of
Arthurian romance in Middle High German, also
wrote three crusading songs, either for the Third Crusade or for the German Crusade of 1197. The lord
whose death he laments in this song may be Berthold
IV, duke of Zähringen (d. 1186), or Emperor Frederick I Barbarossa (d. 1190), or Emperor Henry VI (d.
1197). This song gives a rare glimpse into personal
motivations for taking the cross.

"Ich var mit iuweren hulden, herren unde mage"

I set off with your kind leave, lords and kinsmen. May land
and people flourish! There is no need for anyone to ask
where I am going, I shall tell you in truth what journey it is.
Love took me prisoner and set me free on parole. Now she
has commanded me by her love that I go off to war. There
is no way out, my departure is urgent. How loath I should
be to break my oath of loyalty!

Many a man boasts what he does for love's sake. Where
are the deeds?—all I hear are the words. Yet I'd be glad to
see her ask any one of them to serve her as I shall serve her.
That is real love when someone leaves his home behind for
love's sake. Now see how she takes me over the sea from my
native land. And if my lord were alive, Saladin and all his
army would not bring me a foot away from Germany.

You singers of love songs, you are bound to come to grief;
what does you harm is your vain hopes. I dare boast that I
can confidently sing of love, since love possesses me and I
her. What I desire, see, that desires me just as much. You
continually find your vain hopes dashed. You strive for
pleasure that wants no part of you. Why can't you poor creatures love such a love as I do?

Source

Des Minnesangs Frühling, ed. Hugo Moser and Helmut
Tervooren, 36th ed. (Stuttgart: Hirzel, 1977), pp. 428–429.

D. Walther von der Vogelweide

Walther von der Vogelweide was the greatest medieval
German lyric poet, active between 1190 and 1230. A
clerically educated professional singer, he was the
first nonchivalric German poet of crusade.

"Her keiser, ich bin fronebote" = Ottenton, 1212 (L12,6)

In this song Walther urges Otto IV, Holy Roman
emperor, after his coronation in 1209, to fulfill his

imperial duty and lead a crusade to liberate Christ's earthly kingdom.

Lord Emperor, I am God's envoy and bring you his message. You have sway over the earth as he does over heaven. He bade me lament to you, his regent, how the heathen rise up in his son's kingdom in defiance against you both. You will be eager to restore his rights. His Son is called Christ. Make a solemn bond with him. Where he is regent, he will grant you your rights, even though your adversary were the devil from hell.

Source

Walther von der Vogelweide: Leich, Lieder, Sangsprüche, ed. Christoph Cormeau (Berlin: De Gruyter, 1996), p. 18.

"Ahi wie kristenliche nu der babest lachet" = Unmutston, 1213 (L34,4 and 34,14)

Walther von der Vogelweide's "Songs of Discontent" attack the caricatured Pope Innocent III for the crusade tax of 1213, which, Walther alleges, the Roman Curia will misappropriate for its own corrupt ends. Rivalry between pope and Holy Roman Emperor for control of the crusade is a long-running theme of Walther's political lyrics in the first three decades of the thirteenth century.

Ah, what a Christian smile the pope wears when he tells his Italian pals, "I've done it!" What he says, he should never even have thought. He reckons, "I've made two Tedeschi wear one crown, so that they disrupt and lay waste the kingdom. While they're at it, we'll fill our purses. I've yoked them both beneath my offertory chest; all they have shall be mine. Their German silver trickles into my cash box. My priests, eat your chicken and sup your wine and let those Germans . . . fast!"

Tell us, friend Alms Chest, has the pope sent you here, so you can make him rich and beggar us Germans? When the full loot reaches the Lateran, he'll play the same mean trick he's played before. He'll tell us how the empire will stay in chaos till every parish has filled up the chest a second time. I reckon little of this silver will ever go to help God's Holy Land. It's rare that a cleric's hand gives away largesse. Friend Alms Chest, you've been sent here to do mischief, to make fools and ninnies of German folk.

Source

Walther von der Vogelweide: Leich, Lieder, Sangsprüche, ed. Christoph Cormeau (Berlin: De Gruyter, 1996), pp. 64–65.

"Owe war sint verswunden alliu miniu jar?" = Elegy, traditionally dated 1227–1228 (L124,1)

Walther von der Vogelweide's best-known song of crusade is traditionally associated with the crusade of Emperor Frederick II in 1228–1229 and interpreted as a protest against Frederick's excommunication by Pope Gregory IX for failing to arrive in the Holy Land by the date laid down by papal ultimatum. However, the internal evidence of the song could point at least as relevantly to the excommunication of Duke Leopold V of Austria by Pope Celestine III in 1195 and to the ensuing German Crusade of 1197–1198.

Alas, where have all my years vanished to? Did I dream my life, or is it true? What I always thought was real, was it truly so? Then I must have slept and know nothing more of it. Now I have woken up, and what I once knew like the palm of my hand I recognize no more. People, the land I was brought up in, they are as foreign to me as if they were figments. My playmates and friends are weary and old. The fields are ploughed, the forest hewn down. If it were not that the river flows as it ever did, truly I would deem my misfortune great. Many greet me wearily who once knew me well. All the world is full of misery. When I think back to many a glorious day vanished as utterly from me as a slap of the hand in the sea—ever more, alas.

Alas, how miserably young people behave, whose hearts were once open to all that was new. They can do nothing but worry; alas, how can they be so? Wherever I turn in the world, no one is happy. Dance and song decay into care. Never did a Christian witness such grievous times. See now how ladies wear their headdress, how proud knights wear rustic clothes. Harsh letters have reached us from Rome. We are permitted only sorrow, and all joy is denied us. That grieves me to the core—we fared so well till now—that instead of laughter I now must choose to weep. Our lamentation makes the wild birds mourn. No wonder that it makes me despair. But what am I saying, foolish man, in my misguided anger? Whoever is seduced by these joys forfeits those in the life to come. Evermore, alas.

Alas, how we have been poisoned by sweet things. I see the bitter gall that floats in the honey. The world is outwardly fair, white, green, and red, and inwardly pitch black, dark as death. If it has led you astray, see your salvation. By small penance you may be redeemed from great sin. Think upon it, knights, it is your very own vocation. You wear shining helmets and hard-forged mail, you carry stout shields and consecrated swords. Would to God that I were worthy of such victory. Then, needy man as I am, I would earn rich reward. Nor do I mean lands or princes' gold. I would wear a crown myself and for eternity. A soldier might win it with his spear. If I might make the precious journey overseas, then I would sing for joy and nevermore "alas."

Source

Walther von der Vogelweide: Leich, Lieder, Sangsprüche, ed. Christoph Cormeau (Berlin: De Gruyter, 1996), pp. 264–265.

6. The Crusade of Emperor Frederick II in Freidank's *Bescheidenheit*

Translated by Jeffrey R. Ashcroft

Freidank was a didactic poet who gave an eyewitness account of the city of Acre (mod. 'Akko, Israel) during the Crusade of Emperor Frederick II (1227–1229) in his ethical compendium *Bescheidenheit* ("Wise Judgment"). His satirical verses attack the avarice and irreligious behavior of the Franks of the Holy Land, they deplore Pope Gregory IX's hostility to Frederick II, they express Freidank's disquiet over Frederick's negotiated truce with al-Kāmil, the Ayyūbid sultan of Egypt, but despite all misgivings they assert the continuing validity of pilgrimage and crusade.

I have heard many a man express the wish: "If I might get to Acre, and just see the Holy Land, I would not care if I died there on the spot." Now I see these folk glad to be alive and anxious to get back to their homeland.

I advise those who intend to come here after us to be well equipped: the first shock comes when you buy or exchange something. Acre has gobbled up silver, gold, horses, and clothes, and whatever a man may possess, nothing eludes their clutches. Now they mock us and say, "*Allez*—off you go home across the sea." And if thirty armies came to Acre, they would fare as we have fared; the locals would treat them as they've treated us.

In Rome and Acre it's the same business, which always finds enough fools to exploit. In no time at all they've gobbled so much treasure that I'm amazed it doesn't burst out of the houses.

Since Acre won't relent, it's better to be sheared than skinned: if you get away with your hide intact, you can sing for joy.

Acre is rich in diseases, death is quite at home there, and if thousands died there every day, you'd hear nobody lamenting for long.

The first question they ask when someone's died is, "Sir, where's his money?" (And that's the last word of mourning. God send us a speedy end!)

If anyone doesn't want to live long, I advise him to hurry off to Acre.

There's no difference between the Christians and the heathen in Acre: all the crusaders' might won't disturb their friendly alliance. Young and old all speak the heathen tongue. They prefer the company of one heathen to two or three Christians. So it's no wonder that they're treacherous.

In Acre I'm well acquainted with the food, the climate, people and land: all are bad news to Germans. So many a man slips away to the graveyard—there's a friendly landlord who's never stuck for guests; he does his best to greet all strangers. Acre is the pit of death, where there's naught but death and disease; and a dead donkey would be mourned more in other places than a hundred thousand who die there.

In Acre they live corrupt lives: if the pope has imposed that on them as penance for their sins, then even Judas has hope of salvation.

In Acre the citizens are treacherous: an army of a hundred thousand will be more quickly sold there than ten oxen anywhere else.

The business they are up to in Jaffa is a good bargain for the heathen, but it won't help against the Christians who are in league with the heathen. The allies of this land are showing how far they can be trusted, and if it were up to them, the talks at Jaffa would not be happening.

We were given the cross to protect against sin and to free the Holy Sepulchre. Now the church wants to ban us from doing that. So how shall we save our souls now?

No ban has more force in God's eyes than is justified by a man's guilt. Obedience is only valid if the master acts justly; if the master forces a man to desert God and do wrong, then you must leave the master and cleave to what is right. Though whether the church's ban is wrong or right, it is to be feared, that's true.

It would be fitting if the emperor put a stop to the whispering he and the Sultan have been carrying on. Can that lead to a happy and honorable end without God's help? It's a strange matter, and fools don't believe it—I hear wise folk too say they'll only believe it when they see it.

Mr. Mean and Mr. Stingy were supposed to share three marks: Mean wanted the bigger half, Stingy wouldn't give up. The two misers still haven't settled their quarrel. That's just how the emperor and the sultan are behaving.

When did an emperor ever go on a crusade banned by the pope and without the princes' support? And now he's reached a land where neither God nor man ever found a loyal friend. And without treasure to help him he's met much opposition—may God settle it.

I don't care how, so long as I glimpse the Holy Sepulchre: then I'd return to Acre, stuff myself full of good food, and be happy to board the first ship I found. I deplore all that's ever been told of this land, whether it was true or false; they've enticed many a band of crusaders here.

I'd gladly go back over the sea and send another army here—but I never want to return myself, because of the treachery that goes on here.

What can an emperor achieve when heathen and clerics alike fight against him? Solomon's wisdom would be inadequate there. Treachery is a birthright in this land, and the natives have sworn to reinforce it with false counsel. Treachery, arrogance, and enmity never run short in Syria. If the emperor's might is demonstrated here, all lands will fear him; his honor will either soar or sink to the depths through what happens here.

Whatever the emperor achieves here without sufficient support, the help and cunning of the locals will be pitted against him, so far as they dare.

Many an army has come to Acre, and all, I've been told, perished without achieving honorable victory. The pope's ban and the cunning tricks of many Christians here wanted to thwart us of success. Now God has won his own honor. He was able to ensure without their help that sinners shall see the Holy Sepulchre.

God and the emperor have freed that tomb and brought comfort to all Christians. Since the emperor has done the best he ever could, he should be released from the ban—but I guess those in Rome don't want that. If something good happens without their consent, they don't wish it to endure—and now it's happened against their wishes. All sinners agree that no one should breach the peace treaty. Rome could do us no greater honor than to affirm that too. Those who must live and survive in this land, they did not want to be given it back. What if a miracle happens and their arrogance is taken

way from them? Treachery will come to their rescue.

God has liberated the city that is the joy of our faith. What more do sinners need but the Holy Sepulchre and the honor of the cross? If those who tried to cheat him of his honor had stood by the emperor, the Sepulchre and all this land would have been in his hands: Nazareth and Bethlehem, the Jordan and Jerusalem, and many a holy place where God's own feet trod, Syria and Judaea, many a fair land besides. The roads all lie open before us that lead to the holy places.

It grieves the false hearted that the emperor did not let so many armies be betrayed that would have perished defenseless here. If a lord has men, might, and wealth and gives these for God's cause, it is a grievous sin when anyone gives treacherous counsel.

A ban has no force if it is imposed out of enmity; a ban that harms the faith can do no good. Acre has banned kettle and frying pan, boiled meat and roast; may God provide for us! The masters of our faith rant and rave. Lord God, where shall we praise you, since we are banned from your city, in which you, Lord Christ, were martyred and buried? The honor of your faith is extinguished; sinners are deprived of comfort; how shall we be rid of sin? All Christendom despairs. Lord God, have pity on this inexcusable scandal. This ban will bring scorn on the Sepulchre and all Christendom; disbelief will prosper for it.

I witnessed Christ's own land left without visible defense. When we should be reconquering it, no one was prepared to defend it. The devil has succored this land because no one prevented it. It was the devil's cunning that stopped more of it from being won back. God punish those who are guilty for us Germans being the laughing stock of the Franks. And if the Germans might win back the land today, the Franks hate them so much they would much rather the heathen kept it.

If anyone comes sick and poor to Acre, he will readily get a lodging there—one seven feet long, where he can do penance for his sins.

Nothing was ever better against sin than a pure-hearted pilgrimage across the sea. Even if you never glimpse the Holy Sepulchre, your reward is none the less for that. Anyone who with devout intent bears his cross over the sea (this is my firm belief) shall be freed from sin. Acre roasts the body yet brings comfort to the soul. Have no doubt of this: if you die a righteous death there, you shall be saved!

Source

Kreuzzugsdichtung, ed. Ulrich Müller (Tübingen: Niemeyer, 1979), no. 72, pp. 102–109.

7. *The World's Reward,* by Konrad von Würzburg

Translated by Alan V. Murray

Der Werlte Lôn (*The World's Reward*) is a poem in Middle High German by Konrad von Würzburg, written in rhyming couplets. Konrad was born around the year 1235 and died in 1287. He was probably a professional poet who was active in the Upper Rhine area from around 1260, writing love poetry and moral and religious lyrics as well as longer poems.

Although *The World's Reward* is a fictional account, its central character is a historical individual, a German knight called Wirnt von Gravenberg, who between 1210 and 1220 composed an Arthurian romance, *Wigalois*, or *Der Ritter mit dem Rade. The World's Reward* has a certain similarity to works of the *exemplum*, a prose genre that narrates a purportedly true event in order to bring out a moral. A factor in the choice of Wirnt von Gravenberg as hero may have been the fact that his own subject, *Wigalois*, is characterized as "the knight with the wheel," that is, the Wheel of Fortune, which could be regarded as applying to the character of Wirnt in Konrad's poem.

Sir Wirnt is introduced as the epitome of secular chivalry, skilled and finding delight in deeds of arms and in leisure pursuits such as hunting, music, literature, and chess. He is keen to win honor, that is, to maintain and increase his reputation in the estimation of the society in which he lived. Above all, it was ladies who provided him with inspiration to undertake deeds of knighthood and who praised him when he had performed them. The idea of service to a lady was a central part of the literary chivalric culture of the twelfth and thirteenth centuries and was particularly appealing to many knights since it employed the same vocabulary of service that was used to describe their military and administrative obligations to their lords.

It is this relationship of service that characterizes Sir Wirnt's mysterious female visitor, who insists that he has served her all of his life; the confused knight is certain he has never seen her before but is so smitten by her appearance that he is prepared to freely offer her his service for the rest of his life. The revelation of the name and identity of the beautiful, mysterious stranger forms the climax of the poem. The conclusion describes an act of conversion: the only hope for Wirnt's salvation is a form of knighthood very different from that which he has pursued all of his life. Taking the cross, he becomes a crusader and leaves home with the purpose of serving God by fighting the heathen; Konrad's phrasing implies a journey to the Holy Land, known to the medieval West as Outremer (the land beyond the sea). This model of religious knighthood involves renouncing every vestige of his previous life, even to the extent of abandoning his wife and children, and doing penance for his past sins. The message of *Der Werlte Lôn* is one of uncompromising criticism of the lifestyle and ideology of secular chivalry, but it nevertheless presents the crusade as a route to salvation.

All you who love the world, listen to this story of the fortunes of a knight who constantly strove to achieve the world's reward. Often he considered how he might go about obtaining the reward of worldly honor. He knew how to enhance his reputation everywhere, and both in word and in deed his life was so accomplished that he was counted among the best in the German lands. His whole life long he had kept himself free from disgrace; he was courteous and wise, handsome and full of all the virtues. Whatever prize of honor a man might pursue, this knight knew how to obtain it. This fine man was to be seen wearing choice clothing. He was a skilled and active hunter, with hounds, with hawks, and on horseback. Chess and music were his leisure pursuits. If deeds of knighthood were announced over a hundred miles distant, he would have ridden there and gladly fought to gain the reward of love. He was so devoted to well-mannered ladies that he served them with such constancy all of his days that all happy women praised this delightful man. As the books relate and as I found written, this knight was called Sir Wirnt von Gravenberg. He had done worldly deeds all of his days, and his heart burned after love, both secret and open.

This celebrated man was sitting in a chamber with all kinds of diversion, holding open a book that contained adventures of love. With this he occupied his day until evening, and he found great pleasure in the charming story he was reading. As he was sitting like this, there entered a woman such as was his heart's desire, and of such a lovely form that no one had ever seen a more beautiful lady. Her beauty quite surpassed that of all of today's ladies. Such a lovely child had never before slipped from a woman's breast. I declare upon my baptism that she was far more beautiful than Venus or Athene and all the goddesses of love. Her countenance and her complexion were both as bright as a mirror. Her beauty gave off such an aura and such splendor that the very palace was illuminated by her. Perfection had skimped with none of her skills on her, but deployed her fullest powers. Whatever one might have to say about beautiful women, she surpassed them all; a more lovely woman could not be seen on earth. Furthermore, she was magnificently dressed. The clothes and the crown that this elegant lady was wearing were so rich that no one could have bought them, even had they been for sale. Sir Wirnt von Gravenberg drew back from her in shock as she strode in. Her arrival caused him to turn pale, for he was quite surprised that such a lady should come in. Shocked and pale, the charming man sprang to his feet and welcomed the lovely lady as courteously as he was able, saying, "Welcome, lady! Whatever ladies I have ever known, you surpass them all." The lady replied gracefully,

May God reward you, my dear friend. Do not be so alarmed, for I am that same lady whom you willingly serve and whom you have always served. However much you may be alarmed at my presence, I am that same woman for whom you have repeatedly risked body and soul. Your heart does not weary, because it gains joy through me. You have been courtly and noble all of your days. Your fair, sweet body has striven for me, and spoken and sung as well of me as it can; you were my vassal in the evening and the morning, and you knew how to win the greatest praise and the most worthy prizes; you blossom like a flower in May in numerous virtues. From the time of your youth you have borne the garland of honor, and your loyalty to me has always been true and complete. Most worthy and excellent knight, this is why I have come here, so that you can view my excellent body, both front and back, to your heart's content, and see how lovely I am, how perfect. The great rewards and rich benefits that you may receive in my service, these you should examine closely. I will gladly let you see what reward you may expect, since you have served me so well.

The virtuous, noble lord thought the lady's words amazing,

for he had never seen her before, and yet this very lady had said that he had been her vassal. He said,

If it please you, my lady, if I have ever served you, then I am not aware of it. I must say without deceit that I have never set eyes on you. But since you declare me to be your servant, blessed lady, then my heart and my body are ready for your service until my dying day. You have such grace and such virtue that your joy-bearing youth may bring me a reward. Happy I am that I have lived this day! I rejoice, lovely lady, that you are willing to accept my service. Most virtuous lady, by the joy-bearing fortune that is in you, please reveal this to me: let me know from where you come or what your name is, so that I might know for certain whether I ever heard tell of you.

Courteously, the lady replied,

My dear friend, that shall be done. I will gladly reveal to you my highly praised name. You should never be ashamed that you are in my service. Everything of wealth and property on earth serves me. I am so exalted that the emperor and the sons of kings are subject to my crown, while counts, free lords, and dukes have knelt down before me and obey my command. I fear no one but God, who has power over me. I am called "the World," and am that which you have striven after for so long. You shall be granted a reward from me, as I shall show you. I have come to you, now look!

With that, she turned her back on him. All over it was adorned and hung with worms and snakes, with toads and adders; her body was full of sores and horrible cancers, with flies and ants squatting on it, and maggots eating away at the flesh down to the bone. She was so foul that there went forth from her suppurating body a smell that no one could endure. Her rich clothing was in a pitiful state: on her back it was but a shoddy rag. Her lovely bright complexion now had the color of pale ashes.

And so she departed. May she be cursed by me and all Christendom! When he had seen this wonder, the noble, free knight knew in his heart that anyone in her service would be ruined. Straightaway he bade farewell to his wife and children; he put the cross upon his clothing and traveled across the wild sea to aid God's army fighting against the heathen.

There the virtuous knight did constant penance. This he did at all times until he died, so that his soul would find repose.

Now all you who are children of this wild world, take note of this story: its truth is such that one should be glad to hear it. The World's reward is full of grief: this you should have understood. Now I have come to the end: whoever is found serving her will never receive the joy that God in his constancy has prepared for the chosen.

I, Konrad von Würzburg, give all of you this advice: only you who abandon the World will keep your soul.

Source

English translation based on *Kleinere Dichtungen Konrads von Würzburg,* 1: *Der Welt Lohn – Das Herzmaere – Heinrich von Kempten,* ed. Edward Schröder, 2d ed. (Berlin, 1930), pp. 1–11.

General Bibliography

This bibliography lists works that provide general orientation on the crusades and the main geographical areas affected by them; it is not intended to be a comprehensive listing and its emphasis is on works in English. For bibliography on more specific topics, such as individual crusades, people, places, texts, institutions, and event, the reader should consult the relevant entries in the A–Z section of the encyclopedia.

Bibliographies

Atiya, Aziz S., *The Crusade: Historiography and Bibliography* (Bloomington: Indiana University Press, 1962).

Hunyadi, Zsolt, "A Bibliography of the Crusades and the Military Orders," in *The Crusades and the Military Orders: Expanding the Frontiers of Medieval Latin Christianity,* ed. Zsolt Hunyadi and József Laszlovszky (Budapest: Department of Medieval Studies, Central European University, 2001), pp. 501–588.

International Medieval Bibliography, ed. Alan V. Murray et al. (Turnhout: Brepols, 1967–).

Mayer, Hans Eberhard, *Bibliographie zur Geschichte der Kreuzzüge,* 2d ed. (Hannover: Hahn, 1965).

———, "Literaturbericht über die Geschichte der Kreuzzüge," *Historische Zeitschrift* Sonderheft 3 (1969), 641–731.

Mayer, Hans Eberhard, and Joyce McLellan, "Select Bibliography of the Crusades," in *A History of the Crusades,* ed. Kenneth M. Setton et al., 2d ed., 6 vols. (Madison: University of Wisconsin Press, 1969–1989), 6:511–664.

Murray, Alan V., "Crusade and Conversion on the Baltic Frontier, 1150–1500: A Bibliography of Publications in English," in *Crusade and Conversion on the Baltic Frontier, 1150–1500,* ed. Alan V. Murray (Aldershot, UK: Ashgate, 2001), pp. 277–285.

Atlases

Atlas de la Reconquista: La frontera peninsular entre los siglos VIII y XV, ed. Jesús Mestre Campi and Flocel Sabaté (Barcelona: Peninsula, 1998).

Atlas of the Crusades, ed. Jonathan Riley-Smith (London: Times Books, 1991).

An Historical Atlas of Islam / Atlas historique de l'Islam, ed. Hugh Kennedy, 2d ed. (Leiden: Brill, 2001).

The New Penguin Atlas of Medieval History, ed. Colin McEvedy (London: Penguin, 1992).

Reference Works

Andrea, Alfred J., *Encyclopedia of the Crusades* (Westport, CT: Greenwood, 2003).

Bacharach, Jere L., *A Middle East Studies Handbook* (Cambridge: Cambridge University Press, 1984).

Bosworth, Clifford Edmund, *The New Islamic Dynasties* (Edinburgh: Edinburgh University Press, 1996).

The Coptic Encyclopedia, ed. Aziz S. Atiya, 8 vols. (New York: Macmillan, 1991).

Encyclopaedia of Islam, ed. Hamilton A. R. Gibb et al., 10 vols. and supplements, new ed. (Leiden: Brill, 1960–2001).

Encyclopedia of the Middle Ages, ed. André Vauchez, Barrie Dobson, and Michael Lapidge, 2 vols. (Cambridge: Clarke, 2000).

Εγκυκλοπαιδικο Προσωπογραφικο Λεξικο Βυζαντινης Ιστοριας και Πολιτισμου/ Encyclopaedic Prosopographical Lexicon of Byzantine History and Civilisation, ed. Alexios G. C. Savvides (Athinai: Metron, 1996–).

Lexikon des Mittelalters, ed. Norbert Angermann et al., 9 vols. (München: LexMA, 1977–1998).

Lock, Peter, *The Routledge Companion to the Crusades* (London: Routledge, 2006).

Oxford Dictionary of Byzantium, ed. Alexander P. Kazhdan, 3 vols. (New York: Oxford University Press, 1991).

Periodicals

Al-Masāq: Islam and the Medieval Mediterranean (1988–)

Archives de l'Orient latin (1881–1884)

Crusades (2002–)

Mediterranean Historical Review (1985–)

Revue de l'Orient latin (1881–1911)

Zeitschrift für Ostforschung (1952–1994) and *Zeitschrift für Ostmitteleuropa-Forschung* (1995–)

Surveys of Research

Balard, Michel, "L'historiographie des croisades au XX siècle (France, Allemagne, Italie)," *Revue historique* 302 (2000), 973–999.

Claverie, Pierre-Vincent, "Les dernières tendances de l'historiographie de l'Orient latin (1995–1999)," *Le Moyen Age* 106 (2000), 577–594.

Constable, Giles, "The Historiography of the Crusades," in *The Crusades from the Perspective of Byzantium and the Muslim World,* ed. Angeliki E. Laiou and Roy Parviz Mottahedeh (Washington, DC: Dumbarton Oaks, 2001), pp. 1–22.

Ekdahl, Sven, "Crusades and Colonisation in the Baltic: A Historiographic Analysis," in *XIX Rocznik Instytutu Polsko-Skandynawskiego 2003/2004,* ed. Eugeniusz S. Kruszewski (Kopenhaga: Instytut Polsko-Skandynawski, 2004), pp. 1–42.

Flori, Jean, "De Clermont à Jérusalem: La première croisade dans l'historiographie récente (1995–1999)," *Le Moyen Age* 105 (1999), 439–455.

Hehl, Ernst-Dieter, "Was ist eigentlich ein Kreuzzug?" *Historische Zeitschrift* 259 (1994), 297–336.

Housley, Norman, "Insurrection as Religious War, 1400–1536," *Journal of Medieval History* 25 (1999), 141–154.

Jaspert, Nikolas, "Ein Polymythos: Die Kreuzzüge," in *Mythen in der Geschichte,* ed. Helmut Altrichter, Klaus Herbers, and Helmut Neuhaus (Freiburg im Breisgau: Rombach, 2004), pp. 203–235.

Mayer, Hans Eberhard, "America and the Crusades," *Dumbarton Oaks Papers* 125 (1981), 38–45.

Möhring, Hans, "Kreuzzug und Dschihad in der mediaevistischen und orientalischen Forschung, 1965–1985," *Innsbrucker historische Studien* 10–11 (1988), 361–386.

Palgrave Advances in the Crusades, ed. Helen Nicholson (Basingstoke, UK: Palgrave Macmillan, 2005).

Richard, Jean, "De Jean-Baptiste Mailly à Joseph-François Michaud: Un moment de l'historiographie des croisades (1774–1841)," *Crusades* 1 (2002), 1–12.

Riley-Smith, Jonathan, "History, the Crusades and the Latin East, 1095–1204: A Personal View," in *Crusaders and Muslims in Twelfth-Century Syria,* ed. Maya Shatzmiller (Leiden: Brill, 1993), pp. 1–17.

———, "Islam and the Crusades in History and Imagination, 8 November 1898–11 September 2001," *Crusades* 2 (2003), 151–167.

Zaborov, M. A., Историография крестовых походов: Литература XV-XIX вв. (Moskva: Nauka, 1971).

Collections of Essays (Conference Proceedings, Festschriften, and Collected Reprints)

Abulafia, David, *Italy, Sicily and the Mediterranean, 1100–1400* (London: Variorum, 1987).

———, *Commerce and Conquest in the Mediterranean, 1100–1500* (London: Variorum, 1993).

Autour de la Première Croisade: Actes du Colloque de la Society for the Study of the Crusades and the Latin East (Clermont-Ferrand, 22–25 juin 1995), ed. Michel Balard (Paris: Publications de la Sorbonne, 1996).

Barber, Malcolm, *Crusaders and Heretics, 12th–14th Centuries* (Aldershot, UK: Variorum, 1995).

Brundage, James A., *The Crusades, Holy War and Canon Law* (London: Variorum, 1991).

Carr, Anne Weyl, *Cyprus and the Devotional Arts of Byzantium in the Era of the Crusades* (London: Variorum, 2004).

Chemins d'outre-mer: Etudes sur la Méditerranée médiévale offertes à Michel Balard, ed. Damien Coulon, Catherine Otten-Froux, Paul Pagès, and Dominique Valérian, 2 vols. (Paris: Publications de la Sorbonne, 2004).

La Chrétienté au peril sarrasin: Actes du colloque de la Section Française de la Société internationale Rencesvals (Aix-en-Provence: CUER MA Université de Provence, 2000).

Christians and Christianity in the Holy Land: from the Origins to the Latin Kingdoms, ed. Ora Limor and Gedaliahu G. Stroumsa (Turnhout: Brepols, 2006).

Le Concile de Clermont de 1095 et l'appel à la croisade: Actes du Colloque Universitaire International de Clermont-Ferrand (23–25 juin 1995) (Rome: L'Ecole française de Rome, 1997).

Cowdrey, H. E. John, *The Crusades and Latin Monasticism, 11th–12th Centuries* (Aldershot, UK: Ashgate, 1999).

La Cristianizzazione della Lituania: Atti del Colloquio internazionale di storia ecclesiastica in occasione del VI centenario della Lituania cristiana, Roma, 24–26 giugno 1987, ed. Paulius Rabikauskas (Città del Vaticano: Pontificio Comitato di Scienze Storiche, 1989).

La Croisade—Réalités et fictions: Actes du Colloque d'Amiens, 18–22 mars 1987, ed. Danielle Buschinger (Göppingen: Kümmerle, 1989).

Cross Cultural Convergences in the Crusader Period: Essays Presented to Aryeh Grabois on His Sixty-fifth Birthday, ed.

Michael Goodich, Sophia Menache, and Sylvia Schein (New York: Lang, 1995).

Crusade and Conversion on the Baltic Frontier, 1150–1500, ed. Alan V. Murray (Aldershot, UK: Ashgate, 2001).

Crusade and Settlement: Papers Read at the First Conference of the Society for the Study of the Crusades and the Latin East and Presented to R. C. Smail, ed. Peter W. Edbury (Cardiff: University College Cardiff Press, 1985).

Crusaders and Muslims in Twelfth-Century Syria, ed. Maya Shatzmiller (Leiden: Brill, 1993).

The Crusades: The Essential Readings, ed. Thomas F. Madden (Oxford: Blackwell, 2002).

The Crusades and Other Historical Essays Presented to Dana C. Munro by His Former Students, ed. Louis J. Paetow (New York: Crofts, 1928).

The Crusades and the Military Orders: Expanding the Frontiers of Medieval Latin Christianity, ed. Zsolt Hunyadi and József Laszlovszky (Budapest: Department of Medieval Studies, Central European University, 2001).

The Crusades and Their Sources: Essays Presented to Bernard Hamilton, ed. John France and William G. Zajac (Aldershot, UK: Ashgate, 1998).

The Crusades from the Perspective of Byzantium and the Muslim World, ed. Angeliki Laiou and Roy Parviz Mottahedeh (Washington, DC: Dumbarton Oaks Research Library and Collection, 2001).

Crusading in the Fifteenth Century: Message and Impact, ed. Norman Housley (Basingstoke, UK: Palgrave Macmillan, 2004).

De Sion exibit lex et verbum domini de Hierusalem: Essays on Medieval Law, Liturgy, and Literature in Honour of Amnon Linder, ed. Yitzhak Hen (Turnhout: Brepols, 2001).

Dei Gesta per Francos: Etudes sur les croisades dédiées à Jean Richard / Crusade Studies in Honour of Jean Richard, ed. Michel Balard, Benjamin Z. Kedar, and Jonathan Riley-Smith (Aldershot, UK: Ashgate, 2001).

Dickson, Gary, *Religious Enthusiasm in the Medieval West: Revivals, Crusades, Saints* (Aldershot, UK: Variorum, 2000).

East and West in the Crusader States: Context—Contacts— Confrontations, ed. Krijnie Ciggaar, Herman Teule, and A. Davids (Leuven: Peeters, 1996).

East and West in the Crusader States: Context—Contacts— Confrontations, II, ed. Krijnie Ciggaar and Herman Teule (Leuven: Peeters, 1999).

East and West in the Crusader States: Context—Contacts— Confrontations, III, ed. Krijnie Ciggaar and Herman Teule (Leuven: Peeters, 2003).

The Eastern Mediterranean Lands in the Period of the Crusades, ed. Peter M. Holt (Warminster, UK: Aris and Phillips, 1977).

Edbury, Peter, *Kingdoms of the Crusaders: From Jerusalem to Cyprus* (London: Variorum, Ashgate, 1999).

Elm, Kaspar, *Umbilicus Mundi: Beiträge zur Geschichte Jerusalems, der Kreuzzüge, des Kapitels vom Hlg. Grab in Jerusalem und der Ritterorden* (Sint-Kruis: Sint-Trudo-Abdij, 1998).

Les Epopées de la Croisade: Premier Colloque international (Trèves, 6–11 août 1984), ed. Karl-Heinz Bender and Hermann Kleber (Stuttgart: Steiner, 1987).

Der Erste Kreuzzug 1096 und seine Folgen: Die Verfolgung von Juden im Rheinland (Düsseldorf: Archiv der Evangelischen Kirche im Rheinland, 1996).

The Experience of Crusading, ed. Marcus Bull, Norman Housley, Peter Edbury, and Jonathan Phillips, 2 vols. (Cambridge: Cambridge University Press, 2003).

The First Crusade: Origins and Impact, ed. Jonathan P. Phillips (Manchester, UK: Manchester University Press, 1997).

Flori, Jean, *Croisade et chevalerie, XIe–XIIe siècles* (Bruxelles: De Boeck Université, 1998).

Forey, Alan, *Military Orders and Crusades* (London: Variorum, 1994).

From Clermont to Jerusalem: The Crusades and Crusader Societies, 1095–1500, ed. Alan V. Murray (Turnhout: Brepols, 1998).

Gendering the Crusades, ed. Susan B. Edgington and Sarah Lambert (Cardiff: University of Wales Press, 2001).

Governing the Holy City: The Interaction of Social Groups in Medieval Jerusalem, ed. Johannes Pahlitzsch and Lorenz Korn (Wiesbaden: Reichert, 2004).

Hamilton, Bernard, *Monastic Reform, Catharism, and the Crusades (900–1300)* (London: Variorum, 1979).

———, *Crusaders, Cathars and the Holy Places* (London: Variorum, 2000).

Historians of the Middle East, ed. Bernard Lewis and Peter M. Holt (London: Oxford University Press, 1962).

The Holy Land, Holy Lands, and Christian History, ed. R. N. Swanson (Woodbridge, UK: Boydell, 2000).

The Holy War, ed. Thomas Patrick Murphy (Columbus: Ohio State University Press, 1976).

The Horns of Hattin, ed. Benjamin Z. Kedar (Jerusalem: Yad Izhak Ben-Zvi Institute, 1992).

Housley, Norman, *Crusading and Warfare in Medieval and Renaissance Europe* (Aldershot, UK: Ashgate, 2001).

Gli Inizi del cristianesimo in Livonia-Lettonia: Atti del colloquio internazionale di storia ecclesiastica in occasione dell'VIII centenario della Chiesa in Livonia (1186–1986), Roma, 24–25 giugno 1986, ed. Michele Maccarrone (Città del Vaticano: Libreria Editrice Vaticana, 1989).

Innocent III: Vicar of Christ or Lord of the World?, ed. James M. Powell, 2d ed. (Washington, DC: Catholic University of America Press, 1994).

International Mobility in the Military Orders (Twelfth to Fifteenth Centuries): Travelling on Christ's Business, ed. Helen J. Nicholson and Jochen Burgtorf (Cardiff: University of Wales Press, 2005).

Jacoby, David, *Recherches sur la Méditerranée orientale du XIIe au XVe siècle: Peuples, sociétés, économies* (London: Variorum, 1979),

———, *Studies on the Crusader States and on Venetian Expansion* (Northampton, UK: Variorum, 1989).

———, *Trade, Commodities and Shipping in the Medieval Mediterranean* (Aldershot, UK: Variorum, 1997).

———, *Byzantium, Latin Romania and the Mediterranean* (Aldershot, UK: Variorum, 2001).

———, *Commercial Exchange across the Mediterranean: Byzantium, the Crusader Levant, Egypt and Italy* (Aldershot, UK: Variorum, 2005).

Jerusalem im Hoch- und Spätmittelalter: Konflikte und Konfliktbewältigung—Vorstellungen und Vergegenwärtigungen, ed. Dieter Bauer, Klaus Herbers, and Nikolas Jaspert (Frankfurt am Main: Campus, 2001).

The Jihad and Its Times: Dedicated to Andrew Stefan Ehrenkreutz, ed. Hadia Dajani-Shakeel and Ronald A. Messier (Ann Arbor: Center for Near Eastern and North African Studies, University of Michigan, 1991).

Journeys toward God: Pilgrimage and Crusade, ed. Barbara N. Sargent-Baur (Kalamazoo, MI: Medieval Institute Publications, 1992).

Kedar, Benjam Z., *The Franks in the Levant, 11th to 14th Centuries* (Aldershot, UK: Ashgate, 1993).

Die Kreuzzüge: Kein Krieg ist heilig, ed. Hans-Jürgen Kotzur, Winfried Wilhelmy, and Brigitte Klein (Mainz: Von Zabern, 2004).

Η Κύπρος και οι Σταυροφορίες / Cyprus and the Crusades, ed. Nicholas Coureas and Jonathan Riley-Smith (Nicosia: Cyprus Research Centre, 1995).

Latins and Greeks in the Eastern Mediterranean after 1204, ed. Benjamin Arbel, Bernard Hamilton, and David Jacoby (Ilford, UK: Cass, 1989).

Little, Donald, *History and Historiography of the Mamlūks* (London: Variorum, 1986).

Lourie, Elena, *Crusade and Colonization: Muslims, Christians and Jews under the Crown of Aragon* (London: Variorum, 1990).

Luttrell, Anthony, *Latin Greece, the Hospitallers and the Crusades, 1291–1440* (London: Variorum, 1982).

———, *The Hospitallers of Rhodes and Their Mediterranean World* (London: Variorum, 1992).

———, *The Hospitaller State on Rhodes and Its Western Provinces, 1306–1462* (Aldershot, UK: Ashgate, 1999).

Mayer, Hans Eberhard, *Kings and Lords in the Latin Kingdom of Jerusalem* (London: Variorum, 1994).

———, *Kreuzzüge und lateinischer Osten* (London: Variorum, 1983).

———, *Probleme des lateinischen Königreichs Jerusalem* (London: Variorum, 1983).

McCrank, Lawrence J., *Medieval Frontier History in New Catalonia* (London: Variorum, 1996).

Medieval Christian Perceptions of Islam: A Book of Essays, ed. John V. Tolan (New York: Garland, 1996).

The Medieval Crusade, ed. Susan Ridyard (Woodbridge, UK: Boydell, 2004).

Medieval History Writing and Crusading Ideology, ed. Tuomas M. S. Lehtonen and Kurt Villads Jensen (Helsinki: Finnish Literature Society, 2005).

The Meeting of Two Worlds: Cultural Exchange between East and West during the Period of the Crusades, ed. Vladimir P. Goss (Kalamazoo, MI: Medieval Institute, 1986).

Mendicants, Military Orders, and Regionalism in Medieval Europe, ed. Jürgen Sarnowsky (Aldershot, UK: Ashgate, 1999).

The Military Orders, 1: *Fighting for the Faith and Caring for the Sick,* ed. Malcolm Barber (Aldershot, UK: Variorum, 1994).

The Military Orders, 2: *Welfare and Warfare,* ed. Helen Nicholson (Aldershot, UK: Ashgate, 1998).

Militia Christi e Crociata nei secoli XI–XIII (Milano: Vita e Pensiero, 1992).

Militia Sancti Sepulcri: Idea e istituzioni, ed. Kaspar Elm and Cosimo Damiano Fonseca (Città del Vaticano: Ordine Equestre del Santo Sepolcro di Gerusalemme, 1998).

Montjoie: Studies in Crusade History in Honour of Hans Eberhard Mayer, ed. Benjamin Z. Kedar, Jonathan Riley-Smith, and Rudolf Hiestand (Ashgate, UK: Variorum, 1997).

Muslims under Latin Rule, 1100–1300, ed. James M. Powell (Princeton, NJ: Princeton University Press, 1990).

Nicol, Donald M., *Byzantium: Its Ecclesiastical History and Relations with the Western World* (London: Variorum, 1972).

Nicolle, David, *Warriors and Their Weapons around the Time of the Crusades: Relationships between Byzantium, the West and the Islamic World* (Aldershot, UK: Variorum, 2002).

Outremer: Studies in the History of the Crusading Kingdom of Jerusalem Presented to Joshua Prawer, ed. Benjamin Z. Kedar, Hans Eberhard Mayer, and R. C. Smail (Jerusalem: Yad Izhak Ben-Zvi Institute, 1982).

Palgrave Advances in the Crusades, ed. Helen Nicholson (Basingstoke, UK: Palgrave Macmillan, 2005).

Pope Innocent III and His World, ed. John Moore (Aldershot, UK: Ashgate, 1999).

Porphyrogenita: Essays on the History and Literature of Byzantium and the Latin East in Honour of Julian Chrysostomides, ed. Charalambos Dendrinos, Jonathan Harris, Eirene Harvalia-Crook, and Judith Herrin (Aldershot, UK: Ashgate, 2003).

La Primera Cruzada, Novecientos Anos Después: El Concilio de Clermont y los Oríenes del Movimento Cruzado, ed. Luis García-Guijarro Ramos (Madrid: Amat Bellés, 1997).

Pringle, Denys, *Fortification and Settlement in Crusader Palestine* (Aldershot, UK: Ashgate, 2000).

Pryor, John, *Commerce, Shipping and Naval Warfare in the*

Medieval Mediterranean (London: Variorum, 1987).

Richard, Jean, *Croisés, missionaires et voyageurs: Perspectives du monde latin médiéval* (London: Variorum, 1983).

———, *Croisades et états latins d'Orient: Points de vue et documents* (London: Variorum, 1992).

———, *Francs et Orientaux dans le monde des croisades* (Aldershot, UK: Ashgate, 2003).

———, *Orient et Occident au Moyen Age* (London: Variorum, 1976)

The Sweet Land of Cyprus: Papers Given at the Twenty-fifth Jubilee Spring Symposium of Byzantine Studies, Birmingham, March 1991, ed. Anthony Bryer and George Georghallides (Nicosia: Cyprus Research Centre, 1993).

Tolerance and Intolerance: Social Conflict in the Age of the Crusades, ed. Michael Gervers and James M. Powell (Syracuse, NY: Syracuse University Press, 2001).

War and Society in the Eastern Mediterranean, 7th–15th Centuries, ed. Yaacov Lev (Leiden: Brill, 1997).

The Crusades: General Histories

Crusades: The Illustrated History, ed. Thomas F. Madden (Ann Arbor: University of Michigan Press, 2004).

Flori, Jean, *Les Croisades* (Paris: Gisserot, 2001).

———, *La Guerre sainte: La formation de l'idée de croisade dans l'Occident chrétien* (Paris: Aubier-Flammarion, 2001).

———, *Le Crociate* (Bologna: Il Mulino, 2003).

———, *La Guerra santa: La formazione dell'idea di crociata nell'Occidente cristiano* (Bologna: Il Mulino, 2003).

France, John, *The Crusades and the Expansion of Catholic Christendom, 1000–1714* (London: Routledge, 2005).

Grousset, René, *Histoire des croisades et du royaume franc de Jérusalem,* 3 vols. (Paris: Plon, 1934–1936).

Hamilton, Bernard, and Asa Briggs, *The Crusades* (Stroud, UK: Sutton, 1998).

Hillenbrand, Carole, *The Crusades: Islamic Perspectives* (Edinburgh: Edinburgh University Press, 1999).

A History of the Crusades, ed. Kenneth M. Setton et al., 2d ed., 6 vols. (Madison: University of Wisconsin Press, 1969–1989).

Housley, Norman, *The Avignon Papacy and the Crusades* (Oxford: Oxford University Press, 1999).

———, *The Later Crusades, 1274–1580: From Lyons to Alcazar* (Oxford: Oxford University Press, 1992).

———, *The Italian Crusades: The Papal-Angevin Alliance and the Crusades against Christian Lay Powers, 1254–1343* (Oxford: Clarendon, 1999).

Jaspert, Nikolas, *The Crusades* (London: Routledge, 2006).

———, *Die Kreuzzüge* (Darmstadt: Wissenschaftliche Buchgesellschaft, 2003).

Jensen, Kurt Villads, *Politikens Bog om Korstogene* (København: Politikens forlag, 2005).

Jotischky, Andrew, *Crusading and the Crusader States* (Harlow, UK: Pearson Longman, 2004).

Kedar, Benjamin Z., *Crusade and Mission: European Approaches toward the Muslims* (Princeton: Princeton University Press, 1984).

Madden, Thomas F., *A Concise History of the Crusades* (Lanham, MD: Rowman and Littlefield, 1999).

———, *The New Concise History of the Crusades* (Lanham, MD: Rowman and Littlefield, 2005).

Mayer, Hans Eberhard, *Geschichte der Kreuzzüge,* 10th ed. (Stuttgart: Kohlhammer, 2005).

———, *The Crusades,* 2d ed. (Oxford: Oxford University Press, 1988).

The New Cambridge Medieval History, vol. 4: *c. 1024–c. 1198,* ed. David Luscombe and Jonathan Riley-Smith (Cambridge: Cambridge University Press, 2004).

The New Cambridge Medieval History, vol. 5: *c. 1198–c. 1300,* ed. David Abulafia (Cambridge: Cambridge University Press, 1999).

The New Cambridge Medieval History, vol. 6: *c. 1300–c. 1415,* ed. Michael Jones (Cambridge: Cambridge University Press, 2000).

The New Cambridge Medieval History, vol. 7: *c. 1415–c. 1500,* ed. Christopher Allmand (Cambridge: Cambridge University Press, 1998).

Nicholson, Helen J., *The Crusades* (Westport, CT: Greenwood, 2004).

Oxford Illustrated History of the Crusades, ed. Jonathan Riley-Smith (Oxford: Oxford University Press, 1995).

Phillips, Jonathan, *The Crusades, 1095–1197* (Harlow: Longman, 2002)

Richard, Jean, *Histoire des croisades* (Paris: Fayard, 1996).

———, *The Crusades, C. 1071–c. 1291* (Cambridge: Cambridge University Press, 1999).

Riley-Smith, Jonathan, *The Crusades: A History,* 2d ed. (London: Continuum, 2005)

———, *The Crusades: A Short History* (London: Athlone, 1987).

———, *What Were the Crusades?,* 2d ed. (Basingstoke, UK: Macmillan, 1992).

Runciman, Steven, *A History of the Crusades,* 3 vols. (Cambridge: Cambridge University Press, 1951–1954).

Tyerman, Christopher, *The Invention of the Crusades* (Basingstoke, UK: Macmillan, 1998).

———, *Fighting for Christendom: Holy War and the Crusades* (Oxford: Oxford University Press, 2004).

The Crusades: Origins

Blake, Ernest O., "The Formation of the 'Crusade Idea'," *Journal of Ecclesiastical History* 21 (1970), 11–31.

Charanis, Peter, "Byzantium, the West and the Origin of the First Crusade," *Byzantion* 19 (1949), 17–36.

Cowdrey, H. E. John, "Pope Urban II's Preaching of the First Crusade," *History* 55 (1970), 177–188.

———, "The Papacy and the Origins of Crusading,"

Medieval History 1 (1991), 48–60.

———, "Pope Urban II and the Idea of Crusade," *Studi medievali*, ser. 3, 36 (1995), 721–742.

———, "The Reform Papacy and the Origin of the Crusades," in *Le Concile de Clermont de 1095 et l'appel à la croisade: Actes du Colloque Universitaire International de Clermont-Ferrand (23–25 juin 1995)* (Rome: L'Ecole française de Rome, 1997), pp. 65–83.

Daniel, Norman, "The Legal and Political Theory of the Crusade," in *A History of the Crusades,* ed. Kenneth M. Setton et al., 2d ed., 6 vols. (Madison: University of Wisconsin Press, 1969–1989), 6:3–38.

Erdmann, Carl, *Die Entstehung des Kreuzzugsgedankens* (Stuttgart: Kohlhammer, 1935).

———, *The Origin of the Idea of Crusade* (Princeton: Princeton University Press, 1977).

Flori, Jean, "L'église et la guerre sainte de la 'Paix de Dieu' à la 'croisade'," *Annales ESC* 47 (1992), 453–466.

———, "Réforme, reconquista, croisade: L'idée de reconquête dans la correspondance pontificale d'Alexandre II à Urbain II," *Cahiers de Civilisation Médiévale* 40 (1997), 317–335.

Gilchrist, John T., "The Erdmann Thesis and Canon Law, 1083–1141," in *Crusade and Settlement: Papers Read at the First Conference of the Society for the Study of the Crusades and the Latin East and Presented to R. C. Smail,* ed. Peter W. Edbury (Cardiff: University College Cardiff Press, 1985), pp. 37–45.

Hehl, Ernst-Dieter, "Was ist eigentlich ein Kreuzzug?" *Historische Zeitschrift* 259 (1994), 297–336.

The Holy War, ed. Thomas P. Murphy (Columbus: Ohio State University Press, 1976).

McCormick, Michael, "Liturgie et guerre des Carolingiens à la première croisade," in *"Militia Christi" e Crociata nei secoli XI–XIII* (Milano: Vita e Pensiero, 1992), pp. 209–240.

Munro, Dana C., "Did the Emperor Alexius Ask for Aid at the Council of Piacenza?" *American Historical Review* 27 (1922), 731–733.

Partner, Peter, "Holy War, Crusade and Jihad: An Attempt to Define Some Problems," in *Autour de la Première Croisade: Actes du Colloque de la Society for the Study of the Crusades and the Latin East (Clermont-Ferrand, 22–25 juin 1995),* ed. Michel Balard (Paris: Publications de la Sorbonne, 1996), pp. 333–343.

———, *God of Battles: Holy Wars of Christianity and Islam* (London: HarperCollins, 1997).

Riley-Smith, Jonathan, *The First Crusade and the Idea of Crusading* (London: Athlone, 1986).

Russell, Frederick H., *The Just War in the Middle Ages* (Cambridge: Cambridge University Press, 1975).

Tyerman, Christopher J., "Were There Any Crusades in the Twelfth Century?" *English Historical Review* 110 (1995), 553–577.

The Muslim World

Agadzhanov, Sergei G, Государство Селджукидов и Средняя Азия в XI-XII веках (Moskva: Nauka, 1991).

——— [given as Agadshanow], *Der Staat der Seldschukiden und Mittelasien im 11–12. Jahrhundert* (Berlin: Schletzer, 1994).

Bartlett, W. B., *The Assassins: The Story of Islam's Medieval Secret Sect* (Stroud, UK: Sutton, 2001).

Cahen, Claude, "La première pénétration turque en Asie Mineure (seconde moitié du XIe s.)," *Byzantion* 18 (1948), 5–67.

———, *Pre-Ottoman Turkey: A General Survey of the Material and Spiritual Culture and History, c. 1071–1330* (London: Sidgwick and Jackson, 1968).

———, "The Turkish Invasion: The Selchükids," in *A History of the Crusades,* ed. Kenneth M. Setton et al., 2d ed., 6 vols. (Madison: University of Wisconsin Press, 1969–1989), 1:135–176.

———, "The Turks in Iran and Anatolia before the Mongol Invasions," in *A History of the Crusades,* ed. Kenneth M. Setton et al., 2d ed., 6 vols. (Madison: University of Wisconsin Press, 1969–1989), 1:661–692.

———, *La Turquie pré-ottomane* (Istanbul: Divit, 1988).

The Cambridge History of Iran, vol. 5: *The Saljuq and Mongol Periods,* ed. J. A. Boyle (Cambridge: Cambridge University Press, 1968).

The Crusades from the Perspective of Byzantium and the Muslim World, ed. Angeliki Laiou and Roy Parviz Mottahedeh (Washington, DC: Dumbarton Oaks Research Library and Collection, 2001).

Daftary, Farhad, "The Isma'ilis and the Crusaders: History and Myth," in *The Crusades and the Military Orders: Expanding the Frontiers of Medieval Latin Christianity,* ed. Zsolt Hunyadi and József Laszlovszky (Budapest: Department of Medieval Studies, Central European University, 2001), pp. 21–44.

Egypt and Syria in the Fatimid, Ayyubid and Mamluk Eras, ed. Urbain Vermeulen and Daniel de Smet (Leuven: Peeters, 1995).

El-Azhari, Taef Kamal, *The Saljūqs of Syria during the Crusades, 463–549 A.H./1070–1154 A.D.* (Berlin: Schwarz, 1997).

Gibb, Hamilton A. R., "The Aiyubids," in *A History of the Crusades,* ed. Kenneth M. Setton et al., 2d ed., 6 vols. (Madison: University of Wisconsin Press, 1969–1989), 2:693–714.

———, "The Career of Nur ad-Din," in *A History of the Crusades,* ed. Kenneth M. Setton et al., 2d ed., 6 vols. (Madison: University of Wisconsin Press, 1969–1989), 1:513–527.

———, "The Rise of Saladin," in *A History of the Crusades,* ed. Kenneth M. Setton et al., 2d ed., 6 vols. (Madison: University of Wisconsin Press, 1969–1989), 1:563–589.

———, "Zengi and the Fall of Edessa," in *A History of the Crusades,* ed. Kenneth M. Setton et al., 2d ed., 6 vols.

(Madison: University of Wisconsin Press, 1969–1989), 1:449–463.

Hazard, Harry W., "Moslem North Africa, 1049–1394," in *A History of the Crusades,* ed. Kenneth M. Setton et al., 2d ed., 6 vols. (Madison: University of Wisconsin Press, 1969–1989), 3:457–485.

Hillenbrand, Carole, *The Crusades: Islamic Perspectives* (Edinburgh: Edinburgh University Press, 1999).

Hitti, Philip Khuri, "The Impact of the Crusades on Moslem Lands," in *A History of the Crusades,* ed. Kenneth M. Setton et al., 2d ed., 6 vols. (Madison: University of Wisconsin Press, 1969–1989), 5:33–58.

Hodgson, Marshall G. S., *The Order of Assassins: The Struggle of the Early Nizari Ismailis against the Islamic World* ('s-Gravenhage: Mouton, 1955).

Holt, Peter M., *The Age of the Crusades: The Near East from the 11th Century to 1517* (London: Longman, 1986).

Humphreys, R. Stephen, *From Saladin to the Mongols: The Ayyubids of Damascus, 1193–1260* (Albany: State University of New York Press, 1977).

———, *Islamic History: A Framework for Inquiry,* 2d ed. (London: Tauris, 1991).

Irwin, Robert, *The Middle East in the Middle Ages: The Early Mamluk Sultanate, 1250–1382* (London: Croom Helm, 1986).

Köprülü, Mehmed Fuad, *The Seljuks of Anatolia: Their History and Culture according to Local Muslim Sources* (Salt Lake City: University of Utah Press, 1992).

Lev, Yaacov, *State and Society in Fatimid Egypt* (Leiden: Brill, 1991).

———, "Regime, Army and Society in Medieval Egypt, 9th–12th Centuries," in *War and Society in the Eastern Mediterranean, 7th–15th Centuries,* ed. Yaacov Lev (Leiden: Brill, 1997), pp. 115–152.

Lewis, Bernard, *The Assassins: A Radical Sect in Islam* (London: Weidenfeld and Nicolson, 1967).

———, "The Isma'ilites and the Assassins," in *A History of the Crusades,* ed. Kenneth M. Setton et al., 2d ed., 6 vols. (Madison: University of Wisconsin Press, 1969–1989), 1:99–132.

Morgan, David O., *Medieval Persia, 1040–1797* (London: Longman, 1988).

Vryonis, Speros Jr., *The Decline of Medieval Hellenism in Asia Minor and the Process of Islamization from the Eleventh through the Fifteenth Century* (Berkeley: University of California Press, 1971).

Walker, Paul E., *Exploring an Islamic Empire: Fatimid History and Its Sources* (New York: Tauris, 2002).

Ziada, Mustafa M., "The Mamluk Sultans, 1291–1517," in *A History of the Crusades,* ed. Kenneth M. Setton et al., 2d ed., 6 vols. (Madison: University of Wisconsin Press, 1969–1989), 3:486–512.

The Byzantine World

Alexios I Komnenos, ed. Margaret Mullett and Dion Smythe (Belfast: Belfast Byzantine Enterprises, 1996).

Angold, Michael, *A Byzantine Government in Exile: Government and Society under the Lascarids of Nicaea, 1204–1261* (London: Oxford University Press, 1975).

———, *Church and Society in Byzantium under the Comneni, 1081–1261* (Cambridge: Cambridge University Press, 1995).

———, *The Byzantine Empire, 1025–1204: A Political History,* 2d ed. (London: Longman, 1997).

Brand, Charles, *Byzantium Confronts the West, 1180–1204* (Cambridge, MA: Harvard University Press, 1968).

Bredenkamp, François, *The Byzantine Empire of Thessalonike, 1224–1242* (Thessaloniki: Thessaloniki Municipality History Center, 1996).

Browning, Robert, *The Byzantine Empire* (London: Weidenfeld and Nicolson, 1980).

Charanis, Peter, "The Byzantine Empire in the Eleventh Century," in *A History of the Crusades,* ed. Kenneth M. Setton et al., 2d ed., 6 vols. (Madison: University of Wisconsin Press, 1969–1989), 1:177–219.

Cheynet, Jean-Claude, *Pouvoir et contestations à Byzance (963–1210)* (Paris: Publications de la Sorbonne, 1990).

The Crusades from the Perspective of Byzantium and the Muslim World, ed. Angeliki Laiou and Roy Parviz Mottahedeh (Washington, DC: Dumbarton Oaks Research Library and Collection, 2001).

Geanakoplos, Deno J., "Byzantium and the Crusades, 1261–1354," in *A History of the Crusades,* ed. Kenneth M. Setton et al., 2d ed., 6 vols. (Madison: University of Wisconsin Press, 1969–1989), 3:27–38.

———, "Byzantium and the Crusades, 1354–1453," in *A History of the Crusades,* ed. Kenneth M. Setton et al., 2d ed., 6 vols. (Madison: University of Wisconsin Press, 1969–1989), 3:69–103.

———, *Byzantium: Church, Society, and Civilization Seen through Contemporary Eyes* (Chicago: University of Chicago Press, 1984).

Harris, Jonathan, *Byzantium and the Crusades* (London: Hambledon, 2003).

Jenkins, Romilly, *Byzantium: The Imperial Centuries; A.D. 610 to 1071* (London: Weidenfeld and Nicolson, 1966).

Karpov, Sergei, *L'Impero di Trebisonda, Venezia, Genoa e Roma, 1204–1461: Rapporti politici, diplomatici e commerciali* (Roma: Il Veltro, 1986);

———, Средневековий Понт (Lewiston, NY: Mellen, 2001).

Lilie, Johannes R., *Byzantium and the Crusader States (1096–1204)* (Oxford: Clarendon, 1993).

Magdalino, Paul, *The Empire of Manuel I Komnenos, 1143–80* (Cambridge: Cambridge University Press, 1993).

Nicol, Donald M., *The Despotate of Epiros* (Oxford: Blackwell, 1957).

———, *The Despotate of Epiros, 1267–1479* (Cambridge: Cambridge University Press, 1984).

———, *The Last Centuries of Byzantium (1204–1453)* (Cambridge: Cambridge University Press, 1993).

Ostrogorsky, Georg, *History of the Byzantine State* (Oxford: Blackwell, 1984).

Runciman, Steven, *The Fall of Constantinople, 1453* (Cambridge: Cambridge University Press).

Savvides, Alexios G. C., *Byzantium in the Near East: Its Relations with the Seljuk Sultanate of Rūm in Asia Minor, the Armenians of Cilicia and the Mongols, A.D. c. 1192–1237* (Thessaloniki: Byzantine Research Centre, 1981).

Outremer and Cyprus

Amouroux-Mourad, Monique, *Le comté d'Edesse, 1098–1150* (Paris: Geuthner, 1988).

Asbridge, Thomas, *The Creation of the Principality of Antioch, 1098–1130* (Woodbridge, UK: Boydell, 2000).

Baldwin, Marshall W., "The Decline and Fall of Jerusalem, 1174–89," in *A History of the Crusades,* ed. Kenneth M. Setton et al., 2d ed., 6 vols. (Madison: University of Wisconsin Press, 1969–1989), 1:590–621.

———, "The Latin States under Baldwin III and Amalric I, 1143–1174," in *A History of the Crusades,* ed. Kenneth M. Setton et al., 2d ed., 6 vols. (Madison: University of Wisconsin Press, 1969–1989), 1:513–562.

Boas, Adrian, *Crusader Archaeology: The Material Culture of the Latin East* (London: Routledge, 1999).

———, *Jerusalem in the Time of the Crusades: Society, Landscape and Art in the Holy City under Frankish Rule* (London: Routledge, 2001).

Cahen, Claude, *La Syrie du Nord à l'époque des croisades et la principauté franque d'Antioche* (Paris: Geuthner, 1940).

Crusade and Settlement: Papers Read at the First Conference of the Society for the Study of the Crusades and the Latin East and Presented to R. C. Smail, ed. Peter W. Edbury (Cardiff: University College Cardiff Press, 1985).

Crusaders and Muslims in Twelfth-Century Syria, ed. Maya Shatzmiller (Leiden: Brill, 1993).

East and West in the Crusader States: Context—Contacts—Confrontations, ed. Krijnie Ciggaar, Herman Teule, and A. Davids (Leuven: Peeters, 1996).

East and West in the Crusader States: Context—Contacts—Confrontations, II, ed. Krijnie Ciggaar and Herman Teule (Leuven: Peeters, 1999).

East and West in the Crusader States: Context—Contacts—Confrontations, III, ed. Krijnie Ciggaar and Herman Teule (Leuven: Peeters, 2003).

Edbury, Peter W., *The Kingdom of Cyprus and the Crusades, 1191–1374* (Cambridge: Cambridge University Press, 1991).

———, "The Crusader States," in *The New Cambridge Medieval History,* vol. 5: *C. 1198–c. 1300,* ed. David Abulafia (Cambridge: Cambridge University Press, 1999), pp. 590–606.

———, "The State of Research: Cyprus under the Lusignans and Venetians, 1991–1998," *Journal of Medieval History* 25 (1999), 57–65.

Ellenblum, Ronnie, *Frankish Rural Settlement in the Latin Kingdom of Jerusalem* (Cambridge: Cambridge University Press, 1998).

Fink, Harold S., "The Foundation of the Latin States, 1099–1118," in *A History of the Crusades,* ed. Kenneth M. Setton et al., 2d ed., 6 vols. (Madison: University of Wisconsin Press, 1969–89), 1:369–409.

Furber, Elizabeth C., "The Kingdom of Cyprus, 1191–1291," in *A History of the Crusades,* ed. Kenneth M. Setton et al., 2d ed., 6 vols. (Madison: University of Wisconsin Press, 1969–1989), 2:599–629.

Hardwicke, Mary Nickerson, "The Crusader States, 1192–1243," in *A History of the Crusades,* ed. Kenneth M. Setton et al., 2d ed., 6 vols. (Madison: University of Wisconsin Press, 1969–1989), 2:522–556.

Hill, George, *A History of Cyprus,* 4 vols. (Cambridge: Cambridge University Press, 1940–1952).

The Horns of Hattin, ed. Benjamin Z. Kedar (Jerusalem: Yad Izhak Ben-Zvi Institute, 1992).

Η Κύπρος και οι Σταυροφορίες / *Cyprus and the Crusades,* ed. Nicholas Coureas and Jonathan Riley-Smith (Nicosia: Cyprus Research Centre, 1995).

Luke, Harry, "The Kingdom of Cyprus, 1291–1369," in *A History of the Crusades,* ed. Kenneth M. Setton et al., 2d ed., 6 vols. (Madison: University of Wisconsin Press, 1969–1989), 3:340–360.

———, "The Kingdom of Cyprus, 1369–1489," in *A History of the Crusades,* ed. Kenneth M. Setton et al., 2d ed., 6 vols. (Madison: University of Wisconsin Press, 1969–1989), 3:361–395.

Mayer, Hans Eberhard, *Die Kanzlei der lateinischen Könige von Jerusalem,* 2 vols. (Hannover: Hahn, 1996).

———, *Das Siegelwesen in den Kreuzfahrerstaaten* (München: Bayerische Akademie der Wissenschaften, 1978).

———, *Varia Antiochena: Studien zum Kreuzfahrerfürstentum Antiochien im 12. und frühen 13. Jahrhundert* (Hannover: Hahn, 1993).

Murray, Alan V., *The Crusader Kingdom of Jerusalem: A Dynastic History, 1099–1125* (Oxford: Prosopographica et Genealogica, 2000).

Nicholson, Robert L., "The Growth of the Latin States, 1118–44," in *A History of the Crusades,* ed. Kenneth M. Setton et al., 2d ed., 6 vols. (Madison: University of Wisconsin Press, 1969–1989), 1:410–448.

Outremer: Studies in the History of the Crusading Kingdom of

Jerusalem Presented to Joshua Prawer, ed. Benjamin Z. Kedar, Hans Eberhard Mayer, and R. C. Smail (Jerusalem: Yad Izhak Ben-Zvi Institute, 1982).

Phillips, Jonathan, *Defenders of the Holy Land: Relations between the Latin East and the West, 1119–1187* (Oxford: Oxford University Press, 1996).

Prawer, Joshua, "The Settlement of the Latins in Jerusalem," *Speculum* 27 (1952), 490–563.

———, "Social Classes in the Crusader States: The Franks," in *A History of the Crusades,* ed. Kenneth M. Setton et al., 2d ed., 6 vols. (Madison: University of Wisconsin Press, 1969–1989), 5: 117–192.

———, "Social Classes in the Crusader States: The 'Minorities'," in *A History of the Crusades,* ed. Kenneth M. Setton et al., 2d ed., 6 vols. (Madison: University of Wisconsin Press, 1969–1989), 5:59–116.

———, *The Latin Kingdom of Jerusalem: European Colonialism in the Middle Ages* (London: Weidenfeld and Nicolson, 1972).

———, *Crusader Institutions* (Oxford: Clarendon, 1980).

Richard, Jean, *The Latin Kingdom of Jerusalem,* 2 vols. (Amsterdam: North-Holland, 1979).

———, "The Political and Ecclesiastical Organisation of the Crusader States," in *A History of the Crusades,* ed. Kenneth M. Setton et al., 2d ed., 6 vols. (Madison: University of Wisconsin Press, 1969–1989), 5:193–250.

———, *Le comté de Tripoli sous la dynastie toulousaine (1102–1187),* 2d ed. (Paris: Geuthner, 2000).

———, Латино-Иерусалемское королевство (Sankt-Peterburg: Evrazya, 2002).

Riley-Smith, Jonathan, *The Feudal Nobility and the Kingdom of Jerusalem, 1174–1277* (Basingstoke, UK: Macmillan, 1973).

Runciman, Steven, "The Crusader States, 1243–91," in *A History of the Crusades,* ed. Kenneth M. Setton et al., 2d ed., 6 vols. (Madison: University of Wisconsin Press, 1969–1989), 2:557–599.

Russell, Josiah C., "The Population of the Crusader States," in *A History of the Crusades,* ed. Kenneth M. Setton et al., 2d ed., 6 vols. (Madison: University of Wisconsin Press, 1969–1989), 5:295–314.

Schein, Sylvia, *Gateway to the Heavenly City: Crusader Jerusalem and the Catholic West (1099–1187)* (Aldershot, UK: Ashgate, 2005).

The Sweet Land of Cyprus: Papers Given at the Twenty-fifth Jubilee Spring Symposium of Byzantine Studies, Birmingham, March 1991, ed. Anthony Bryer and George Georghallides (Nicosia: Cyprus Research Centre, 1993).

The Latin Empire of Constantinople and Frankish Greece

Jacoby, David, "Social Evolution in Latin Greece" in *A History of the Crusades,* ed. Kenneth M. Setton et al., 2d ed., 6 vols. (Madison: University of Wisconsin Press, 1969–1989), 6:175–221.

———, *La Féodalité en Grèce médiévale* (Paris: Mouton, 1971).

———, "The Encounter of Two Societies: Western Conquerors and Byzantines in the Peloponnese after the Fourth Crusade," *American Historical Review* 78 (1973), 873–906.

Latins and Greeks in the Eastern Mediterranean, ed. Benjamin Arbel and David Jacoby (Ilford, UK: Cass, 1989).

Lock, Peter, *The Franks in the Aegean, 1204–1500* (London: Longman, 1995).

Longnon, Jean, *L'Empire latin de Constantinople et la principauté de Morée* (Paris: Payot, 1949).

———, "The Frankish States in Greece, 1204–1311," in *A History of the Crusades,* ed. Kenneth M. Setton et al., 2d ed., 6 vols. (Madison: University of Wisconsin Press, 1969–1989), 2:235–276.

Setton, Kenneth M., "The Catalans and Florentines in Greece, 1380–1462," in *A History of the Crusades,* ed. Kenneth M. Setton et al., 2d ed., 6 vols. (Madison: University of Wisconsin Press, 1969–1989), 3:225–277.

———, "The Catalans in Greece, 1311–1380," in *A History of the Crusades,* ed. Kenneth M. Setton et al., 2d ed., 6 vols. (Madison: University of Wisconsin Press, 1969–1989), 3:167–224.

Topping, Peter, "The Morea, 1311–1364," in *A History of the Crusades,* ed. Kenneth M. Setton et al., 2d ed., 6 vols. (Madison: University of Wisconsin Press, 1969–1989), 3:104–140.

———, "The Morea, 1364–1460," in *A History of the Crusades,* ed. Kenneth M. Setton et al., 2d ed., 6 vols. (Madison: University of Wisconsin Press, 1969–1989), 3:141–165.

Wolff, Robert L., "The Latin Empire of Constantinople, 1204–1261," in *A History of the Crusades,* ed. Kenneth M. Setton et al., 2d ed., 6 vols. (Madison: University of Wisconsin Press, 1969–1989), 2:187–274.

Iberia

Bishko, Charles Julian, "The Spanish and Portuguese Reconquest, 1095–1492," in *A History of the Crusades,* ed. Kenneth M. Setton et al., 2d ed., 6 vols. (Madison: University of Wisconsin Press, 1969–1989), 3:396–456.

Bisson, Thomas N., *The Medieval Crown of Aragón. A Short History* (Oxford: Oxford University Press, 1986).

Burns, Robert Ignatius, *The Crusader Kingdom of Valencia,* 2 vols. (Cambridge, MA: Harvard University Press, 1967).

Catlos, Brian A., *The Victors and the Vanquished: Christians and Muslims of Catalonia and Aragon, 1050–1300* (Cambridge: Cambridge University Press, 2004).

Fletcher, Richard, "Reconquest and Crusade in Spain, c. 1050–1150," *Transactions of the Royal Historical Society,* ser. 5, 37 (1987), 31–48.

Hillgarth, Jocelyn, *The Spanish Kingdoms, 1250–1516,* 2 vols. (Oxford: Clarendon, 1976–1978).

Lomax, Derek W., *The Reconquest of Spain* (London: Longman, 1978).

MacKay, Angus, *Spain in the Middle Ages: From Frontier to Empire, 1000–1500* (New York: St. Martin's, 1977).

O'Callaghan, Joseph F., *A History of Medieval Spain* (Ithaca, NY: Cornell University Press, 1993).

———, *Reconquest and Crusade in Medieval Spain* (Philadelphia: University of Pennsylvania Press, 2002).

The Baltic Lands and Russia

Blomkvist, Nils, *The Discovery of the Baltic: The Reception of a Catholic World-System in the European North (AD 1075–1225)* (Leiden: Brill, 2004).

Burleigh, Michael, "The Military Orders in the Baltic," in *The New Cambridge Medieval History,* vol. 5: *C. 1198–c. 1300,* ed. David Abulafia (Cambridge: Cambridge University Press, 1999), pp. 743–753.

Christiansen, Eric, *The Northern Crusades: The Baltic and the Catholic Frontier, 1100–1525,* 2d ed. (London: Penguin, 1997).

La Cristianizzazione della Lituania: Atti del Colloquio internazionale di storia ecclesiastica in occasione del VI centenario della Lituania cristiana, Roma, 24–26 giugno 1987, ed. Paulius Rabikauskas (Città del Vaticano: Pontificio Comitato di Scienze Storiche, 1989).

Crusade and Conversion on the Baltic Frontier, 1150–1500, ed. Alan V. Murray (Aldershot, UK: Ashgate, 2001), pp. 3–20.

Ekdahl, Sven, "Crusades and Colonization in the Baltic," in *Palgrave Advances in the Crusades,* ed. Helen J. Nicholson (Basingstoke, UK: Palgrave Macmillan, 2005), pp. 172–203.

Fennell, John, *The Crisis of Medieval Russia, 1200–1304* (London: Longman, 1993).

Gli Inizi del cristianesimo in Livonia-Lettonia: Atti del colloquio internazionale di storia ecclesiastica in occasione dell'VIII centenario della Chiesa in Livonia (1186–1986), Roma, 24–25 giugno 1986, ed. Michele Maccarrone (Città del Vaticano: Libreria Editrice Vaticana, 1989).

Johnson, Edgar N., "The German Crusade on the Baltic," in *A History of the Crusades,* ed. Kenneth M. Setton et al., 2d ed., 6 vols. (Madison: University of Wisconsin Press, 1969–1989), 3:545–585.

Krötzl, Christian, *Pietarin ja Paavalin nimissä: Paavit, lähetystyo ja Euroopan muotoutuminen (500–1250)* (Helsinki: Suomalaisen Kirjallisuuden Seura, 2004).

Lind, John H., Carsten Selch Jensen, Kurt Villads Jensen, and Ane L. Bysted, *Danske korstog—krig og mission i Østersøen* (København: Høst og Søn, 2004).

Rowell, Stephen C., *Lithuania Ascending: A Pagan Empire within East-Central Europe, 1294–1345* (Cambridge: Cambridge University Press, 1994).

———, "Baltic Europe, c. 1300–c. 1415," in *The New Cambridge Medieval History,* vol. 6: *C. 1300–c. 1415,* ed. Michael Jones (Cambridge: Cambridge University Press, 2000), pp. 695–734.

Urban, William L., *The Baltic Crusade,* 2d ed. (Chicago: Lithuanian Research and Studies Center, 1994).

———, *The Prussian Crusade,* 2d ed. (Chicago: Lithuanian Research and Studies Center, 2000).

———, *Tannenberg and After: Lithuania, Poland, and the Teutonic Order in Search of Immortality,* rev. ed. (Chicago: Lithuanian Research and Studies Center, 2003).

———, *The Teutonic Knights: A Military History* (London: Greenhill, 2003).

———, *The Livonian Crusade,* 2d ed. (Chicago: Lithuanian Research and Studies Center, 2004).

Index

About the Editor

Dr Alan V. Murray studied Medieval History, German Language and Literature, and Folk Studies at the universities of St Andrews, Salzburg and Freiburg, and taught at the universities of Erlangen, St Andrews and Leeds. He is currently Lecturer in Medieval Studies at the University of Leeds. He has written and edited numerous works on the crusades, the history of Outremer, and medieval historiography, including the monograph *The Crusader Kingdom of Jerusalem: A Dynastic History, 1099-1125* (2000), and the edited collection *Crusade and Conversion on the Baltic Frontier, 1150-1500* (2001).